GLOBAL
FINANCIAL
MARKETS

Ian H. Giddy
Stern School of Business
New York University

D. C. Heath and Company
Lexington, Massachusetts   Toronto

Address editorial correspondence to:

D. C. Heath and Company
125 Spring Street
Lexington, MA 02173

Developmental Editor: Stephen Wasserstein
Production Editor: Bryan Woodhouse
Designer: Alwyn Velásquez
Art Editor: James Roberts
Production Coordinator: Charles Dutton
Permissions Editor: Margaret Roll

To my family—
Rachel, Julia, and Laura—
for their love and tolerance

Preface

This book examines the financial markets that multinational corporations, government agencies, and banks use in conducting their business. It combines a solid foundation of theory with a state-of-the-art analysis of today's domestic and international markets. Although financial management per se is not its subject, *Global Financial Markets* does explain much about the markets in which corporate international financial managers deal.

The international financial markets include the market for foreign exchange, the Eurocurrency and related money markets, the Eurobond and global equity markets, the commodity markets, and (of no less importance) the markets for forward contracts, options, swaps, and other derivatives. In recent years profound changes have swept the markets and institutions of international finance. In key ways the institutions that in earlier decades dominated global finance—commercial banks and supranational organizations like the International Monetary Fund—have been displaced by direct, private finance.

To some extent, expertise and market power have moved away from banks and toward corporations. Industrial companies increasingly issue commercial paper, bonds, and medium-term notes, and they manage their financial risks internally. Some have created finance subsidiaries that in their own right have become powerhouse financial-service firms.

In response, the functions of commercial banks have broadened, too: a few have become more like investment banks, underwriting and distributing securities to investors rather than lending money themselves. Many banks have developed capabilities in such risk-management instruments as options, swaps, and more complex derivatives.

All successful market participants now need a more sophisticated understanding of financial risks and of the tools to manage them. The asset-liability management task in commercial banks has become more complex as the variety of products, both on and off their balance sheets, proliferates. As a result, clients of banks have more choices, and bank regulators have more headaches.

The International Monetary Fund, originally designed to resurrect the world's monetary system following the chaos of World War II, has become a lender to less-developed countries in financial distress; it is no longer a player in the main arena of international finance. National capital markets have gained importance, to some extent at the expense of external markets like the Eurobond market, as barriers erode and domestic institutions face the harsh winds of international competition.

All of these changes make the field one of continual excitement, a case study that never ends. *Global Financial Markets* reflects my view that learning at its best is an active process, not passive absorption. A foundation in the principles of finance, frequent examples, case studies, and illustrations afford the reader the opportunity to view the field from the perspectives of practicing bankers and corporate financial officers. In many instances the case studies are thinly disguised real-life dilemmas that companies and banks encounter, and they invite the reader to work through the situations by proxy. Doing so helps to develop the mental skills and familiarity with techniques that are this book's true goals.

You will undoubtedly favor some topics more than others and thus may be tempted to skip to what you consider the more interesting material. That's fine, but keep in mind that each chapter has a sequence of logic and exposition, with later explanations often heavily dependent on earlier ones. One effective reading strategy would be first to skim a whole chapter to focus on topics of interest but to return to the earlier parts as needed.

As indicated in the table of contents, the book consists of five major Parts. Part 1, "A Framework for International Finance," introduces the international financial system and its basic "foundation" markets, the foreign-exchange and international money markets. A newcomer to the field should certainly read Part 1 first, because much of the rest of the book relates to the practices and principles described here. Concluding this Part, Chapter 5 ties together some well-known foreign-exchange market relationships. It provides a good starting point for Part 2, "Foreign-Exchange Prediction and Hedging Tools," which consists of three chapters dealing with currency forecasting and hedging instruments, such as forwards, futures, and options. The chapters in Part 2 provide essential reading on the tools and techniques that corporations use to manage their foreign-exchange risk.

Part 3, "International Banking and Credit Markets," analyzes credit instruments in the arena of international banking. These instruments include multiple-option loan facilities, money-market instruments such as Eurocommercial paper, and less-developed-country debt. Part 4, "International Capital Markets," contains chapters on the global bond markets, the equity and commodity markets, and the burgeoning market for currency and interest-rate swaps. Borrowers and investors worldwide have come to rely increasingly on the swap and capital markets described in these chapters, and all kinds of financial institutions are hastening to develop capabilities in the design and trading of capital-market and derivative instruments.

Part 5, "International Financing," considers the use of the international money, capital, and derivative markets by corporations and other borrowers. It offers a logical framework for selecting among the myriad choices available to major borrowers in today's global market. Chapter 17 explains the role of financial innovations, including hybrid Eurobonds, in international corporate financing and gives the reader numerous chances to learn how the techniques work and how firms and banks employ them in practice. Part 6, "Review Section," briefly recaps the book's key concepts. A comprehensive glossary completes the text.

Acknowledgments

I have been helped enormously by a number of people through several years and numerous drafts of this book. Special mention must be made of my friend, mentor, and frequent coauthor, Gunter Dufey. I often find it difficult to separate which ideas are his and which are mine. Others that made substantive contributions include Peter Bossaerts, Catherine Bonser-Neal, Kevin Chang, Chitru Fernando, Jack Glen, Dick Herring, Robert Hodrick, Antonio Mello, Michael Moffett, Carol Osler, Lee Remmers, Dean Taylor, and Bernie Yeung. Yungeng Hu and Soonpoong Park, translators of the Chinese and Korean editions, respectively, made numerous helpful comments. My students at Wharton and NYU and in Helsinki drew my attention to errors or lack of clarity on many occasions, and I am grateful to them. I especially thank Carlos Abadi, Craig Bamsley, Stephen Fletcher, George Hongchoy, and Christian Nanu.

The following people also reviewed the manuscript and offered valuable comments that helped shape the book:
Catherine Bonser-Neal, University of Washington
Peter Bossaerts, California Institute of Technology

Reid W. Click, Brandeis University
Janamitra Devan, Middlebury College
Joseph E. Finnerty, University of Illinois at Urbana-Champaign
Daniel Himarios, University of Texas, Arlington
Robert J. Hodrick, Northwestern University
Philippe Jorion, Columbia University
Evi Kaplanis, London Business School (England)
Coleman S. Kendall, University of Illinois at Chicago
Nalin Kulatilaka, Boston University
Richard M. Levich, New York University
Mya Maung, Boston College
Antonio S. Mello, Massachusetts Institute of Technology
Carol L. Osler, Federal Reserve Bank of New York
Frank Pedersen, Aarhus Business School (Denmark)
Knut Sagmo, Norwegian School of Management (Norway)
Bernard Yeung, University of Michigan

Many of the practical insights in the book are attributable to former colleagues at Drexel Burnham Lambert or to friends at JP Morgan, Citibank, Chase Manhattan Bank, Bank of America, Chemical Bank, Credit Suisse, Deutsche Bank, Royal Bank of Canada, Banca Commerciale Italiana, and the World Bank group. I am grateful as well to my editors at D. C. Heath, notably George Lobell, Stephen Wasserstein, and Bryan Woodhouse, for their patience and help. My greatest debt, as reflected in the dedication to this book, is to my family.

Ian Giddy

About the Author

Ian Giddy was born in South Africa and received his Ph.D. from the University of Michigan. A U.S. citizen, he currently teaches at the New York University Stern School of Business and is a Senior Fellow of the NYU Salomon Center. He has taught at the Wharton School of the University of Pennsylvania, Columbia University, the University of Michigan, the University of Chicago, and Georgetown University.

Dr. Giddy has served the U.S. government in the Office of the Comptroller of the Currency and at the Board of Governors of the Federal Reserve System. He has acted as a consultant to a number of multinational corporations and financial institutions, including Credit Suisse, Yamaichi Securities, Banca Commerciale Italiana, Barclay's Bank, Deutsche Bank, JP Morgan, First Boston, Morgan Stanley, and Citibank. As Director of the International Product Group at Drexel Burnham Lambert, a securities firm, Professor Giddy was responsible for swap-related deals as well as for the introduction of several index-linked and other hybrid bond structures for the firm's international clients.

Dr. Giddy's twenty years of practical and academic experience reflect his interest in international finance, financial markets, and risk management. Besides lecturing around the world, he has participated in studies for the U.S. Treasury, the U.S. Congress, and the World Bank. The author or coauthor of more than fifty articles in the field of international finance, he is a contributor to *Euromoney* and to *The Journal of Financial and Quantitative Analysis*. Professor Giddy is also coauthor of *The International Money Market* and *Cases in International Finance* and coeditor of the two-volume *International Finance Handbook*.

Contents

PART 2   FOREIGN-EXCHANGE PREDICTION AND HEDGING TOOLS   143

CHAPTER 8   *Foreign-Exchange Options*   207

To the Instructor

An instructor's support package is available to all those adopting the book for courses. These materials, all of which I have written and will periodically update, include modifications and additions based on information not available at the time the book went to press. These instructional materials include the following:

Instructor's Guide. For each text chapter, the *Instructor's Guide:*

- describes the key concepts in each chapter and offers tips for presenting them in class.
- provides solutions to all questions and problems in the textbook, and discussion guidelines for the applications.

The *Instructor's Guide* also includes a set of transparency masters for presenting lecture points, key tables, and other information in the classroom.

Electronic Updates. A WordPerfect update on an IBM-compatible diskette keeps *Global Financial Markets* current as events unfold. It will be made available several times a year, free to instructors who adopt the textbook and to others for a small charge to cover mailing and handling.

Computerized Test Questions. I have prepared test questions (with answers) that instructors may wish to use in teaching the course; they are available free of charge on IBM diskette to all instructors who request it.

FOG: A Trading Game. This computer-based foreign-exchange trading game has been used successfully in many courses and seminars, both at universities and in banks.

Please contact D.C. Heath for information about any of these instructional materials. Address your request to your local Heath sales representative or call, fax, or write to: D.C. Heath and Company, College Marketing Department, 125 Spring Street, Lexington, Massachusetts 02173 (telephone: 1-800-242-8807; fax 1-800-860-1587).

Phone orders for the *Instructor's Guide* and the computerized test questions cannot be accepted. Please contact your Heath sales representative or write or fax D.C. Heath on your departmental letterhead with the following information:

- name and position;
- institution, department, address, and/or telephone number;
- name of course in which *Global Financial Markets* is being used, semester and academic year in which it is offered, and number of students enrolled;
- bookstore(s) through which you have ordered *Global Financial Markets* for student purchase.

If you are using this textbook in a course, you will doubtless find places where you think that a topic could be explained more clearly, or where you simply disagree. I'd like very much to hear from you. Call me at New York University at 212-998-0704, or write to P.O. Box 147, Rhinecliff, New York 12574.

I.H.G.

To the Student

This book is intended to be useful to both the newcomer and the working professional. To get the most out of it, be an active—not a passive—reader. When you begin a chapter, read the contents and the introductory paragraph for a preview. Skim through the chapter, looking for a key idea or fact under each heading. Form the habit of framing a question as you read the heading, and try to look quickly for the answer in the section. Use the figures and tables: the captions are designed to convey information, not merely to act as labels. If you find an unfamiliar term, look it up in the Glossary. Bold type indicates the first occurrence of terms that appear in the Glossary; italics are used for emphasis.

The Conceptual Questions at the end of each chapter test your understanding. If you're uncertain about your answer, look back in the chapter. The questions are roughly in order of topic coverage in the body of the chapter. Armed with a calculator or computer spreadsheet program, work through the numerical examples in the chapter.

These are my suggestions; use whatever method works best for you. I hope that you learn, and I welcome suggestions; many improvements have already resulted from students' comments. You can contact me at the address given in the To the Instructor section.

I.G.

Electronic Updates. A WordPerfect update on an IBM-compatible diskette keeps *Global Financial Markets* current as events unfold. It will be made available several times a year, for a small charge. Your bookstore manager can order it for you. In the United States, you can also call the D. C. Heath Distribution Center toll-free at 1-800-428-8071.

A Framework for International Finance

1
An Introduction to the World of International Finance

International finance is concerned with the global dimensions of financial markets, institutions, instruments, and techniques, and with the public policy issues arising from the markets and techniques. This chapter seeks to introduce, in a nontechnical fashion, the key ideas that we will later develop in this book. The reader will find that even though much of modern international finance revolves around foreign exchange, private market participants today employ a rich array of techniques, including the cross-border use of one another's national money and capital markets, and use of international markets such as the Eurocurrency and Eurobond markets.

What Are the Global Financial Markets?

A market is where things are bought and sold. Currencies and financial claims are bought and sold in much the same way as tomatoes are, except that more currencies—about half a trillion dollars' worth—are traded every day than vegetables. Financial markets deal with the exchange of different monies, the means by which people pay one another in different countries. In addition, financial markets trade claims—promises to pay in the future—and a variety of contingent contracts, where payments or exchanges depend on some future event. Claims include stocks and bonds, mortgage loans, bank deposits, and many other instruments, whereas contingent contracts include futures and options, letters of credit, and forward contracts, among other things.

And what about the *global* financial markets? To be honest, none of these financial markets is truly global in that it penetrates every nook and cranny of the globe. But many have become global, in the sense that the buyers and sellers of certain financial instruments readily trade beyond their national boundaries. Some instruments, like **Eurodollars**, have been designed specifically to trade internationally; others, like U.S. Treasury bonds, were once domestic but are now traded in a global marketplace.

In this book the term *global financial markets* means the *foreign-exchange* markets, where pounds are exchanged for pesos, and so forth; the *external* or "Euro" financial markets, where financial claims are bought and sold outside the jurisdiction of the currency in which they are denominated; and certain *domestic* financial markets, which by dint of having substantial international participation can be considered global. The derivative markets, where these instruments are traded for future delivery (futures, options, forwards, and the like), are nowadays an integral part of the global financial market.

A Bit of History

For as long as there has been international trade, there has been international finance. When an Egyptian merchant wished to import fine fabrics from Babylon, he had to exchange his currency for that of the exporter, or pay in a mutually acceptable currency. The former would represent the elements of a foreign exchange market; the latter, a commonly accepted "vehicle" currency. If the exporter allowed the Egyptian merchant to defer payment, an international extension of credit had taken place.

The present international capital market, however, has its roots in the nineteenth-century proliferation of stocks and bonds that were issued in the Americas, China, and other countries, for sale in Europe. Most of these financed the railroads, canals, and other infrastructure projects in what were then the developing countries. Not only were these financings essential to the development of the United States, Australia, and other nations, but the instruments and the problems stemming from them gave rise to a set of norms and laws governing private international finance. Simultaneously governments were experimenting with paper money and the gold exchange standard, whereby currencies' values were fixed by the willingness of governments to offer gold in exchange for a fixed amount of paper currency. But the system proved somewhat rigid, and in the early twentieth century costly lessons were learned in the arena of public monetary policy, culminating in the Great Depression and the competitive devaluation of currencies in the 1930s.

By 1944, toward the end of World War II, the allied leaders were weary of war, economic and otherwise. At a famous meeting at **Bretton Woods**, New Hampshire, they established some fundamental rules aimed at stabilizing international monetary relations. The core of the agreement that was hammered out contained two key elements: (1) to facilitate trade, governments should insofar as possible allow people to freely convert one currency into another;[1] (2) to forestall the use of currency exchange rates to gain a temporary export advantage, governments should fix their currencies' external values, using the U.S. dollar as the keystone unit.

By the late 1960s this "dollar standard" came under strain as a result of U.S. inflation and the general divergence of monetary policies among the industrial countries, and in 1971 the U.S. dollar was officially devalued. Two decades of floating exchange rates ensued, until by the early 1980s, with vast capital flows driving currencies far from their perceived fundamental values, governments began to yearn for the external monetary discipline that fixed exchange rates offer. Whereas some sought to link their currencies to the U.S. dollar or the Japanese yen, others were attracted by the gradual, if erratic, move toward monetary union in Europe, the **European Monetary System**, or EMS. In Chapter 4 we revisit the EMS and the issues of exchange-rate policy in general, always seeking an answer to the question, *Fixed or floating—which is better?*

Key Themes of This Book

For many, the subject of international finance has a forbidding aspect. How can one make sense of the confusion of currencies, policies, instruments, and rules and regulations? Professionals in the field also help perpetuate the myth of complexity by using jargon such as SDR, EMU, multicurrency option facility, and Matador bond. If the truth be

---

[1]In fact, it was thirty years before this became a reality even for the major developed countries.

known, making our subject seem a little bit mysterious helps keep us employed. A fundamental theme of this book is that *international finance is much more comprehensible than people think,* especially if you keep in mind two maxims:

1. Do not expect to learn how to forecast exchange rates. Although this book seeks to make sense of what factors influence currencies, it makes no pretense of providing any easy way of knowing when and by how much the factors' influence will be felt.
2. Most aspects of global finance follow exactly the same principles as domestic finance. A **Eurobond** denominated in Spanish pesetas is still a bond, and apart from some minor institutional details, it follows precisely the same rules as domestic bonds. So where's the mystery? The basic approach is to assume the international market is the same as the domestic one and then to focus on the question, What, if anything, is different about this so-called international market?

Of course there's no escaping the fact that at home we only have to deal with one currency, and going international involves *currency exchange.* Wouldn't it be nicer if there was only one world currency, or at least if the major currencies were fixed against one another so that there was no uncertainty about what they were worth? Not necessarily: if you want to buy wine in Portugal, and domestic inflation has eroded the purchasing power of the escudo, then wine will seem very expensive unless the government allows the foreign-exchange value of the escudo to fall to a level that make Portuguese wine reasonably priced once again. We will learn in Chapter 4 that *one fundamental reason that currencies fluctuate is that different governments pursue different domestic monetary policies.* Some place a high priority on price stability; others find themselves politically unable to resist inflationary pressures.

So different national economic priorities go a long way toward explaining why we have fluctuating currencies. National priorities also cause governments to place restrictions on the flow of funds into and out of their money and capital markets. However, no national financial market of any significance is totally isolated from the rest of the world. As we will discuss throughout this book, national financial markets have different conditions, and this fact leads to an incentive to profit by arbitrage between the markets. The markets are, to some degree, linked, allowing such arbitrage to occur; but they are also partially segmented, because regulations, taxes, and exchange controls prevent perfect arbitrage. So the incentive to seek a better way to arbitrage among national markets persists.

Domestic financial market imperfections are what gave rise to the so-called Euromarkets (such as the Eurodollar banking market, where dollar deposits are taken and loans are made outside the jurisdiction of the U.S. authorities). Because the Eurocurrency and Eurobond markets are relatively unrestrained, and securities can be denominated in almost any currency, we will have an excellent way to study intercurrency arbitrage and unfettered financial creativity at work in these markets.

Thus global finance encompasses an odd combination of the world's most perfect money and capital markets (the Euromarkets and the free foreign-exchange markets) and the world's most imperfect markets (some domestic capital markets whose development is stunted by heavy-handed restrictions and in which exchange controls severely limit competition from the outside).

The Euromarkets were a breakthrough in separating the currency of denomination from the country of jurisdiction of securities. Now, other aspects of financial claims can be separated and traded on their own. In the past, one might invest in a Swiss-franc bond whose interest rate was fixed. Today, one can buy and trade the bond and the interest-rate fixity aspect separately. The latter is done in the interest-rate swap market, one of the many derivative markets that nowadays are the source of some of the most exciting developments in the global financial marketplace.

These themes will reappear more than once throughout the book. Most underpinnings of the global markets are the same as in the domestic context. Foreign-exchange fluctuations, arising from different economic conditions and policies, must be understood and managed, but the book contains no formula for predicting currency movements. *Currency markets are efficient, but many national capital markets are not; these national markets are partially, but not wholly, linked to the global market.* The core of the global market may be said to be the Eurocurrency and Eurobond markets. The creativity of these markets comes from participants' constant efforts to overcome market imperfections, and from constraints on borrowers or investors. These efforts are now more effective, thanks to the burgeoning range of futures, options, swaps, and other derivative instruments available to the international financier. This book seeks to explain the principles and pricing of these instruments, and offers numerous examples of how they can be used by banks, corporations, and governments.

The Foreign-Exchange Market

Currencies are bought and sold in exchange for one another in a 24-hour over-the-telephone market by individuals, companies, securities firms, and central banks, all of which deal with the foreign-exchange traders at commercial banks. The liquidity of the market stems from the readiness of such banks to trade with other banks as well as with nonbanks. Probably over 95 percent of trading occurs between the banks themselves, as they continuously adjust and readjust their positions. Foreign-exchange traders must anticipate changes in government actions by buying and selling currencies for future (**forward**) or immediate (**spot**) delivery. The market rates that companies face in doing international business change each time news or expectations of futures events alter the outlook for a currency.

Understanding a currency's movements involves fundamental economic analysis, political prognostication, and technical analysis that studies the patterns of movement in the currency itself. Modern finance theory, on the other hand, regards these efforts as self-defeating—any method that works will become disseminated and used to the point where it no longer works! The market will respond more and more rapidly to new information, and in time an *efficient market* will prevail: exchange rates will behave as randomly as the arrival of unanticipated information.

Not all currencies behave this way, of course. Some are fixed to other currencies, as the German mark is fixed to the Dutch guilder. Some governments fix or influence their currencies' values by either open-market buying or selling, pushing the price up or down. Others control supply and demand by placing restrictions on who can buy or sell foreign exchange, and for what purpose.

In the chapters that follow, we will encounter fixed and floating exchange rates, and currencies traded in a free market as well as those whose market is so closely regulated as to be not really a market at all.

Some currencies, such as the pound and the yen, are traded for deferred settlement—forward delivery—in one month or more—as well as the more normal spot delivery—settlement within two business days. Thus a corporation can purchase Japanese yen for delivery not today but, say, in three months' time.[2] This technique, commonly used to protect the value of foreign currency payments, is called a forward foreign-exchange contract. It also provides a linkage among the different Eurocurrency markets.

Domestic and International Money Markets

The 1970s and 1980s saw enormous growth in the Eurodollar market and its offshoots in other currencies. These are markets for *credit* outside the country of the currency in which the credit instrument is denominated. **Eurodollars** are the money market gypsies, living side-by-side with their more domesticated neighbors. They are simply bank time deposits, denominated in U.S. dollars, but deposited in a bank outside the United States. Euroyen, Eurosterling, and so forth are similarly deposits in banks located outside the jurisdiction of the country in whose currency the instrument is denominated. The **Eurocurrency market**, in other words, permits the separation of the currency of denomination from the country of jurisdiction.

In the past, investors and borrowers of short-term money were limited to their home markets and currencies. Now the international investor can place any of the major currencies in almost any of the major financial centers. Euromarkets now dominate domestic money markets, setting the standards.

As we will learn in Chapter 2, money-market traders actively arbitrage among instruments in the Eurocurrency market denominated in different currencies. For example, it is common for banks to borrow in French francs and invest the money in U.S. dollars, to take advantage of different interest rates in the two currencies. To protect itself from exchange risk, the bank will cover itself by means of a forward-exchange contract. An equilibrium will be established when the cost of the "forward cover" precisely offsets the interest-rate differential. Hence interest rates in different currencies are linked, because Eurocurrency deposits, as well as other credit instruments, can be arbitraged between one another through the spot and forward foreign-exchange markets. Chapter 5 offers a simple framework for understanding the linkages among interest rates, exchange rates, and other key variables of international finance.

Domestic and International Capital Markets

The international capital market consists of the global bond and equity markets, the market for those many instruments that lie somewhere in between bonds and equity, and the market for derivatives of these financing instruments. By far the most mature of these markets is the **international bond** market, which comprises the Eurobond and foreign bond markets, and those markets such as the U.S. market that actively encourage global

---

[2]The price for forward delivery will differ from the spot price. Some currencies, like the yen, typically cost more for forward delivery (they are trading at a "premium"), while others, such as the pound sterling, cost less (they trade at a "discount"). Premium or discounted prices are determined by the "cost of carry"—that is, by the net cost (or benefit) from borrowing in one currency and depositing the funds in the other. The forward premium or discount, therefore, is a function of relative interest rates in the two currencies—another expression of the interest-rate-parity relationship.

participation. The *Eurobond* market's distinctive feature is that the bonds are issued and sold in a jurisdiction outside the country of the currency of denomination. This makes the market freer of certain constraints (such as registration requirements and withholding taxes) than the domestic markets. *Foreign bonds,* unlike Eurobonds, are issued within the domestic market of the currency of denomination, but they are issued by nonresident borrowers. Eurobonds are quite distinct from Eurodollars, because bond markets enable final borrowers to issue securities to investors directly. In the Eurobond market, there are no intermediaries between borrower and lender (except during the underwriting and distribution process). Eurobonds represent direct claims on corporations, governments, or governmental entities.

Nowadays, as the reader will learn in the latter half of the book, much of the international bond market has become merged with the domestic bond market. National regulations in the United States, Japan, and France, for example, have been altered to make the domestic capital markets more competitive with the international market. Yet the Eurobond market continues to set the pace of financial innovation. In this fertile ecosystem of finance, a sort of Darwinian mutation and evolution is continually at work, as banks fight for ascendancy and survival.

The Global Derivatives Market

Many of the financial techniques peculiar to the global market have thrived because national regulations limited the growth and variety of financing and investment vehicles within domestic markets. The global derivatives market is no exception. While futures and options flourished in the United States in the 1970s, other countries soon offered rival contracts and many private "off balance sheet" contracts flourished in the 1980s. Many of these today serve as integral adjuncts to Euromarket securities issues.

Derivatives are contracts for future performance derived from cash instruments such as bonds, stocks, and deposits. The "original" derivative contract of international finance is the *forward exchange contract,* which evidences two parties' agreement to exchange two currencies in the future at a fixed exchange rate. The forward exchange market has, since the 1960s, played the role of linking international interest rates. Today, however, forward contracts have to share the stage with other instruments and markets for arbitrage and for hedging. These newer derivative instruments include futures, options, and swaps.

Futures markets for currencies and Eurodeposits have sprung up in most of the global trading centers. A futures contract is the common man's forward contract; while forwards are available only to banks and others with high credit standing, futures contracts minimize credit risk by daily repricing, called marking to market, of each party's gains or losses. As a result, futures can be purchased or sold by anyone who has sufficient funds to open a margin account. Because they are virtually equivalent, currency futures track currency forwards almost perfectly. Both forwards and futures entail a commitment to exchange two currencies at a certain rate on a given future date. *Currency options,* on the other hand, give the holder the right, but not the obligation, to purchase (or sell) a currency at a prearranged exchange rate in the future.

More recent, but in many respects more important than futures and options, is the market for *interest-rate and currency swaps.* A French airline wishes to obtain long-term, fixed-rate French-franc financing for equipment purchases, but finds that its most efficient access to funds is in the form of dollar-denominated borrowing from banks on a floating-rate basis. By entering into a currency swap, the airline can convert the floating-rate,

U.S.-dollar debt into fixed-rate, French-franc debt. The importance of the swap market in international bond financing, as well as in general financial risk management, will be seen in Chapter 13.

Beyond the Money and Bond Markets: International Equity and Commodity Markets

Previous books on this subject made great strides in recognizing the economic linkages between national and international markets, but practice has now gone two steps further. Equities are now incorporated, in various guises, into global portfolios, and commodities are now used not only as components of investment portfolios but also as hedging and financing vehicles. To keep pace with these innovations, this book will show how the international equities and commodities markets link into the global capital market.

International equity investment, always important, has assumed added significance in recent years for at least three reasons:

1. Modern portfolio theory has unequivocally demonstrated that the investor in equities can obtain a clearly superior combination of lower risk and higher return by diversifying internationally rather than only domestically.
2. Cross-border mergers and acquisitions are more evident as the world economy, with Europe at the forefront, becomes more integrated.
3. The performance of foreign markets such as Tokyo means that no modern institutional investor can afford to ignore the opportunities presented by the fast-growing countries of Asia and elsewhere. Because some of these markets suffer from restrictions and illiquidity, many investors have chosen to purchase shares in one of the hundred or more funds or trusts devoted to international investment.

On the *financing* side, some firms now list their shares on several exchanges to facilitate round-the-clock trading, although there is no distinct "Euro-equity" market.

Commodities are becoming more and more integrated into financing as well as investment portfolios, as commodity users do "gold swaps" and other swaps, and as bonds are sometimes linked to a commodity price. So today the Canadian utility company, Hydro Quebec, might issue a bond in the Eurobond market denominated in its home currency, Canadian dollars, or in U.S. dollars, the currency of the global energy market. Alternatively, the bond might be in effect denominated in oil (that is, the interest and principal is linked to the oil price), the key raw-material benchmark price of the global energy market!

Using the Global Capital Markets

This is not a "how-to" book. It seeks to impart understanding rather than simply enumerating procedures. Nevertheless, it has been written on the assumption that most who read it approach the subject of global finance as a potential participant—to invest money internationally, to borrow from international banks or issue securities in the international capital markets, to use one or more of the many hedging techniques so important in the management of financial risk today.

With this in mind, one way to approach the chapters that follow is to ask, How can I or my organization benefit from participating in the global financial market? Without going into specifics, I believe you will discover benefits of three kinds:

1. *Competition* drives out monopolistic practices and inflated margins, and the global market offers unfettered competition that rivals any domestic market. Those depositors and borrowers who have not discovered the joys of Eurodollars will find, like many before them, that Eurocurrency bank deposits offer better deposit rates and lending terms than many domestic banks provide. The global markets in general have lowered costs and improved returns for investors and borrowers alike.

2. The financial world has already seen a dramatically increased participation by portfolio managers in international investments. The chief reason is *diversification*. Risk can be reduced without a sacrifice of expected return if investments are diversified internationally as well as domestically. From a borrower's viewpoint, two factors—access to funding denominated in different currencies and the availability of a much broader range of investor groups with different preferences—offer substantial risk reduction.

3. While the growth of the global financial market has yielded benefits in the areas of pure cost and in more efficient portfolio diversification, the most telling improvement in the lives of the professional investment manager and in that of the corporate or governmental borrower comes not from cost reduction but from *innovation* in financing and investment technologies. A decade ago the British institutional investor might have been able to choose from several department store companies if she wished to hold long-term sterling bonds. Today her choices might number several dozen. One of these, for example, could be a Japanese company offering a sterling-denominated Eurobond which, at the investor's option, is convertible into common stock of the issuing company *or* puttable back to the issuer at one or more dates during the life of the bond. Chapter 12, on the international bond market, introduces the reader to several hybrid bonds of this genre, while Chapter 17 specifically addresses the use of hybrid bonds from the point of view of the international borrower. In sum, the global market's prime contribution is innovations that lead to greater choice by investors and issuers to solve a variety of financial problems.

SUMMARY

The international financial system revolves around the foreign-exchange market. This market links prices in different countries, and governments waver between floating and fixing their exchange rates to manage this interdependence. Domestic money markets are today linked through the Eurocurrency market, which permits the separation of currency of denomination from country of jurisdiction. National interest rates each reflect the time value of their own money, and the forward foreign-exchange market reflects the time value of the exchange rate between the two monies. Thus the foreign-exchange market links national interest rates, inflation rates, and monetary policies. Currency swaps, used in connection with international bond financing or investment, are the long-term counterparts of the forward-exchange market. Both allow the separation of the currency and interest rate risks of an asset from the asset itself.

Today's global financial technologies offer still-greater separability of the attributes of financial claims. These manifest themselves in the derivative securities, in new forms of bank lending, and in the international bond market. Eurobonds may be the most innovative instruments of the global financial market; they are subject to fewer constraints than the new derivative instruments, and they are frequently packaged with future- and optionlike features to match investor and issuer needs in the international capital market. This innovation exemplifies a recurring theme of international finance: because national markets are constrained, international markets evolve to intermediate between them, creating partial but not perfect linkages between them.

CONCEPTUAL QUESTIONS

1. What markets are encompassed in the term *global financial markets*?
2. What considerations might lead a country to fix its exchange rates rather than letting the currency's value be determined in free trading?
3. What does the "efficient markets" theory say about the predictability of exchange rates?
4. Through what instruments are interest rates linked to one another?
5. Is there an important distinction between foreign-exchange forward contracts, futures, and options?
6. How does the Eurobond market differ from the Eurodollar market?
7. What are the three key benefits of the global financial markets, from the perspective of those using them?

SELECTED REFERENCES

Aggarwal, Raj. *The Literature of International Business Finance: A Bibliography*. New York: Praeger, 1984.

Aliber, Robert F. *The International Money Game*. New York: Basic Books, 1987.

Eiteman, David K., and Arthur I. Stonehill. *Multinational Business Finance*. 5th ed. Reading, Mass.: Addison-Wesley, 1989.

Friedman, Milton, and Robert V. Roosa. "Free Versus Fixed Exchange Rates: A Debate." *Journal of Portfolio Management*. (Spring 1977): 68–73.

George, Abraham, and Ian H. Giddy. *International Finance Handbook*. Vols. I and II. New York: Wiley, 1983.

Krugman, Paul R., and Maurice Obstfeld. *International Economics*. 2nd ed. New York: HarperCollins, 1991.

Lessard, Donald R. *International Financial Management: Theory and Applications*. 2nd ed. New York: Wiley, 1987.

Levi, Maurice. *International Finance: Financial Management and the International Economy*. 2nd ed. New York: McGraw-Hill, 1989.

Shapiro, Alan C. *Multinational Financial Management*. 3rd ed. Boston: Allyn and Bacon, 1990.

Solnik, Bruno. *International Investments*. 2nd ed. Reading, Mass.: Addison-Wesley, 1991.

2
The Foreign-Exchange and Eurocurrency Markets

The foreign-exchange market is fundamental to international finance. It is also one of the most interesting aspects of the field. This chapter is intended to immerse the reader in the hurly-burly of money movements and currency trading as quickly as is feasible. The chapter also introduces the Eurocurrency market, which has become an integral part of the modern foreign-exchange market and is today the core of international borrowing and lending. In short, the chapter is about the key markets for international payments and international credit.

The currency market and the international money market together constitute the cornerstone of the global financial market and are tightly integrated with one another. Eurodollars and other Eurocurrency deposits are traded and priced simultaneously within a single dealing room in most international banks. Figure 2.1 illustrates the fact that the

Figure 2.1 **_Eurocurrency Market Linkages._** Each Eurocurrency market is tied to the others through the foreign-exchange market, and each is linked to its home market.

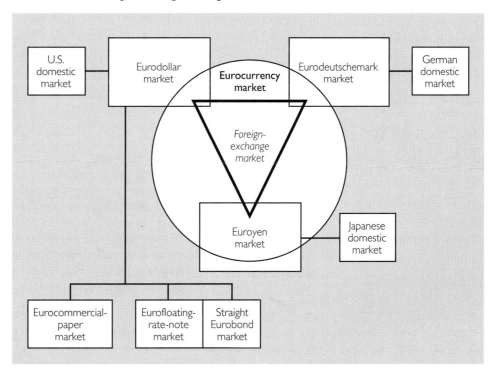

Author's note: I wish to acknowledge Gunter Dufey's important contributions to this chapter.

foreign-exchange market is what binds different segments of the Eurocurrency market together. Each segment of the Eurocurrency market—Eurodollars, Euromarks, and so forth—is also linked to its home-country money market, and the whole market is in turn tied to the international bond market. Together, these markets form the essence of the global financial market.

Some Terms and Concepts

The *foreign-exchange market* is the means by which payments are made across national boundaries, jurisdictions, and currencies; it is also the market in which one currency is traded for another, and hence sets the price for one currency in terms of the other. The **Eurocurrency market** is the market for bank time deposits and loans made outside the country of the currency. It is the means by which credit is provided and obtained in various individual currencies, outside of the normal jurisdiction of the country in which that currency originates.

Foreign exchange, as most people know, is the means by which one currency is exchanged for another, and the foreign-exchange market is the "place" where such exchanges occur. But what's special about the Eurocurrency market? First, the international money market consists of the Eurodollar market and the other money markets to which it is linked. Prime among these are the other Eurocurrency markets—Eurodeutschemarks, Euroyen, Euro-French francs, and so forth. Later we will show in detail how these markets are bound to one another through the spot and forward foreign-exchange markets. Each Eurocurrency sector is in turn linked by back-and-forth flows to its home money markets and to financial conditions in that market, unless those ties are weakened by exchange restrictions. Finally, the Eurocurrency market, as a market for bank deposits and loans, operates hand-in-hand with the markets for direct financing—the Euro-commercial paper and Eurobond markets.

Both the terminology and the concepts pertaining to the international money market reflect the confusion surrounding this phenomenon. The term *Eurocurrency market(s)* itself gives rise to at least two misleading associations: (1) it implies that it is a market for foreign currencies similar or closely related to the foreign-exchange market, and (2) the term implies either that the market is located in Europe or that it deals primarily in European currencies. Both these implications are incorrect or misleading.

Table 2.1 offers a scheme for classifying financial markets in general. Let us begin with the distinction between markets for *means of payments* (money) and markets for *credit* (the use of funds over time).

Despite global use, the dollar and other major currencies retain their national character: each unit is produced by a national government, which carefully guards its prerogative to do so. Its acceptability is ensured by "legal tender" laws, which give national money the power to discharge debt legally. But this ability is strictly limited by the nation's borders. There is no uniquely international money; instead, the exchange of national monies is normally necessary to effect payments in another country. This is the rationale for the market for foreign exchange, the market in which different national means of payments are traded.

In contrast to the foreign-exchange market, credit markets deal in the allocation of claims over time. The saver, whose income exceeds his use of funds in a particular period, makes the additional output that he has created (earned) temporarily available to the (ultimate) investor, whose need for funds is greater than the resources available during that period.

Table 2.1   *Classification of Financial Markets.*   International markets include foreign markets (issues by nonresidents in a domestic market) and Euromarkets (outside of the country of the currency).

I. MARKETS FOR MEANS OF PAYMENT
   Example: The foreign-exchange market

II. MARKETS FOR CREDIT

	National	International	
	Domestic examples	Foreign examples	"Euro" examples
Direct	U.S. corporate-bond market	Swiss-franc foreign-bond market	Euroyen bond market
Intermediated	U.S. bank loan market	Bank loans within U.S. to foreign borrowers	Eurosterling deposit and loan market
	Internal		External

    The scheme used here for classifying credit markets, shown in Table 2.1, is different from the usual distinction between money and capital markets, according to which the maturity of the instruments involved is the major distinguishing criterion. Instead, we ask *how and where* the process of transferring funds from savers to investors is effected.

    The big difference between the Eurocurrency and domestic markets, for instruments in a partcular currency, is that all transactions done within the domestic market are directly subject to the rules and institutional arrangements of the local financial system. To illustrate, when Australian investors purchase securities in Tokyo, they do so according to the rules, market practices, and regulatory guidelines that govern such transactions in Japan. The same applies to those who place their funds in Japanese banks. The Korean borrower who approaches a Swiss bank or insurance company for a Swiss franc loan borrows at rates and conditions imposed by the financial institutions of Switzerland and is directly affected by the Swiss authorities' policy toward lending to foreign residents. Likewise, a Swedish borrower who wishes to issue bonds in a domestic market such as Finland must follow the rules and regulations of this market—and often these rules simply say "no."

    Let us summarize the definitions of certain terms:

- *Eurodollar* or *Eurocurrency* refers to bank time deposits denominated in a currency other than that of the country in which the bank or bank branch is located. Similarly, the Eurocurrency market is the market for such bank deposits.
- *Eurobonds* are bonds issued outside the country of the currency in which such bonds are denominated. Dollar-denominated Eurobonds are sometimes referred to as Eurodollar bonds, and a similar practice applies to other currencies.
- *Foreign bonds* are bonds issued within a particular country and denominated in the currency of the country, but the issuer is a nonresident.
- *The Euromarkets* is a term that loosely includes Eurocurrency deposits, Eurobonds, Eurocommercial paper, and other instruments issued outside the country of the currency of denomination.

In many cases, these definitions become fuzzy, because regulatory practices do not fall into neat categories. For example, foreign-currency bonds issued in the United States are subject to all domestic regulations and thus are, for all intents and purposes, domestic bonds. Bonds issued in Switzerland are treated much like Eurobonds even if they are denominated in Swiss francs. And in many countries foreign-currency-denominated deposits are subject to the same constraints as domestic deposits, so they cannot really be considered part of the Eurocurrency market.

Differences in interest rates, practices, and terms that exist between domestic and external (Euro) markets arise primarily from the extent to which regulatory constraints can be avoided by doing business outside the country of the currency, in certain favorable jurisdictions. As long as these differences persist, there will be plenty of business for the international money-market trader. Let us now try to gain a picture of the context in which the trader operates.

The trading, or "treasury," business in a major international bank has evolved from two much more limited activities. Lending, the core activity of most commercial banks, has to be funded through deposits. To manage this funding and to match it to the bank's needs, the treasurer must actively seek deposits (or place funds temporarily) in the interbank market. This transfer has now become a profitable activity in its own right, called *deposit dealing,* and when it involves deposits in currencies outside the participant's home country, it is called *Eurocurrency deposit dealing.*

Similarly, foreign-exchange trading evolved as a natural outcome of corporate customers' needs to make international payments for export–import business. Eventually, banks with frequent transactions in foreign exchange transformed a rather dull activity into today's risk-taking, profit-seeking *foreign-exchange dealing* desks.

The Dealing Room: Foreign Exchange and Eurocurrency

The foreign-exchange and money-market dealing-room activities are depicted schematically in Figure 2.2 Although funding or "treasury" activities and customer foreign-exchange services remain part of the dealing room's goals, the main show now lies in the self-sufficient business of interbank foreign-exchange and Eurocurrency trading. In this section and the next the reader will learn a little of what these traders do, and why, and how they relate to one another.

Foreign exchange is the exchange of one currency for another. An *exchange rate* is simply the price of one currency in terms of another. For example, the British pound is priced at 2.4515 German marks. We say the sterling/deutschemark exchange rate is DM2.4515.[1] Trading or "dealing" in each pair of currencies consists of two markets, *the spot market,* where payment (delivery) is made "right away" (usually the second business day), and *the forward market.* The rate in the forward market is a price for foreign currency set at the time the transaction is agreed to but the actual exchange, or delivery, takes place at a specified time in the future. The amount of the transaction, the value date, the payments procedure, and the exchange rate are all determined in advance, but *no exchange of money takes place until the actual settlement date.* This commitment to exchange currencies at a previously agreed exchange rate is usually referred to as a *forward contract.*

---

[1] If a pound sterling is worth 2.4515 deutschemarks, then one deutschemark is worth the reciprocal, 1/2.4515, or 0.4079, pounds sterling.

Figure 2.2 *Diagram of a Dealing Room.* Foreign-exchange and Eurocurrency dealing are interrelated activities and so are done on the same trading floor.

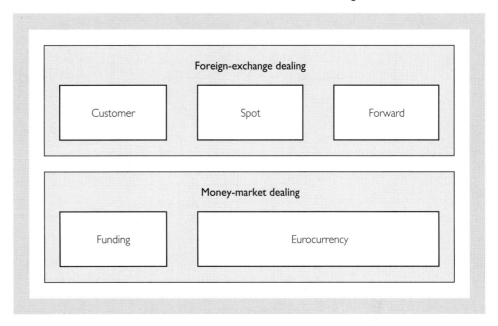

In Figure 2.2, the box showing the spot traders is separate from that showing the forward traders, because in practice the two functions are separated. Spot traders concentrate on the *level* of the exchange rate, while forward (or "FX swap") traders concentrate on the *difference* between the spot and forward rates. In absolute terms, this difference is called the *swap rate* or *swap points*. In relative terms, the forward premium, or **discount**, is the annualized percentage difference between the spot and forward exchange rates. It is calculated as:

$$\frac{n\text{-day forward rate} - \text{spot rate}}{\text{spot rate}} \times \frac{365}{n} \times 100$$

where the exchange rate is defined as domestic currency units per unit of foreign currency, such as $1.50 per pound sterling. For example, at the time of writing, the pound was trading at a discount against the U.S. dollar in the three-month forward market. The forward discount was:

$$\frac{1.5386 - 1.5530}{1.5530} \times \frac{365}{91} \times 100 = -3.72\% \text{ per annum}$$

If this annualized difference between spot and forward is positive, meaning the foreign currency is worth *more* in the forward market, we say that the foreign currency is trading at a *forward premium;* if it's worth *less* in the forward market, it is trading at a *discount.*

The spot market is, and probably will always be, the most liquid segment of the foreign-exchange market. Yet as Figure 2.3 shows, the volume of forward transactions in centers such as London now rivals spot-transactions volume. The forward-exchange market is used by companies to "cover" or protect their future cash flows in foreign currencies. For example, if Mitsubishi Corporation wishes to protect the Japanese yen value of revenues from Australia, it will sell Australian dollars forward in exchange for yen.

Figure 2.3   *Foreign-Exchange Transactions Volume in London, April 1992*

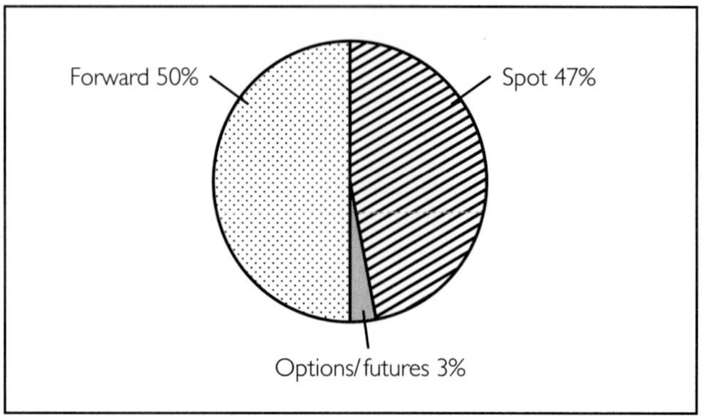

Source: Bank of England.

The forward contract guarantees an exchange rate at which currencies will be sold or bought, and so eliminates the chance of exchange-rate losses for any particular transaction. The forward rate that a corporation agrees upon will depend, among other things, on its expectations regarding the future behavior of the exchange rate.[2] Under normal circumstances, the forward rate is strongly influenced by market participants' best guess as to the future spot exchange rate. If this were not the case, and if, for example, many believed that the future spot rate would be below the prevailing forward rate, they would tend to offer more for forward delivery and drive the forward rate down toward the expected future rate.

The spot traders buy and sell foreign currencies. In the forward market, on the other hand, traders deal in the *difference* between spot and forward rates: they trade foreign-exchange swaps.[3] A *foreign-exchange (FX) swap* is a transaction in which a spot transaction and an opposite forward transaction are both agreed upon simultaneously. Swaps of this kind are commonly employed by banks to offset "outright" forward-exchange deals done with corporations.[4]

As shown in Figure 2.2, most major banks' dealing rooms are organized to reflect the difference between interbank and corporate dealing. Corporate liaison dealers, referred to as *advisors* or *FX sales people,* deal directly with clients. They provide not only information about rates but also general market information, news, and sometimes, courageously, forecasts. They base their prices on quotes obtained from the interbank traders and, in turn, provide interbank traders with feedback information about the demand-and-supply forces emanating from the corporate sector. (Figure 2.9 illustrates the institutional relationships of the interbank and corporate foreign-exchange markets.) In reality, the demarcation line between "corporate" and "interbank" trading is not so neat. Some

---

[2]For a bank, the forward rate that it is willing to quote depends on the spot-exchange rate and on the interest differential rather than on the bank's currency expectations; we will discuss this topic in more detail later.

[3]Throughout this book we use the term "foreign-exchange swap" to mean the (usually) short-term simultaneous spot purchase and forward sale of a currency. This is different from a "currency swap," which is the periodic exchange of interest rates and final principal in two currencies, is often associated with longer-term bond issues, and is dealt with later in the book. In practice, unfortunately, market participants commonly just say "swap," so that only the context can tell you which of the two kinds they mean. Such is the English language.

[4]The reader will learn more about spot, "outright" forward, and foreign-exchange swap trading in Chapter 7.

smaller banks are plugged into the interbank market via the traders at larger banks, while some large international corporations employ professional traders in their treasury departments who demand two-way quotes and have a tendency to deal directly through brokers. At the same time, large securities companies have built up professionally staffed foreign-exchange departments whose personnel trade not only to accommodate international investors but also for their own account.

Consider the role of the corporate dealing desk. These are the people who deal directly with corporations, government agencies, and other noncommercial bank participants in the market. A corporate dealer, for example, may enter into a forward contact to sell 10 million Swiss francs to BMW. It is now the task of the interbank dealers to come up with the Swiss francs at the designated time. Having agreed to deliver Swiss francs to a customer at the end of May, the dealer could, in principle, enter a forward-exchange contract to buy Swiss francs from some other bank. However, the interbank market for such "outright" forwards is less well developed than those for spot and swap deals, and for Eurodeposits. Hence the trader will normally buy the Swiss francs for spot delivery; then, because he will not actually need the francs until May 31, he can (and will) enter a spot-sale-and-future-repurchase arrangement with another bank—in other words, he will do a swap.

Alternatively, our interbank dealer could use the Eurocurrency market to achieve the same objective. This is the cue for the people on the Eurocurrency dealing desk to come on stage. The foreign-exchange dealer needs the Swiss francs later; but he could get them now and hold them on deposit until needed. To do this, he would call over to the funding desk and have them borrow dollars, which he would then change into francs in the spot market, and hold them in a Swiss-franc deposit until the end of May. Having bought the Swiss francs spot with, say, borrowed Eurodollars, the trader would ask the Eurocurrency dealer to put them into a bank deposit at Credit Suisse in London—a Euro–Swiss-franc deposit, in fact—maturing on May 31. He would then have the Swiss francs ready to deliver to his customer on that day. Such a transaction is termed a **money-market hedge**. A numerical example is given in the final section of this chapter.

The cost of this money-market hedge is the difference between the Eurodollar interest rate paid and the Swiss franc interest rate earned. The dealer could instead have used the foreign-exchange swap technique, the cost of which would have been the difference between the spot and forward rates—the swap rate or swap points. At the margin, the two should be equal. This suggests that the Eurodeposit market is a counterpart to the foreign-exchange swap market. Indeed, swaps are rooted in deposits and neither Eurodeposits nor foreign-exchange swaps can be efficiently traded without the assistance of the others. That's why they're together in one dealing room. (If it's not yet clear how all these transactions work, don't worry. We've done no more than introduce the players at this point. We'll meet them again.) But first let's go backstage to learn a little more about the fundamentals of this business, to see how money actually moves internationally.

The Mechanism of Foreign-Exchange Transfers

When a corporate treasurer needs to make a payment abroad, she will invariably deal with a commercial bank. Banks around the world are central to the foreign-exchange market simply because their demand liabilities (sight deposits, or "current account" balances) serve as the principal means of payments within any financial system. In all but the most primitive economies, the overwhelming majority of all payments are effected through a transfer of ownership of demand deposits from payer to payee, by sending instructions to the banks involved via check, written transfer orders, phone, telegraphic instruction (wire transfer), or, increasingly, linked computer networks.

Hence the treasurer making or intending to make payment to someone in another country needs first to obtain ownership, directly or indirectly, of a demand deposit in a bank in the foreign country, which can subsequently be transferred to the foreign recipient of the funds. Even very large companies rarely maintain current accounts in foreign countries, and there is really no need for it. Most major banks maintain demand-deposit accounts with their foreign correspondent banks, preferably those that are members of the respective national clearing system. They make funds in these accounts available to their clients and transfer them to the foreign payee according to the instructions of the client.

EXAMPLE 2.1 **A Foreign-Exchange Transfer**

Here's an example of such a transaction. Assume a Hong Kong–based firm, Wing On Company, wishes to pay its Singaporean supplier S$1 million. An officer of the treasury department of Wing On will ask a foreign-exchange trader (the "corporate dealer") at his bank, Hang Seng Bank, to "sell" him S$1 million.[5] The bank will quote a rate, say, HK$21 per Singapore dollar. It will then initiate two simultaneous transfers:

1. Hang Seng Bank will debit Wing On's current account in Hong Kong for HK$21,000,000 (and credit that amount to its correspondent bank's account).
2. It will instruct its correspondent bank in Singapore (one in which it keeps a current account balance) to debit Hang Seng's account and credit the amount to the account of the Singaporean firm within the banking system of Singapore.

This illustrates the fact that international transactions really involve two simultaneous payments involving each national system. In our example, there was a transfer of funds in the Hong Kong system from the payer to his bank, and a parallel payment within Singapore from the Hong Kong bank's account with the Singaporean bank to that of the payee. Of course, the receipt of foreign funds would involve two transfers in the opposite direction.

We have seen that the clearing of foreign-exchange transactions takes place after the conclusion of a deal. The date of the "delivery" for the actual payment of funds is called the **value date**, by convention two business days after the trade date. This is when funds are debited from the account of the seller and credited to that of the buyer. How is this actually done?

Strictly speaking, payments themselves do not move internationally. Instead, domestic payments are made for international transactions. In a foreign-exchange transaction, a payment in one national system is related to a payment in another. This requires a system of correspondent accounts, just as domestic check or giro payments[6] make it

---

[5]In reality, the employee may call several banks in order to get the best rate—that is, the lowest U.S.-dollar price for S$1 million. For an interesting review of "shopping practices," see Laura White Dillon, "The Education of U.S. Multinationals," *Institutional Investor* (International ed.), Jan. 1980, pp. 79–84.

[6]In a check-transfer system, funds are transferred only when the payee deposits a check sent by the payor. In a giro payments system, the payor instructs his bank to transfer the funds to the payee's bank.

necessary that payer and payee have demand accounts with banks that in turn are plugged into a national clearing system. The essence of such a clearing system is a carefully structured network of working balances that banks keep with each other—so-called *correspondent relationships*. The structure is designed to minimize account relationships and the number of transactions, and yet provide the account holder with some alternative, so that competition assures a satisfactory level of service. The banks where the accounts are held get compensated, through idle balances or fees, for the bookkeeping chores that they perform.

For international payments, the same principles apply. Banks engaged in international transactions maintain account relationships with banks abroad. At first sight, this might require that all full-service banks maintain at least one, or probably several, accounts in virtually every country of the world. In reality, very few banks do this. Banks can and do use the accounts of their *correspondents* abroad. This system minimizes the number of accounts to be held. However, the tying up of expensive funds in "nostro accounts" (demand accounts held in a foreign country)[7] becomes a much more significant phenomenon: the subsequent need to minimize account relationships explains the phenomenon of *vehicle currency,* whereby one currency acts as the exchange vehicle for the others. (See Box 2.1.)

In an attempt to minimize both the number of accounts as well as the funds tied up therein, internationally active banks have a natural tendency to concentrate their accounts in one country, using that country's banking system to clear international transactions. Consider three currencies: the Japanese yen, the Malaysian ringgit, and the Thai baht.

BOX 2.1

Vehicle Currencies

The U.S. dollar is the currency of choice for many international transactions. Clearly, there is nothing in the world financial system that says that the U.S. dollar has to continue in this role. Indeed, in Europe a substantial amount of trading is done against the German mark instead of against the dollar, and in Asia the yen is often used as a vehicle currency. How do international banks agree on the country in which they will maintain their accounts? Three factors seem to influence which currency will be chosen as the vehicle currency:

1. Banks tend to concentrate their accounts in the country with which they do a relatively large volume of transactions anyway. In other words, a country is a prime candidate for being selected as a place to hold balances if it has a large economy that gives rise to a correspondingly large volume of international transactions, not only in terms of traditional exports and imports but also in terms of borrowing, lending, and service transactions.

2. A country's attractiveness is enhanced if it facilitates the management of working balances. Because payments and disbursements are uncertain and working balances are costly to maintain, a country is in an advantageous position if it has good facilities available to meet the bank's unexpected needs. (For example, a bank may want to borrow additional funds on short notice, at reasonable rates, when a given working balance is deficient, or to lay off funds profitably when liquid balances are unexpectedly large.) In short, a country with an efficient market that provides depth, breadth, and liquidity is more likely to be where balances are held.

---

[7]The accounts held by a bank abroad are called "nostro accounts" or *due from* accounts; those held by foreign banks with a domestic bank are known as "vostro accounts" or *due to* accounts.

3. The country should exhibit a pattern of political and economic stability. Foreign owners of working balances are particularly concerned that they be able to enter into transactions without interference of any kind from the local authorities. The technical term for this freedom is *nonresident convertibility*. Nonresident account holders seek the freedom to increase or decrease their balances in the course of transactions with other nonresidents. Therefore, law and order, communication facilities, and commercial contracts must be upheld consistently by the local government. As a part of political and economic stability, it helps to have stable prices, interest rates, and exchange-rate conditions.

The selection of a country by the international banking community does not happen through an organized vote, but through the long-term drift of account relationships. For many centuries, London and the British pound sterling have served the international financial community well. However, since World War I, New York and the U.S. dollar have gradually taken over and remained prominent since World War II. Any potential competitor to the dollar would have to provide a better service to the international community in terms of the criteria listed above.

Banks from Malaysia and Thailand do not need to hold working balances with each other as long as they both have accounts in Japan. Consider how Bumiputra Bank, in Malaysia, can sell ringgit for baht (which it needs, to make a payment to Bangkok Bank in Thailand). Bumiputra will use its own currency to purchase yen, and simultaneously sell yen for Thai baht in order to make the payment. To effect these two transactions, the following clearing transfers are necessary: (1) an international transfer from Malaysia to Japan, involving the debiting and crediting of accounts in Kuala Lumpur and Tokyo, respectively; (2) a transfer within the clearing system of Japan involving the debiting and crediting of accounts that Bumiputra and Bangkok maintain with banks in Japan; (3) an international transfer between Japan and Thailand, involving the debiting of Bangkok Bank's account in Tokyo and a credit to an account in Thailand. In the end there is no need for banks to have account relationships anywhere but in Japan. Of course, the greater the number of countries in the system, the greater the saving if they all decide to hold their working balances in one country.

The economics of clearing and the pattern of account relationships have also affected foreign-exchange trading practices. *Today, most foreign exchange is traded against the U.S. dollar.* To a certain extent this trend has become reinforcing: because most institutions hold dollar accounts, most transactions in a given currency will be done against dollars; thus, the market is so active and liquid that traders find it advantageous to go through the dollar whenever they want to obtain a third currency. The dollar's position is further reinforced by the fact that the U.S. banking system provides opportunities for adjusting cash balances until late in the "world business day" that begins in mid-Pacific.

CHIPS

Technology is now central to the clearing of transactions. In the United States, where almost all foreign-exchange transactions are cleared, a computer-based **Clearing House Interbank Payments System** (CHIPS) handles tens of thousands of payments representing transactions worth several hundred billion dollars each day. CHIPS can be thought of as a sort of international bankers' play money. During the day, all international banks making dollar payments to one another pass this CHIPS money to one another in lieu of real money. At the end of the day the game-master totals up everybody's CHIPS money to see the net amount that is owed by who to whom, and real money ("Fed funds") is transferred in that amount.

EXAMPLE 2.2   A Payment Through CHIPS

The working of CHIPS can best be explained using an example. Assume an Italian businessman needs to pay U.S. dollars for a shipment of Brazilian coffee. He would contact his local bank, Credito Italiano, to make arrangements for the transfer. Credito Italiano will cable the New York correspondent bank with whom it has an account relationship to credit the bank of the Brazilian coffee exporter. For simplicity, assume that the exporter's bank has as a correspondent one of the more than 100 CHIPS members, say Citibank.

Figure 2.4 shows in flow chart form how a hypothetical payment between Credito Italiano and the Banco do Brasil would run through the U.S. clearing system. Citibank either confirms that Credito Italiano has sufficient funds, or, through authorization by its

Figure 2.4   *Payments Clearing in the Foreign-Exchange Market*

International Payments and U.S. Clearing

Abroad		New York
Early in the day	Prior to 4:30 P.M. East coast time	After 6:30 P.M. East coast time

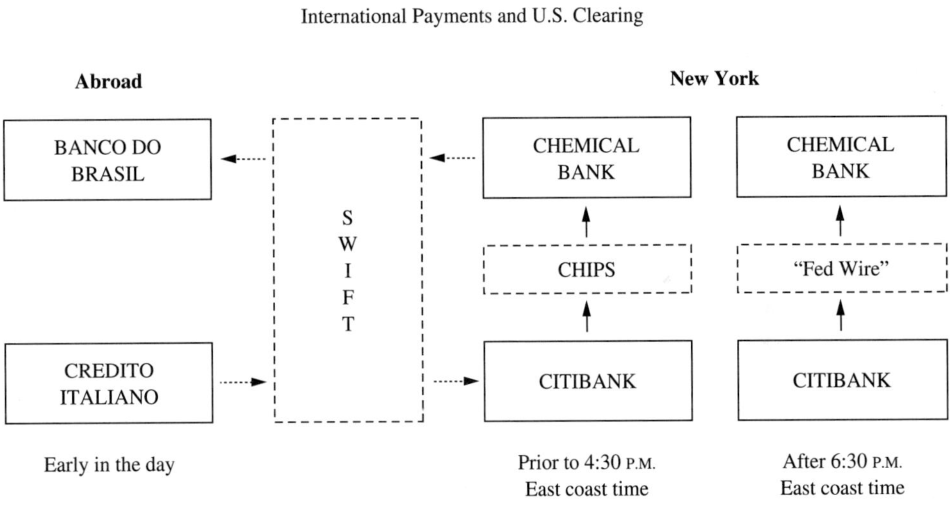

Steps in the transfer of funds resulting from a foreign-exchange transaction:

1. Credito Italiano instructs Citibank — using SWIFT — to debit its account and transfer the dollar funds to Chemical Bank "for credit to the account of Banco do Brasil."

2. Citibank debits Credito Italiano's account and transfers the funds through CHIPS. In effect, it sends the equivalent of an electronic check to CHIPS, where Chemical Bank's account is credited the very same day.

3. At the end of the day any debits and credits between Citibank and Chemical are settled by a transfer of "fed funds" — i.e., deposits held by member banks at various branches of the Federal Reserve System.

4. Chemical credits Banco do Brasil's account and notifies that bank through the SWIFT system.

NOTE: Dotted lines indicate information flows, while solid arrows indicate a transfer of funds.

Source: Adapted from Ian H. Giddy, "Measuring the World Foreign Exchange Market," *Columbia Journal of World Business,* Winter 1979, pp. 36–48.

credit officer, extends credit to it. In either case, the computer prompts payment of the appropriate amount to the correspondent bank of the payee's bank, for example, Chemical Bank, within minutes or at least within hours, depending on how long the bank's internal decision and approval process takes.

In earlier times, the relay mechanism outlined in Example 2.2 used to be handled by check, but nowadays a computer-based facility merely requires a few entries into the system. Each bank has a code number; all the relevant information about the payment is entered into a computer terminal, and the authenticity of the payment is checked. At the end of the day, the CHIPS clearing-house funds get netted out and real money is paid (see Box 2.2, Clearing House Funds Versus Fed Funds in the U.S. Market).

In addition to providing a tabulation for all the member banks of CHIPS at the end of the day, the system also permits members to look at those payments that are "on-line" (in storage, awaiting approval), so that better information on available funds can be used for the member bank's credit decisions. If a credit officer knows that a certain account will be credited later in the day, he or she may be more willing to grant credit. Although its operating procedures are highly technical, CHIPS operations have important economic implications: (1) The role of the U.S. dollar as a world vehicle currency is influenced by the relative operating efficiency and safety of its payment mechanism. (2) Its handling of failures to settle accounts, which have the potential to initiate a chain reaction leading to a worldwide liquidity crisis, makes such occurrences isolated events. (3) The specific roles of individual banks in the dollar clearing system have important implications for worldwide correspondent banking relationships and, therefore, market share and profits.

The improvement in the domestic U.S. clearing system utilized for international transactions has been followed by improvement in international bank communications that link national clearing systems. After seven years of cooperative efforts, banks from 17 countries formed the Society for Worldwide Interbank Financial Telecommunications (**SWIFT**) that began operations at the end of 1977. SWIFT consists of national data concentration centers, which are connected by leased telephone lines to operating centers in Belgium, the Netherlands, and the United States. Computer terminals at the participating banks are linked to the national concentration centers. With SWIFT, a message can be sent from one bank to another as speedily as with Telex but error free, more securely, and at lower cost. SWIFT has largely replaced interbank transfers made by check or draft because of the advantage of speed while at the same time providing for immediate verification of accuracy and authenticity. The system has over a thousand members in several dozen countries, giving it essentially global coverage. Ultimately, there may be provisions for nonbank clients to plug directly into the SWIFT system of a bank, in order to eliminate the remaining source of errors in international money transfers. In essence, SWIFT provides member banks that operate through correspondents the same payment service as that available to the few multinational banks that have an extensive network of wholly owned affiliates.

We have seen that in order to service clients, banks maintain accounts ("working balances") with banks abroad. The management of these working balances is at the core of modern foreign-exchange trading.

Working balances maintained by traders can be viewed as inventories of foreign currency assets and are known as *long* positions. Because these foreign currency assets have to be bought with another currency—for instance, the domestic currency—the bank is *short* with respect to the domestic currency. A long position in a certain foreign currency always implies a short position in another currency. What determines the size of a trader's

BOX 2.2

Clearing-House Funds Versus Fed Funds in the U.S. Market

Because of the significance of the U.S. dollar in foreign-exchange transactions, the student of foreign-exchange markets should be aware of an institutional oddity that exists in the U.S. payment system. Unlike other countries, the United States has a two-stage clearing process for certain payments. U.S. banks that are members of the Federal Reserve System submit checks for collection to the local clearing house and receive credit in so-called clearing-house funds. It is only on the next day that these credits are then settled by transferring balances on the books of the respective federal reserve bank (in fed funds). Such funds count as required reserves and can be lent to other banks at interest, the "fed funds rate." They are, therefore, more useful than clearing-house funds.

In the United States all transactions were settled in this way. There was no problem, because most transactors received and paid out the same volume of funds. However, foreign-exchange transactions that involved the clearing of funds in two different systems resulted in an institutional phenomenon variously referred to as the weekend effect, the Wednesday effect, or the Thursday-Friday effect.

When spot foreign exchange was sold (or bought) on a Wednesday, delivery of funds was on the second business day, that is, on Friday. Assume such a transaction involved a sale of deutschemarks (DM) for dollars. On Friday, the buyer of the marks received the amount specified in the form of a credit to his account in Frankfurt, and the funds could be used on the very same day to make payments or to lend them out at interest.

The receiver of the dollar funds also obtained a credit, but in the form of a balance in the local U.S. clearing house. He now had to wait until the next business day to obtain "good" funds, that is, fed funds. The next business day after Friday, however, was Monday. This time lag allowed the seller of the dollar to use the funds another two days over the weekend before he had to settle in fed funds. Thus the buyer of the deutschemarks had a special incentive for doing the transaction on a Wednesday; on any other day, the score would have been equalized. To compensate the seller of the deutschemarks (who was the receiver of the dollars) the buyer had to give him a somewhat better rate—that is, more dollars per DM—in order to make up the loss of interest that the seller incurred by trading dollars on Wednesday.

Prior to 1981, all payments were done on this basis. Since then, however, wire payments through the Clearing House Interbank Payments System (CHIPS) are settled after 4:30 P.M. Eastern Standard Time on the same day; fed funds transactions are cleared for banks until 6 P.M. through the Fed Wire system. Payments by check, however, still follow the two-stage clearing process.

foreign-currency position? First, working balances are a function of (a) the size of the transactions in each currency and (b) the uncertainty associated with the flow of disbursements (debits) and receipts (credits). Second, the size of the position is also influenced by (c) the cost of holding the funds and (d) the opportunities for profit from holding these balances.

The cost of maintaining a long position is essentially the cost of the domestic funds that the bank must acquire on the liability side of the balance sheet to finance the foreign assets. Thus opportunities for profit stem from the possibility that the position held will appreciate as the foreign currency increases in relative value (after adjusting for different interest rates), from the ability to service customers at competitive rates, and, perhaps, from ancillary business (such as money transfers with float and trade financing).

Foreign-Exchange Dealing and Quotations

The foreign-exchange market has no physical location—it is a telephone market, working directly between banks and their clients, sometimes with specialized brokers bringing parties together. The bulk of activity occurs between banks located in London, New York, and Tokyo, as Figure 2.5 shows.

Changes in net foreign-exchange positions arise continuously as banks deal with their corporate clients. In order to accommodate those customers effectively without holding large inventories, banks rely on the *interbank market*.[8] Indeed, interbank trading for most major banks accounts for 90 percent or more of total transactions volume. This phenomenon comes about because of liquidity and information requirements. Only a bank that is active in the interbank market can buy and sell foreign exchange in substantial amounts—that is, adjust its positions quickly by having ready access to many counterparties. Furthermore, profitable foreign-exchange trading requires the acquisition of timely and relevant information. Although traders are provided with expensive monitoring equipment, in the final analysis, detailed and timely information about the state of the market and the actions of the various players comes only from continuous, active, individual participation. It is only the traders' access to detailed information and their skill in interpreting it that allows them to take positions that are profitable over time.

Figure 2.5   *Foreign-Exchange Market Turnover in Some Major Centers*

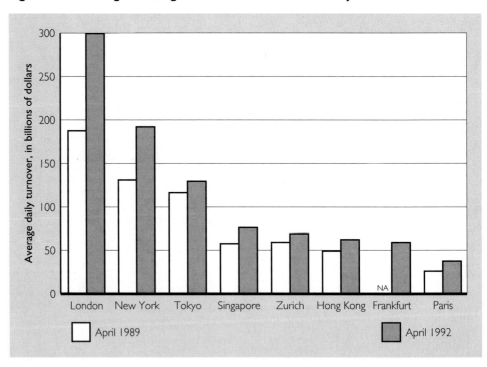

Source: Bank of England.

---

[8]For greater detail, see Thomas M. Campfield and John G. O'Brien, "Foreign Exchange Trading Practices: The Interbank Market," in Abraham George and Ian Giddy, eds., *International Finance Handbook* (New York: Wiley, 1983), vol. 1; or Julian Walmsley, *The Foreign Exchange Handbook* (New York: Wiley, 1983).

Banks seek to control the risks they take. Most do so by limiting the size of positions that traders can take. The allocation of these limits is influenced mainly by the bank's strategic objectives with respect to foreign-exchange trading, by currencies, by the credit-worthiness of counterparties, and by each dealer's track record. Regulatory capital requirements imposed by the Federal Reserve, the Bank of England, and other banking authorities increasingly play a role in the determination of trading-position controls. Application 2.3, entitled At the End of the Day, offers a simplified example of the development of a trading-risk limit based on the volatility of exchange rates.

The foreign-exchange market moves with the sun (see Box 2.3). Technically, the trading day starts in Tokyo, although traders there will be in touch early in the morning with their colleagues on the West Coast of the United States to obtain closing prices and information regarding market conditions. Thus foreign-exchange rates are continually changing; the market never sleeps. As foreign-exchange positions are always subject to risk, banks have a policy of keeping their overnight positions at the end of the day much smaller than those during the day, often referred to as *daylight limits*. Because many large international banks now have affiliates and trading operations in financial centers around the globe, attempts have been made to avoid the constraints on trading imposed by the necessity to reduce positions (inventories) toward the end of the trading day by passing on any ending positions to the "next" affiliate; it becomes that unit's starting position. In this case, decisions to buy and sell are not constrained by the necessity to reduce or build up inventories in various currencies to levels that are optimal from a trading standpoint. However, difficulties with profit allocations among various affiliates and related problems with tax and other governmental regulations have made the implementation of the concept of global foreign-exchange books elusive.[9]

BOX 2.3

The Global Foreign-Exchange Market

"A 24-hour market knowing no national boundaries without any central meeting place." This description is true of the foreign-exchange market. But it is also a market in which a large part of the business is concentrated in three financial centers—New York, London, and Tokyo—each striving to increase its share.

By most counts London remains the leader. Despite the relative stability of the intra-European currency relationships, volume continues to increase. A large part of the market in French francs, Swiss francs, Italian lira, and Spanish pesetas is in London. One factor favoring London over New York is the increasing number of transactions that are going directly between European currencies: French francs exchanged for German marks, for example, instead of through the U.S. dollar. Still, probably between 80 and 90 percent of all deals continue to be conducted in dollars.

Tokyo dominates in the Asian time zone, and is replaced by Frankfurt, Switzerland, Paris, and London as the sun moves west. The day's trading reaches its peak during European waking hours. New York, five hours behind London, is most active during the morning when Europe is open, but during the afternoon the market quietens, spreads widen, and rates become more volatile. Foreign-exchange managers know that among the worst times to trade is after New York closes but before Sydney has taken up the baton.

---

[9]An example can be seen in Citibank's transactions in the 1970s, in which foreign-exchange positions were passed on to the Nassau Branch and "parked" overnight, allegedly to circumvent the foreign-exchange controls and tax regulations of certain European countries. For an account, see "Close Encounters," *The Wall Street Journal*, Sept. 14, 1982, p. 1.

In share of trading, the rising star is yen/mark dealing, which may have reached fifth place in volume. The busiest markets are those trading in dollar/mark, dollar/yen, dollar/sterling, and dollar/Swiss franc.

There is no systematic measurement system for the world's foreign-exchange market, although the Bank for International Settlements in Basle conducts a survey from time to time. The results of one such survey are summarized in the accompanying table.

Foreign-Exchange Market Turnover
(billions of dollars)

Country	Net turnover (monthly total)	Share (of 10-country total)
United Kingdom	$3,740	27.8%
United States	2,580	19.2
Japan	2,300	17.1
Switzerland	1,140	8.5
Singapore	1,100	8.2
Hong Kong	931	6.9
Australia	570	4.2
France	520	3.9
Canada	300	2.2
Netherlands	260	1.9

Source: Bank for International Settlements. Data are for April 1989.

Foreign-exchange quotations provided by a trader reflect both market conditions and the trader's desire to buy or sell the currency. For example, the senior traders in any dealing room might get a feel for the market by reviewing the news on their terminals. If markets are volatile they might get up especially early and call from their homes colleagues in dealing rooms of the bank that are several time zones ahead to discuss the news and the market's reaction. After discussions with management inside and contacts outside the bank, and after checking markets for gold and various financial instruments, traders might arrive at their own quotes on the basis of the desired position in the currency (or currencies) for which they have primary responsibility. Of course, the experienced trader will make sure that her intent is not too obvious in order to avoid giving counterparties useful information.

How do traders communicate quotes in the market? Foreign-exchange dealings are conducted by banks over the "wire"; there is no central meeting place. Thus efficient information regarding rates and information that has a bearing on rates is required. Indeed, the investment in the costly communication facilities of any major trading operation is a significant aspect of the business. Traders usually give two numbers when quoting foreign-exchange rates. For example, in a DM/$ quote by a *European* bank of 17060/17070, the deal would indicate commitment to buy dollars at DM1.7060 per U.S. dollar and sell dollars at DM1.7070, following the classic trader's principle: "buy low, sell high."

Prior to 1978, a U.S. bank would have quoted the DM at US$0.5858 bid/0.5862 offer, if it had the same view of the market. Unfortunately for novices in foreign exchange, the advent of international brokerage and worldwide data systems like Reuters caused the transition to an indirect, or "European" way of quoting foreign exchange in the U.S.

market, too. This means that a quote of 1.7060/70 by a U.S. dealer signals his interest in buying deutschemarks at 1.7070 per dollar and selling them for 1.7060. To compound the confusion, 1.7060 is still referred to as "bid" rate for U.S. dollars, 1.7070 the "offer" (or "ask"). (To avoid going broke, the dealer must obtain more DMs per dollar than he sells.) Unfortunately, this practice causes difficulties for students of foreign-exchange markets in the United States. To make things worse, there are exceptions: pounds sterling, Irish punts, and the European Currency Unit (the ECU), for example, are quoted in "direct" terms (for example, US$1.72 per pound).

With modern telecommunications, dealers obtain rate information through the FX "page" of one of the data transmittal services, such as Reuters, Telerate, and others. Table 2.2 depicts a typical foreign-exchange screen and explains how outright forward rates can be calculated from spot quotations and "swap points." The rule for banks is to buy low, sell high, and seek a higher spread in the forward market than in the spot, because of less liquidity in the former.

When on the phone, traders will not quote the full rate but simply the last two decimal points—for example, "60 and 75"—as professionals know perfectly well what numbers come in front at any moment in time. Suppose in response to a Swiss franc/ U.S. dollar quote of SF1.5360/75 per dollar, a corporation sells the trader in Zurich $1 million. Before filling out the purchase voucher,[10] the trader will say loudly to his colleagues, "We get 1 million U.S. at 60," upon which the chief trader might adjust the rates to, perhaps, 55/70 if he wants to avoid further purchases of dollars. Quotes among

Table 2.2   ***Foreign-Exchange Quotations.***   Quotations would be shown in this manner on a typical monitor in a foreign-exchange dealing room.

INTERBANK FOREIGN EXCHANGE					
	SPOT	I MO	3 MOS	6 MOS	12 MOS
1113 DMK	182 40/50	39/37	107/105	202/198	290/282
1114 SFC	153 60/75	32/29	96/93	197/191	372/352
1112 FFL	607 10/20	113/121	345/365	675/700	1265/1340
1115 DFL	206 10/30	38/37	105/102	199/195	281/271
1116 YEN	153 08/18	27/25	85/82	172/168	280/270
1110 CAN	133 22/25	11/13	25/28	86/92	180/200
1111 STG	154 15/25	57/56	162/160	293/289	589/590
1117 ECU	113 22/32				

Because time is money, dealers use a kind of shorthand to quote rates. Typically, the trader will say: "Marks are 40/50, 39/37, 107/105, 202/198, 290/282." This means that the spot rate for one US$ is DM1.8240/50 and the 1-, 3-, 6-, and 12-month forward rates for the U.S. dollar, from a German bank's perspective, are DM 1.8201 bid, 1.8213 offer; 1.8133 bid, 1.8145 offer; etc. These rates are obtained by subtracting the "points" 39/37, 107/105, etc., from the bid and ask prices for spot U.S. dollar. A descending order of the points means they should be subtracted from the spot rate (the dollar is trading at a discount on the forward market). If the U.S. dollar is worth more in the forward market (trading at a premium), traders would quote the lower adjustment points first, signaling that they would have to be added to spot bid/ask rates. The logic is that bid/ask spreads tend to become wider for longer maturities. (This fact can be used to double-check forward rate quotations.)

---

[10]Also referred to as the *ticket;* this procedure is becoming more and more automated as the use of minicomputers spreads in trading rooms.

traders of major banks are good for up to $5 million or the equivalent if it is a major currency. Otherwise traders will specify the amount. If a trader is unwilling to commit himself he will add, ''for indication only.''

The difference between the buy and sell rates is the **spread** for the trader. If he is not interested in dealing at all, he will quote with a very wide spread between bid and ask. If he wishes to purchase a currency, he will raise the bid price, and likewise, if he is interested only in selling, he will lower the sell (or ask) price. If he is interested in volume, dealing on both sides of the market, he would naturally quote in such a way as to show very narrow spreads between bid and ask. Still, the extent to which traders will reduce their spreads is limited, because the spread is one source of trading profit.

Not only does information flow among banks and other foreign-exchange market participants in a given market—say, New York—but foreign exchange is traded frequently among banks in many national markets. For instance, a bank in New York that is looking for Canadian dollars may check quotes for that currency not only with other U.S. banks, but also with banks in Canada as well as selected banks in, say, London. Because of time differences, London banks have been trading foreign exchange for five or six hours prior to the opening of the New York market. In turn, banks in the Middle East, particularly Bahrain and Kuwait, have been trading even earlier, and they are preceded by those in the Far East countries, particularly Singapore, Hong Kong, and Tokyo. Indeed, foreign exchange is being traded 24 hours a day, somewhere in the world.

Cross Rates

Quotations for rates between third currencies—such as the number of Mexican pesos per Canadian dollar—are called **cross-rate** quotations. These are easily calculated from direct quotations and are best explained by means of an example. Cross-rate calculations are provided daily by financial publications; an example is the table taken from the May 5, 1993, *Wall Street Journal* (see Table 2.3).

Table 2.3   *Cross-Rates for Major Currencies*

Key Currency Cross Rates Late New York Trading May 4, 1993

	Dollar	Pound	SFranc	Guilder	Yen	Lira	D-Mark	FFranc	CdnDlr
Canada	1.2710	1.9906	.89476	.71844	.01153	.00086	.80657	.23943	....
France	5.3085	8.314	3.7371	3.0007	.04815	.00361	3.3688	....	4.1766
Germany	1.5758	2.4680	1.1093	.89074	.01429	.00107	....	.29684	1.2398
Italy	1470.0	2302.3	1034.85	830.93	13.333	....	932.86	276.91	1156.6
Japan	110.25	172.67	77.614	62.320	....	.07500	69.964	20.769	86.74
Netherlands ...	1.7691	2.7708	1.2454	....	.01605	.00120	1.1227	.33326	1.3919
Switzerland	1.4205	2.2248	....	.80295	.01288	.00097	.90145	.26759	1.1176
U.K.	.63849	....	.44948	.36091	.00579	.00043	.40518	.12028	.50235
U.S.	....	1.5662	.70398	.56526	.00907	.00068	.63460	.18838	.78678

Source: Telerate

Source: *The Wall Street Journal*, May 5, 1993.

EXAMPLE 2.3 **A Cross-Rate Calculation**

From the US$-based quotations for the New Zealand dollar (NZ$) and the Indonesian rupiah (IR), we can calculate a *cross rate* for the NZ$ in terms of the rupiah. The *Straits Times* of Singapore quoted the following rates on January 13, 1993:

New Zealand dollar	1.9552 NZ$/US$
Indonesian rupiah	2054 IR/US$

From these, we calculate the cross rate by dividing the rate for the rupiah by the rate for the New Zealand dollar:

$$\frac{2054 \text{ IR/US\$}}{1.9552 \text{ NZ\$/US\$}} = 1050.5 \text{ IR/NZ\$}$$

In reality, a trader would take into account transactions costs, notably the bid and offer spreads, in calculating a cross-rate bid or offer rate. For example, if P.T. Astra, an Indonesian company, wanted to buy New Zealand dollars, ANZ Bank might calculate its quotation from the following bid and offer rates:

New Zealand dollar	1.9535–1.9560 NZ$/US$
Indonesian rupiah	2050–2075 IR/US$

We can calculate the cross rate by dividing the offer rate for the rupiah by the bid rate for the New Zealand dollar:

$$\frac{2075 \text{ IR/US\$}}{1.9535 \text{ NZ\$/US\$}} = 1062.2 \text{ IR/NZ\$}$$

The principle is that the dealer who gives the quotation must assume he has to purchase at the more expensive rate and sell at the lower rate. Put differently, the dealer gives the quotations as if he had to do two separate trades: selling U.S. dollars to Astra (for rupiah), and then selling New Zealand dollars to Astra (for U.S. dollars).

Triangular Arbitrage

Foreign exchange is traded in dozens of locations, so it should not be surprising that inconsistencies can arise from time to time. **Triangular arbitrage** helps eradicate some of these anomalies. This kind of profit-seeking entails using one currency to buy a second, using that to buy a third, and using the latter to buy the first: a triangle that leaves you where you started, perhaps with a bit of profit for your efforts.

Opportunities for triangular arbitrage arise from inconsistencies between **direct quotations** (in terms of the US$) and cross-rate quotations (third currencies against one another). Consider the following situation:

Direct quotations	Dutch guilders per US dollar	1.8315 DFl/US$
	Australian dollars per US dollar	1,4870 A$/US$
Cross-rate quotation	Dutch guilders per Australian dollar	1.2380 DFl/A$

Calculation of the implied cross-rate between guilders and Australian dollars gives 1.2317 DFl/A$, so there is apparently a triangular arbitrage opportunity between the guilder and the Australian dollar (the "Aussie"). The steps required to exploit the opportunity are sketched in Figure 2.6.

Figure 2.6   ***Triangular Arbitrage.***   This opportunity occurs when inconsistent quotations between three markets allow a profitable "round trip." The cross rate implied by dollar rates is DFI1.2317/A$, making it cheaper to exchange DFI for A$ through the US$ than directly.

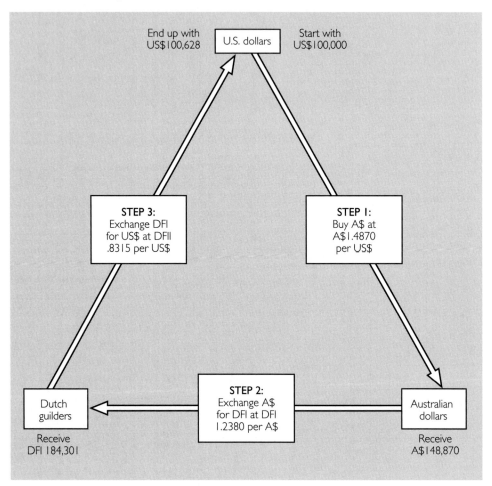

How Profits Are Made in the Trading Room

Arbitrage opportunities of the kind just described are rare; bid–offer spreads and other transactions costs eliminate most possibilities. How, then, do banks make profits in the trading room?

Trader talk is largely about the direction of the market, about supply and demand pressure, government actions, and market sentiment affecting, say, the value of the Japanese yen. It is not surprising that outsiders suppose that the great bulk of profits must be made from speculative positioning. This supposition is a myth. Yet another prevalent fallacy is that the profitability of trading can be measured by the bid–offer spread. Although some money can be made by positioning based on a "view" of the market's direction, and even though some fraction of the bid–offer spread can be earned by big interbank dealers, the bulk of trading profits of the bulk of trading rooms comes in fact from *customer business*. Let us examine each of these propositions in turn.

In the theater of finance, the trader is often the central character in the comedy of foreign exchange. Believing the myth himself, the trader thinks that his skill lies in understanding short-term trends in the market, that the best of his kind are able to anticipate the movements of foreign-exchange rates, interest rates, and the like. Profits, this theory holds, come from a better-than-average ability to "beat the market." Yet even in the best of circumstances, the evidence suggests, betting on price movements is not a sound business proposition.[11] Even the trading rooms of the best-regarded banks do not seem to be able to consistently position on the right side of the market. The foreign-exchange market is simply too efficient. Sometimes, when there is a continual slide or rise in a currency, dealers do seem to be able to make money. That is because they all gradually imitate those who have got it right, until the trend reverses itself. And few have been able to call the timing of the turn. So it is only in the midst of such a sustained trend that one seems to be able to make positioning profits. Occasionally a trader gains access to new information before everyone else, and sometimes a dealing room with a large share of the market seems to be able to influence prices. In both cases, however, the ability to make money comes from customers rather than from the bank's proprietary traders' skills.

Foreign-Exchange Brokers

Information on foreign-exchange rates is communicated to others either directly, or through a system of brokers that exists in many countries, including the United States and Canada. In the United States, dealing in foreign exchange in the interbank market may involve only U.S. domestic banks or may involve commercial banks abroad. To give an example, a large U.S. bank may receive in its network £6 million from U.S. exporters and, at the same time, experience a demand for £11 million from U.S. importers of British goods. The net requirement for the bank in this instance is £5 million. The U.S. bank will approach one or more brokers who specialize in the £/$ market for quotes on the £/$ rate. The value of the broker is in knowing "where the market is," that is, at which rates various banks are willing to sell sterling (and to purchase dollars).

Brokers also know who will deal with whom ("who will take which names"), as any bank is willing to deal with only a limited number of other banks, and each bank has limits on how much business it will do with any other bank. The setting of such limits is a credit decision made by bank officers responsible for evaluating the bank's exposure to defaults.[12]

The use of brokers provides anonymity to the participants until a rate is agreed upon, because knowing the other party may give dealers an insight into whether the other party is "long" or "short." Also, the use of brokers allows banks to economize on their contact with other market participants. Instead of calling half a dozen competitors, the trader will call one broker who is in contact with other banks to whom he will "show the quote." The broker is compensated by a commission. In the U.S. market, that commission has been traditionally 1/32 of 1 percent of the amount. Bills for commissions are presented separately, split between buyer and seller.

Many of the brokers, most of which are London based, have opened offices in the United States and the financial centers in the Far East. The advent of reliable and affordable international communication facilities via satellites and improved undersea cables has

---

[11]Alberic Braas and Charles N. Bralver, "An Analysis of Trading Profits: How Most Trading Rooms Really Make Money," *Journal of Applied Corporate Finance*, vol. 2, no. 4, 1990, pp. 85–90.

[12]The credit risk stems from the possibility that the other bank may be unable to deliver if it goes out of business.

Figure 2.7　　*The Foreign-Exchange Market: Brokers, Banks, and Clients*

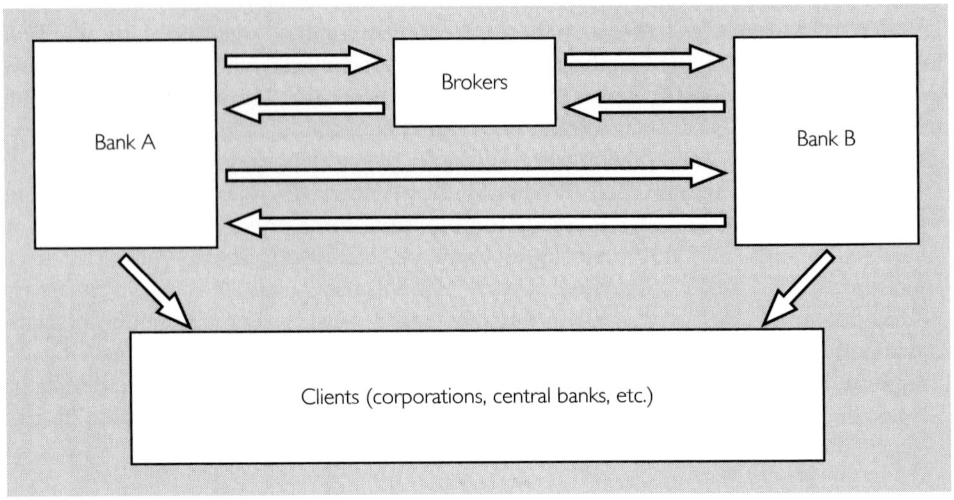

allowed them to link their offices through "open lines" and "squawkboxes." This puts brokers in centers thousands of miles apart virtually in the same room—and with their client banks who, in turn, have open lines to their brokers' offices.

Figure 2.7 illustrates the role of brokers in the foreign-exchange market.

New Foreign-Exchange Technology

Foreign-exchange market participants have traditionally communicated by telephone and telex, but changes in information technology have affected trading practices significantly. At the time of writing, a number of systems had been introduced to improve the information flow among bank participants in the foreign-exchange market. One, for example, provides a video retrieval system through which the principal banks who are subscribers flash their currency quotations on the screen. These services are an important source of price information for nonbanks, too, taking away some of the advantages of bank dealers. Most bank traders still conclude deals through the system of brokers or through direct contact, because screen quotes are "for information only."

The next logical advancement, not yet adopted to any significant degree, would be automation of foreign-exchange dealings, permitting traders to conclude their transactions electronically. Systems that automatically execute matching bids and offers, and even generate hard copy, post-trade confirmations, and payment and delivery instructions, have been proposed. Rate information is increasingly supplied in digital form, permitting analysis by special computer-software packages. The capital investment in modern workstations for dealers reportedly approaches $100,000 per dealer, representing a significant factor in dealing-room economics.

This concludes our look at the foreign-exchange market. We have seen that although some of the business is driven by international trade and investment, the great bulk of trading occurs among professional traders. In the so-called interbank market, trading occurs at a rapid pace, in very stylized fashion, and governed by a largely unwritten code of professional behavior. We now turn to a closely related market, in which transactions are conducted side by side with foreign exchange: the Eurocurrency dealing business.

The Mechanics of the Eurodollar Market

It's time to return to the traders on the other side of the dealing room, those whose focus is the money market, the market for short-term depository, and other instruments. Their incentives and behavior are similar to those on the foreign-exchange side, but their basic product is different: it is the handling of bank time deposit rather than the transfer of current account balances. The fundamental instrument of the international money market is the Eurodollar deposit. Let's see how one is created, and what is done with it. In the next few pages we shall trace through the steps in the creation of a Eurodollar deposit, of interbank deposits between Eurobanks, and of a Eurodollar loan to a corporation.

First, let us suppose that Fosters Brewing, an Australian beverage company, decides that the slightly better rate that it can earn on a Eurodollar deposit in Sakura Bank's London branch[13] warrants shifting $1 million out of its Los Angeles bank time deposit and into a time deposit with that Eurobank in London. We use simple T-accounts to represent this transaction, starting with Table 2.4.

Upon maturity of its time deposit, Fosters Brewing gets money—a demand deposit—in its Los Angeles bank, Wells Fargo. Fosters than acquires a time deposit in Sakura Bank, London branch, by transferring ownership (payment) of the demand deposit in the U.S. bank to London (as shown in Table 2.5). A Eurodollar deposit has been created, substituting for an equivalent time deposit in a U.S. bank. To repay the time deposit, of course, the Los Angeles bank would have to reduce its loans by roughly $1 million.

Table 2.4   ***Mechanics of the Market: Step 1.***   Initial situation— Fosters Brewing's time deposit sits in a U.S. bank.

UNITED STATES Wells Fargo Bank	
	$1 million demand deposit
	$1 million time deposit due to Fosters Brewing

Table 2.5   ***Mechanics of the Market: Step 2.***   After a shift of funds into the Eurobank, a Eurodollar deposit has been created, substituting for the U.S. time deposit.

UNITED STATES Wells Fargo Bank		LONDON Sakura Bank	
	$1 million demand deposit due to Sakura Bank	$1 million demand deposit in Wells Fargo Bank	$1 million Eurodollar time deposit due to Fosters Brewing

---

[13]Chapter 3 explains why Eurocurrency deposits may pay higher rates than domestic deposits.

Back to Sakura Bank, whose dollar-deposit dealer has realized that he would be foolish to leave idle funds in a U.S. bank. If he does not immediately have a commercial borrower or government to which he can loan the funds, Sakura Bank's dealer will "place" the $1 million in the Eurodollar interbank market. In other words, he will deposit the funds in some other Eurobank. (Sakura Bank may also keep some portion of the $1 million in a U.S. bank as a working balance, but this portion is likely to be so small that we can neglect it.) The resulting situation is shown in Table 2.6.

We should perhaps emphasize that what has crossed the Atlantic to find a European home is not a demand deposit, but rather an interest-bearing time deposit, although with a maturity that may be as short as one day ("overnight"). Despite their name, Eurobanks tend not to perform one of the prime functions of banks—that is, they tend not to offer checking accounts. The Euromarket has no particular competitive advantage in the payments transfer function of banks, which continues to be done through the domestic payments system of each currency of denomination in the Euromarket. What Eurobanks do best is pure financial intermediation—taking fixed-term deposits and making loans, and in the process performing maturity transformation.

Notice that the role of the demand deposits held in U.S. banks is simply that of transferring funds from one party to another. Nobody holds on to these balances for very long; indeed, New York's CHIPS enables banks throughout the world to initiate and settle transfers of dollars within a matter of hours, with no loss of interest as a result of idle overnight balances.

If Barclay's Bank cannot immediately use the funds to make a loan, it will redeposit them in the interbank market. This process of redepositing may proceed through several Eurobanks before the $1 million finds its way to a final borrower. At each stage, the next bank will have to pay a slightly higher rate than the previous bank paid. However, the margins involved in the interbank market are very small, of the order of ⅛ of 1 percent. As a general rule, larger, better-known banks will receive initial deposits, whereas smaller banks will have to bid for deposits in the interbank market (that is, they will borrow from better-known banks).[14]

Table 2.6   *Mechanics of the Market: Step 3.*   Redeposit of funds in another Eurobank.

UNITED STATES Wells Fargo Bank		LONDON Sakura Bank	
	$1 million demand deposit due to Barclay's Bank	$1 million Eurodollar deposit in Barclay's Bank	$1 million Eurodollar time deposit due to Fosters Brewing
		Barclay's Bank	
	$1 million demand deposit in Wells Fargo Bank	$1 million Eurodollar time deposit due to Sakura Bank	

---

[14]This interbank redepositing of an initial Eurodollar deposit merely involves the passing of funds from bank to bank; it does not add to the final extension of credit in the financial markets. Only when the $1 million is lent to a borrowing corporation is credit effectively extended. So when one seeks to evaluate the credit-granting capacity of the Eurodollar markets, one has to net out interbank deposits.

The final step occurs when a Eurobank needs the funds to lend to a borrower. For the sake of simplicity, let us assume that Barclay's Bank uses the funds to make a loan to Ladbroke, the British betting and property concern. Barclay's Bank would make the loan by drawing on its newly acquired balance in a U.S. bank and giving ownership of $1m to Ladbroke. (In all likelihood Ladbroke would be drawing down on a previously made commitment from Barclay's Bank and will use the funds immediately to make payments.) Immediately after the loan is made, the position would be as shown in Table 2.7.

Loans made by Eurobanks are, in principle, quite similar to larger loans made domestically by U.S. banks. Borrowers can and do obtain very large amounts by borrowing from a syndicate of banks from different countries when the amount needed is greater than one Eurobank is willing to provide, and often have the option of borrowing in any of several currencies. Euroloans may be short term, for working capital or trade financing, or have maturities as long as 10 years. The latter would be designated as medium-term Eurocredits, although conceptually they are no different from their short-term counterparts. When a Eurocurrency loan or commitment has a maturity of more than six months, the interest rate is usually set on a "roll-over" basis: at the start of each three- or six-month period, it is reset at a fixed amount, say 1 percent, above the prevailing London interbank offer rate.

The upshot of the process described above is a shift from domestic to external financial intermediation. It is, however, by no means an automatic process, because three conditions have to exist before such a sequence of transactions can occur: (1) Eurodollar deposit interest rates must be high enough relative to domestic rates for Fosters Brewing to shift their funds to the Eurobank. (2) Eurodollar loan rates must be low enough to induce Ladbroke to borrow from Barclay's Bank rather than, say, from a U.S. bank. (3) The spread between Eurodollar deposit and loan rates must be sufficient to enable the Eurobanks to borrow and lend profitably. In addition, borrowers, depositors, and banks must have relatively free access to the market. Only if these conditions are present will the market continue to exist and grow along with the expansion of credit in general.

Table 2.7 *Mechanics of the Market: Step 4.* Funds are loaned to a final borrower.

UNITED STATES Wells Fargo Bank		LONDON Sakura Bank	
	$1 million demand deposit due to Ladbroke	$1 million demand deposit in Barclay's Bank	$1 million Eurodollar time deposit due to Fosters Brewing
		Barclay's Bank	
		$1 million loan to Ladbroke	$1 million Eurodollar time deposit due to Sakura Bank
		Ladbroke Company	
		$1 million demand deposit in Wells Fargo Bank	$1 million due to Barclay's Bank

Arbitrage Between the Foreign-Exchange and Eurocurrency Markets

This section is a prelude to Chapter 3, which explores the relationship between currencies and interest rates in greater detail. The most fundamental link between Eurocurrency interest rates and the foreign-exchange market is the so-called interest-rate parity theorem that results from arbitrage between the spot and forward markets and the Eurocurrency deposit markets. **Covered-interest arbitrage**, undertaken by large international banks, involves the rapid movement of funds between securities denominated in different currencies in order to profit from different *effective* rates of interest in different currencies after taking hedging costs into account. In the earlier section, The Dealing Room, the reader was introduced to the idea of a *money-market hedge*—where the foreign-exchange "swap" trader used a Eurocurrency deposit to hedge a forward-exchange contract, creating a link between the two markets. Returning to the dealing room, we will now see how the Eurodeposit trader can use the spot and forward foreign-exchange markets to hedge a Eurocurrency funding. This is a form of arbitrage designed to obtain cheaper funds by exploiting a market imperfection.

A typical arbitrage of this kind might occur where a Eurocurrency dealer borrows money for three months in one currency and invests the funds in a different currency. To avoid exchange risk, the dealer hedges the repayment of the currency borrowed by means of a forward-exchange contract. This will occur if and only if the cost of borrowing the foreign currency, adjusted for the cost of hedging, is lower than the cost of funds in the currency in which the funds are being invested.

An Example of Arbitrage

Assume, for example, that Banco de Bilbao's Brussels branch has just agreed to make a three-month loan in Belgian francs to a customer at Belgian franc LIBOR (London Interbank Offer Rate) plus ¼ percent, which works out to be 9⁷⁄₁₆ percent. A request is sent up to the dealing room's funding desk: "We need to fund BF25 million as cheaply as possible!" The funding manager asks the Eurocurrency trader about the rate at which Bilbao could borrow francs: "9⁵⁄₁₆ percent" is the reply. Then the Eurodollar trader cries out, "I can get U.S. dollar funds at 6 percent flat!"

"Let's see what that swaps into in Belgian francs," says the funding manger. He calls over to the franc-swap trader on the foreign-exchange desk. "What swap rate can you give us on three-month Belgian?"

"21–25 centimes. That means that if you want to buy francs spot and sell them forward, the swap points would be BF0.25. My spot bid price for Belgian is BF36.30."

Pause for a moment and reflect on what's being proposed in this example. Bilbao needs Belgian francs to make the loan, and will be paid back, with interest, in three months. As an alternative to funding this loan by borrowing francs at 9⁵⁄₁₆ percent, it may borrow the equivalent amount of U.S. dollars at 6 percent. The dollars will be sold for francs at the spot rate. At the same time the bank will buy dollars forward to lock in the exchange rate, because the Belgian francs to be received on the loan will be used to repay the dollars borrowed. Together these two transactions, sell spot and buy forward, constitute a *foreign-exchange swap* of the kind described earlier (hence the need for a quotation from the swap trader.) The effective cost, in Belgian franc terms, of the dollar funding can be measured by adjusting the dollar interest rate by the swap points, expressed as a percentage, as follows:

Step 1

Forward premium ($+$) or discount ($-$)

= [(forward − spot)/spot]

= [swap points/spot]

(Note that in this calculation, the exchange rates must be defined as number of local currency per unit of foreign currency.)

Step 2

Effective cost of foreign currency funding, hedged with a swap

= [1 + foreign interest rate] · [1 + forward premium or discount] − 1

Now let us apply this reasoning to the problem at hand. We are going to borrow dollars at 6 percent, change the money into francs at the spot rate of BF36.30 per dollar, and at the end repay the dollars (plus interest) by buying dollars forwards. The forward purchase of dollars will be at a higher cost, because the dollar is trading at a *premium* in the foreign-exchange market. (Remember the rule of thumb: if the swap points quoted are increasing, add the points to the spot to get the forward.) Thus the adjusted interest rate will be higher than 6 percent. But will it be more expensive or cheaper than straightforward franc borrowing? Here is the calculation:

Step 1

Forward premium ($+$) or discount ($-$)

= [swap points/spot]

= .25/36.30

= .0069

Step 2

Effective cost of foreign currency funding, hedged with a swap

= [1 + foreign interest rate] · [1 + forward premium or discount] − 1

= [1 + .06/4] · [1 + .0069] − 1

= .022

= 8.80% per annum

(Note that we had to express the foreign interest rate as a quarterly fraction, and then at the end annualize the result to compare it with the annual interest rate conventionally used.)

The result is that funding is cheaper if Bilbao funds itself in a different currency and uses the foreign-exchange swap market to eliminate any exchange risk! Banks routinely compare the cost of funding in this fashion. Eventually, of course, markets will eliminate any opportunity to profit from such arbitrage. An equilibrium would be produced so that the cost of funding is the same in both currencies. By a similar computation,

[1 + interest rate in currency X] · [1 + forward premium or discount] − 1

= interest rate in currency Y

To a close approximation this can be simplified as follows:[15]

Effective interest rate in Eurocurrency Y

= interest rate in Eurocurrency X + forward-exchange premium (positive) or discount (negative)

---

[15]For a detailed explanation, see Chapter 3.

This last statement is the *interest-rate parity theorem*. It says that covered-interest arbitrage equalizes effective interest rates in different currencies. For example, the interest rate on a dollar deposit must equal the interest rate on a German mark deposit covered in the forward market. We will encounter the interest-rate parity theorem in a number of different guises in this book. It is a key relationship in international finance, because it defines the link between the international money market and the foreign-exchange market. And it forms an important element in the structure of international interest rates, to be discussed in the next chapter.

SUMMARY

The foreign-exchange market is the means by which payments are made across national boundaries, jurisdictions and currencies; it is also the market in which one currency is traded for another, and hence sets the price for one currency in terms of the other. The Eurocurrency market is the means by which credit is provided and obtained in various individual currencies, outside of the normal jurisdiction of the country in which that currency originates. This chapter described how each is traded, and how the forward-exchange market provides a linkage between interest rates denominated in different currencies, setting the stage for a more detailed explanation of the relationship among interest rates in the global financial market.

CONCEPTUAL QUESTIONS

1. Explain the difference between the foreign-exchange market for European currencies and the Eurocurrency market.
2. What is a money-market hedge in the context of foreign-exchange trading?
3. What factors influence the choice of a currency as a vehicle currency?
4. What would you identify as the key source of profit making in the foreign-exchange dealing room?
5. Describe the role of brokers in the interbank foreign-exchange market.
6. Clarify the distinction between the functions of SWIFT and CHIPS.
7. Briefly explain the mechanics of a Eurodollar interbank deposit.
8. What is a foreign-exchange swap, and how is it used by Eurocurrency deposit dealers?
9. Explain the term *triangular arbitrage*. What costs might limit profitable exploitation of apparent opportunities for triangular arbitrage?

PROBLEMS

1. China Light, wishing to buy 10,000 British pounds, receives a quotation of US$1.6710–1.6750. How many U.S. dollars would the sterling cost the company? (Remember that the pound is quoted in U.S. dollars per pound sterling.)
2. Svenska Handelsbank provides the following quotation to Volvo for the Swedish krone: 6.3550–6.3600 kronor per dollar. How many dollars would Volvo receive if it made a 10-million-kronor investment in the United States?
3. Canadian dollars are normally quoted as number of C$ per US$. If Toronto Dominion Bank gives a quote of 1.1465–75, what quote would it give if asked to quote in "U.S. terms"?
4. Gunter Roeling, an Austrian entrepreneur, has been asked to give a quote on a sale of ski wax to the United States. Before he can do that, he wants to know how many Austrian schillings he would receive for every dollar he is paid. He would get paid $125,000 in either one or three months, depending on terms to be negotiated. His treasurer calls her bank, Creditanstalt Bankverein, and receives the following bid-offer quotations for schillings per U.S. dollar: spot 12.4300–12.4400, one month .0335–.0375, three months .0920–.1040. What should she tell Roeling?
5. Swiss Bank Corporation quotes bid-asked rates of SF2.5110–2.5140/$ and ¥245–246/$. What ¥/SF bid and asked cross rates would the bank quote?

6. WestDeutsche Landesbank quotes bid/ask spot rates of DM3.2446–3.2456/$ and BF35.30–35.40/$. What would WestLB's bid price for the Belgian franc in terms of deutschemarks?

7. You work for Société Générale, a French bank. One of your customers, a French perfume company that exports to Switzerland, would like to sell Swiss francs against French francs. Market rates are:

   (a) FF4.0340–4.0350/US$
   (b) SF1.6010–1.6020/US$

   Your customer would like an SF -rate from you. What rate would you quote?

8. If Intel, a U.S. firm, has DM liabilities whose present value is DM 3 million and it has DM assets whose present value is DM 2 million, how much does Intel gain or lose if the dollar depreciates from the current rate of DM2.5227/$ to DM2.2704/$ (a 10% depreciation?)

9. The Eurocurrency dealer at National Westminster Bank in London provides the following quotations for six-month Eurosterling deposits to the Central Bank of Taiwan: $11\frac{1}{16}$–$10\frac{15}{16}$. What rate could Taiwan expect to receive on funds placed with Natwest?

10. If the treasury department at Mitsubishi Bank in London is quoting the yen/pound exchange rates at 234–235 spot, $2\frac{1}{8}$–2 three months forward, would you expect that the same bank's Euroyen quotations to be above, below, or the same as its Eurosterling quotations?

11. Standard Chartered Bank in Hong Kong needs to fund a U.S. dollar loan. It obtains the following quotations: three-month Eurodollars $6\frac{1}{4}$–$6\frac{1}{8}$, three-month Euroyen $7\frac{3}{4}$–$7\frac{11}{16}$, yen/$ spot 140.25–140.35, three-month forward points .049–.052. Which is the cheapest way of funding the loan? Explain carefully how it would be done.

12. AT&T has a known cash payment of 50,000,000 Swiss francs to be made to a Swiss supplier in 100 days. The company wishes to fix or lock in the nominal dollar price of this payment using currently available rates. The spot rate available to AT&T is SF2.50/$, the forward rate for maturity in 100 days is SF2.465/$, and the company faces a dollar interest rate of 12 percent and a SF interest rate of 6 percent. Given this information, what is the smallest dollar price on its SF50,000,000 that AT&T can lock in with certainty? Explain the procedure the company will follow to obtain this price.

13. Sakura Bank in London is currently quoting 9% on 12-month Eurodollar deposits. It is also quoting 5 FF/$ and 5.25 FF/$ for spot and 12-month forward French francs, respectively. If a customer asks for a quote on depositing French francs, what interest rate should the bank quote? (choose one):

    (a) 9.25%
    (b) 4.25%
    (c) 4.00%
    (d) 14.45%

14. Using the quotations of spot rates and forward points listed in the accompanying table, calculate the *outright* one-month and three-month bid and offer forward rates for the German mark, the Japanese yen, and the ECU.

DOLLAR SPOT - FORWARD AGAINST THE DOLLAR						
May 18	**Day's spread**	**Close**	**One month**	**% p.a.**	**Three months**	**% p.a.**
UK†	1.5235 - 1.5340	1.5310 - 1.5320	0.41-0.39cpm	3.13	1.14-1.11pm	2.94
Ireland†	1.4970 - 1.5085	1.5005 - 1.5015	0.60-0.57cpm	4.68	1.70-1.65pm	4.46
Canada	1.2715 - 1.2780	1.2725 - 1.2735	0.16-0.20cdis	-1.70	0.61-0.67dis	-2.01
Netherlands .	1.8105 - 1.8250	1.8200 - 1.8210	0.63-0.66cdis	-4.25	1.74-1.80dis	-3.89
Belgium	33.20 - 33.50	33.30 - 33.40	11.00-13.00cdis	-4.32	31.00-35.00dis	-3.96
Denmark	6.1965 - 6.2480	6.2425 - 6.2475	2.50-3.70oredis	-5.96	7.50-10.00dis	-5.60
Germany	1.6140 - 1.6285	1.6235 - 1.6245	0.64-0.65pfdis	-4.77	1.75-1.77dis	-4.33
Portugal	154.65 - 155.75	154.70 - 154.80	143-153cdis	-11.48	410-450dis	-11.11
Spain-.........	123.40 - 123.95	123.70 - 128.80	90-100cdis	-9.21	260-290dis	-8.89
Italy	1476.25 - 1486.00	1476.75 - 1477.25	9.50-10.30liredis	-8.04	27.00-28.00dis	-7.45
Norway	6.8360 - 6.8960	6.8800 - 6.8850	2.50-3.05oredis	-4.84	6.80-7.80dis	-4.24
France	5.4410 - 5.4885	5.4775 - 5.4825	2.18-2.28cdis	-4.88	5.87-6.03dis	-4.34
Sweden	7.3250 - 7.3890	7.3675 - 7.3725	3.10-3.800redis	-5.62	9.10-10.20dis	-5.24
Japan	111.20 - 111.90	111.50 - 111.60	par-0.01ydis	-0.05	par-0.01dis	-0.02
Austria	11.3600 - 11.4500	11.4275 - 11.4325	3.90-4.20grodis	-4.25	10.90-11.70dis	-3.95
Switzerland .	1.4650 - 1.4820	1.4785 - 1.4795	0.25-0.28cdis	-2.15	0.71-0.76dis	-1.99
Ecu†	1.1990 - 1.2085	1.2025 - 1.2035	0.51-0.50cpm	5.04	1.37-1.35pm	4.52

Commercial rates taken towards the end of London trading. † UK, Ireland and Ecu are quoted in US currency. Forward premiums and discounts apply to the US dollar and not to the individual currency.

Source: *Financial Times*, May 19, 1993.

Application 2.1 | AUNT HELEN

Your aunt, who lives in Holly, Michigan, has been reviewing possibilities for investing profits from trading silver options and wants to take advantage of your new-found expertise. She has been reading the financial press and is intrigued by frequent reference to "Eurodollars." In a letter to you, she asks you to clarify which of the following are unequivocally Eurodollars:

- Dollar-denominated bonds issued by American banks such as First Chicago outside the United States
- Dollar-denominated bonds issued within the United States but issued by foreign borrowers such as Olivetti and Hitachi
- Any deposit in a branch of a U.S. bank located in Paris
- A dollar deposit in the Detroit branch of Swiss Bank Corporation
- A French-owned dollar deposit in a bank in New York
- U.S. Treasury bills owned by the Monetary Authority of Singapore
- Dollar deposits in London owned by Korean exporters

Application 2.2 | CROSS-RATE CLARITY

"Pick it up, will ya?"

"Huh? Me?" you may well ask, since you don't even work here. You are on an interview at Gotham Global Bank's foreign-exchange dealing room, and your interviewer's still too busy to talk to you. But the little light on the bank of telephone buttons has been flashing impatiently.

"Yes, you," the busy interviewer replies. "It's Clarence from Clarendon in London. He wants clarification on our bid quote for Swissies in terms of DM. Here you are: these are your direct quotes. Work out the bid cross rate for him, and tell him it's good for twenty."

She scribbles something on a bit of paper and hands it to you. It reads:

German marks	DM1.6860–1.7000/$
Swiss francs	SF1.5350–1.5500/$

"Give it a try!"

Can you calculate quickly a clear cross-rate quote for Clarendon's Clarence?

Application 2.3 | AT THE END OF THE DAY

It is the end of the trading day at Gotham Global Bank, and your interview is coming to an end. But it seems they like you, for your interview with the head FX/Eurocurrency dealer has concluded with her giving you a little task. The room, she says, has a net long position in French francs of FF90 million, which at the current spot rate of 5.80 francs to the dollar comes to over $15 million. What, she wonders, would be the probability distribution of the unit's gains or losses if the position is left uncovered overnight?

In response to your questions, the trader has said that the franc is moving sideways (zero expected change) but that the bank has found the overnight standard deviation is about 0.5 percent and that the exchange rate follows roughly a normal probability distribution. She suggests you provide potential gains and losses corresponding to 1, 2, and

3 standard deviations, and the probabilities of each. Enter your information in the box provided below.

Now assume you wish to set *limits* for the trading desk's position. The limit should be such that the probability of being wiped out is less than 1 percent. If the capital assigned to the French franc trading unit is $10 million, what limit would you set for the bank's French franc position? Enter your answers in the box below.

	Maximum long position	Maximum short position	Probability of a loss that exceeds assigned capital
French franc position			

Application 2.4 | FUJI ERUPTS

You are a financial analyst with KPMG Peat Marwick International, and your new task is to look at Fuji Bank's past problems in the currency trading area with an eye toward making sure that, in the future, the bank retains control over its foreign-exchange exposure (see the memo to the Fuji team for background). Your assignment is to devise guidelines or rules that give Tokyo sufficient information and control to limit risks and losses from foreign-exchange activities in its overseas branches. On the other hand, you must not prevent this leading Japanese bank from taking the risks necessary to provide its customers with a full and flexible range of foreign-exchange services. You also cannot recommend centralizing everything, because that would make their treasury operations too unwieldy.

Can you list some recommendations that will achieve these objectives? If so, you should be prepared to defend them in front of a critical committee of experienced Fuji traders who are determined to test you as a new employee.

MEMORANDUM TO FUJI TEAM

On November 7 Fuji Bank revealed that Mr. Jahimu Nakazawa, the chief foreign-exchange dealer in its New York branch, had lost ¥11.5 billion ($47.9 million at current exchange rates) this summer when he bet that the dollar would crash against the yen. After keeping his losses secret for three months, our client fired him. All Fuji's board members have taken a 20 percent pay cut for the next six months to emphasize their remorse.

How did such a thing happen? From what we understand, in April Nakazawa-san became convinced that America's huge trade deficit made a devaluation of the dollar inevitable. With the dollar at ¥226, he bought huge amounts of yen in the forward market—about $500 million worth, or so the magnitude of his losses would indicate. The dollar promptly strengthened, eventually reaching ¥249. Nakazawa was, our client says, breaking Fuji's internal rules on trading limits; and to conceal his position-taking, he made deals after hours with banks outside New York. He was helped, Fuji Tokyo says, by the fact that his branch's computer system was being replaced at the time, and the bank's normal accounting system had become temporarily confused.

Fuji says that this event will not affect the profit figures that the bank has been forecasting, because it has been able to sell securities to plug the hole.

SELECTED REFERENCES

Riehl, Heinz, and Rita Rodriguez. *Foreign Exchange and Money Markets*. Englewood Cliffs, N.J.: Prentice-Hall, 1989.

Stigum, Marcia. *The Money Markets*. Homewood, Ill.: Dow Jones Irwin, 1988.

Walmsley, Julian. *The Foreign Exchange Handbook*. New York: Wiley, 1986.

3

Interest Rates in the Global Money Market

The Global Financial Market

What is the global financial market? The term *market* implies a single market in which all instruments compete with one another for buyers' and sellers' attention. Yet much of the world's capital market remains segmented, so instruments and rates are not strictly comparable. On the other hand, so much of world finance now takes place in the major domestic and Euromarkets that a coherent world structure of interest rates can be said to exist, and those markets that are isolated can be regarded as exceptions rather than the rule. Figure 3.1 shows a stylized schematic of the global financial market. It starts with the domestic government bill (short-term) and bond (long-term) markets. Building on these are the other domestic money and bond markets in each country, including the market for bank deposits and corporate bonds. Then come international markets in that country's currency—the foreign markets and the famous Euromarkets introduced in the last chapter. Finally, each Euromarket relates to each other Euromarket through the currency structure of interest rates. Table 3.1, excerpted from *The Economist* magazine, illustrates the variety of interest rates that can be found within this framework at one particular point in time. We'll return to this framework as we progress with our analysis.

The *global money market* consists of the domestic and Eurocurrency markets for instruments and means of lending (or investing) and borrowing funds for relatively short periods, typically regarded as from one day to one year. Such means and instruments include short-term bank loans, Treasury bills, bank certificates of deposit, commercial paper, bankers' acceptances and repurchase agreements, and other short-term, asset-backed claims. In this chapter, we focus on the purely international segment of the global money market, the Eurocurrency market, and its linkages to domestic money markets.

The Two Kinds of Rate Linkages

This chapter attempts to provide two things essential to an understanding of international interest rates. First, it gives an analysis that identifies and integrates the determinants of domestic and Eurocurrency interest rates. Then it presents a framework that enables the borrower or investor of funds (1) to compare interest rates in the domestic and external money markets, and (2) in the external markets themselves, to compare interest rates on funds denominated in dollars, French francs, German marks, and so forth.

The theme of the chapter is simply that *there are close interdependencies between national and Eurocurrency interest rates, between interest rates in different currencies, and between the spot and forward exchange markets that link those currencies.*

Note: Portions of this chapter are excerpted from *The International Money Market,* 2d ed., by Gunter Dufey and Ian H. Giddy (Englewood Cliffs, N.J.: Prentice-Hall, 1994).

Figure 3.1   *The Domestic and Offshore Markets*

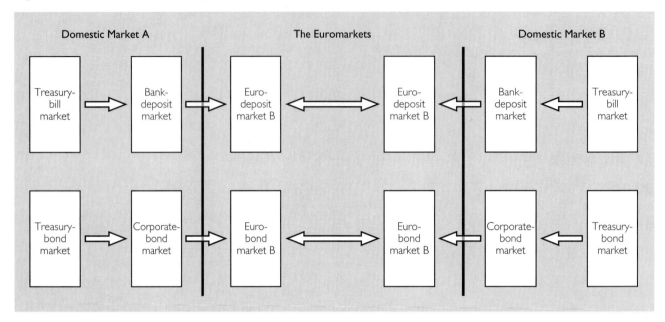

Table 3.1   *Global Money and Bond-Market Rates*

MONEY AND INTEREST RATES Germany's Bundesbank eased its monetary policy again; its securities repurchase rate fell from 7.71% to 7.6%. Canada's broad-money growth edged down to 7.2% in the year to April. French banks cut their prime lending rate to 9%.

	money supply‡			interest rates % p.a. (May 11th 1993)							
	% rise on year ago			money market		commercial banks		bond yields		eurocurrency	
	narrow (M1)	broad		overnight	3 months	prime lending	deposits 3 months	gov't long-term	corporate	deposits 3 months	bonds
Australia	+20.8	+ 8.9 Feb		5.13	5.13	9.50	5.13	7.52	7.75	4.94	na
Belgium	− 0.7	+ 6.6 Dec		7.31	7.19	11.50	6.63	7.46	7.90	7.25	6.98
Canada	+12.1	+ 7.2 Apr		4.50	5.05	6.00	4.50	8.16	9.30	5.00	8.45
France	+ 0.9	+ 5.2 Feb		8.19	7.69	9.00	7.63	7.30	7.70	7.75	6.83
Germany	+10.0	+ 7.6 Mar		7.80	7.50	10.25	6.83	6.76	6.70	7.50	6.31
Holland	+ 5.7	+ 6.4 Feb		7.43	7.10	9.75	7.10	6.69	7.53	7.13	6.32
Italy	+ 4.1	+ 7.1 Mar		11.13	11.06	12.38	na	10.94	11.28	10.69	10.75
Japan	+ 0.6	− 0.3 Mar		3.16	3.20	4.00	3.00	4.47	5.31	3.25	4.55
Spain	− 1.9	+ 7.4 Mar		16.29	15.04	13.75	8.00	11.50	12.33	15.88	11.90
Sweden	na	+ 4.6 Mar		9.25	9.06	11.00	8.95	9.12	10.09	8.95	8.35
Switzerland	+ 8.2	+ 4.1 Feb		5.00	5.00	7.13	4.50	4.75	4.97	4.94	4.68
UK	+ 4.9	+ 3.6 Mar		4.31	5.88	7.00	5.88	8.49	9.69	5.94	7.59
USA	+10.7	− 1.3 Mar		2.98	3.09	6.00	3.05	6.81	7.53	3.13	5.26

Other key rates in London: 3-mth Treasury bills 5.6%, 7-day interbank 5.6%. Eurodollar rates (LIBOR): 3 mths 3.1%, 6 mths 3.2%.

‡ M1 except UK M0; M3 except Belgium, Holland, Italy and Sweden M2, Japan M2 plus CDs, Spain M3 plus other liquid assets, UK M4. Definitions of interest rates quoted available on request. Sources: Banco Bilbao Vizcaya, Belgian Bankers' Association, Chase Manhattan, Credit Lyonnais, Bank Nederland, Royal Bank of Canada, Svenska Handelsbanken, Westpac Banking Corp, CSFB, The WEFA Group. These rates cannot be construed as offers by these banks.

Source: *The Economist*, May 15, 1993, p. 128.

Thus the chapter is concerned with interest-rate relationships of two types:

- competition between the domestic and external credit markets in a particular currency
- competition between pairs of external markets for credit denominated in different currencies[1]

In dealing with these and related questions, we rely on the *efficient markets argument:* that competition will tend to equalize expected rates of return on similar securities, and that effective interest-rate differentials will persist only if the securities possess different risk attributes or if barriers such as capital controls prevent arbitrage between two markets. In the first three sections of this chapter, therefore, we argue that there is nothing particularly special about the Eurocurrency markets and that, other things being equal, one would expect arbitrage to ensure equality between bank interest rates in the domestic and external markets. We then show why Eurobanks tend to offer more attractive loan and deposit rates than do domestic institutions, and how arbitrage between internal and external markets may be inhibited by controls on international capital flows or other market imperfections.

Arbitrage between deposits in the same Eurobanking center, but denominated in different currencies, is not subject to capital control. Hence interest rates differ only because of expected exchange-rate changes. If exchange rates were fixed, rates on different Eurocurrencies would be identical. In a later section we will employ this notion to show how Eurocurrency interest-rate differentials adjust so as to approximate the expected rate of change of the exchange rate, which in turn equals the forward-exchange premium or discount. We will also show how this relationship is consistent with the interest-rate-parity theorem, which says that arbitrage ensures equality between interest-rate differentials and the forward premium or discount.

The chapter ends with a look at the term structure of Eurocurrency interest rates—rates at different maturities.

Our initial focus will be the nature of the competition and arbitrage between each national money market (such as the New York market) and the corresponding external market (such as the dollar-denominated portion of the Eurocurrency market). We then turn to the linkages among markets denominated in different currencies.

Competing Internal and External Credit Markets

One way to understand the Eurodollar market is to think of it as merely one segment, albeit a very important one, of the market for short-term, U.S. dollar–denominated instruments. As Figure 3.2 illustrates, Eurodollar rates can be found in the money-rates section of U.S. financial newspapers. The numbers provide evidence of the relationship between interest rates on different instruments in the dollar money market. In particular, observe where Eurodollar rates lie in relation to domestic CD and Treasury-bill rates. One may also see a widening of the bid-offer spreads in the longer, more thinly traded, maturities.

---

[1]For the purpose of establishing the basic linkages in this chapter, however, such costs are unimportant. In covered interest arbitrage, for example, the total transactions costs have been estimated to be 0.15 percent or less. See Jacob A. Frenkel and Richard M. Levich, "Covered Interest Arbitrage: Unexploited Profits?" *Journal of Political Economy,* April 1975, pp. 325–338.

Figure 3.2   *Eurodollar and U.S. Money Market Rates.*   Arbitrage ensures a close linkage among the federal funds rate, the domestic CD rate, and the Eurodollar rate.

MONEY-MARKET RATES

Key U.S. and foreign interest rates. These are indicative rates only.

U.S. PRIME RATE: 11.5% The base rate for corporate loans made by large U.S. money-center banks.

CALL MONEY: 9 1/4% to 9 1/2%. Rate charged by banks for short-term loans made on the basis of stock-exchange collateral.

FEDERAL FUNDS RATE: 10% to 10 3/8%. Overnight interbank loans made between banks, in the form of reserves held at the Federal Reserve.

TREASURY BILLS: 13 weeks 8.03%; 26 weeks 8.12%. Results of previous Monday's auction of short-term U.S. government obligations, sold at a discount from face value and quoted as a discount rate.

COMMERCIAL PAPER: 30 days 8.35%; 60 days 8.30%; 90 days 8.30%. Unsecured notes issued by major, high-grade corporations in large amounts and sold through dealers.

BANKERS ACCEPTANCES: 30 days 8 1/4%; 60 days 8 1/ 4%; 90 days 8.15%; 120 days 8.15%; 180 days 8.10%. Negotiable trade-credit instruments, usually financing exports or imports, supported by a bank letter of credit.

U.S. CERTIFICATES OF DEPOSIT: One month 8 1/4%; two months 8.30%; three months 8.30%; six months 8.35%; one year 8.70%. Rates quoted by major banks in the U.S. on new issues of negotiable deposit instruments, usually on amounts of $1 million or more.

LONDON LATE EURODOLLARS: One month 8 9/16% to 8 7/16%; two months 8 9/16% to 8 7/16%; three months 8 1/2% to 8 3/8%; six months 8 3/4% to 8 7/8%.

LONDON INTERBANK OFFERED RATE (LIBOR): Three months 8 5/8%; six months 8 3/4%. The average of interbank rates for offerings of dollar deposits in London based on quotations at 5 major banks.

LONDON LATE EURODOLLARS refers to the closing <u>offer</u> (eg. 8 9/16%) and <u>bid</u> (eg. 8 7/16%) interest rates on large deposits as of 5 P.M. London time, i.e. noon New York time.

LONDON INTERBANK OFFERED RATES (LIBOR) refers to the standard benchmark Eurodollar rate, used for loan, floating-rate note and Euronote interest rates, usually provided by prime banks at 11 A.M. London time.

Table 3.2   *Eurocurrency Interest Rates*

EURO-CURRENCY INTEREST RATES

May 17	Short term	7 Days notice	One Month	Three Months	Six Months	One Year
Sterling	$6\frac{3}{8} - 6\frac{1}{8}$	$6\frac{1}{8} - 6$	$6\frac{1}{8} - 6$	$6\frac{3}{16} - 6\frac{1}{16}$	$6\frac{1}{16} - 6\frac{1}{16}$	$6\frac{5}{8} - 6\frac{3}{8}$
US Dollar	$3\frac{1}{4} - 3\frac{1}{8}$	$3\frac{1}{8} - 3$	$3\frac{1}{8} - 3$	$3\frac{1}{4} - 3\frac{1}{8}$	$3\frac{3}{8} - 3\frac{1}{4}$	$3\frac{5}{8} - 3\frac{1}{2}$
Can. Dollar	$4\frac{3}{8} - 4\frac{1}{8}$	$4\frac{1}{4} - 4$	$4\frac{1}{4} - 4\frac{1}{2}$	$5\frac{1}{8} - 4\frac{7}{8}$	$5\frac{5}{8} - 5\frac{3}{8}$	$6\frac{1}{4} - 6$
Dutch Guilder	$7\frac{7}{8} - 7\frac{5}{8}$	$7\frac{3}{8} - 7\frac{1}{4}$	$7\frac{1}{4} - 7\frac{1}{8}$	$7 - 6\frac{7}{8}$	$6\frac{11}{16} - 6\frac{9}{16}$	$6\frac{3}{8} - 6\frac{1}{4}$
Swiss Franc	$5\frac{1}{4} - 5$	$5\frac{1}{4} - 5$	$5\frac{3}{16} - 5\frac{1}{16}$	$5\frac{1}{16} - 4\frac{13}{16}$	$4\frac{7}{8} - 4\frac{3}{4}$	$4\frac{5}{8} - 4\frac{1}{2}$
D–Mark	$8 - 7\frac{7}{8}$	$7\frac{7}{8} - 7\frac{3}{4}$	$7\frac{13}{16} - 7\frac{11}{16}$	$7\frac{3}{8} - 7\frac{1}{4}$	$7\frac{1}{8} - 7$	$6\frac{5}{8} - 6\frac{1}{2}$
French Franc	$8\frac{1}{4} - 8$	$8\frac{1}{4} - 8$	$8 - 7\frac{3}{4}$	$7\frac{5}{8} - 7\frac{1}{2}$	$7\frac{3}{8} - 7\frac{1}{8}$	$7\frac{1}{16} - 6\frac{13}{16}$
Italian Lira	$12\frac{1}{2} - 10\frac{1}{2}$	$10\frac{3}{4} - 10\frac{3}{8}$	$10\frac{7}{8} - 10\frac{1}{2}$	$10\frac{5}{8} - 10\frac{1}{4}$	$10\frac{5}{8} - 10\frac{1}{4}$	$10\frac{1}{2} - 10\frac{1}{4}$
Belgian Franc	$7\frac{7}{8} - 7\frac{5}{8}$	$7\frac{1}{2} - 7\frac{3}{8}$	$7\frac{3}{8} - 7\frac{1}{4}$	$7\frac{1}{4} - 7\frac{1}{8}$	$7 - 6\frac{7}{8}$	$6\frac{13}{16} - 6\frac{11}{16}$
Yen	$3\frac{3}{16} - 3\frac{1}{8}$	$3\frac{1}{4} - 3\frac{3}{16}$	$3\frac{1}{4} - 3\frac{3}{16}$	$3\frac{1}{4} - 3\frac{3}{16}$	$3\frac{3}{32} - 3\frac{7}{32}$	$3\frac{11}{32} - 3\frac{7}{32}$
Danish Krone	$9\frac{3}{4} - 9$	$10 - 9\frac{3}{4}$	$9\frac{3}{4} - 9$	$8\frac{1}{2} - 8$	$8\frac{1}{8} - 7\frac{5}{8}$	$7\frac{5}{8} - 7\frac{1}{8}$
Asian $Sing	$3\frac{1}{4} - 2\frac{1}{4}$	$3\frac{1}{4} - 2\frac{1}{4}$	$3\frac{1}{2} - 2\frac{1}{2}$	$3\frac{1}{2} - 2\frac{1}{2}$	$3\frac{1}{2} - 2\frac{1}{2}$	$3\frac{3}{4} - 2\frac{3}{4}$
Spanish Peseta	$12\frac{5}{8} - 12\frac{1}{8}$	$12\frac{5}{8} - 12\frac{1}{8}$	$12\frac{3}{8} - 12\frac{1}{8}$	$12\frac{1}{8} - 11\frac{7}{8}$	$11\frac{5}{16} - 11\frac{5}{16}$	$11\frac{5}{16} - 11\frac{5}{16}$
Portuguese Esc	$15\frac{1}{4} - 14\frac{3}{4}$	$16\frac{1}{4} - 15\frac{1}{4}$	$15\frac{3}{8} - 14\frac{5}{8}$	$15 - 14$	$14 - 13\frac{1}{2}$	$13\frac{3}{4} - 13\frac{1}{4}$

Long term Eurodollars: two years $4\frac{3}{16}$-$4\frac{1}{16}$ per cent; three years $4\frac{11}{16}$-$4\frac{9}{16}$ per cent; four years $5\frac{1}{8}$-5 per cent; five years $5\frac{7}{16}$-$5\frac{5}{16}$ per cent nominal. Short term rates are call for US Dollar and Japanese Yen; others, two days' notice.

Source: *Financial Times*, May 18, 1993.

Table 3.2 provides a different view, one of the Eurocurrency market as a whole. In papers such as the London *Financial Times* and the *International Herald Tribune* one finds data on Eurorates for deposits in a number of currencies. Observe the differences between currencies: in rate levels, in bid-offer spreads, and across maturities. Note also that banks in London offer daily quotations for deposits in "currency baskets:" the SDR (Special Drawing Right) and ECU (European Currency Unit).

In Chapter 2 we noted that U.S. and Eurodollar banking is similar in most respects. The currency of denomination is the same; the banks doing business are the same; and the terms and conditions of the instruments are almost identical. The only thing that differentiates Eurodollar from domestic banking, then, is the fact that they take place in *different locations* with correspondingly different regulations and, perhaps, different risks arising from the jurisdictions in which the units operate.

The answers to issues concerning onshore-offshore rate relationships are consistent with the view of the Eurodollar market expressed in Chapter 2—that it can be regarded as simply a segment of the larger market for dollar-denominated deposits and loans. Three questions about relative rates may be raised; the answers lead to a picture of the Eurodollar market like that in Figure 3.3:

1. *Which market dominates?* Because the total market for short-term assets and liabilities in the United States is large and resilient, rates in any smaller, competing market tend to be dominated by U.S. rates on both the deposit and the loan sides of the market. Thus we have chosen to draw Figure 3.4 under the assumption that Eurodollar rates are constrained by U.S. rates, and not vice versa.

Figure 3.3   ***The Eurodollar Market.***   This schematic shows the boundaries within which Eurodollar rates normally fluctuate.

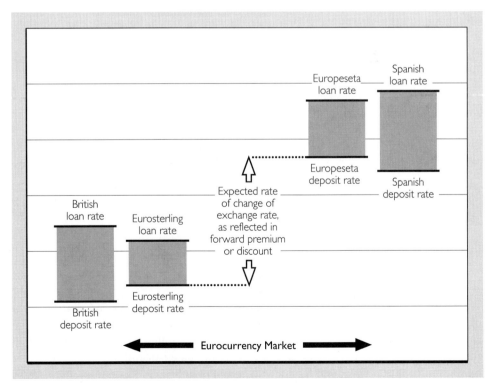

Figure 3.4   ***Eurodollar and U.S. Deposit Rates.***   Over a five-year period, Eurorates exceeded U.S. rates most of the time, but by amounts that varied with perceived risk and the cost of regulation.

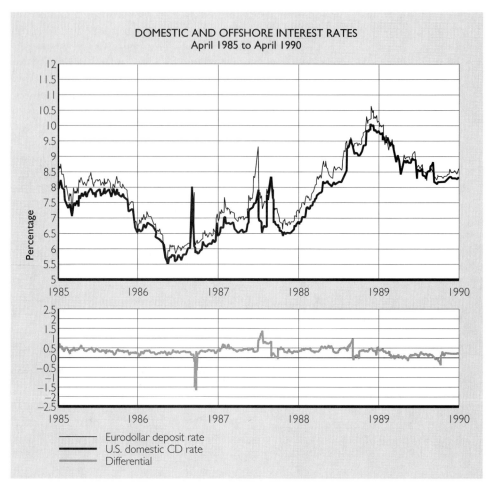

2. *What is the relationship between Eurodollar and U.S. deposit rates?* Briefly, Eurodollar deposits must normally pay a rate at least as high as in the United States. Otherwise, why would a depositor entrust his dollar–denominated time deposit to a financial institution outside the United States instead of a bank in the United States?

Although familiarity, similar business hours, and in special circumstances the desire for political anonymity may occasionally account for such deposits being offered to financial institutions outside the United States, in the vast majority of cases Eurobanks could not offer lower deposit rates than are offered by U.S. banks without losing the deposit. In other words, the supply of deposits to Eurobanks becomes infinitely elastic at the U.S. deposit rate.

3. *How are Eurodollar and U.S. lending rates linked?* Similar considerations apply. Because borrowers consider a loan from a U.S. bank to be as good as, if not better than, a loan from a Eurobank, foreign institutions can compete successfully only if they offer loan rates that are no higher than the effective rates charged by U.S. banks. Factors such as familiarity, business hours, and communications may again play a role. But in the world

of sizable transactions (seldom in units of less than $5 million), where the transactors are large banks, public entities, and corporations that have resident operations in many countries, modern communications technology makes the impact of such factors minimal. The demand for Eurodollar loans becomes infinitely elastic at the U.S. loan rate, thus serving as an upper boundary for the movement of the Eurodollar loan rate.

These constraints establish rough boundaries for Eurodollar interest rates.

The Behavior of Eurodollar Interest Rates

Do Eurodollar interest rates in fact differ significantly from domestic rates? And if so, why?

On the lending side, Eurodollar interest rates at one time had to be noticeably below their domestic counterparts, prime-rate loans, to attract borrowers away from their domestic banking relationships. As corporations' knowledge of available alternatives grew during the 1970s, however, they began to realize that a dollar is a dollar wherever you get it, so why not take the cheapest loan you can get? Domestic loan practice began to incorporate the Euromarket principles of roll-over, cost-plus pricing—and both markets were influenced by the fact that the best borrowers had the alternative of borrowing directly, by issuing short-term commercial paper.

In practice, effective loan rates are difficult to pin down; loan rates include a premium for the risk specific to a borrower, and bankers are creative people when it comes to disguising the true cost of funds, through various fees and (sometimes) compensating balance requirements. Nevertheless, it is safe to say that today the effective rates on a U.S. loan are seldom much above what the same borrower would pay for a Eurodollar loan. As a practical matter, the cost of commercial paper issued by U.S. corporations, plus the cost of maintaining lines of credit to back up the paper, may be the best proxy for the U.S. lending rate. It has the advantage of being objective, although at times it may deviate from the loan rates because the commercial-paper market becomes very thin in periods when corporate liquidity becomes a major concern of investors. We shall return to Eurodollar loan pricing practices in Chapter 9.

What about the deposit side? A glance at Tables 3.1 or 3.2 will verify that on any given day, the Eurodollar deposit rate is higher than the domestic rate. Interest rates on Eurodollar *deposits,* in contrast, do exceed those on domestic bank deposits by a substantial and persistent margin. This is shown vividly in Figure 3.4, which traces three-month Eurodollar deposit rates and 90-day domestic CD rates over a typical five-year period.[2] The raw differential is shown at the bottom of the chart; it averages about 1 percent per annum. Why?

A clue to the answer lies in old-fashioned supply-and-demand principles. The Eurodollar market grows to the point at which both Eurodollar depositors and Eurobanks are satisfied with the interest rate paid on that particular quantity of deposits. In other words, it is *supply and demand,* both of which are directly competitive with the domestic money market, that determines the size of the Eurodollar market and the premium of Eurodollar deposits. The premium is one that represents both risk and relative cost; it is high enough to induce depositors to willingly hold some of their funds in Eurobanks,

---

[2]It is frequently supposed that the absence of taxes plays a role in depositors' choice of an offshore deposit. This is usually true only for those seeking to evade taxes through anonymity. Otherwise, U.S. residents are subject to income tax on both domestic and offshore interests, and nonresidents are not subject to withholding tax on either kind of bank deposit.

and it is low enough to persuade banks to obtain funds in the Euromarket instead of the domestic market.

But what determines the demand? And the supply? The "market-price-of-risk" view emphasizes the demand side, holding that the Eurodollar deposit rate should lie above the domestic rate at a level given by the risk premium demanded by depositors. Because depositors can readily arbitrage between domestic and offshore assets of equivalent risk, the Eurodollar premium should *only* be determined by relative risks. Because no one will hold a risky instrument if he can purchase a less risky one bearing the same return, the yields on risky assets will be driven up, and on safe assets down, until there is a well-defined hierarchy of risks and returns. The additional yield required for an additional unit of risk is the market price of risk.[3]

Presumably, depositors would be indifferent between holding domestic deposits at the U.S. deposit rate and holding Eurodeposits at the U.S. rate plus the market-risk premium. At this level, depositors' supply of funds to the Eurodollar market would become infinitely elastic.

The other extreme is the "cost-of-regulation" view, which says that the Eurodollar premium is purely and solely determined by the regulatory costs, such as taxes and reserve requirements, of offering domestic rather than offshore deposits. Banks, in this view, are indifferent between obtaining funds in the United States, Nassau, or other Eurobanking centers, except for the regulatory cost differential, which is primarily the cost of holding non-interest-bearing reserve requirements. Banks will shift all their funding offshore if the cost of deposits is lower in the Euromarket than in the domestic market (after adjusting for reserve requirements), and vice versa.

If this cost is X percent, and if the U.S. and Eurodollar interest rates are I_{US} and $I_{E\$}$ respectively, then banks would be indifferent between obtaining funds in the Eurodollar market at $I_{E\$}$ and borrowing in the United States at an effective cost of $I_{US} + X$.

The logical implication of this view is that changes in risk perception, familiarity with the market, and other factors will not change the Eurodollar premium. No matter how much, or how little, depositors are prepared to offer at various interest rates, they always get the same rate relative to the U.S. rate. Conclusion? The Eurodollar premium is bank determined, and (for a given cost differential) the Eurodollar market's size is depositor determined.

Even though the market-price-of-risk approach is more solidly grounded in modern asset-pricing theory, the cost-of-regulation view has the support of many observers of the market. Arbitrage seems to be undertaken much more rapidly and in much larger amounts by banks than by individuals, governments, or even corporate depositors. Eurocurrency traders act on the presumption that the Eurodeposit rate differs from the domestic rate almost entirely because of the cost of reserve requirements.

A simple empirical test of these models suggests itself. If the cost-of-regulation theory were correct, then changes in the U.S.–Eurodollar interest rate gap should be a function *only* of changes in the relative costs of borrowing onshore and offshore. Among the various additional costs of funding through domestic deposits are:

- Reserve requirements,
- Federal Deposit Insurance Corporation fees, and
- State and local taxes.

---

[3]Precisely how the market defines and measures price risk is another issue. Adherents of the market-price-of-risk theory would tend toward the theory that investors have a range of assets and asset combinations to choose from, and that the special risk of Eurodollar deposits is that component of risk that one cannot diversify away by holding Eurodeposits in combination with other assets.

Figure 3.5   *Eurodollar and Adjusted Domestic CD Rates.*   The effective cost of domestic funds is found by adjusting for regulatory costs: Cost = (CD Rate + FDIC Fees)/ (1 − Reserve Requirement).

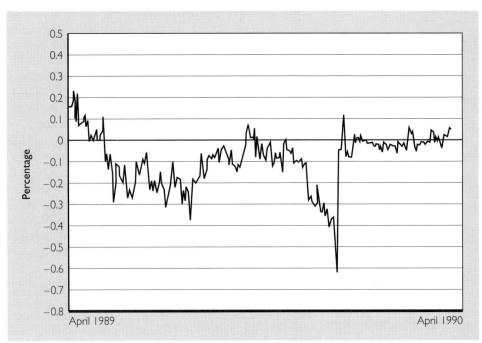

Of these, reserve requirements are by far the most important. They are also the most varied, because the effective cost of holding interest-free reserves changes with the opportunity cost of the funds, while taxes and fees of the Federal Deposit Insurance Corporation (FDIC) are relatively stable.

Figure 3.5 plots the differential between the Eurodollar and domestic CD bid rates, adjusted for the estimated cost of reserve requirements and FDIC fees. As an example of the calculation, say a U.S. bank receives $100 in domestic deposits and the reserve requirement is 5 percent. The *effective funds received* amount to only $95. But the bank must pay an interest rate of (for example) 15 percent on the full $100 plus estimated FDIC fees and additional taxes. Ignoring difficult-to-measure state and local taxes, the *effective cost of funds* to the bank is therefore

$$\text{Effective cost of domestic deposit} = \frac{\text{interest rate } + \text{ FDIC fees}}{1 \ - \ \text{reserve requirement}}$$
$$= \frac{15\% \ + \ \frac{1}{12}\%}{1 \ - \ 0.05}$$
$$= 15.88\%$$

Thus the additional cost of the reserve requirements is 88 basis points—and this is the extra amount the bank can afford to pay on Eurodollar deposits to achieve the same cost of funds.

If the cost-of-regulation theory were absolutely correct, and our measurements free of error, then the adjusted differential would be zero. In fact, in Figure 3.5, the differential wiggles closely around the zero line for much of the time, suggesting that the Eurodollar premium is dominated, at least in normal times, by the relative costs of regulation.

On the other hand, the same chart manifests significant deviations from zero during certain periods. What explains them? In the past, capital controls have inhibited arbitrage. The U.S. capital control of 1963–1973 produced a positive adjusted gap in 1972 and 1974. The adjusted Euro/domestic differential rose above zero again in 1974–1975, but for a different reason: the perceived risk of Eurodollars rose following the failure of Germany's Herstatt Bank and other international banking problems that occurred during that period. Similar concerns were present in the years 1979–1983, following the global recession and collapse of commodity prices, and again in the late 1980s, as the country's debt burden took its toll. In the early 1990s, egregious circumvention of laws and regulations by BCCI, a bank with its headquarters in Luxembourg, shook the financial community.

These examples verify the fact that bank regulatory costs alone are insufficient to fully explain the Eurodollar premium. Although relative costs of regulation dominate the Euro/domestic differential, there are times when the risk premium demanded by depositors rises above the cost differential.

Another way to look at this issue is to consider the difference between the overnight Eurodollar deposit rate and the overnight federal funds rate. Banks in America regard these two sources of very short-term funds as virtually interchangeable, because federal funds are interbank loans and as such not subject to reserve requirements or deposit-insurance assessments. (The reasoning is that these regulatory costs were incurred by the first bank that obtained deposits from the public, and should not be reimposed when the funds are relent in the interbank market.) The bank placing the funds will of course do so only at a rate sufficient to recoup the reserve requirement and other costs; hence the fed funds rate already reflects these regulatory costs. Thus the cost-of-regulation theory would predict that the raw difference between the overnight Eurorates and the fed funds rate would be approximately zero.

> *Hence under normal market conditions, both domestic interbank placements and Euro-deposits are exempted from reserve requirements and therefore bear interest rates that exceed the domestic nonbank deposit rate by an amount equal to the relative costs of regulation.*

To sum up: the data provide rough confirmation of the theory that the relative costs of regulation dominate arbitrage between the domestic and offshore markets, except when unusual risks or exchange controls inhibit such arbitrage, and except for temporary supply and demand factors and measurement problems.

Let us continue to explore the basic framework of how Eurocurrency interest rates are linked—and how, sometimes, they can be uncoupled from their domestic engines. Three factors producing such uncoupling—capital controls, risk differences, and market imperfections—are discussed in the next section.

Capital Controls and Divided Credit Markets

The essence of the Eurocurrency market is external financial intermediation: financial institutions (Eurobanks) outside the domestic banking system compete for dollar-denominated deposits and loans.

For depositors and borrowers who reside outside the United States, the choice between the domestic U.S. market and the external dollar market involves a choice of jurisdiction governing the transaction and its attendant obligations. Even when foreigners contract with Eurobanks within their own jurisdiction—for example, a Swiss corporation obtaining a Eurodollar loan from a Swiss bank—an international financial transaction occurs: the borrower receives the loan proceeds in New York because only the U.S. banking system offers dollars as means of payments. Thus all such transactions are, legally, international transactions, as they involve either the extension of credit or the effecting of a payment in a foreign jurisdiction.[4] Similarly, for a U.S. resident, every Eurodollar transaction involves an international credit transaction.

Legal restrictions on international transactions come in many different forms, shapes, and sizes.[5] But they all have the same effect on the relationship between internal (domestic) and external (Euro) markets: they cut the external market off from its internal base. Such controls, to the extent that they are effective, insulate a particular Eurocurrency market from the influence of domestic credit conditions, making exchange-rate expectations in conjunction with foreign credit conditions the essential determinants of the currency's Eurorates.

Let us take a closer look at this relationship. We have seen that, in the *absence* of tight controls on international financial transactions, there will be arbitrage between the external and internal segments of the market for dollar credit. This keeps Eurodollar lending and deposit rates within a margin determined by effective domestic lending rates (the upper limit) and domestic deposit rates (the lower limit). But when controls prevent capital outflows, Euromarket rates can exceed domestic interest rates by an amount much greater than the normal bounds allow (Figure 3.6).

In a similar fashion, controls limiting depositor arbitrage may cause rates in the external market to fall below corresponding domestic deposit rates, when effective capital controls prevent an inflow of funds. Germany and Switzerland are cases in point. Both countries at various times during the 1970s imposed controls on the inflow of foreign funds, promptly causing the external deposit rate to fall below the equivalent domestic deposit rate, which would otherwise represent an effective "floor" for the Euro–Swiss franc or Euro–German mark rate.

Perhaps the most dramatic instance of divided credit markets is that of the Euro–French franc market in the early 1980s, following the accession to power of a socialist government in the spring of 1981. The external payments situation in France had been under pressure for many years, even prior to the franc's entry into a polygamous liaison with the German mark and other currencies under the European Monetary System (instituted in 1979). A paramount aim of the French authorities had accordingly become to restrict the scope for speculation against the French franc by both residents and nonresidents. Banks' net foreign-currency positions were strictly limited and residents were prohibited from holding liquid external foreign-currency assets. The latter were required to repatriate and dispose of any foreign currency receipts within a very short period of time, and advance payment for imports and forward-exchange cover were also severely

---

[4]From the perspective of economic analysis, however, not all Eurodollar transactions involve international capital flows. To illustrate, funds deposited in a Eurobank by a U.S. resident may simply be loaned to another U.S. resident. This round trip of funds through external intermediaries instead of domestic institutions does not involve any of the effects that are germane to international capital flows, such as changes in the monetary base, domestic liquidity, and credit conditions.

[5]For details, see Michael R. Rosenberg, "Foreign Exchange Controls: An International Comparison," in Abraham George and Ian Giddy, eds., *International Finance Handbook* (New York: Wiley, 1983), vol. 1; David T. Llewellyn, "How To Control Capital Flows?" *The Banker,* July 1973, pp. 764–68, Rodney H. Mills, Jr., "Regulations on Short-Term Capital Movements: Recent Techniques in Selected Industrial Countries," *Federal Reserve Board Discussion Paper,* Washington, D.C., November 6, 1972; Organization for Economic Cooperation and Development, *Regulations Affecting International Banking Operations* (Paris: OECD, 1981).

Figure 3.6   ***Breaking the Bounds.***   U.S. capital outflow controls allowed Eurodollar lending
rates to move above the theoretical limit set by the U.S. lending rate.

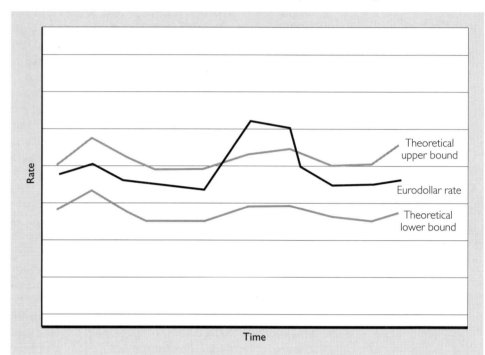

restricted. To limit nonresident sales of French francs in exchange for foreign currencies, bank and nonbank French-franc loans abroad other than in connection with export finance were forbidden.

Banks were even prohibited from entering into forward foreign-exchange contracts with foreign banks in which the latter would be selling francs forward. In effect, therefore, the Eurofranc market was cut off from virtually all domestic supplies of funds. The limited pool of Euro–French francs available to nonresidents and the awkward restrictions on forward cover combined to make the Euro–French franc market a shallow, illiquid one, unable to easily absorb large borrowings or lendings without the rates moving substantially. In effect, French exchange controls created two separate credit markets, with two separate interest-rate structures—and two separate forward-exchange markets, with different forward rates being quoted on the internal franc forward market and the external one.[6] Because the primary influence on Euro–French franc rates could not be the domestic market, external franc deposit rates were much more closely linked to the Eurodollar market and the forward-exchange market. Euro–French franc rates equaled Eurodollar rates adjusted for the cost of cover in the forward market for francs. The forward rate was in turn dominated by currency expectations. When, as happened time and again, nonresidents sought to borrow French francs (or sell francs forward) in anticipation of a

---

[6]According to dealers in the Eurocurrency market, there were days when the external French franc forward rate was at a discount, while the internal forward rate was at a premium against the U.S. dollar. This could be observed by rates quoted on a Reuters monitor by a domestic French bank such as Credit Agricole and by a similar bank in London or New York. See Julian Walmsley, "Euromarket Dealing," in Abraham George and Ian Giddy, *International Finance Handbook* (New York: Wiley, 1983), vol. 1.

Figure 3.7 ***Strange Days in Euroland.*** Anticipating a French-franc devaluation, Euro–French-franc borrowers drove rates to unheard-of heights, possible because exchange controls prevented domestic funds from flowing out.

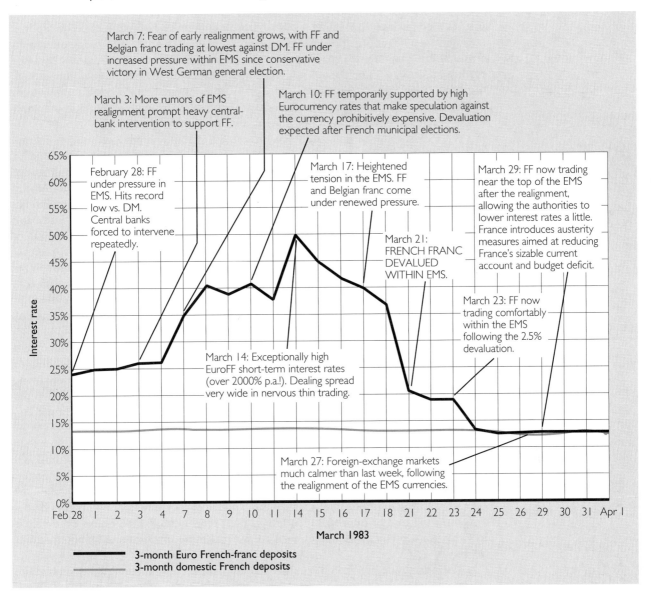

March 7: Fear of early realignment grows, with FF and Belgian franc trading at lowest against DM. FF under increased pressure within EMS since conservative victory in West German general election.

March 3: More rumors of EMS realignment prompt heavy central-bank intervention to support FF.

March 10: FF temporarily supported by high Eurocurrency rates that make speculation against the currency prohibitively expensive. Devaluation expected after French municipal elections.

February 28: FF under pressure in EMS. Hits record low vs. DM. Central banks forced to intervene repeatedly.

March 17: Heightened tension in the EMS. FF and Belgian franc come under renewed pressure.

March 29: FF now trading near the top of the EMS after the realignment, allowing the authorities to lower interest rates a little. France introduces austerity measures aimed at reducing France's sizable current account and budget deficit.

March 21: FRENCH FRANC DEVALUED WITHIN EMS.

March 23: FF now trading comfortably within the EMS following the 2.5% devaluation.

March 14: Exceptionally high EuroFF short-term interest rates (over 2000% p.a.!). Dealing spread very wide in nervous thin trading.

March 27: Foreign-exchange markets much calmer than last week, following the realignment of the EMS currencies.

Interest rate

65% 60% 55% 50% 45% 40% 35% 30% 25% 20% 15% 10% 5% 0%

Feb 28 | 1 | 2 | 3 | 4 | 7 | 8 | 9 | 10 | 11 | 14 | 15 | 16 | 17 | 18 | 21 | 22 | 23 | 24 | 25 | 26 | 29 | 30 | 31 | Apr 1

March 1983

———— 3-month Euro French-franc deposits
———— 3-month domestic French deposits

devaluation, they would willingly pay interest rates (or forward rates) far in excess of those prevailing (but unobtainable!) in the domestic market.

The giddiness of this market reached new heights when, in March 1983, Euro–French franc interest rates of up to 5,000 percent per annum were paid reportedly on overnight deposits. Speculators and hedgers seemed willing to pay almost anything to borrow French francs and invest them in a strong currency. Figure 3.7, based on three-month deposit rates in the domestic French and the Euro–French franc market, provides a truncated picture of those strange days in the life of Euromarket dealers. In addition to the huge premium of Euro over domestic rates that appeared, the market's thinness and trading risks at the time produced extraordinarily wide Euromarket bid-offer spreads.

Risk Differences Between Domestic and External Money Markets

Risk in credit markets lies in the nonzero probability that an obligation to repay funds at a certain interest rate (in the case of a deposit agreement) or to lend funds on certain terms (in the case of a loan facility) will not be honored. In the international financial markets, this risk is closely associated with the presence or absence of government regulations and control. Because, from a regulatory point of view, all Eurodollar transactions are international transactions, this means that each and every such transaction is subject to the potential intervention of not one but two (or more) sovereigns.

A U.S. depositor in the Eurodollar market, for example, holds a claim in one jurisdiction (say, London) but receives payment in another (the United States). He could be deprived of his funds at maturity by an action of either the British government or the U.S. government. In the case of a domestic deposit, only actions by the U.S. authorities matter.[7] For a depositor residing in the United Kingdom the situation is quite similar. He may own a dollar-denominated time deposit in (1) a U.S. bank, directly, (2) a Eurobank operating in Luxembourg, or (3) a London-based Eurobank. In all three cases, the safety of his funds depends ultimately on the expectation that the United States will not restrict the disposition and transfer of foreign-held dollar funds (that is, that the United States will continue to observe "nonresident convertibility"). In comparison to the situation of our U.S. investor, the U.K. investor will face a greater risk, to the extent that the U.S. government may restrict nonresident convertibility more readily than it interrupts domestic bank transfers.[8]

What of risk from the point of view of the borrower of Eurodollars? To the extent that the U.S. government may place quantitative restrictions on U.S. banks' lending to foreigners or some other class of borrowers, these borrowers may feel safer borrowing from the unregulated Eurodollar market. Thus the fear of capital controls, as well as the controls themselves, could allow Eurodollar lending rates to rise above those in the domestic market.

In summary, the risk on external dollar deposits and loans is somewhat greater than on deposits in, and loans from, U.S. domestic banks. The major risks in Eurodollar transactions stem from (1) the removal of nonresident convertibility by the United States, (2) the seizing of the assets and liabilities of the Eurobanks by the authorities where they operate, and (3) the possibility that central banks may not function as "lenders of last resort" in the case of Eurobanks. Although the probability of these events occurring is low, they are of sufficient importance to warrant close examination by international depositors.

There has certainly been a secular decline in the interest-rate incentive required to attract depositors and borrowers from the domestic into the external market. Still, espe-

---

[7]Of course, in countries where new capital outflow controls on residents are feared, external deposits may well be considered less risky by residents who wish to purchase foreign goods.

[8]Residents of offshore banking centers constitute a special case. In the situation represented by example (3), the depositor may well perceive more risk than in either the first or second cases, because he is subject to the direct control of his own country regarding foreign currency holdings.

The other special case is that of depositors from countries which are confronted by the risk of selective (political) interference with their assets in particular countries. The concrete example in the 1970s was that of dollar deposits owned by the government of Iran: these may be somewhat less subject to risk of government seizure when held in Swiss banks rather than in banks in the United States. Iranian investors may, therefore, be willing to accept a lower return on dollar-denominated time deposits in banks outside the United States. But these are minor exceptions relative to the bulk of investors whose transactions maintain Eurodollar deposit rates in excess of domestic rates.

cially on the loan side, it has been found that U.S. rates appear not to react in a rapid and unbiased fashion to changes in credit conditions and abnormally high or low margins seem not to adjust very rapidly to market conditions.[9] These imperfections arise from (1) regulatory restraints, such as interest-rate ceilings; (2) institutional and perceptual factors, such as the tradition of adjusting the quantity rather than the price of loans when credit conditions change, partly because of the political visibility of the prime rate; and (3) oligopolistic market conditions that result from barriers to entry in the U.S. banking system. Interest rates in the Eurodollar market, on the other hand, are free of governmental or competitive restraints and therefore react with alacrity to changes in credit conditions. As a result, during "tight" credit conditions in the United States, lending-rate differentials become smaller, while those on the deposit side widen.

Competing Eurocurrency Markets: Interest–Rate Arbitrage and Currency Expectations

The last two sections described the relationship between Eurorate and corresponding domestic rates. Although the discussion focused on the U.S. and Eurodollar markets, the same set of relationships applies to the internal and external markets for credit in each major currency. Just as Eurodollar loan and deposit rates are constrained by U.S. rates, so are interest rates on Eurosterling, Euro–Swiss francs, Eurodeutschemarks (Euromarks), and Euroguilders bounded by corresponding domestic rates *except* when capital controls inhibit arbitrage, as for example in the case of Euro–French francs. The next question, therefore, is, *What is the relationship between rates in different segments of the Eurocurrency market?* For example, how do Euromark rates influence Eurosterling rates, and vice versa?

Each Eurorate influences, and is influenced by, the level of interest rates in other Eurocurrency markets and hence by the level of rates in the corresponding domestic credit markets. Other things being equal, a rise in German interest rates, for example, will immediately result in a parallel rise in the Euromark interest rate, which in turn will tend to raise interest rates in other currencies, such as Euro–Dutch guilders.

But it is *forward exchange rates* that keep interest rates between Eurocurrency markets different and that temper the influence of a change in one currency's rates on those in other currencies. For example, other things being equal, a shift in the market's expected rate of change in the pound/French-franc exchange rate will change the forward premium or discount, producing an interest-rate change in the Eurosterling market, or in the Euro–French-franc market, or (as is more likely) both. The mutual influences of Eurocurrency interest rates, currency expectations, and forward-exchange rates, illustrated in Figure 3.8, may be summarized as follows:

1. Through the process of *covered interest arbitrage,* interest-rate differentials tend to equal the forward premium or discount.
2. Through *speculation,* the forward premium or discount tends to equal the expected rate of change of the exchange rate.
3. Also through speculation, the expected rate of change of the exchange rate tends to equal the Eurocurrency interest-rate differential.

---

[9]Ian Giddy, Gunter Dufey, and Sangkee Min, "Interest Rates in the U.S. and Eurodollar Markets," *Weltwirtschaftliches Archiv,* vol. 115, No. 1 (1979), pp. 51–67.

Figure 3.8   ***Eurocurrency Rates and Forward Exchange.***   Arbitrage and speculative capital ensure linkages among Eurocurrency interest differentials, the forward premium, and currency expectations.

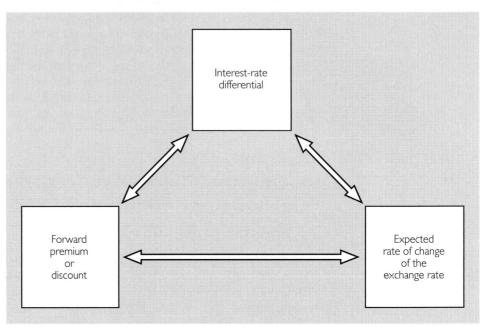

These relationships are not only compatible but are, as we shall see, simply different aspects of the same phenomenon. How these processes work is the subject of this and the next section. We shall study the relationship between Eurocurrency interest rates and the foreign-exchange markets by looking at the behavior of borrowers and lenders, who are considering the use of alternative Eurocurrency markets, and at the behavior of bankers, who are willing at any time to move funds from one market to another in order to make profits. As exchange rates, interest rates, and currency expectations change, profit opportunities appear, and banks and companies are quick to take advantage.

Interest-Rate Parity

We have already encountered the fundamental relationship between interest rates and spot and forward exchange rates. The *interest-rate parity theorem,* as we saw in Chapter 2, results from arbitrage between the spot and forward markets and the Eurocurrency deposit markets. *Covered-interest arbitrage,* undertaken by large international banks, involves the rapid movement of funds between securities denominated in different currencies in order to profit from different *effective* rates of interest in different currencies after taking hedging costs into account:

Effective interest rate on a foreign currency deposit
          = nominal interest rate + cost of forward cover
          = interest rate + forward premium (positive) or discount (negative)

This interest-rate parity theorem says that covered-interest arbitrage equalizes the return (adjusted for the cost of eliminating exchange risk by means of a forward contract) in different currencies. For example, the interest rate on a dollar deposit must equal the interest rate on a German mark deposit covered in the forward market. More specifically, the following relationships hold true. Here $I_{E\$}$ and I_{EDM} represent the Eurodollar and Eurodeutschemark interest rates, respectively.

$$
\begin{array}{l}
\text{Value at } (t + n) \text{ of} \\
\text{\$1 earning dollar} \\
\text{interest rate } I_{E\$}
\end{array}
=
\begin{array}{l}
\text{value at } (t + n) \text{ of \$1 converted into foreign} \\
\text{currency and earning foreign currency interest rate} \\
I_{EDM}, \text{ until } (t + n), \text{ when foreign currency is converted} \\
\text{back into dollars at the prearranged forward rate, } F_t^n
\end{array}
$$

$$
\$1(1 + I_{E\$}) = \$1\left(\frac{1 + I_{EDM}}{S_t}\right)F_t^n
$$

where S_t is the spot exchange rate (dollars per German mark) and F_t^n is the forward rate.

$$
\frac{1 + I_{E\$}}{1 + I_{DM}} = \frac{F_t^n}{S_t}
$$

Subtracting 1 from each side gives the **interest-rate parity relationship:**

$$
\frac{I_{E\$} - I_{EDM}}{1 + I_{EDM}} = \frac{F_t^n - S_t}{S_t}
$$

For a period of n days, the right-hand side must be converted to an annualized percentage:

$$
\frac{I_{E\$} - I_{EDM}}{1 + I_{EDM}} = \left(\frac{F_t^n - S_t}{S_t}\right)\left(\frac{365}{n}\right)
$$
$$
= \text{Forward premium or discount}
$$

and if I_{EDM} is small, then, to a close approximation,

$$
(I_{E\$} - I_{EDM}) = \left(\frac{F_t^n - S_t}{S_t}\right)\left(\frac{365}{n}\right) 100
$$

That is, *the interest-rate differential equals the forward premium or discount.*

Because banks take advantage of such covered-interest arbitrage opportunities as they arise, they seldom last very long. As shown in Example 3.1, Euromark deposit rates would be driven down, \$/DM spot rates bid up, and \$/DM forward rates bid down to the point at which the arbitrage opportunity no longer exists once the (small) bid-offer spreads and transactions costs were taken into account. In other words, interest-rate parity would soon prevail. That is,

Eurodollar interest rate = Euromark interest rate + Premium or discount

or

Interest-rate differential = forward premium or discount in the dollar/mark foreign-exchange market

EXAMPLE 3.1   **A Covered-Interest Arbitrage Transaction**

A foreign-exchange dealer, in the course of constantly monitoring interest rates and exchange rates quoted by different banks around the world, notices that the following combinations of rates are available:

> 90-day interest rates (percent per annum)
>   Euromark: 4.75 (bid) 5.00 (offer)
>   Eurodollar 6.625 (bid) 6.75 (offer)

> Exchange rates (dollars per German mark)
>   Spot: 0.3801 (bid) 0.3802 (ask)
>   90-day forward: 0.3821 (bid) 0.3823 (ask)

Realizing that when she borrows funds or buys a currency she will have to pay the higher (offer or ask) of the two rates, and realizing that when she deposits funds or sells a currency she will receive the lower of the two rates, the trader makes the following calculation:

$$\text{\textit{Cost} of borrowing Eurodollars} = 6.75 \text{ percent per annum}$$

Return from buying marks in the spot market, depositing them in a Euromark deposit, and simultaneously selling them in the forward market

$$= \text{Euromark rate} + \text{Forward premium}$$
$$= 4.75 + \frac{(0.3821 - 0.3802)}{0.3802} \times \frac{365}{90} \times 100$$
$$= 4.75 + 2.03$$
$$= 6.78 \text{ percent per annum}$$

Hence, by borrowing Eurodollars and depositing them in the Euromark market while covering them forward, the bank can earn 0.03 percent per annum, which, for a $10 million transaction, is $750.

Interest-rate parity also results from the fact that Eurobanks stand ready to offer loans or deposits in any Eurocurrency but are usually unwilling to have a net exposed position in loans or deposits. If, for example, a Eurobank offers both Eurodollar and Euromark deposits and loans, and funds itself with an imbalance of loans and deposits in each currency, it will cover this net imbalance through use of the forward market.

The purpose of covering the net exposed dollar assets is to protect the bank from being adversely affected should the dollar have weakened relative to the German mark by the time the deposits and loans mature. But if the dollar is expected to weaken, the bank will face a premium for the forward purchase of German marks. Hence the bank will only be willing to convert Euromark deposits into dollar loans if the Euromark deposit rate *plus* the $/DM forward premium is equal to or lower than the cost of dollar deposits. Similarly, banks hedging a net exposed asset position in German marks will be willing to convert Eurodollar deposits into mark loans only if the Eurodollar deposits rate *minus* the $/DM forward discount is equal to or lower than the cost of mark deposits. In equilibrium, then, the forward premium or discount will tend to settle at a rate exactly equal to the interest-rate differential between two Eurocurrencies.

In conclusion, interest-rate parity holds extremely well in the Eurocurrency markets. It does *not* always apply when comparing domestic interest rates, as is explained in Box 3.1.

Interest-rate parity does not always hold when comparing domestic, as opposed to Eurocurrency, interest rates. As noted earlier, capital controls can divide credit markets, thereby preventing arbitrage. In fact, a widely accepted measure of the effectiveness of capital controls is the **covered-interest differential**, the difference in interest rates that is not explained by the forward premium of discount. Another reason is that instruments are not always as alike as they seem. Treasury bills, for example, may be free of credit risk, have different tax treatments, liquidity, day count, pricing conventions, and institutional arrangements. Moreover, the arbitrageur cannot borrow at the risk-free Treasury-bill rate: all that can be done is *quasi-arbitrage*—that is, choosing between two different investments, one of which would be covered with a forward-exchange contract. Finally, because the forward contract itself is not risk free, unadulterated covered-interest arbitrage between Treasury bills is not really possible.

Forward-Exchange Rates, Relative Interest Rates, and Exchange-Rate Expectations

The second relationship is that between the forward- and spot-exchange rates and exchange-rate expectations.

The forward premium or discount reflects not only covered interest arbitrage but also exchange-rate expectations, because commercial and financial transactors who expect to receive future revenues in currencies other than that which they wish to hold will tend to agree to forward-exchange transactions only at an exchange rate close to that which they expect to prevail in the future. In general, the forward exchange rate is strongly influenced by the market's expectations about the future exchange rate, as people's currency expectations change as the result of new information, so the forward premium or discount will adjust to equal the expected rate of change of the exchange rate (expressed as an annualized percentage), adjusted, perhaps, for a risk premium. We will discuss this risk premium in detail in Chapter 6; for simplicity's sake, we'll assume it's zero. Then

Forward premium or discount

= Expected annual rate of change of the exchange rate

That is,

$$P_{\$/DM} = E(R_{\$/DM})$$

where $P_{\$/DM}$ is the dollar/German-mark forward premium or discount as before, and $E(R_{\$/DM})$ is the annual rate at which the market expects the dollar/German-mark exchange rate to change. This relationship between the forward rate and the exchange-rate expectations may be termed the "unbiased forward-rate theorem."

Let us stop for a moment and compare the two relationships identified so far. The first said that the interest-rate differential equals the forward premium or discount; the second, that the forward premium or discount equals the expected rate of change of the exchange rate. Clearly, the two are compatible if and only if interest-rate differentials between Eurocurrencies equal the expected rate of change of the exchange rate. It is reasonable to suppose that there is such a tendency, because banks and corporations will seek to invest in currencies expected to appreciate, and to borrow currencies expected to depreciate, to the point at which the expected gain from an exchange rate change is offset by the interest rate differential. For example, when in 1993 market participants expected the Irish punt to devalue against the German mark, the interest rate on short-term interbank Irish punt deposits was driven to levels that made speculation against the punt uneconomic.

So if we ignore the possible premium necessary for taking speculative risk, the incentive for depositing in strong currencies and borrowing in weak currencies will disappear only when the Euromark rate has been bid up and the punt/mark exchange rate bid down to the point at which the Euromark rate plus the expected rate of depreciation of the punt approximates the Europunt rate.

Because any pair of Eurocurrencies will quickly adjust to borrowing and depositing pressures of the kind just described, one would expect that the following relationship would normally hold to a close approximation:

Interest rate in one Eurocurrency market	*minus*	Interest rate in other Eurocurrency market	*equals*	Expected annual rate of change of exchange rate

That is,

The interest rate differential equals the expected annual rate of change of the exchange rate.

If both Eurocurrency markets are closely linked to their respective domestic markets, then domestic as well as Eurocurrency interest rates are linked to one another through the spot- and forward-exchange rates, and adjustments that occur in Eurocurrency rates must also occur in domestic credit markets. This relationship, which is sometimes termed the **International Fisher Effect**, shows how the two notions of how the forward premium of discount is determined (*the covered-interest arbitrage theory* and *the forward-rate-equals-expected-future-spot-rate theory*) are consistent, compatible, and indeed two sides of the same coin.

The three theorems that have been described may now be brought together and summarized in a single statement of the normal relationship between Eurocurrency rates,

Figure 3.9   *Money and Foreign-Exchange Market Linkages.*   The interest-rate differential equals the forward premium or discount, which tends also to equal the expected exchange-rate change.

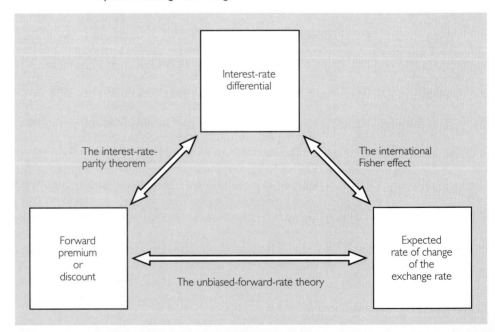

spot– and forward–exchange rates, and exchange-rate expectations: *The borrowing, lending, and hedging actions of banks and corporations tend to ensure that the interest-rate differential between two Eurocurrency markets equals the forward premium or discount and also equals the expected exchange-rate change expressed as an annual rate.*

In the absence of capital controls, risk premiums, or other barriers, all credit markets are linked to one another through arbitrage and currency expectations. The final situation will resemble that illustrated in Figure 3.9.

The Term Structure of Eurocurrency Interest Rates

The term structure of interest rates is the relationship between interest rates and time to maturity. Typically this relationship is depicted as the **yield curve,** a plot of U.S. Treasury yields at a particular point in time. As in Figure 3.10, the interest rate is plotted on the vertical axis and time to maturity on the horizontal axis. Term-structure theory is concerned with why the yield curve has a particular shape at a particular time. Although there is some dispute as to the role of institutional constraints and liquidity preference in

Figure 3.10   *A Snapshot of Eurocurrency Yield Curves*

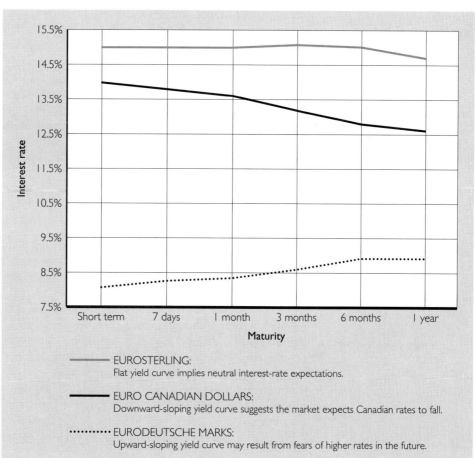

EUROSTERLING:
Flat yield curve implies neutral interest-rate expectations.

EURO CANADIAN DOLLARS:
Downward-sloping yield curve suggests the market expects Canadian rates to fall.

EURODEUTSCHE MARKS:
Upward-sloping yield curve may result from fears of higher rates in the future.

influencing the yield curve, all agree that expectations of future short-term rates play a dominant role in determining the level of longer-term rates.

For our purposes it suffices to observe that whatever explanation of the term structure holds for the domestic market should also hold for the external or Euromarket. In the absence of capital controls, arbitrage would ensure the virtual equality of internal and external rates at each maturity, and whatever holds for the domestic market would also hold for Eurorates. In other words, there is normally no independent Eurodollar term structure of interest rates.

If capital controls were in place and affected all maturities equally, the internal term structure might not be identical to the external one. But since Eurorates would tend to be at the same position relative to the internal rates at each maturity, a nearly identical term structure would hold. If capital controls affected some maturities but not others, the term structure should still be identical as long as expectations of future rates were the same, because the expectations theory at work, along with arbitrage in one maturity, would bring external rates in other maturities into alignment with internal rates. If, for example, internal–external arbitrage were possible between short-term but not long-term deposits, identical forecasts for future short-term rates in both the internal and external credit markets should result in identical long-term rates in both markets.

What about the relationships between the term structures of interest rates in different Eurocurrency markets? Because there can be no capital controls separating the Euromarkets, the primary influence keeping yield structures different is the expectation of exchange-rate changes, which in turn are based in large part on inflation expectations. The relationship between the term structures of two Eurocurrency markets, such as the Eurodollar and Euromark term structures, reflects the forward premium of discount and currency expectations at each period in the future. In other words, by comparing the term structure of interest rates in two Eurocurrency markets, one may infer the term structure of exchange-rate expectations.

Of course, if well-developed forward markets exist for all maturities, the term structure of exchange-rate expectations may be derived directly from the series of forward-exchange rates, assuming these give an unbiased expectation of future spot rates. For most markets, however, longer-term forward markets are nonexistent or too thin to be reliable. In such cases it may be useful to employ the term structure of interest rates in two credit markets to deduce the term structure of exchange-rate expectations.

Summary

In this chapter the major determinants of international interest rates were identified as (1) domestic and foreign credit conditions, (2) forward-exchange rates and exchange-rate expectations, and (3) three sets of factors that might inhibit arbitrage—capitol controls, risk factors, and transactions costs.

External (or Euro) interest rates, it was argued, are always linked through arbitrage to internal rates, although capital controls can weaken this linkage. In the absence of capital controls, external loan and deposit rates are bounded by loan and deposit rates in the internal credit market. Eurocurrency rates are linked to one another through covered-interest arbitrage in such a way that the interest-rate differential equals the forward premium or discount between two currencies. In addition, market transactors, through the process of borrowing and lending in different currencies, cause the forward premium or discount and the interest-rate differential to approximate the expected rate of change of the exchange rate. As a result, the path of exchange-rate changes that the market expects can be deduced by comparing the term structures of interest rates in two Eurocurrency markets.

The reader will recognize that these relationships do not necessarily hold at all times in exactly the form described here. We showed that interest-rate parity does not necessarily hold when comparing domestic interest rates, even when they are rates on seemingly equivalent instruments. It is not certain, for example, that the forward rate is always an unbiased predictor of the future spot exchange rate; indeed, some evidence points to the existence of a bias attributable to a risk premium, as we shall see in Chapter 6. But the relationships as presented have enough generality to explain a wide range of phenomena in the international money market.

In the Eurocurrency market, the relationships between interest and foreign-exchange rates described in this chapter result from a continual process of simultaneous interaction among international currency and credit dealers. Any deviation from interest-rate parity, for example, will set in motion a number of transactions that will change interest rates and exchange rates, and this change will trigger further transactions until interest-rate parity between Eurocurrency and foreign exchange is reestablished. The interest-rate-parity theorem describes an ex post relationship toward which rates will tend to move. However, which part of the total readjustment is actually accomplished by changes in which rate cannot be determined a priori; this depends on the relative sizes of the credit markets involved, on exchange-rate expectations, on the degree of institutional flexibility and efficiency in the market, and, of course, on government regulations and intervention.

CONCEPTUAL QUESTIONS

1. Define the two key relationships among interest rates in the international money market.
2. What are the upper and lower boundaries for Eurodollar interest rates, based on their relationship with the domestic money market?
3. What considerations influence the choice of depositing funds in the Eurocurrency rather than in the domestic money market?
4. What considerations influence a borrower's choice of whether to borrow from a bank in its domestic market rather than in the same currency in the Euromarket?
5. Why have Eurodollar rates historically exceeded domestic U.S. bank deposit rates? Would you expect this to continue?
6. Contrast the *market-price-of-risk* with the *cost-of-regulation* explanations of the Eurodollar premium.
7. In what way are domestic interbank placements in the United States like Eurodollar deposits?
8. How can the imposition of controls on capital outflows influence Eurocurrency interest rates?
9. Is a deposit in Royal Bank of Canada's Hong Kong branch as safe as an equivalent deposit in its Toronto headquarters? Explain your answer.
10. Which is more important in explaining Eurocurrency interest-rate differentials: covered interest arbitrage or exchange-rate expectations?
11. If capital controls separated the Eurocurrency market from the domestic money market, would you expect the term structure of Eurocurrency interest rates to be different from, the same as, or similar to the domestic term structure?

PROBLEMS

1. The U.S. bank deposit rate is now 5.35 percent, and the Eurodollar deposit rate 5.60 percent. Assuming that the entire differential is attributable to the Fed's reserve requirement on bank deposits, what is likely to happen to the Eurodollar rate if the U.S. rate rises by one percentage point?
2. If the U.S. three-month bank deposit rate is 10 percent, the reserve requirement is 3 percent, and FDIC fees are 0.20 percent, what would you expect the Eurodollar rate to be?

3. The relationship between domestic and Eurodeposit interest rates is best explained by

(a) exchange-rate expectations.   (d) relative regulatory costs.

(b) the forward premium or discount.   (e) relative risks, as perceived by depositors.

(c) both (a) and (b).   (f) both (d) and (e).

4. Based on the Eurocurrency interest rates in Table 3.2, which currencies might be expected to fall against the French franc?

5. Show, by means of an example using actual market rates, why the interest-rate differential roughly equals the forward-exchange premium or discount.

6. A bank in London is currently quoting 9 percent on 12-month Eurodollar deposits. It is also quoting 5 FF/$ and 5.25 FF/$ for spot and 12-month forward French francs, respectively. If a customer asks for a quote on depositing French francs, what interest rate should the bank quote? (Choose one.)

(a) 9.25%

(b) 4.25%

(c) 4.00%

(d) 14.45%

7. If the dollar is trading at 130 yen in the spot market, and the six-month Eurodollar and Euroyen rates are 10 percent and 7.5 percent respectively, what is the six-month yen/dollar forward-exchange rate?

(a) 127.045

(b) 131.567

(c) 128.452

(d) 133.023

(e) 127.500

8. On one day in early 1993, the rates shown below were quoted on the Reuters screen. Can you identify a covered interest-rate differential (in other words, a deviation from interest-rate parity)? What factors might account for this deviation from parity?

3-Month interest rates	Treasury-bill rate	Domestic interbank deposit rates
London (sterling)	6 3/4–6 11/16	7 5/16–7 3/16
Paris (French francs)	11 1/8–11	12 1/8–11 3/8

Exchange rates against pound	Spot	3-month forward points
French franc	5.3395–53405	11.00–12.00 centimes discount

Application 3.1 | THE MOMU PRESENTATION

You are Missouri Mutual's investment banker. Study the Momu case below, in preparation for your presentation to Momu on their choices of hedging methods for their sterling investment.

Develop a presentation on the advantages and disadvantages of

1. doing nothing.
2. implementing a forward hedge.
3. implementing a "spot" hedge (using the money market).

Think about the principles involved. Use the numbers in the table entitled Money and Interest Rates to check your logic. Then prepare a clear, nontechnical presentation to Momu's Investment Committee.

THE MOMU FUND

Missouri Mutual, known in the industry as Momu, is a U.S. insurance company whose funds managers have, in the past, specialized in beating the averages by identifying special opportunities in the fixed-income market. As a result of a research report produced by their investment advisors, FNB Securities Inc., the company decided on September 3, 1985, to invest in two "Zebras"—essentially U.K. Treasury bonds ("gilts") that had been stripped of their coupons. The exchange rate at the time was $1.31 per pound sterling, and Missouri Mutual paid FNB $106,800 and $934,300 for the two Zebras that would mature on October 30, 1985, and January 31, 1986, respectively. These were funded in the U.S. at an estimated cost of 9 percent per annum.

On October 27, 1985, as Momu's portfolio manager was considering what to do with the £83,000 to be received in three days' time, she observed that Momu had, as hoped, made a gain on the bonds.

But Momu's Investment Committee was now nervously urging her to think about hedging the company's foreign-currency exposure to the £750,000 Zebra maturing in January. One alternative was to avoid any involvement with foreign exchange by doing nothing. The fact that the pound sterling had appreciated to $1.4286 and was expected to remain strong as a result of a recent central-bank intervention agreement reinforced those favoring this choice.

A second choice was simply to lock in the future exchange rate through a forward-exchange contract. The Reuters screen was quoting three-month forward sterling at $1.4170–1.4180. In effect, this would lock in a loss compared to what sterling was worth now.

As a third possibility, Momu's portfolio manager considered a so-called spot, or money market, hedge. This would involve borrowing in the United Kingdom and changing the money into dollars right away. The cost of this would be the lower interest rate that could be obtained in U.S. investments compared to the cost of borrowing in Britain.

Money and Interest Rates

	Money supply % rise on year ago		Interest rates (percent per annum)							
			Money market		Commercial banks		Bond yields		Eurocurrency	
	Broad	Narrow (M1)	Overnight	3-month T bills	Prime lending	3-month deposits	Gov't. long-term	Corporate	3-month deposits	Bonds
Australia	+ 16.1	+ 18.7	15.75	16.25	18.50	16.00	13.78	14.78	15.66	13.18
Belgium	+ 2.5	+ 6.8	7.85	9.35	12.00	8.80	10.64	10.95	9.13	na
Canada	+ 7.0	+ 4.9	8.63	9.05	10.13	9.10	11.10	11.07	8.81	11.51
France	+ 7.7	+ 8.2	9.38	9.56	10.85	9.56	10.84	12.21	10.38	11.40
Germany	+ 4.1	+ 4.7	4.55	4.65	7.50	4.23	6.80	6.60	4.44	6.77
Holland	+ 6.1	+ 6.5	5.63	5.81	7.50	5.81	6.93	7.35	5.89	7.04
Italy	+ 13.8	+ 14.3	14.25	14.25	16.00	11.50	13.85	13.08	12.75	na
Japan	+ 5.0	+ 8.3	6.25	6.31	5.50	3.50	5.98	6.52	6.44	7.18
Sweden	na	+ 2.7	15.00	15.15	15.25	14.93	13.50	13.50	15.56	na
Switzerland	− 1.2	+ 4.4	10.63	4.50	7.50	4.00	4.72	5.02	4.50	5.16
UK	+ 18.3	+ 13.6	12.25	11.10	12.50	11.25	10.54	11.30	11.38	10.77
U.S.	+ 10.4	+ 8.9	7.86	7.70	9.50	7.90	10.77	11.55	8.13	10.38

Other key rates in London 11.1%, 7-day interbank 11.9%. Eurodollar (LIBOR): 3-month 8.2%, 6-month 8.4%.

Application 3.2 | A YEN FOR PROFIT

One o'clock in the afternoon is sometimes slow in the dealing rooms of banks in Tokyo. New York has gone to bed, London is not yet awake, and many of the senior staff are out to lunch. It was such an afternoon when Hiroki Uenishi, a junior trader at Sanyo Bank, thought he would take advantage of the lull. The previous week, on a visit to Tokyo, he had noticed that Eurodollar deposits in Singapore (sometimes called Asian dollar deposits) sometimes yielded more than their London equivalents. Sanyo, he knew, could often obtain one-month yen deposits about ⅛ percent cheaper than the market's quoted bid rates. Could he perhaps initiate a covered-interest arbitrage program, borrowing in yen and investing in U.S. dollars? The accompanying Reuters screen gave him the necessary Eurocurrency rates.

REUTERS EUROCURRENCY INTEREST-RATE SERVICE

	1 MONTH	3-MONTH	6-MONTH	1 YEAR
STERLING	15 3/32–15 1/16	15 3/32–15 1/16	15–14 7/8	14 5/8–14 1/2
U.S. DOLLAR	8 3/8–8 1/4	8 5/16–8 3/16	8 5/16–8 3/16	8 5/16–8 3/16
CAN DOLLAR	12 1/8–11 7/8	12 3/16–11 15/16	11 15/16–11 11/16	11 3/4–11 1/2
DUTCH GUILDER	8 15/16–8 13/16	8 15/16–8 13/16	8 15/16–8 13/16	8 15/16–8 13/16
SWISS FRANC	9 13/16–9 11/16	9 1/2–9 3/8	9 1/4–9 1/8	9 1/16–8 15/16
DEUTSCHEMARK	8 1/8–8	8 7/16–8 5/16	8 5/8–8 1/2	8 11/16–8 9/16
FRENCH FRANC	11 1/4–11 1/8	11 5/8–11 1/2	11 5/8–11 1/2	11 5/8–11 1/2
ITALIAN LIRA	13–12 1/2	13–12 1/2	13–12 5/8	13 1/4–13
BELG. FRANC	10 9/16–10 7/16	10 9/16–10 7/16	10 9/16–10 7/16	10 9/16–10 11/16
YEN	6 11/16–6 9/16	6 15/16–6 13/16	7–6 7/8	7–6 7/8
DANISH KRONE	12 5/16–12 1/16	12 5/16–12 1/16	12 1/8–11 15/16	11 7/8–11 3/4
ASIAN $ SING.	8 3/8–8 1/4	8 3/8–8 1/4	8 5/16–8 3/16	8 5/16–8 3/16

To get spot and forward foreign-exchange rates, Uenishi buzzed the FX traders across the room. The reply came from the dollar/yen spot trader. "Spot 143.70–143.80." Then the swap trader piped in, "Swap rate, one month dollar-yen, 0.23–0.21 premium."

Is there an arbitrage opportunity? Specify the steps that would have to be taken to undertake such arbitrage.

Application 3.3 | TEA IN CANADA

You are an investment manager/trader at Steinhardt Partners, an aggressive New York investment-management firm. Evaluate the attached trade recommendation. Can you explain briefly the reason why such an arbitrage opportunity might arise? And before you rush to do the trade, be sure to list its possible disadvantages, if any.

Again from the point of view of Steinhardt as money managers, what merit might there be to using futures instead of a forward contract to effect this transaction?

TEA IN CANADA WITHOUT PAYING THE BILL
AUGUST 20, 1987

Recommendation

Swap U.S. T-Bills into fully hedged Canadian dollar T-Bills. Yield pickup on 6-month and 1-year maturity investments is approximately 70 basis points over Treasury.

Analysis

The Canadian dollar forward discount against the dollar is determined by the arbitrage conditions in the offshore interbank market. In circumstances where U.S. bank credit risk increases relative to Canadian bank credit risk, the Canadian dollar discount in the forex market can decline. This creates a virtually riskless arbitrage opportunity in the Canadian Treasury Bill hedged into U.S. dollars. The beauty of the trade lies in the fact that the investor can earn a significant spread over U.S. T-Bills while holding the credit risk of the Canadian government!

In May this year the opportunity was greatest when Citicorp wrote off a portion of its LDC debt. This signaled higher credit risk in the Eurodollar deposit market. In Diagram 1 we plot the spread between 6-month LIBOR and T-Bills as a measure of U.S. bank credit risk. In diagram 2 we plot the spread between 3-month Canadian bank acceptances and T-Bills as a measure of Canadian bank risk. While U.S. bank credit risk has increased since 1986, Canadian bank risk has been volatile but trendless. Diagram 3 plots the spread between Canadian T-Bills hedged into dollars against U.S. T-Bills. It is evident that this spread is highly correlated with U.S. bank credit risk (relative to Canadian bank credit risk). While in May an investor could have earned 136 basis points swapping U.S. T-Bills from hedged Canadian bills, this declined precipitously to zero in July. The decline in bank risk eliminated the arbitrage opportunity. In August the opportunity arose again as U.S. bank risk widened.

> **Execution of the basic trade**
> 1. Sell U.S. Treasury Bills
> 2. Buy spot Canadian dollars with dollars
> 3. Buy Canadian T-Bills
> 4. Sell Forward Canadian dollars to lock in dollar return

The optimal timing of the trade is at the peak of a U.S. bank credit crisis. One leading indicator of this would be a persistent decline in U.S. bank stocks (relating to the DJ index) or a continuous rise in the TED spread. At this time, not only does the investor pick up the lower discount on the Canadian T-Bills but also can sell his U.S. bills at a top price due to a flight into quality paper.

In Exhibits A and B we fully describe the flow of funds from purchasing the hedged T-Bills for 1 year and 6 months, respectively, and holding the bills to maturity. The face value of the Canadian T-Bill is assumed to be C$10 million. An alternate strategy is to unwind the transaction as the spread over T-Bills narrows. This could occur if the "bank credit" problem is resolved. For example, had the above arbitrage been carried out on May 27 and closed out on July 28, an investor would have earned 136 basis points in two months. On a Canadian T-Bill with face value of C$10 million, an investor would have earned US$185,901 or a 16.10% return on the value of the swapped U.S. T-Bill. (See Exhibit C for details of this swap.)

EXHIBIT A

1-Year Arbitrage

Canadian T-Bill

			BID	OFFER
Face Value:	100			
Discount:	9.052%		BID	OFFER
Price:	90.97298725	Canadian Spot:	1.3309	1.3314
Principal Amt.:	10,000.000	Premium(Disc):	(0.026)	(0.0275)
Actual Days:	364	Canadian Forward:	1.3569	1.3589

		Canadian Cash Flows	Hedged Net US Cash Flows
Settlement:	Aug. 21, 1987	(9,097,299)	($6,835,449)
Maturity:	Aug. 19, 1988	10,000,000	$7,358,893
Yield:		9.950%	7.679%

Spread over U.S. T-Bill: 69 Basis Points

EXHIBIT B

6-Month Arbitrage

Canadian T-Bill

			BID	OFFER
Face Value:	100			
Discount:	9.027%		BID	OFFER
Price:	95.40912216	Canadian Spot:	1.3309	1.3314
Principal Amt.:	10,000,000	Premium(Disc):	(0.0145)	(0.0149)
Actual Days:	182	Canadian Forward:	1.3454	1.3463

		Canadian Cash Flows	Hedged Net US Cash Flows
Settlement:	Aug. 21, 1987	(9,540,912)	($7,168,767)
Maturity:	Feb. 19, 1988	10,000,000	$7,427,765
Yield:		9.650%	7.246%

Spread over U.S. T-Bill: 71 Basis Points

EXHIBIT C

Investor swaps U.S. T-Bills (face value: C$10 mil.) for Canadian T-Bills on May 27, 1987, and then unwinds the position on July 28, 1987.

DATA	May 27, 1987	July 28, 1987
Spot Rate	1.3426	1.335
Forward Rate	1.3568	1.3587
U.S. 1-Year T-Bill Rate		
(Simp. Yld 365 days)	0.0708	0.0866
CN 1-Year T-Bill Rate	0.0960	0.0910

DIAGRAM 1   **6-Month LIBOR–6-Month US T-Bill(Disc), July 1986 to Present**

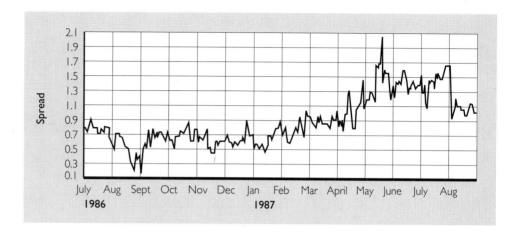

DIAGRAM 2   **3-Month Canadian B.A.–3-Month Canadian T-Bill, July 1986 to Present**

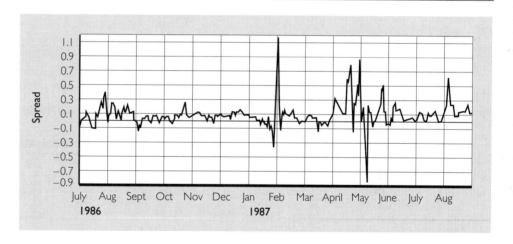

DIAGRAM 3   **1-Year Canadian T-Bill Hedged Forward ($)–1-Year U.S. T-Bill, July 1986 to Present**

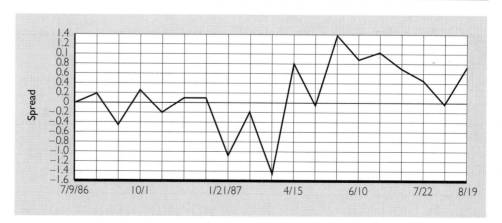

Face CN$: 100	*May 27, 1987*		*July 28, 1987*	
May 27, 1987	C$	US$	C$	US$
1) Sell U.S. T-Bill		67.96		
2) Buy Spot C$	91.24	(67.96)		
3) Buy CN T-Bill (face: 100)	(91.24)			
4) Sell 100 C$ FWD				
July 28, 1987				
1) Sell CN T-Bills			92.98	
2) Buy Spot US$			(92.98)	69.65
3) Buy back orig. US$ Bills				(67.89)
4) Unwind FWD Forex Contract				.10
			TOTAL PROFIT	**1.86**

Profits on the arbitrage are US$185,901 on C$10 MIL. Face Value.

Application 3.4

TEA IN ENGLAND

Lisa Donneson, County Natwest's international fixed-income portfolio advisor, had heard from the manager of the Momu Fund that, from time to time, opportunities arose to arbitrage the Treasury bill markets in the United States and the United Kingdom. She decided to check on this. "First," she thought, "Momu would have to use the forward-

Exhibit I ***Excerpts from the Currency and Interest-Rate Page in the*** **Financial Times**

EXCHANGE CROSS RATES

May.20	£	$	DM	Yen	F Fr.	S Fr.	N Fl.	Lira	C$	B Fr.	Pta.	Ecu
£	1	1.556	2.510	172.0	8.465	2.280	2.818	2284	1.971	51.60	191.4	1.286
$	0.643	1	1.613	110.5	5.440	1.465	1.811	1468	1.267	33.16	123.0	0.826
DM	0.398	0.620	1	68.53	3.373	0.908	1.123	910.0	0.785	20.56	76.25	0.512
YEN	5.814	9.047	14.59	1000.	49.22	13.26	16.38	13279	11.46	300.0	1113	7.477
F Fr.	1.181	1.838	2.965	203.2	10.	2.693	3.329	2698	2.328	60.96	226.1	1.519
S Fr.	0.439	0.682	1.101	75.44	3.713	1	1.236	1002	0.864	22.63	83.95	0.564
N Fl.	0.355	0.552	0.891	61.04	3.004	0.809	1	810.5	0.699	18.31	67.92	0.456
Lira	0.438	0.681	1.099	75.31	3.706	0.998	1.234	1000.	0.863	22.59	83.80	0.563
C $	0.507	0.789	1.273	87.27	4.295	1.157	1.430	1159	1	26.18	97.11	0.652
B Fr.	1.938	3.016	4.864	333.3	16.41	4.419	5.461	4426	3.820	100.	370.9	2.492
Pta	0.522	0.813	1.311	89.86	4.423	1.191	1.472	1193	1.030	26.96	100.	0.672
Ecu	0.778	1.210	1.952	133.7	6.582	1.773	2.191	1776	1.533	40.12	148.8	1.

Yen per 1,000: French Fr. per 10: Lira per 1,000: Belgian Fr. per 100: Peseta per 100.

EURO-CURRENCY INTEREST RATES

May 20	Short term	7 Days notice	One Month	Three Months	Six Months	One Year
Sterling	$5\frac{1}{2} - 5\frac{3}{8}$	$5\frac{3}{4} - 5\frac{5}{8}$	$6\frac{1}{16} - 5\frac{15}{16}$	$6\frac{1}{16} - 5\frac{15}{16}$	$6\frac{1}{8} - 6$	$6\frac{1}{4} - 6\frac{1}{8}$
US Dollar	$3 - 2\frac{7}{8}$	$3\frac{1}{16} - 2\frac{15}{16}$	$3\frac{1}{8} - 3$	$3\frac{1}{4} - 3\frac{1}{8}$	$3\frac{3}{8} - 3\frac{1}{4}$	$3\frac{11}{16} - 3\frac{9}{16}$
Can. Dollar	$3\frac{7}{8} - 3\frac{5}{8}$	$4 - 3\frac{7}{8}$	$4\frac{5}{8} - 4\frac{3}{8}$	$5\frac{1}{8} - 4\frac{7}{8}$	$5\frac{1}{2} - 5\frac{1}{4}$	$6 - 5\frac{3}{4}$
Dutch Guilder	$7\frac{3}{8} - 7\frac{1}{4}$	$7\frac{5}{16} - 7\frac{3}{16}$	$7\frac{1}{4} - 7\frac{1}{8}$	$6\frac{15}{16} - 6\frac{13}{16}$	$6\frac{11}{16} - 6\frac{9}{16}$	$6\frac{3}{8} - 6\frac{1}{4}$
Swiss Franc	$5\frac{1}{4} - 5$	$5\frac{1}{4} - 5$	$5\frac{1}{8} - 5$	$5\frac{1}{8} - 5$	$4\frac{15}{16} - 4\frac{13}{16}$	$4\frac{11}{16} - 4\frac{9}{16}$
D-Mark	$8 - 7\frac{7}{8}$	$7\frac{7}{8} - 7\frac{3}{4}$	$7\frac{11}{16} - 7\frac{9}{16}$	$7\frac{3}{8} - 7\frac{1}{4}$	$7\frac{1}{8} - 7$	$6\frac{5}{8} - 6\frac{1}{2}$
French Franc	$8\frac{1}{4} - 8$	$8\frac{1}{4} - 8$	$8 - 7\frac{3}{4}$	$7\frac{9}{16} - 7\frac{7}{16}$	$7\frac{1}{4} - 7$	$6\frac{7}{8} - 6\frac{5}{8}$
Italian Lira	$12\frac{1}{2} - 10\frac{1}{2}$	$10\frac{3}{4} - 10\frac{3}{8}$	$10\frac{5}{8} - 10\frac{1}{4}$	$10\frac{1}{2} - 10\frac{1}{8}$	$10\frac{1}{2} - 10\frac{1}{8}$	$10\frac{1}{4} - 10$
Belgian Franc	$7\frac{7}{16} - 7\frac{5}{16}$	$7\frac{7}{16} - 7\frac{5}{16}$	$7\frac{5}{16} - 7\frac{3}{16}$	$7\frac{3}{16} - 7\frac{1}{16}$	$6\frac{7}{8} - 6\frac{3}{4}$	$6\frac{3}{4} - 6\frac{5}{8}$
Yen	$3\frac{5}{16} - 3\frac{1}{4}$	$3\frac{5}{16} - 3\frac{1}{4}$	$3\frac{5}{16} - 3\frac{1}{4}$	$3\frac{5}{16} - 3\frac{1}{4}$	$3\frac{3}{8} - 3\frac{5}{16}$	$3\frac{7}{16} - 3\frac{3}{8}$
Danish Krone	$9\frac{1}{2} - 9$	$9\frac{1}{2} - 9$	$9\frac{1}{4} - 8\frac{1}{2}$	$8\frac{1}{2} - 8$	$8 - 7\frac{1}{2}$	$7\frac{1}{2} - 7$
Asian $Sing	$3\frac{1}{4} - 2\frac{1}{4}$	$3\frac{1}{4} - 2\frac{1}{4}$	$3\frac{1}{2} - 2\frac{1}{2}$	$3\frac{1}{2} - 2\frac{1}{2}$	$3\frac{1}{2} - 2\frac{1}{2}$	$3\frac{3}{4} - 2\frac{3}{4}$
Spanish Peseta	$12\frac{5}{8} - 12\frac{1}{8}$	$12\frac{5}{8} - 12\frac{1}{8}$	$12\frac{1}{16} - 11\frac{13}{16}$	$11\frac{9}{16} - 11\frac{5}{16}$	$11 - 10\frac{3}{4}$	$11 - 10\frac{3}{4}$
Portuguese Esc.	$14\frac{1}{2} - 13\frac{1}{2}$	$14\frac{1}{2} - 13\frac{1}{2}$	$14\frac{1}{4} - 13\frac{1}{4}$	$13\frac{3}{4} - 12\frac{3}{4}$	$13\frac{3}{4} - 12\frac{3}{4}$	$13\frac{1}{2} - 12\frac{1}{2}$

Long term Eurodollars: two years $4\frac{3}{8}$-$4\frac{1}{4}$ per cent; three years $4\frac{13}{16}$-$4\frac{11}{16}$ per cent; four years $5\frac{1}{4}$-$5\frac{1}{8}$ per cent; five years $5\frac{5}{8}$-$5\frac{5}{16}\frac{1}{2}$ per cent nominal. Short term rates are call for US Dollar and Japanese Yen; others, two days' notice.

LONDON MONEY RATES

May 18	Overnight	7 days notice	One Month	Three Months	Six Months	One Year
Interbank Offer	$6\frac{5}{8}$	$6\frac{1}{4}$	$6\frac{1}{8}$	$6\frac{1}{8}$	$6\frac{3}{16}$	$6\frac{3}{8}$
Interbank Bid	5	$5\frac{3}{4}$	$5\frac{7}{8}$	6	$6\frac{1}{16}$	$6\frac{1}{4}$
Sterling CDs.	-	-	$5\frac{31}{32}$	$5\frac{31}{32}$	6	$6\frac{3}{32}$
Local Authority Deps.	$6\frac{1}{2}$	$6\frac{1}{4}$	$6\frac{1}{8}$	$6\frac{1}{8}$	$6\frac{3}{16}$	$6\frac{3}{8}$
Local Authority Bonds	-	-	-	-	-	-
Discount Mkt Deps	$6\frac{1}{4}$	6	-	-	-	-
Company Deposits	-	-	-	-	-	-
Finance House Deposits	-	-	$6\frac{3}{32}$	$6\frac{1}{8}$	$6\frac{3}{16}$	$6\frac{3}{16}$
Treasury Bills (Buy)	-	-	$5\frac{11}{16}$	$5\frac{11}{16}$	$5\frac{9}{16}$	-
Bank Bills (Buy)	-	-	$5\frac{23}{32}$	$5\frac{23}{32}$	$5\frac{23}{32}$	-
Fine Trade Bills (Buy)	-	-	-	-	-	-
Dollar CDs.	-	-	2.94	2.98	3.07	3.33
SDR Linked Dep. Offer	-	-	$4\frac{11}{16}$	$4\frac{5}{8}$	$4\frac{9}{16}$	$4\frac{9}{16}$
SDR Linked Dep. Bid	-	-	$4\frac{9}{16}$	$4\frac{1}{2}$	$4\frac{7}{16}$	$4\frac{7}{16}$
ECU Linked Dep. Offer	-	-	$8\frac{1}{8}$	$7\frac{3}{4}$	$7\frac{1}{2}$	$7\frac{3}{16}$
ECU Linked Dep. Bid	-	-	$7\frac{7}{8}$	$7\frac{1}{2}$	7	$6\frac{15}{16}$

MONEY RATES

NEW YORK — Treasury Bills and Bonds

4pm					
		One month	2.90	Three year	4.48
		Two month	2.99	Five year	5.28
Prime rate	6	Three month	3.09	Seven year	5.76
Broker loan rate	5	Six month	3.21	10-year	6.13
Fed.funds	$2\frac{13}{16}$	One year	3.40	30-year	7.08
Fed.funds at intervention	$3\frac{1}{16}$	Two year	4.04		

Source: *Financial Times*, May 21, 1993.

exchange market, so I'd better find out what the spot- and forward-exchange rates are, and what yields can be obtained on Treasury bills in the two countries. I'll get the data from the newspaper (see Exhibit I) and organize it in a little table."

	U.S. Bid-Offer	U.K. Bid-Offer
Spot exchange rate, $ per £		
Forward exchange rate, $ per £		
Eurocurrency interest rates		
Treasury bill yields		

"Hmm, it looks like some information is missing. I guess I'll have to calculate it, being careful to use bid and offer rates in the correct manner. Now that I've done that, what covered-interest arbitrage opportunity is there between the U.S. and the U.K. treasury bill markets?"

Can you help Ms. Donneson find an opportunity to profit? How much could she make?

SELECTED REFERENCES

Dufey, Gunter, and Ian H. Giddy. *The International Money Market.* 2d ed. Englewood Cliffs, N.J.: Prentice-Hall, 1994.

Bank for International Settlements, *Annual Report,* various issues.

Frankel, Jeffery A. "Measuring International Capital Mobility: A Review." *American Economic Association Papers and Proceedings* (May 1992):197–202.

4
Exchange-Rate Systems

This chapter is about how a country's domestic economy is tied to its international trade and capital flows, and, through its exchange rate and the foreign-exchange market, to the world economy. It confronts the problem countries face: Should we have a freely floating exchange rate, or a fixed rate, or something in between? The chapter concludes by looking at the answer sought by the European Monetary System.

The Issues in Brief

What is the so-called international monetary system? Is it a system at all, or is it a haphazard collection of monetary and exchange-rate choices that individual countries happen to make? No country today is forced by any global institution to have a fixed exchange rate, or a floating one, so there is certainly no *system* in the sense of a centralized ordering of countries' international monetary relations. However noble the goals of the International Monetary Fund (IMF), that institution has no coercive power, especially over countries that are not borrowers in need. Yet there *is* a system in the biological sense that certain natural limits order the ways things turn out in fact. The idea that countries choose their exchange-rate mechanism willy-nilly cannot be correct, for their choices are severely constrained by economic circumstances and domestic policies.

Consider the world's economy. Countries buy goods from and sell goods to one another; they borrow from and lend to one another; and they invest in or receive investments from one another. This sounds like profit-maximizing business, and by and large it is. Except for aid or other politically motivated economic interactions, the same principles governing personal business govern the international economy. People buy goods from other countries only if the products are desirable and reasonably priced, so a country's prices and its exchange rate must be consistent with those in the rest of the world. If circumstances change, and someone else's products become more attractive or cheaper (or the other way round), a country will have to adjust accordingly, just as a business would have to. Nobody can borrow forever, so at some point borrower (deficit) countries have to reduce consumption or increase production to make the money to repay debt. Because countries have to live with these economic realities, they usually (not always!) adopt international economic policies, including the choice of an exchange-rate regime, that facilitate rather than hinder such adjustments.

So what natural order prevails? We can break the answer into two parts: (1) the *economic circumstances* that prevail, and (2) the *economic policies* the country has chosen. Each set of factors will have a strong influence on the kind of exchange-rate system the country has, and together they help make sense of the variety of currency types that prevail today.

The following economic circumstances are likely to constrain a country's choice of an exchange-rate system:[1]

---

[1]Adapted from H. Robert Heller, "Choosing an Exchange Rate System," *Finance and Development,* vol. 14 (June 1977), 23–27.

- *Openness.* Relatively closed economies—characterized by a small foreign-trade sector, such as Japan—may find it costly to adjust to external imbalances via domestic inflation (more on this later), so are more likely to have flexible exchange rates, whereas relatively open economies with a large foreign-trade sector will tend to prefer fixed exchange rates.
- *Size.* Small countries tend to adhere to fixed exchange rates, whereas large countries often find floating exchange rates more suitable. The reason is that in small and relatively homogeneous economies, it may be possible to tailor economic policy much more closely to the needs of the economy than in a diversified, large economy in which significant regional and sectoral differences exist.
- *Commodity concentration.* A country highly dependent upon exports of one or a few commodities will probably find it advantageous to peg its currency and to add to, or deplete, reserves rather than to let erratic changes in export receipts have a disruptive effect on the domestic economy.
- *Capital-market integration.* Because capital flows can have an overwhelming effect on exchange rates, countries with large and relatively open capital markets have considerable difficulty maintaining a fixed exchange rate.

These criteria help one to gain a picture of the kind of country that will tend to have a fixed exchange rate. Yet none of these matter much if the country's *inflation rate* is substantially out of line with that of its trading partners. Inflation is not simply an economic condition; it is the result of economic policies. So let's turn to that aspect of our "systematic" view of exchange-rate mechanisms.

Imagine that you are the governor of the Central Bank of Bulgovia. As the country has a small, nondiversified economy, you think it might be best to fix the Bulgovian grud against the U.S. dollar at 3 gruds to the dollar. This would help maintain certainty for business transactions and give foreign investors confidence in the currency's value. But, given the present recessionary conditions, you are under pressure from the Grey House, the Presidential quarters, to help stimulate the economy. Specifically, the President needs funds to pay for the recent rise in wages that the military insisted upon. This means another "temporary" loan to the government—that is, printing more money. The money supply has been growing at 23 percent per annum for the past six months, and inflation has reached 16 percent per annum, compared to about 6 percent in the rest of the world. The bank lending rate is 18 percent.

Can a fixed exchange rate be sustained? Probably not, for the higher inflation rate means that imports look more and more attractive to Bulgovians, while your exporters are screaming for relief because of their deteriorating price competitiveness in world markets. Unless you can bring inflation down sharply, you will probably have to let the grud devalue. (The alternative is to cut the country off from the influence of foreign trade and capital flows, by imposing increasingly severe controls on the external transactions.) A fixed exchange rate cannot be sustained indefinitely in a country whose inflation rate deviates significantly from those of its trading partners. Something has to give—either the exchange rate or the policy. Thus apart from basic economic conditions, the policies, monetary and fiscal, that a government chooses to pursue can constrain the choice of fixed or floating exchange rates. In general, if the economy is reasonably open, *the choice to fix the exchange rate against another country's currency implies giving up monetary policy independence.*

Strangely enough, giving up monetary autonomy may be precisely what the country wants. Back in Bulgovia, suppose that the government, with great fanfare, announces that the grud will henceforth be fixed against the European Currency Unit, the ECU. To maintain the exchange rate, wage settlements will have to be brought into line with those of the European Community and you, the governor, will have to hold the reins on the money supply. Businessmen will have no excuse for raising prices, which means that they will have to keep wage and cost increases to a moderate pace or go out of business. Inflation creates costs and uncertainties, so in the end the country will be better off; but getting through the transition period, the adjustment process, is difficult—politically difficult. So why not rally external forces to help achieve the desired result? In other words, *some countries adopt a fixed exchange rate to force external monetary discipline on the domestic economy.*

These, then, are the influences governing the basic choice of an exchange-rate policy. They are clearly bound in with other aspects of international economic policy, such as the freedom (or lack of it) of trade and capital movements. In practice, the choices are not quite so clear cut, and the solutions a little more varied (see Box 4.1). And in practice,

---

BOX 4.1

Exchange-Rate Systems: The Choices

To fix or not to fix—that seems to be the question. In fact, there is a wide spectrum of exchange-rate practices between the extremes of a rigid peg on the one hand and a clean float on the other. First, if a currency is pegged to another currency, then it is presumably floating against all others, except those that are pegged to the same currency. (So the currency in question would really be pegged to a *group* of currencies.) Along the same lines, some currencies are fixed to a weighted average of several other currencies: a *basket peg*. And fixed does not always mean *fixed*. For instance, the Austrian schilling is supposedly pegged to the deutschemark but in fact is permitted to fluctuate within a fairly wide margin. Other countries may adjust the peg so frequently that their currencies resemble floaters (the Jamaican dollar, for example). On the other hand, the Canadian dollar is, at the time of writing, nominally freely floating, but in practice tracks the U.S. dollar closely. This is an extreme example of a **managed float.**

Countries with high inflation, like Brazil, give a degree of predictability to their devaluations by adopting the **crawling peg system,** in which the currency is allowed to depreciate weekly or monthly by a well-accepted amount or percentage. When inflation is really high, as in Brazil or Argentina, the rate of currency depreciation may track an inflation index so as to keep the "real" exchange rate constant.

The accompanying diagram illustrates the spectrum of choices in exchange-rate policy.

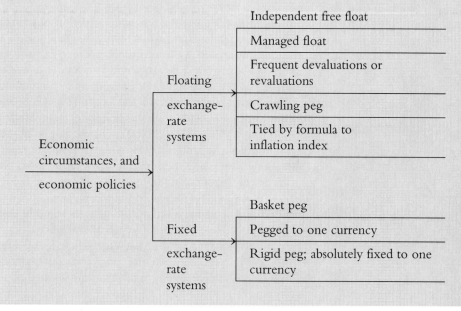

the variant that a country has adopted at any particular time may have less to do with rational selection than with historical evolution. It would help us, therefore, to gain a little historical perspective on the present international monetary system.

Gold and the Bretton Woods System

Until the mid-nineteenth century, international monetary arrangements centered around the commerce and investment of the colonial powers. Private financial instruments had been developed long before. The Italian Renaissance, for example, stimulated international trade and the instruments of trade, such as bills of exchange—documents with legal status conferring the holder's right to get paid a certain amount in the future, in a certain currency. Many modern financial techniques, including stock exchanges, were developed in Italy and the Netherlands, after the Middle Ages. The seventeenth and eighteenth centuries saw the rise of the British Empire and with it the East India Company, the Bank of England (the world's first central bank), and private merchant bankers. Because the pound sterling was the strongest and most widely accepted of national currencies, it became the de facto *vehicle currency* of international trade and investment. London became the center of the international financial community, and the British merchant banking houses provided essential export and import credit facilities and foreign-currency-exchange facilities. These were the elements of today's international banking, providing the means of (1) making payments at a distance, indeed across national boundaries, and (2) making payments in different currencies.

In the nineteenth century, the industrial revolution and Britain's export success meant that the country ran a large surplus in its balance of trade, as Japan has in more recent times. Britain was selling more than it was buying, so it had plenty of savings looking for good returns. Investment abroad was the answer—indeed, it was the necessity, for the developing world needed to borrow from Britain in order to pay for all the imports. As international trade gave rise to international investment, the merchant bankers of Europe organized the issuance of stocks and bonds to finance development in America, South Africa, Argentina, and the other colonies.

The more world commerce grew, the greater were the demands on the major currencies. Britain's currency remained a bastion of stability in part because it was backed by gold. The **gold standard**, adopted in 1821, simply meant that the Bank of England said that one could walk into the Bank any day and exchange the paper money for a fixed weight of gold. They meant it, so confidence in sterling paper money was sustained even during the mid-nineteenth century, when a number of bank notes proved worthless as their issuers went under. In the late nineteenth century, most of the major countries followed Britain's lead and undertook to fix the value of their currencies in terms of gold.

We have noted that a fixed exchange rate may mean the sacrifice of autonomy in economic policies, and so it was with the gold standard. Governments pursued contractionary policies when their gold reserves came under pressure and expansionary policies as the reserves accumulated. Policy was adjusted to the monetary standard rather than the money's *par value* in terms of gold being revised to accommodate domestic political objectives. The result was a period of price stability that we have never seen since, and as close as we have come to a single world currency.

The system collapsed during World War I. A postwar attempt to restore fixed rates failed, and in fact some attribute the precipitous economic decline that we now call the Great Depression to overly rigid monetary policy in the face of dramatically changed economic conditions and national priorities. Following the Depression, some countries tried to stimulate exports by devaluing their currencies, only to encounter competitive devaluations by trading partners that left both worse off.

Figure 4.1 illustrates the connection between a similarity of inflation rates and periods of fixed exchange rates in the century leading up to the floating of exchange rates in the early 1970s.

The end of World War II provided a clean slate on which to redesign the system and a degree of political and economic leadership on the part of the United States that made reform of the international monetary system a reality. Memories of the interwar period persuaded the powers that independent, beggar-thy-neighbor policies were anathema, so that a high priority had to be put on *coordination* and *openness*. Trade and capital flows eventually had to be freed, and currencies had to become convertible. Fixed exchange rates were far more desirable than competitive devaluations. On the other hand, the major nations no longer wanted to be rigidly nailed to "a cross of gold," as it was described by the nineteenth-century politician William Jennings Bryan. The system that emerged would have to accommodate some differences in economic policies, and that meant the possibility of exchange-rate changes.

In 1944, at an historic conference at Bretton Woods in New Hampshire, national representatives reached an agreement to establish such a system with the U.S. dollar as its pivot. It was, in effect, a *dollar exchange standard*. Currencies were pegged to the U.S. dollar at a fixed rate of exchange, plus or minus one percent, while the dollar itself was fixed to, and convertible into, gold. The **International Monetary Fund (IMF)** was conceived, its goal being to document, monitor, and encourage appropriate policies. In the interests of stability, the members of the IMF undertook to realign their currencies only after consultation with the Fund. The IMF would have access to a pool of funds that could be drawn upon by member countries experiencing temporary payments difficulties. (The emphasis was on *temporary* difficulties.) The IMF's job was to ease adjustment so that countries would not have to devalue or revalue their currencies except when a permanent change in conditions had occurred. The **World Bank** was established at

Figure 4.1   *Inflation Divergence and the Exchange-Rate System.*   When inflation has been similar in the four leading countries, fixed exchange rates prevailed, but inflation divergence has been accompanied by flexible exchange rates.

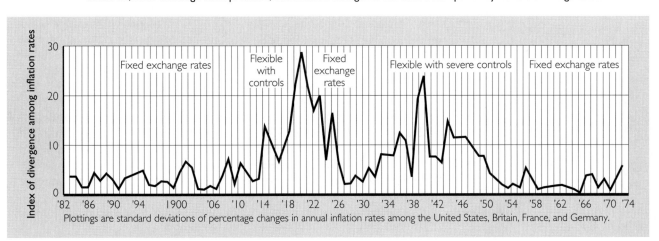

Source: *Citibank Money International,* June 30, 1975, p. 4.

the same time, but its task was reconstruction and development financing of a more permanent nature (see Box 4.2).

The manner in which countries agreed to fix their exchange rates was through intervention in the foreign-exchange market, buying their currency when its dollar value fell more than 1 percent below the par value, and selling it when it rose 1 percent above the par value. In practice, a number of countries fixed an official rate and instructed all banks to channel sales and purchases of foreign exchange through the central bank. To undertake this intervention, or to provide for an excess demand for foreign currency, governments had to have some reserves of foreign exchange and gold. Such reserves had to be freely available and transferable, and because the dollar was the only currency that met these requirements, it became the primary reserve currency. An additional amount of borrowing was made possible via a mechanism called **Special Drawing Rights (SDRs)**, which were in essence a means by which a deficit country could borrow hard currency from surplus countries for short periods.[2]

BOX 4.2

The IMF and the World Bank

The central institution of the international monetary system is the International Monetary Fund. The IMF's stated role is to facilitate adjustment to balance-of-payments imbalances that are rectifiable by macroeconomic policy changes. It does so by conducting studies (called "missions") and recommending changes in areas such as monetary, tariff, and exchange-rate policies. The IMF has funds that it can use for the temporary financing of a deficit; these are made available conditional upon the country's agreement to make certain policy changes. In recent years, the temporary financing has been stretched out further and further, so that it is becoming less credible to call the IMF merely a facilitator of the adjustment process. Instead, the IMF has taken an active role in longer-term efforts to solve the third-world debt problem. Today the IMF retains very little influence over the macroeconomic policies of the industrial countries.

The International Bank for Reconstruction and Development, commonly known as the World Bank, is the leading institution for long-term development financing. Using its own funds and substantial amounts borrowed in the international capital markets, the World Bank lends for infrastructure, industrial, and agricultural purposes in the developing countries. Many of the Bank's technical experts remain in the borrower country to help implement the projects. The World Bank Group includes the **International Financing Corporation** (IFC) whose lending and equity investing is confined to the *private sector* in developing countries. Both the IMF and the World Bank provide extensive statistical information and research reports, which are available to the public. A readable summary of IMF/World Bank research is contained in *Finance and Development,* published monthly.

Other development banks include the **Asian Development Bank (ADB),** the **African Development Bank (AfBD),** the Inter-American Development Bank, and the recently created **European Bank for Reconstruction and Development (EBRD),** whose focus is on Eastern Europe. The banks invest their funds regionally but are funded in large part by the industrial countries such as Japan, Germany, and the United States.

---

[2]The term *Special Drawing Rights* has also come to mean the IMF's unit of account, a basket of currencies similar in concept to the ECU discussed later.

The dollar standard was fine as long as the dollar was stable, but by the late 1960s, U.S. inflation had weakened the U.S. dollar's credibility. Also, other countries' economies had grown to the point where they were less willing to tie their domestic policies to the exigencies of a fixed exchange rate. In 1971, President Richard Nixon suspended the convertibility of the dollar into gold, effectively devaluing the U.S. currency. This was followed a short time later by the widespread adoption by the industrial countries of flexible exchange rates. Many developing countries still found it advantageous to peg their currencies to the dollar, the French franc, or some other currency. And the **European Economic Community (EEC)**,[3] established in 1958 primarily to create a free-trade grouping, began the long process of currency union. We will return to that subject later in this chapter.

The Seventies and Eighties

With the devaluation of the dollar and the abandonment of the Bretton Woods system of fixed exchange rates, no one currency was paramount. The German mark, the Swiss franc, and the Japanese yen proved stronger than the dollar because those countries were able to hold the line on inflation. Gold's role declined. In the academic world, many adopted reality as desirable; floating exchange rates were seen as reflecting market forces rather than the artificial defense of a currency by the government. A country that did not need to intervene to support its currency would not need foreign-exchange reserves—one less worry. In 1977 the IMF members formalized some rules for the new floating-exchange-rate system and asked the IMF to monitor adherence to the guidelines. The United States experienced its worst bout of inflation in decades, and the dollar plummeted. But by the end of the 1970s, the floating-exchange-rate system was legitimized.

Oddly, the pendulum had already begun to swing. The turn of the decade saw the old "loose money" days give way to anti-inflationary monetary discipline. A minority of academics began to argue that the floating-exchange-rate system had not cured all the world's ills, and that, in any case, few if any currencies were truly freely floating. Most countries had a managed float, also known as a "dirty" float; they intervened if and when they felt the currency was out of line. Moreover, the aggregate of governments' foreign-exchange reserves had *increased,* not decreased. And average inflation in the OECD (Organization for Economic Cooperation and Development) countries was significantly higher than when exchange rates had been fixed. Currencies' values were determined not by the fundamental forces of purchasing power parity but by the speculators and arbitragers of the international money market. The other major feature of the 1980s, extending into the 1990s, was the widespread dismantling of controls on capital flows, depicted in Figure 4.2. One result was that international trade became overwhelmed by international flows of funds as a determinant of exchange rates. On the other hand, countered some advocates of freely floating rates, if governments know better than the market where an exchange rate belongs, then they should, on average, be able to make a profit—buying when a currency is undervalued and selling when it is overvalued. Yet the evidence demonstrated the opposite: central-bank intervention seemed to be mistimed, losing more often than winning.

Meanwhile, policymakers vacillated. They liked the freedom for domestic policy that flexible rates allowed but acknowledged that some seemed prone to abuse that freedom. Italian unions appeared to use every fall in the lira as an excuse for wage hikes while never making concessions if the currency rose. In 1979, a second attempt at European monetary

---

[3]Now simply called the European Community or European Union.

Figure 4.2   *Capital Controls in Industrial and Developing Countries, 1985–1991 (number of measures).*   These measures do not purport to indicate the economic significance of the measures taken over the period; however, they can provide an overall sense of whether member countries are taking more or less restrictive measures.

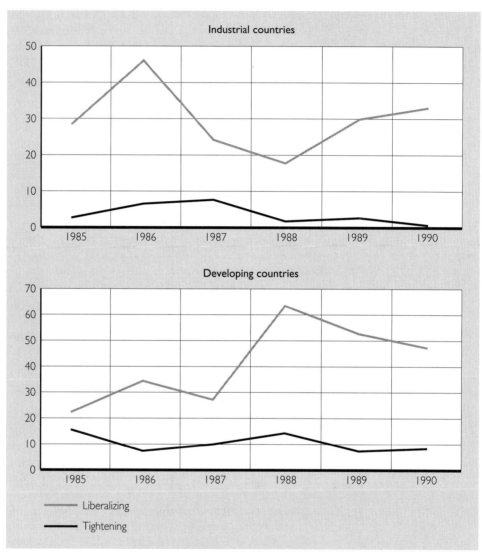

Source: International Monetary Fund, *AREAER,* 1986, 1987, 1988.

union was made, with the establishment of the **European Monetary System**, but currency weakness in Italy, Britain, France, and elsewhere meant that it was a stumbling start. In 1985, the Plaza Agreement of the major industrial countries initiated concerted intervention to bring down the seemingly overvalued dollar. The dollar did fall, but the consensus remains today that such massive intervention by central banks can work only if they reinforce what the market participants are prone to believe anyway, because the volume of private capital available for speculation far exceeds the combined reserves of the world's central banks.

One thing we now know clearly. Flexible rates do not really bring complete independence for economic policy. Countries still have to do whatever is necessary to survive in a competitive world economy. Flexible exchange rates, or whatever the melange we have now may be called, do *not* substantially ease the adjustment process. When a country inflates, or when a country runs a trade deficit, it must pay the price one way or another. In the author's view, the main benefit of more flexible exchange rates was to remove the incentive for exchange controls. But they have not proved a panacea. In fact, once exchange controls have been removed, the best solution for many countries would seem to be that of pegging their currencies to a nice stable unit like the deutschemark or the Japanese yen, bringing external discipline to bear on domestic macroeconomic policy. That, basically, was what persuaded France, Italy, and finally Britain to join the exchange-rate mechanism of the European Monetary System. The experiment has not always been successful, and the EMS came under enormous strains in the early 1990s, strains that in effect derailed progress toward monetary union, which had been planned for 1997.

Table 4.1, extracted from an annual survey published by the IMF called *Developments in International Exchange and Payment Systems,* lists summary features of the official exchange and trade systems of countries that were members of the International Monetary Fund in 1992.

Multiple Exchange Rates and Black Markets

Some countries have different exchange rates for different purposes. One exchange rate may be for exports and imports, and another for financial transactions. The latter is typically more market determined. In fact, it may be designed as a transition from a controlled to a freer exchange-rate regime, assuming some of the role of the parallel or **black market** in foreign exchange.

Multiple exchange-rate practices, such as those described in Box 4.3, are used not only as a way to manipulate the exchange rate to help the balance of payments but also as a method of taxation and subsidization. As in the case of all taxes and subsidies, multiple rates simultaneously influence the distribution of income and the pattern of production and consumption and will, therefore, have budgetary, monetary, and balance-of-payments consequences. Multiple rates distort domestic prices and output and make it more difficult for the authorities to resist pressure for special treatment of a given commodity or class of economic agents. The intervention creates what has been termed *by-product distortions.* That is, the attempt to correct a given market imperfection creates, as a by-product, new and possibly more serious distortions elsewhere in the economy. One such by-product may be the creation of criminal activity in foreign exchange.

The existence of an officially tolerated parallel market or an illegal black market in currency, where the rate is more depreciated than in the official, restricted market, is evidence of the inappropriateness of the official exchange rate or rates. At the time of writing, a parallel or black market existed in about seventy countries, in which access to the official exchange market was restricted, according to IMF estimates.[4]

---

[4]International Monetary Fund, *Developments in International Exchange and Payments Systems,* June 1992, p. 19.

Table 4.1 *Summary Features of Exchange and Trade Systems of IMF Countries in 1992*

Pegged				
Single currency			Currency composite	
U.S. dollar	French franc	Other	SDR	Other
Angola[4]	Benin	Bhutan (Indian rupee)	Burundi	Albania[4, 5]
Antigua and Barbuda	Burkina Faso	Lesotho[4] (South African rand)	Iran, Islamic Rep. of[4]	Algeria
Argentina	Cameroon	Swaziland (South African rand)	Libyan Arab Jamahiriya[8]	Austria
The Bahamas[4]	Central African Rep.	Yugoslavia (deutschemark)	Myanmar	Bangladesh
Barbados	Chad		Rwanda	Botswana
Belize	Comoros		Seychelles	Cape Verde
Djibouti	Congo			Cyprus
Dominica	Côte d'Ivoire			Czechoslovakia
Ethiopia	Equatorial Guinea			Fiji
Grenada	Gabon			Finland[9]
Iraq[4]	Mali			Hungary
Liberia	Niger			Iceland[10]
Mongolia[4]	Senegal			Jordan
Nicaragua[4]	Togo			Kenya[4]
Oman				Kuwait
Panama				Malawi
St. Kitts and Nevis				Malaysia[10]
St. Lucia				Malta
St. Vincent and the Grenadines				Mauritius
Sudan[4]				Morocco[13]
Suriname				Nepal
Syrian Arab Rep.[4]				Norway[14]
Trinidad and Tobago				Papua New Guinea
Yemen				Solomon Islands
				Sweden[16]
				Tanzania
				Thailand
				Tonga
				Uganda[4]
				Vanuatu
				Western Samoa
				Zimbabwe

[1]Current information relating to Cambodia is unavailable.

[2]In all countries listed in this column, the U.S. dollar was the currency against which exchange rates showed limited flexibility.

[3]This category consists of countries participating in the exchange-rate mechanism of the European Monetary System. In each case, the exchange rate is maintained within a margin of 2.25 percent around the bilateral central rates against other participating currencies, with the exception of Spain and the United Kingdom, in which case the exchange rate is maintained within a margin of 6 percent.

[4]Member maintains exchange arrangements involving more than one exchange market. The arrangement shown is that maintained in the major market.

[5]The basic exchange rate of the lek is pegged to the ECU.

[6]Exchange rates are determined on the basis of a fixed relationship to the SDR, within margins of up to ±7.25 percent. However, because of the maintenance of a relatively stable relationship with the U.S. dollar, these margins are not always observed.

Flexibility Limited Vis-à-Vis a Single Currency or Group of Currencies		More Flexible		
Single currency[2]	Cooperative arrangements[3]	Adjusted according to a set of indicators	Other managed floating	Independently floating
Bahrain[6]	Belgium	Chile[4,7]	China, People's	Afghanistan[4]
Qatar[6]	Denmark	Colombia	Rep. of[4]	Australia
Saudi Arabia[6]	France	Madagascar	Costa Rica	Bolivia
United Arab	Germany, Fed.	Mozambique[4]	Ecuador[4]	Brazil[4]
Emirates[6]	Rep. of	Zambia[4]	Egypt	Bulgaria
	Ireland		Greece	Canada
	Italy		Guinea	Dominican Rep.
	Luxembourg		Guinea-Bissau	El Salvador
	Netherlands		Honduras	The Gambia
	Spain		India[7]	Ghana
	United Kingdom		Indonesia	Guatemala
			Israel[11]	Guyana
			Korea	Haiti
			Lao People's	Jamaica
			Dem. Rep.	Japan
			Maldives	Kiribati[12]
			Mauritania	Lebanon
			Mexico	Namibia[4,15]
			Pakistan	New Zealand
			Poland	Nigeria[4]
			Portugal	Paraguay
			Romania	Peru
			Sao Tome and	Philippines
			Principe	Sierra Leone
			Singapore	South Africa[4]
			Somalia[4]	United States
			Sri Lanka	Uruguay
			Tunisia	Venequela
			Turkey	Zaïre
			Vietnam	

[7]The exchange rate is maintained within margins of ±5 percent on either side of a weighted composite of the currencies of the main trading partners.

[8]The exchange rate is maintained within margins of ±7.5 percent.

[9]The exchange rate, which is pegged to the ECU, is maintained within margins of ±3.0 percent.

[10]The exchange rate is maintained within margins of ±2.25 percent.

[11]The exchange rate is maintained within margins of ±5.0 percent.

[12]The currency of Kiribati is the Australian dollar.

[13]The exchange rate is maintained within margins of ±3.0 percent.

[14]The exchange rate, which is pegged to the ECU, is maintained within margins of ±2.25 percent.

[15]The currency of Namibia is the South African rand, pending issuance of Namibia's own national currency.

[16]The exchange rate, which is pegged to the ECU, is maintained within margins of ±1.5 percent.

Source: International Monetary Fund, *Developments in International Exchange and Payment Systems,* June 1992.

Dual or Multiple-Market System

Multiple markets usually consist of an official market, in which the supply of and demand for foreign exchange associated with certain specified transactions are controlled, and a free market that handles all other transactions. The free rate is almost always more depreciated than the official rate. Because they are less selective in their impact than the imposition of individual rates for given transactions, multiple markets typically penalize broad categories of suppliers of foreign exchange to the official market—usually exporters—and subsidize groups of purchasers—often the government or key pressure groups.

Fixed Exchange Rate on Given Transactions

Specific foreign-exchange transactions can be either subsidized or penalized by the authorities, forcing the purchase or sale of exchange at an over- or undervalued exchange rate. This practice is often used to hold down official expenditures on the servicing of government-guaranteed debt, to encourage migrant labor to repatriate foreign earnings, or to penalize profit remittances abroad of foreign companies or travel abroad by residents.

Taxes and Subsidies on the Value of Transactions

Similar in impact to fixing the exchange rate for given transactions and equally selective, these practices typically target current-account transactions. Examples include export bonuses or subsidies, mandatory advance import deposits (which pay no interest or less than market rate of interest), taxes on remittances abroad, and taxes on sales of exchange by commercial banks.

Excessive Spreads

Multiple currency practices result when the central bank prescribes buying and selling rates for spot foreign-exchange transactions with a spread of more than 2 percent of their midpoint rate.

Source: International Monetary Fund, *Developments in International Exchange and Payments Systems,* June 1992, p. 18.

The Balance of Payments: Flows of International Trade and Capital

A country is in some respects like a business: its main job is to produce and sell things and get something useful in return. Sometimes, when sales are booming and it does not need or want to consume right now (a "trade surplus"), the excess earnings can be hoarded by the government ("international reserves") or invested outside by the private sector ("capital outflows").

People export, import,[5] invest, and borrow abroad voluntarily—and do so only to get something in exchange. Every time something is sent abroad, something (perhaps just a cash balance in a bank) is received from abroad. To keep people happy, the value of what is received must equal the value of what is given. In accounting terms, debits must equal credits. The **balance of payments** is just the sum of all these international transactions: the imports and exports, the inward and outward investments, and the government's accumulation or depletion of foreign assets. Because debits must equal credits individually, the inflows must equal the outflows in the aggregate balance of payments.

Thus to talk of a balance-of-payments deficit is in a sense foolish. Except for foreign aid, we get something back for everything we give away. (Moreover, in a reversal of conventional logic, we seem to worry more when we're getting more than we're giving than the other way around.)

It does make at least accounting sense to talk of a trade deficit, a situation in which imports exceed exports. For a trade deficit to have occurred some importers must not have paid in real goods or there weren't enough aggregate exports to pay for all the imports. So we must have gotten some of the imports on credit or by depleting some of the cash or other assets we held abroad. (Or perhaps government assets are affected if the country is helping to pay for the excess of imports.) In either case, we can describe this situation as selling financial assets to foreigners. "Selling financial or real assets to foreigners" is called a *capital inflow;* "buying assets from foreigners" is called a *capital outflow.*

Hence, unless the government chooses to intervene, private capital inflows must be sufficient to equal the trade deficit. (Private capital inflows occur when foreigners lend to us, or invest here, or we draw down on assets held abroad.) More generally, the net foreign capital inflow must be sufficient to offset the export shortfall. Table 4.2 contains

Table 4.2 *Transylvania's Balance of Payments*

	Debits	Credits	
Exports (goods sold to foreigners)		11	
Imports (goods bought from foreigners)	− 16		
Net			**− 5 Trade Balance**
Services, like tourism (and interest paid or received)	− 2	3	
Aid (a plug category)		1	
			− 3 Current Account Balance
Financial and real assets sold to foreigners (capital inflows)		3	
Financial and real assets bought from foreigners (capital outflows)	− 2		
			− 2 Overall Balance
Government's financial assets sold (foreign-exchange reserves reduced)		3	
Government's financial assets bought (foreign-exchange reserves increased)			
Errors and omissions (a plug category)	− 1		
TOTAL	**− 21.00**	**21.00**	

[5]The theory of comparative advantage helps explain why it benefits all countries to engage in international trade. Even the poorest and most inefficient of countries have a *comparative* advantage in *something,* and even the strongest and most efficient of countries can save effort and profit by importing those things in which they are relatively less efficient. Both types of countries gain from trade.

a stylized **balance-of-payments** structure. The general rule is: *When residents sell something (goods, services, assets) to nonresidents, it is a credit; when residents buy something from nonresidents, it is a debit. Value given must equal value obtained.* In the table, "Aid" and "Errors and Omissions" are both plug categories inserted to make the balance balance; in this table, "Errors and Omissions" could well represent capital outflows that went unrecorded.

The term *overall balance-of-payments deficit* refers to the government's intervention. Private exports plus capital inflows *must* equal private imports plus capital outflows, unless the government chooses to help the private sector pay for some of those imports of goods (or financial assets) by drawing down on its international reserves. When it does so, private purchases of goods and assets from abroad (imports plus capital outflow) exceed private sales of goods and assets to the rest of the world (exports plus capital inflows), and we say there is a balance-of-payments deficit.

Let us stress this once more. *Without government intervention, credit transactions must equal debit transactions so there cannot be a balance-of-payments deficit or surplus.* If there is an overall surplus or deficit, it can only be to the extent of intervention by the central bank. Thus to the extent that the central bank's reserves have decreased, there was an overall deficit. To the extent that the central bank's reserves have increased, there was a surplus. If the central bank's reserves are unchanged, as would be the case where the government chose not to intervene in the foreign-exchange market, payments are in overall balance.

The External Deficit and the Internal Deficit

How does a deficit in the balance of trade relate to a domestic budgetary deficit? Is there any necessary connection? To make one thing clear, there have been and are countries with trade and balance-of-payments surpluses that simultaneously have serious domestic budget deficit problems—Japan is such a country now. There are also countries, such as the United Kingdom, which have made major progress in reversing domestic budgetary shortfalls while their external deficit was accumulating. However, the two problems are often linked.

We will show, by using some simple national-income equations, how a country's balance-of-trade surplus equals the difference between private savings and the government deficit.[6] The fundamental national-income equation says that everything that's produced must be used in some fashion. In two versions of this equation—one showing how a whole country allocates its national product according to different segments of "demand," and the other showing how individuals, taken together, allocate their incomes—these terms are used: Y is national product, C is private consumption, I is private investment, G is government expenditure, S is personal saving, T is taxation, and X and M are exports and imports.

National production	=	National demand		

$$Y = C + I + G + (X - M)$$ How the nation spends its production

Also,

$$Y = C + S + T$$ How individuals allocate their incomes

---

[6]It is important to understand that what follows is a set of accounting equations; it does not predict what causes what. The variables, Y, C, S, T, X, and M are *endogenous*, not exogenous.

From these,

$$C + S + T = C + I + G + (X - T)$$

Let's rearrange to put the current account surplus on the left:

$$X - M = (S - I) - (G - T)$$

In other words,

Current account surplus	=	Net private sector savings	−	Net government deficit

Consider a practical application of this conclusion. Japan has a high personal savings rate, in the region of 20 percent. About a quarter of this is to be invested in the private sector, in the form of new capital equipment, accumulation of inventory, and so forth. This leaves net private-sector savings at, say, 15 percent of national income. But the Japanese government is spending heavily, indeed running a deficit of about 10 percent of national production (gross domestic production—GDP). So total national savings, the private surplus minus the government shortfall, is 5 percent of GDP. What isn't used at home must be sent abroad, and it follows that Japan will run a current account surplus in the region of 5 percent of GDP.

What of a country in which the national savings rate is insufficient to meet both private investment requirements and the government's need to borrow? Then total national spending will exceed national production, and the difference will have to be imported from abroad. In the United States, private-sector savings of 6 percent minus real investment of 4 percent leaves only 2 percent to finance the government budget deficit that is in the region of 5 percent of GDP, so the country runs a current account deficit of about 3 percent of national income. One way of looking at this is to think of the U.S. government and U.S. companies as competing for the private sector's savings; because there is "too much borrowing chasing too little lending," interest rates will tend to be driven sufficiently high to attract foreign lending, resulting in a capital inflow. And from our earlier discussion we know that the net capital inflow equals the current account deficit.

> *Moral: A country with a domestic budget deficit will run a trade deficit unless the domestic private sector is willing to make up the difference through lending their savings to the government.*

The Adjustment Process

In the long run, no business or country wants to go on selling more than it's receiving forever; even the Japanese want to consume the spoils of their export success at some point, or what's the point? The other side of the coin is that a trade-deficit country is by definition accumulating debts, for its excess of imports had to be accompanied by capital inflows. Moreover, the creditors or investors will at some point wonder about whether the country can continue to service its increasingly leveraged capital structure. So someday, by choice or by necessity, forces will be put into motion that will reverse a balance-of-payments surplus or deficit. These forces, and the domestic changes they entail, make up what we call the *adjustment process*. (Sometimes, as Box 4.4 illustrates, the International Monetary Fund is called in, to help the process with money—and conditions.)

The effects are easiest to picture when a currency is fixed but overvalued.

BOX 4.4

IMF Medicine

In 1988 Morocco found, to its dismay, that with a weaker market for phosphates and diminishing OPEC aid, its foreign debt amounted to more than its gross national product. It was not the first country to find itself in that unfortunate situation, nor was it the last. Like other countries whose balance of payments had sunk into chronic deficit, it called in the IMF. The IMF brought money, but the money was accompanied by a set of economic-reform prescriptions that typify the role that the IMF has played in facilitating balance-of-payments adjustments in the developing world in recent years. IMF remedies have included:

- the gradual elimination of government budget deficits.
- the removal of subsidies.
- the floating of currencies, because artificially high parities encourage consumption and imports.
- the payment of real rates of interest by the banks, to encourage saving and discourage capital outflow.
- privatization of loss-making public enterprises and, in general, the greater involvement of the private sector.

As countries such as Egypt know well, however, prescriptions of this kind have political costs. People who are told that their country is bankrupt and that the prices of commodities upon which they depend are to be raised are likely to vent their anger on their governments. Countries that have had a measure of success tend to be those with strong dictatorships (Chile) or strong democracies (Mexico). Others with more fragile polities, such as Brazil and Argentina, have from time to time rejected the IMF's terms and money, and retained the distortions that keep the system intact.

Repercussions of an Overvalued Currency

Fixed Exchange Rate

Let's look at the fixed and floating exchange-rate situations separately. Picture a country. The government has fixed the official level of the exchange rate (the price of the currency), but it is widely agreed that the true value of the currency is less than the official rate. People are trying to unload what currency they hold, and exporters complain that at the current level, no one wants to buy the country's goods. But don't despair—there's an adjustment mechanism that will tend to help things right themselves. Here's how it works:

We begin with the assumption that the currency is "overvalued," meaning that the exchange rate is being held at a level that puts the value of the currency (in terms of other currencies) higher than would be if the market were to clear. The way in which the government fixes the currency is by purchasing it in the foreign-exchange market, using the country's official foreign-exchange reserves, whenever its price tends to fall. What now happens?

The fact that the currency is overvalued implies that inflation at home has been higher than abroad, making the country's goods less competitive. Foreign importers drop off purchases of our goods, so the supply of foreign exchange tendered by exporters to the central bank drops. Domestic importers find foreign goods a bargain, so imports tend to rise, placing more demands on the central bank for the dwindling stock of foreign-exchange reserves. Also, aware of the currency's weakness, corporations, banks, and individuals sell the currency, so its price tends to fall.

The government has to prop up the currency by further purchases, so its foreign-exchange reserves decline. But by now the foreign-exchange actions are having an effect on the domestic economy. While paying out foreign exchange, the central bank is receiving domestic money in exchange. This is high-powered money, being the cash that banks hold in their clearing or reserve accounts at the central bank. Thus commercial banks' reserves at the central bank decline. (This money is, in effect, withdrawn from circulation.) If high-powered money declines, the domestic money supply will also decline, by a multiple of the decline in the monetary base (the "money multiplier").

(This reduction in the monetary base can be offset by central banks' action in the domestic money market—open market operations in which the central bank buys domestic assets and gives out domestic money. This is called *sterilized intervention,* and forestalls the impetus of the adjustment that would otherwise have occurred through the monetary mechanism.)

The contraction of the domestic money supply will tend to dampen inflation (less money chasing the same amount of goods). A smaller money supply, or at least slower growth in the money supply, will mean tighter credit. Unless there is **sterilization**, short-term interest rates will tend to rise. But long-term interest rates will tend to fall (or at least rise less than short-term rates) as lenders gain more confidence that, with less inflation, their returns won't be eaten away by a declining purchasing power of the dollar.

The tighter money supply and rise in short-term interest rates may not be what the politicians want, especially if they have employment and election problems, so the temptation is to either impose exchange controls or to "let the damn currency fall" and try again at a lower level. In the EMS, the first action undermines the commitment to a stable set of parities, and the latter is not permitted, because it represents the very antithesis of what the EEC is trying to achieve.

The converse tends to happen in a surplus country—the accumulation of reserves resulting from an undervalued currency under fixed rates tends to increase the rate of growth of the money supply, pushing inflation, inflationary expectations, and longer-term interest rates up (as happened, for example, in Germany in 1989–1990). If the government does not like this, there is nothing it can do short of quitting intervention (doling out money) or sterilizing the intervention (which may be self-defeating) or imposing capital-inflow controls.

Floating Exchange Rate

When the government lets its currency find its own level in the foreign-exchange markets, and refrains from more than occasional intervention to prop up or restrain the currency's international value, the exchange rate must itself do much of the work in rectifying a payments imbalance. In fact, as long as the authorities keep their distance from the currency market and other private financial markets, a trade surplus and deficit can, in principle, persist as long as it likes with no cause for concern. After all, international traders and investors are adults and if they choose to sell or buy or invest or borrow at certain prices, who's to say they shouldn't? The balance of payments will balance, of course, not because the central bank is making up any difference between private flows, but because nobody will sell to us unless they are satisfied with the goods or financial assets that they are getting in return.

In practice, things will not stay in such blissful equilibrium for very long, for the moment somebody says our prices are too high or our interest rates too low, they will cease to purchase our currency in the foreign-exchange market and the dollar will fall. Then more repercussions will begin. Interest rates will tend to rise as foreigners withdraw their money, making it harder to borrow, until the point at which interest rates are high enough to attract sufficient capital to pay for the excess of imports. *Or,* on the trade side, with the value of the currency falling in the forex market, imports may prove too costly for some and the adjustment will take place through a reduction of imports. Or the adjustment might occur through an increase in exports, as foreigners find our goods cheap at this low exchange rate.

Meanwhile, adjustments are taking place in the surplus (undervalued currency) country as well. And all these changes in trade and capital flows are not occurring in isolation but also have effects on domestic financial markets and on the domestic real economy as well.

EXAMPLE 4.1   The Adjustment Process in Practice

In this example we shall visit the Baltic Sea to illustrate monetary adjustment under either fixed or floating exchange rates. At the start, let's assume that trade between Germany and Sweden is balanced, so that the value of Swedish exports to Germany equals the value of German exports to Sweden. What do you think would happen to the exchange rate between the Swedish krona and the German mark over time? The answer depends on inflation rates, which in turn depend on monetary policies.

Assume that Germany's real output and money stock both are growing at 4 percent a year, so that German inflation is zero, and that the same holds true of Sweden. The exchange rate is then determined by the absolute price levels in the two countries. Trade and currency flows between them are balanced, so these flows cause no change in the real output or money stocks of either country, and inflation is still zero in both. Because neither country runs a deficit with the other, no pressures develop that would change the exchange rate. So it makes no substantive difference whether the exchange rate is fixed or flexible. It will not budge.

But what if inflation rates differ? Suppose that, in Sweden, the money stock's growth outruns real output much faster than in Germany. If Sweden's inflation rate is 10 percent

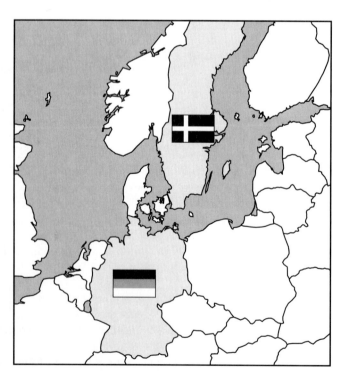

a year while Germany's is 5 percent, German goods will become cheaper than Sweden's. Germany will export more goods to Sweden and import more kronor in return. And it will matter a great deal whether the exchange rate is fixed or flexible.

If the exchange rate is *fixed,* the outflow of kronor through Sweden's payments deficit will tend to contract the Swedish money stock, or slow its growth. But it will expand the German money stock, because the Bundesbank will place more marks in circulation, paying them out to German exporters in exchange for the flood of kronor they receive from the Swedish. *Sweden's inflation rate will fall and Germany's will rise because of these monetary flows.* The process ends only when inflation rates become equal between the two countries.

There are two ways in which countries try to resist this process and still stay in the fixed-rate game. One way is for the Bundesbank to intervene in the German money markets to sterilize the excess funds accumulated there. It might sell some of its assets and withdraw from circulation the money it receives in payment. In real life, this technique never works for long, because funds flow in faster than they can be sterilized. The other way is to impose trade and exchange controls to check the flow of goods and money. However, unless the two countries again align their rates of money growth—and thus their inflation rates—the controls will have to be tightened until trade is stopped dead.

But what if the exchange rate is *flexible?* With inflation 10 percent in Sweden and 5 percent in Germany, Germany's goods once again become cheaper than Sweden's. Once again, more kronor stream into the exchange markets. But as the flow of kronor rises, the exchange rate moves, cutting the price of kronor in terms of marks. This lowers the price of Swedish goods in marks. Sweden's exports will rise and Germany's will fall until trade flows are back in balance and the excess of kronor is gone. (Of course, if the inflation difference persists, the excess of kronor will reappear and the Swedish currency will have to continue its fall.)

Now to the practical application. In early 1991, Sweden announced that it would fix its currency to the European Currency Unit (explained in the section entitled The ECU). Now Sweden wants to keep the krona fixed against the ECU, and hence against the German mark. What conclusions can we draw from this example?

- An exchange rate can be held fixed over the long run only when monetary conditions are similar in the two countries concerned—or when both let their payments balances determine these conditions. This can happen only when both share similar economic policy goals.
- If these goals are different, divergent policies will cause their monetary conditions—and inflation rates—to diverge. In that event, either trade must be halted or the fixed rate must change and eventually give way to a flexible rate.
- A return to similar monetary conditions—and inflation rates—is a prerequisite for the return to a fixed exchange rate.

The European Monetary System

In March 1957, France, Germany, Italy, Belgium, the Netherlands, and Luxembourg signed a formal treaty in Rome calling for the creation of a large free trade area, or customs union, the **European Economic Community** (EEC). Within a generation, membership in the community expanded to include 12 nations.

The EEC was principally intended to create a common market for goods and services. This goal having been achieved in large measure by the early 1970s, Europe's economic leadership turned its attention to monetary unification. Several false starts in the 1970s culminated in 1979 in the formation of the **European Monetary System** (EMS), a system that, despite initial tensions and significant modifications, remains in place today.

The EMS's key feature, the **Exchange-Rate Mechanism (ERM),** links the member currencies to one another. The EMS's long-term goal is monetary unification, perhaps accompanied by a common currency, the ECU. Let us briefly review the context in which these aims are being pursued.

The European Community and the "Single Market"

The EMS is but one facet of the goal of economic unification in Europe and should be seen in context. Among the most important aspects of European unity is a series of initiatives known as the "Single Market" plan, of which the monetary system is but one element. To the extent that unification is advanced in difficult areas, such as competition in services, monetary unification will be made easier. The effort continues well beyond the original target date of 1992, by which time the European Community had planned to "complete the internal market" and to remove barriers to the free circulation of goods and services and factors of production.

Let us look at the three measures required in order to achieve free movement of goods and services within the EC. The first is the abolition of border controls, which are used to enforce national quantitative restrictions that restrain imports from the rest of the world. The intent is to convert these restraints into Community-wide restrictions.

The second measure is the elimination of technical barriers to trade by mutual recognition of most barriers and harmonization of others, such as health, safety, and environmental regulations. The principle of mutual recognition implies that products legally marketed in one member state, whether manufactured in the EC or imported into the EC, can circulate freely throughout the Community.

The third measure is the opening up of public procurement in four areas not already covered by existing international trade agreements:[7] energy, telecommunications, transportation, and water supply.

The ECU

At present the ECU, or European Currency Unit, is not really a currency in the conventional sense. It is not issued by any national government as a means of payment, nor does it have any domestic clearing system of the kind discussed in Chapter 2. Most payments in Europe continue to be made in national currencies, and one may expect that this will be the case for some time to come. Instead, the ECU is an artificial unit, an index or "basket" of the currencies of the member countries of the European Community. Nevertheless, the ECU has come into increasing use as a *currency of denomination* of financial contracts, such as bonds and deposits. It is even possible to make payments between some banks in ECU. In fact, the official institutions of the European Community keep their accounts and make payments in ECU.

The ECU is a basket of currencies. It is like a portfolio of different amounts of the individual currencies, including some deutschemarks, some French francs, some pounds sterling, and so on (see Table 4.3). The quantities of each currency in the ECU stay the same while exchange rates fluctuate, although as a result of these fluctuations, the values and therefore the weightings of the various currencies may change. It does not change even when there is a big move in the EMS currencies occasioned by a *realignment* of the relative value of the EMS currencies. This stability in the portfolio is important, because the ECU is used as a currency of denomination, and one really would like to know what one's buying if one buys (or issues) a contract denominated in ECU.

Once in a while the composition is changed. A reconstitution or *revision* of what's in the basket can occur every five years, or if new members are accepted into the EC. At the time of writing, the ECU basket had been changed twice, in 1984 and in 1989. Table 4.3 reflects the composition following the 1989 inclusion of the Spanish peseta and the Portuguese escudo in the basket.

Because the ECU is composed of 12 currencies, its value changes constantly with the market value of those 12 currencies. To calculate the market value of the ECU in terms of any one of its 12 constituent currencies (or, for that matter, against any other currency that can be used

Table 4.3 *Composition of the ECU*

Currency	Fixed amount of currency in the ECU
DM	0.6242
FF	1.332
£	0.08794
Lire	151.8
DFl	0.2198
BFr/LUF	3.431
DKr	0.1976
I£	0.00855
Dr	1.440
Pta	6.885
Esc	1.393

---

[7]Most existing international trade agreements fall under GATT, the General Agreement on Tariffs and Trade.

as a numeraire, such as the U.S. dollar) at any point in time, you take the fixed amounts of each currency in the ECU and the market exchange rate of each component currency against the chosen numeraire currency. These are used to get the value of each of the component currencies in terms of the currency of interest. Add them all up and you have the value of one ECU.

EXAMPLE 4.2   As an example of finding the value of the ECU in terms of a component currency, we will calculate the value of the ECU in terms of German marks as of June 19, 1991. Look at Table 4.4. The data in the first two columns were obtained from the following morning's *Financial Times*. Take the fixed amount of each component currency (column a) and divide by the market exchange rate of the German mark (column b). This gives column (c), the value of the fixed quantity of each component currency in terms of the German mark. Sum those values. The result is the ECU's total value—expressed in terms of the German mark—of DM/ECU 2.059.[8]

We could undertake a similar exercise to calculate the value of the ECU in terms of French francs or another European currency, but it's easier to do it directly from the same table. One ECU is worth 2.059 German marks, and each mark is worth 3.404 French francs. So the ECU is worth 2.059 × 3.404 = 7.0088 French francs.

The last column in Table 4.4 gives the weights of each currency in the ECU. Note that while the physical quantities of each of the 12 currencies normally remain fixed for five-year periods, the currency weights in terms of any one currency vary, depending on the currencies' relative strength. But because relative changes are limited by the intervention

Table 4.4   *Calculating the Value of the ECU in Terms of the German Mark*

	Amount of each currency in the ECU basket	Market exchange rates for one German mark on June 19, 1991		Value of component currencies in DM terms	Weight as of June 19, 1991
	(a)	(b)		(c) = (a)/(b)	(d) = (c)/2.059377
Deutschemark	0.6242	1,000		0.6242	30.3%
French franc	1.332	3.404	FF/DM	0.391304	19.0%
Pound sterling	0.08784	0.342	GBP/DM	0.256842	12.5%
Italian lira	151.8	745.900	LIT/DM	0.203513	9.9%
Dutch guilder	0.2198	1.126	NG/DM	0.195126	9.5%
Belgian franc	3.301	20.650	BF/DM	0.159855	7.8%
Danish krone	0.1976	3.859	DKR/DM	0.051209	2.5%
Irish punt	0.008552	0.374	IRP/DM	0.022873	1.1%
Luxembourg franc	0.13	20.650	LF/DM	0.006295	0.3%
Greek drachma	1.44	62.917	DRA/DM	0.022887	1.1%
Spanish peseta	6.885	62.917	PTA/DM	0.10943	5.3%
Portuguese escudo	1.393	87.93	ESC/DM	0.015842	0.8%
	Value of one ECU in terms of DM			**2.059377**	**100.0%**

---

[8]At least that's what it should be. In fact, if you get a quote on ECU from a foreign-exchange dealer, you'll get whatever supply and demand dictates. But arbitrage will ensure the ECU never deviates more than a small fraction from its theoretical value.

agreement of the exchange-rate mechanism, large changes in the weightings tend to occur only when there are *realignments* of the European currencies. To learn about these we turn to the exchange-rate mechanism.

The ERM

The Exchange-Rate Mechanism (ERM), a key part of the EMS, is an attempt to link the currency values (and hence the monetary and economic policies) of Europe to one another, to create, in effect, a "mini" fixed-exchange-rate system within Europe. This is done through two sets of rules, the parity grid and the divergence indicator.

The **parity grid** rule says that each currency is supposed to remain fixed against each other currency, within limits. For example, in early 1994, the value of the deutschemark was supposed to remain fixed at 3.3539 French francs, although it was allowed to fluctuate by 15 percent above or below that level. There is a set "central rate" for each EMS currency against each other one, as illustrated in Table 4.5.

If, say, the French franc falls to its lower limit against *any* one of the currencies of the EMS (such as the Dutch guilder), the French central bank is obliged to intervene in the foreign-exchange market, buying francs and selling guilders. The Dutch government is similarly supposed to intervene, selling guilders and buying francs.[9] This is known as *marginal intervention* (because the action happens at the margins of the parity grid). Central banks may also intervene before the margins are reached—intramarginal intervention. The central "cross rates" are set at a point in time, namely whenever there is a realignment of the EMS currency values. The central cross rates can be calculated from each currency's central rate against the ECU (see Table 4.6).

If one or more currencies is under too much pressure, the member countries may agree to undertake a *realignment* and set new parities (and therefore a new parity grid) that are regarded as more realistic. Realignments have to be agreed to by all ERM member countries, with final decisions being taken by the finance ministers and central bank governors. They have tended to take place on weekends, when markets are closed. In the interest of stability, realignments are agreed to only reluctantly; when they do occur, they must be of sufficient magnitude to remove pressure, but not so great as to distort competitive relations among member states. A more extreme measure is to suspend the currency's participation in the exchange-rate mechanism, as the pound sterling and Italian lira did following a crisis in the ERM in September 1992.

To determine whether there's pressure on a currency in the EMS, all one has to know is how much it has fallen (from the central rate in the grid) against the strongest currency, or how much it has risen against the weakest currency. Then see if it's approaching the allowed limit. Experience suggests that once a cross rate actually reaches its ERM limits, it can be extremely difficult for the central banks to head off an avalanche of market speculation about a possible realignment—that is, a devaluation of the weak currency.

The divergence indicator is the second major rule keeping the EMS currencies together. This indicator measures how far a currency is out of line with respect to an average of all the other currencies. The ECU, with some adjustments, is used as a proxy for this average. The extent to which the individual currency has moved from its central rate against the ECU, relative to its allowed divergence, is regarded as an indicator of

Table 4.5   *Example of the European Parity Grid*

	DM	FF	DFI
DM	I	3.3539	1.1267
FF	0.2982	I	0.3360
DFI	0.8875	2.9762	I

---

[9]In practice, the burden of adjustment and intervention falls on the currency at the bottom of its band, for it has limited foreign-exchange reserves with which to buy its own currency. It is also obliged to buy back, at a later date, however much of its currency has been acquired by the strong-currency central bank.

Table 4.6 *EMS European Currency Unit Rates*

	Ecu Central Rates	Currency Amounts Against Ecu Aug 24	% Change from Central Rate	% Spread vs Weakest Currency	Divergence Indicator‡
Dutch Guilder	2.19672	2.16386	-1.50	7.84	-
D–Mark	1.94964	1.92425	-1.30	7.63	-
Irish Punt	0.808628	0.812764	0.51	5.69	-3
Belgian Franc	40.2123	40.5046	0.73	5.46	-5
Spanish Peseta	154.250	155.562	0.85	5.33	-6
Portuguese Escudo	192.854	195.956	1.61	4.54	-11
French Franc	6.53883	6.70116	2.48	3.65	-21
Danish Krone	7.43679	7.89981	6.23	0.00	-43

Ecu central rates set by the European Commission. Currencies are in descending relative strength. Percentage changes are for Ecu; a positive change denotes a weak currency. Divergence shows the ratio between two spreads: the percentage difference between the actual market and Ecu central rates for a currency, and the maximum permitted percentage deviation of the currency's market rate from its Ecu central rate.
‡Indicative values only. Divergence indicators are based on 15% band limitations but do not show the 2.25% band between the Dutch Guilder and D–Mark.

Source: *Financial Times*, August 25, 1993.

how badly the country is deviating from the weighted average of the others. When the limit is approached, the country is supposed to undertake *monetary and fiscal* actions to change domestic economic conditions so that its currency behaves more like the others. The hope is that such actions, if taken in a sufficiently timely manner, will forestall the need for a realignment and further the cause of policy coordination.

The divergence indicator, expressed as a percentage of the allowed divergence, is shown in Table 4.6, excerpted from the *Financial Times* of August 25, 1993. As of that date no country seemed to be under great pressure to change its policies. But even if the divergence indicator did suggest that action was needed, there would be only a presumption that corrective action would be taken, not an absolute requirement.

To summarize: the *parity grid* rule has to do with the exchange rate of each country against each other country; the remedy, if the limit is approached, is intervention in the foreign-exchange market. The *divergence-indicator* rule concentrates on the exchange rate of each country against the ECU; the prescription is economic policy changes to bring inflation and monetary conditions back into line with those of the other members.

The Obstacle-Strewn Path to Monetary Union

By the early 1990s, all the European Community members had agreed that the ultimate goal of the currency linkages with the ERM was European monetary union. They even have an acronym for it: EMU.[10] But what that elusive beast looks like depends on whom you ask. It seems that it would entail the transfer of monetary power from national governments to a new central bank, dubbed "Eurofed." This European central bank would set Europe's interest rate. And the EC finance ministers have said that Eurofed "*should be explicitly committed to price stability.*" That much is agreed.

But how long before such a transfer of sovereignty occurs? And what path should it take? And should all the Community's currencies be permanently glued at set exchange

---

[10]Strictly speaking, EMU stands for economic and monetary union.

BOX 4.5

The Stages of European Monetary Union

The Delors Committee of the European Commission in Brussels set out three stages of economic and monetary union.

- *Stage One* includes the removal of all obstacles to financial integration. All monetary and financial instruments circulate freely, and banking, securities, and insurance services are offered uniformly throughout the Community. On the broader economic front, this stage sets forth the "1993 goals": a complete removal of all physical, technical and fiscal barriers to economic transactions in a free internal market.
- *Stage Two* is envisaged as a brief transition in which a common central bank, Eurofed, is established and collective decision-making is practiced.
- *Stage Three* is the culmination of the monetary union process, including a European currency to be issued by a European central bank, Eurofed. (It is not yet clear whether national currencies would continue to be issued, but if they were, they would have to be irrevocably tied to the European unit.)

rates, or should the ECU replace national currencies? (See Box 4.5.) The next few years will see the debate continue, with some wanting a fast track to monetary union, insisting on a common currency even before monetary policies have been properly coordinated, while others caution that hard political choices of economic unit must precede the final stage of union. Margaret Thatcher, the former Prime Minister of Britain, put it more dramatically, "It is to give up for all time the rights of the banks of England and Scotland and our Treasury to issue our own currency, backed by our own economic policy, answerable to our own Parliament."[11] Certainly the Eurofed will have to make decisions on monetary growth, interest rates, and the like in the context of a consensus on economic priorities. Divergence of monetary and growth policies in mid-1992 led to a partial break-up of the ERM, one that centered around the German central bank's unwillingness to compromise its anti-inflationary stance. Later that year, the following Christmas carol was making the rounds of London's dealing rooms:

God make ye merry, Bundesbank,

You cause so much dismay;

Why don't you give us all a break

And cut your rates today?

To save the troubled ERM

And keep the slump away,

All because of Frankfurt and Bonn

Our industry's gone—

All because of Frankfurt and Bonn.[12]

The French might have cried a similar lament in the summer of 1993 when German anti-inflationary credit policies, coupled with recessionary conditions in France, led speculators to short the French franc and other currencies in the belief that current parities were unsustainable. After spending a reported $35 billion to defend the EMS parities, Europe's central-bank governors met to resolve the recurrent crisis. What could be done

---

[11]Quoted in *The Economist,* June 29, 1991, p. 49.

[12]Thanks to Mike Connelly for this verse.

to keep the EMS alive, help economic recovery, and remove the incentives to speculate? According to one report, six options were under consideration:[13]

- Continue central-bank intervention to support existing parities
- The German mark and the Dutch guilder, the two strong currencies, leave the ERM indefinitely
- Widen all the currency fluctuation bands to 6 percent
- Introduce wider bands just for the German mark and the Dutch guilder against other currencies
- Permanently fix the exchange-rate parities of the "core" ERM members— Germany, France, and the Benelux countries—for a rapid move towards mini-European Monetary Union
- Suspend the system entirely

The choice was a variation of the fourth option: intervention bands for all but the mark and guilder were widened to 15 percent. This preserved the Exchange-Rate Mechanism, but in name only, because most agreed that the long-fought battle for a "franc fort" had been lost. Although some bemoaned the ensuing incapacitation of the EMS as destroying the dream of European unity, others maintained that the ERM, with fixed parities and Bundesbank anti-inflationary leadership, had performed a useful function in the 1980s, and perhaps would do so again.[14] An unwavering peg to the German mark in times of divergent and recessionary conditions involves too much of a sacrifice for present-day European polities.

If the final stage of monetary union is ever reached, Europe will be a very different place politically for a simple reason.[15] The power to create money will now reside with the Eurofed. Unless this institution were to abandon its mandate of price stability, there would have to be no monetary financing of public deficits. *So only a state's creditworthiness will determine its ability to borrow.*

Treasury bonds in Europe will become like municipal bonds in Britain or the United States, by no means the perfect credit risk. In a sense, EMU means turning over power not to Brussels but to the man in the street. The reason is threefold: (1) National central banks will no longer have the power to avoid formal default by printing more currency. Every centime that they spend will have to come from taxation or borrowing. (2) Their ability to borrow will be limited by their ability to get the means to repay. This follows from the loss of the printing press and because an explicit part of the monetary union plans excludes a Community bailout of profligate borrowers. (3) The single market will put an effective cap on oppressive taxation. Because European citizens will possess the four freedoms—free movement of people, goods, service, and capital—they can readily vote with their feet by migrating to an EC state with a more favorable tax regime if they're not getting their money's worth. Already the market discriminates among sovereign borrowers in Europe when they issue debt in a currency other than their own, as the credit ratings in Table 4.7 confirm.

Table 4.7 *Credit Ratings of EC Member States*

	Moody's	Standard & Poors
France	Aaa	AAA
Germany	Aaa	AAA
Holland	Aaa	AAA
Britain	Aaa	AAA
Luxembourg	Aaa	NR*
Italy	Aaa	AA +
Belgium	Aa1	AA +
Denmark	Aa1	AA
Spain	Aa2	AA
Ireland	Aa3	AA −
Portugal	A1	A
Greece	NR	BBB

*NR means not rated.

[13]*Financial Times,* August 2, 1991, p. 1.

[14]Olivier Blanchard, Rudiger Dornbusch, Stanley Fischer, Franco Modigliani, Paul Samuelson and Robert Solow, "Why the EMS Deserves an Early Burial," *Financial Times,* July 29, 1993, p. 9.

[15]An elaboration of this argument is given by Graham Bishop in "The Creation of an EC 'Hard Money' Union," Salomon Brothers, *1992 and Beyond* Series, July 1990.

SUMMARY

The international monetary system consists of a set of arrangements for currency values and for financial linkages between countries. In this chapter we saw that the central issue in the choice between fixed and floating exchange rates is one of monetary and economic policy independence. In the past century, the major countries have vacillated between more-or-less fixed rates, and more-or-less floating rates. When monetary policies are similar and inflation rates converge, a fixed exchange-rate system is possible; otherwise, it is not.

In either case, when payments are out of balance, when capital flows do not willingly match an imbalance between exports and imports, then the country must make certain adjustments. These adjustments can be initiated by public policy, or by the inevitable monetary contraction or expansion that results from capital flows under fixed exchange rates, or by an exchange-rate change.

Although the industrial world moved decisively toward a flexible exchange-rate system in the 1970s and 1980s, a countermove occurred in Europe in the form of the European Monetary System. The first decade of experience with this system has demonstrated that where the political will is present to reduce inflation, a currency bloc can achieve economic coordination and monetary discipline. Having achieved their major goals on the inflation front, however, the countries of Europe found strict monetary union to be incompatible with autonomy in domestic monetary policy. When economic conditions diverge sharply, the costs of maintaining fixed exchange rates can reach an unacceptable level.

CONCEPTUAL QUESTIONS

1. Identify the basic choices of exchange-rate regime that face a country.
2. What considerations are likely to persuade a country that pegging its currency to the U.S. dollar makes sense?
3. What is a crawling peg exchange rate?
4. Contrast the gold standard with the Bretton Woods system.
5. "Since debits must equal credits individually, balance of payments inflows must equal outflows." If this statement is true, how can we say that a country has a balance-of-payments deficit?
6. Can there be a balance-of-payments deficit if the country's currency is freely floating? Why or why not?
7. Does a balance-of-trade deficit in any way imply a government budget deficit?
8. Why is sterilized intervention in the foreign-exchange market likely to be ineffective?
9. When does a rise in the British interest rate mean that the pound will be strong?
10. What can occasion a change in the composition of the basket of currencies that comprise the ECU?
11. What is the difference between the parity grid and the divergence indicators of the European exchange-rate mechanism?

PROBLEMS

1. Under the Bretton Woods system, if the par value of the pound was $2.40, what was the permitted band of fluctuation?
2. Under the Bretton Woods system, if the par value of the pound was $2.40 and that of the French franc $0.15, what was the maximum and minimum value of the pound in terms of French francs?
3. The Finnish markka is fixed against the ECU. If Finland doubles its export surplus, what is likely to happen to the money stock in Finland?

4. Choose the most accurate completion statement: A country can be said to be running a balance-of-payments surplus when

   (a) the country's currency is rising.
   (b) the central bank or exchange authority is gaining reserves, defined as gold foreign exchange and special drawing rights (SDRs).
   (c) exports exceed imports.
   (d) exports (including services and interest) exceed imports similarly defined.
   (e) exports (including services, interest, and long-term capital inflows) exceed imports (including services, interest, and long-term capital outflows).
   (f) none of the above.

5. Choose the most accurate completion statement: Reversal of the U.S. trade deficit must involve

   (a) a reduction of the U.S. government budget deficit (including state and local government budgets).
   (b) an increase in the growth of domestic output.
   (c) an increase in the U.S. personal savings rate (plus a reduction in the U.S. personal consumption rate).
   (d) all of the above.
   (e) any of the above.

6. Assume that New Zealand decides to fix the New Zealand dollar (NZ$) against the U.S. dollar. Then, because of a global surplus of sheep, New Zealand suffers an export shortfall. Explain how this might affect New Zealand's foreign-exchange reserves, money supply, inflation rate, and long-term interest rates.

7. In 1986, Gondwana faced a shut-off of new international loans and bond issues. Which of the following most likely resulted? (Pick one or more.)

   (a) Capital inflows in the form of direct investment increased.
   (b) The country's current account improved. (It ran a current account surplus or the deficit was reduced.)
   (c) The government's foreign-exchange reserves increased.
   (d) The government's foreign-exchange reserves decreased.
   (e) The money supply increased (assuming no sterilization).
   (f) The money supply decreased (assuming no sterilization).

8. Explain, by means of a simple equation, the link between the external deficit and the internal deficit—in other words, between the balance-of-trade deficit and the budget deficit.

9. On July 20, 1985, the Italian lira was "devalued by 6 percent" in the EMS. Other participating currencies were "revalued upward by 2 percent." EMS central rates were as follows:

Currency	Currency/ECU (before)	Currency/ECU (after)
DM	2.24184	2.2384
Italian lira	1403.49	1520.6138

   Verify that Italian lira/DM rate has changed by about 8 percent. How does this percentage change compare to actual percentage changes in ECU central rates?

10. An Italian company exports to Germany and has DM850,000 due in three months. How much could it lose, assuming Germany and Italy adhere to the two sets of EMS rules with a 2.25% band?

11. If the DM is trading at 78 yen and the ECU is valued at DM2.02, what is the value of the ECU in terms of yen?

12. Based on the composition of the ECU shown in Table 4.4, what is likely to happen to the weightings in the ECU if sterling rises significantly versus the German mark?

Application 4.1

THE EXOTICS

This roundup of the world's currencies includes a number that currency traders shun, calling them "exotics." From the table and your own knowledge, can you identify (1) a

FT GUIDE TO WORLD CURRENCIES

The table below gives the latest available rates of exchange (rounded) against four key currencies on Monday, May 24, 1993 . In some cases the rate is nominal. Market rates are the average of buying and selling rates except where they are shown to be otherwise. In some cases market rates have been calculated from those of foreign currencies to which they are tied.

COUNTRY		£ STG	US $	D-MARK	YEN (X 100)
Afghanistan	(Afghani)	99.25	64.6579	39.5024	58.641
Albania	(Lek)	168.41	109.713	67.0288	99.5036
Algeria	(Dinar)	34.355	22.3811	13.6736	20.2983
Andorra	(Fr Fr)	8.4575	5.5097	3.3661	4.997
	(Sp Peseta)	191.35	124.658	76.1592	113.058
Angola	(New Kwanza)	6154.09	4009.18	2449.39	3636.09
Antigua	(E Carr $)	4.1337	2.6929	1.6452	2.4423
Argentina	(Peso)	1.5310	0.9973	0.6093	0.9045
Aruba	(Florin)	2.7405	1.7853	1.0907	1.6192
Australia	(Aus $)	2.2130	1.4416	0.8807	1.3075
Austria	(Schilling)	17.685	11.5211	7.0388	10.449
Azores	(Port Escudo)	238.50	155.375	94.9253	140.916
Bahamas	(Bahama $)	1.5350	1	0.6109	0.9069
Bahrain	(Dinar)	0.5767	0.3757	0.2295	0.3407
Balearic Is	(Sp Peseta)	191.35	124.658	76.1592	113.058
Bangladesh	(Taka)	61.5498	40.0975	24.4974	36.3662
Barbados	(Barb $)	3.0793	2.006	1.2255	1.8193
Belgium	(Belg Fr)	51.65	33.6482	20.5572	30.5169
Belize	(B $)	3.0620	1.9947	1.2187	1.8091
Benin	(CFA Fr)	422.875	275.489	168.308	249.852
Bermuda	(Bermudian $)	1.5350	1	0.6109	0.9069
Bhutan	(Ngultrum)	47.819	31.1524	19.0324	28.2534
Bolivia	(Boliviano)	6.4685	4.214	2.5745	3.8218
Botswana	(Pula)	3.6093	2.3513	1.4365	2.1325
Brazil	(Cruzeiro)	60060.35	39127.3	23904.6	35486.2
Brunei	(Brunei $)	2.4748	1.6122	0.9849	1.4622
Bulgaria	(Lev)	37.88	24.6775	15.0766	22.381
Burkino Faso	(CFA Fr)	422.875	275.489	168.308	249.852
Burma	(Kyat)	9.4750	6.1726	3.7711	5.5982
Burundi	(Burundi Fr)	363.25	236.645	144.577	214.623
Cambodia	(Riel)	5358.5	3490.88	2132.74	3166.03
Cameroon	(CFA Fr)	422.875	275.489	168.308	249.852
Canada	(Canadian $)	1.9390	1.2631	0.7717	1.1456
Canary Is	(Sp Peseta)	191.35	124.658	76.1592	113.058
Cp. Verde	(CV Escudo)	113.60	74.0065	45.2139	67.1196
Cayman Is	(CI $)	1.3014	0.8478	0.5179	0.7689
Cent.Afr. Rep	(CFA Fr)	422.875	275.489	168.308	249.852
Chad	(CFA Fr)	422.875	275.489	168.308	249.852
Chile	(Chilean Peso)	631.67	411.511	251.411	373.217
China	(Renminbi Yuan)	8.9175	5.8094	3.5492	5.2688
Colombia	(Col Peso)	1304.03	849.531	519.017	770.476
CIS ♣	(Rouble)	0.8899o	0.5797	0.3541	0.5257
		1451.55m	945.635	577.731	857.637
Comoros	(CFA Fr)	422.875	275.489	168.308	249.852
Congo (Brazz)	(CFA Fr)	422.875	275.489	168.308	249.852
Costa Rica	(Colon)	211.57	137.831	84.2069	125.004
Côte d'Ivoire	(CFA Fr)	422.875	275.489	168.308	249.852
Croatia	(Dinar)	3526.03	2297.09	1403.4	2083.33
Cuba	(Cuban Peso)	1.1596	0.7554	0.4615	0.6851
Cyprus	(Cyprus £)	0.7386	0.4811	0.2939	0.4363
Czech Rep.	(Koruna)	44.441c	28.9517	17.6879	26.2576
		43.02t	28.026	17.1223	25.418
Denmark	(Danish Kroner)	9.6125	6.2622	3.8258	5.6794
Djibouti Rep	(Djib Fr)	270.0	175.896	107.463	159.527
Dominica	(E Carrib $)	4.1337	2.6929	1.6452	2.4423
Dominican Rep	(D Peso)	19.9030	12.9661	7.9215	11.7595
Ecuador	(Sucre)	2933.40o	1911.01	1167.52	1733.18
		2893.59a	1885.07	1151.68	1709.65
Egypt	(Egyptian £)	5.11	3.3289	2.0338	3.0192
El Salvador	(Colon)	13.3809	8.7171	5.3257	7.9059
Equat'l Guinea	(CFA Fr)	422.875	275.489	168.308	249.852
Estonia	(Kroon)	19.89	12.9576	7.9164	11.7518
Ethiopia	(Ethiopian Birr)	7.5796	4.9378	3.0167	4.4783
Falkland Is	(Falk £)	1.00	0.6514	0.398	0.5908
Faroe Is	(Danish Kroner)	9.6125	6.2622	3.8258	5.6794
Fiji Is	(Fiji $)	2.3445	1.5273	0.9331	1.3852
Finland	(Markka)	8.4518	5.506	3.3639	4.9936
France	(Fr)	8.4575	5.5097	3.3661	4.997
Fr. Cty/Africa	(CFA Fr)	422.875	275.489	168.308	249.852
Fr. Guiana	(Local Fr)	8.4575	5.5097	3.3661	4.997
Fr. Pacific Is	(CFP Fr)	152.0	99.0228	60.4975	89.8079
Gabon	(CFA Fr)	422.875	275.489	168.308	249.852
Gambia	(Dalasi)	13.0135	8.4778	5.1795	7.6889
Germany	(D-Mark)	2.5125	1.6368	1	1.4844
Ghana	(Cedi)	922.38	600.899	367.116	544.981
Gibraltar	(Gib £)	1.00	0.6514	0.398	0.5908
Greece	(Drachma)	339.575	221.221	135.154	200.635
Greenland	(Danish Krone)	9.6125	6.2622	3.8258	5.6794
Grenada	(E Carr $)	4.1337	2.6929	1.6452	2.4423
Guadaloupe	(Local Fr)	8.4575	5.5097	3.3661	4.997
Guam	(US $)	1.5350	1	0.6109	0.9069
Guatemala	(Quetzal)	8.5301	5.557	3.395	5.0399
Guinea	(Fr)	1243.61	810.169	494.969	734.777
Guinea-Bissau	(Peso)	7655.0	4986.97	3046.77	4522.9
Guyana	(Guyanese $)	192.91	125.674	76.78	113.979
Haiti	(Goude)	18.3720	11.9687	7.3122	10.8549
Honduras	(Lempira)	9.3085	6.0641	3.7048	5.4998
Hong Kong	(HK $)	11.8373	7.7115	4.7113	6.9939
Hungary	(Forint)	134.91	87.8892	53.6955	79.7104
Iceland	(Icelandic Krona)	99.20	64.6254	39.4825	58.6115
India	(Indian Rupee)	47.819	31.1524	19.0324	28.2534
Indonesia	(Rupiah)	3209.33	2090.77	1277.35	1896.21
Iran	(Rial)	2503.0	1630.62	996.219	1478.88
Iraq	(Iraqi Dinar)	0.5936	0.3867	0.2362	0.3507
Irish Rep	(Punt)	1.0285	0.67	0.4093	0.6076
Israel	(Shekel)	4.175	2.7198	1.6616	2.4667
Italy	(Lira)	2279.50	1485.02	907.264	1346.82
Jamaica	(Jamaican $)	33.988	22.142	13.5275	20.0815
Japan	(Yen)	169.25	110.261	67.3631	100
Jordan	(Jordanian Dinar)	1.0518	0.6852	0.4186	0.6214
Kenya	(Kenya Shilling)	97.2185	63.3345	38.6939	57.4407
Kiribati	(Australian $)	2.2130	1.4416	0.8807	1.3075
Korea North	(Won)	3.2917	2.1444	1.3101	1.9448
Korea South	(Won)	1234.78	804.417	491.455	729.56
Kuwait	(Kuwaiti Dinar)	0.4620	0.3009	0.1838	0.2729
Laos	(New Kip)	1102.32	718.124	438.734	651.297
Lebanon	(Lebanese £)	2660.06	1732.94	1058.73	1571.68
Lesotho	(Maluti)	4.8970	3.1902	1.949	2.8933
Liberia	(Liberian $)	1.5350	1	0.6109	0.9069
Libya	(Libyan Dinar)	0.4515	0.2941	0.1797	0.2667
Liechtenstein	(Swiss Fr)	2.2575	1.4706	0.8985	1.3338
Luxembourg	(Lux Fr)	51.65	33.6482	20.5572	30.5169
Macao	(Pataca)	12.2227	7.9626	4.8647	7.2216
Madagascar	(MG Fr)	2794.07	1820.24	1112.07	1650.85
Madeira	(Port Escudo)	238.50	155.375	94.9253	140.916
Malawi	(Kwacha)	6.5565	4.2713	2.6095	3.8738
Malaysia	(Ringgit)	3.9308	2.5607	1.5644	2.3224
Maldive Is	(Rufiya)	18.3337	11.9437	7.2969	10.8323
Mali Rep	(CFA Fr)	422.875	275.489	168.308	249.852
Malta	(Maltese Lira)	0.5621	0.3661	0.2237	0.3321
Martinique	(Local Fr)	8.4575	5.5097	3.3661	4.997
Mauritania	(Ouguiya)	174.24	113.511	69.3492	102.948
Mauritius	(Maur Rupee)	25.9338	16.8949	10.3219	15.3227
Mexico	(Mexican Peso)	4.7813	3.1148	1.903	2.8249
Miquelon	(Local Fr)	8.4575	5.5097	3.3661	4.997
Monaco	(French Fr)	8.4575	5.5097	3.3661	4.997
Mongolia	(Tugrik)	229.65	149.609	91.4029	135.687
Montserrat	(E Carr $)	4.1337	2.6929	1.6452	2.4423
Morocco	(Dirham)	13.4569	8.7667	5.3559	7.9509
Mozambique	(Metical)	4204.63	2739.17	1673.48	2484.27
Namibia	(S A Rand)	4.8970	3.1902	1.949	2.8933
Nauru Is	(Australian $)	2.2130	1.4416	0.8807	1.3075
Nepal	(Nepalese Rupee)	71.23	46.4039	28.3502	42.0856
Netherlands	(Guilder)	2.8125	1.8322	1.1194	1.6617
N'nd Antilles	(A/Guilder)	2.8255	1.8407	1.1245	1.6694
New Zealand	(NZ $)	2.8175	1.8355	1.1213	1.6646
Nicaragua	(Gold Cordoba)	9.3471	6.0893	3.7202	5.5226
Niger Rep	(CFA Fr)	422.875	275.489	168.308	249.852
Nigeria	(Naira)	38.275	24.9348	15.2338	22.6144
Norway	(Nor. Krone)	10.6075	6.9104	4.2218	6.2673
Oman	(Rial Omani)	0.5894	0.3839	0.2345	0.3482
Pakistan	(Pak. Rupee)	40.4811	26.372	16.1118	23.9179
Panama	(Balboa)	1.5350	1	0.6109	0.9069
Papua New Guinea	(Kina)	1.4920	0.9719	0.5938	0.8815
Paraguay	(Guarani)	2640.97	1720.5	1051.13	1560.4
Peru	(New Sol)	3.010	1.9609	1.198	1.7784
Philippines	(Peso)	40.05	26.0912	15.9402	23.6632
Pitcairn Is	(£ Sterling)	1.00	0.6514	0.398	0.5908
	(NZ $)	2.8175	1.8355	1.1213	1.6646
Poland	(Zloty)	26343.0	17161.6	10484.8	15564.5
Portugal	(Escudo)	238.50	155.375	94.9253	140.916
Puerto Rico	(US $)	1.5350	1	0.6109	0.9069
Qatar	(Riyal)	5.5765	3.6328	2.2195	3.2948
Reunion Is. de la	(F/Fr)	8.4575	5.5097	3.3661	4.997
Romania	(Leu)	986.47	642.651	392.625	582.848
Rwanda	(Fr)	219.95	143.29	87.5422	129.956
St Christopher	(E Carr $)	4.1337	2.6929	1.6452	2.4423
St Helena	(£)	1.00	0.6514	0.398	0.5908
St Lucia	(E Carr $)	4.1337	2.6929	1.6452	2.4423
St Pierre	(French Fr)	8.4575	5.5097	3.3661	4.997
St Vincent	(E Carr $)	4.1337	2.6929	1.6452	2.4423
San Marino	(Italian Lira)	2279.50	1485.02	907.264	1346.82
Sao Tome	(Dobra)	367.44	239.375	146.245	217.099
Saudi Arabia	(Riyal)	5.7423	3.7409	2.2854	3.3927
Senegal	(CFA Fr)	422.875	275.489	168.308	249.852
Seychelles	(Rupee)	7.808	5.0866	3.1076	4.6132
Sierra Leone	(Leone)	826.74	538.593	329.051	488.473
Singapore	($)	2.4748	1.6122	0.9849	1.4622
Slovakia	(Koruna)	44.441c	28.9517	17.6879	26.2576
		43.02t	28.026	17.1223	25.418
Slovenia	(Tolar)	171.233	111.552	68.1524	101.172
Solomon Is	($)	4.9060	3.196	1.9526	2.8986
Somali Rep	(Shilling)	4011.22	2613.17	1596.51	2370
South Africa	(Rand)	4.8970c	3.1902	1.949	2.8933
		7.1038g	4.6278	2.8273	4.1972
Spain	(Peseta)	191.35	124.658	76.1592	113.058
Spanish Ports in N Africa	(Sp Peseta)	191.35	124.658	76.1592	113.058
Sri Lanka	(Rupee)	73.3828	47.8063	29.207	43.3576
Sudan Rep	(Dinar)	19.903	12.9661	7.9215	11.7595
Surinam	(Guilder)	2.7328	1.7803	1.0876	1.6146
Swaziland	(Lilangeni)	4.8970	3.1902	1.949	2.8933
Sweden	(Krona)	11.2050	7.2996	4.4597	6.6203
Switzerland	(Fr)	2.2575	1.4706	0.8985	1.3338
Syria	(£)	32.916	21.4436	13.1008	19.4481
Taiwan	($)	39.625	25.8143	15.7711	23.4121
Tanzania	(Shilling)	541.97	353.075	215.709	320.219
Thailand	(Baht)	38.65	25.1791	15.383	22.836
Togo Rep	(CFA Fr)	422.875	275.489	168.308	249.852
Tonga Is	(Pa Anga)	2.2120	1.441	0.8803	1.3069
Trinidad/Tobago	($)	8.7298	5.6871	3.4745	5.1579
Tunisia	(Dinar)	1.5065	0.9814	0.5996	0.8901
Turkey	(Lira)	15618.65	10175	6216.38	9228.15
Turks & Caicos	(US $)	1.5350	1	0.6109	0.9069
Tuvalu	(Australian $)	2.2130	1.4416	0.8807	1.3075
Uganda	(New Shilling)	1849.91	1205.15	736.283	1093
U A E	(Dirham)	5.6235	3.6635	2.2382	3.3225
United Kingdom	(£)	1.00	0.6514	0.398	0.5908
United States	(US $)	1.5350	1	0.6109	0.9069
Uruguay	(Peso Uruguayo)	5.8362	3.802	2.3228	3.4482
Vanuatu	(Vatu)	184.59	120.254	73.4686	109.064
Vatican	(Lira)	2279.50	1485.02	907.264	1346.82
Venezuela	(Bolivar)	134.03	87.3159	53.3452	79.1905
Vietnam	(Dong)	16152.05	10522.5	6428.68	9543.31
Virgin Is-British	(US $)	1.5350	1	0.6109	0.9069
Virgin Is-US	(US $)	1.5350	1	0.6109	0.9069
Western Samoa	(Tala)	3.9166	2.5515	1.5588	2.314
Yemen (Rep of)	(Rial)	25.26	16.456	10.0537	14.9246
Yemen (Rep of)	(Dinar)	0.7056	0.4596	0.2808	0.4168
Yugoslavia	(New Dinar)	123363.4	80367	49099.9	72888.3
Zaire Rep	(Zaire)	4688600.0	3054463	1866109	2770222
Zambia	(Kwacha)	796.12	518.645	316.864	470.381
Zimbabwe	($)	9.7984	6.3833	3.8998	5.7893

Special Drawing Rights May 21, 1993 United Kingdom £0.909425 United States $1.41170 Germany D Mark 2.29359 Japan Yen155.993
European Currency Unit Rates May 24, 1993 United Kingdom £0.780588 United States $1.19446 Germany D Mark 1.95891 Japan Yen132.238

Abbreviations: (a) Free rate; (b) Banknote rate; (c) Commercial rate ; (d) Controlled rate; (e) Essential imports; (g) Financial rate; (h) Exports; (i) Non commercial rate; (j) Business rate; (k) Buying rate; (l) Luxury goods; (m) Market rate; (n) Public transaction rate; (o) Official rate; (p) preferential rate; (q) convertible rate; (r) parallel rate; (s) Selling rate; (t) Tourist rate (u) Currencies fixed against the US Dollar (v) Floating rate ; ♣ CIS applies to states in the Rouble Zone.
Some data supplied by Bank of America, Economics Department, London Trading Centre. Enquiries: 071 634 4360/5.
Monday May 24, 1993

country whose currency is freely floating with no intervention by the central bank, (2) a currency that uses its neighbor's currency as its own legal tender, (3) a currency that is tied to the French franc, and (4) a country that has two different exchange rates? What would be the purpose of having two rates?

Application 4.2

STERLING TAKES A POUNDING

The time is early September 1989. During the past week, the British pound has suffered while the U.S. dollar has proved far stronger than most observers expected. As of September 5, one pound cost $1.5385 on the wholesale market, down from its summer levels in the $1.65 range. (See the accompanying article and tables from the London *Financial Times*.) This weakness occurred despite the fact that British short-term interest rates were almost 5 percent above equivalent U.S. rates.

Sterling's tumble is now provoking criticism of the U.K. authorities' apparent reluctance to make any sort of policy response. The trade-weighted index of sterling's value has fallen another 2.6 percent since the last hike of base rates to 14 percent in late May. As one economist says, "The longer sterling is allowed to slide, the greater the worry that the authorities have quietly abandoned their firm exchange-rate policy."

FOREIGN EXCHANGES

Dollar up despite intervention

Co-ordinated central bank intervention was only partially successful in stemming the dollar's rise yesterday. The US Federal Reserve was followed by 12 other central banks in selling dollars. The rise started in Far East markets despite intervention by the Bank of Japan estimated as at least $500m.

The firmer tone came after comments from leading bankers in the US expressing concern about the possible need for higher interest rates to control inflation. This was seen as providing a thinly veiled excuse for buying the US unit anyway. Comments such as these do not necessarily reflect Fed policy but were enough to spark off further dollar gains.

The US unit broke through resistance levels in Tokyo, and many traders expected a resulting sell off and had taken short positions accordingly. However, there was no sell off, and in the scramble to cover short positions, the US unit was pushed through resistance levels.

The firmer tone continued after the start of trading in London, and the US unit broke through the DM1.99 level but failed to hold above resistance at DM1.9920. At this point, most investors were holding back, waiting for the start of trading in New York after the long weekend break. But central banks took advantage of the market's hesitancy, sensing that the lack of any further advancement reflected caution and indecision. Nevertheless, the intervention by most central banks failed to dampen enthusiasm, and the dollar managed to finish close to the day's high at DM1.9910 from DM1.9875 and Y147.05 from Y145.90. Elsewhere, it closed at SFr1.7180 from SFr1.7095 and FFr6.7125 compared with FFr6.6725. On Bank of England figures, the dollar's exchange rate index rose to 72.7 from 72.2.

Sterling suffered at the hands of a stronger dollar and also lost ground against the D-Mark and other EMS currencies. The pound fell through support levels at $1.5450 and $1.5425, and is now expected to trade down to a floor level of $1.5225. There were no fresh economic factors to influence trading, and yesterday's decline tended to add weight to the argument that sterling has recently been a convenient parking lot for funds, in the absence of a better trading opportunity. High interest rates are a supporting factor but tend to be ignored if there is a stronger and quicker capital gain to be made elsewhere.

On Bank of England figures, the pound's exchange rate index closed at 90.7, down from 91.0 at the opening and 91.2 on Monday. Against the dollar, sterling fell to $1.5380 from $1.5540 and DM3.0625 compared with DM3.0750. It was also lower in yen terms at Y226.25 from Y226.75. Elsewhere, it finished at SFr2.6425 from SFr2.6575 and FFr10.3250 from FFr10.3700.

CURRENCY MOVEMENTS

Sep. 5	Bank of England Index	Morgan Guaranty Changes %
Sterling	90.7	− 19.7
U.S. Dollar	72.7	− 6.5
Canadian Dollar	105.4	+ 1.5
Austrian Schilling	106.2	+ 9.4
Belgian Franc	105.6	− 6.2
Danish Krone	103.1	− 1.8
Deutsche Mark	112.1	+ 19.8
Swiss Franc	106.6	+ 15.7
Guilder	109.8	+ 12.9
French Franc	99.3	− 15.4
Lira	99.4	− 18.6
Yen	136.7	+ 66.4

Morgan Guaranty changes: average 1980–1982 = 100. Bank of England Index (Base Average 1985 = 100). Rates are for Sep. 1.

POUND SPOT- FORWARD

Sep. 5	Day's spread	Close
US	1.5375–1.5470	1.5375–1.5385
Canada	1.8180–1.8300	1.8180–1.8190
Netherlands	3.44¼–3.46¼	3.44½–3.45½
Belgium	63.95–64.35	64.00–64.10
Denmark	11.87¼–11.92¼	11.87¼–11.88¼
Ireland	1.1465–1.1520	1.1490–1.1500
W. Germany	3.05–3.07¼	3.05¼–3.06½
Portugal	254.70–256.70	254.70–255.70
Spain	191.05–192.15	191.15–191.45
Italy	2192¼–2202¼	2194½–2195½
Norway	11.11½–11.17½	11.11¼–11.12¼
France	10.31¼–10.36½	10.32–10.33
Sweden	10.29½–10.36½	10.29½–10.30½
Japan	225¼–227½	225¼–226¼
Austria	21.54–21.60	21.54–21.57
Switzerland	2.63¼–2.65½	2.63¼–2.64¼
ECU	1.4730–1.4775	1.4760–1.4770

What is *your* opinion after reading the article? Why should the U.K. authorities have a "firm exchange rate policy" in the first place, rather than letting the currency find its own level in free market trading? What sort of choices do the authorities have?

| **Application 4.3** | UNDERGROUND ECONOMICS |

Traveling in the New York subway, you find yourself jostled by a group of rowdy, argumentative high school kids. You cannot help overhearing their dispute. It appears that the *Village Voice* has reported that the Canadian and U.S. central banks have both undertaken to peg their currencies with respect to each other at an exchange rate that undervalues the Canadian dollar relative to the U.S. dollar. The students all agree that there is free trading in both currencies, so that to fix the exchange rate the authorities will have to engage in foreign-exchange intervention, but they are quarreling about the likely result. Here are the different opinions you hear:

"Canadian reserves will increase!"

"But the Fed is more likely to intervene in the foreign-exchange market, which means that U.S. reserves will fall!"

"The Canadian monetary base will increase!"

"According to the *Voice,* the U.S. monetary base will decrease and M1 will decrease even more!"

"I think Canadian long-term interest rates will tend to fall!"

"You're *all* right!"

"You're all wrong!"

Suddenly they notice you looking at them. "Hey, what's your opinion?" the biggest one asks.

| **Application 4.4** | DOUBLE DEFICITS |

At a recent meeting of the OLS (Occasional Lunch Society), a group of private-sector international economists, an oft-repeated lament was heard. As a nation, the story goes, the United States has a low savings rate relative to the rest of the world. Some even blame the U.S. trade deficit on this inadequate savings, saying that "because we cannot save here, the rest of the world is forced to lend to us." Be that as it may, it is a truism (resulting from the national accounting equation $X - M = S - [I + (G - T)]$) that the trade balance must equal the amount by which private saving exceeds private investment plus the government deficit. Hence, if savings is inadequate to meet the country's investment and budget deficit needs, we must borrow from abroad.

So what does this mean for the U.S. trade deficit? Which of the following, in your opinion, is necessary for reversal of the U.S. trade deficit (choose one):

1. A reduction of the U.S. government budget deficit (including state and local government budgets)
2. An increase in the growth of domestic output
3. An increase in the U.S. personal savings rate (plus a reduction in the U.S. personal consumption rate)
4. All of the above
5. Any of the above

Application 4.5

IMBALANCED

Excerpts from Aunt Helen's postcard from Japan:

The Nihon Keizai Shinbum talks a lot about the Japanese surplus and the U.S. balance-of-payments deficit. But what does it mean? The *balance of payments,* we all know, consists of a summary of a country's international transactions in goods, services, and capital flows, plus the government's intervention. The *current account* records all exports and imports of goods and services, including interest and foreign aid. The *capital account* comprises all flows of financial assets vis-a-vis the rest of the world. Either can be out of balance by itself. But tell me, which of the following indicates that this country is running an overall balance-of-payments surplus?

1. The Japanese yen is rising.
2. The central bank, the Bank of Japan, is gaining reserves, defined as gold foreign exchange and special drawing rights (SDRs).
3. Exports from Japan exceed imports.
4. Exports (including services and interest) exceed imports similarly defined.
5. Exports (including services, interest, and long-term capital with flows) exceed imports (including services, interest, and long-term capital outflows).
6. None of the above.

Application 4.6

THE EEC YANKEE BOND

You own ECU 100,000 face value of the EEC "Yankee" bond (see Exhibit I). You bought them in January 1988 at the issue price. At that time, the composition of the ECU had remained unchanged since 1984. The spot exchange rates of the member country currencies were then as follows:

1 USD (U.S. dollar) =	35.0525	BFR/LFR	(Belgian franc/Luxembourg franc)
	6.424	DKR	(Danish krone)
	1.6774	DM	(deutschemark)
	133.65	DRA	(Greek drachma)
	113.85	PTA	(Spanish peseta)
	5.655	FF	(French franc)
	0.63091	IRL	(Irish punt)
	1235.25	LIT	(Italian lira)
	1.8838	HFL	(Dutch guilder)
	137.105	ESC	(Portuguese escudo)
	0.56529	UKL	(British pound)

(Source: *Eurostat,* published by the European Economic Community in Brussels.)

1. Assuming interest rates have not changed, what would your bonds be worth now in U.S. dollars? Is this a gain or a loss? To obtain today's exchange rates, use the accompanying extract from the *Financial Times* (Exhibit IIa, page 113).
2. What, if anything, is the likely effect of the "single market" on the value of your bonds?
3. What is the likely effect of a realignment of the EMS currencies on the value of your bond?

(Questions continued on page 115.)

EXHIBIT I

P R O S P E C T U S

ECU 200,000,000

European Economic Community

9 ⅞% Bonds Due December 1, 1996

Interest payable on June 1 and December 1

PURCHASERS OF THE BONDS WILL BE REQUIRED TO PAY FOR THE BONDS IN ECU (EUROPEAN CURRENCY UNITS). PRINCIPAL OF AND INTEREST ON THE BONDS WILL BE PAYABLE ONLY IN ECU. AS SET FORTH HEREIN. FOR INFORMATION AS TO THE LIMITED FACILITIES IN THE UNITED STATES FOR CONVERSION OF ECU, CHANGES IN THE RELATIVE VALUE OF THE U.S. DOLLAR AND THE ECU AND CERTAIN ECONOMIC AND TAX CONSEQUENCES TO PURCHASERS OF THE BONDS, SEE "IMPORTANT INFORMATION", "DESCRIPTION OF THE ECU", "DESCRIPTION OF THE BONDS" AND "TAXATION".

The 9⅞% Bonds Due December 1, 1996 (the "Bonds") are unconditional, direct, general obligations of the European Economic Community (the "EEC"), for the payment and performance of which the full faith and credit of the EEC is pledged. The Bonds will bear interest from December 6, 1984. The Bonds are issuable in fully registered form only. The EEC will redeem, or in the case of the last installment pay at maturity ECU 20,000,000 aggregate principal amount of Bonds on December 1 in each of the years 1987 through 1996, in each case at the principal amount thereof plus accrued interest. The Bonds are not otherwise subject to redemption at the option of the EEC.

THESE SECURITIES HAVE NOT BEEN APPROVED OR DISAPPROVED BY THE SECURITIES AND EXCHANGE COMMISSION NOR HAS THE COMMISSION PASSED UPON THE ACCURACY OR ADEQUACY OF THIS PROSPECTUS. ANY REPRESENTATION TO THE CONTRARY IS A CRIMINAL OFFENSE.

	Price to the Public(1)	Underwriting Discounts and Commissions	Proceeds to the EEC(1)(2)
Per Bond	99.50%	1.125%	98.375%
Total	ECU199,000,000	ECU2,250,000	ECU196,750,000

(1) Plus accrued interest, if any, from December 6, 1984.

(2) Before deduction of expenses payable by the EEC estimated at ECU 626,500, including ECU 135,000 payable to the Underwriters in partial reimbursement of their expenses.

Investors are advised to read this Prospectus and to retain it for future reference.

The Bonds are offered by the several Underwriters when, as and if issued by the EEC and accepted by the Underwriters and subject to their right to reject orders in whole or in part. It is expected that the Bonds will be ready for delivery in New York City on or about December 6, 1984.

Bear, Stearns & Co.

The First Boston Corporation

Morgan Stanley & Co.
Incorporated

The date of this Prospectus is November 29, 1984.

DESCRIPTION OF THE ECU

Introduction

The ECU is a composite currency, consisting of specified amounts of currencies of each of the ten Member States of the EEC. Although the ECU's primary role initially related to the European Monetary System (the "EMS") and the operations of the EEC institutions, commercial use of the ECU by other governmental bodies and private entities has developed rapidly over the past several years. Because the ECU is a composite currency, its exchange rate tends to be more stable than those of its component currencies, since changes in the latter may offset each other in the ECU exchange rate. Interest rates on ECU denominated debt have tended to reflect the weighted average interest rates of borrowing in each of the component currencies.

The ECU Within the European Banking System. Although there is no central bank which issues ECU bank notes, the ECU is increasingly recognized in the international financial markets as a freely convertible foreign currency. To facilitate the growth of the ECU for private commercial transactions, certain European banks have established a clearing mechanism for the ECU, thus enabling the transfer of ECU without necessarily having to make separate transactions in each of the component currencies. Banks are also able to cover open ECU positions by undertaking transactions in the component currencies.

Many financial institutions, primarily in the Benelux countries, Britain, France, Denmark and Italy, make both spot and forward markets in the ECU against the U.S. dollar and other currencies. These exchange rates are published in most European daily financial publications and through several news services. There is also an ECU market for overnight investments and investments with maturities of up to one year.

The Use of the ECU for Denominating International Debt Issues. The first ECU denominated debt issue was underwritten early in 1981. The ECU is now a significant currency for denominating international debt issues in the Eurobond markets. At October 31, 1984, there were at least 5.7 billion principal amount of outstanding public ECU denominated securities issued in the Eurobond markets. In addition, a substantial amount of ECU denominated securities have been placed privately.

The following table sets forth the statistical compilations of the Commission of the European Communities (the "Commission") of the number and aggregate principal amount (in millions of ECU) of public ECU bond issues in the Eurobond markets for each of the calendar years 1981 through 1983 and for the ten months ended October 31, 1984:

	1981	1982	1983	October 31, 1984
ECU borrowings by the European Communities, their institutions and public and private issuers in the Member States	150	572	1,330	1,522
ECU borrowings by public and private issuers in non-Member States, the World Bank and others	40	150	605	1,294
Total	190	722	1,935	2,816
Number of issues	5	17	33	53

Such compilations of public debt issues show that during the first ten months of 1984 the ECU has been the third most utilized currency for issuance of bonds on the Eurobond markets (after the U.S. dollar and the German mark), as determined by amount of the indebtedness raised.

There is a well developed secondary market for ECU denominated public issues in Europe, and most issues trade on a daily basis in the Eurobond market.

The Use of the ECU for Other Commercial Transactions. The ECU is increasingly used for pricing, invoicing and settling commercial transactions within the EEC and with other European countries.

Definition and Composition

Following the Resolution of December 5, 1978, of the Council of the European Communities (the "Council"), concerning the establishment of the EMS and the role of the ECU in the EMS, the ECU was defined by the Council Regulation of December 18, 1978, as the sum of specified amounts of the currencies of the Member States. The ECU's composition, and thus its value, were identical to those of the European Unit of Account ("EUA"), which had been used in the EEC's accounts since 1975. Following adoption of the ECU in the EMS framework, the ECU replaced the EUA in all EEC uses, effective January 1, 1981.

Since 1978, the specified amounts of the currencies that make up the ECU have only been changed once in September 1984 when, following the reexamination required every five years, the Council changed the composition of the ECU and incorporated the Greek drachma as required by the treaty of accession of Greece to the EEC and their other European communities. In addition to the inclusion of the Greek drachma, the principal revisions were to decrease the amounts of German marks and Dutch guilders included in the ECU and to increase the amounts of Italian lire and French francs. These changes were made mainly to bring the weights of the component currencies in line with underlying economic criteria and had the effect of compensating for the appreciation of the German mark and the Dutch guilder and the depreciation of the French franc and the Italian lira over the previous five-year period. As a result, since September 17, 1984, the ECU is defined by Council Regulation as the sum of the following amounts of the currencies of the Member States:

0.719	German marks	3.71	Belgian francs
0.0878	United Kingdom pounds	0.14	Luxembourg francs
1.31	French francs	0.219	Danish kroner
140.00	Italian lire	0.00871	Irish pounds
0.256	Dutch guilders	1.15	Greek drachmas

It is important to differentiate between the composition of the ECU as legally defined, which is fixed and subject to change only under strict conditions, and the exchange rate of the ECU, which can vary on a day-to day basis. As discussed below, and as is the case with most other currencies, the exchange rate of the ECU fluctuates against each component currency as well as non-component currencies.

Circumstances in Which the Composition of the ECU May Change

The 1978 Council Resolution requires that the relative weights (at then prevailing exchange rates; see table) of the component currencies of the ECU be examined every five years and, if necessary, the specified amounts of the component currencies be revised. This resulted in the September 1984 revision. In addition, any Member State may request a reexamination if the weight of a currency in the ECU has changed at least 25% since the previous revision.

In either event a revision can occur only by unanimous decision of the Council. Any revision is to be made in line with underlying economic criteria. While the 1978 Council Resolution does not specify the economic criteria to be considered, the principal criteria used in the September 1984 revision were the relative gross domestic products of and trade among the Member States. In making the revision, the Council also took into account the need to ensure the continued smooth functioning of the ECU markets.

The 1978 Council Resolution requires that any revision not, in and of itself, modify the exchange rate of the ECU. This is accomplished by choosing a set of specified amounts of the component currencies which ensures that, on the day of calculation, the exchange rate of the ECU under its revised composition is identical to its exchange rate under the superseded composition. For example, the exchange rate of the ECU against the U.S. dollar as of the day of calculation for the September 1984 revision remained at 1 ECU = $0.742589 under both the revised and the superseded compositions. Because of the revised composition, however, the exchange rate will differ over time from what it would have been under the superseded composition.

While changes in exchange rate of the currencies of the Member States, including revaluations and devaluations, do not affect the fixed composition of the ECU, the exchange rate of the ECU in subsequent trading may change because of the increased or reduced exchange rates of its components.

The following table sets forth the relative weights of the component currencies in the ECU, based on the prevailing exchange rates on March 13, 1979 (when the EMS became operative), at each subsequent year-end and at October 31, 1984 (reflecting the revision of the ECU implemented on September 17, 1984). The weight of a currency in the ECU is the ratio in percentage terms between the specified amount of that currency in the ECU and the value of the ECU in terms of that currency. The weights fluctuate as the relevant currency strengthens or weakens on the foreign-exchange markets.

	March 13, 1979	December 31, 1979	1980	1981	1982	1983	October 31, 1984
German mark	32.9%	33.2%	32.3%	33.9%	36.0%	36.7%	32.3%
French franc	19.9	19.9	19.4	18.5	17.6	16.7	19.2
United Kingdom pound	13.4	13.7	16.1	15.6	14.7	15.5	14.5
Italian lira	9.5	9.4	8.9	8.4	8.2	7.9	10.1
Dutch guilder	10.5	10.4	10.2	10.7	11.3	11.3	10.2
Belgian franc	9.2	9.1	8.9	8.8	8.1	7.9	8.2
Luxembourg franc	0.4	0.4	0.3	0.3	0.3	0.3	0.3
Danish krone	3.1	2.8	2.8	2.7	2.7	2.7	2.7
Irish pound	1.1	1.1	1.1	1.1	1.1	1.0	1.2
Greek drachma	—	—	—	—	—	—	1.3
	100.0%	100.0%	100.0%	100.0%	100.0%	100.0%	100.0%

It is expected that in the event of the entry of Spain and Portugal into the European Communities, the currencies of those two countries will at some date be included in the ECU.

Functions of the ECU Within the EMS

The ECU plays a central role in the functioning of the EMS, which aims to foster close monetary cooperation among the Member States with the intention of making the EEC a zone of monetary stability. The EMS provides for an exchange rate mechanism based on taking appropriate actions to limit exchange rate fluctuations among currencies of the participating Member States within a narrow range around their parity rates. In this context, the ECU is used as a reference point for the calculation of these parities, as a denominator for the claims and liabilities among the participating central banks and as a reserve and settlement instrument created against gold and dollar deposits by those banks. All Member States except the United Kingdom and Greece participate in the EMS stabilization mechanism. The mechanism established under the EMS is limited to stabilization of exchange rates of the currencies of the participating Member States and does not provide for stabilization of those currencies against any other currencies.

Exchange Rate of the ECU

Since the ECU is composed of specified amounts of Member State currencies, a value for the ECU can be determined at any time by using the current market rate of each component. For example, the value of the ECU in terms of the Dutch guilder may be calculated by adding to the specified amount of the Dutch guilder in the ECU the amounts of all the other components after having converted them into the Dutch guilder at market rates. A similar procedure is followed to determine the ECU's value in terms of noncomponent currencies.

The Commission calculates daily ECU exchange rates for official use in terms of most of the world's major currencies, including the U.S. dollar, based on the rates in effect at 2:30 p.m. Brussels time, on the exchange markets of the component currencies. These rates are published daily in the Official Journal of the European Communities. They are used for internal purposes of the European Communities and are not necessarily rates at which commercial transactions in ECU can be effected.

The following table sets forth, for the periods and dates indicated, certain information concerning the exchange rate of the ECU in terms of the U.S. dollar, determined by the Commission as described above, for the period from March 13 to December 31, 1979, for the calendar years 1980, 1981, 1982 and 1983 and for the period from January 1 to October 31, 1984.

	At End of Period	Average Rate (1)	High	Low
1979	$1.43839	$1.37442	$1.44443	$1.31113
1980	1.30963	1.39233	1.45302	1.26638
1981	1.08517	1.11645	1.33166	0.97759
1982	0.96767	0.97972	1.09601	0.90589
1983	0.82737	0.89022	0.98310	0.81333
1984 (through October 31)	0.73574	0.79933	0.87944	0.70976

(1) The average of the exchange rates on each trading day during the period.

EXHIBIT IIA

POUND SPOT - FORWARD AGAINST THE POUND

May 18	Day's spread	Close	One month	% p.a.	Three months	% p.a.
US	1.5235 - 1.5340	1.5310 - 1.5320	0.41-0.39cpm	3.13	1.14-1.11pm	2.94
Canada	1.9415 - 1.9595	1.9480 - 1.9490	0.28-0.19cpm	1.45	0.53-0.39pm	0.94
Netherlands	2.7735 - 2.7925	2.7825 - 2.7925	1_8-3_8cdis	−1.08	1_2-3_4dis	−0.90
Belgium	50.85 - 51.20	51.00 - 51.10	2-7cdis	−1.06	11-16dis	−1.06
Denmark	9.5020 - 9.5700	9.5600 - 9.5700	1_2-4_8oredis	−3.53	4-6_8^5dis	−2.22
Ireland	1.0135 - 1.0195	1.0185 - 1.0195	0.11-0.14cdis	−1.47	0.33-0.40dis	−1.43
Germany	2.4740 - 2.4900	2.4850 - 2.4900	1_4-3_8pfdis	−1.51	5_8-7_8dis	−1.21
Portugal	236.35 - 238.10	236.35 - 237.35	179-198cdis	−9.55	460-478dis	−7.92
Spain	188.80 - 189.55	189.00 - 189.30	86-112cdis	−6.28	252-295dis	−5.78
Italy	2261.50 - 2270.40	2261.50 - 2262.50	8-10liredis	−4.77	24-27dis	−4.51
Norway	10.5030 - 10.5450	10.5350 - 10.5450	1_2-2_4^1oredis	−1.57	2_8^1-4dis	−1.16
France	8.3320 - 8.3975	8.3875 - 8.3975	1-1_2^1cdis	−1.79	2_8^5-3_4^1dis	−1.40
Sweden	11.2360 - 11.2925	11.2825 - 11.2925	1_2^1-3_8^5oredis	−2.72	5_2^1-7_4^1dis	−2.26
Japan	170.20 - 171.25	170.25 - 171.25	1_2-3_8ypm	3.07	1_8^3-1_8^1pm	2.93
Austria	17.38 - 17.49	17.46 - 17.49	1-2grodis	−1.03	2_8^7-4_8^7dis	−0.89
Switzerland	2.2450 - 2.2800	2.2600 - 2.2700	1_4-1_8cpm	0.99	3_4-1_2pm	1.10
Ecu	1.2665 - 1.2730	1.2720 - 1.2730	0.20-0.23cdis	−2.03	0.46-0.52dis	−1.54

Commercial rates taken towards the end of London trading. Six-month forward dollar 2.17-2.12pm . 12 Month 3.85-3.75pm.

DOLLAR SPOT - FORWARD AGAINST THE DOLLAR

May 18	Day's spread	Close	One month	% p.a.	Three months	% p.a.
UK†	1.5235 - 1.5340	1.5310 - 1.5320	0.41-0.39cpm	3.13	1.14-1.11pm	2.94
Ireland†	1.4970 - 1.5085	1.5005 - 1.5015	0.60-0.57cpm	4.68	1.70-1.65pm	4.46
Canada	1.2715 - 1.2780	1.2725 - 1.2735	0.16-0.20cdis	-1.70	0.61-0.67dis	-2.01
Netherlands .	1.8105 - 1.8250	1.8200 - 1.8210	0.63-0.66cdis	-4.25	1.74-1.80dis	-3.89
Belgium	33.20 - 33.50	33.30 - 33.40	11.00-13.00cdis	-4.32	31.00-35.00dis	-3.96
Denmark	6.1985 - 6.2480	6.2425 - 6.2475	2.50-3.70oredis	-5.96	7.50-10.00dis	-5.60
Germany	1.6140 - 1.6285	1.6235 - 1.6245	0.64-0.65pfdis	-4.77	1.75-1.77dis	-4.33
Portugal	154.65 - 155.75	154.70 - 154.80	143-153cdis	-11.48	410-450dis	-11.11
Spain	123.40 - 123.95	123.70 - 123.80	90-100cdis	-9.21	260-290dis	-8.89
Italy	1476.25 - 1486.00	1476.75 - 1477.25	9.50-10.30liredis	-8.04	27.00-28.00dis	-7.45
Norway	6.8360 - 6.8960	6.8800 - 6.8850	2.50-3.05oredis	-4.84	6.80-7.80dis	-4.24
France	5.4410 - 5.4885	5.4775 - 5.4825	2.18-2.28cdis	-4.88	5.87-6.03dis	-4.34
Sweden	7.3250 - 7.3890	7.3675 - 7.3725	3.10-3.80oredis	-5.62	9.10-10.20dis	-5.24
Japan	111.20 - 111.90	111.50 - 111.60	par-0.01ydis	-0.05	par-0.01dis	-0.02
Austria	11.3600 - 11.4500	11.4275 - 11.4325	3.90-4.20grodis	-4.25	10.90-11.70dis	-3.95
Switzerland .	1.4650 - 1.4820	1.4785 - 1.4795	0.25-0.28cdis	-2.15	0.71-0.76dis	-1.99
Ecu†	1.1990 - 1.2085	1.2025 - 1.2035	0.51-0.50cpm	5.04	1.37-1.35pm	4.52

Commercial rates taken towards the end of London trading. † UK, Ireland and Ecu are quoted in US currency. Forward premiums and discounts apply to the US dollar and not to the individual currency.

Source: *Financial Times,* May 19, 1993.

EXHIBIT IIB.   The chart shows the two constraints on European Monetary System rates. The upper grid, based on the weakest currency in the system, defines the cross-rates from which no currency (except the lira) may move more than 2¼ percent. The lower chart gives each currency's divergence from the "central rate" against the European Currency Unit (ECU), a basket of European currencies.

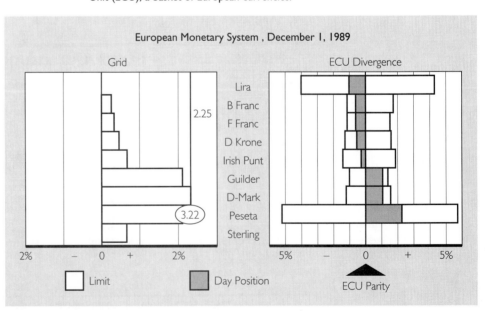

Source: *Financial Times,* December 2, 1989.

4. What effect, if any, would an increase of the number of countries participating in the EMS have on your bonds? (See Exhibit IIb for the chart labeled ECU Divergence for a list of currencies currently participating in the EMS.)
5. What would you anticipate would happen to the value of your bonds if other countries were to join the European Community, assuming that any new member's currency would be included in the basket comprising the ECU? (Remember all those homeless neighbors that might seek shelter?)

SELECTED REFERENCES

Andrews, Michael D. "A Primer on the European Monetary System and Its Exchange Rate Mechanism." *Currency and Bond Market Trends*. Merrill Lynch (January 24, 1991).

Bishop, Graham. "The Creation of an EC 'Hard Money' Union." New York: Salomon Brothers, July 1990.

Dornbusch, Rudiger. *Open Economy Macroeconomics*. New York: Basic Books, 1980.

Frenkel, Jacob A., and Morris Goldstein. "Europe's Emerging Economic and Monetary Union." *Finance and Development* (March 1991): 2–5.

Friedman, Milton, and Robert V. Roosa. "Free Versus Fixed Exchange Rates: A Debate." *Journal of Portfolio Management* (Spring 1977): 68–73.

Krugman, Paul R., and Maurice Obstfeld. *International Economics*. 2d ed. New York: HarperCollins, 1991.

5

Exchange Rates, Interest Rates, and Inflation Rates: An Integrated Framework

This chapter serves as a recap and integration of key elements of the global financial economy that we have covered so far. In a somewhat simplified manner, it provides a framework for understanding the linkages among inflation rates, interest rates, and spot- and forward-exchange rates. The framework is illustrated in Figure 5.1.

The reader should be cautioned that the precise nature of each of the relationships to be described is the subject of considerable controversy. Questions can be raised about both the assumptions and the empirical verification of each relationship. If the relationships hold at all, they do so only under the assumption that the markets for goods, capital, and currencies reasonably meet the requirements for perfect markets, especially in respect to governmental regulations and restrictions. However, at this point, the concern is not so much with empirical validation as with presenting a simple, consistent, and comprehensive set of ties that can serve as a point of departure for further analysis of exchange rates, inflation, and interest rates. We begin with six key linkages among these variables.

Figure 5.1 **_An Integrated Framework._** The diagram summarizes the relationships among money, inflation, interest rates, and exchange rates.

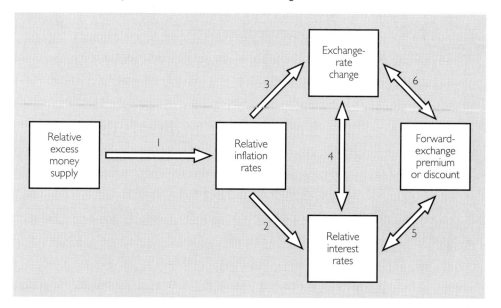

Author's note: Thanks to Guy Hurley for comments. The core of this chapter is based on I. H. Giddy, "An Integrated Theory of Exchange Rate Equilibrium," *Journal of Financial and Quantitative Analysis* (Dec. 1976), 883–892.

Link 1: Money and Inflation

The secret wish of every scholar in the field of international finance is to discover what really determines exchange rates. Even though that pot of gold remains elusive, many models begin with the idea that *the exchange rate is a monetary phenomenon.* That makes sense when one realizes that any exchange rate is, after all, just the relative price or value of two monies. The value of most things, including money itself, is a function of supply and demand.

If the supply of money exceeds the demand for money, its price, as measured by how much it buys, will fall. We call this loss of purchasing power *inflation.* Internationally, differences in the rates of growth of excess money cause (relative) price-level changes.

Figure 5.2   ***The Monetary Theory of Inflation.*** When the supply of money exceeds the demand for money, its value falls.

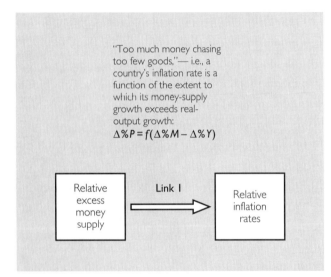

"Too much money chasing too few goods,"— i.e., a country's inflation rate is a function of the extent to which its money-supply growth exceeds real-output growth:

$$\Delta\%P = f(\Delta\%M - \Delta\%Y)$$

Relative excess money supply — Link I → Relative inflation rates

This relationship is shown, in a one-country context, in Link 1 (Figures 5.1 and 5.2). To be precise, the relationship implies that the rate of change in the general price level (inflation) in a country is determined by the differences between the rate of growth in real goods and services and the growth in the supply of money.

The underlying idea is that when the rate of change in the money supply differs from the need for liquidity resulting from changes in real output, the general level of prices in the economy will change. The real need for money changes because of changes in the level of output of goods; if more goods are produced, then more money is needed to trade them at the existing price levels. If the money supply changes at a rate greater than the rate of increase in output of goods, it can only be absorbed by an increase in prices such that the new output at new (higher) prices requires the new (higher) amount of money supply. As a consequence, an excessive increase in the money supply will cause prices to rise. Eventually, it can be argued, relative excess money growth will feed through to the exchange rate; but we'll defer discussion of models of this kind to the next chapter.[1]

Link 2: The Fisher Effect

The second link identifies the relationship between changes in interest rates and changes in price levels.[2] In a theory generally attributed to Irving Fisher,[3] interest rates have two components: a real return plus an adjustment for price-level changes. If the holders of loanable funds are to be induced to give up their funds for a period of time, they must receive some compensation. This compensation is the higher purchasing power of the

---

[1]For a different view see Richard A. Meese and Kenneth Rogoff, "Was It Real? The Exchange Rate–Interest Differential Relation Over The Modern Floating-Rate Period," *Journal of Finance,* vol. 43, no. 4 (1988), 933–948.

[2]For a comprehensive review of these issues in a deterministic framework, see Ronald L. Teigen, "The Demand and Supply of Money," in W. L. Smith and R. L. Teigen, eds., *Readings in Money, National Income, and Stabilization Policy* (Homewood, Ill.: Richard Irwin, 1970).

[3]Irving Fisher, *The Theory of Interest,* Reprint ed. (New York: Macmillan, 1980).

funds in the period in which they are returned. This compensation is necessary because, without it, the holders of funds have no incentive to forgo current consumption and, in addition, be exposed to the risk of default. This compensation is termed the *real return* to the lenders of money.

If prices do not change, this return would represent the increase in the purchasing power of the loaned funds. But when prices are expected to rise, and when lenders are aware of that, they will demand compensation for inflation to protect the real rate of return. This demand will be met by including a factor for the expected rate of inflation in the interest rate. Thus the interest rate will include a real return that increases the purchasing power of the loaned funds plus a return that offsets the loss of purchasing power due to inflation. The nominal interest rate i, then, can be represented formally by the following equation,[4]

$$(1 + i) = (1 + c)(1 + \Delta\%P)$$

or

$$i = c + \Delta\%P$$

where i, the nominal rate of interest, provides a return on the investment equal to that given by a real rate of interest, c, after the expected rate of inflation, $\Delta\%P$, has been taken into consideration. This relationship is approximately valid for small values of the product of c and $\Delta\%P$. That is,

$$\frac{\text{Nominal interest}}{\text{rate}} = \frac{\text{Real interest}}{\text{rate}} + \frac{\text{Expected}}{\text{inflation rate}}$$

Because the nominal interest rate must be determined before prices have actually increased, the expected price change, rather than the actual price change, is incorporated into the nominal rate. Ex post, the price change will not equal the expected value in most cases, but if the financial markets in the country utilize all the available information correctly, i will include the best possible estimate of $\Delta\%P$. (For simplicity, a possible risk premium due to uncertainty about the future price level is omitted.)

In Figure 5.3, Link 2 between price level changes and interest rates implies that as the price level is expected to change (as, for example, because of excessive money supply), the interest rate will change, so that changes in i completely offset $\Delta\%P$. The change in interest rates will thus be equal to the percentage change in expected price levels, which equals the rate by which the increase in the money supply exceeds the real needs of the economy.

It should be clear by now that if, by the end of the time period, prices have changed more than was expected, the rate of interest would have been underestimated and borrowers would have gained at the expense of lenders. Similarly, lenders would have gained if the price changes had been overestimated.

Figure 5.3   *The Fisher Effect*

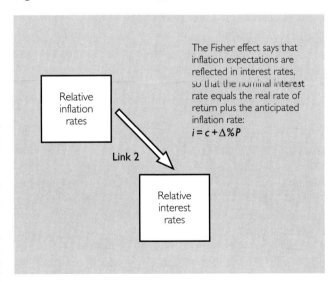

The Fisher effect says that inflation expectations are reflected in interest rates, so that the nominal interest rate equals the real rate of return plus the anticipated inflation rate:

$i = c + \Delta\%P$

Relative inflation rates

Link 2

Relative interest rates

---

[4]Throughout this book, the symbol $\Delta\%$ (delta percent) is used to denote *percentage change* in the value of a variable. Thus $\Delta\%P$ represents percentage change in P from one period to another, whereas ΔP would denote the absolute change in P.

Figure 5.4   *Purchasing Power Parity*   **Figure 5.5**   *The International Fisher Effect*

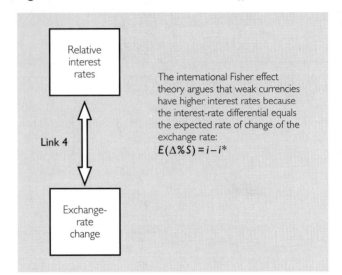

Given the process by which interest-rate changes are determined in a national economy, how do differentials in interest rates between different countries come about? Two additional relationships, shown in Figure 5.1 as Links 3 and 4, will contribute to the explanation. The first of these relates price-level changes in different countries to exchange-rate changes; it is usually referred to as the *purchasing-power-parity theorem* (see figure 5.4). The other link, which relates differences in interest rates between different countries to expected changes in the exchange rates, is sometimes referred to as the *international Fisher effect* to distinguish it from the relationship between price-level changes and interest rates in a closed economy; see Figure 5.5.

Link 3: Purchasing Power Parity

The purchasing-power-parity theorem can be stated in different ways, but the most common representation links the changes in exchange rates to those in relative price indexes in two countries.

Rate of change of exchange rate = Difference in inflation rates

The relationship can be restated as follows. *In the absence of trade restrictions, changes in the exchange rate mirror changes in the relative price levels in the two countries.* Why? Under conditions of free trade, prices of similar commodities cannot differ between two countries, because arbitragers will take advantage of such situations until price differences are eliminated. We can state this as a simple equation showing that the foreign price (p_t^*) times the exchange rate (S_t) equals the domestic price (p_t).

$$p_t^* S_t = p_t$$

This so-called *law of one price* leads logically to the idea that what is true of one commodity should be true of the economy as a whole, that the price level in two countries should be linked through the exchange rate—and hence to the notion that exchange-rate changes are tied to inflation-rate differences.

Thus Link 3 in Figure 5.4 relates expected changes in exchange rates to the expected differences in inflation rates. The reader will recognize that this statement, like all simple relationships, is based on some strong assumptions. One is that consumers in all countries have the same consumption basket and that all goods are equally tradable, so that the relative price changes are not possible within only one country. If these conditions are not met, the postulated relationship between the respective inflation rates and the exchange rate will hold only approximately.

These relationships can be stated more precisely. If at time t the price levels in two countries are P_t and P_t^* and the exchange rate[5] (the price of the foreign currency) is S_t, then prices in the two economies must be equated through the price levels and

$$S_t = \frac{P_t}{P_t^*}$$

From this we can derive the relationship between inflation rates and the exchange rate. This is approximately

$$\Delta\%S_t = \Delta\%P_t - \Delta\%P_t^*$$

That is, the rate of change in the exchange rate equals the difference in inflation rates.

For more insight into purchasing power parity, including its shortcomings as a predictive relationship in international finance and economics, see the section later in this chapter entitled Purchasing Power Parity: Absolute and Relative.

Link 4: The International Fisher Effect

The relationship between the interest rates in two countries and the expected exchange-rate changes has already been discussed in general terms. Now the linkage between these rates can be treated more explicitly. In the absence of effective controls on capital flows, "risk neutral" investors will employ their funds wherever the (expected) return is the highest. Thus if the interest rates between two countries are unequal, investors will transfer their funds to the country in which the interest rate is higher. Will the higher interest rate not come down under the influence of these flows? According to the international Fisher effect, the interest-rate differential will exist only if the exchange rate is expected to change in such a way that the advantage of the higher interest rate is offset by the loss on the foreign-exchange transactions.

In plain words, this international Fisher effect can be stated as follows:

Expected rate of change of the exchange rate = Interest rate differential

The relationship is illustrated as Link 4 in Figure 5.5. In practical terms, it implies that while an investor in a low-interest country can convert his funds into the currency of the high-interest country and get paid a higher rate, his gain (the interest-rate differential) will be offset by his expected loss because of foreign-exchange-rate changes. This effect can now be stated more formally by equating the returns, after explicitly taking the

---

[5]In this section, and by convention throughout the book, the exchange rate S is the spot rate in *domestic currency units per unit of foreign currency*. For example, if the United States is the "domestic" country and Switzerland the "foreign" country, the exchange rate S might be $0.65 per Swiss franc.

expected exchange-rate changes into account. In equilibrium, the following statement of the international Fisher effect holds true:

Value at $t + 1$ of an original investment earning interest at a rate of i $=$ Value of an equal amount converted to a foreign currency at t, invested at an interest rate of t^* and converted back into domestic currency at $t+1$

where

i = rate of interest in the home country, and
i^* = rate of interest in a foreign country.

If the investment is \$1, then the left-hand side is equal to $(1 + i)$. And if S_t is the exchange rate at time t and $E(S_{t+1})$ the expected future exchange rate, then the right-hand side is equal to $1/S_t$ times $(1 + i^*)$ times $E(S_{t+1})$. So

$$1 + i = \frac{1}{S_t}(1 + i^*)E(S_{t+1})$$

or, rearranging and subtracting 1 from both sides,

$$\frac{E(S_{t+1})}{S_t} - 1 = \frac{1 + i}{1 + i^*} - 1$$

or

$$\frac{E(S_{t+1}) - S_t}{S_t} = \frac{i - i^*}{1 + i^*}$$

If the time period is short or the foreign interest rate low, then the denominator on the right-hand side is close to 1 and a useful approximation of the international Fisher effect is:

$$E(\Delta\%S_t) = i - i^*$$

That is, *the expected rate of change of the exchange rate equals the interest-rate differential.* People don't invest in a depreciating currency unless they are compensated by a higher interest rate, high enough to offset the anticipated exchange-rate change (plus a premium for risk, which, for the sake of simplicity, we ignore here, deferring discussion to the next chapter).

Link 5: The Interest-Rate-Parity Theorem

The IRPT (*interest-rate-parity theorem*), which we have already encountered, says that covered-interest arbitrage equalizes effective interest rates in different currencies. For example, the interest rate on a dollar deposit must equal the interest rate on a German mark deposit covered in the forward market.

Interest-rate parity is probably the most basic relationship in international finance. Like the international Fisher effect, it describes the linkage among interest rates in different countries. But while the international Fisher effect is purely an ex ante, *expectations-based theory,* not subject to direct proof, the IRPT is an *arbitrage relationship* that is demonstrably true under the right conditions. The reason is that the interest-rate parity substitutes a known forward rate for the unknown expected future exchange rate. This forward rate, just like interest rates, is a contractual rate. According to this theorem, the observed differences in the interest rates will be equal to the premium or the discount of the

Figure 5.6 ***The Interest-Rate-Parity Theorem***

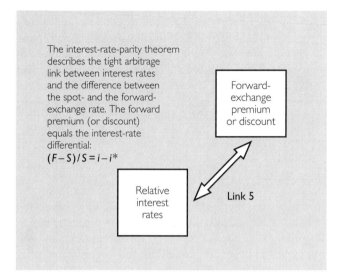

The interest-rate-parity theorem describes the tight arbitrage link between interest rates and the difference between the spot- and the forward-exchange rate. The forward premium (or discount) equals the interest-rate differential:

$(F-S)/S = i - i^*$

Forward-exchange premium or discount

Relative interest rates

Link 5

forward-exchange rate over the spot rate. This relationship, represented by Link 5 in Figure 5.6, was already encountered in Chapter 2 in the context of the operation of foreign-exchange and Eurocurrency markets, and again in Chapter 3. It is produced by covered-interest arbitrage.

Covered-interest arbitrage, undertaken by large international banks and corporations, involves the rapid movement of funds between securities denominated in different currencies in order to profit from different *effective* rates of interest in different currencies, after having taken hedging costs into account. The effective interest rate in the domestic currency is simply the interest rate (compounded, if necessary). The effective interest rate on a foreign currency is, loosely speaking, the foreign interest rate plus the forward premium or minus the forward discount. Recall that the forward premium or discount is $(F - S)/S$ or, as an annualized percentage, $[(F - S)/S](365/\text{days})(100)$.

More specifically,

Value at $t + 1$ of an original investment earning interest at a rate of i = Value of an equal amount converted to a foreign currency at t, invested at an interest rate of i^* and converted back into domestic currency at $t + 1$ at the prearranged forward rate, F_t

$$1 + i = \frac{1}{S_t}(1 + i^*)F_t$$

or, rearranging and subtracting 1 from both sides,

$$\frac{F_t}{S_t} - 1 = \frac{1 + i}{1 + i^*} - 1$$

or

$$\frac{F_t - S_t}{S_t} = \frac{i - i^*}{1 + i^*}$$

If the time period is short or the foreign interest rate low, then the denominator on the right-hand side is close to 1. Therefore, an approximation of the interest-rate-parity theorem is the following equation:[6]

$$\frac{F_t - S_t}{S_t} = i - i^*$$

For a period of n days, the right-hand side must be converted to an annualized percentage:

$$\left(\frac{F_t - S_t}{S_t}\right)\left(\frac{365}{n}\right)100 = i - i^*$$

The conclusion:

The forward premium or discount is equal to the interest rate differential.

---

[6]Does this look vaguely familiar? Of course! It's exactly the same as the international Fisher effect, except that the forward rate replaces the expected future spot rate.

Banks take advantage of such covered-interest arbitrage opportunities as soon as they arise, so any aberration seldom lasts very long. The process is exemplified most tellingly in the Eurocurrency market, in which U.S. dollar and German mark deposits, for example, differ *only* in terms of currency of denomination. If the Eurodeutschemark rate, covered in the forward market, were to exceed the Eurodollar rate, then in the blink of an eye, Euromark deposit rates would be driven down, $/DM spot rates bid up, and $/DM forward rates bid down to the point at which the arbitrage opportunity no longer existed, once the (small) bid-offer spreads and transactions costs were taken into account. In other words, interest-rate parity would soon prevail.

Link 6: The Unbiased-Forward-Rate Theory

The theory that the forward-exchange rate is the best, unbiased estimate of the expected future spot-exchange rate is widely assumed and also widely disputed as a precise explanation. We will return to this dispute in Chapter 6. However, for the present, we will give a general statement of the principle and show how it ties into the interest-rate-parity theorem and the international Fisher effect. This will complete our tour of the basic parity relationships in international finance.

An example may clarify the concept. Richard Marston, Treasurer of the Red Herring Canning Company, is scheduled to receive £550,000 from a British customer in two months' time. He can lock in the dollar value of the pound sterling by selling them at the going forward rate of $1.50 per pound; in other words, by forward hedging. If he has confidence in his forecasting ability, he will leave the receivable unhedged if he expects sterling to be above $1.50 in two months. He will sell sterling forward if he expects the pound to be below $1.50. Doing so will tend to drive the pound down; and if a lot of other people agree with Marston, the forward rate will be driven down until the rate roughly equals the level the financial community expects to prevail in two months. Similarly, a currency expected to reach a level above the prevailing forward-exchange rate will attract buyers until the forward rate approximates the expected future spot rate. This "expected" rate is only an average, but the theory of rational expectations tells us that it is an *unbiased* expectation—that there is an equal probability of the actual rate's being above or below the expected value.

The unbiased-forward-rate theory, diagrammed in Figure 5.7, can be stated simply in words or in algebra:

Figure 5.7   *The Unbiased Forward-Rate Theory*

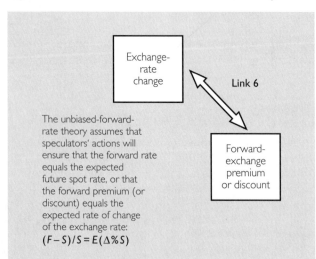

The unbiased-forward-rate theory assumes that speculators' actions will ensure that the forward rate equals the expected future spot rate, or that the forward premium (or discount) equals the expected rate of change of the exchange rate:

$(F-S)/S = E(\Delta\%S)$

Expected exchange rate = Forward exchange rate

$$E(S_{t+1}) = F_t$$

(Notice that this equality is what makes the international Fisher effect consistent with the interest-rate-parity theorem.) Alternatively, we can express each side as a percentage deviation from the current spot rate:

$$\frac{E(S_{t+1}) - S_t}{S_t} = \frac{F_t - S_t}{S_t}$$

Another way of putting it is that if the international Fisher effect *and* interest-rate parity hold, then the expected rate of change of the exchange rate equals the forward premium or discount.

Summary of Discussion So Far

Interest-rate differences and exchange-rate changes, we have seen, are linked in two ways: first, through the international Fisher effect, which is based on expectations; and second, through the interest-rate-parity theorem, which reflects an actual, ex post, arbitraged relationship in the market. Interest rates are driven by inflation expectations as well as real returns, and inflation is largely a monetary phenomenon.

The six linkages explained in the preceding sections represent an integration of certain ideas that are fundamental to an understanding of international finance. We'll meet each one of them again. In summary:

1. Monetary theory links different rates of excess money supply and changes in price levels.
2. Changes in price levels and changes in interest rates are linked by the Fisher effect.
3. Changes in price levels and changes in foreign-exchange rates are linked by the purchasing-power-parity theorem.
4. Two countries' interest rates and *expected* exchange rates are linked by the international Fisher effect.
5. Interest rates in two countries and *forward*-exchange rates are linked according to the interest-rate-parity theorem.
6. The forward rate is linked to the expected future spot rate via the unbiased-forward-rate theory.

As noted at the beginning of this chapter, those familiar with economic theory will recognize that the precise nature of each of these relationships continues to be the subject of considerable dispute. Questions can be raised about both the assumptions and the empirical verification of these relationships. If these relationships hold at all, they do so only under the assumption that the markets for goods, capital, and currencies reasonably meet stringent requirements for perfect markets and for no risk aversion. The purpose has been to present a simple, consistent, and comprehensive set of relationships that can serve as a point of departure for further analysis.

The starting point of international trade and finance, and a key relationship in our little framework, is the idea that people can trade goods and services among different countries, and so eventually bring prices into line with one another. If they're not in line, distortions in international competitiveness may result. So let's take a closer look at purchasing power parity and deviations from it.

Purchasing Power Parity and a Nation's International Competitiveness

From the common-sense idea that a pound of flesh should cost the same whether denominated in rubles or ringgit comes a complex measure of a nation's competitiveness called the **real effective exchange rate**. This is a measure of the deviation of a currency from its purchasing-power-parity level, and is used by governments worldwide to guide exchange-rate policies. It can have a profound effect on an international company's anticipated profitability. The remainder of this chapter shows how we get from here to there.

Purchasing Power Parity Is a Simple Idea

If I have a thousand dollars to spend, it should buy roughly the same amount of goods and services whether I spend it in Baltimore or Berlin. That's the idea of **purchasing power parity** (PPP). It begins with the notion that one can buy individual goods—oil, cameras, wine, and so forth—at home or abroad. Competition, if permitted, should ensure that they cost about the same, when translated at the current exchange rate, in all countries. Taken as an aggregate, the cost of a consumer's basket of goods should be priced approximately the same in each country. If they don't there will be a tendency for prices in the high-cost country to rise less rapidly than prices in the low-cost country; or if the prices of the goods themselves don't adjust, the exchange rate will. In other words, if one country's inflation rate is higher than another (making its goods prices move out of line), then its currency's value will tend to fall by an amount sufficient to restore parity. The exchange-rate change will tend to equal the inflation-rate differential.

This notion of arbitrage and parity of prices between nations is fundamental to an understanding of international economics and trade. It is at the core of the theory of how exchange rates are determined, and of how balance is reached in flows of goods and money between countries. The following sections will explore several different ways of looking at purchasing power parity. The common idea is that different currencies have purchasing power over goods and services, and that exchange rates equalize this power.

The Law of One Price

The whole notion of purchasing power parity stems from the **law of one price (LOP)**, which says that identical items cost the same, translated at the spot-exchange rate, in two different markets. For example, if a bottle of Remy Martin costs £20 in Britain, it should cost the same in Japan, that is, £20 converted to Japanese yen at the going exchange rate. If the exchange rate is £1 = ¥240, the price of Remy Martin in Japan would be ¥4800.

Let us state this proposition more formally. We'll call p the price of any particular good in the "domestic" country (say Britain), and p^* the price of the same good in the "foreign" country (say Japan). S is the exchange rate between the two currencies—in this case between British pounds and Japanese yen—expressed in pounds sterling per yen. Then

$$p = Sp^*$$

As before, the exchange rate S is defined as the price of a unit of foreign currency, again expressed in domestic units per unit of foreign currency.

EXAMPLE 5.1   On one day in 1992, gold was trading at $387.75 on the London Bullion Exchange. On the same day, an ounce of gold was quoted in sterling terms in London at £202.00. The dollar/sterling exchange rate was $1.9195. Any deviation from the law of one price?

$$£202 \times 1.9195 = \$387.74$$

So the law of one price seems to hold for gold. Turning to tin, prices could be found for three different markets—New York, Malaysia (a big tin producer), and London. The law appeared not to hold as tightly; not only transportation costs, but also timing differences may account for the discrepancies.

The Price of Tin

In New York	On the Kuala Lumpur Market	On the London Metal Exchange
273¢ per lb. = US$6.02 per kilogram[a]	15.37 ringgit per kilogram = US$5.70 per kilogram[b]	US$5830 per ton = US$5.83 per kilogram[c]

[a]1 avoirdupois pound = 0.45359 kilograms
[b]US$1 = 2.6965 Malaysian ringgit on the date of calculation
[c]1 tonne = 1000 kilograms

All data taken from the commodities section of the London *Financial Times*.

Some economists argue that the law of one price holds as a tautology. If the goods being compared are identical in *every possible respect,* then the price will be the same irrespective of what currency it's denominated in. If there are transportation costs to arbitrage, then they can't be in the same place, so they differ on one dimension: location! A more reasonable statement is that the prices will differ only by the cost of arbitrage, such as transportation and transaction costs, and only as long as there are no barriers to trade such as tariffs or labeling requirements. Looked at this way, the law of one price holds up well for fairly uniform, tradable commodities such as precious metals, oil, agricultural goods, and even certain standard manufacturing components.

For example, the going price of a 1-megabyte SIMMS chip set in the United States at the time of writing was US$57.[7] The same item could be obtained by mail from Canada for C$66. The exchange rate that would equate these two prices would therefore be $0.8636. The spot Canadian dollar was actually US$0.8643—close enough!

On the other hand, the LOP can become meaningless as an empirical relationship if the ostensibly similar items have a large location-contingent service or convenience component (such as fast food) or if they are much more heavily taxed in one country than another (such as cigarettes or petroleum). *The Economist* magazine makes an occasional joke of the law of one price by publishing the translated prices of several items in different countries. Box 5.1 contains an excerpt.

BOX 5.1

Big MacCurrencies

It is time for our annual burgernomics binge. *The Economist*'s Big Mac index was first launched in 1986 as a rough and ready guide to whether currencies were at their correct exchange rate. It is not intended to be a precise predictor of currency movements, but as a tool to make exchange-rate theory more digestible.

Big Mac watchers rely on the theory of purchasing-power parity (PPP). This argues that the exchange rate between two currencies is in "equilibrium" when it equalises the prices of identical bundles of traded goods and services in both countries. Supporters of PPP argue that, in the long run, currencies tend to move towards their PPP.

---

[7]I bought some. They said "Made in Korea." The difference in shipping costs between the United States and Canada was negligible. As for price, there was far more variation *within* the United States than between the United States and Canada.

For simplicity, our "bundle" is a McDonald's Big Mac. Celebrating its 25th birthday this year, it is the perfect universal commodity, produced locally in 66 countries. The Big Mac PPP is the exchange rate that leaves hamburgers costing the same in all countries. Comparing a currency's actual exchange rate with its PPP signals whether the currency is under- or overvalued against the dollar.

For example, the average price of a Big Mac in four American cities is $2.28 (including sales tax). In Japan, Big Mac fans have to fork out ¥391 for this feast. Dividing the yen price by the dollar price gives a Big Mac PPP of ¥171. Yet in the currency markets on April 13th, yen-holders could buy a dollar for only ¥113. This implies that the yen is 51% overvalued against the dollar. Economists who forecast that the yen will rise further, towards ¥100 to the dollar, need to chew this over.

Repeating the exercise for a British Big Mac gives a sterling PPP of $1.27, against a current rate of $1.56–ie, the pound is 23% overvalued against the dollar. The other EC currencies are also too strong.

What about parities within Europe itself? Dividing the Frankfurt price by the London price gives a sterling PPP of DM2.57. Thus, at its current rate of DM2.44, the pound is undervalued against the D-mark. By contrast, most of the surviving members of the European exchange-rate mechanism seem to be overvalued against the D-mark—the French franc by 19% and the Danish krone by 46%.

The second column of the table shows the prices of burgers in dollars. The cheapest Big Mac is in Moscow (only $1.14); the dearest is in Copenhagen ($4.25). This is just another way of saying that the rouble is the most undervalued currency in the table against the dollar, whilst the Danish krone is the most overvalued. . . .

A stronger objection to using the Big Mac is that the theory of PPP assumes no trade barriers. Yet farm produce, the main component of a Big Mac, is particularly prone to protectionism. To some extent, therefore, the Big Mac hamburger standard may be picking up the degree of farm subsidy in different countries—i.e., currencies appear most overvalued in countries which keep out cheap beef imports, such as Japan.

. . . Nevertheless, the fact remains that economists who try to calculate PPPs by more sophisticated means seem to be coming up with strikingly similar results.

Most estimates of the dollar's PPP against the yen lie within the ¥140–180 range, depending on the method used; likewise, dollar PPPs for the D-mark lie between DM1.80 and DM2.20, and for sterling, around $1.30–1.40. Our Big Mac PPPs fall comfortably near these estimates.

PPPs can be viewed as an equilibrium only in the very long run. In the shorter term, exchange rates are influenced by other factors, such as interest rates. Yet investors would be foolish to ignore burgernomics altogether.

Excerpted from *The Economist*, April 17, 1993.

The hamburger standard

	Big Mac prices		Actual exchange rate 13/4/93	Implied PPP† of the dollar	Local currency under (-)/ over (+) valuation**,%
	Prices in local currency*	Prices in dollars			
UNITED STATES‡	$2.28	2.28	—	—	—
Argentina	Peso3.60	3.60	1.00	1.58	+58
Australia	A$2.45	1.76	1.39	1.07	-23
Belgium	BFr109	3.36	32.45	47.81	+47
Brazil	Cr77,000	2.80	27,521	33,772	+23
Britain	£1.79	2.79	1.56‡‡	1.27‡‡	+23
Canada	C$2.76	2.19	1.26	1.21	-4
China	Yuan8.50	1.50	5.68	3.73	-34
Denmark	DKr25.75	4.25	6.06	11.29	+86
France	FFr18.50	3.46	5.34	8.11	+52
Germany	DM4.60	2.91	1.58	2.02	+28
Holland	Fl5.45	3.07	1.77	2.39	+35
Hong Kong	HK$9.00	1.16	7.73	3.95	-49
Hungary	Forint157	1.78	88.18	68.86	-22
Ireland	I£1.48	2.29	1.54‡‡	1.54‡‡	0
Italy	Lire4,500	2.95	1,523	1,974	+30
Japan	¥391	3.45	113	171	+51
Malaysia	Ringgit3.35	1.30	2.58	1.47	-43
Mexico	Peso7.09	2.29	3.10	3.11	0
Russia	Rouble780	1.14	686 §	342	-50
S. Korea	Won2,300	2.89	796	1,009	+27
Spain	Ptas325	2.85	114	143	+25
Sweden	SKr25.50	3.43	7.43	11.18	+50
Switzerland	SwFr5.70	3.94	1.45	2.50	+72
Thailand	Baht48	1.91	25.16	21.05	-16

Source: McDonald's   *Prices may vary locally   †Purchasing-power parity: local price divided by price in United States
**Against dollar   ‡Average of New York, Chicago, San Francisco and Atlanta   ‡‡Dollars per pound   §Market rate

Purchasing Power Parity: Absolute and Relative

Let us assume for the moment that price equality holds for all individual goods and services, at least to a good approximation. Then price parity should hold for the whole economy, for the *price levels* of two countries, shouldn't it? That at least is what the **absolute purchasing power parity** theory claims:

$$\text{Price level of domestic economy} = \begin{array}{l}\text{Price level of another economy,}\\ \text{translated at the spot-exchange rate}\end{array}$$

$$L = SL^*$$

where L and L^* are the domestic and foreign aggregate price levels of the whole economies in the two countries.

The catch is that the two countries' price levels are not comparable, because the prices are *weighted differently*. The price levels are defined as follows:

$$L = \sum_i w_i p_i \qquad \text{Domestic price level}$$

$$L^* = \sum_j w_j^* p_j^* \qquad \text{Foreign price level}$$

where w_i and w_j are the weights of individual goods in the domestic and foreign economies, respectively.

Look at L and L^*. They are not likely to be equal *even if the law of one price holds for every individual good* unless the weights are the same in both countries. Moreover, not every item is tradable—you cannot arbitrage an aerobics class between Britain and Japan—so economists often distinguish between tradable and nontradable goods in examining the validity of purchasing power parity. So absolute PPP is an implausible theory, and no self-respecting economist pays much attention to it. More interesting is **relative purchasing power parity**.

Relative PPP, as the name implies, deals with relative prices over time—with inflation rates, in fact. Inflation is measured by looking at the change in a price *index*, which is like a price level but includes only a sample of prices in the economy rather than everything. Let P designate the price index. Relative PPP equates the price-index ratio at home to that abroad through the exchange-rate ratio:

$$\frac{P_{t+1}}{P_t} = \left(\frac{S_{t+1}}{S_t}\right)\left(\frac{P_{t+1}^*}{P_t^*}\right)$$

Now we get to inflation rates. Let's rearrange to put the exchange-rate ratio on the left, and then express the price ratios as inflation rates:

$$\frac{S_{t+1}}{S_t} = \frac{\dfrac{P_{t+1}}{P_t}}{\dfrac{P_{t+1}^*}{P_t^*}} = \frac{1 + I}{1 + I^*}$$

Subtracting 1 from both sides yields an equation similar to those we've seen earlier in the chapter:

$$\frac{S_{t+1} - S_t}{S_t} = \frac{I - I^*}{1 + I^*}$$

This is relative purchasing power parity, stated in terms of inflation rates.

Neglecting the I^* in the denominator gives us the quick and dirty version of relative purchasing power parity, one that we've already seen earlier in the chapter. In other words, *the rate of change of the exchange rate equals the inflation rate differential.*

EXAMPLE 5.2   Let's try the relative version of PPP, using some actual inflation rates. Back in 1990 the inflation rate in the Netherlands was 2.3 percent per annum, while that in Australia was 7.7 percent. During the year, the exchange rate fell from 1.70 Dutch guilders per Australian dollar to 1.45. *Did relative purchasing power parity hold?*

From the inflation rates, the exchange-rate change should have been

$$\frac{I^{\text{Neth}} - I^{\text{Aust}}}{1 + I^{\text{Aust}}} = \frac{.023 - .077}{1 + .077} = -.05$$

The actual exchange-rate change was

$$\frac{S_{t+1} - S_t}{S_t} = \frac{1.45 - 1.70}{1.70} = -.15$$

So the Aussie fell 15% when it was supposed to fall only 5 percent.

Recent academic research has examined more refined concepts of purchasing power parity. Because deviations from PPP seem to be persistent, one may ask whether they are *predictable.* This inquiry leads to tests of *ex-ante* PPP: as Huang puts it, "the expected rate of change in nominal exchange rates between two countries equals the expected differential in their inflation rates over the same holding period." Ex-ante PPP leads to the prediction that percentage changes in real exchange rates should be serially uncorrelated. This idea, among other issues, is the subject of empirical tests of PPP such as those described in the next section.

Purchasing Power Parity: Empirical Evidence

We might as well be honest about it: purchasing power parity, even the relative version based on relative inflation rates, does not hold up very well for the major currencies. They're too skittish to adhere to the comparatively slow movements in prices indexes. For the two decades of the 1970s and 1980s, for example, the standard deviation of monthly changes in the Japanese yen/German mark exchange rate was 3.01 percent, while the same measure of variability of the relative inflation rates was 0.79 percent. The exchange rate is free to move daily, weekly, and monthly in response to short-term capital flows. Wages and prices are often sticky, since it is costly to change price lists because of prior contracts, oligopolistic price-setting, and government restraints.

Nevertheless, PPP has been a focus of extensive research for decades. For a number of reasons, people are searching for *some* empirical regularity in the link between inflation and a currency's value.

- Most modern theories of exchange-rate determination accord a central role to the connection between the exchange rate and the price level.
- Central bankers, seeking some anchor for their currency intervention, need a guide as to whether, and by how much, the currency is overvalued or undervalued—some measure that abstracts from the daily speculative pressure of market supply and demand.

- International organizations, such as the OECD, that measure international competitiveness and compare the GNP of nations need to know the extent to which current exchange rates have deviated from their competitive-equilibrium level.
- For an international company, the extent to which the exchange rate can move while input or sales prices remain unchanged can be fundamental to the potential profitability of a plant heavily dependent on exports or imports.
- Finally, private forecasters want to know if there is a tendency for exchange rates that seem to be grossly out of line with prices in different countries to return to more reasonable levels.

So let us see what the data tell us. We shall look at the inflation–exchange rate link from three points of view: in the "shortish" run (month to month); in the longer run; and in the special case of a high-inflation country.

We shall begin with three major currencies: the pound sterling, the French franc (both against the U.S. dollar), and the Japanese yen (against the German mark). The results of a graphical comparison of each month's relative inflation with that month's rate of change of the exchange rate are shown in Figures 5.8, 5.9, and 5.10. In the case of the

Figure 5.8 **_Relative Purchasing Power Parity: The British Pound–U.S.-Dollar Relationship._** This scatter graph shows monthly percentage changes in the value of each currency versus monthly changes in the ratio of price levels in the two countries. Data are for the period 1973–1989.

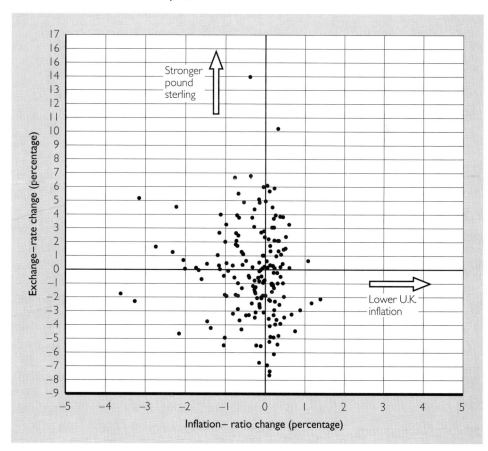

Figure 5.9   *Relative Purchasing Power Parity: The French-Franc–U.S.-Dollar Relationship.*   This scatter graph shows monthly percentage changes in the value of each currency versus monthly changes in the ratio of price levels in the two countries. Data are for the period 1973–1989.

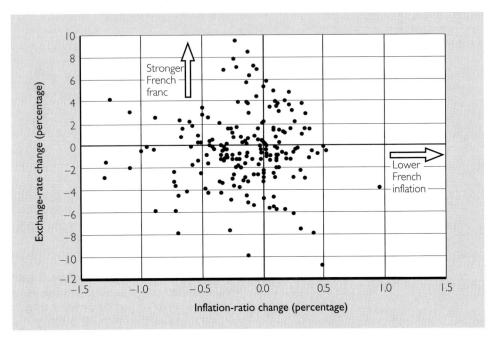

British pound in Figure 5.8, the horizontal axis shows relative inflation, which is measured as follows:

$$\frac{\dfrac{P^{US}_{t+1}}{P^{US}_t} - \dfrac{P^{UK}_{t+1}}{P^{UK}_t}}{\dfrac{P^{UK}_{t+1}}{P^{UK}_t}}$$

where P, as before, is the price index. The vertical axis measures the rate of change of the exchange rate:

$$\frac{S_{t+1} - S_t}{S_t}$$

where S measures the exchange rate in U.S. dollars per pound sterling. The other axis quantities in Figures 5.9 and 5.10 are measured analogously.

The scatter graphs for Figures 5.8–5.10 give data for 1973–1989. If relative PPP held perfectly for every month during the period studied, the points would lie on an upward-sloping 45-degree line passing through the origin. As a general observation those points falling in the upper-right and lower-left quadrants are consistent with the PPP tendency, while the others are not.

In the U.K. case (Figure 5.8), nothing can be said about month-to-month purchasing power parity except that there are many, many fairly large exchange-rate changes that are accompanied by little or no change in relative price ratios. As Figures 5.9 and 5.10 show, the franc/dollar and yen/mark relationships fare little better, although with a little bit of imagination you might agree that there is preponderance of points in the right

Figure 5.10 **_Relative Purchasing Power Parity: The Japanese Yen–German Mark Relationship._** This scatter graph shows monthly percentage changes in the value of each currency versus monthly changes in the ratio of price levels in the two countries. Data are for the period 1973–1989.

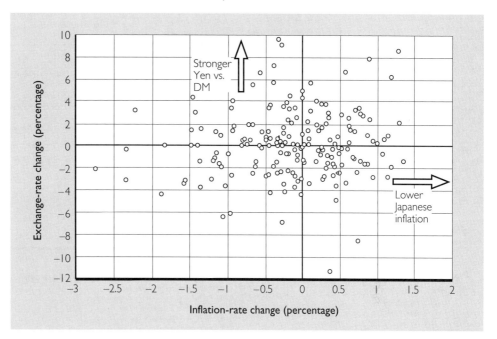

quadrants. And most of the really big exchange-rate movements seem to correspond to larger-than-normal relative price movements. The overall pattern, however, confirms what you probably suspected already: that *relative purchasing power parity does not hold in the short run.*

But there's a significant exception to this statement, as exemplified by the data on the Turkish lira shown in Figure 5.11. During the 1970s, Turkey had a fixed exchange rate (or rather one that was temporarily tied to the U.S. dollar but subject to frequent devaluations). Meanwhile, Turkey underwent increasingly severe bouts of inflation. As that inflation occurred and the currency remained fixed, there would be naturally sharp deviations from PPP. A devaluation would follow and parity would be more or less restored. This pattern repeated itself until the 1980s, when the devaluations were so frequent that they closely followed the inflation trend. This demonstrates the following idea: *when inflation is severe and persistent, the currency eventually follows the price level and purchasing power parity holds very well.*

These results confirm the consensus of empirical research that PPP does not hold in the short run.[8] Even so, isn't there a tendency for the exchange rate to return to its parity level in the *long run?* We address that question in Figures 5.12 through 5.14. These show the *actual exchange rates* for a 17-year period, and then the *purchasing-power-parity exchange rate* indexed to begin at the same level. In all cases, the actual and PPP levels diverge for years on end; but, in the case of France and Germany, the two do seem to converge

---

[8]For a summary, see M. Adler and B. Lehmann, "Deviations from Purchasing Power Parity in the Long Run," *Journal of Finance,* Dec. 1983, 1471–1487. For further evidence, some of which contradicts Adler and Lehmann, see Abuaf and Jorion, *Journal of Finance,* March 1990.

Figure 5.11   ***Purchasing Power Parity: Turkey Versus United States.***   For high-inflation countries, purchasing power parity holds more precisely the longer inflation persists.

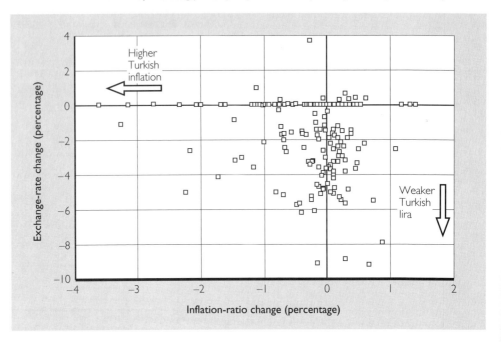

Figure 5.12   *Long-Run Purchasing Power Parity: French Franc Versus U.S. Dollar*

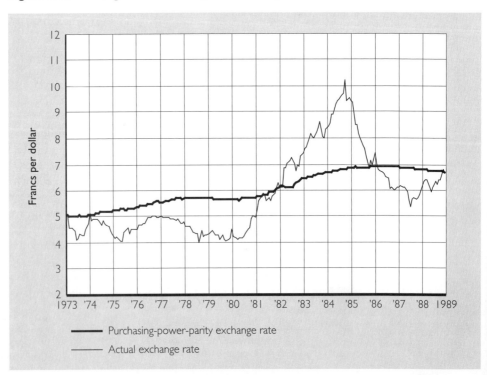

Figure 5.13   *Long-Run Purchasing Power Parity: German Mark Versus U.S. Dollar*

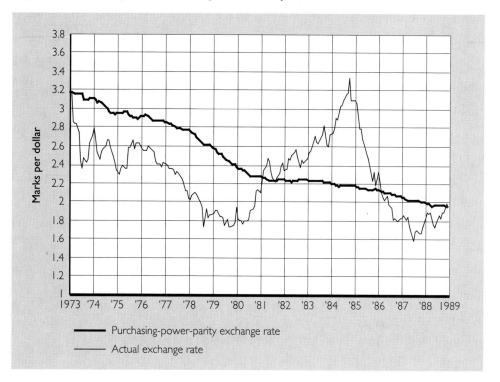

Figure 5.14   *Long-Run Purchasing Power Parity: Yen Versus U.S. Dollar*

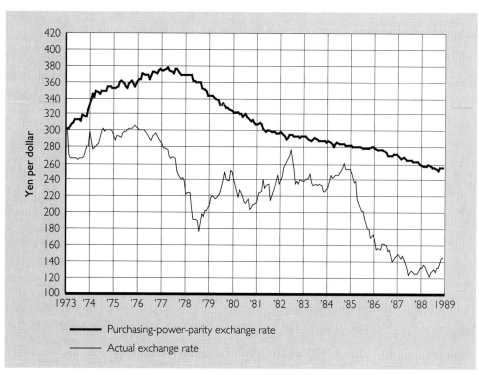

toward the end. (Later on they diverged severely again!) In Japan, convergence is less evident, although a careful look at Figure 5.12 shows that there is clear tendency for the trend of relative prices and the exchange rate to be in the same direction. But until and unless you see much higher and more persistent levels of inflation in one of the two countries, you are not likely to find much stronger evidence of convergence to parity than is shown here. The issue of long-run purchasing power parity is tied in with the stability of the *real exchange rate*.

The Real Exchange Rate

The **real exchange rate** is a measure of the extent of deviation from purchasing power parity, given some starting point at which rough parity is assumed to have held. It is used as a measure of the extent to which movements in the exchange rate are improving or reducing the competitiveness of a country's exports.

In an *absolute* sense, the real exchange rate R_t is defined as the ratio of the home price level to the foreign price level, the latter translated at the current exchange rate:

$$R_t = \frac{P_t}{S_t P_t^*}$$

In practice, the real exchange rate can be regarded as an *index*. If absolute PPP holds, the index equals 1. Assume it does; we may then measure *deviations* from PPP using price indices and the exchange-rate change over time. At any future date, the index of the real exchange rate will be:

$$R_{t+n} = \frac{\dfrac{P_{t+n}}{P_t}}{\left(\dfrac{S_{t+n}}{S_t}\right)\left(\dfrac{P_{t+n}^*}{P_t^*}\right)}$$

As long as you started at parity, if relative PPP has held over time, then this measure R_{t+n} will still be 1. If the domestic currency has fallen faster than should be the case given relative inflation, then the country's goods are cheaper than they were in world markets, and the country has gained competitiveness. If the domestic currency has risen faster than is dictated by relative inflation, then $R_{t+n} > 1$, and the country has lost competitiveness.

One way to use the real exchange rate as a test of purchasing power parity was pioneered by Richard Roll.[9] This method asks whether there are systematic, persistent deviations from PPP or whether, in contrast, the real exchange rate follows a random walk. If the latter is true, then

$$E(R_t) - 1 = 0$$

Roll's work and subsequent evidence confirm that this is the case.

The real exchange rate has been at the center of international economic policy discussions in the past decade for at least two reasons: (1) Because this relative price affects a country's competitive position, deviations may have serious economic costs. During a period of undervaluation, tradable-goods industries are stimulated and tend to overex-

---

[9]Richard Roll, "Violations of Purchasing Power Parity and Their Implications for Efficient International Commodity Markets," in M. Sarnat and G. Szego, eds., *International Finance and Trade*, Vol. 1 (Cambridge, Mass.: Ballinger, 1979).

pand. If this period is followed by one of overvaluation, the result can be layoffs, plant closings, and bankruptcies in exporting and import-competing industries. (2) Real exchange rates have been more variable in the floating-rate period than in the preceding era of fixed exchange rates. Research has as yet failed to identify clear-cut determinants of the real exchange rate, or even whether it has a tendency to return over time to a fixed value, the long-run-equilibrium real exchange rate.[10]

Figure 5.14 can be used as a measure of the real exchange rate for Japan (compared with the United States), assuming that equilibrium held in 1973 when the series started. According to relative PPP theory, the exchange rate should have been in the ¥280 range in 1989. Instead, it had reached 150 or better! By this theory, Japan should have suffered a severe decline in competitiveness over this period. As we know, this apparent loss of competitiveness was more than compensated for by improvements in productivity and other factors not captured in a raw consumer price index.

Finally, even the real exchange rate as a concept is eclipsed by a better measure of a nation's *overall* competitiveness, the **real effective exchange rate**. In this context, the effective rate simply means an average of the country's exchange rates with its trading partners, weighted by the proportion of trade done with each. So the real effective exchange rate is an index just like the one-currency real rate, but it averages all the bilateral real rates, weighted by trade proportions.[11]

SUMMARY

This chapter has drawn together several of the major broad-brush variables of international finance: monetary conditions, inflation, interest rates, and spot- and forward-exchange rates. We demonstrated a set of principles that make sense of the huge variety of financial-market conditions around the world. We then proceeded to undermine the credibility of one of the key conditions—purchasing power parity—which, we saw, tends to hold only in the very long run (or in fairly extreme conditions), and even then, imperfectly. Nevertheless, the integrated framework presented in this chapter provides a very powerful paradigm for participants in the global markets, and always serves as a useful point of departure.

CONCEPTUAL QUESTIONS

1. What is the Fisher effect?
2. Describe the relative purchasing-power-parity theory.
3. What is the international Fisher effect?
4. If relative purchasing power parity does not hold in the short run, what does this imply for the validity of the international Fisher effect as applied to three-month Eurocurrency interest rates?
5. Explain how the international Fisher effect differs from the interest-rate-parity theorem.
6. Describe the unbiased-forward-rate theory.
7. If the forward rate is not an unbiased estimator of the expected future spot-exchange rate, what does this imply for the validity of the international Fisher effect as applied to three-month Eurocurrency interest rates?

---

[10]R. Dornbusch, "Real Exchange Rates and Macroeconomics," *Scandinavian Journal of Economics,* issue 2, 1989, 401–432.

[11]For a survey, see J. A. Whitt, Jr., "Purchasing Power Parity and Exchange Rates in the Long Run," *Federal Reserve Bank of Atlanta Economic Review,* July–Aug. 1989, 18–32.

8. Are there any reasons to believe purchasing power parity may not hold even in the long run?

9. Explain the difference between the real exchange rate and the real *effective* exchange rate.

10. How might the real effective exchange rate be useful to a government trying to decide whether or not to fix its currency?

PROBLEMS

1. The international Fisher effect is (choose one)

   (a) the choice between goods and financial assets.

   (b) the choice between goods and financial assets denominated in two different currencies.

   (c) a relationship between interest rates in two different countries that reflects relative recent inflation rates in the two countries.

   (d) equivalent to the interest-rate-parity relationship, except that it is riskier because it does not involve forward-exchange contracts.

2. The annualized interest rates in the United States and Switzerland are 10 percent and 4 percent, respectively, and the current spot rate for the Swiss franc is $0.3864.

   (a) What is the 90-day forward rate if interest-rate parity holds?

   (b) You observe that the 90-day Swiss franc is being quoted at $0.3902. Is there an arbitrage opportunity? Specify the steps you would take to undertake such an arbitrage.

3. Suppose that, in the course of one year, inflation in Gondwana has been 17 percent and in Nirvana 8 percent. Then, on the basis of relative PPP, which of the following would we expect to find? (Choose the most accurate.)

   (a) The Gondwana dinar price of the Nirvana ducat rose by 9 percent.

   (b) The Gondwana dinar price of the Nirvana ducat fell by 9 percent.

   (c) The Gondwana dinar price of the Nirvana ducat will rise by 9 percent.

   (d) The Gondwana dinar price of the Nirvana ducat will fall by 8.33 percent.

   (e) The Gondwana dinar price of the Nirvana ducat rose by 8.33 percent.

   (f) The Gondwana dinar price of the Nirvana ducat fell by 7.69 percent.

4. Which of the following defines real exchange rate?

   (a) the sum of the rate of inflation and a "real" component that represents the return to capital in the absence of inflation

   (b) the change in the exchange rate, adjusted for the interest-rate differential

   (c) an index designed to measure deviations from purchasing power parity

   (d) an index of the exchange rate constructed by weighting each foreign currency by the country's share in trade with the home country

   (e) your own definition (write it here)

5. "Botswana's real exchange rate has risen" implies that

   (a) Botswana's competitiveness in international markets has declined.

   (b) Botswana's competitiveness in international markets has improved.

   (c) Botswana's foreign-exchange reserves have been declining.

   (d) Botswana's foreign-exchange reserves have been increasing.

   (e) Relative purchasing power parity does not hold.

   Which statement or statements are the most accurate?

Application 5.1 | THE DEVIANT ECONOMIST

Take a look at the attached Economic and Financial Indicators section from the back pages of *The Economist*.

ECONOMIC AND FINANCIAL INDICATORS 1

OUTPUT, DEMAND AND JOBS America's industrial production rose by only 0.1% in April, but was 3.5% higher than a year earlier. Britain's industrial output increased by 1.5% in the 12 months to March. British retail sales rose by 2.4% in the year to April but slipped 0.3% from the previous month's level. Germany's retail sales fell by 2.0% in the 12 months to March. German unemployment increased to 8.0% of its workforce in April; Italy's rose to 10.4% and Sweden's to 7.7%.

% change at annual rate

	industrial production		GDP		retail sales (volume)		unemployment % rate	
	3 mths†	1 year	3 mths†	1 year	3 mths†	1 year	latest	year ago
Australia	+12.4	+ 3.5 Feb	+ 2.8	+ 2.5 Q4	− 1.0	+ 2.0 Q4	10.7 Apr	10.4
Belgium	+ 0.3	+ 0.6 Oct	na	+ 1.6 1991**	+ 2.1	nil Nov	9.2 Apr	8.1
Canada	+ 5.4	+ 4.2 Feb	+ 3.5	+ 1.3 Q4	+ 2.4	+ 2.6 Feb	11.4 Apr	11.0
France	−11.9	− 2.4 Feb	− 2.0	+ 0.7 Q4	+ 1.0	− 4.1 Feb	10.7 Mar	10.1
Germany††	−13.8	−10.5 Mar	− 3.3	+ 0.2 Q4	−18.3	− 2.0 Mar	8.0 Apr	6.5
Holland	− 5.1	+ 0.1 Feb	− 0.3	+ 0.5 Q4	− 1.1	− 1.2 Jan‡	5.2 Apr‡‡	4.4
Italy	− 2.7	− 4.5 Feb	− 2.3	− 0.3 Q4	−16.8	+ 1.3 Aug‡	10.4 Apr	10.1
Japan	− 1.2	− 2.2 Mar	− 0.3	+ 0.2 Q4	− 7.7	− 5.6 Jan	2.3 Mar	2.1
Spain	−17.2	− 7.0 Feb	na	− 0.2 Q4	−23.3	− 8.5 Jan‡	16.5 Apr*	15.0
Sweden	−12.2	− 3.7 Feb	−10.8	− 3.6 Q4	− 6.0	− 7.4 Jan	7.7 Apr*	4.6
Switzerland	−15.5	− 3.3 Q4	− 1.3	− 0.9 Q4	− 5.9	− 1.0 Feb	5.0 Apr*	2.6
UK	+ 1.1	+ 1.5 Mar	+ 1.1	+ 0.6 Q1	+ 5.4	+ 2.4 Apr	10.5 Mar	9.4
USA	+ 4.0	+ 3.5 Apr	+ 1.8	+ 2.9 Q1	− 1.5	+ 2.7 Mar	7.0 Apr	7.3

† Average of latest 3 months compared with average of previous 3 months, at annual rate. ** GNP. ‡Value index deflated by CPI.‡‡ Average of latest 3 months.

PRICES AND WAGES America's 12-month rate of consumer-price inflation rose to 3.2% in April. In the same month, Spain's inflation rate quickened to 4.6% and Sweden's to 5.1%. Japan's producer prices fell by 2.8% in the year to April. German workers had a pay rise of 4.2% in the year to March, exactly in line with consumer-price inflation. In the same period Japanese workers' pay rose by 1.4%, a rise of only 0.2% in real terms.

% change at annual rate

	consumer prices*		producer prices*		wages/earnings‡	
	3 mths†	1 year	3 mths†	1 year	3 mths†	1 year
Australia	+ 3.8	+ 1.2 Mar	+ 1.3	+ 2.6 Jan	+13.6	+ 2.5 Feb*
Belgium	+ 3.4	+ 2.9 Apr	− 1.6	− 0.2 Dec	− 3.1	+ 5.0 Q3*
Canada	+ 2.9	+ 1.9 Mar	+ 4.0	+ 3.6 Mar	+ 7.7	+ 3.0 Feb
France	+ 3.3	+ 2.2 Mar	− 6.7	− 1.5 Q4	+ 2.3	+ 3.5 Q1*
Germany††	+ 3.5	+ 4.3 Apr	+ 0.3	+ 0.3 Mar	+ 2.6	+ 4.2 Mar
Holland	+ 1.2	+ 2.3 Apr	+ 0.8	− 0.5 Apr	+ 3.7	+ 3.9 Mar‡
Italy	+ 3.8	+ 4.1 Apr	+ 8.8	+ 4.4 Feb	+ 2.4	+ 2.4 Dec*
Japan	nil	+ 1.2 Mar	− 3.9	− 2.8 Apr	− 6.8	+ 1.4 Mar
Spain	+ 4.6	+ 4.6 Apr	+ 3.1	+ 1.8 Feb	+ 7.2	+ 7.8 Q4
Sweden	+10.6	+ 5.1 Apr	+17.7	+ 5.3 Mar	+ 1.8	+ 4.4 Mar
Switzerland	+ 5.6	+ 3.8 Apr	+ 2.2	+ 0.2 Apr	na	+ 7.4 Oct‡
UK	− 2.6	+ 1.9 Mar	+ 7.2	+ 3.8 Apr	+ 3.0	+ 4.5 Feb
USA	+ 4.0	+ 3.2 Apr	+ 2.6	+ 2.4 Apr	+ 2.0	+ 2.6 Apr

‡ Hourly earnings for all employees except: Australia, weekly earnings; Belgium, Sweden, industrial hourly earnings; Canada, manufacturing hourly earnings; Holland, hourly wage rates; Italy, manufacturing hourly wage rates; Japan, Switzerland, manufacturing monthly earnings; Spain, quarterly earnings; UK, monthly earnings. † Average of latest 3 months compared with average of previous 3 months, at annual rate.‡1991.‡‡ New series

The Economist **COMMODITY PRICE INDEX** The platinum market was in surplus by only 20,000 ounces last year. According to Johnson Matthey, a metals trader, supplies fell by 8% to 3.8m ounces, thanks to a 30% fall in Russian exports. The jewellery industry took a record 1.5m ounces. The car industry also used more platinum in 1992, but manufacturers drew on stocks, so less was bought in the market. Johnson Matthey expects car makers to use even more of the metal this year. All new EC cars must now be fitted with catalysts, most of which still employ platinum. Nevertheless new platinum supplies are coming on stream in South Africa, so prices may not rise from today's $390 an ounce.

1985=100

	May 11th‡	May 18th‡	% change on	
			one month	one year
Dollar index				
All items	106.3	107.2	− 0.5	− 3.7
Food	93.3	95.0	+ 5.9	+ 6.7
Industrials				
All	119.2	119.3	− 5.1	−10.6
Nfa ‡‡	127.8	130.0	− 9.7	+ 2.5
Metals	113.1	111.7	− 0.9	−19.2
Sterling index				
All items	88.3	89.7	+ 0.1	+15.6
Food	77.5	79.5	+ 6.6	+28.2
Industrials				
All	99.1	99.8	− 4.4	+ 7.3
Nfa ‡‡	106.2	108.8	− 9.0	+23.1
Metals	94.0	93.5	− 0.2	− 3.0
SDR index				
All items	76.5	77.4	+ 0.4	− 4.0
Food	67.1	68.6	+ 7.0	+ 6.5
Industrials				
All	85.8	86.1	− 4.1	−10.9
Nfa ‡‡	91.9	93.8	− 8.7	+ 2.3
Metals	81.4	80.6	nil	−19.4
Gold				
$ per oz	356.45	370.25	+ 8.8	+ 9.8
Crude oil North Sea Brent				
$ per barrel	19.11	18.35	− 2.5	− 4.4

‡ Provisional ‡‡ Non-food agriculturals

■ **ICELAND** Inflation has been virtually eliminated in Iceland, thanks to smaller wage rises and plunging domestic demand. According to new forecasts by the Paris-based OECD, the rich-countries' club, consumer prices will rise by just 0.2% next year. As recently as 1989, inflation was a hefty 22%. Unfortunately good news on inflation is partly the result of a punishing 3.3% fall in GDP in 1992. The economy is forecast to shrink again this year, by 1.8%. Fish exports have been hit by tighter quotas imposed to protect shrinking stocks. Foreign demand for the country's aluminium has also slumped. Once boasting one of the OECD's lowest jobless rates, Iceland is also suffering from growing unemployment, expected to reach 5.3% of the workforce this year.

GDP
% change on a year earlier

Iceland's:
$bn — trade balance — current-account deficit

Consumer prices
% increase on a year earlier

Unemployment
as % of labour force

Source: OECD

*Private-consumption deflator †Forecast

Footnotes applicable to all tables. All figures seasonally adjusted except * not seasonally adjusted. na not available. ††western Germany: consolidated figures for Germany not yet available.

ECONOMIC AND FINANCIAL INDICATORS   2

■ **INTERNATIONAL BANKING** According to the Bank of England's latest *Quarterly Bulletin*, London remains the leading centre for cross-border bank lending, with 17% of the total. Japan is second with 14%. In 1984, by contrast, Britain accounted for 24% of external lending and Japan only 9%. If Japan's lending had continued to expand at the same pace as in recent years it would have overtaken Britain in 1992. Instead, lending from Japan fell by $59 billion last year, whilst lending from Britain increased by $88 billion. America's share of external lending has slumped over the past eight years, to 9%, but lending from continental Europe has soared. In 1984 lending from Britain was more than double that of France, Germany and Switzerland combined. Last year their 20% of total lending was well ahead of Britain's 17% share.

WORLD BOURSES Madrid was this week's star performer. Hopes of lower interest rates after the peseta's devaluation lifted share prices by 6.1% to a 1993 high. Hong Kong, Singapore and Zurich hit record highs. But Tokyo dipped 3.4% and the world index finished 1.2% lower.

Stock price indices

		1993 high	1993 low	one week	one year	record high	Dec 31st 1992 in local currency	Dec 31st 1992 in $ terms
	May 18th							
Australia	1677.9	1710.1	1495.0	− 0.6	+ 0.7	−27.2	+ 8.3	+ 8.8
Belgium	1212.4	1269.1	1125.5	+ 1.8	− 0.8	− 4.5	+ 7.6	+ 7.3
Canada	3826.9	3826.9	3275.8	+ 1.2	+ 13.0	− 7.0	+14.2	+14.1
France	505.5	547.4	471.2	− 1.3	− 8.2	−10.5	+ 4.3	+ 5.2
Germany	1628.5	1717.4	1516.5	− 0.8	− 7.6	−17.3	+ 5.4	+ 5.1
Holland	217.0	223.5	198.6	− 1.2	+ 2.8	− 2.9	+ 9.6	+ 9.5
Hong Kong	7149.3	7149.3	5437.8	+ 4.5	+ 26.7	nil	+29.7	+29.9
Italy	544.2	547.3	446.3	+ 2.4	+ 15.1	−40.1	+21.9	+21.6
Japan	20229.4	21054.7	16287.5	− 3.4	+ 7.9	−48.0	+19.5	+34.3
Singapore	1878.0	1878.0	1531.1	+ 4.7	+ 27.8	nil	+23.2	+25.0
South Africa	4469.9	4645.0	4333.0	+ 2.0	− 2.0	− 4.7	+ 2.3	+ 5.7†
Spain	256.9	256.9	215.6	+ 6.1	− 1.1	−21.9	+19.9	+11.0
Sweden	1083.2	1083.2	879.1	+ 2.0	+ 8.5	−21.1	+18.7	+13.9
Switzerland	2226.9	2226.9	2049.5	+ 1.6	+ 15.5	nil	+ 5.7	+ 4.7
UK	2847.3	2957.3	2737.6	+ 0.4	+ 5.4	− 3.7	nil	+ 1.2
USA	3444.4	3482.3	3242.0	− 0.7	+ 1.4	− 1.1	+ 4.3	+ 4.3
World‡	553.5	565.2	488.6	− 1.2	+ 7.9	− 3.1	+11.3	+11.3

‡ Morgan Stanley Capital International. † Converted at financial rate.

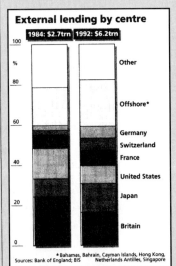

External lending by centre

1984: $2.7trn   **1992: $6.2trn**

Other
Offshore*
Germany
Switzerland
France
United States
Japan
Britain

* Bahamas, Bahrain, Cayman Islands, Hong Kong, Netherlands Antilles, Singapore
Sources: Bank of England; BIS

MONEY AND INTEREST RATES America's narrow-money growth quickened to 10.8% in the year to April, but its broad-money supply fell by 1%. During the same period Spain's broad money increased by 7.2%. France's broad money grew by 4.8% in the 12 months to March.

	money supply‡ % rise on year ago narrow (M1)	money supply‡ % rise on year ago broad	money market overnight	money market 3 months	commercial banks prime lending	commercial banks deposits 3 months	bond yields gov't long-term	bond yields corporate	eurocurrency deposits 3 months	eurocurrency bonds
Australia	+20.8	+ 8.9 Feb	5.25	5.15	9.50	5.15	7.60	8.46*	4.94	na
Belgium	− 0.7	+ 6.6 Dec	7.13	7.19	11.00	6.63	7.38	7.31	7.19	6.91
Canada	+12.1	+ 7.2 Apr	4.13	5.03	6.00	5.13	8.30	9.41	5.00	8.39
France	+ 0.6	+ 4.8 Mar	8.13	7.44	9.00	7.38	7.26	7.62	7.44	6.84
Germany	+10.0	+ 7.6 Mar	7.90	7.40	10.00	6.73	6.78	6.69	7.31	6.29
Holland	+13.5	+ 9.3 Mar	7.31	6.90	9.50	6.90	6.67	7.47	6.94	6.28
Italy	+ 4.1	+ 7.1 Mar	10.69	10.75	12.25	na	10.63	11.27	10.44	10.44
Japan	+ 0.6	− 0.3 Mar	3.16	3.20	4.00	3.00	4.65	5.36	3.22	4.76
Spain	− 3.8	+ 7.2 Apr	12.66	12.02	12.25	8.00	10.94	12.19	11.44	10.80
Sweden	na	+ 4.6 Mar	9.00	8.60	11.00	8.60	8.84	9.83	8.45	8.09
Switzerland	+ 8.2	+ 4.1 Feb	5.13	5.25	7.13	4.75	4.70	4.92	5.06	4.76
UK	+ 4.9	+ 3.6 Mar	5.81	6.06	7.00	5.97	8.50	9.69	6.25	7.58
USA	+10.8	− 1.0 Apr	2.97	3.15	6.00	3.13	7.02	7.47	3.38	5.46

interest rates % p.a. (May 18th 1993)

Other key rates in London: 3-mth Treasury bills 5.7%, 7-day interbank 6.0%. Eurodollar rates (LIBOR): 3 mths 3.2%, 6 mths 3.3%.

‡ M1 except UK M0; M3 except Belgium, Holland, Italy and Sweden M2, Japan M2 plus CDs, Spain M3 plus other liquid assets, UK M4. Definitions of interest rates quoted available on request. Sources: Banco Bilbao Vizcaya, Belgian Bankers' Association, Chase Manhattan, Credit Lyonnais, Bank Nederland, Royal Bank of Canada, Svenska Handelsbanken, Westpac Banking Corp, CSFB, The WEFA Group. These rates cannot be construed as offers by these banks. *new series

TRADE, EXCHANGE RATES AND RESERVES America's visible-trade deficit rose to $10.2 billion in March, lifting its 12-month deficit to $93.8 billion. Germany's 12-month trade surplus fell to $21.9 billion in February; its current-account deficit narrowed to $27.3 billion in the same period. Following last week's 8% devaluation of the Spanish peseta within the ERM, it fell 4% in trade-weighted terms.

	trade balance‡ $bn latest month	trade balance‡ $bn latest 12 months	current-account balance $bn latest 12 mths	trade-weighted‡‡ exchange rate 1985=100 latest	trade-weighted‡‡ exchange rate 1985=100 year ago	currency units per $ latest	currency units per $ year ago	currency units per £	currency units per DM	currency units per ecu	foreign reserves†† $bn Mar	foreign reserves†† $bn year ago
Australia	− 0.50 Mar	+ 1.1	− 10.9 Mar	76.2	84.5	1.45	1.32	2.21	0.89	1.74	9.3*	13.6
Belgium	− 0.77 Dec	− 2.0	+ 5.1 Q3	115.2	111.6	33.4	32.8	51.1	20.5	40.2	13.2	11.1
Canada	+ 0.58 Mar	+ 9.1	− 23.7 Q4	94.3	99.5	1.27	1.20	1.95	0.78	1.53	12.7	14.7
France	+ 1.00 Dec	+ 5.8	+ 3.1 Q4	109.5	104.8	5.48	5.35	8.39	3.37	6.59	33.0*	32.7
Germany	+ 0.79 Feb	+ 21.9	− 27.3 Feb	123.9	118.9	1.62	1.59	2.49	—	1.95	70.3	61.6
Holland	+ 0.27 Dec	+ 5.7	+ 6.7 Q4	119.0	114.6	1.82	1.79	2.79	1.12	2.19	27.3	16.6
Italy	− 0.75 Dec	− 10.3	− 26.6 Q3	82.8	98.8	1477	1197	2262	909	1784	26.4	42.7
Japan	+12.51 Mar	+137.1	+126.7 Mar	170.0	140.1	112	129	171	68.7	134	73.0	71.2
Spain	− 1.60 Mar	− 31.2	− 24.0 Dec	91.9	108.3	124	99.7	189	76.1	149	44.4	65.8
Sweden	+ 0.51 Apr	+ 6.5	− 4.9 Feb	79.3	96.1	7.37	5.73	11.3	4.54	8.86	19.7*	22.4
Switzerland	+ 0.19 Mar	+ 0.9	+ 15.5 Q4	110.1	105.0	1.48	1.46	2.27	0.91	1.78	31.4	27.1
UK	− 2.71 Dec	− 24.1	− 20.7 Dec	80.2	93.0	0.65	0.54	—	0.40	0.79	38.1*	40.9
USA	−10.20 Mar	− 93.8	− 62.4 Q4	64.5	63.0	—	—	1.53	0.62	1.20	63.2	63.6

‡ Australia, France, Canada, Japan, UK and USA imports fob, exports fob. All others cif/fob. ‡‡ Bank of England, Reserve Bank of Australia indices. †† Excluding gold. * February

1. Consider the French franc–deutschemark relationship. Can you identify any deviations from relative purchasing power parity based on the past year's data?
2. What are the prospects for the franc/DM exchange rate, based on purchasing power parity and (a) wage and (b) money supply pressures?
3. To compare long-term interest rates in France and Germany, which pair of rates would you use? What do these relative long-term interest rates signal?
4. Based on Eurocurrency deposit rates, what is the three-month forward rate (FF per DM)? How does this deviate from what you might expect based on your answers to the earlier questions?

Application 5.2 | MACPARITY

As Director of Planning for Scott Paper Company, Dick Thompson does not typically have to get into arguments with the firm's accountants. Recently, however, his efforts to give Scott's manufacturing subsidiaries in Europe and Japan more financial independence had been frustrated by the V.P. of Finance, who pointed to the losses these subsidiaries had sustained during the past six months. The reason was not in dispute: because of the U.S. dollar's rise of almost 7 percent against most other currencies, the translated value of the foreign subsidiaries had fallen.

Dick's argument was that the loss was fictional, a "paper loss" resulting from the fact that the firm's accountants were ignoring the value of the overseas operations' fixed assets and future revenues. "Because of purchasing power parity," he said, "foreign prices tend to rise, relative to U.S. prices, by an amount sufficient to offset the currency change. For example, if you were to take a few representative goods in the United States, and compare the prices of identical goods in Japan and Europe, translated into U.S. dollars at the current rate, you'd find they're similar."

"Is that so? Prove it!" retorted the chief accountant. "I'd bet that if you compared the price of a Big Mac, or a gallon of gasoline, or any other comparable commodity in a couple of different countries, you'd find that there's no practical relationship between prices and exchange rates."

Who is right? Can you identify the prices of one or more comparable consumer goods in at least three different countries? Are their prices the same in U.S. dollars, and if not, what is the percentage deviation from the law of one price? Please identify your sources!

Application 5.3 | GOBBLE GOBBLE

Jeremy Symonds, arriving at his office at Midland Bank's headquarters in London, found the following fax lying on his desk, with a note attached saying, "This came from Sykes Wilford in Ankara. As you know, Surrey is a good client. Would you kindly fax him a reply?"

What should Jeremy Symonds state in his reply fax?

Hotel Istanbul, Ankara, Turkey
Telephone (90) 1-42-88-00
Facsimile (9) 1-42-88-36

TO: Jeremy Symonds
        Midland Bank

FROM: Sykes Wilford

Jeremy, I need your advice. At dinner last night the Deputy Minister of Finance mentioned to me that it might be possible to convert some of our local funds into Greek drachmas. He also said that, for the forthcoming year, inflation in Turkey is projected to be 17%, while inflation in Greece is expected to continue at an 8% rate. On this basis, he said, one should expect the drachma price of the lira to fall by 9%. This sounds right, but before I make any arrangements I would like to hear your comments on this statement. If you have any reservations, please state them concisely and fax them to me ASAP.

Sykes

SELECTED REFERENCES

Baillie, Richard T., and Patrick C. McMahon. *The Foreign Exchange Market: Theory and Econometric Evidence.* Cambridge University Press, 1989.

Coughlin, Cletus C., and Kees Koedijk. "What Do We Know About the Long-Run Real Exchange Rate?" *Federal Reserve Bank of St. Louis Review* (Jan./Feb. 1990): 36–48.

Huang, Roger D. "Risk and Purchasing Power in International Banking." *Journal of Money, Credit and Banking,* vol. 22, no. 3 (August 1990): 338–356.

PART 2

Foreign–Exchange Prediction and Hedging Tools

6
Currency Prediction Versus Market Efficiency

This chapter introduces some leading ideas about what determines exchange rates, and how those rates may or may not be helpful in forecasting currency values in light of the highly efficient nature of the foreign-exchange markets.

Competing Theories of Exchange-Rate Determination

The sad truth is that no theory of exchange rates can yet purport to provide a complete explanation of past exchange-rate behavior, never mind forecast the future with any degree of accuracy. Nevertheless, the past two decades' research has yielded a clearer understanding of how exchange rates are set. The relationship between spot- and forward-exchange rates and Eurocurrency interest rates is beyond dispute. And a consensus of theoreticians and empirical researchers on exchange rates may be summarized in four fairly well accepted propositions:

1. Foreign exchange is a financial asset that behaves very much like other financial assets, such as stocks and bonds, in that its price is determined in the context of risk, returns, and most of all, expectations.
2. Recent research has nevertheless confirmed repeatedly that although the foreign-exchange market is broadly efficient, short-run technical models can often beat the odds.
3. Movement in the exchange rate between two currencies is fundamentally a monetary phenomenon, determined by the basic factors underlying the demands for and supplies of each national money.
4. However, it is clear that "real" factors such as economic growth and monetary aberrations do exert a strong influence on a currency's value.

The models described below assume a floating exchange rate, but the same forces generally apply if the exchange rate is fixed. The difference is that the government, through administrative controls or by means of intervention in the foreign-exchange market, can postpone the currency's change. This delay can perhaps allow the government time to undertake fundamental adjustments in order to avert the need for the exchange-rate change altogether. A section entitled Forecasting in a Fixed-Rate System in this chapter is devoted to forecasting exchange rates under a fixed-but-adjustable regime.

Author's note: Thanks to Jack Glen for comments on the content of this chapter.

Exchange Rates, Trade, and the Balance of Payments

The most basic theory of exchange-rate determination, and one that accords with common sense as well as with the theory of international trade discussed earlier, is that the equilibrium exchange rate is the one that equates exports with imports between two countries. Explaining this requires a brief revisit to the balance of trade. Australia, for example, trades with New Zealand. Assume the exchange rate is 1:1, that is, one Australian dollar (A$) per one New Zealand dollar (NZ$). Australians import 20 million crates of kiwis per annum at a total cost of NZ$2 billion, and export 30 million barrels of beer for which they charge A$3 billion. For the value of exports to equal the value of imports, the exchange rate must be A$1.50 = NZ$1.00. Then Australia's exports of A$3 billion equal its imports of NZ$2 billion (2 billion times 1.50 = A$3 billion). In this simple model, *the exchange rate is determined by equilibrium in the balance of trade.* The model is admittedly oversimplified, because it takes no account of the capital flows that invariably form part of what determines a currency's value, but it still underlies how many reasonable people think about exchange-rate determination. Indeed, trade equilibrium is the central tenet of the *elasticities approach* to exchange-rate determination.

The elasticities approach to the exchange rate recognizes that exports, imports, and the exchange rate interact in a complex way to reconcile supply and demand of exports and imports between two countries. If trade is out of equilibrium, the exchange rate will adjust to reestablish export-import equality. For example, if New Zealanders' demand for Australian beer declines, the Australian dollar will likely fall in relation to the New Zealand dollar. This fall will persuade some Australians to import less and export more, and vice versa in New Zealand. But how much the currency needs to change to achieve equilibrium depends on the *price elasticity of demand for imports* and the *price elasticity of the supply of exports* on the two countries. How readily can domestic goods be substituted for imported goods? If there is no domestic substitute, the country's currency may have to fall a lot to reduce imports to the equilibrium point. (This is one reason that many developing countries importing oil and capital goods have objected to the IMF recommendations that the exchange rate be freed to restore the proper incentives as a precondition to concessional loans.)

The exchange-rate change will also make one country better off and the other country worse off; in other words, national income will change in each. For example, when the pound sterling dropped out of the exchange-rate mechanism of the European community, U.K. residents had to give up more of their income to pay for exports. When people's income declines, they tend to consume less, so less will be imported, and more domestic production will be freed for exports. These, in turn, will influence the exchange rate. But how much change will occur depends on the *income elasticity of demand* for imports and for exportable goods.

The early literature on exchange rates and the balance of payments, especially for Keynesians who tend to pay more attention to income and growth than to purely monetary factors, devoted a lot of study to these elasticities and their effects on imports, exports, and exchange rates. Their results proved somewhat inconclusive. Perhaps this should not surprise anyone, because the elasticities approach totally neglects capital flows and the speculative influences that accompany them.[1] Yet the version of "trade-flow"

---

[1]To be fair, the elasticities models were not originally intended to be full-fledged models of exchange-rate determination; rather, they were designed to help policymakers understand how a given exchange-rate change affects trade.

theory that still has the most appeal of all is the simplest! This is the **purchasing-power-parity** (PPP) theory of exchange-rate determination.

We have already encountered purchasing power parity in Chapter 5, so we need allude only briefly to its implications for the theory of exchange-rate determination. The theory says that the exchange rate must be set at a level that equates *aggregate* prices between two countries, so the exchange rate is the ratio of the home and foreign countries' price levels, which are weighted-average prices of all goods and services in the economy:

$$S_t = \frac{L_t}{L_t^*}$$

Better still, because price levels themselves are not measured, the present rate relative to the past rate equals the ratio of inflation rates in the two countries:

$$\frac{S_t}{S_{t-1}} = \frac{1 + I^*}{1 + I}$$

As before, S is the spot exchange rate in home currency units per unit of foreign currency, L is the price level and I is the inflation rate. An asterisk designates the foreign country.

However appealing the relative-inflation approach, we know that there is a very poor short-term relationship between inflation and the exchange rate. Today, therefore, the role of PPP in exchange-rate determination takes one of the following two forms:

- Some models incorporate the exchange rate–inflation link as a *tendency* to which exchange rates revert over time. PPP is a moving target, but other factors determine short-term fluctuations.
- Other models say that relative inflation *does* have an immediate effect, but that it is not today's inflation, nor yesterday's, but rather anticipated future inflation, that is captured in short-term currency fluctuations.

But in talking of expectations we are anticipating our later discussion of the efficient-markets approach to exchange-rate changes.

Monetary and Portfolio-Balance Models

The two models in this section share the view that the exchange rate is fundamentally a monetary phenomenon. The exchange rate is, by definition, the relative price of two national monies. It is determined by the basic factors underlying the demand for, and supply of, the national money stocks. The government *supplies* the money, perhaps to pay for a budget deficit or to stimulate the economy. The public's *demand* for money depends, among other things, on real income and the interest rate. The interest rate itself, we have seen, is in part a product of inflationary expectations.

The foundations of the **monetary approach** to exchange-rate determination lie in purchasing power parity and the quantity theory of money. The latter says that the public's demand for real money balances, M/L, is a function of real income Y, the interest rate R, and other factors designated as K. The income variable is a proxy for the volume of real transactions effected with the aid of money and therefore represents the transactions demand for money. The greater is real income, the stronger the demand for money. The nominal interest rate represents the opportunity cost of holding money instead of interest-bearing assets. One way of expressing this relationship is

$$\frac{M}{L} = KYR^{-a}$$

where a is a constant referred to as the *interest elasticity of demand for money,* assumed to be the same in both countries. In the other country,

$$\frac{M^*}{L^*} = K^*Y^*R^{*-a}$$

so, from the purchasing-power-parity equation,

$$S = \frac{L}{L^*}$$

we get the basic monetary model of the exchange rate:

$$S = \left(\frac{M}{M^*}\right)\left(\frac{K^*}{K}\right)\left(\frac{Y^*}{Y}\right)\left(\frac{(R^*)^{-a}}{(R)^{-a}}\right)$$

For purposes of testing this model, one can take logarithms of both sides:

$$s = (m + m^*) + (k^* - k) + (y^* - y) + a(r - r^*)$$

where lowercase letters represent the natural logarithm of the same variable in uppercase letters. For example, s means $\ln S$. Assuming the k's are equal, they cancel out.[2]

Looked at this way, it becomes clear what the monetary models claim: that the value of the foreign currency s rises if that country's relative money supply falls, if its relative real income rises, or if its interest rate falls.

The monetary model seems to work well during periods dominated by monetary shocks, such as hyperinflation. In the long run, too, currencies with high nominal interest rates (such as those of Australia and the United Kingdom) have been characterized by currency depreciation, while currencies with low nominal interest rates (such as those of Germany and Switzerland) have had a secular increase in the value of their currencies. In the post-1973 developed world, however, monetary shocks have often taken second place to *real* shocks such as booms, busts, and commodity-market disruptions. Also the simple monetary approach does not seem to be able to explain why exchange rates are so volatile—that is, why they vary much more than commodity prices in response to economic disturbances. To explain this, the short-term capital market and the participants' expectations play pivotal roles.

One of the simplifying assumptions of the pure monetary model is that real interest rates are stable, so that an (unexpected) change in monetary policy, for example, will affect only nominal rates. This assumes that prices of goods and services will adjust instantaneously to changes in financial markets. Obviously, they do not. Prices for goods and services tend to be much more sticky than prices of financial assets because of the existence of contractual relationships and especially because of the prevalence of market imperfections (unions, large corporations, technological advantages). As a result, there will be transitory changes in real interest rates that may persist for some time when the change in monetary policy is not expected to last.

A number of variants of the model have accordingly tried to take into account the stickiness of prices and the lag in purchasing power parity, as well as the possibility that a rise in short-term interest rates can increase the real interest rate, attracting funds, and causing the currency to rise. An "overshooting" model by Dornbusch[3] shows that an

---

[2]An example of a model of this kind may be found in Thomas M. Humphrey and Thomas A. Lawler, "Factors Determining Exchange Rates: A Simple Model and Empirical Tests," *Federal Reserve Bank of Richmond Economic Review* (May/June 1977), 10–15.

[3]See R. Dornbusch, "Expectations and Exchange Rate Dynamics," *Journal of Political Economy,* 84 (1976), 1161–1176.

unanticipated change in the money supply leads to exchange-rate overshooting because consumer prices cannot move immediately to reflect the money-supply change. Thus in the short run, the exchange rate responds to *capital flows* (see Box 6.1). Along similar lines, Frankel[4] modified the simple monetary model to take account of real interest differentials; he used an equation like the logarithm equation given earlier but supplemented by relative long-term interest rates, representing inflation expectations, and financial wealth as a further determinant of the demand for money.

> *The pure monetary approach thus claims that high nominal interest rates imply a falling currency because they incorporate an inflationary premium. Models incorporating capital flows, in contrast, argue that a high interest rate can represent a high real rate, thus attracting foreign capital and causing the currency to appreciate.*

We seek to reconcile this contrast in the next section. The one major flaw of most monetary models is the assumption that real, inflation-adjusted, interest differentials cannot persist. Many now believe that they can, because, after all, people do arbitrage between nominal, not real, interest rates. This concept has been shown in a simple but ingenious fashion by Jeffery Frankel.[5] He decomposes the real interest differential into a *country premium* and a *currency premium* as follows. Begin by defining the real interest differential as

$$r_R - r_R^* = [r_N - E(I)] - [r_N^* - E(I^*)]$$

BOX 6.1

Exchange-Rate Overshooting

One influential view of why exchange rates are more volatile than the underlying economic variables is the *exchange-rate dynamics theory,* which argues that prices of *financial assets* adjust quickly to equate asset demands and supplies, while prices of *goods* adjust slowly. Here's an illustration of how currency volatility results:

> *Consider the instantaneous versus long-run impacts on the exchange rate of a one-time money supply increase. As in the simple version of the monetary approach, in each country money demand is determined by the level of domestic income and the domestic interest rate. Given instantaneous clearing in asset markets, money supply must continuously equal money demand. With income fixed in the short run owing to sluggish goods market adjustment, a 1 percent money supply increase must lower instantaneously the domestic interest rate (to increase money demand to absorb the greater liquidity). Assuming domestic and foreign interest are equal initially, the continuous (uncovered) interest parity assumption implies that the (lower) domestic interest rate equals the (fixed) foreign interest rate minus the expected rate of future appreciation of the home currency. Yet in the long run, the assumption of PPP ensures that the home currency depreciates proportionately to the money supply increase. How can an eventual 1 percent depreciation of the home currency be reconciled with an instantaneous expectation of appreciation over time of the home currency toward its long run value? These two facts are reconciled if the exchange rate instantaneously "overshoots" its long run value—that is, the home currency depreciates immediately by more than 1 percent and appreciates over time toward the long-run exchange rate value consistent with PPP.*

From Jeffrey H. Bergstrand, "Selected Views of Exchange Rate Determination After a Decade of 'Floating'," *New England Economic Review,* Federal Reserve Bank of Boston (May/June 1983), 14–29.

---

[4] J. A. Frankel, "The Mystery of the Multiplying Marks: A Modification of the Monetary Model," *Review of Economics and Statistics* 64 (1982), 515–519.

[5] "Measuring International Capital Mobility: A Review," *AEA Papers and Proceedings* (May 1992), 197–202.

where r_R and r_N are real and nominal interest rates, respectively, and $E(I)$ is the expected inflation rate. Real interest rates are nominal rates minus the expected inflation rate. Now decompose the right-hand side into three parts:

$$r_R - r_R^* = [r_N - r_N^* - FD] + [FD - E(s)] + [E(s) - E(I) - E(I^*)]$$

where FD is the forward discount on the domestic currency and $E(s)$ is the expected depreciation of the domestic currency.

The first term $[r_N - r_N^* - FD]$ is the covered interest differential. It can be called the *country premium* because it captures barriers to arbitrage attributable to national boundaries: transactions costs, information costs, present and expected capital controls, taxes, and default risk. The second term $[FD - E(s)]$ is the deviation from the international Fisher effect, or the *exchange-risk premium*. The third term, $[E(s) - E(I) - E(I^*)]$, is the expected real depreciation. Frankel calls the last two together the *currency premium* because they pertain to differences in assets attributable to the currency of denomination rather than the country of jurisdiction. Only if one believes that all of these are zero, or that they coincidentally offset one another, would one expect that real interest rates are equal between countries.

The *currency-substitution approach* supplements the monetary models by allowing each country's residents to hold the other country's currency. Then the aggregate demand for money will be the sum of domestic and foreign components. This accords with reality for the major countries, and may help explain why certain actively used currencies seem to continue to rise when money growth and other indicators suggest they should be falling. If a currency is considered more convenient or secure for transactions, people from a number of other countries will demand it and its price will rise. There is evidence in Europe, for example, of a growing elasticity of substitution between German marks and other currencies.

Although the currency-substitution model itself adds little to the explanatory power of the monetary model, it does provide the insight that even if both currencies are equal in terms of their own return and risk, residents of each country will tend to hold some of the others' currency for diversification, as long as returns are not perfectly correlated. Its shortcoming is that it does not go far enough.

A **portfolio-balance approach** takes account of the fact that people can hold an array of risky financial assets as well as money denominated in their own or other currencies.[6] In the portfolio-balance model, demand in the foreign-exchange market for currencies is determined largely from demand for financial assets. The wealthier a country, the more demand there will be for assets denominated in its currency, and the stronger its currency will be. One source of a wealth increase is a current account surplus (implying an accumulation of foreign assets). Thus the portfolio-balance approach is able to incorporate international trade versus capital flows as part of the explanation of exchange-rate movements. Unfortunately, its variables are hard to measure. (Who knows the composition of Europeans' portfolios?) It also has had very little empirical predictive power.

Indeed empirical tests of all of these models have failed to bring the debate to a satisfactory conclusion. One comprehensive study compared several competing exchange-rate models, including a monetary approach, using in-sample data to estimate the models and out-of-sample data to test them.[7] The authors concluded that even when

---

[6]See, for example, P. R. Allen and P. B. Kenen, *Asset Markets, Exchange Rates and Economic Integration* (Cambridge University Press, 1980).

[7]R. Meese and K. Rogoff, "Empirical Exchange Rate Models of the Seventies: Do They Fit Out of Sample?" *Journal of International Economics* 14 (February 1983), 3–24. See also C. P. Wolff, "Time-Varying Parameters and the Out-of-Sample Forecasting Performance of Structural Exchange Rate Models," *Journal of Business and Economic Statistics* (January 1987), 87–97.

the models worked well in-sample, they performed poorly in the post-sample period and failed to outperform the random-walk model or the forward rate in forecasting the spot rate.

Fundamental Models in Forecasting

For many, the value of an exchange-rate model lies not in whether it meets the academic criteria of consistency and statistical significance but whether it can be usefully employed in exchange-rate forecasting. Meeting this standard is much harder than might appear at first blush. The reason is that even if we were able to find a good model, and upon testing it out-of-sample find that its properties were robust, we would still have to insert values for the independent variables that enter the model. And that often means making assumptions about government policy actions.

Let's take an example. One version of Frankel's real interest-differential model, when fitted to actual data for the dollar/mark exchange rate, resulted in the following equation:

$$s = .80 + .31(m - m^*) - .33(y - y^*) - .259(r - r^*) + 7.72(\pi - \pi^*)$$

where

$m - m^*$ = natural logarithm of German M1/U.S. M1
$y - y^*$ = natural logarithm of German production/U.S. production
$r - r^*$ = short-term German–U.S. interest-differential
$\pi - \pi^*$ = expected German–U.S. inflation-differential, proxied by long-term government bond differential

The equation fits the data quite well, with an $R^2 = .91$. But now think of how one would use it to forecast, say, the dollar/mark exchange rate at the end of next quarter. We would have to plug in *forecasted* values not only for industrial production but also for the money supply in each country. And both short-term and long-term interest rates would have to be predicted before one could get anywhere with the model. Both money supplies and interest rates are policy variables, and both may well depend on exchange-market pressures! Brave indeed are those who tread this minefield.

In practice, those who use models seldom rely on the models alone. Because so much judgment is involved in estimating the independent variables in the models, the forecasters typically temper the model's results with their own common-sense evaluations. Thus model-based forecasts are often melded with *judgmental forecasts*.

Interest Rates, Exchange Rates, and Inflation

A simple example of the use of judgment in exchange-rate forecasting, one that depends on both the international Fisher effect and the monetary/overshooting models of exchange-rate determination and also depends on assumptions concerning government policy, is given by one of the puzzles of international finance:

- Does a high dollar interest rate (relative to other currencies) mean the dollar will be strong?
- Does a high dollar interest rate (relative to other currencies) mean the dollar will be weak?

The answer to both questions is yes, or perhaps no! In fact, it depends. It depends on whether the high dollar interest rate reflects tight monetary policies, designed to reduce inflation, or whether the high rate merely reflects inflationary expectations, as predicted by the Fisher effect. It also depends on whether one is talking about the long run or the short run.

Common wisdom holds that raising the interest rate strengthens the currency of a country. Figure 6.1 shows that several major increases in the interest-rate gap between two currencies do appear to have caused a rise in the currency with the higher interest rate. Such a rise occurred frequently in the 1970s and 1980s when a country, seeing its currency actually or potentially falling, tightened the credit reins, thus raising interest rates and attracting funds into the currency. In such a situation, traders are prepared to take advantage of the higher interest rates because they do not expect the currency to fall to offset the interest-rate gain.

On the other hand, the same graph shows that there are at least as many instances—often in the same currencies—when a higher interest rate means a *weaker currency*. When interest rates are high because of a high expected rate of inflation, then people also expect the currency to fall. Indeed, according to the PPP theory, the currency might be expected to fall by an amount equal to the inflation-rate differential, on average. Thus any gain from the higher interest rate would tend to be offset by the currency depreciation.

Figure 6.1   *The Interest-Rate Gap: When a Currency Rises If Its Interest Rate Rises.* Tight credit raises interest rates and can support a currency. But the opposite seems to be true as well. What explains this paradox?

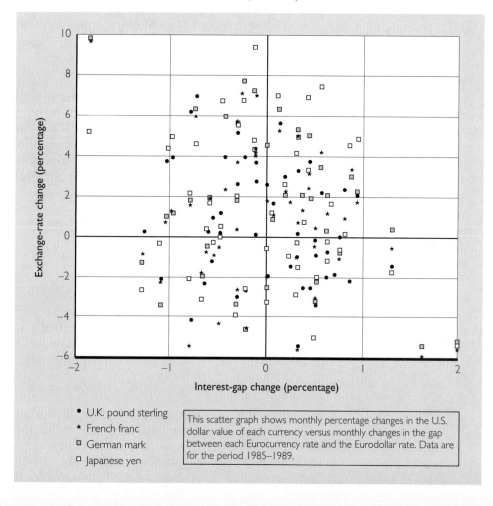

- U.K. pound sterling
- French franc
- German mark
- Japanese yen

This scatter graph shows monthly percentage changes in the U.S. dollar value of each currency versus monthly changes in the gap between each Eurocurrency rate and the Eurodollar rate. Data are for the period 1985–1989.

This opposite phenomenon is illustrated in Figure 6.2, which traces the course of interest rates in the major Eurocurrencies for one particular year. In general, it is the currencies with higher inflation rates and weaker currencies—the French franc and the pound sterling, for example—that exceed the interest rates on strong currencies with lower inflation rates, such as the Japanese yen and German mark. In general, consistently high rates of inflation lead to higher interest rates and falling currencies, but temporary deviations from the interest-rate–inflation-rate link can induce capital flows to the country whose rate has risen.

The United States and Argentina are two examples of the contrasting effect of interest rates on exchange rates. In the early 1980s, the United States had a high interest rate, which led to a very strong dollar value against other currencies. On the other hand, Argentina had a much higher interest rate (often exceeding 100 percent) and a very weak currency. As these two extreme examples illustrate, in order to reconcile the two seemingly opposed views of how interest rates and exchange rates are related, one must look *behind* the interest rate, at

1. changes in interest rates that are *real* versus those that are *nominal*.
2. the *timing* of inflation's effect on interest rates.

Thus the difference between the cases of the United States and Argentina might only be a matter of the magnitude and rapidity with which interest rates respond to inflation expectations. In both countries, the exchange rate reacts positively to an increase in the real interest rate. The question to consider is, When something—such as an expansion

Figure 6.2 **_The Interest Gap and Inflation._** Consistently higher rates of inflation lead to higher interest rates and weakening currencies.

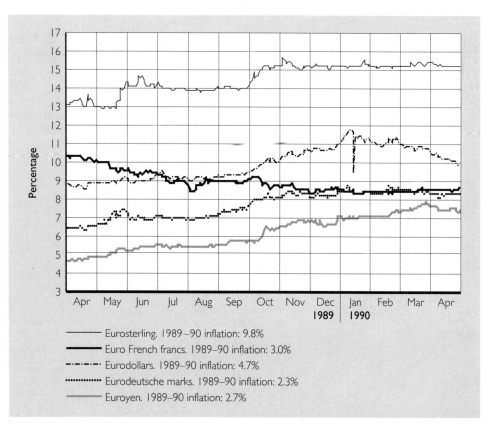

of the money supply—increases a country's inflation rate, how readily do prices, interest rates, and exchange rates react? A reasonable rule of thumb is:

- *Prices of goods* (inflation) tend to react slowly, in part because commodity arbitrage across time periods requires storage and is expensive.
- *Prices and rates in financial markets,* where arbitrage is cheap, change rapidly, and information dissemination permits future effects to be fully anticipated; expected future rate changes happen immediately.

The slow adjustment of the price level following a one-shot monetary expansion means that at first interest rates and the exchange rates *both fall;* later they *both rise.* But once inflation has fully set in, interest rates will have risen and exchange rates will have fallen enough to offset the inflation.

Subtracting the expected inflation rate from the nominal interest rate gives the **real interest rate.** According to a simplified version of the Dornbusch overshooting model, the sequence following a monetary expansion is roughly as follows:

- At first, the drop in interest rates occurs without any drop in prices. This is a drop in the *real* interest rate, and corresponds to a fall in the exchange rate.
- Later, as the liquidity effect dissipates, the interest rate rises to reflect the inflation that has set in. Because the interest rate must rise to a point *above* its original level, it climbs by more than anticipated inflation, so part of the interest-rate rise is a real increase, and it is accompanied by a *partial rise* in the exchange rate.
- Over the whole period, the net rise in the interest rate is offset by inflation and so is only a *nominal rise,* and over the whole period, the exchange rate falls by the inflation rate.

The basic decision rule is illustrated in Figure 6.3. Suppose Australia increases the money supply; the short-term interest rate will fall. Perceiving this as a real drop, market partic-

Figure 6.3   *A Road Map for the Exchange-Rate–Interest-Rate Puzzle.* The key lies in understanding the source of the interest-rate change. Is it just a nominal rate change, or has monetary policy altered the real rate?

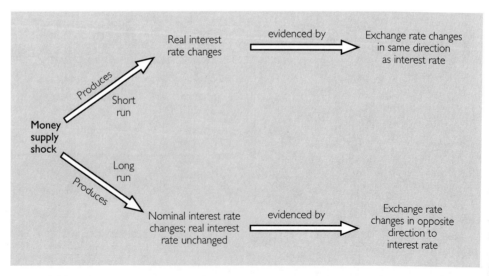

ipants will sell Australian dollars and the currency will fall. But a credit squeeze in Australia could also cause rates to drop in the long run, by diminishing inflation; then the Australian dollar might rise. The main point is that the effect of a change in the interest rate on the exchange rate depends on the *source* of the interest-rate change. If the interest rate falls because of a monetary-policy short-term effect, or because the government is keeping the rate down, it is a *drop in the real interest rate;* inflation has not fallen and the exchange rate falls. But if the interest rate falls because of a monetary contraction, as will eventually happen as inflation expectations fall, the market will recognize that the *real interest rate is unchanged,* and the currency will not fall.[8]

Finally, a real interest-rate change can occur as a result of the imposition or removal of interest rate and exchange *controls.* Especially in a country with high inflation and devaluation, when the rate rises to approach market levels, capital and the exchange rate could respond positively (as in Argentina); conversely, a too-low rate might precipitate a devaluation.

Exchange-Rate Determination in a Fixed-Rate System

If the exchange rate is fixed, it's going to stay where it is, isn't it? The answer is, Not necessarily, because a fixed-exchange-rate system remains so only as long as the government undertakes policy measures that ensure that the currency remains pegged to its benchmark. So forecasting a devaluation or revaluation of an ostensibly fixed rate is to a large extent a matter of forecasting two factors:

1. The economic pressures that can provoke a parity change.
2. The response of governments to them.

Let us begin with a model or concept of how the exchange rate is determined in a particular country. Let's assume the exchange rate could float but let's abstract from temporary expectations-driven variability. In the long run, our basic monetary framework suggests, fundamental factors like relative money growth, output, inflation, and investment opportunities determine the equilibrium level of the currency. For considerable periods of time, however, governments can resist the fundamental forces and fix the exchange rate at a "disequilibrium" level. This can be done in the open market, through a commitment to exchange domestic money for foreign assets at a fixed exchange rate. (EMS currencies are fixed in this way.) Or the exchange rate can be fixed by administrative means, by means of controls on currency exchange and on trade and capital flows. Many developing countries have adopted a mix of measures, with an emphasis on the administrative approach, because of their limited foreign-exchange resources.

The exchange rate being fixed at a non-market-clearing level does not necessarily mean that the rate has to change, nor need the disequilibrium persist. As the EMS has demonstrated, governments committed to fixed exchange rates can sustain them by allowing or encouraging adjustment to occur in the *domestic* economy rather than through

---

[8]One sign of a situation in which high interest rates accompany falling inflation and portend a stronger currency is a negatively sloped yield curve. For example, in early 1989, West Germany's short-term interest rates exceeded 10-year bond yields because the market expected inflation to be held down. A year later, however, the yield curve sloped upwards because of the risks caused by German unification and the impact that monetary union might have on future inflation.

the exchange rate. (A discussion of how this adjustment works was included in Chapter 4.) In order to understand exchange rates in a fixed-rate system, we have to address the following questions.

- *How much* adjustment is needed to eliminate underlying pressures?
- *When* will the pressures reach the critical point at which an exchange-rate change, or some other drastic measure, must be made?
- *Will* the exchange rate be changed? Or will some other policy measure prove economically and politically feasible?

This set of questions allows us to break the analysis of fixed exchange rates into four parts for purposes of forecasting.

Forecasting in a Fixed–Rate System

The framework illustrated in Figure 6.4 allows us to break the forecasting task into four steps:

1. Estimate the market-clearing level of the exchange rate, given accumulated inflation, pent-up investment demand, and other economic conditions.

Figure 6.4   ***Exchange-Rate Forecasting in a Fixed-Rate System.***   Forecasting in a fixed-rate system involves estimating the pressure on a currency, how long it can be resisted, and what alternative policy options are open to the government.

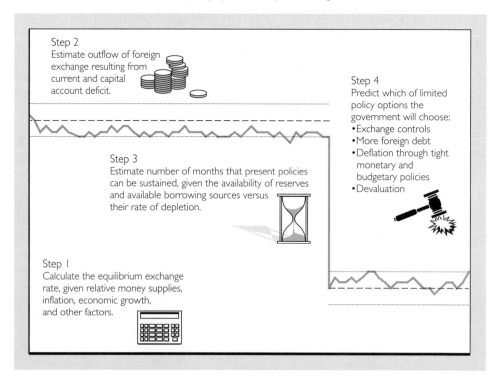

Step 2
Estimate outflow of foreign exchange resulting from current and capital account deficit.

Step 4
Predict which of limited policy options the government will choose:
- Exchange controls
- More foreign debt
- Deflation through tight monetary and budgetary policies
- Devaluation

Step 3
Estimate number of months that present policies can be sustained, given the availability of reserves and available borrowing sources versus their rate of depletion.

Step 1
Calculate the equilibrium exchange rate, given relative money supplies, inflation, economic growth, and other factors.

2. Predict the rate of depletion of reserves, given the excess of imports over exports, debt service, and other private and non–central bank transactions.
3. Use this information—in conjunction with the level of gold and foreign-exchange reserves, supplemented by potential borrowing from the IMF and other sources—to estimate how long the present conditions can be sustained without a devaluation or some other radical action.
4. Use political as well as economic analysis to judge what policy actions might be taken when the government has the gun to its head. Will it reform (by austerity), resist (with more controls), or realign (with devaluation) to a new parity with a new band of intervention?

EXAMPLE 6.1   ## Sweden on the Precipice

Should we hedge our DM borrowings? Volvo's treasurer wondered. He was a deliberate man who resisted getting swept away by panicky thinking. There was no doubt that the rumor mill at Volvo's headquarters was in high gear. The chairman, Mr. Per Gyllenhammar, was said to be furious at the effects that Sweden's deteriorating competitiveness in Europe was having on Volvo's sales. In a morning meeting he had ranted that the country was facing a "cost crisis" and that all Volvo's managers should be prepared for the inevitable economic adjustments that would soon be forced on the government. If Volvo in Sweden could not improve its flagging productivity, he had said, the company would be forced to move even more of its production abroad.

That Sweden faced balance-of-payments difficulties was beyond dispute. In the past 12 months Sweden had had to borrow SKr450 billion to finance its estimated current account deficit of SKr50 billion, to support a large increase in direct corporate investments abroad, and to pay for purchases of foreign securities. (The Stockholm stock market had fallen almost 25 percent in the past year.)

In recent weeks, pressure on the currency had intensified. Foreigners had been selling the krona on speculation that Sweden would have to devalue in order to restore growth to its deteriorating economy, which seemed headed for a period of stagflation. Sweden had lost SKr12 billion in foreign-exchange reserves during the past week alone. The previous day Sweden's central bank, the Riksbank, raised short-term market interest rates for the second time in a week, to 17 percent, the highest level since 1981. The rise was achieved by increasing the overnight lending rate to banks and through intervention in the market for six-month government bills. "We want to show the foreign-exchange market that we are serious in our support for the krona," said Bengt Dennis, the Riksbank governor. He also reminded the market that the Social Democratic government was actively negotiating with other political parties and labor groups on an anti-inflation package that would be announced the following week.

The Stockholm bourse was swept by rumors that the economic package could include a Swedish link to the European Monetary System as well as a long-term freeze on local government taxes, stiffer rules on worker sickness benefits, and a cap on wage growth in the next year.

Volvo's immediate concern was DM300 million worth of accounts payable and bank debt that had recently been raised to meet seasonal needs. The average rate on this debt was about 8.5 percent. Hedging it would entail selling krona forward for DM. In the three-month forward market, the krona traded at a discount of almost 8 percent per annum. Was it worth it?

To help you decide whether or when a devaluation of the krona is likely, some recent economic statistics on Sweden are shown in the accompanying table.

Economic Indicator	Sweden	U.S.	Germany
Spot rate vs US$	5.615%/$	—	1.515%/$
Spot rate, 1 year ago	6.50%	—	1.90%
3-month forward rate	5.73%	—	1.516%
3-month Eurodeposit rate	N.A.	8.125%	8.625%
10-year government bond rate	15.75%	8.78%	9.05%
Broad money supply, 1-year percentage change	+8.0	+1.9	+4.0
Consumer prices, 1-year percentage change	+11.1	+5.6	+3.0
Wholesale prices, 1-year percentage change	+3.9	+3.6	+1.9
Wages, 1-year percentage change	+13.8	+4.0	+5.7
Average hourly wages, US% equivalent, 1990 (and 1986)	$20.30 ($12.60)	$14.90 ($13.40)	$21.25 ($13.30)
Real GNP 1-year percentage change	+0.1	+1.0	+3.4
Unemployment, latest	1.8%	5.7%	7.1%
Unemployment, 1 year ago	1.5%	5.3%	7.8%
Current account balance, past 12 months, US$ equivalent in billions	−$2.7	−$97.8	+$50.3
Foreign reserves, latest month, US$ equivalent in billions	$12.7	$66.8	$62.5
Foreign reserves, 1 year ago, US$ equivalent in billions	$8.4	$52.4	$56.9

Technical Analysis

The inability of what one might call "fundamental" models to explain short-run exchange-rate behavior has led many practitioners to seek other solutions. Some have concentrated on developing tools for the management of exchange risk, on the grounds that exchange-rate forecasting is fruitless. For the many who believe that currency prediction is necessary and useful, "technical" models offer some appeal.

A *technical model* is one that predicts an exchange rate by using some interpretation of the series of past exchange rates but without any reference to outside information, such as monetary or trade statistics, except perhaps for trading data such as volume or open interest. Some of these models are complex and thoroughly tested; others are more basic because they carry greater intuitive plausibility. Let us see how one technical model, the moving average, might be used.

Figure 6.5 displays a series of monthly exchange rates and a 3-month and 12-month moving average of past rates. An n-month moving average is simply the average of the past n periods' values, updated each period to reflect the latest n periods. There are at least two ways in which market participants interpret such a chart.

1. There is a general view that technical models help the trader to distinguish between temporary, erratic movements and the overall trend; the moving average does just that. As one can see from the 12-month moving average line, the general direction of movement is clearly distinguished from the seemingly random jiggles. The implication is that the exchange

Figure 6.5   *Moving Averages.*   Technical models such as the moving averages shown here ignore exchange-rate economics, seeking instead to discover patterns in past data.

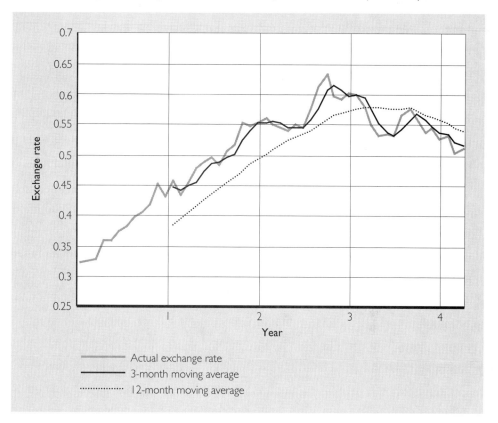

rate will tend to return to the trend line, as measured by one or other of the moving-average graphs.

2. A technical model can also be used to look for confirming signals. For example, if both the 3-month and the 12-month moving averages point to a movement in the same direction, and if other technical indicators confirm this, then it may be time to "buy" or to "sell," which brings us to an important point: most technical models do not pinpoint a forecasted exchange rate; rather they indicate whether the currency is moving up or down. Such models are designed to provide a signal for trading action, not to provide a precise forecast.

Do these methods work? Efficient market theory says technical models should not beat the market, except in a very narrow sense. And as we shall see, the more a particular kind of model is used, the more useless it should become. Yet the past decade has seen a surge of interest in technical models, to the point where no trading room is without at least one person who devotes part of his day to poring over graphs or over a PC keyboard to extract a little more information from the data. Some claim they do it because their customers use the models; others say that it is the influence of the futures market, populated by traders who focus on time series because they know very little about exchange-rate theory or markets, that makes technical models an important indicator of trading behavior. Whatever the reason, there are enough market participants who consistently over the years have devoted resources to this kind of model that one cannot dismiss them out of hand, as academics once did.

A variant of the technical model is the *chartist model,* which refrains from building any quantitative model at all, preferring instead to construct visual patterns from past trading levels. Like all technical models, chartist models are vulnerable to the charge that they do not use all available information. And a basic criticism that can be levied against any technical model is that it is not grounded in the fundamental determinants of a currency. For instance, the moving-average model may indicate a level of .55 for the DM, but there is no mystical force that pushes it in that direction. Indeed, if one could discover any repetitive behavior with a good reason behind it, and if this led to above-normal profit opportunities, the rate would quickly adjust to this level with no lag.

Today, exchange-rate forecasters also employ theories and techniques developed in branches of science far removed from the financial markets. They use *neural networks* (networks of computer processing units whose interaction is meant to replicate the learning process of the human brain), *genetic algorithms* (a method of generating better hypotheses about how currency markets work by starting with a wide range of assumptions and using them to evolve, in a Darwinian fashion, new and better models), and *chaos theory,* which holds that it is often possible to identify short-term patterns in seemingly chaotic natural and human phenomena. Whether this generation of financial technology survives the test of time and of careful academic scrutiny remains to be seen.

Evaluating the Performance of the Forecasters

For anyone involved in the currency game, it is a difficult task to decide whether to use professional forecasting services, and then how to choose among those available. Levich[9] has examined over 11,000 individual forecasts to test their performance against that of the forward rate. Let us see how he did it.

Levich starts with the assumption that the forward rate represents the market's expectation of the future spot rate (for more on this assumption, see the next section, entitled Efficient Markets). But how are we to compare the forward rate with the professionals' performance? One way would be to examine the size of the forecast error, defined as

$$\text{Forecast error} = \text{Predicted exchange rate} - \text{Actual exchange rate}$$

But there is no necessary relationship between the magnitude of forecast errors and the cost of forecast errors to investors. It depends on how the investor uses the forecast. A similar argument can be made about evaluating forecasting performance by calculating the stream of returns that an investor could earn by following the forecast. Investors use forecasts very differently, often with caution, for they recognize that forecasts are seldom perfect. Levich's studies distinguish between *accurate* forecasts and *correct* forecasts, where he defines accuracy to be a measure of the size of errors. Levich finds that, on average, exchange-rate forecasts have not been as accurate as the forward-rate prediction, which itself is not very accurate at all, as measured by mean-squared error (MSE). The mean-squared error is

$$\text{MSE} = \frac{1}{n}\sum_{1}^{n}(\text{Forecast} - \text{Actual})^2$$

---

[9]R. M. Levich, "Evaluating the Performance of the Forecasters," in Richard Ensor, ed., *The Management of Foreign Exchange Risk,* 2nd ed. (London: Euromoney Publications, 1982), 121–134.

Yet the professional services may be better than the forward in producing *correct* forecasts. They exhibit significant expertise in predicting whether the spot rate will appreciate or depreciate relative to the forward rate, the key for corporate hedging strategies. Even better forecasting performance along these lines can be obtained from a composite of professional forecasts. These results are obtained by ignoring the *magnitude* of forecast errors, and concentrating on the proportion of times in which the forecast correctly predicts the *direction* of currency movement.

Let S_p and S_a be the predicted and actual spot exchange rates, respectively, and F the lagged forward rate. Then $(S_p - F)$ is the forecaster's bias, and $(S_a - F)$ the market's error. If both have the same sign—both positive, or both negative—then the forecast is correct, in the sense that it has given the right signal for trading. The fraction

$$p = \frac{\text{Correct forecasts}}{\text{Total forecasts}}$$

estimates the probability of correct advice in any one period. The null hypothesis is that $p = .5$. (Even a monkey has a 50–50 chance of getting it right half the time.) The conclusion? As a group, the forecasters did not exhibit expertise above a level that could have occurred by chance. Individual forecasters, however, seemed to perform far better than chance would suggest. Users of these forecasts who made all-or-nothing hedge decisions would have come out ahead. But to do so, they had to take risks, and the profits earned by those who use successful services may only represent a fair return for the extra foreign-exchange risk incurred. So the success of a number of forecasting services is not necessarily inconsistent with market efficiency, a topic to which we now turn.

Efficient Markets

"Currency forecasters who do their job well will eventually put themselves out of business." That's one interpretation of the famous random-walk approach to foreign-exchange and other speculative markets. The theory claims that exchange rates fluctuate randomly and are therefore unpredictable. The reasoning is simple and logical. First, there are certainly profits to be made from successful prediction, so market participants will invest resources in gathering and interpreting information that will improve their predictive accuracy—and they will act on that information. Currencies will be bid up when they are expected to rise, and sold when they are expected to fall, until the current price reflects a market consensus. At this point the "best and the brightest" (or best-capitalized risk takers) will have "given it their all." They will have used all information available to them, public and private, and interpreted that information using the most accurate available models.

But the best models will not be able to provide an advantage for very long. The better the models, the richer their users will become, and the more others will try to imitate them. Pretty soon the bulk of trading, at the margin, will be dominated by traders using the best models, or variants of them. So the models will no longer give anyone an edge. The market price will quickly come to represent what the models say, as soon as anything is known to change the perceived equilibrium exchange rate.[10]

So the only time the dominant participants' forecasts are likely to change is when something new arises—some news, some unexpected information. From now on, the

---

[10]Good models drive out the bad. But good models themselves become bad in a speculative market like the foreign-exchange market.

exchange rate will react only to unpredictable or random events. But if the rate moves only when the unanticipated occurs, then the movements themselves must be unpredictable, or "random."

Efficient market theory is thus based on the notion that current prices reflect all available information, including market participants' expectations about future prices and, further, that all new information that is received by the market is analyzed and immediately incorporated into expectations about future prices. From these expectations, decisions to buy and sell are made, and thus the expected prices are converted into current prices.[11]

A literal application of the random-walk theory of asset prices to the exchange rate would produce the conclusion that the spot-exchange rate itself should follow a random walk. Because all changes in the spot rate result from unanticipated information, each and every future change in a currency's value should be unpredictable. (See Figure 6.6.) The spot rate itself would be the best available predictor of the future spot rate:

$$S_t = E(S_{t+1})$$

The trouble with this approach is that it takes no account of the expected return inherent in the interest-rate differential or the forward rate. If the pure random-walk theory were correct, one could profit on average by investing in, or buying forward, any currency trading at a discount from spot in the forward market, and selling any currency trading

Figure 6.6   ***The Random-Walk Theory.***   This exchange-rate theory maintains that the spot rate can move up or down with equal probability.

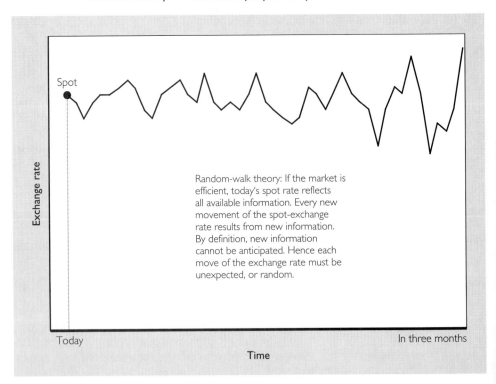

Random-walk theory: If the market is efficient, today's spot rate reflects all available information. Every new movement of the spot-exchange rate results from new information. By definition, new information cannot be anticipated. Hence each move of the exchange rate must be unexpected, or random.

---

[11]An extension of the efficient-market theory is the theory of **rational expectations,** which says that all economic decision makers, including not only foreign-exchange speculators but also consumers and wage earners, take into account all available information about the economy, including any available information on the probable future actions of policymakers. The information set even includes the economist's model!

at a premium. A more persuasive argument is that the current spot rate reflects an equilibrium *level* of the exchange rate, while the forward premium or discount represents the market's expectations about the future *rate of change* of the exchange rate. It follows that the forward rate would equal the expected future level of the spot rate. Because the forward rate is a contractual price, it offers opportunities for speculative profits for those who correctly assess the future spot price relative to the current forward rate. Specifically, risk-neutral players will seek to make a profit whenever their forecast differs from the forward rate, so if there are enough such participants, the forward rate will always be bid up or down until it equals the expected future spot. This is the unbiased-forward-rate theory encountered in earlier chapters:

$$F_t = E(S_{t+1})$$

Because expectations of future spot rates are formed on the basis of presently available information (historical data) and an interpretation of its implication for the future, they tend to be subject to frequent and rapid revision. As previously noted, the actual future spot rate may therefore deviate markedly from the expectation embodied in the present forward rate for that maturity. In addition, *the actual exchange rate may deviate from the expected by some random error*. These forecast errors, which are known only after the fact, will be designated e. So the future spot rate can be described as

$$S_{t+1} = E(S_{t+1}) + e_{t+1}$$

and according to the unbiased-forward-rate theory, the error will be the difference between the forward and the actual rate:

$$e_{t+1} = S_{t+1} - F_t$$

As is indicated in Figure 6.7, in an efficient market the forecasting error will be distributed randomly, according to some probability distribution, with a mean equal to zero. An

Figure 6.7 **The Unbiased-Forward-Rate Theory.** If the forward rate follows a random walk, then in effect, the spot rate follows a random walk with drift.

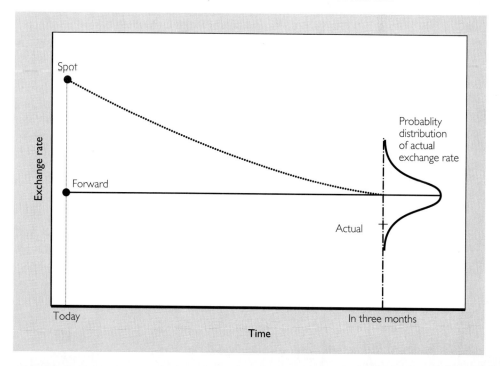

implication of this theory is that today's forecast, as represented by the forward rate, is equal to yesterday's forward rate plus some random amount. In other words, the forward rate itself follows a random walk.[12]

Another way of looking at these errors is to consider them as speculative profits or losses: What you would gain or lose if you consistently bet against the forward rate? Can they be consistently positive or negative? Deductive reasoning suggests that they should not. Otherwise, one would have to explain why consistent losers do not quit the market, or why consistent winners are not imitated by others or do not increase their volume of activity, thus causing adjustment of the forward rate in the direction of their expectation. Barring such explanation, one would expect that the forecast error is sometimes positive, sometimes negative, alternating in a random fashion, driven by unexpected events in the economic and political environment. Over sufficiently long periods of time, allowing a large number of decisions, e_{t+1} should average out to zero. This is the statistical basis for the view that the forward rate is an unbiased forecast of the future spot rate, and that the error is random.

Just as models of exchange-rate determination have come to recognize that people hold more than money in their portfolios, so the theory of foreign exchange has evolved toward a *portfolio view* of market efficiency. Decisions to speculate in foreign exchange, the story goes, are made on the basis of risk as well as expected return. Even if there is money to be made from speculation, people may not act unless the profit is commensurate with the risk of taking an open position in a currency. Instead, the forward rate will differ from the expected future spot rate by a **risk premium,** γ (gamma):

$$F_t = E(S_{t+1}) + \gamma + e_{t+1}$$

This proposition, illustrated in Figure 6.8, sounds reasonable; even speculators are risk averse, and will refrain from exploiting a profit opportunity if the expected return is too low. But now comes the hard part: How big is the risk premium? Is it positive or negative? And what factors determine the risk premium?

Modern portfolio theory offers a logical starting point for the analysis of the nature and price of risk in foreign-exchange speculation. Portfolio theory says that there is a linear relationship between risk and return—the higher the risk, the higher the expected return—but that investors do not get rewarded for taking risk that is diversifiable. According to the theory, anyone can diversify by combining a particular asset (such as foreign exchange) with the "market portfolio," so it would be the degree of covariance with investors' feasible market portfolio that would determine the risk premium in the forward-exchange rate. Therefore, to understand the pricing of any risk premium, we must address the issue of diversifiable versus nondiversifiable risk in the broader context of an international capital-asset pricing model. It would, for example, be risky to hold securities denominated in a currency whose value is positively correlated with that of other assets: the securities are afflicted with a risk that cannot be diversified away and a risk premium would be required (see Box 6.2). But difficult questions arise as to the definition of "other assets" and the relevant investment universe, as well as the consumption patterns of international investors.

On the latter subject, any investor in foreign fixed-interest securities faces a purchasing-power risk, because of the uncertainty of future inflation. So long as inflation

---

[12]Note that when we say the forward rate follows a random walk, we mean the forward for a given delivery date, not the rolling three-month forward. The only published measure of a forward rate for a given delivery date is the price of a futures contract, so the latter serves as a proxy to test the proposition that the forward rate should fluctuate randomly.

Figure 6.8   ***The Risk-Premium Theory.***   In this view, the forward rate may differ from the market's forecast of the future spot rate by a risk premium, γ.

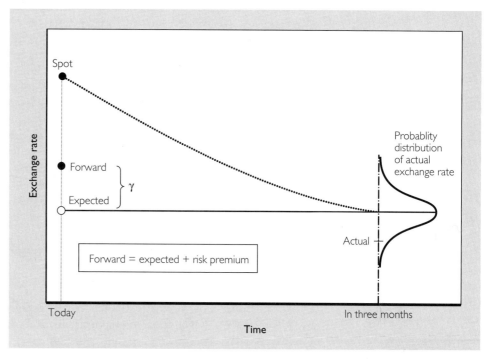

rates are not perfectly (positively) correlated among countries, it would pay to diversify portfolios internationally. In portfolio balance, therefore, it is theoretically possible that real return expectations differ from domestic and foreign securities because of residual

<table>
<tr><td>

BOX 6.2

The Risk Premium and Hedging

</td><td>

The size, direction, and nature of the risk premium, if any, in the forward rate are fundamental to the practice of international finance. If there is a risk premium, then it is very important to know something about it; otherwise we have no way of determining the exchange rate of the market's "consensus" forecast. We have no criterion for evaluating any forecasting method, nor can we satisfactorily test the market's efficiency (see the section entitled Tests of Market Efficiency). On the other hand, if the risk premium is negligible, the forward rate is, in effect, an unbiased predictor of the future spot rate. If the forward rate is unbiased, then anyone engaged in international business who takes an open, speculative position in a currency has the same long-run expected return as those who consistently hedge, covering their exposure, using forward contracts.

If there is a risk premium, it will be "paid" by transactors on one side of the market and "received" by transactors on the other. For example, assume that the dollar/sterling forward rate is determined by the expected rate, plus a risk premium, $\gamma_£$. Then buyers of pounds are paying more than the expected future spot rate for their hedge, while sellers of the pounds are receiving more dollars for a hedged position than they would expect, on average, to receive if they were unhedged!

</td></tr>
</table>

purchasing-power risk.[13] Put somewhat differently, systematic deviations from the international Fisher relationship are possible when one or the other country has issued an "excessive" amount of government debt[14] relative to its share in the minimum-variance, internationally diversified portfolio.[15] Accordingly, a premium above and beyond the expected depreciation could be explained as compensation for investors to increase their holdings of foreign currency assets, of which "excessive" amounts have been issued.

Further, for a risk premium to exist, the risk of holding a foreign-currency asset must be nondiversifiable. With risk-neutral investors, any risk premium will be competed away, because it represents expected excess profits. If there is a systematic risk premium on, say, dollar-denominated securities (perhaps because too many dollar-denominated securities have been issued by the U.S. government) then it might pay, in terms of lower nominal and expected real interest cost, to issue securities in other currencies.

From this analysis we can see that deviations of the forward rate from the expected future spot rate can be attributed to a number of different factors that themselves interact in complex ways. Although this ambiguity might be frustrating, it may prove comforting to the analyst to know that even international investors do not get excess returns very easily.

Technical Factors

One of the sources of systematic differences is a technicality known in the literature as the Siegel paradox, which is based on a mathematical concept called Jensen's inequality. If residents of two countries consume a common basket of goods, the foreign-exchange rate will generally lie between the expectation of the future rate defined in terms of one currency and the expectation of the future rate defined in terms of the other currency. However, the practical significance of the Siegel paradox is negligible when the (expected) variance of the exchange rate is not excessive, and it disappears altogether when PPP holds.[16]

Transactions costs incurred by speculators who are buying or selling foreign currency forward are another potential source of bias. If the expected future spot rate is given by $E(S_{t+1})$, the current forward rate for that maturity is F_t, and T is the per-unit transaction cost (all quoted as dollars per foreign currency unit), then a risk-neutral speculator will sell foreign currency forward so long as

$$E(S_{t+1}) - F_t < T$$

and speculative profits are eliminated when

$$E(S_{t+1}) - F_t = T$$

Similarly, speculators will buy foreign currency forward as long as

$$F_t - E(S_{t+1}) < T$$

---

[13]There should be no residual exchange risk because there is a perfect negative correlation for deviation from purchasing power parity for any two currencies—guaranteeing, in principle, complete diversifiability.

[14]Government, rather than private, debt is necessary for a risk premium, for with private debt, gains to borrowers will be losses to lenders, and the perfect negative correlation of such returns permits the complete elimination of this risk through an appropriate diversification strategy.

[15]See, for instance, Rudiger Dornbusch, "Exchange Rate Economics: Where Do We Stand?" *Brookings Papers on Economic Activity* 1 (1980), 143–185.

[16]For a thorough analysis of this phenomenon see Michael Beenstock, "Forward Exchange Rates and 'Siegel's Paradox,'" *Oxford Economic Papers* 37 (1985), 298–305.

and in the process establish

$$E(S_{t+1}) - F_t = T$$

When the spot-exchange rate is rising and is expected to continue doing so, then the forward rate is likely to underestimate the future spot rate, and vice versa for a falling spot rate. Unless there is a secular trend in the exchange rate, a sufficiently large number of observations would eliminate any measurable bias attributable to transaction cost.

Tests of Market Efficiency

Levich[17] distinguishes between tests of the efficiency of the spot market and tests of forward-market efficiency. One might suppose that the forward market, not the spot market, is the proper instrument of speculative activity. In practice, however, spot and forward exchange rates are sufficiently highly correlated that if you can make money in one you can probably make money in the other.

Rigorous studies of filter rules in foreign exchange have been conducted by Dooley and Shafer.[18] A **filter rule** is a technical model in that it uses only past exchange-rate data to mechanically produce buy or sell signals. An x-percent filter rule might be the following trading strategy: "Buy a currency whenever it rises x percent above its most recent low; sell the currency (or short it) whenever it falls x percent below its most recent peak." Profits could result if the currency's value has momentum, in which significant moves in one direction persuade traders to push it further in the same direction. Dooley and Shafer found that small filters ($x = 1$, 3, or 5 percent) would have been profitable for all nine currencies that they examined for the floating-rate period of the 1970s, even after adjusting for interest expense, interest income, and for bid-offer spreads. Similar results have been found subsequently by others.[19] Technical analysis of a certain kind, it seems, does work. However, in all these studies, it is clear that from time to time the trader following the rules would have lost money, so trading rules are not risk free. To undertake such speculation, you have to have capital, and there is some chance that capital will be reduced or even wiped out. So to use these rules, one has to persuade investors that the profits are high enough to compensate for the risk. The latter profit criterion has not, as far as one can tell, been satisfied.

Other tests have focused on the relationship between the current n-period forward rate, $F_{t,n}$ and the actual future spot rate, S_{t+n}. The simple efficiency or **unbiased-forward-rate hypothesis** is

$$F_{t,n} = E(S_{t+n})$$

If this hypothesis is true, then deviations between $F_{t,n}$ and S_{t+n} should have a mean of zero and be serially uncorrelated.

---

[17]R. M. Levich, "Empirical Studies of Exchange Rates," in R. W. Jones and P. B. Kenen, *Handbook of International Economics,* Vol. 2 (New York: Elsevier Science Publishers, 1985).

[18]M. P. Dooley and J. R. Shafer, "Analysis of Short-Run Exchange Rate Behavior. March, 1973 to November, 1981," in D. Bigman and T. Taya, eds., *Exchange Rate and Trade Instability* (Cambridge, Mass.: Ballinger, 1983).

[19]C. S. Hakkio, "Does the Exchange Rate Follow a Random Walk? A Monte Carlo Study of Four Tests for a Random Walk," *Journal of International Money and Finance* (June 1986), 221–229.

Initial studies by Giddy and Dufey,[20] Cornell,[21] and Levich[22] could not reject the simple-efficiency hypothesis. In recent years, however, researchers have developed more rigorous tests that make the fullest possible use of historical data. Market efficiency does not require that the forward rate be unbiased. Investors may demand a risk premium, γ, on forward contracts. The test of efficiency can be restated as a regression equation of the form

$$S_{t+n} = a + bF_{t,n} + c\gamma + e_t$$

where c, the coefficient of the risk premium, is nonzero. (Simple efficiency would dictate that $a = 0$, $b = 1$, and $c = 0$.) For example, a study by Hsieh[23] found that lagged variables play a role in explaining forward-rate forecasting errors. In this study, the simple efficiency hypothesis was rejected; but is the market really inefficient, or can this deviation be explained by a risk premium?

Unfortunately, tests of market efficiency test two propositions jointly: (1) the underlying model that generates foreign-exchange rate, and (2) the proposition that participants indeed set the forward rate equal to the level dictated by the model. Thus conclusive empirical verification of the existence of market efficiency or of an identifiable risk premium is virtually impossible to achieve. For the existence of a risk premium, the empirical evidence is ambiguous. Cornell[24] and Frankel,[25] using rather different methodologies, came to the conclusion that, with respect to the currencies and sample periods used in their studies, the existence of a risk premium cannot be either supported or denied. On the other hand, Meese and Singleton[26] find evidence of a time-variant risk premium for the Canadian dollar and the German mark, but not for the Swiss franc, during 1976–1979. More recently Frankel and Chinn, using survey data from a panel of seventeen countries, found that the exchange-risk premium was important but highly variable in all

---

[20]I. H. Giddy and G. Dufey, "The Random Behavior of Flexible Exchange Rates," *Journal of International Business Studies,* vol. 6, no. 1, 1–32.

[21]B. Cornell, "Spot Rates, Forward Rates and Exchange Market Efficiency," *Journal of Financial Economics,* vol. 5, 55–65.

[22]R. M. Levich, "On the Efficiency of Markets for Foreign Exchange," in R. Dornbusch and J. Frenkel, eds., *International Economic Policy: An Assessment of Theory and Evidence* (Baltimore: Johns Hopkins University Press, 1979).

[23]Hsieh, David A., "Testing for Nonlinear Dependence in Daily Foreign Exchange Rates," *Journal of Business,* vol. 62, no. 3 (1982), 339–368. Other econometric studies that draw similar conclusions include L. P. Hansen and J. Hodrick, "Forward Exchange Rates as Optimal Predictors of Future Spot Rates: An Econometric Analysis," *Journal of Political Economy,* vol. 88 (1980), 829–853; R. E. Cumby and M. Obstfeld, "A Note on Exchange Rate Expectations and Nominal Interest Rate Differentials: A Test of the Fisher Hypothesis," *Journal of Finance,* vol. 36 (1981), 697–703; C. S. Hakkio "Expectations and the Forward Exchange Rate," *International Economic Review,* vol. 22 (1981), 663–678; and D. Longworth, "Testing the Efficiency of the Canadian Exchange Market Under the Assumption of No Risk Premium," *Journal of Finance,* vol. 36 (1981), 43–50.

[24]Bradford Cornell, "Spot Rates, Forward Rates, and Exchange Market Efficiency," *Journal of Financial Economics* 5 (1977), 55–65.

[25]Jeffrey A. Frankel, "A Test of the Existence of the Risk Premium in the Foreign Exchange Market vs. the Hypothesis of Perfect Substitutability," Federal Reserve System, International Finance Discussion Papers, no. 149 (Aug. 1979).

[26]Richard A. Meese and Kenneth J. Singleton, "Rational Expectations, Risk Premia, and the Market for Spot and Forward Exchange," Federal Reserve System, International Finance Discussion Papers, no. 165 (July 1980).

but a few of the countries.[27] Given the difference in models, statistical techniques, currencies, and sample periods, not to mention the fact that exchange-rate expectations are not directly observable, this inconclusive state of affairs is not surprising. However, once the effect of variances in statistical techniques is removed, the different results for different currencies and sample periods can be plausibly explained by changes in the respective countries' net indebtedness. This factor appears to be one major explanatory variable of risk premium. Because net indebtedness changes over time, one should expect to find a risk premium that is equally unstable.[28] In conclusion, the consensus of research seems to be that there is evidence of a risk premium, but that it is unstable.[29]

SUMMARY

Research in the foreign-exchange markets has come a long way since the days when international trade was thought to be the dominant factor determining the level of the exchange rate. Monetary variables, capital flows, rational expectations and portfolio balance are all now understood to factor into the determination of currencies in a floating-exchange-rate system. Many models have been developed to explain and to forecast exchange rates. No model has yet proved to be the definitive one, perhaps because the structures of the world's economies and financial markets are undergoing such rapid evolution.

Yet there is strong empirical support for the role of arbitrage in global financial markets, and for the view that exchange rates exhibit behavior that is characteristic of other speculative-asset markets. Exchange rates react quickly to news. Rates are far more volatile than changes in underlying economic variables; they are moved by changing expectations, and hence are difficult to forecast. Frankel, in a review of research on exchange rate changes, states that

> *the proportion of exchange rate changes that are forecastable in any manner—by the forward discount, interest rate differential, survey data, or models based on macroeconomic fundamentals—appears to be not just low, but almost zero.*[30]

[27]Jeffery Frankel and Menzie Chinn, "Exchange Rate Expectations and the Risk Premium: Tests for a Cross-Section of 17 Currencies," National Bureau for Economic Research (Cambridge, MA) Working Paper No. 3806, August 1991. See also the survey in Jeffrey Frankel, "Quantifying International Capital Mobility in the 1990s," in D. Bernheim and J. Shoven, eds., *National Saving and Economic Performance* (Chicago: University of Chicago Press, 1991), 227–260.

[28]For a comprehensive review of exchange-rate behavior during the 1970s, see G. Hacche and J. C. Townsend, "A Broad Look at Exchange Rate Movements for Eight Currencies, 1972–80," *Bank of England Quarterly Bulletin* (Dec. 1981), 489–509. For a review of the literature and the theory on exchange-risk premium, see also Jerome L. Stein, M. Rzepczynski, and R. Selvaggio, "A Theoretical Explanation of the Empirical Studies of Futures Markets in Foreign Exchange and Financial Instruments," *The Financial Review* 18 (February 1983), 1–32.

[29]E. Fama, "Forward and Spot Exchange Rates," *Journal of Monetary Economics,* November 1984; and R. J. Hodrick and S. Srivatava, "An Investigation of Risk and Return in Forward Foreign Exchange," *Journal of International Money and Finance* (April 1984). Various empirical results are summarized in R. T. Baillie and P. C. McMahon, *The Foreign Exchange Market: Theory and Econometric Evidence* (Cambridge University Press, 1989).

[30]Jeffery Frankel, "Flexible Exchange Rates: Experience Versus Theory," *Journal of Portfolio Management* (Winter 1989), 45–54.

In a broad sense they are efficient, but tests of efficiency face inherent obstacles in testing the precise nature of this efficiency directly. Rigorously tested academic models have cast doubt on a naive, unbiased-forward-rate theory of efficiency and demonstrated the presence of speculative profit opportunities (for example, by the use of "filter rules"). However, it is also logical to suppose that speculators will bear foreign-exchange risk only if they are compensated with a risk premium. Are the above-zero expected returns excessive in a risk-adjusted sense? Given the small size of the bias in the forward-exchange market, and the magnitude of daily currency fluctuations, the answer is "probably not."

CONCEPTUAL QUESTIONS

1. According to the elasticities approach to exchange-rate determination, what will happen if the economy grows faster, causing more imports? How does this prediction differ from that of the monetary approach to the exchange rate?
2. How does the monetary approach to the exchange rate say the interest rate affects the exchange rate? Why?
3. Explain the difference between the standard monetary approach to the exchange rate and that of Frankel, based on real interest differentials.
4. Under what circumstances is the monetary approach to exchange-rate determination likely to provide a good explanation of exchange-rate behavior?
5. What does it mean to say the foreign-exchange market is "efficient"?
6. Does the efficient market theory imply that the forward rate is a good predictor of the actual spot exchange rate?
7. Does the efficient market theory say that the forward rate is an unbiased predictor of the exchange rate?
8. Why might you expect that the spot exchange rate does *not* follow a random walk?
9. One way of testing for market efficiency is to compile a series of spot and forward exchange rates and see whether the difference between the forward rate and the actual spot rate averages out to zero, with an equal probability of positive and negative errors. What problems might you see with this method of examining the efficiency of the foreign-exchange market?

PROBLEMS

1. Assume that the following is a good model of the determinants of the value of the kwacha (Zambia's currency):

$$s = 1.3(m - m^*) + .5(y^* - y) + .8(r - r^*)$$

where m and y represent natural logs of the money supply and real GNP, and r is the Eurokwacha rate, respectively, in Zambia, and the asterisks represent the corresponding U.S. variables. As before, s is the natural log of the exchange rate, in units of domestic currency per unit of foreign currency.

(a) Can you determine whether the kwacha will rise if the Lusaka government reduces the money supply by 5 percent, thus raising short-term interest rates from 10 percent to 10.5 percent, bringing down the inflation rate without slowing economic growth?
(b) What additional variables might you want to include in this model?

2. You have just conducted a test of the efficiency of the forward-exchange market for Canadian dollars and have estimated the following regression equation:

$$S_{t+n} = .11 + 1.09F_{t,n} + .6\gamma$$

The term γ (gamma) is a risk-premium factor, measured by the percentage surplus (positive) or deficit (negative). You observe that in recent years the trade balance has been in surplus. You may assume that all the coefficients are statistically significant.

Now you are asked to advise a Canadian exporter whether it would pay, in the long run, for him to hedge all his U.S.-dollar-denominated export receivables. Should he? What would he gain or lose by doing so?

3. You are Dutch. Rabobank has set you up with DFl20 million capital to speculate in the foreign-exchange market. Today's spot rate is 1.720 Dutch guilder per U.S. dollar, and the one-month forward is 1.715. The one-month Eurocurrency rates are 9 percent and 7.375 percent in dollars and guilders, respectively. Combining a technical model with your own intuition, you have concluded that the most likely level for the guilder in a month's time is 1.705.

(a) How would you use forward contracts to profit from your prediction?
(b) How would you use the money markets to profit?
(c) Comment on which is the preferred way to profit.

| Application 6.1 | SWEDISH MATCH |

SWEDISH MATCH

You work for Swedish Match. For the past year the company has been subscribing to the Wharton Econoclastics forecasting service to help decide when to hedge its exposure generated from sales to Japan. Now you have been asked to help decide whether to continue with the service. From a pile of fading faxes that were sent monthly from Philadelphia to Stockholm, you have compiled the service's monthly yen/dollar forecasts for the past year.

1. Identify two alternative methods for evaluating the merits of the forecasting service.
2. Using these methods, provide quantitative measures of the forecasting service.
3. What does the performance of the service imply for a company's hedging activities?

Forecast dates		Forecast on "From" date for "To" date	1-month forward rate on "From" date	Spot rate on "To" date	Method 1	Method 2
From	To					
1 Jan	1 Feb	130	127.21	125.4		
1 Feb	1 Mar	131	124.57	124.85		
1 Mar	1 Apr	131	123.85	125.25		
1 Apr	1 May	128	124.17	132.4		
1 May	1 Jun	134	131.30	132.55		
1 Jun	1 Jul	133	131.37	135		
1 Jul	1 Aug	131	133.84	134.55		
1 Aug	1 Sep	131	133.32	125.75		
1 Sep	1 Oct	128	124.48	121.75		
1 Oct	1 Nov	127	120.32	125.85		
1 Nov	1 Dec	129	124.43	129.15		
1 Dec	1 Jan	130	127.63	127		

| **Application 6.2** | MY CURRENCY, RIGHT OR WRONG |

From a financial newspaper (dated no more than five days ago), cut out a journalist's or economist's remarks on the near-term outlook for a particular exchange rate such as DM/$, DM/£, or ¥/$. Use *The Wall Street Journal, The New York Times, The Financial Times, The Economist,* or an equivalent newspaper as your source.

Assignment: Comment on the recent "street" forecast that you selected in one page or less. Attach a copy of the forecast to your answer.

In your analysis, look for consistency among the following:

1. The particular central banks' intervention in the FX market
2. Domestic monetary policy, as indicated by domestic interest-rate actions
3. Economic indicators (such as wage and price pressures described in the back pages of *The Economist*)
4. A "market forecast" indicator

SELECTED REFERENCES

Baillie, Richard T., and Patrick C. McMahon. *The Foreign Exchange Market: Theory and Econometric Evidence.* Cambridge University Press, 1989.

Bergstrand, Jeffrey H. "Selected Views of Exchange Rate Determination After a Decade of 'Floating'." *New England Economic Review.* Federal Reserve Bank of Boston (May/June 1983): 14–29.

Dornbusch, Rudiger. "Exchange Rate Economics: Where Do We Stand?" *Brookings Papers on Economic Activity,* vol. 1 (1980): 143–185.

Frankel, Jeffery A. "On the Mark: A Theory of Floating Exchange Rates Based on Real Interest Differentials." *American Economic Review* (Sept. 1979): 610–622.

Frankel, Jeffery. "Flexible Exchange Rates: Experience Versus Theory." *Journal of Portfolio Management* (Winter 1989): 45–54.

Levich, Richard M. "Empirical Studies of Exchange Rates: Price Behavior, Rate Determination and Market Efficiency," in R. W. Jones and P. B. Kenen, eds., *Handbook of International Economics* (New York: Elsevier Science Publishers, 1985): 979–1040.

Levich, Richard M. "Evaluating the Performance of the Forecasters," in Richard Ensor, ed., *The Management of Foreign Exchange Risk,* 2nd ed. (London: Euromoney Publications, 1982): 121–134.

7

Currency Forwards and the Futures Market

In this chapter we return to foreign-exchange trading. The forward market, we will find, is distinguished by its default risk in addition to market risk. We will see how dealers use the short-term "swap" market to hedge their positions in the forward market. We will learn of some alternative approaches to hedging and the link to the Eurocurrency market. This analysis helps show why it is difficult to hedge long-dated forwards with precision, and why bid-offer spreads are so much wider in the forward market. We will then turn to the futures market—an ingenious alternative to the forward market whenever credit risk is a problem.

EXAMPLE 7.1

Paul Newhart, Foreign Exchange Manager at E.I. du Pont de Nemours & Co., was informed that du Pont was importing 25,000 tons of naphtha from Canada at a total cost of C$11,500,000, to be paid upon delivery in two months' time. To protect his company, he arranged to purchase 11.5 million Canadian dollars *forward* from the Royal Bank of Canada. The two-month forward-contract price was US$0.8785 per Canadian dollar. Two months and two days later, Newhart paid Royal US$10,102,750 in exchange for C$11,500,000. The latter sum was then paid to du Pont's supplier.

The Forward Contract

The example above shows how a forward foreign-exchange contract, used in this case to hedge a future payment in a foreign currency, entails delivery of a certain amount of one currency in exchange for a certain amount of another currency at a certain future date.

A more general definition of a **forward-exchange contract** is a fixed-price contract made today for delivery of a certain amount of a currency at a specified future date. The specified date is the **settlement date.** (See Box 7.1.) The agreed-upon price is termed the **forward rate.** A simple forward contract is illustrated in Figure 7.1.

Typically in such contracts, *no money changes hands today.*[1] The exchange takes place on a future date. Also typically, the

> **BOX 7.1**
> **Settlement-Date Conventions**
>
> By convention, the settlement date for spot transactions is two business days after the trade date. The settlement date for a forward contract is a certain number of days or months *after the spot date.* Thus a three-month forward contract settles in three months plus two business days' time.

---

[1] No money need change hands because the contract is done at an agreed-upon forward rate that both parties think is fair—as long as it's done at the prevailing market rate. If for some reason they arrange to do it at a rate different from the prevailing market rate, an up-front payment will be required. This arrangement may be made, for example, to "unwind" a pre-existing forward contract.

Figure 7.1   *A Forward Transaction Illustrated.*   No money changes hands on the trade date. On the settlement date, either the full amounts are exchanged or the net value paid.

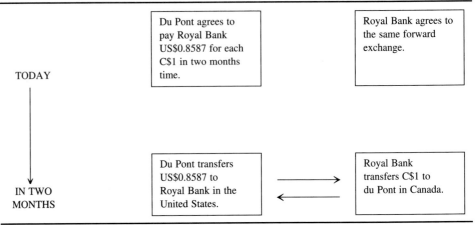

forward contract stipulates that the full amount need not be exchanged on the settlement date. Instead, because the purpose is to hedge against change in the exchange rate, only the difference between the forward rate and the spot rate prevailing on the settlement date will be paid.

Forward-exchange contracts may be used, as in the du Pont example, to *hedge* a future import payment or export receipt. A forward contract can also be used selectively, by companies and others, to implement a view on a currency's direction—in other words, for *speculation*. A bank may engage in a forward contract as a service to a customer such as du Pont; the bank will then offset the forward, seeking to profit from the spread between currency bought and currency sold. A money-market trader may use forwards to *arbitrage* between instruments denominated in one currency and similar instruments denominated in another currency. And a forward combined with a financial asset or liability can effectively transform the currency of denomination of that asset or liability, thus creating *synthetic securities*. We'll encounter each variety in this chapter. They are all variations on a theme—financial-market participants seeking to take advantage of an apparent inefficiency in the currency or money markets.

Forward-exchange contracts are amazingly versatile. They are available in two dozen or more currencies, and for maturities ranging from one week to several years. Yet many market participants shun them. Bond issuers and investors prefer currency swaps because, as we'll see in Chapter 13, they're tailored to coupon-bearing instruments. Banks prefer to hedge with short-term foreign-exchange swaps, because they're more liquid. And many individuals and even institutions are drawn to the currency-futures market, because it entails far less default risk. It is to the latter subject that we must now turn.

Default risk in forward contracts arises because such a contract is a commitment for future performance, and one or the other party may be unwilling or unable to honor that commitment. What would either party have to gain from nonperformance? The answer is that on the settlement date, one party in effect owes the other party a net amount. The net amount, and who owes whom, cannot be determined in advance—it depends on the direction and extent to which the currency has moved in the interim. To see this effect more clearly, let's use a simplified example.

On March 1, A agrees to buy one pound sterling from B three months forward at a price of $1.75. A is doing this to hedge against any movement in the pound during the next quarter. As a convenience to both, they agree that on the settlement date (June 3) only the *net amount* will be exchanged. The net amount is defined to be the difference between the forward rate ($1.75) and the spot rate, whatever it is, in three months' time (June 1). If the pound is above $1.75, B pays A the difference; if the spot rate turns out to be below $1.75, A pays B the difference. Either way, the payment will take place in dollars—again, as a convenience. Table 7.1 shows the possible outcomes.

Today's three-month forward rate is F_0, in domestic units per unit of foreign currency, and S_t is the spot rate on day t.[2] The principal amount of the transaction is Q units of the foreign currency.

On the settlement date B owes A $(S_t - F_0)Q$ or A owes B $(F_0 - S_t)Q$, depending on whether the spot rate is above or below the prearranged forward. If the latter, and if A is a company and B a bank, it's just as though the bank had loaned A some money that was now due for repayment. The risk of default on the amount $(F_0 - S_t)Q$ is the same as though it were a maturing loan. So it is easy to see why bankers think of forward contracts as involving "credit risk," and why they evaluate and limit the extent to which they are willing to expose themselves to default by the counterpart in any forward-exchange agreement. (See Box 7.2 for more details.)

So not everyone qualifies to enter into forward contracts. The little guy, or small company, cannot establish a significant credit line.[3] Even large firms such as investment

Table 7.1   *The Forward Contract*

Time	Agreement between A and B		General forward contract	
Today (time 0); Trade date	A buys £1 forward from B at $1.75		A buys Q units forward from B at forward rate F_0	
In 3 months (time t)	If spot = $1.79	If spot = $1.72	If $S_t > F_0$	If $S_t < F_0$
In 3 months and 2 days (time $t + 2$); Settlement date	Then B pays A $0.04	Then A pays B $0.03	Then B pays A $(S_t - F_0)Q$	Then A pays B $(F_0 - S_t)Q$

---

[2]In an actual forward-exchange agreement, the contract would allow the parties to decide whatever forward rate and settlement date they chose, but would take care to specify which reference spot rate is used at time of settlement. It might be the average of the bid-and-ask spot-rates (two-day delivery) quoted by a prominent bank at a specified location and time, for example, Barclay's London 11 A.M. spot sterling rate.

[3]One way for a smaller concern to obtain a forward trading line is to pledge collateral, in the form of marketable assets such as receivables or cash balances, but that ties up scarce resources.

BOX 7.2

Paperwork and Legalese

Because a forward contract on settlement date resembles a loan at maturity, the lawyers tell banks and their clients to put a lot of credit language into the contracts and to be specific about the terms and conditions of each individual deal. Here are some of the steps involved:

- *Before a trade can take place,* the counterparties have to approve one another's credit. For a bank, this means establishing an internal "line" or limit that authorizes the dealing desk to enter into certain transactions with the customer, perhaps broken down by maturity, settlement date, and other risk-related variables.
- *Once a line is established,* a "master agreement" may be signed by both parties, governing future transactions. This agreement will describe the reference spot rate, events of default, interest to be paid on delinquent payments, and so forth.
- *On the trade date,* the bank trader and her customer reach a verbal agreement on the terms of the trade: "My word is my bond, and I have a tape recording of it to prove what we agreed."
- *Following the trade,* a written confirmation is sent by the bank to the customer by telex or fax.
- *Some time later,* the party or parties to receive payment must specify where they want it (which bank and branch, and account number) if they have not already done so.
- *Two days before the settlement date,* the reference spot rate is obtained and the net amount payable is communicated, and instructions given for two-days-later settlement. (This step is skipped if the full amounts are to be exchanged.)
- *On the settlement date,* the amount or amounts to be paid are transferred by debit and credit of bank accounts.

banks hate to tie up scarce lines of credit granted them by commercial banks. So many people turn to the currency-futures market, which reduces default risk on both sides to a minimum, as a substitute for forward foreign exchange. We'll look at how that market works later in this chapter. Meanwhile, we shall learn more about the forward market, beginning with its use in hedging, speculation, and arbitrage.

Nontransferability and Reversal of Forward Contracts

In principle, forward-exchange contracts could be "securitized" like so many other financial instruments, so that they could be traded in a secondary market. All one would have to do is include a clause in the original agreement stating that the rights and obligations of the contract could be assigned to a third party. This has not happened, for a simple reason: default risk. No bank wants to get up one morning and find that IBM's forward contracts have been sold to Moonlight Tours, a fly-by-night outfit. Transferability without the hazard of deteriorating counterparty creditworthiness would require the other party's approval—that is, establishment of a line of credit, before any transfer could be made effective. This arrangement would be more cumbersome than simply engaging a new contract with the buying party.

On the other hand, corporations do want to get out of forward contracts from time to time, so their master agreement generally specifies how this can be done and at what cost. Briefly, what happens is that the two parties agree on the "net value" of the outstanding forward contract, and a payment is made from one party to the other. Assume, for example, that A and B have entered into a forward contract to sell X million pula (the currency of Botswana) to B at a price of F_0. Sometime before maturity A wishes to cancel the contract. The prevailing forward rate for the same settlement date has risen to F_m. From B's point of view, the contract is "in the money," and he will have to be compensated for canceling it now. The minimum net amount that A will have to pay B is the present value of the difference between the two rates, or $PV(F_m - F_0)$.

If B still grumbles, or if the forward contract lacked cancelation provisions, A can still achieve an *effective cancellation* of the contract without B's cooperation. He does this by going to another bank, say C, and buying X million pula forward at the going rate, F_m. The forward contract has been *reversed*. He has now locked in a future purchase at F_m and sale at F_0, guaranteeing a loss of $F_m - F_0$. In today's dollars, the cost of reversing the forward contract is $PV(F_m - F_0)$.

Forwards in Hedging

Hedging foreign-exchange risk means doing something that reduces one's **foreign-exchange exposure,** or risk of loss from currency fluctuations. The forward-exchange contIract is the classic way to do this, but it is by no means the only one. Money-market instruments, futures, options, and swaps can also be used. As long as the market is efficient, they will all cost about the same. But when imperfections do prevail, the forward-exchange market usually turns out to be the cheapest way to hedge exchange risk. Transactions costs are low, the market is reasonably liquid, and only one cash flow is necessary. There are three kinds of hedging applications:

1. *Hedging transactions exposure* in the forward market simply entails buying or selling foreign exchange for future delivery to match a *known foreign currency payment or receipt,* as in the Figure 7.1 example of du Pont and the Royal Bank. This kind of hedging can also be termed monetary, or contractual, hedging. Both terms convey the idea that the forward sale or purchase is designed to match and offset a foreign-currency cash flow of known amount and date. The forward contract guarantees conversion at a known rate, locking in the amount of domestic currency to be paid or received.

2. *Hedging balance-sheet exposure* means using short-term forward contracts to offset "paper" gains and losses on the long-term assets and liabilities of foreign subsidiaries. The balance sheets, the assets and liabilities, of foreign subsidiaries are valued according to accounting principles applied fairly uniformly across companies, but differing between countries. Depending on the type of business the company is in, the balance sheet may not be a good reflection of the true gains or losses arising from foreign-exchange fluctuations. Nevertheless, these do get recorded as gains or losses in year-end financial statements, and so corporate foreign-exchange managers frequently must hedge part or all of this exposure.

3. *Hedging economic exposure* is trickier than either of the above. It entails estimating neither immediate transactions nor the accounting exposure but rather the effect of an exchange-rate change on the firm's overall profitability. Only that risk then gets hedged. Although the analysis of economic exposure is beyond the scope of this book, the idea is a common-sense one. The economic purpose of an exchange-rate change is to alter consumers' and producers' incentives. Thus a devaluation could stimulate exporters' revenues and those of import-competing companies, *regardless of the currency of denomination of their short-term assets and liabilities.* Economic exposure asks, How might my customers,

my potential customers, my suppliers, and my competitors be affected by an exchange-rate change? Answering this, or attempting to do so, will give an estimate of the true risk that a company faces from a currency movement, and therefore an indication of what to hedge.

EXAMPLE 7.2   The location is St. Louis; the date is July 13. David Guthrie, manager of foreign exchange in Monsanto's treasury department, is seeking to hedge 25 million Norwegian krone to be received from the company's distributor in Perth on August 15. At the spot-exchange rate of NKr6.02 per U.S. dollar, this is worth $4,152,824. A bank has quoted the krone for one-month forward delivery at 6.0345–6.0400. Because Guthrie would be buying dollars, he'd pay the higher of the two prices, namely NKr6.04000, to reap $4,139,073. This is less than the spot-market equivalent, because the krone is trading at a discount in the forward market. Deciding that it's not worth the risk of leaving the receivable un-hedged, Guthrie calls the dealer at Bergen Bank to sell the full 25 million krone for August 15 delivery. He has hedged his long krone position.

EXAMPLE 7.3   Olympia and York, the troubled Canadian property company, owned several buildings in midtown Manhattan in the early 1990s. These were kept on the books as U.S.-dollar-denominated assets, so when the Canadian dollar rose against the U.S. dollar, a loss would be registered. This loss was equal to the assets' value, minus the U.S.-dollar mortgage debt used to finance the properties, times the change in the U.S. unit's value. Rather than suffer such losses, Olympia and York chose to hedge their balance sheet exposure by selling U.S. dollars forward in the one-to-three-month forward market. When these contracts reached maturity, Olympia and York would book the gain or loss and replace the expiring contracts with new ones.

Forwards in Speculation

Nobody speculates. Everybody speculates. Anyone involved in international financial transactions must sooner or later make a decision as to whether and when an exposed position should be covered in the forward market. Forward contracts are thus being used selectively to gain from anticipated rises or falls in a currency's value. Given a firm's "natural" exposure, such as payables from the import of raw materials and receivables from the export of photographic emulsions, the firm's treasury department may decide to leave the exposure unhedged on the grounds that the cost of hedging is too high. This means that an asset is denominated in a foreign currency whose forward rate is at a discount, or a liability is denominated in a currency trading at a premium in the forward market. In effect, the corporate official is saying that he disagrees with the forward mar-ket's assessment of the currency's future. He thinks that the actual rate will be above the forward rate (if he has an asset in the currency) or he thinks the spot will end up below today's forward rate (if he has a liability denominated in the currency). The decision to add or remove forward cover is simply a decision to go long, short, or neutral on the currency, just as one would do if only forward contracts were traded.

Banks claim they do not assume exposure in the forward market the way corporations do. "We match asset and liability positions, purchases, and sale of forward foreign exchange every day." True; but during the day, perhaps only for minutes at a time, currency dealers are of necessity speculators, deciding when and how to hedge an exposed position. The difference lies in their time horizon—and in the fact that they break exposure down into finer components, such as spot risk and swap risk, than do their corporate counterparts.

EXAMPLE 7.4   At Kodak's Rochester headquarters in upstate New York, David Fiedler was assessing the company's exposure to the Japanese yen. For the past month Fiedler had been bullish on the currency, expecting tighter monetary policies on the part of the Bank of Japan. Now, he felt, interest rates had peaked and the hike in oil prices would weaken the Japanese currency. This opinion was reinforced by several short-term technical indicators of the yen's probable movements. Accordingly, he hedged not only Kodak's existing receivables in yen but also shorted another ¥20 billion in the three-month forward market, in anticipation of further receivables that the company would soon obtain.

Forwards in Arbitrage

Covered-interest arbitrage—haven't we seen that before somewhere? Yes, we saw it in Chapter 2, in the context of Eurocurrency trading; in Chapter 5 it was one of the key linkages of international finance; and in Chapter 3 it played a role in the structure of Eurocurrency interest rates. Here we illustrate its role in the determination of the forward-exchange rate. The forward rate is kept in place by those who detect any exploitable deviation from interest-rate parity, in particular those banks whose lines with one another allow them to undertake large forward-exchange transactions rapidly. These transactors can borrow in one currency, convert the funds into the other currency in the spot market, and invest in the other currency. To eliminate exchange risk, they sell the proceeds of the foreign-currency investment forward. If they can do this at a profit they've conducted true arbitrage. *True arbitrage* is a self-contained, profitable set of transactions, which in combination is free of market risk (but perhaps not free of default risk). This is the kind of arbitrage that we encountered in earlier chapters. The technique is illustrated in the accompanying diagram.

Covered-Interest Arbitrage Technique

Borrow in dollars at interest rate $r_\$$ for n days

$$Cost:\ 1\ +\ \frac{r_\$}{360/n}$$

and then:

- change the dollars into deutschemarks at the spot rate S_0
- invest the DM in an n-day instrument at rate r_{DM}
- sell the DM principal and interest forward for settlement in n days' time at forward rate F_0.

$$Revenue:\ \frac{1}{S_0}\left(1\ +\ \frac{r_{DM}}{360/n}\right)F_0$$

At maturity, use the dollar proceeds of the forward sale of DM to repay the dollars borrowed. If the arbitrage is successful, there will be a profit left over.

The profit from the above transaction will be the investment proceeds minus the debt repayment:[4]

$$\Pi = \frac{F_0}{S_0}\left(1 + \frac{r_{DM}}{360/n}\right) - \left(1 + \frac{r_\$}{360/n}\right).$$

At a second level, international investors and borrowers use forward contracts to undertake arbitrage of a different kind: choosing among fixed-income investments or debt denominated in different currencies, made equivalent by covering the foreign-currency cash flows in the forward market. If one is better than the other, a kind of arbitrage profit has been made. But this does not mean anyone can do it; this kind of arbitrage depends on an existing asset or liability being improved upon. It is not a stand-alone transaction entailing both borrowing and lending; rather it is a substitution of one kind of lending or borrowing for another. For this reason we can call it *quasi-arbitrage*.

EXAMPLE 7.5   The dealer at Bergen Bank (Example 7.2) who entered into a forward contract with Monsanto to hedge the company's Norwegian krone exposure decides to use it in a profitable covered-interest-arbitrage transaction. He is able to fund the arbitrage with one-month interbank NKr deposits at 11.14 percent per annum. Using the covered-interest-arbitrage method given above, the dealer's cost in kroner is

$$1 + \frac{.1114}{12} = 1.009283$$

The borrowed kroner are converted into U.S. dollars at the best spot rate he is able to obtain in the market, namely 6.019 kroner per dollar. (Observe that this is his home-currency price for one unit of foreign currency.) The funds are placed in the Eurodollar market for one month at 8 percent per year, and at maturity converted back at the forward rate he quoted Guthrie, 6.04. The proceeds for this are

$$\frac{6.04}{6.019}\left(1 + \frac{.08}{12}\right) = 1.010179$$

The net profit is 0.000896 per krone, or about NKr22,388 for a 25-million-kroner transaction. This is about $3700 in U.S. dollars. Not a fortune, but not bad for ten minutes' work.

EXAMPLE 7.6   Our friend Guthrie has been placing Monsanto's surplus cash in the domestic U.S.-Treasury-bill market. Recently he noticed that U.K.-Treasury-bill rates are much higher: at the three-month maturity, for example, U.K. bills pay 14⅜ compared to 7.36 for U.S. bills. The best spot quotes he has been able to get are 1.8890–1.8900, and the best forward quotes are 1.8564–1.8698. As usual, sterling is quoted in dollars per pound.
    Is there an opportunity to improve his profit without additional risk?

    Answer: For a correct comparison, Guthrie must assume money that would otherwise earn 7.36 percent per annum in the United States would instead be converted into pounds at $1.89, invested at 14.375 percent, and reconverted forward at $1.8564. If left in the

---

[4]Note that this formulation assumes, in accordance with money market convention, simple interest calculations. This works as long as no interest is paid prior to maturity. If interest is paid, it must be compounded.

United States, each dollar would be worth $1.0184 at maturity. If invested in U.K. bills and hedged in the forward market, it would be worth $1.01752 at maturity. So there's no advantage to the switch this time.

Pricing a Forward Contract from Relative Interest Rates

In the last section we talked about true arbitrage, which is easiest to do in the Eurocurrency market. As a result, opportunities for profitable arbitrage seldom (if ever) appear, at least from an outsider's point of view. Indeed, it is clear from the way in which dealers price their quotations and hedge their forward contracts (with swaps, or in the Eurocurrency market) that *forward rates are priced in such a way as to obey covered-interest parity*. So we can take the two sides of the basic arbitrage transaction described in the previous section and set the profit to zero. Therefore we can write

$$1 + \frac{r_\$}{360/n} = \frac{F_0}{S_0}\left(1 + \frac{r_{DM}}{360/n}\right)$$

and solve for the forward rate:

$$F_0 = S_0 \frac{1 + \dfrac{r_\$}{360/n}}{1 + \dfrac{r_{DM}}{360/n}}$$

EXAMPLE 7.7   While sitting with a customer at a tavern in Athens, Sotirios Sikelianos faced an unexpected question. Roughly what rate, the customer wanted to know, could Sotirios' bank quote for three-month forward sale of drachma? The banker paused. The Greek drachma was trading spot at 204.60 to the U.S. dollar. Three-month rates were 8.125 percent in the Eurodollar market and 20.5 percent in the Athens interbank market. Now what was that formula again?

Answer:

$$204.6 \; \frac{1 + \dfrac{.205}{4}}{1 + \dfrac{.08125}{4}} = 210.80 \text{ drachma per dollar}$$

The formula for the forward rate F_0 can be seen as describing the fundamental way in which that rate is determined. It is nothing more than the spot rate, with an adjustment for relative interest rates. Although the interest-rate adjustment takes up most of the space in the formula, it's actually the spot rate that is the most important component. *The spot rate fluctuates far more radically than does the adjustment for the interest-rate differential.* The latter, called the "swap points" by dealers, is the forward premium or discount when expressed as an annualized percentage. This relationship is demonstrated in Figure 7.2, which plots the spot rate and the forward rate on the same graph, along with the forward premium or discount below.

Figure 7.2   *The Forward Rate Tracks the Spot Rate.* The forward premium is shown on a different scale from the spot and forward rates.

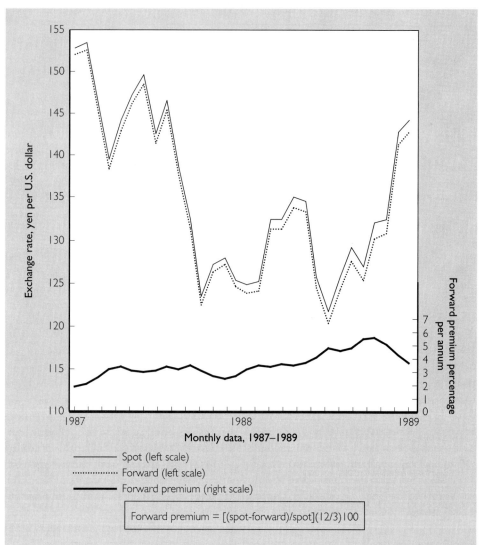

Monthly data, 1987–1989

———— Spot (left scale)
············· Forward (left scale)
━━━━ Forward premium (right scale)

Forward premium = [(spot-forward)/spot](12/3)100

Forwards and Foreign-Exchange Swaps

In Chapter 2 we learned that professional foreign-exchange dealers do not normally use forward contracts to hedge their own exposures; instead, they typically employ a combination of a spot transaction and a foreign-exchange "swap." A swap in this context means a simultaneous agreement to buy spot and sell forward, or vice versa. Let us review briefly how this is done, and why.

Assume that a bank foreign-exchange dealer has just agreed to purchase deutsche-marks in exchange for dollars for delivery in six months from a customer. From the very moment that the transaction is agreed to, when the dealer says "Done!" his bank is at risk. The dealer has an *open position*. Perhaps this is deliberate; perhaps he thinks the mark will rise. But the magnitude and unpredictability of unexpected news will normally persuade a dealer to hedge the bulk of his open positions within hours, if not minutes, of the transaction. The chief dealer will normally impose guidelines as to what magnitude of risk may be taken, and by whom. From our discussion on the forward rate and from Figure 7.2, we see that fluctuations in the forward rate are attributable to two variables:

1. Fluctuations in the spot rate, which account for most of the risk.
2. Fluctuations in the swap points, arising from slower-moving changes in relative interest rates.

The dealing room separates the management of these two kinds of risk. Following the dealer's forward purchase of DM, he faces substantial currency risk. His immediate concern is to eliminate the most important component of his risk—the component attributable to the spot-rate fluctuations. Therefore, he enters into a *spot* contract equal and opposite to his *forward* contract. In other words, having bought DM forward for six months delivery), he sells DM spot (for two-day delivery). Breathing easier, he can now deal with the other component of the risk: the "basis" between the spot and forward rates, the swap points.

To hedge changes in the swap points, a dealer engages in a swap contract. Where's the best place to find someone to enter simultaneously into a spot purchase and forward sale of foreign exchange? Why, it's among those who do covered-interest arbitrage between deposits denominated in different currencies, namely the Eurocurrency traders. Indeed, there is a subspecialty of people who trade not foreign exchange per se, not plain Eurocurrency deposits, but the *difference* between Eurocurrency rates linking the spot and forward exchange markets. These are called *FX swap dealers*. The DM dealer's job is to do a swap that entails buying DM spot and selling DM six months forward. Then both components of this risk will be hedged, with any luck, at a profit. The second half of his swap contract, selling DM forward in exchange for dollars, will match the forward purchase that started this process

To sum up, the foreign-exchange dealer undertook a total of three transactions:

- He bought DM forward (six-month delivery).
- He sold DM spot (two-day delivery).
- He did a swap, spot against six months, meaning a spot purchase (two-day delivery) and a forward sale (six-month delivery).

In two days' time, the spot sale and the spot purchase that are part of the swap will offset one another, leaving the dealer with the forward purchase and countervailing sale.

That's how an FX swap works in forward contracts. The swap is such an integral part of forward contracts that, as noted, it has its own traders, and forward rates are not quoted "outright" but rather as a number of points above or below the spot rate. We saw how to interpret them in Chapter 2. As a reminder, a swap screen is reproduced in Table 7.2.

Swap dealers trade not the currency itself but the *difference* between the spot and forward rate. This difference is determined by the interest-rate differential between two Eurocurrency markets. So swap traders are more concerned about Eurocurrency interest rates than they are about the foreign-exchange market. Any movement in the Eurodollar or the Eurodeutschemark six-month rate would affect the swap quotation that our dealer would encounter in the transaction outlined above. How, precisely? To answer that, let's derive the swap points for the formula for the forward rate given earlier.

$$\text{Swap points} = \text{Forward} - \text{Spot}$$

$$\text{Swap points} = S_0 \left[\frac{1 + \dfrac{r_{\$}}{360/n}}{1 + \dfrac{r_{\text{DM}}}{360/n}} - 1 \right]$$

Table 7.2   *Foreign-Exchange Quotations.*   This is a typical monitor in a foreign-exchange dealing room.

```
              INTERBANK FOREIGN EXCHANGE

                    SPOT        1 MO      3 MOS      6 MOS      12 MOS

      1113  DMK   182  40/50    39/37    107/105    202/198    290/282

      1114  SFC   153  60/75    32/29     96/93     197/191    372/352

      1112  FFR   607  10/20   113/121   345/365    675/700   1265/1340

      1115  DFL   206  10/30    38/37    105/102    199/195    281/271

      1116  YEN   153  08/18    27/25     85/82     172/168    280/270

      1110  CAN   133  22/25    11/13     25/28      86/92     180/200

      1111  STG   154  15/25    57/56    162/160    293/289    589/590

      1117  ECU   113  22/32
```

As usual the spot rate is defined in dollars per unit of the foreign currency, so the swap points will be quoted that way, too. If the spot rate used in the above equation is quoted in European terms, such as guilders per U.S. dollar, the result in swap points will be in fractions of the guilder.

EXAMPLE 7.8   One morning in London the ECU was quoted spot at 1.3375–1.3385 (dollars per ECU). Quotations for three-month Eurodollar and Euro-ECU were 8⅛–8 and 10⅛–10, respectively. What bid and offer swap points should a dealer quote? Be conservative; that is, assume you have to buy at the offer price and sell at the bid price.
Answer: The actual swap points quoted were .0070–.0068 from the *Financial Times*.

The Dealer's Book

To keep track of its various transactions and the risks they entail, the foreign-exchange dealing room maintains a "book" or accounting of outstanding positions. A simplified position book representing a dealer's French-franc position is shown below.

DEALING ROOM: FRENCH-FRANC POSITION

Long		Short	
FF-deposits owned	XX	FF-deposits issued	XX
FF bought spot	XX	FF sold spot	XX
FF bought forward	XX	FF sold forward	XX
Total Long	XX	**Total Short**	XX

Figure 7.3 *Profit-Profile Diagram.* This graph shows the gains and losses on a forward contract arising from currency movements.

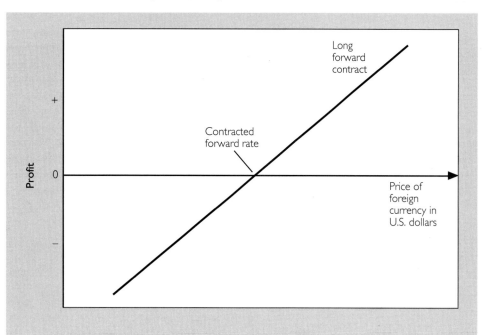

From the table one can see that a "long" position is like an asset, and a "short" position is like a liability. When you own something you gain if its price rises; when you owe something, you gain when its price falls. Thus we can define the two positions as follows:

> A **long position** is any contract whose value rises when the underlying instrument's price rises, and vice versa.
>
> A **short position** is any contract whose value rises when the underlying instrument's price falls, and vice versa.

Any short position can be used to offset any long position of equal amount, to provide a rough hedge. Of course, a three-month deposit owned is not going to behave exactly like French francs sold spot, so one is not perfectly hedged simply by matching long and short positions in French francs. The relative movements of different long or short positions depend in large part on movements in interest rates. Matching hedges the gross movements in the spot value of the currency. As shown in the previous sections, this spot movement accounts for most of the risk in a currency position that entails future delivery.

A useful way to look at the dealer's position in any particular instrument, including spot, forward, deposit, futures, and options positions, is the *profit-profile diagram*. Figure 7.3 profiles the potential gains or losses from a long forward contract in French francs. If the market forward rate is above the contracted forward rate, the dealer has a profit; if below, a loss. The amount of gain or loss is the present value of the difference between the contracted forward rate and the prevailing forward rate for the same delivery date.

Hedging a Forward Position

We can use the stylized position sheet and the profit-profile diagram to show how a dealer might use the swap market to hedge a forward contract.

Our FX dealer starts the day by agreeing to buy 10 million Swiss francs forward, for settlement in six months, from a customer. Her initial position is shown in the position sheet and profit profile in Figure 7.4. The obvious way to hedge this forward position is by means of an equal and opposite forward contract. If she were able to find one quickly, where she could sell Swissies at a higher price than what she paid for them, that would be great. The position sheet would show a "Sold 6 mo forward SF10m" on the short side, and the dealer's market risk will have been eliminated. The trouble is that the market for outright forward contracts is somewhat illiquid, so the dealer might have to wait a few hours or even days before a profitable contract comes along, perhaps from another customer who wants to buy Swiss francs. Meanwhile the market is moving; if the Swiss franc falls, the dealer will have lost proportionately. Her book is "marked to market" at least daily, showing any gain or loss in the value of her positions from day to day. (You don't wait until maturity in this business to find out whether you're a winner or a loser!)

So we must find a way to hedge the position more quickly. The spot market is the most liquid of the foreign-exchange markets, so that's the place to turn. Even though it does not perfectly offset the forward contract on her book, selling the same amount of currency spot will match long and short positions and, we have seen, take care of the bulk of the risk. (See Figure 7.5.)

The next step is to hedge the differential between the spot rate and the forward rate. This difference is the swap rate. The easiest way to hedge the swap rate is with a swap contract. So our dealer enters into a swap contract with another dealer or perhaps with her own Eurocurrency trading desk, which frequently has need of a swap to be able to take deposits in one currency and place them in another. The swap means buying spot and simultaneously selling forward. She's now fully hedged, as is shown in Figure 7.6. After two days, the spot contracts will have cleared and all that remains is the two mutually offsetting forward contracts.

Figure 7.4   *Hedging a Forward Position: Step 1*

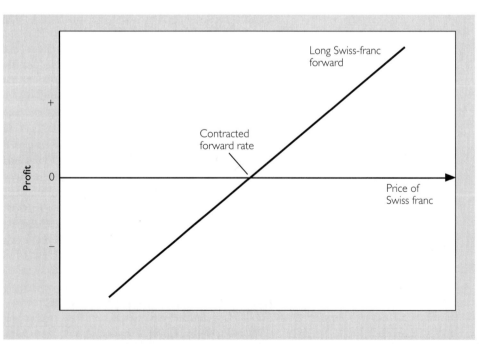

Figure 7.5 *Hedging a Forward Position: Step 2*

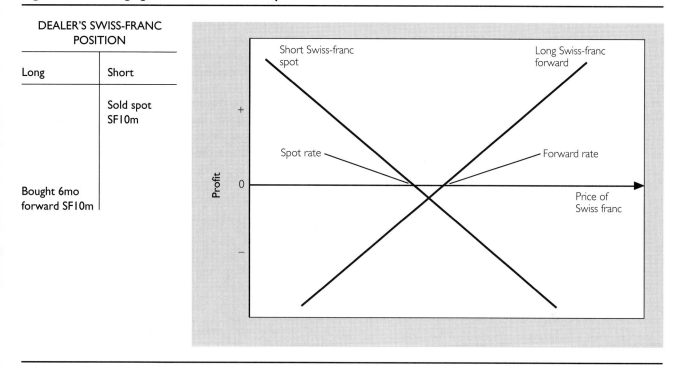

DEALER'S SWISS-FRANC POSITION

Long	Short
	Sold spot SF10m
Bought 6mo forward SF10m	

Short Swiss-franc spot

Long Swiss-franc forward

Spot rate

Forward rate

Profit

0

+

−

Price of Swiss franc

Figure 7.6 *Hedging a Forward Position: Step 3*

DEALER'S SWISS-FRANC POSITION

Long	Short
Swap: Bought spot SF10m	Sold spot SF10m
	Swap: Sold 6 mo forward SF10m
Bought 6mo forward SF10m	

The Swap:
Short forward and long spot

Short Swiss-franc spot

Long Swiss-franc spot

Spot rate

Forward rate

Profit

0

+

−

Price of Swiss franc

Net effect: neutral

Six Ways to Hedge

At this point we have discussed two alternative ways in which the dealer could hedge her Swiss-franc position: selling francs forward, or by a spot-plus-a-swap transaction. Her choices are not limited to these. Depending on price and liquidity, two other well-accepted methods could be used. These are the money-market hedge and the roll-over hedge.

1. The **money-market hedge** is perhaps the most obvious alternative: it is nothing other than covered-interest arbitrage in the Eurocurrency market, using an advantageously priced forward contract as the starting point. In execution it is the same as the spot-plus-swap hedge, except that for the swap we substitute borrowing in one Eurocurrency and placing the funds in another. As one can see from Figure 7.7, at maturity the banker will be receiving dollars and paying Swiss francs, precisely offsetting the customer forward.

2. The **rollover hedge** uses a spot transaction, plus a swap, but instead of using a six-month swap to match the six-month forward, the dealer does a one- or three-month swap and "rolls it over" (replaces it with a new one) at the initial swap's maturity. Figure 7.8 illustrates the technique. The rationale is again liquidity: the short-term swap market is more liquid than longer-term swap markets. There is slightly more risk, because the swap rate may have changed as a result of a change in the interest differential, but this may also be what the dealer anticipates. The swap dealer's job is to understand and manage interest-differential risk.

The dealer can, and sometimes will, hedge an outright forward by using *currency futures* or even a combination of *currency options*. But we'll discuss the methods and risks of these later.

Figure 7.7   *The Money-Market Hedge*

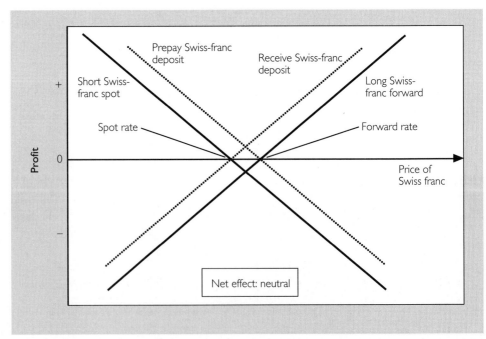

DEALER'S SWISS-FRANC POSITION	
Long	Short
Euro-SF deposit: Receive SF10m	Sold spot SF10m
Bought 6mo forward SF10m	Euro-SF deposit: Repay SF10m

Figure 7.8 *Rolling Over a Swap to Hedge a Forward Contract*

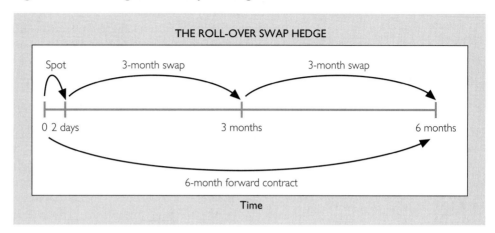

Long-Dated Forwards

The active forward and foreign-exchange swap markets are in the short maturities. Few dealers quote rates beyond a year's maturity and the most liquid markets are in the one-to-three-month range. Quotations are given for as long as 10 years out, as shown in Table 7.3. The table shows a set of actual quotations; these are indicative of the quotes that are used in deals typically done on an ad hoc basis.

There are several reasons for the dearth of long-dated forward contracts:

1. *Credit risk.* The further out you go, the more likely it is that unanticipated circumstances might undermine the ability of your counterparty to honor his contract, and the more is at risk, because longer time means the exchange rate can move more.
2. The *difficulty of hedging.* The bank providing the contract can find the spot component of the hedge easily enough, but long-term FX swaps are scarce because covered interest arbitrage in the Eurocurrency market is inactive beyond a year or two.

Table 7.3 *Long-Dated Forward-Exchange Quotations.* These quotations exhibit bid-offer spreads much wider than in the shorter maturities, and liquidity is low.

METROBANK LONG-DATED FX

	SPOT	2 YEAR	3 YEAR	4 YEAR	5 YEAR	7 YEAR	10 YEAR
STG	1.8900/10	1625/1525	2200/2000	2650/2425	3000/2750	3800/3200	5000/4100
SF	1.3080/90	200/50	500/250	800/500	1180/775	1950/1350	3000/2000
DM	1.5760/70	100/200	25/200	−150/+100	300/P	900/200	1300/400
JY	143.75/85	120/P	295/145	550/350	875/650	1750/1150	1800/1900
FFR	5.1700/50	1800/1950	2300/2650	2600/3100	2800/3400		
HFL		100/200	P/200	−100/+200	−300/+100		

3. *Money- and bond-market instruments that might be used to hedge a long-dated position normally carry periodic interest rates.*[5] This means that the interest payment, which is not matched by the forward contract, must be hedged separately or left unhedged, making the deal more complicated and risky. In the early 1980s, the currency-swap technique emerged as a means by which the principal and coupons on an interest-bearing instrument could be hedged.[6]

4. For many purposes, *the currency swap market does the job better.*

This said, long dates, as they are called by some, still serve a useful function. They are the best available instruments for hedging a precise amount at a precise date in the future. A Japanese utility, for example, might wish to hedge the dollar cost of a long-term oil-supply contract by selling dollars for yen several years into the future. Another common application is to convert the principal payment of a dual-currency bond—one where the interest payments are one currency, but the principal is in another.

Hedging Long-Dated Forwards

Those few foreign-exchange dealers willing to make a market in long-dated forwards hedge them in much the same way as ordinary forward contracts, except that it is much more of a headache to do so, and more risky. Consequently, spreads in the long-dated market far exceed those in the near-term markets. As is exemplified in Figure 7.9, bid-offer spreads in the ten-year market can exceed 5 percent, compared to one-twentieth of one percent in the spot market for sterling.

Beginning with hedging like with like, if it's hard to find a ready counterparty for a near-term forward, it's doubly so for a long-dated forward. Moreover, unlike in the short dates, there is virtually no interbank market for foreign-exchange swaps beyond a year or so.

Certainly the *money-market hedge* is a possibility. The dealer would issue a liability in one currency, change the funds spot, invest in the second currency, and use the existing long-dated forward contract to hedge the repayment of the liability. But when we get a little further out in maturities, this means issuing debt that is equivalent to a bond, and then tying up the bank's funds for a not-insignificant period. In today's environment of more severe capital standards, this would require more equity or other forms of subordinated capital to be assigned to the dealer's needs, which might make the profitability of the deal questionable.

The *currency-swap technique* (discussed in Chapter 13) involves the exchange of coupons and principal in one currency or coupons and principal in another. It avoids some of the capital burden imposed by actual assets and liabilities while mimicking their behavior, so it is not uncommon for the long-dated forward book to be merged in some fashion with the currency-swap position in some dealing rooms.

Even if the asset-and-liability approach were not undesirable for other reasons, there is the problem of interest payments mentioned earlier. The bank will be receiving interest in one currency and paying it in another, with all the exchange risk that entails. It would be better to do a money-market hedge as it's done in the money market—with *zero-coupon claims*. But that means searching an even smaller universe for suitable assets and liabilities.

---

[5]Eurocurrency deposits, for example, typically pay interest semiannually.

[6]See Chapter 13 on currency swaps.

Figure 7.9 *Bid and Offer Quotations in the Long-Dated Forward Market.* Note how the spread widens, from .05% to 6.34%, as the contract maturity lengthens.

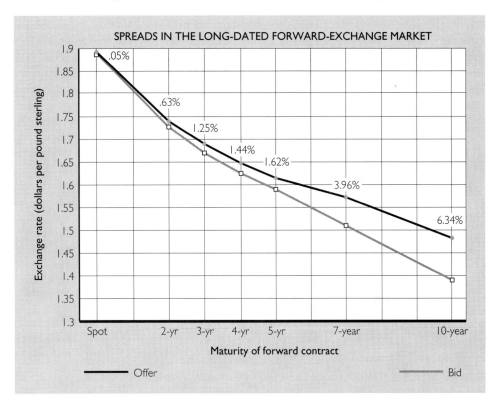

Consequently, the dealer who takes on a long-dated forward contract must almost certainly employ an imperfect hedge. The usual approach is a *rollover hedge,* using short-term swaps repeatedly rolled over or short-term money-market hedges, when available. This means a fairly high degree of risk of interest-differential changes. To cushion these risks, banks must necessarily quote disproportionately wide bid-offer spreads in the long-dated forward market.

Currency Futures

Outside of the interbank forward market, the best-developed market for hedging exchange-rate risk is the currency-futures market. Currency futures are widely used by corporations, banks, and securities firms, sometimes in preference to forward contracts. This section aims to show why this may be the case, and to establish the link between the forward and the futures market.

We may define the **futures contract** as a standardized agreement with an organized exchange to buy or sell some item, such as a currency or commodity, at a fixed price at a certain date in the future. Some contracts, notably foreign-currency futures, provide for cash delivery; others, such as Eurodollar futures, are based on some reference price and allow only for cash settlement at maturity. The purpose of futures is not to obtain delivery but to replicate, without credit risk, the gains or losses that would occur from an equivalent forward contact. In principle, currency futures are similar to foreign-exchange forwards in that they are contracts for delivery of a certain amount of a foreign currency at some future date and at a known price. In practice, most futures contracts are terminated prior to maturity and they differ from forward contracts in other important ways, as summarized in Table 7.4.

A forward contract is like a tailored suit, available only to those with good credit. Futures are like off-the-rack suits, designed and priced for the man in the street. Foreign-exchange forwards are typically done in amounts of $5 million and above, while futures contracts cover amounts in the $50,000–$100,000 range. On the other hand, many of the features that make futures suitable for individual traders make them useful to professionals, too.

Figure 7.10 contains a reproduction of the currency-futures quotations that may be found in most business newspapers. These futures are contracts for delivery of a standard amount of a foreign currency in exchange for delivery of a given amount of U.S. dollars at some future date. The funds to be exchanged may be, for example, 125,000 German marks in exchange for the equivalent value in dollars. The figure offers a guideline for interpretation of published futures quotations. As in the forward market, each delivery takes place in the country of the currency,[7] although as a matter of practice few deliveries actually occur. The futures contract can be used to hedge, speculate, or perform arbitrage in much the same way as forwards are used. Many commercial and investment banks are members of the major futures exchanges and are able to buy currencies in the forward market and sell them in the futures markets, and vice versa, ensuring that futures prices stay in line with forward prices for the same delivery date.

Table 7.4   *Comparison of Forward and Futures Contracts*

	Forward Contract	Futures Contract
Size	Tailored to needs; generally $5 million equivalent or more	Standardized; typically in the range of $50,000–$100,000
Range of Currencies	Approximately fifty currencies, including most European and Pacific Basin currencies; in principle, any currency for which an accessible money market exists	Only major, liquid currencies. For example, on the Chicago International Monetary Market: yen, German mark, Canadian dollar, sterling, Swiss franc, and Australian dollar.
Maturity	Tailored to needs; from 1 week to 10 years	Standardized; typically four settlement dates per year
Settlement	Actual delivery, or offset with cash settlement	Usually by cash settlement; even when physical delivery is possible, few actually settle
Cost	No fee. Cost is spread between market maker's buy and sell price	No spread. Negotiated brokerage commissions for executing trades
Regulation	Self-regulating (apart from normal prudential supervision of banks)	Regulated by exchange rules and by some form of government agency
Credit	Credit risk of future delivery can be substantial; requires lines of credit	Credit risk largely eliminated by use of margin deposit and daily cash settlement of profits or losses

---

[7]For more details, see Chapter 2.

Figure 7.10   ***Currency Futures Dissected.***   This chart explains the components of a currency futures listing.

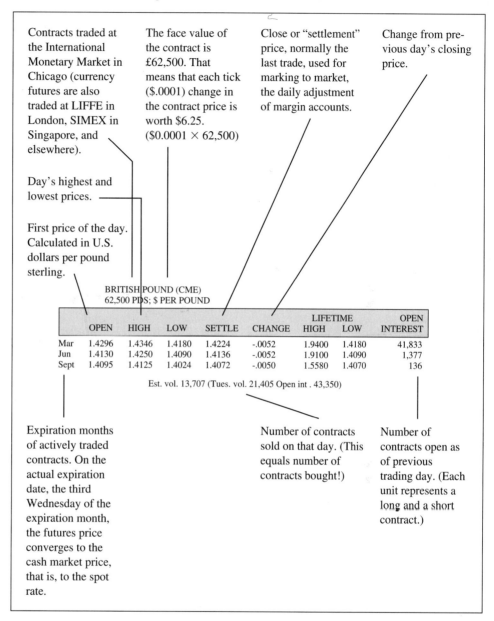

Contracts traded at the International Monetary Market in Chicago (currency futures are also traded at LIFFE in London, SIMEX in Singapore, and elsewhere).

The face value of the contract is £62,500. That means that each tick ($.0001) change in the contract price is worth $6.25. ($0.0001 × 62,500)

Close or "settlement" price, normally the last trade, used for marking to market, the daily adjustment of margin accounts.

Change from pre-vious day's closing price.

Day's highest and lowest prices.

First price of the day. Calculated in U.S. dollars per pound sterling.

BRITISH POUND (CME)
62,500 PDS; $ PER POUND

	OPEN	HIGH	LOW	SETTLE	CHANGE	LIFETIME HIGH	LOW	OPEN INTEREST
Mar	1.4296	1.4346	1.4180	1.4224	-.0052	1.9400	1.4180	41,833
Jun	1.4130	1.4250	1.4090	1.4136	-.0052	1.9100	1.4090	1,377
Sept	1.4095	1.4125	1.4024	1.4072	-.0050	1.5580	1.4070	136

Est. vol. 13,707 (Tues. vol. 21,405 Open int . 43,350)

Expiration months of actively traded contracts. On the actual expiration date, the third Wednesday of the expiration month, the futures price converges to the cash market price, that is, to the spot rate.

Number of contracts sold on that day. (This equals number of contracts bought!)

Number of contracts open as of previous trading day. (Each unit represents a long and a short contract.)

An important advantage of futures contracts is liquidity, and liquidity requires stan-dardization. Forwards are for any amount, as long as it's big enough to be worth the dealer's time, whereas futures are for standard amounts, each contract being far smaller than the average forward transaction. Futures are also standardized in terms of delivery date. The normal currency futures delivery dates are March, June, September, and De-cember, whereas forwards are private agreements that can specify any delivery date that the parties choose. Both of these features allow the futures contract to be tradable.

Another difference is that forwards are traded by phone and telex and are completely independent of location or time. Futures, on the other hand, are traded in organized exchanges such as the LIFFE in London, SIMEX in Singapore, the IMM in Chicago,

Figure 7.11   *Trading Volume on Futures Exchanges.*   This graph shows the percentages of the average daily total volume of 1.6 million contracts in 1990.

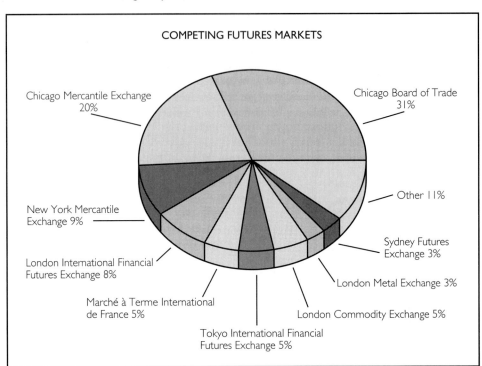

the MATIF in Paris, the DTB in Frankfurt, the HKFE in Hong Kong, and exchanges in Australia and New Zealand. (Figure 7.11 provides an idea of the relative volume of futures contracts of all kinds traded in different markets around the world.) Futures traders reach agreements with one another, but the counterparty in all trades is not the other trader but rather the "clearing house," the association of members of the exchange.

The most important feature of the futures contract is not its standardization or trading organization but the *time pattern of the cash flows* between parties to the transaction. In a forward contract, whether it involves full delivery of the two currencies or just compensation of the net value, the transfer of funds takes place once: at maturity. With futures, cash changes hands every day during the life of the contract, or at least every day that has seen a change in the price of the contract. *This daily cash-compensation feature largely eliminates default risk.*

Futures as Daily Recontracted Forwards

Let us explain this important point more fully. Futures contracts evolved from forwards. When commodities futures exchanges first came into existence in the 1860s in the midwest of America, the exchange was merely a centralized location where traders could come together to buy or sell specified forward contracts on agricultural goods—agreements to deliver or receive specific amounts of agricultural commodities at future dates at prices fixed now. In time, the exchanges began to play an intermediary role and to develop more efficient means of settlement and risk management over the life of the contract. Today, the difference between the forward and futures markets is that in the forward market, a profit (or loss) is realized on the maturity date, whereas in the futures market all profits and losses must be settled on a daily basis. This procedure, called **marking to market,** requires that funds change hands each day. The funds are added to, or subtracted from, a mandatory **margin** account that traders are required to maintain. In contrast, in the forward market no money changes hands until delivery occurs at maturity.

In an earlier section we learned that a forward contract can have a *value*. The value is determined by the difference between the original forward rate and the forward rate prevailing today for the same delivery date. More precisely, it is the present value of that difference, multiplied by the face amount of the contract. If a forward contract is terminated, the party who has gained (the forward is "in the money") pays the party who has lost (the forward is "out of the money"). Now assume that on Monday you and I agree to enter into a forward contract at $0.85 per Canadian dollar for delivery on December 15. On Tuesday we cancel the contract and I pay you (or you pay me) the value, as determined by the change in the forward rate for December 15 delivery. That same day we reenter into the same contract again. On Wednesday we settle the gain or loss and recontract for December 15 delivery once again! We continue this cumbersome procedure every day until the delivery date. Thus we are, in effect, "marking to market" the forward contract daily, making a cash compensation, *and reducing our credit exposure to one day's movement in the exchange rate*. That is precisely what a futures contract does. The daily payment is equal to the change in value of the forward rate for the given delivery date. The change in value is determined by the closing price—that is, by the price at which the last trade was done at the end of each trading day. In summary, futures contracts are forward-exchange contracts that are recontracted daily.

A forward contract that is recontracted daily in this way, with daily cash settlement, reduces the two counterparties' exposure to default risk to one day's movement in the forward-exchange rate. To eliminate even this risk, the futures exchanges take two further steps: (1) They require that both parties to a trade place funds or securities in a *margin account* to which each day's gains will be added or from which losses will be subtracted. The size of this margin account is based on the maximum potential daily movement in the currency. (2) Once the price of the trade is agreed, the exchange itself, backed by members' capital, becomes the legal counterparty to each party to the trade.[8] These steps ensure that nobody entering into a futures contract has to be concerned with the creditworthiness of the person or firm on the other side of the trade.

In summary, futures contracts provide a means of managing currency risk without also incurring credit risk, unlike the forward technique. Similarly, when you use futures, you are not asking a bank to take on *your* credit risk.

Margin and Marking to Market

Assume a buyer of a DM future contract agrees on a price with a seller. Once the deal is struck, the buyer and the seller each pay to the exchange an initial deposit or margin that the exchange will hold as security against each party's market position. The margin account is designed to be sufficient to meet the largest possible day's loss, so the size of this initial deposit varies with the volatility of the instrument.

---

[8]More specifically, the **clearing house** is an organization that holds exchange members' accounts and clears trades and marked-to-markets payments. Once a trade is confirmed, the clearing house guarantees fulfillment of each contract. To support this guarantee, the clearing house sets membership standards, operates a margining system, monitors daily positions, and maintains a guarantee fund that can be called upon in the event of default of one or more members (not an unheard-of event).

If the initial margin falls to a pre-set level, the trader is asked to replenish his margin account to its previous level. This additional margin is called **variation margin.**

Many exchanges operate a system of price limits and trading halts. If the price of a futures contract moves by an unusually large amount during the trading day, thereby reaching the *price limit* set by the exchange, additional variation margin is immediately called and trading may be halted for a short period. The purpose of such a price limit is to ensure that variation margin is collected more frequently when the market is moving rapidly, thus reducing the risk of a default. The value of limits is doubtful, however, because participants may panic as they perceive that they will be unable to trade when the limit is hit, so they try to get out earlier than they would otherwise. This puts additional pressure on the system and drives the price further toward the limit.

Two business days before settlement date, the futures price must equal the cash (spot) price of the currency, because at that point both contracts specify delivery of the same thing on the same day. Hence the payment required on the maturity date to buy the underlying currency is simply its spot price at that time. The futures trader's total gain or loss will equal the difference between the futures price (or forward rate) and the spot-exchange rate on the date of maturity of the contract, multiplied by the amount of the contract.

Contract positions may be reversed or closed out at any time by an offsetting transaction, so that a buyer of a futures contract can eliminate his obligation to ultimately buy the currency by selling an equal number of identical contracts, and a seller can eliminate his obligation to sell by buying contracts. Indeed, only a small number are actually held to delivery.

EXAMPLE 7.8   Let us demonstrate the marking-to-market and margin-account features with an example, illustrated in Figure 7.12.

You are the assistant treasurer of Underware, a U.S. software company. Assume you have a payment of DM2.5 million coming in one month from now. Rather than use up your scarce lines of credit with your bank, you'll use the futures market to hedge. Your DM receivable is a long position in marks, so to hedge you must sell, or go short, the German-mark futures contract.

You call a discount broker to open a futures account. He tells you that for each "round trip" (purchase and sale, or sale and purchase) in DM futures you will pay a commission of $25 per contract. He also asks for some money to keep in your "margin account," out of which payments will come and into which receipts will be placed. (At this time the amount is $2000 per contract, each contract being for DM125,000.) You send him the money and ask him to sell 20 German-mark futures contracts for March delivery. He reminds you that as a futures trader, you do not have to worry about any other trader's creditworthiness, because you are dealing with the exchange. The exchange itself minimizes its credit exposure by insisting on daily settlement of gains and losses, so the maximum it can be owed is one day's price movement.

A future on DM125,000 is quoted in dollar terms—that is, as 0.XXXX U.S. dollars per German mark. The contract has a minimum permissible price movement (known as a tick) of 0.01 cents. This represents $12.50 for each DM125,000 contract, so multiplying the number of ticks by $12.50 gives the dollar change in a DM contract's value.

The broker calls back to tell you that he has sold 20 March contracts for you at 6456 (at $0.6456 per German mark). The March contract has 25 trading days to run before delivery. He explains that if the value of the German-mark futures contract falls during the course of a day, you, the seller of a futures contract, receive cash in the amount of the fall multiplied by the number of contracts you sold. If it rises, you lose, and must pay

Figure 7.12 *The Marking to Market of a Futures Contract.* Settlement of the gains and losses is done daily.

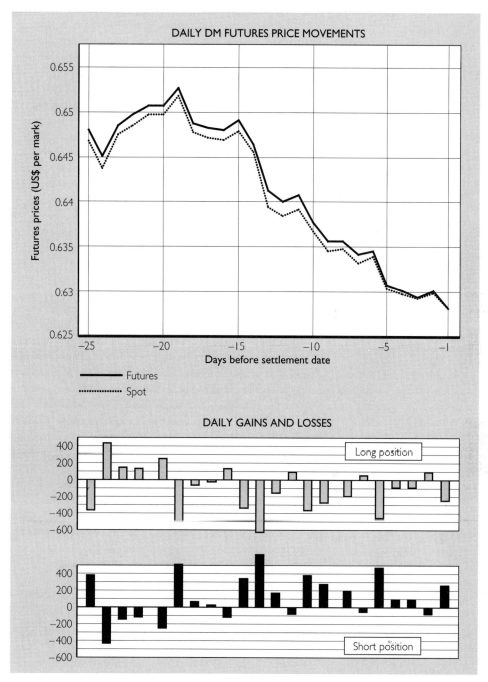

the loss to the clearing house, which transfers it to someone who has bought DM futures. This settlement happens every day for the day's change in price up to the final day of the contract.

Over the course of the 25 trading days, as the diagram in Figure 7.12 illustrates, the DM fluctuates both down and up. Each time it moves down, your account is credited and the person who bought the contract, who has a long position, has his account debited. When the DM futures price rises, you are debited and the "long" is credited. The changes in your account, and that of the opposite party, are shown in the lower part of Figure 7.12. On the first day the mark moves down, and your account is credited. For the next three days the currency rises, and your account is debited. At the end, the sum of the individual changes equals the total move in the currency. It is in this manner that the future contract hedges you against an adverse move in the German mark. In fact, over the whole 25 days the mark futures fell from $0.6456 to $0.6290.

The total profit or loss realized by the long trader who buys a contract at time *0* and closes, or reverses, it at time *t* is equal to the change in the futures price over the period $F_t - F_0$. Symmetrically, the short trader earns $F_0 - F_t$. Because the future contract does its job of hedging against the bulk of your currency risk by means of daily debits and credits, there is no need for you to deliver the German marks or take delivery of the dollars, and you decide to buy 20 DM futures three days before the March settlement day, thus eliminating your position. You are able to do so at a price of 6300. In all, the contract has moved down a total of 156 ticks, giving you a gain of $1950 per contract. This offsets the loss you have taken on your outstanding DM-denominated receivable.

Basis Risk in Futures Hedging

By reducing credit risk to a minimum, the futures market allows the participation of a much wider range of institutions and even individuals in the currency market. Because futures are standardized and have a limited number of delivery dates, trading is concentrated in a few contracts, and in many cases liquidity may be better than some forward contracts. The tradeoff is that futures contracts cannot be tailored to the particular needs of firms and financial institutions. Glaxo, the British pharmaceutical company, may have payables in deutschemarks for payment on July 30; however, the DM futures contracts on LIFFE, the London futures exchange, have mid-June and mid-September delivery dates but nothing in July. So Glaxo would have to take some June and some September contracts, rolling the June contracts into more September contracts as the June delivery date approached. This rollover would provide a reasonably good hedge, but there would be no assurance that the June and September futures prices would move precisely like the forward contract for delivery on July 30. Thus Glaxo would face basis risk.

Basis risk can be defined as the deviation between the price of the item being hedged and the price of the hedging instrument. Banks have to take basis risk explicitly into account when they arbitrage between the futures and the forward markets.

Interest-Rate Forwards and Futures

Forward and futures contracts on interest-bearing instruments, notably on Eurodollar and Eurocurrency deposits, are widely used in international finance. FRAs, or **forward-rate agreements,** are over-the-counter bilateral contracts to fix an interest rate for one period in the future. They are effected by means of cash compensation. For example, Banque Indosuez may agree to fix PIBOR (the Paris interbank rate) for Alcatel, the French telecommunications company, "in 6 for 3" at 7 percent. This means that Indosuez has entered into a six-month forward contract, an FRA, on three-month PIBOR. If in six months' time PIBOR exceeds 7 percent, Indosuez will pay Alcatel the difference. If PIBOR is less than 7 percent, Alcatel will pay Indosuez the difference.

Figure 7.13 **Interest-Rate Futures Contracts.** They operate very much as do currency-futures contracts.

EURODOLLAR (CME) – $1 million; pts of 100%

	Open	High	Low	Settle	Chg	Yield Settle	Chg	Open Interest
June	96.70	96.73	96.68	96.72	+ .03	3.28	– .03	256,862
Sept	96.52	96.60	96.52	96.59	+ .06	3.41	– .06	265,432
Dec	96.03	96.16	96.02	96.14	+ .10	3.86	– .10	313,295
Mr94	95.90	96.03	95.90	96.01	+ .10	3.99	– .10	214,288
June	95.60	95.69	95.56	95.68	+ .09	4.32	– .09	150,245
Sept	95.28	95.36	95.23	95.36	+ .08	4.64	– .08	126,258
Dec	94.84	94.91	94.80	94.91	+ .07	5.09	– .07	95,299
Mr95	94.75	94.82	94.73	94.82	+ .07	5.18	– .07	86,950
June	94.53	94.60	94.51	94.59	+ .07	5.41	– .07	65,581
Sept	94.31	94.40	94.30	94.38	+ .07	5.62	– .07	49,827
Dec	93.99	94.06	93.97	94.05	+ .06	5.95	– .06	47,842
Mr96	93.96	94.03	93.95	94.02	+ .05	5.98	– .05	43,799
June	93.77	93.82	93.74	93.82	+ .04	6.18	– .04	29,432
Sept	93.64	93.67	93.61	93.67	+ .03	6.33	– .03	25,236
Dec	93.39	93.42	93.37	93.42	+ .02	6.58	– .02	21,572
Mr97	93.39	93.41	93.36	93.41	+ .01	6.59	– .01	18,230
June	93.26	93.26	93.21	93.25	....	6.75	....	14,146
Sept	93.12	93.14	93.10	93.11	....	6.86	....	12,517
Dec	92.92	92.93	92.90	92.93	– .01	6.07	+ .01	10,554
Mr98	92.92	92.92	92.90	92.93	– .01	....	....	5,200

Est vol 380,574; vol Tues 364,787; open int 1,852,565, +4,314.

EURODOLLAR (LIFFE) – $1 million; pts of 100%

	Open	High	Low	Settle	Change	Lifetime High	Low	Open Interest
June	96.70	96.71	96.70	96.71	....	96.83	91.50	8,297
Sept	96.56	96.57	96.54	96.55	....	96.76	92.50	3,979
Dec	96.06	96.07	96.05	96.07	– .01	96.70	92.24	3,948
Mr94	95.94	95.94	95.90	95.94	– .01	96.30	92.20	952
June	95.61	95.61	95.61	95.60	– .07	95.98	93.36	349
Sept	....	....	....	95.28	– .05	95.30	93.76	126

Est vol 2,505; vol Tues 2,190; open int 17,696, +230.

STERLING (LIFFE) – £500,000; pts of 100%

	Open	High	Low	Settle	Change	Lifetime High	Low	Open Interest
June	93.98	94.00	93.94	93.97	+ .03	94.88	87.58	56,123
Sept	93.98	94.07	93.96	94.05	+ .11	94.94	87.20	76,131
Dec	93.90	93.99	93.90	93.97	+ .11	94.81	88.95	68,016
Mr94	93.64	93.71	93.62	93.69	+ .11	94.53	89.87	36,897
June	93.34	93.40	93.32	93.39	+ .11	94.23	89.78	29,316
Sept	93.00	93.04	92.95	93.02	+ .09	93.91	90.10	17,457
Dec	92.68	92.71	92.64	92.69	+ .08	93.55	90.10	10,457
Mr95	92.46	92.49	92.43	92.45	+ .06	93.20	90.70	7,727
June	92.24	92.31	92.24	92.25	+ .04	92.95	91.73	3,088
Sept	92.07	92.07	92.01	92.04	+ .04	92.58	91.65	3,881

Est vol 62,792; vol Tues 40,023; open int 309,063, +3,130.

LONG GILT (LIFFE) – £50,000; 32nds of 100%

	Open	High	Low	Settle	Change	Lifetime High	Low	Open Interest
June	104-02	104 14	104-01	104-11	+ 0-07	107-18	100-04	78,627
Sept	103-05	103-16	103-05	103-13	+ 0-18	106-30	102-16	1,525

Est vol 49,491; vol Tues 34,436; open int 80,152, +726.

EUROMARK (LIFFE) – DM 1,000,000; pts of 100%

	Open	High	Low	Settle	Change	Lifetime High	Low	Open Interest
June	92.86	92.91	92.77	92.78	– .10	93.99	90.86	131,909
Sept	93.64	93.68	93.54	93.54	– .11	94.29	91.12	125,813
Dec	94.09	94.12	94.02	94.03	– .07	94.62	91.31	117,869
Mr94	94.47	94.50	94.40	94.41	– .06	94.77	91.53	73,438
June	94.55	94.57	94.48	94.49	– .07	94.80	91.71	43,014
Sept	94.54	94.55	94.45	94.45	– .07	94.00	91.81	33,606
Dec	94.32	94.33	94.23	94.24	– .08	94.61	91.83	22,123
Mr95	94.30	94.30	94.20	94.21	– .09	94.60	92.45	11,800
June	94.18	94.18	94.07	94.07	– .11	94.52	93.15	7,063
Sept	94.01	94.01	94.01	93.95	– .11	94.23	93.62	1,677

Est vol 134,854; vol Tues 89,944; open int 568,312, +4,862.

EUROSWISS (LIFFE) – SFr 1,000,000; pts of 100%

	Open	High	Low	Settle	Change	Lifetime High	Low	Open Interest
June	95.01	95.04	94.94	94.95	– .04	95.75	92.02	22,336
Sept	95.38	95.43	95.31	95.34	– .04	96.11	93.35	12,980
Dec	95.67	95.68	95.63	95.62	– .05	96.11	94.83	5,342
Mr94	95.76	95.76	95.71	95.71	– .05	96.16	95.71	900

Est vol 6,784; vol Tues 11,890; open int 41,558, +1,969.

GERMAN GOV'T. BOND (LIFFE)
250,000 marks; pts of 100%

	Open	High	Low	Settle	Change	Lifetime High	Low	Open Interest
June	94.38	94.50	94.06	94.19	– .24	97.90	91.28	144,585
Sept	94.59	94.72	94.33	94.42	– .23	97.64	91.65	25,582

Est vol 122,690; vol Tues 118,430; open int 170,167, +4,832.

ITALIAN GOVT. BOND (LIFFE)
ITL 200,000,000; pts of 100%

	Open	High	Low	Settle	Change	Lifetime High	Low	Open Interest
June	99.52	99.92	99.26	99.53	+ .16	99.92	92.74	40,254
Sept	99.40	99.69	99.10	99.33	+ .17	99.69	95.45	2,155

Est vol 25,576; vol Tues 29,807; open int 42,409, +2,438.

FT–SE 100 INDEX (LIFFE) – £25 per index point

	Open	High	Low	Settle	Change	Lifetime High	Low	Open Interest
June	2859.	2862.	2818.	2821.	– 36.0	3001.5	2634.	40,604
Sept	2865.5	2865.5	2842.	2844.5	– 36.0	2987.	2804.	10,177

Est vol 16,423; vol Tues 9,308; open int 50,793, +400.

Source: *The Wall Street Journal*, May 19, 1993, p. C14.

Eurodollar futures (which fix LIBOR, the London interbank rate) and futures on other instruments play a similar role: they allow hedging or positioning on a rise or fall in certain key interest rates or fixed-income instrument prices such as Treasury bills and bonds. Some newspaper quotations of important interest-rate futures prices are reproduced in Figure 7.13. The Chicago Eurodollar futures contract is among the most actively traded of any in the world, and allows the hedging of borrowing costs or investment returns as many as five years into the future.

Eurodollar futures contracts operate very much as do the currency futures described earlier. They lock in a forward interest rate and are marked to market daily as that forward rate changes. They are quoted as a price that is nothing more than 100 minus the fixed add-on yield. For example, referring to Figure 7.13, Alcatel could hedge anticipated three-month U.S.-dollar borrowing for the period September through December of the current year by selling the September Eurodollar futures contract at a price of 96.59—that is, at an interest rate of 3.41. If LIBOR rises, the price will fall and Alcatel will make a gain, paid through daily cash compensation, of an amount equal to the change in the forward rate (multiplied by the one million dollars face value of the contract).

Futures on long-term instruments, such as German government bonds ("bunds"), are commonly used to hedge against the price risk of investment portfolios or against the interest-rate risk of future bond issuance. One application of bond futures is demonstrated in Application 7.5, "Kleinwort's Bulldog Hedge," at the end of this chapter.

Summary

The forward market is a versatile market for the delayed delivery of currencies at a known rate. It is characterized by both default risk and market risk. The chapter showed how forwards can be used in hedging, in exploiting a view, and in arbitrage. The latter, covered-interest arbitrage, enables one to derive the forward rate with great precision from the spot rate and Eurocurrency interest rates.

We saw how dealers use the short-term swap market to hedge their positions in the forward market. We learned, too, of some alternative approaches to hedging, including use of the Eurocurrency market itself. This analysis helped show why it is difficult to hedge long-dated forwards with precision, and why bid-offer spreads seem to widen with increasing maturity.

We then turned to the futures market—an alternative to the forward market but linked to it by active arbitrage and by the fact that futures contracts can be seen as merely forward contracts that are recontracted, with cash compensation, daily. This feature, along with collateral accounts sufficient to absorb daily price movements and the fact that the futures exchange serves as mutual counterparty to trades, largely eliminates the credit-risk problem. Like an off-the-rack suit, the futures contract does not always fit perfectly, but for many participants in the foreign-exchange market, it serves the purpose. The task of the professional is to match the instrument to the need. The same consideration governs the choice between symmetrical instruments, such as forwards and futures, and asymmetrical instruments, such as options.

CONCEPTUAL QUESTIONS

1. Forward contracts entail default risk because either party could walk away from its obligation at the contract's maturity. From a bank's point of view, is this default risk greater or less than a loan of the same face amount?
2. Why are forward contracts nontransferable?
3. How can one get out of a forward contract?
4. Why do traders use two transactions instead of just one to hedge a forward-exchange contract?
5. Identify the different ways in which a foreign-exchange dealer can hedge a forward transaction. State briefly how each is done.
6. Why is the long-dated forward market less active than the short-dated market?
7. List the ways in which futures contracts differ from forward contracts.
8. Explain the connection between daily cash compensation of gains and losses in the futures market and the risk of default on these contracts.
9. What are the three ways in which futures contracts reduce credit risk?
10. "Futures contracts are like forward contracts, recontracted daily." Explain.
11. Explain the meaning of the term *FRA*.
12. Using the quotations in Figure 7.13, explain how Volkswagen could hedge the cost of issuing three-month commercial paper in Germany for one year. You may assume that the Euromark interest rate exceeds the German commercial paper rate by, on average, 35 basis points. What would be the risk of using futures to hedge the cost of issuing commercial paper?

PROBLEMS

1. You are a foreign-exchange dealer. A customer calls, asking for a three-month forward quotation on the Portuguese escudo. You reply, "137.05, 137.20." He says, "I'll hit your bid for half-a-billion escudos." What steps do you now take to execute the transaction?
2. In judging your bank's credit risk on the transaction in problem 1, how much can you lose if the escudo rises or falls by 5 percent from its present level?
3. Continuing from question 2, what steps would you normally take to hedge your position?
4. From the swap-rate quotation screen in Table 7.1, derive the six-month outright forward bid rate for French francs.
5. Using the long-dated forward-exchange quotations in Table 7.3, compare the bid-offer spread in the two-year and five-year forward Swiss-franc markets.
6. From the foreign-exchange market page of the *Financial Times,* obtain the spot and Eurodeposit rates quoted for one-month Danish kroner. Work out the swap bid and offer rates that you, as an FX swap dealer, might quote.
7. Show, using a numerical example from Table 7.1, how a dealer could profit from matching a six-month forward sale of yen with

   (a) an offsetting forward contract, or
   (b) a spot and a swap.

8. Continuing from question 7, show how a six-month forward sale hedged with two successive swaps (a rollover hedge) can be rendered unprofitable as a result of a change in relative interest rates.
9. Based on the deutschemark futures quotations in Figure 7.7, calculate how much a trader would have gained or lost if he had shorted (sold) 10 deutschemark nearby futures contracts on the previous day.
10. Examine the forward and futures prices for the Canadian dollar reproduced in the accompanying tables. Can you identify an arbitrage opportunity between the over-the-counter forward market and the CME futures market? How, specifically, would a bank exploit this opportunity? What are the risks of doing so?

Currency Futures on the Chicago Mercantile Exchange. Wednesday, Feb. 10, 1993

	Open	High	Low	Settle	Change		Lifetime High	Lifetime Low	Open Interest
JAPAN YEN (CME) – 12.5 million yen; $ per yen (.00)									
Mar	.8258	.8289	.8219	.8261	+	.0008	.8372	.7445	63,699
June	.8284	.8287	.8236	.8264	+	.0008	.8340	.7745	1,361
Sept	....	....	....	.8273	+	.0008	.8260	.7995	1,010
Dec	....	....	....	.8286	+	.0008	.8205	.7970	1,522
Est vol 7851; vol Tues 44,796; open int 67,592, – 12,133.									
DEUTSCHEMARK (CME) – 125,000 marks; $ per mark									
Mar	.6044	.6057	.5988	.5998	–	.0025	.7025	.5724	132,596
June	.5965	.5985	.5920	.5927	–	.0026	.6920	.5890	16,146
Sept	.5928	.5928	.5870	.5874	–	.0026	.6720	.5875	3,095
Est vol. 75,749; vol Tues 37,342; open int 151,858, +942.									
CANADIAN DOLLAR (CME) – 100,000 dlrs.; $ per Can$									
Mar	.7876	.7894	.7869	.7887	+	.0018	.8712	.7610	19,751
June	.7822	.7833	.7815	.7830	+	.0021	.8360	.7532	2,150
Sept	.7760	.7780	.7760	.7776	+	.0022	.8335	.7515	852
Dec	....	....	....	.7726	+	.0023	.8310	.7470	584
Est vol. 3,023; vol Tues 6,121; open int 23,366, – 1,239.									

Spot and Forward Interbank Foreign Exchange Market. Wednesday, February 10, 1993. The New York foreign-exchange selling rates below apply to trading among banks in amounts of $1 million and more, as quoted at 3 p.m. Eastern time by Bankers Trust Co., Telerate, and other sources. Retail transactions provide fewer units of foreign currency per dollar.

Country	U.S. $ equiv. Wed.	U.S. $ equiv. Tues.	Currency per U.S. $ Wed.	Currency per U.S. $ Tues.
Argentina (Peso)	1.01	1.01	.99	.99
Australia (Dollar)	.6727	.6705	1.4865	1.4914
Austria (Schilling)	.08564	.08574	11.68	11.66
Bahrain (Dinar)	2.6522	2.6522	.3771	.3771
Belgium (Franc)	.02916	.02923	34.29	34.21
Brazil (Cruzeiro)	.0000523	.0000532	19110.01	18800.03
Britain (Pound)	1.4260	1.4317	.7013	.6985
30-Day Forward	1.4225	1.4282	.7030	.7002
90-Day Forward	1.4160	1.4215	.7062	.7035
180-Day Forward	1.4090	1.4144	.7097	.7070
Canada (Dollar)	.7913	.7889	1.2637	1.2676
30-Day Forward	.7896	.7871	1.2665	1.2705
90-Day Forward	.7859	.7833	1.2724	1.2767
180-Day Forward	.7803	.7774	1.2815	1.2863

Source: *The Wall Street Journal*, Thursday, February 11, 1993.

Application 7.1	BANCO SANTANDER

PART 1. A FOREX SWAP AT SANTANDER

Banco Santander in Madrid has just sold 500 million pesetas three months forward to Telefonica, its biggest client. The price was 115.20 pesetas per U.S. dollar. How would delivery of the pesetas occur? How would Telefonica deliver dollars to Santander in exchange? What exposure does Santander now have? Explain the means by which the bank would normally cover such an exposure.

PART 2. SANTANDER PRICES A EUROCURRENCY DEPOSIT

Banco Santander's London branch is currently quoting 8 percent on 12-month Eurodollar deposits. It is also quoting 100 pesetas per U.S. dollar and 115 pta per dollar for spot and 12-month forward French francs, respectively. If Telefonica asks for a quote on depositing Spanish pesetas, what interest rate should the bank quote?

Application 7.2	THE PEOPLE'S BANK OF CHINA

The technicians were hard at work getting the systems up and running again, but Li Huifeng, Assistant Manager in the Treasury Department of the People's Bank of China, was frustrated. The bank had adopted a policy of quoting spot- and forward-exchange rates out to one year for the major state-owned enterprises, and with the screens down he found himself unable to give such quotations.

He *had* managed to print out the Reuters screen with Eurocurrency interest rates before the systems crashed (see below), and the spot FX dealer was on the telephone

REUTERS EUROCURRENCY INTEREST-RATE SERVICE

	1 MONTH	3-MONTH	6-MONTH	1 YEAR
STERLING	15 3/32-15 1/16	15 3/32-15 1/16	15-14 7/8	14 5/8-14 1/2
U.S. DOLLAR	8 3/8-8 1/4	8 5/16-8 3/16	8 5/16-8 3/16	8 5/16-8 3/16
CAN DOLLAR	12 1/8-11 7/8	12 3/16-11 15/16	11 15/16-11 11/16	11 3/4-11 1/2
DUTCH GUILDER	8 15/16-8 13/16	8 15/16-8 13/16	8 15/16-8 13/16	8 15/16-8 13/16
SWISS FRANC	9 13/16-9 11/16	9 1/2-9 3/8	9 1/4-9 1/8	9 1/16-8 15/16
DEUTSCHEMARK	8 1/8-8	8 7/16-8 5/16	8 5/8-8 1/2	8 11/16-8 9/16
FRENCH FRANC	11 1/4-11 1/8	11 5/8-11 1/2	11 5/8-11 1/2	11 5/8-11 1/2
ITALIAN LIRA	13-12 1/2	13-12 1/2	13-12 5/8	13 1/4-13
BELG. FRANC	10 9/16-10 7/16	10 9/16-10 7/16	10 9/16-10 7/16	10 9/16-10 11/16
YEN	6 11/16-6 9/16	6 15/16-6 13/16	7-6 7/8	7-6 7/8
DANISH KRONE	12 5/16-12 1/16	12 5/16-12 1/16	12 1/8-11 15/16	11 7/8-11 3/4
ASIAN $ SING.	8 3/8-8 1/4	8 3/8-8 1/4	8 5/16-8 3/16	8 5/16-8 3/16

to Hong Kong getting interbank spot-exchange rates. With these, he should be able to use the interest-rate-parity relationship to calculate 1-, 3-, 6-, and 12-month forward bid and ask quotations.

"Can you give me the interbank spot quotations yet?" Huifeng asked the spot dealer.

"Dollar/yen, spot 103.60–103.70. I'll have the others shortly," came the reply.

To assist Huifeng, calculate bid and ask forward dollar/yen quotes, assuming that the People's Bank can borrow at the offer and deposit at the bid rates quoted. Then set up a spreadsheet to calculate the others once the remaining spot rates arrive.

Application 7.3 | BANCA COMMERCIALE ITALIANA

Earlier today the sterling/dollar corporate trader at Banca Commerciale Italiana in Milan sold Enimont, the Italian chemical firm, £100 million forward for delivery in one year. Despite the efforts of his FX traders, BCI's dealing room manager has been unable to come up with an outright forward purchase of one-year sterling at an acceptable price.

What alternative ways could the foreign-exchange trading manager use to offset this exposure?

The following market data may assist you in listing the possibilities.

Sterling Spot and Forward Versus U.S. Dollar

£ Spot	1 Month Forward (US$)	3 Months Forward (US$)	12 Months Forward (US$)
1.6085–1.6095	.0084–.0083	.0239–.0236	.0838–.0828

Eurocurrency Interest Rates

Short-Term	1 Month	3 Months	12 Months
US$: $8\frac{1}{2}$–$8\frac{3}{8}$ (Call)	$8\frac{3}{8}$–$8\frac{1}{4}$	$8\frac{3}{8}$–$8\frac{1}{4}$	$8\frac{1}{4}$–$8\frac{1}{8}$
UK£: $15\frac{1}{8}$–15 (Two days' notice)	$15\frac{1}{8}$–$15\frac{1}{16}$	$15\frac{1}{8}$–$15\frac{1}{16}$	$14\frac{25}{32}$–$14\frac{21}{32}$

LIFFE £/$ FX Futures

Mar	Jun	Sep	Dec
1.5844	1.5605	1.5410	1.5205

Application 7.4 | THE EYE OF THE JAGUAR

At 10:00 A.M. on January 18, 1992, the vice president of finance for Ford Motor Company International, Ardath Deming, had concluded a transatlantic phone call with Kleinwort Benson, Ford's merchant-banking advisors in London. The sterling "Bulldog" (a corporate bond issued within Britain by a nonresident issuer) market, she had been told, might now provide the opportunity that Deming had been seeking to refinance a portion of Ford's acquisition of Jaguar, the British motor car company. Deming had agreed that Kleinwort would act as lead manager for a £200-million 10-year zero-coupon bond to be issued within the next 72 hours. This was something that had been planned for several weeks; now was the time to do it, and all concerned wanted to take advantage of the market "window." Jaguar's caché would make the bonds a sellout, Kleinwort had said. The issue would be priced to yield 127 basis points over the benchmark 9 percent gilt of 2008, which Deming saw from her Telerate screen was currently trading at 89-08 to yield 10.21 percent.

Because most of the market for Jaguars was outside the United Kingdom, Deming intended to convert the zero-coupon Bulldog into U.S. dollar financing by means of a long-dated forward-exchange contract. This would be arranged as soon as the deal was done and a forward contract of suitable maturity and price could be obtained.

Meanwhile, however, Deming wanted to avoid any possible exchange risks by hedging against a rise in the pound. She wanted something flexible and quick, so she decided to use the Chicago futures market to hedge her currency risk until such time as a long-term forward contract could be arranged. When it was, she would remove the futures hedge.

Given the pound-sterling futures contracts listed in the accompanying table, how should Ardath Deming hedge Jaguar's anticipated funding?

A week later the time came for Ford to replace the futures hedge with a forward contract. The pound had fallen by $0.02. What do you think happened to the futures position that Deming had taken? How should she get out of it?

When Deming sought to enter into a forward contract to convert the Bulldog into U.S.-dollar financing, her bank gave her the following quotation: "Spot 1.8995, ten year swap points 5547 discount."

What was the outright forward rate applicable to Deming's hedge? What was Ford's all-in cost of U.S.-dollar funding?

British Pound (IMM) 62,500 pounds; $ per pound

-Season-			High	Low	Close	Chg.	Open Interest
High	Low						
1.9518	1.5290	Sep	1.9240	1.9054	1.9118	−258	38,062
1.9230	1.6230	Dec	1.8950	1.8740	1.8814	−260	3,294
1.8950	1.6610	Mar	1.8650	1.8450	1.8538	−260	1,554

Last spot 1.9170, off 265.
Est. sales 20,537. Wed's sales 12,232.
Wed's open interest 42,910, off 966.

Application 7.5	KLEINWORT'S BULLDOG HEDGE

On February 11, 1993, the syndicate manager for Kleinworth Benson in London had just agreed to underwrite a ten year, £200 million zero-coupon Bulldog issue for Jaguar with a guarantee from Ford Motor Company. (A Bulldog bond is a corporate bond issued within Britain by a non-resident issuer.) Under pressure from Ford, Kleinwort's corporate finance department had agreed to price the bonds to yield 8.65 percent. Kleinwort's syndicate manager was confident that they could place all the paper at this level, which was equivalent to 55 basis points over the ten-year gilt, the British government bond.

There was a danger in making such an undertaking, however. During the day or so that it would take to syndicate the bonds, Kleinwort Benson would face a risk that the bonds' price might fall as a result of weakness in the U.K.-government bond market. Therefore the syndicate manager wanted to hedge his exposure using interest-rate futures on LIFFE, the London International Futures Exchange.

Look at the futures quotations in the accompanying tables. What should Kleinwort's syndicate manager do?

FINANCIAL FUTURES

LIFFE LONG GILT FUTURES OPTIONS
£50,000 64ths of 100%

Strike Price	Calls-settlements		Puts-settlements	
	Sep	Dec	Sep	Dec
101	3-05	3-14	0-45	1-30
102	2-25	2-41	1-01	1-57
103	1-50	2-09	1-26	2-25
104	1-19	1-45	1-59	2-61
105	0-58	1-21	2-34	3-37
106	0-40	1-02	3-16	4-18
107	0-26	0-50	4-02	5-02
108	0-17	0-37	4-57	5-53

Estimated volume total, Calls 422 Puts 728
Previous day's open int. Calls 9324 Puts 4476

LIFFE EUROMARK OPTIONS
DM1m points of 100%

Strike Price	Calls-settlements		Puts-settlements	
	Jun	Sep	Jun	Sep
9200	0.73	1.42	0	0
9225	0.49	1.18	0.01	0.01
9250	0.25	0.94	0.02	0.02
9275	0.08	0.71	0.10	0.04
9300	0.03	0.50	0.30	0.08
9325	0.01	0.32	0.53	0.15
9350	0	0.19	0.77	0.27
9375	0	0.11	1.02	0.44

Estimated volume total, Calls 4828 Puts 1643
Previous day's open int. Calls 151534 Puts 93363

LONDON (LIFFE)

9% NOTIONAL BRITISH GILT *
£50,000 32nds of 100%

	Close	High	Low	Prev.
Jun	104-07	104-11	103-30	104-04
Sep	103-12	103-12	103-04	103-08

Estimated volume 29630 (64383)
Previous day's open int. 77026 (77924)

US TREASURY BONDS 8% *
$100,000 32nds of 100%

	Close	High	Low	Prev.
Jun	109-29			110-01
Sep	108-22			108-26

Estimated volume 0 (0)
Previous day's open int. 0 (0)

6% NOTIONAL GERMAN GOVT. BOND *
DM250,000 100ths of 100%

	Close	High	Low	Prev.
Jun	93.80	93.87	93.68	93.99
Sep	94.04	94.18	93.93	94.23

Estimated volume 77827 (77188)
Previous day's open int. 164590 (174791)

6% NOTIONAL MEDIUM TERM GERMAN GOVT.
BOND (BOBL) DM250,000 100ths of 100% *

	Close	High	Low	Prev.
Jun	98.35	98.41	98.18	98.51
Sep	98.68	98.71	98.50	98.83

Estimated volume 5154 (5622)
Previous day's open int. 19936 (20041)

6% NOTIONAL LONG TERM JAPANESE GOVT.
BOND Y100m 100ths of 100%

	Close	High	Low
Jun	106.87	106.80	106.72
Sep	105.95	105.98	105.78

Estimated volume 2008 (2136)
Traded exclusively on APT

12% NOTIONAL ITALIAN GOVT. BOND (BTP) *
LIRA 200m 100ths of 100%

	Close	High	Low	Prev.
Jun	99.56	99.75	99.46	99.72
Sep	99.34	99.49	99.34	99.48

Estimated volume 7765 (12178)
Previous day's open int. 41344 (40693)

10% NOTIONAL SPANISH GOVT. BOND (BONOS)
Pta 20m 100ths of 100%

	Close	High	Low	Prev.
Jun	94.07	94.10	94.00	94.25
Sep				

Estimated volume 261 (46)
Previous day's open int. 4986 (4990)

THREE MONTH STERLING *
£500,000 points of 100%

	Close	High	Low	Prev.
Jun	94.00	94.00	93.97	93.95
Sep	94.06	94.09	94.04	94.01
Dec	93.98	94.00	93.96	93.92
Mar	93.72	93.75	93.70	93.67

Est. Vol. (inc. figs. not shown) 34830 (36501)
Previous day's open int. 312588 (315498)

Source: *Financial Times*, May 25, 1993, p. 32.

SELECTED REFERENCES

Giddy, I. H., and A. George, eds. *International Finance Handbook*. New York: Wiley, 1983.

Riehl, Heinz, and Rita Rodriguez. *Foreign Exchange and Money Markets*. New York: McGraw-Hill, 1983.

Smith, Clifford W., Charles W. Smithson, and Sykes Wilford. *Managing Financial Risk*. New York: Harper & Row, 1990.

8

Foreign-Exchange Options

Introduction

Many companies, banks, and governments have extensive experience in the use of forward-exchange contracts. With a forward contract, one can lock in an exchange rate for the future. There are a number of circumstances, however, in which it may be desirable to have more flexibility than a forward provides. For example, a computer manufacturer in California may have sales priced in U.S. dollars as well as in German marks in Europe. Depending on the relative strength of the two currencies, revenues may be realized in either German marks or dollars. In such a situation the use of forward or futures would be inappropriate: there's no point in hedging something you might not have. What is called for is a foreign-exchange option: the right, but not the obligation, to exchange currency at a predetermined rate.

A foreign-exchange option is a contract for future delivery of a specific currency in exchange for another, in which the holder of the option has the right to buy (or sell) the currency at an agreed price, the **strike** or exercise price, but is not *required* to do so. The right to buy is a *call;* the right to sell, a *put.* For such a right the buyer pays a price called the **option premium.** The option seller receives the premium and is obliged to make (or take) delivery at the agreed-upon price if the buyer exercises his option. In some options, the instrument being delivered is the currency itself; in others, it is a futures contract on the currency. American options permit the holder to exercise at any time before the expiration date; European options, only on the expiration date.

EXAMPLE 8.1

Steve Parker of Campbell Soup had just agreed to purchase I£5 million worth of potatoes from his supplier in County Cork, Ireland. Payment of the five million punt was to be made in 245 days' time. The dollar had recently plummeted against all the EMS currencies and Parker wanted to avoid any further rise in the cost of imports. He viewed the dollar as being extremely unstable in the current environment of economic tensions. Having decided to hedge the payment, he had obtained dollar/punt quotes of $2.25 spot, $2.19 for 245 days forward delivery. His view, however, was that the dollar was bound to rise in the next few months, so he was strongly considering purchasing a call option instead of buying the punt forward. At a strike price of $2.21, the best quote he had been able to obtain was from the Ballad Bank of Dublin, which would charge a premium of 0.85 percent of the principal.

Parker decided to buy the call option. "In effect," he reasoned, "I'm paying for downside protection while not limiting the possible savings I could reap if the dollar does recover to a more realistic level. In a highly volatile market where crazy currency values can be reached, options make more sense than taking your chances in the market, and you're not locked into a rock-bottom forward rate."

Figure 8.1   *Call Option on a Currency.*   The option holder can exercise his right to buy at the strike price if the currency rises above it, or to buy the currency in the spot market if that's cheaper.

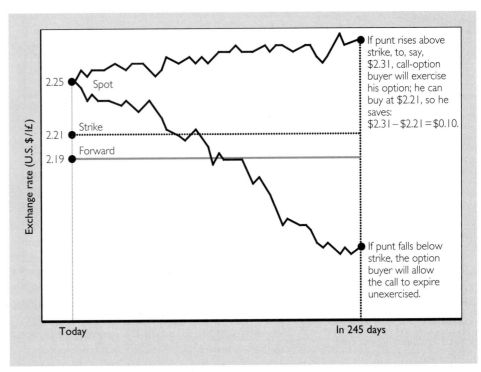

This simple example illustrates the lopsided character of options. Futures and forwards are contracts in which two parties oblige themselves to exchange something in the future. They are thus useful to hedge, or convert, known currency or interest-rate exposures. An option, in contrast, gives one party the *right but not the obligation* to buy or sell an asset under specified conditions while the other party *assumes an obligation* to sell or buy that asset if that option is exercised. Figure 8.1 illustrates the two possible outcomes of an option such as that bought by Steve Parker.

When should a company like Campbell use options in preference to forwards or futures? In the example, Parker had a view on the currency that differed from the forward rate. Taken alone, this would suggest taking a position. But he also had a view on the dollar's volatility. As we will explain later on, options provide the only convenient means of hedging, or positioning "volatility risk." Indeed, the price of an option is directly influenced by the outlook for a currency's volatility: the more volatile, the higher the price. To Parker, the price was worth paying. In other words, he thinks the true volatility is greater than that reflected in the option's price.

The Over-the-Counter Options Market

Multinational companies and international banks have recognized the flexibility of options for many years. Traditionally, international banks have tailored foreign-exchange options to the specific needs of their corporate clients. This OTC market is open only to larger firms because it involves amounts in millions of dollars. The players are banks, the dominant market makers, as well as corporations and securities houses. The customized nature of the market allows for the negotiation of the terms of the contract between the holder and the writer. Although this market provides flexibility in fitting option contracts to the specific needs of a multinational firm, it suffers from several shortcomings:

- The option buyer always faces the risk of nonperformance; in Example 8.1, the option writer, Ballad Bank, is obliged to make good on its contract *if and only if* the market moves in Parker's favor.
- In addition, the holder is directly faced with the risk of default by the writer, so the creditworthiness of the writer had to be evaluated in every instance. On the other hand, there should be no particular reason to prevent the holder of an option from selling it to another party, because the writer faces no counterparty exposure vis-a-vis the holder. Yet this happens only rarely.
- The small number of writers and buyers for any one of such tailor-made arrangements may cause the options to be mispriced because of the absence of a competitive market.
- The amounts of the underlying currency, exercise prices, expiration dates, and premiums vary widely from transaction to transaction. The lack of standardization has severely limited the development of a secondary market for OTC options, and the missing liquidity of the secondary market has in turn limited the scope of this market.

Exchange-Traded Currency Options

Options on currencies were first traded on the Philadelphia exchange in the early 1980s and are now traded worldwide in Chicago, London, Paris, Singapore, and elsewhere. The exchange contracts take two forms: (a) options on so-called physicals—that is, actual currencies, and (b) options on futures (see Box 8.1).

The first currency options were options on spot delivery, which require delivery of the underlying currency contract. Later, in Chicago, options on foreign-exchange futures were introduced; these meshed well with the existing currency-futures market on Chicago's International Monetary Market and are now the most actively traded. Let us see how exchange-traded options work and how they are related to currency futures.

BOX 8.1 **Currency-Exchange Warrants**	In June 1987 a new type of currency option, the currency-exchange warrant (CEW), was introduced on the American Stock Exchange (AMEX). Basically, a CEW is a currency option with a long maturity. By February 1988, all twelve CEWs traded in AMEX were foreign-currency put options (or, alternatively, U.S.-dollar call options) with five years to expiration. For a put warrant-holder, a CEW embodies the right to sell a specified amount of foreign currency for U.S. dollars at a predetermined exercise price during a specified exercise period. Unlike the case of currency options, however, the respective currencies are not exchanged between the issuer and the holder when the warrant is exercised. Instead, the difference between the exercise price and spot price on the day of exercise is paid to the holder of the CEW in a U.S.-dollar "cash settlement." These put CEWs are typically issued in conjunction with a note or bond offering, so that the total costs of financing are lowered, from the issuer's point of view. To hedge the exposed option position, the issuer buys foreign-currency put options (that

is, U.S.-dollar call options) on the OTC market. Because the option premium in the OTC market is substantially lower than the price of CEW, issuers can lock in an arbitrage profit, thus lowering their effective borrowing costs.

A CEW is an attractive instrument for those investors who are unable to participate in the OTC or listed exchange market because of requirements in transaction size. The CEW also offers interesting investment opportunities to those investors who prefer longer maturities. All CEWs currently traded on the AMEX have five-year maturities, while the longest maturities available in the option exchanges—in Philadelphia and Chicago—are for twelve months. However, the investor bears the credit risk of the issuer for up to five years.

Source: This section draws on *International Financing Review*, Feb. 13, 1988, pp. 523–526.

As with over-the-counter options, there are two kinds of listed currency options: puts and calls. A call option gives the holder (or "buyer" because he must pay for his rights) the right to purchase a currency on a certain date, at a certain price, say $0.57 per German mark. If, at expiration, the market price of the DM turns out to be lower than the rate specified in the option contract, say $0.54, it will make sense for the option holder to let the option expire. But if the market exchange rate is $0.59, above the contractual rate, the holder of the DM call option will exercise his right to receive an instrument at the cheaper price. A put option is, conversely, the right to sell a German mark or other currency at a contractual price to the writer (or seller) of the option.

The buyer of any option will, of course, have to pay a cash price, the premium, for the rights he receives. The greater the likelihood of the option's being exercised profitably, the higher the premium.

Figure 8.2 shows the profit-and-loss diagrams for the call buyer, the call seller, the put buyer, and the put seller.

One of the most important distinguishing features between listed options and OTC options is the relationship between the option holder and the option writer. In the OTC market, this relationship is direct and therefore the risk of nonperformance falls squarely on the option holder. In the case of listed options, the Options Clearing Corporation (OCC) guarantees every trade in foreign currency options by positioning itself between the buyer and the seller. The OCC therefore takes the ultimate responsibility both for delivery of the underlying option to the buyer and for payment of the premium to the seller. Therefore, the holder is relieved from the onerous task of evaluating the writer's creditworthiness. Instead, what really matters are the resources of the OCC. The clearing organization's resources are buttressed by stringent *margin requirements*. In exchange-traded options contracts, the margin requirements differ from futures contracts in that the option *holder* is never required to deposit money in a margin account, because he has no obligation to perform after paying the premium. Because the *writer* must perform if the option is exercised, he is required to deposit margin when a position is opened. This deposit is usually the initial margin plus some amount. As in the futures market, the margin account will be marked to market daily to reflect changes in the option's value.

The OCC itself is a nonprofit organization regulated by the Securities and Exchange Commission. Its resources are, in effect, the combined resources of all its clearing members; essentially, this includes the major securities firms in the United States. The OCC ensures the viability of the listed options market by imposing high membership standards, substantial capital requirements, stringent margin requirements, and by maintaining a large clearing fund.

As with currency futures, exchange-traded options are standardized contracts with a face value of (for example) DM125,000 and set expiration dates (on the Chicago IMM,

Figure 8.2 **Payoff at Expiration of Options.** Buying a call produces a gain if the currency (that is, the forward rate or futures price) rises above the strike plus the premium; the call writer's profit profile is the opposite.

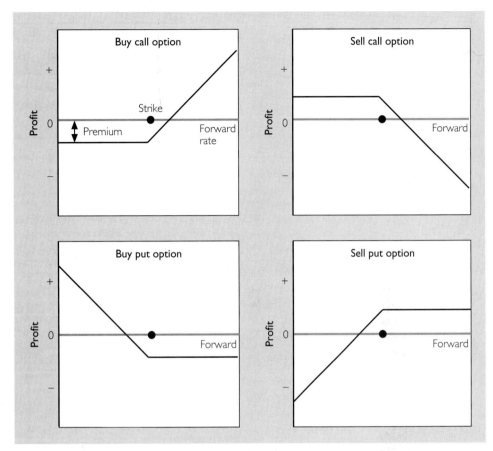

every month). Both the strike price and the price of the underlying currency are quoted in so-called American terms, as the dollar price of a unit of foreign currency. The option price is quoted in U.S. cents per unit of foreign currency. For example, the price of a June German-mark call option with a strike price of 57 cents per DM could be 2.08 cents per DM. A call option gains value, and a put loses value, as the underlying futures price rises. Conversely, if the currency falls a call option loses value while a put gains.

An important feature of the Philadelphia currency option is that it is a **European option,** meaning that the option can only be exercised on the expiration date. For the vast majority of hedging purposes this provides as much protection as the **American option** privilege of early exercise that characterizes the IMM options on futures (and most other traded options). The rules of European options allow users to write options with confidence that they will not be involuntarily liquidated prior to expiration. This feature facilitates certain trading strategies—such as spreads and straddles—and arbitrage between options and forwards or futures by assuring the trader that the position will not be broken prematurely.[1]

---

[1]These considerations aside, the most important consideration for most banks and corporate hedgers is the liquidity of the market. On that score, Chicago wins.

Options on futures are the most actively traded currency options on the organized markets today. With an option on "cash," if you have a call and you choose to exercise it, you actually get funds transferred into a bank account in the country of the currency being purchased, and you must make a corresponding transfer into a bank account of the currency being sold. With an option on futures, the instrument being delivered is a futures contract. If you exercise a call on sterling, you will receive a long sterling-futures contract. If you exercise a put, you'll receive a short contract. Options on futures sound more complicated than options on the currencies themselves, but they are not. If you exercise a futures option, instead of the full amounts of the physical currencies being involved, all that happens is that you are delivered a futures contract that is marked to market, producing a cash gain or loss. For example, if a call option on a Swiss-franc futures contract has a strike price K and if the option is exercised when the current SF futures price F is greater than K, then the party exercising the option acquires a long futures position established at price K. The corresponding seller of the SF call is assigned a short position in the same futures contract. These positions are immediately marked to market, resulting in a cash flow of $F - K$ going from the short to the long.

Also, the futures contract that is deliverable matures at the same time as the option expires. Remember that a futures becomes a spot when it matures. So if you take delivery of a futures contract, you're getting the same effect as if you had a European option—ultimate settlement only occurs at the expiration of the option.

Who Needs Them?

Currency options are useful for anyone who requires a gain if the exchange rate goes one way, but wants protection against loss if the rate goes the other way. The most the holder of an option can lose is the premium he paid for it. Naturally, the option writer faces the mirror image of the holder's picture: if you sell (or "write") an option (call or put), the most you can get is the premium if the option dies for lack of exercise. The writer of a call option can face a substantial loss if the option is exercised: he is forced to deliver a currency-futures contract at a below-market price. If he wrote a put option and the put is exercised, then he is obliged to buy the currency at an above-market price.

Unlike futures, forwards, and currency swaps, therefore, foreign-exchange options represent an asymmetrical risk profile. This lopsidedness works to the advantage of the holder and to the disadvantage of the writer—but that, after all, is what the holder is paying for. When two parties enter into a symmetrical contract like a forward, both can gain or lose equally and neither party feels obliged to charge the other for the privilege. Forwards, futures, and swaps are mutual obligations; options are one-sided. As we saw in Figure 8.2, the holder of a call has a downside risk limited to the premium paid up front; beyond that he gains one-for-one with the price of the underlying security. One who has bought a put option gains one-for-one as the price of the underlying instrument falls below the strike price. Traders who have written or sold options face the upside-down mirror-image profit profile of those who have bought the same options.

From the asymmetrical risk profile of options, it follows that options are ideally suited to offsetting exchange risks that are themselves asymmetrical. The risk of a forward-rate agreement is symmetrical; hence, matching it with a currency option will not be a perfect hedge, because doing so would leave you with an open, or speculative, position. Forward contracts, futures, or currency swaps are suitable hedges for symmetrical risks. Currency options are suitable hedges for situations in which currency risk is already lopsided, and for those who choose to speculate on the direction *and* volatility of rates. An example of a possible use of currency options is given in Example 8.2.

EXAMPLE 8.2 Consider the choices facing a U.S. electronics firm that has been invited to bid on a contract to supply the Swiss power authority with switching systems. Bids are also to be submitted by French and Japanese firms, both of whose governments are keen on winning the contract. The result of the tender will be known some time during the following two months. If its bid is accepted, the American firm will receive an initial payment of two million Swiss francs, with the remainder of the payments made in Swiss francs at fixed dates thereafter.

To submit a bid in Swiss francs, our firm can assume that the current Swiss-franc/dollar exchange rate will remain unchanged and then translate the bid at today's spot rate; this is the "no hedge" assumption. The danger, however, is that if the bid is accepted and the franc falls, the profit margin on the deal can easily be wiped out. Alternatively, the firm can sell the anticipated Swiss-franc receipts in the forward market, at the then-current forward-exchange rate for two-months-and-later delivery dates. However, if its bid is *not* selected, the firm then has a short position in Swiss francs and can lose money.

A third, and preferable, strategy might be to purchase an *option to sell* Swiss francs on the payment dates. This gives the American firm the right to transfer the Swiss francs received at a prearranged exchange rate. If the contract is not won, the firm can allow the option to expire (or even sell the right to someone else) with no further obligation on its part. Note also that even if our firm's bid is accepted, it faces no compulsion to exchange any Swiss francs received at the prearranged rate; if the value of the Swiss currency rises, then the firm may do better by selling the francs in the spot market.

Options are not only for hedgers, but also for those who wish to take a "view." However, for one who is, say, bearish on the deutschemark, a DM put is not necessarily the best choice. One can easily bet on the *direction* of a currency by using futures or forwards. A DM bear would simply sell DM futures, limiting his loss, if wants to do so, via a stop-loss order.[2]

For an investor who has a view on direction *and* on volatility, the option is the right choice. (See Box 8.2.) If you think the DM is likely to fall below the forward rate, and you believe that the market has underestimated the mark's volatility, then buying a put on German marks is the right strategy.

Who needs an American option? Because it offers an additional right—the privilege of exercise on any date up to the expiration date—it gives the buyer greater flexibility and the writer greater risk. American options will therefore tend to be priced slightly higher than European options. Even so, as Example 8.3 illustrates, *the American option is almost always worth more "alive" than "dead," meaning that it pays to sell rather than exercise early.* The reason for this statement lies in the fact that most options trade at a price higher than the gain that would be made from exercising the option. If the pound is worth $1.70, and you have a call option giving you the right to buy at $1.60, then your gain from exercising immediately would be $0.10. This "immediate exercise" gain is called the **intrinsic value** of the option. But typically the call would trade in the market at a price *higher* than this 10-cent intrinsic value. The call option might, for example, have a market price of 13 cents. The amount by which the price exceeds the intrinsic value is called the **time value.** We'll encounter these concepts again later. For now, it should be clear that you would be better off selling the call rather than exercising it early.

---

[2]A stop-loss order is an instruction given by a trader that if an instrument reaches a certain price, his position should be liquidated.

BOX 8.2

When Should a Company Use Currency Options?

Options, futures, forwards, and other instruments can be used to take a view, a speculative position in the currency market. Let us assume, however, that the objective of the firm is to reduce risk arising from the company's natural business. If forward and option contracts are fairly priced, it is best to use forward contracts when foreign-currency transactions exposures are known. When the firm's exposure is unknown—in a case when either the volume or the prices (or both) are unknown—conditions may justify the use of options, although forwards often remain the logical choice. The underlying idea is to offset with the hedging instrument the risk-reward profile of the underlying exposure.

Because a known foreign-currency inflow or outflow has a symmetrical gain-loss profile, it can be offset by a forward or debt contract with an opposite profile. That is, when the quantity of a foreign-currency cash flow is known, forwards should be used or debt-denominated in such a way as to offset this flow. In contrast, combining a known foreign-currency cash inflow or outflow with an option (which has an asymmetrical profile) creates another asymmetrical position. The combined risk profile is not neutral but is asymmetrical itself, so that buying an option in this case is a speculative rather than a hedging strategy. One would adopt it if and only if one had a view on direction and volatility other than that of the market, as reflected in the market price of forwards and options.

EXAMPLE 8.3   A portfolio manager has purchased IMM put options on 10 million German marks to hedge his position in DM Eurobonds. The strike price was $0.52 per mark. Now he wants to sell his bonds and repatriate the funds. The mark has fallen in the spot and futures markets: the DM futures contract has fallen to $0.495 per mark. If he exercises his American option early he will realize 52 cents per mark, or $5.2 million. But the option contract has not expired; because it has time to run, it will be trading at *more* than its intrinsic value—the difference between the futures price and the strike price—of $0.025. This additional *time value* is what makes it more worthwhile to sell the option than to exercise it. Because it still has time to run, the market price would be, say, $0.03 per option. By selling the option the portfolio manager will realize a gain of $0.005 per deutschemark, giving him $5.25 million. By keeping the option alive, he's profited by $50,000.

How to Read the Newspaper

Table 8.1 displays a typical newspaper quotation of currency option prices. Currency options, which are now traded worldwide, are regarded as key instruments of the global foreign-exchange market. Daily quotations can be found both in newspapers and on trading screens such as Reuters and Telerate. Exchanges in Philadelphia, Amsterdam, Chicago, and Montreal began to offer options in the early 1980s in several major currencies. Since then, markets for listed options have grown tremendously in size and trading volume. The Amsterdam, Montreal, and Philadelphia stock exchanges offer options on spot currencies, while the Chicago Mercantile Exchange, LIFFE in London, and SIMEX in Singapore trade in options on foreign-currency futures contracts.

Only exchange-traded options are quoted in the press. These "listed" options are standardized. Each option contract is written for the same foreign-currency amount. For

Table 8.1   ***Currency-Options Quotations.***   Using options, hedgers can lock in the maximum cost of foreign currency (buy calls) or the minimum price received on foreign currency to be sold (buy puts).

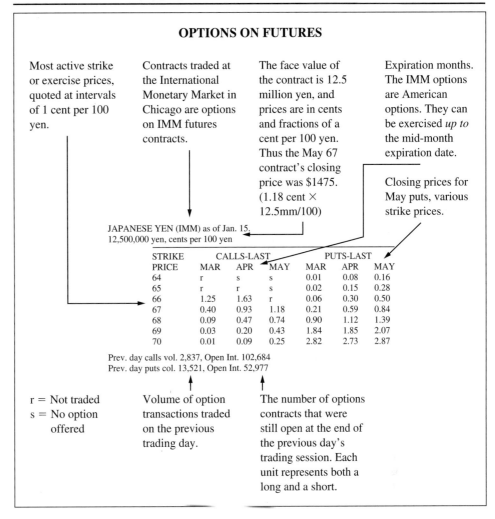

OPTIONS ON FUTURES

Most active strike or exercise prices, quoted at intervals of 1 cent per 100 yen.

Contracts traded at the International Monetary Market in Chicago are options on IMM futures contracts.

The face value of the contract is 12.5 million yen, and prices are in cents and fractions of a cent per 100 yen. Thus the May 67 contract's closing price was $1475. (1.18 cent × 12.5mm/100)

Expiration months. The IMM options are American options. They can be exercised *up to* the mid-month expiration date.

Closing prices for May puts, various strike prices.

JAPANESE YEN (IMM) as of Jan. 15.
12,500,000 yen, cents per 100 yen

STRIKE	CALLS-LAST			PUTS-LAST		
PRICE	MAR	APR	MAY	MAR	APR	MAY
64	r	s	s	0.01	0.08	0.16
65	r	r	s	0.02	0.15	0.28
66	1.25	1.63	r	0.06	0.30	0.50
67	0.40	0.93	1.18	0.21	0.59	0.84
68	0.09	0.47	0.74	0.90	1.12	1.39
69	0.03	0.20	0.43	1.84	1.85	2.07
70	0.01	0.09	0.25	2.82	2.73	2.87

Prev. day calls vol. 2,837, Open Int. 102,684
Prev. day puts col. 13,521, Open Int. 52,977

r = Not traded
s = No option offered

Volume of option transactions traded on the previous trading day.

The number of options contracts that were still open at the end of the previous day's trading session. Each unit represents both a long and a short.

example, the yen option shown in Figure 8.3 is for an amount of exactly ¥12.5 million. The expiration dates are the Saturday preceding the third Wednesday of March, June, September, and December. Listed options are available in maturities of 3, 6, 9, and 12 months only. Today, foreign-exchange options are available in a variety of currencies including Australian dollars, British pounds, Canadian dollars, French francs, Swiss francs, German marks, and Japanese yen. Quotes for these options are listed in *The Financial Times, The Wall Street Journal,* and other financial newspapers daily.

    The options in Table 8.1 are those traded on the IMM in Chicago, where the contract is for options on futures. From such quotations you may see which options are actively traded and perhaps find one that meets your needs. Say, for example, you expect to receive ¥25 million in May and are prepared to pay to be sure of getting at least 68 cents per 100 yen. This implies that you want to buy *two* Japanese-yen put options at a strike price of 68. According to the quotations, this would cost you 1.39 cents per 100 yen, or $1,737.50 per contract.

Figure 8.3   *Option Combinations.* The diagram shows four classic ways of combining an option with a futures to create the opposite option.

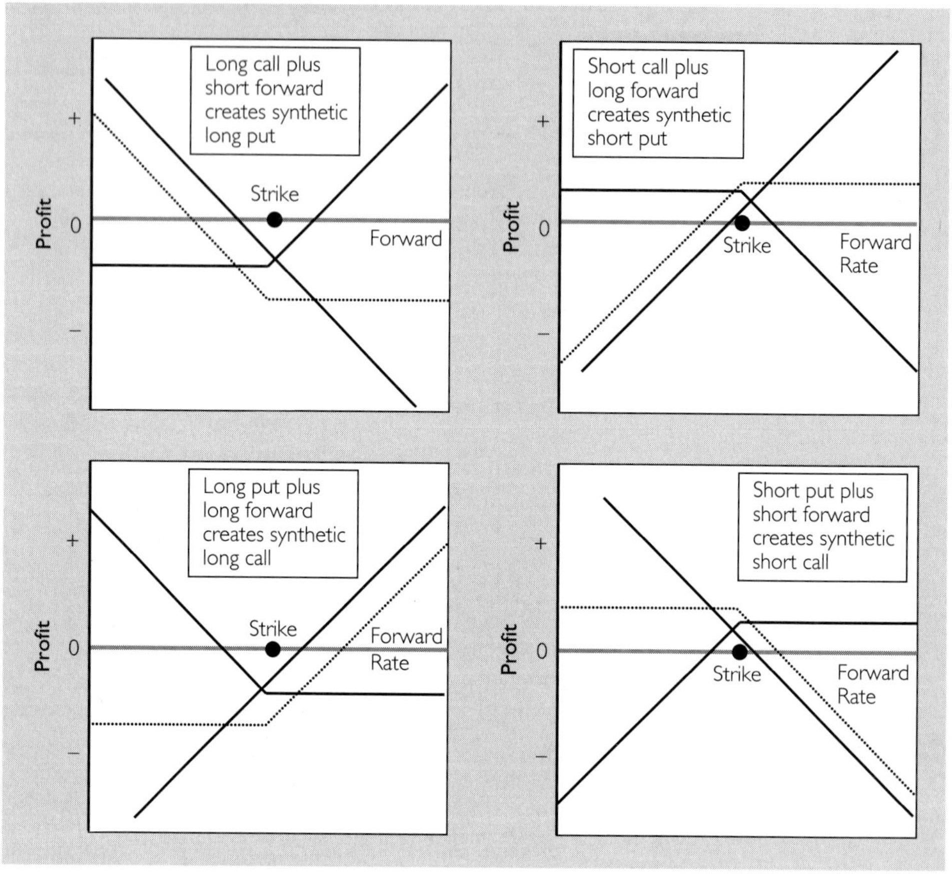

Options Combinations

Options are frequently combined with long or short positions in the underlying currency, sometimes to provide a "hedge." Combining an option, which is an asymmetrical position, with an equal amount of forwards or futures (a symmetrical position), creates another asymmetrical position. *It does not eliminate the risk—it simply changes the risk profile to resemble that of another option.* For example, adding a call option to a short position in the underlying currency creates a "synthetic" put option. (This is what Steve Parker created in Example 8.1.) Figure 8.3 illustrates four classic ways of combining an option with a futures to synthesize the opposite option.)

The two right-hand diagrams in Figure 8.3 help deflate the myth that writing "covered" calls or puts is any less risky than writing "naked" options. A covered-call write, for example, occurs when you sell a call and buy a futures or forward. But this is identical to writing a naked put, which few would claim is riskless.

Put-Call Parity

Although options and futures are distinct instruments, their prices are linked by a fundamental arbitrage relationship called *put-call parity*. The buying of a call and the selling of a put, both for the expiration date and strike price *K,* produces a pattern of gains and losses that duplicates that on a long futures contract with a price of *K.* Think about a trader who buys a call and sells a put on German marks. He will gain dollar-for-dollar on the call by the amount the futures price rises above *K,* or lose dollar-for-dollar on the put by the amount the futures price falls below *K,* just as he could have had he bought a DM futures contract. Of course, he has had to pay for the call (and he has received the put premium). So to figure the price at which the trader has effectively purchased currency forward, one should take into account the difference between the premium *C* paid for the call and the premium *P* received for the put, plus interest *i* on this difference, because *C* and *P* are paid up front. The total picture, taking into account the premiums, is illustrated by the thin line in Figure 8.4. It looks just like a futures!

The net cost of this "synthetic" futures is

$$K + (C - P)(1 + i)$$

If the cost of locking in the future price for DM using this strategy is cheaper than locking it in via a plain old futures at the going futures price *F,* the trader will do an arbitrage

Figure 8.4 **_Put-Call Parity._** The diagram shows how a long call plus a short put can replicate a long futures.

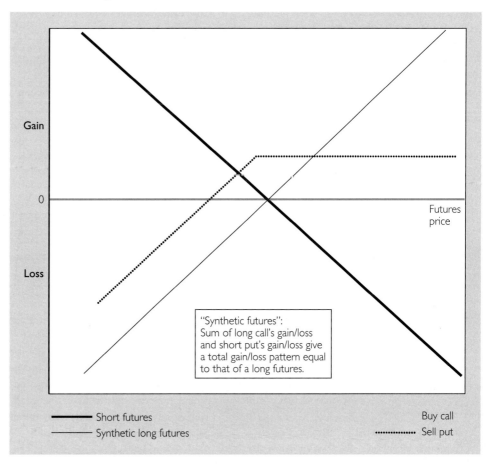

"Synthetic futures":
Sum of long call's gain/loss
and short put's gain/loss give
a total gain/loss pattern equal
to that of a long futures.

——— Short futures   Buy call
——— Synthetic long futures   ············ Sell put

called a **reversal**—couple the long call and short put with a sale of DM futures, earning a profit:

$$\text{Profit from reversal} = F - K - (C - P)(1 + i)$$

What if the opposite is true? What if buying a futures contract is cheaper than locking in the rate by combining puts and calls? Well, the trader will then perform the mirror-image act, one called **conversion.** Here the trader creates an artificial *short futures* position by buying a put, selling a call, and investing (or borrowing) the difference between the two premiums at an interest rate *i*. Coupled with a *long* futures at *F,* the conversion produces a profit:

$$\text{Profit from conversion} = K + (C - P)(1 + i) - F$$

Easy, right? Dream on! Lots of traders read this before you did and rushed to take advantage of any price anomalies between futures and options prices. In doing so they drove call and put prices to the point at which no profits remained. So, the right-hand side of both equations becomes equal to zero. This implies that, in equilibrium, the difference between the call and put premiums for an option with strike price *K* will be equal to the difference between the German-mark futures price *F* and *K,* discounted to the present at the market interest rate *i:*

$$C - P = \frac{F - K}{1 + i}$$

This is the relationship that we call *put-call parity,* or PCP. It defines the relationship between puts and calls. For example, if the option is at the money, meaning the futures price *F* equals the strike price *K,* the put price equals the call price.

For interest, the reader may wish to go back to the newspaper extracts, determine whether put-call parity holds, and imagine how much money he or she could make. The problem with doing so, of course, is that published prices do not necessarily reflect the prices at which you and I could deal; nor were the reported trades in the put, call, and futures contracts concluded at precisely the same time. In fact, one of the problems with doing conversions or reversals, or for that matter any arbitrage, is the difficulty of executing two or more trades simultaneously. Finally, a put-call parity holds only for European options. Under certain circumstances, it can break down for options that can be exercised early.

Currency-Option Pricing

In this section we will give an intuitive view of why some options are priced very cheaply and others are more expensive—in other words, what determines option prices. We will do so with minimal reference to formal option-pricing models, leaving that for the next section. Although our discussion refers to call options, most of what is said applies equally to put options. Moreover, once one knows the price of a call, one can use the put-call-parity equation to calculate the price of a put.

To a large extent, currency options are priced like other kinds of options—stock options, commodity options, interest-rate options, and index options. All options provide the option buyer with downside protection and upside opportunity, and it is the value of this combination that gives the option its value.

Put differently, *the value of any option depends crucially on the probability of the option's being exercised.* A glance back at Table 8.1 will remind us that some of the quoted option contracts are quite likely to be exercised, and others are quite unlikely. When Table 8.1

was compiled, the March futures price was 67.19 cents per 100 yen. A deep-out-of-the-money option, such as the March 70 call, is rather unlikely to be exercised, because there is a pretty trivial probability that the Japanese-yen futures price will rise to 70 by the March 15 exercise date. One shouldn't bet much on that horse; neither, apparently, will the market. Look at Figure 8.5, a diagram of how theoretical currency-option prices change with different currency-futures prices. The deep-out-of-the-money option, on which the strike price far exceeds the current market-level index, is worth next to nothing.

Of course, for out-of-the-money options on which the market price is quite close to the strike price, the upside potential becomes significant and the option becomes more valuable.

Returning now to the table of option prices in Table 8.1, one can easily identify an option whose exercise is a near-certainty. Take the Mar 66 call. Almost sure to win, this option has a price that reflects that fact. Indeed, you could exercise it now, locking in the purchase price of 66 cents per 100 yen and sell the futures to receive 67.19. Because it is such a sure thing, it's almost like a futures or forward contract, the ultimate sure thing. But nobody in his right mind pays an up-front premium for a futures contract; any rational mind will come to the conclusion not to pay much more for the option than its intrinsic value—the gain that could be locked in by exercising it now. That gain is 67.19 − 66 = 1.19. The traded price of the call was 1.25. Thus the market paid only 0.06 cent for the negligible downside protection that is the only thing that differentiates a deep-in-the-money option from a futures contract.

Now that we've taken a look at two rather extreme options—a "nothing" option and a "nothing-but-a-futures" option—we can move toward the middle ground, toward those options whose downside protection and upside potential are significant. As you can guess, those are "at-the-money" options—those whose strike price is equal or close to

Figure 8.5 *Currency-Option Pricing.* This shows the smooth but asymmetrical increase in the value of a call option as the underlying futures price rises.

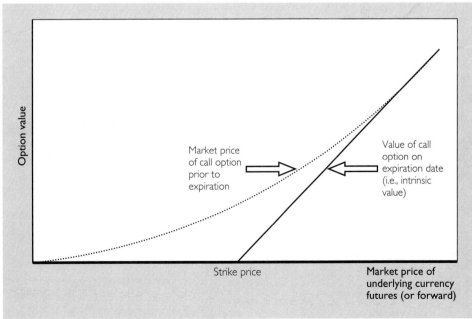

the going market price. Those are the options worth paying for, and their price reflects that fact. To recap, all option prices consist of two parts:

| Price | equals | Money you could lock in now | plus | Value from downside protection plus upside potential |

In options-market parlance:

| Price | equals | Intrinsic value | plus | Time value |

The relative importance of the intrinsic-value and time-value components are summarized in Table 8.2.

So far we've described the way that currency-option prices change as the exchange rate changes, something very important for anyone trading foreign-exchange options. To complete our intuitive survey of option pricing, we must turn to the three other important determinants of options prices: exchange-rate volatility, the time left to expiration of the option, and the risk-free interest rate. Together these determine, for a given level of "inness" or "outness" of the money (that is, for a given point on the x axis in Figure 8.5), what the time value of the option should be.

1. The *time value* depends on how much the exchange rate can move between now and expiration. For this reason time value is perhaps better termed *volatility value*. It is a function of the usefulness of the option. How much downside protection does it provide? How much upside potential does it offer? For a given strike and market price, the answer

Table 8.2   *Breakdown of Intrinsic Value and Time Value in Option Prices*

Kind of Option (Market price relative to strike price)	Intrinsic Value	Time Value
Deep-out-of-the-money option	Zero	Negligible, because of trivial upside potential
Slightly-out-of-the-money option	Zero	Considerable, because of downside protection plus substantial upside potential
At-the-money option	Zero	Maximum, because of greatest downside protection *and* greatest upside potential
Slightly-in-the-money option	Equals difference between strike and futures price	Considerable, because of upside potential plus substantial downside protection
Deep-in-the-money option	Equals difference between strike and futures price; constitutes bulk of option's value	Negligible, because of trivial downside protection relative to futures contract

depends purely on the probability of the market's moving above (or below) the strike between now and the expiration date. That probability depends principally on (1) how much time is left and (2) how volatile exchange rates are. (**Volatility** is defined as the annualized standard deviation of daily price changes.) Obviously, the greater the *time to expiration,* the greater the probability of significant exchange-rate movement and the higher the time value. Other things being equal, the time value drops off sharply as an option approaches maturity, particularly in the last month or so.

2. Time, intrinsic value, and the market interest rate can all be measured quite easily. The hardest thing is *volatility* itself, because what matters is not past but future volatility of exchange rates. Clearly the greater the volatility, the higher is the value of the option, so two traders with a different view of rate volatility will place a different value on the same option. Expected volatility, in short, is the key variable in pricing options. As noted earlier, options prices are not affected by changes in expectations about the level of a currency; only its variability is influenced.

3. The final factor is the *risk-free interest rate.* This is a time-value-of-money factor: the option gain (if any) is reaped at expiration, but the option must be paid for up front. In reality, option prices are normally quite insensitive to the risk-free interest rate.

Putting the market relative to the strike price, the risk-free interest rate, the time to expiration and the expected volatility together to figure out the theoretical option price requires a model, such as modifications of the famous *Black-Scholes Model.* Even though the mathematics of these quantities can be complex, modern option-pricing theory is derived from building blocks of relatively simple arbitrage strategies—arbitrage between options and the underlying instrument—that provide the trader with only the risk-free rate of return. Perhaps the most significant feature of these models is that although expectations of *volatility* of prices is a factor, the models do not rely on expectations regarding the *level* of future prices or rates to determine the correct price of an option.

Fischer Black's Option-Pricing Model

The Black–Scholes model was adapted to non-dividend-paying commodities such as foreign exchange by Fischer Black in 1976.[3] The model has stood the test of time, although it did not find common use in foreign exchange until reinterpreted by Garman and Kohlhagen.[4]

Let's talk for a moment about how one might derive a model of a currency option's value.[5] Remember that the *intrinsic value* of a call option at expiration is $F - K,$ or zero if it's out of the money. Assume we know today what the intrinsic value is going to be at expiration. Then the present value, today's price, of the option would be

$$\text{Max}\{0, PV(F - K)\}$$

This idea is the basis for the Black formula, although the *actual* present value is uncertain, so that the formula represents the present value of the option's *expected* intrinsic value at expiration. Uncertainty implies some probability distribution of the currency's value. We

---

[3]Fischer Black, "The Pricing of Commodity Options," *Journal of Financial Economics,* 1976, vol. 3 (1/2), 167–179.

[4]Mark Garman and Steve W. Kohlhagen, "Foreign Currency Option Values," *Journal of International Money and Finance,* 1983, vol. 2(3), 231–237.

[5]In the discussion that follows we will assume that the option being priced is a European option on a futures or forward contract. A futures or forward is one that matures on the expiration date of the option itself; in effect, this is the same as a European option on spot currency.

typically assume that the natural logarithm of the exchange rate follows a normal distribution. (Nevertheless, studies have found the distribution of daily exchange returns to be "leptokurtic," which means its shape is more peaked around the mean, and the tails are more massive and longer than in a normal distribution.) Figure 8.6 illustrates how the value is found. First we truncate the probability distribution of the log of the forward rate, because the option expires worthless if the currency ends up below the strike price, K. Then we find the expected value of that probability distribution. The call price is the present value of the difference between the expected forward and the strike. Written in symbols, this idea becomes the famous formula

$$C = PV[F \cdot N(d_1) - K \cdot N(d_2)]$$

where

$$d_1 = \frac{\ln(F/K)}{\sigma\sqrt{\tau}} + \frac{\sigma\sqrt{\tau}}{2}$$

$$d_2 = d_1 - \sigma\sqrt{\tau}$$

That's it! Note the similarity of this relationship to the known intrinsic-value formula given earlier. As for the symbols, F is the forward price of the currency, K is the strike price, σ is the volatility (standard deviation) of the forward rate,[6] τ is the time to expiration

Figure 8.6   Value of Call Option.   The value of the option equals the present value of its expected intrinsic value at expiration, given that the forward is above the strike.

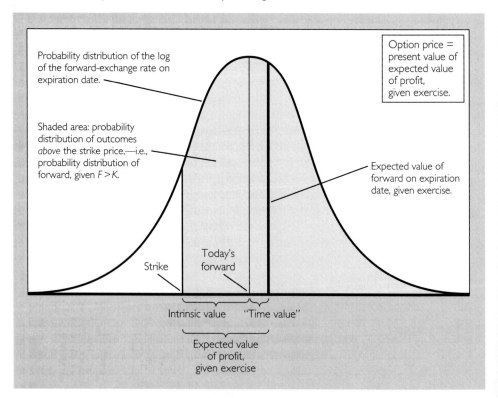

(in years) and $N(d)$ is the cumulative normal probability function.[7] Another variable, the risk-free interest rate, also comes into the formula through the present-value function, $PV()$.[8]

The formula makes intuitive sense as well as being useful. First, split it up into two terms: $C = PV[F \cdot N(d_1)] - PV[K \cdot N(d_2)]$. Keeping in mind that $N(d_1)$ is a probability, the term inside the first square brackets is the expected value of the forward rate, F_τ, at expiration, given that $F_\tau > K$. Similarly, the second term inside the brackets, $K \cdot N(d_2)$, is the expected value of the strike price at expiration, again given that $F_\tau > K$. Thus the *value of the option is the present value of its expected value at expiration.* Another interesting feature is that $N(d_1)$ is the probability that the call will be exercised, and as such gives the *hedge ratio* for a call, the amount of the underlying instrument needed to hedge an options position (see next section). The greater the chance that the writer will have to deliver, the more of the underlying instrument he'd better have purchased to hedge against the likelihood of exercise.

From the Black formula we get the value of a call, and, given the call price, we can easily derive the put price by using the put-call parity equation

$$P = C - PV(F - K)$$

Also, intuitively, when a call is not worth exercising, that is, when $F_\tau < K$, then a put with the same strike *is* worth exercising. Hence the probability of the put's being exercised is one minus the probability of the call's being exercised. So the *put hedge ratio equals 1 minus the call hedge ratio.*

Despite its complexity, the currency-option pricing formula is fairly easy to program on a computer spreadsheet, so that it becomes a useful "black box" in which the user plugs in values for the five parameters (F, K, τ, I, and σ), and the value of the call option, the put option, and their hedge ratios pop out. As such, this model or variations on it are widely used by financial-market practitioners. (See Box 8.3.)

BOX 8.3

Black Shoals

No model is perfect. The Black–Scholes option-pricing model and its variants work well for most purposes, but the following should alert the user to some of its limitations:

- The model's most problematic input variable is volatility. Although it's possible to estimate future volatility from the standard deviation of past data, what's really needed is one's *expectation* of future volatility. Volatility can be just as hard to predict as the exchange rate itself.
- The basic model yields the price of a European option; American options are usually worth a little more, by an amount that cannot be found by any straightforward formula.
- The formula assumes that the natural logarithm of the forward-exchange rate follows a normal distribution. Evidence suggests that the true distribution of exchange rates has considerably more outliers than is implied by the normal distribution.

---

[7]$N(d)$ is the probability that a deviation less than d will occur in a normal distribution with a mean of zero and a standard deviation of 1.

[8]Another way of writing the formula is $e^{-r\tau}[F \cdot N(d_1) - K \cdot N(d_2)]$ where e is the base of the natural logarithm (approximately 2.71828), and r is the risk-free interest rate expressed on a continuously compounding basis. The latter is equal to $\ln(1 + i)$ where i is the simple annual interest rate, expressed as a decimal.

- The model assumes that rates move continuously. Other models, notably Merton's jump-diffusion model, have been developed to allow for abrupt changes.
- The model depends on the forward-exchange rate's being independent of the interest rate. We know this is untrue, although for short-term options it seems not to matter.
- To obtain the value of a put from the call price, we assume that put-call parity holds, but PCP can break down under some unusual circumstances for American options.

How Changes in the Market Price of a Currency Affect an Option's Price

So you want to try your hand at trading options. Fine, but please take a few minutes to learn how changes in certain key variables are likely to affect the call you're about to buy (or the put you plan to sell, or whatever). To do this we'll turn to Figure 8.7, another example of our familiar profit-profile diagram, similar to Figure 8.5. This time, however, we combine it with the probability distribution of the forward price of the underlying instrument. This combination is done in order to show where we get the time-value portion. If today's forward or futures price of the DM is F, then the total option price is $(F - K)$ plus the time value—that is, the intrinsic value plus the time value (or just the time value if the option is out-of-the-money). Now we can see directly how the strike price truncates the probability distribution of the underlying instrument to determine the option's price.

Today's forward rate, F, is at the center of the distribution. If the underlying market moves, so does the whole "bell curve." This produces a change in the option price. The bottom part of Figure 8.7 shows the effect on the call price of an increase in the forward rate. The *intrinsic value* increases by the same amount as the forward. But the *time value* decreases as the market price moves away from the strike price. The reason is that the truncated distribution (the shaded part) now resembles the full distribution more closely, and so the means of the two are closer—that is, $E(F_\tau, \text{ given } F_\tau > K) - F$ (the measure of the time value) is smaller. Similar reasoning applies to puts, except that the time value diminishes and the intrinsic value takes over as the forward rate falls, making the put more in-the-money.

As any option gets deeper in-the-money, the time value diminishes to almost nothing, and the change in the option price is virtually identical to the change in the forward rate or futures price. At the other extreme, as the forward rate moves to make the option further out-of-the-money, there is no intrinsic value, only time value, which symmetrically diminishes toward zero.[9] Thus deep-out-of-the-money options hardly change at all as the forward or futures price changes.

This kind of information is very important for those trying to hedge an options position. People who write options especially want some way to hedge their risk. If you define a trader's risk as the changes in the value of an option she has bought or sold, then

---

[9]The time value is very small when the option is deep out-of-the-money of deep in-the-money and at its maximum when the option is at the money: ⌐‿⌐ .

Figure 8.7   *How a Change in the Forward Rate Changes the Currency-Option Price*

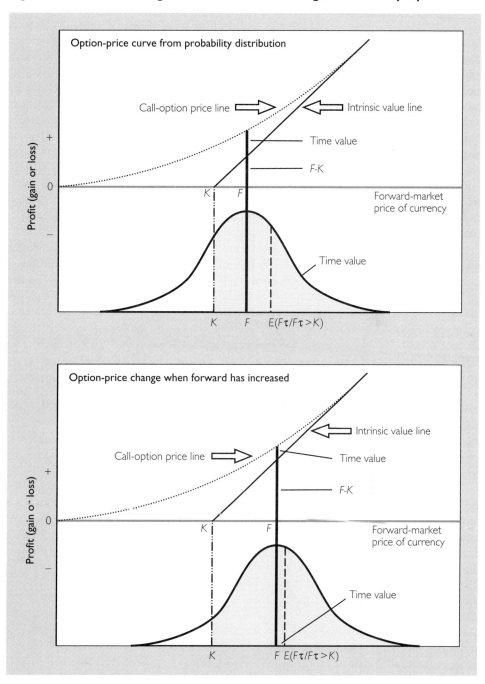

hedging that risk means putting on a position that produces an equal and opposite change. When the option is deep in-the-money, the option price moves virtually one-to-one with the forward or futures price change, so we say that the *hedge ratio* is 1 (or 100 percent). When the option is deep out-of-the-money, the hedge ratio approaches zero because the option price is totally insensitive to changes in the futures price. When the option is at-the-money—that is, when $F = K$—the hedge ratio is 50 percent; at that point, the truncated distribution is exactly half of the full distribution.

Delta Hedging and the Gamma

What do you do if, as a sophisticated options trader, you want a position that protects you against currency risk, but that exposes you to a change in volatility? The measure of the sensitivity of a given options price to the futures price is called the **delta.** (Delta is the Greek mathematical symbol used as shorthand for the hedge ratio.) It tells the trader how many futures contracts to use to offset the price behavior of one options contract. The delta is graphically represented by the *slope* of the option-price line in Figure 8.8. For example, if an option has a delta of .4 (or 40 percent), then 100 options will gain or fall in value like 40 futures contracts. So a bank might write 100 Swiss franc call options[10] for a customer and it might "delta-hedge" itself by buying 40 Swiss-franc futures contracts. In general, the options trader who employs delta hedging will take a futures position opposite to her options position, with the delta determining how many futures contracts are necessary to hedge the options position. The following are examples of the four typical options positions and the futures positions required to hedge them:

- Trader *buys calls* with a delta of 65 percent. To hedge, she *sells futures*. (She sells 65 futures contracts for every 100 calls bought.)
- Trader *sells calls* with a delta of 35 percent. To hedge, she *buys futures*. (She buys 35 futures contracts for every 100 calls sold.)

Figure 8.8   ***The Delta or Hedge Ratio.***   As measured by the slope of the option-price curve, the hedge ratio changes as the underlying price changes.

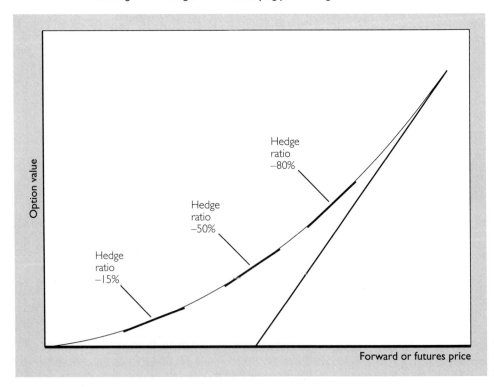

---

[10]Each contract covers 62,500 Swiss francs, so the bank would be writing call options on SF6,250,000.

- Trader *buys puts* with a delta of 17 percent. To hedge, she *buys futures*. (She buys 17 futures contracts for every 100 puts bought.)
- Trader *sells puts* with a delta of 72.3 percent. To hedge, she *sells futures*. (She sells 72 futures contracts for every 100 puts sold.)

As mentioned, the delta can be depicted as the slope of the option-price line. Unfortunately, as can be seen in Figure 8.8, the delta itself changes each time there is a change in the price of the underlying instrument. Hence a delta-hedge approach involves calculating daily, or even more frequently, the proportion of the underlying futures contract that should be held long to hedge a written call (or short, to hedge a written put). Only continual adjustments of this frequency will allow the option writer to hedge his market risks.

The measure of the rapidity with which the delta changes for a given change in the futures price is called the **gamma.** The gamma is represented in the option-price diagram by the *curvature* of the line. (The delta is the first derivative of the option price; the gamma is the second derivative.) To avoid being whipsawed by change in the delta, an option writer can hedge his short option position more precisely by using something that behaves like the instrument he sold—something that has a similar delta *and* a similar gamma. This is called *gamma hedging*. The obvious way to hedge an option, therefore, is with another option. We will cover this topic in more detail in the next section.

How Changes in Time and Volatility Affect an Option's Price

Changes in the currency futures price cause movements *along* the option-pricing curve. In this section we will see how changes in volatility or in time to expiration cause the whole curve to move up or down.

We have already stressed the importance of volatility in the determination of options prices. *Time to expiration* plays a related role. Increased volatility and increased time always increase the value of an option. The intuitive ideas have already been discussed, but we can summarize them as follows:

> *The greater the volatility and the more time there is before expiration, the wider the range of possible movements of the exchange rate.*

For the option buyer, this is desirable: big favorable moves increase his profit potential, whereas big unfavorable moves do not matter, because at worst he can let it expire unexercised. This is another way of saying that the greater the volatility and time, the greater is the expected value of the *truncated* distribution. To show this relationship we'll use another version of the option-pricing diagram shown in the top panel of Figure 8.7. In Figure 8.9, two probability distributions are shown. The wider one means greater volatility (higher standard deviation) or greater time. In that one, the expected value of the truncated distribution has shifted to the right, creating greater time value. Because the time value is greater at every possible forward rate, the whole option-pricing curve has shifted upward.

The sensitivity of an option price to changes in volatility is called the **vega.** For near-the-money options, the relationship between a change in the standard deviation of the forward price and the option price is roughly linear. Volatility sensitivity is generally greatest for long-term at-the-money options.

Long-term options are not very sensitive to changes in the length of time to expiration. As any option's expiration date draws nearer, this value falls faster and faster: it gets more and more sensitive to a change in the time to expiration. The rate of this time decay is called the **theta.** Theta is greatest when an option is near-the-money and close to expiration. Other things being equal, currency options lose most of their value in the last month of their lives.

Figure 8.9   ***Volatility and Time to Expiration.***   Both affect the option price directly, by shifting the price curve up or down.

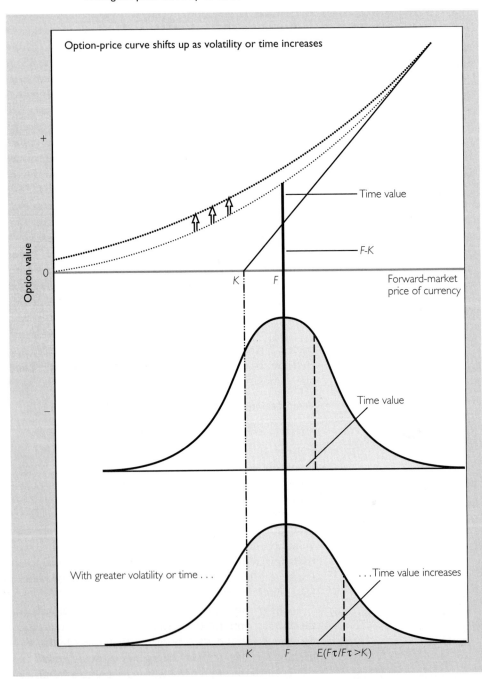

Hedging Options with Futures Versus Hedging Options with Options

We mentioned previously that the technique of hedging options with futures is subject to a serious shortcoming: the number of futures contracts required to hedge a given options position is given by the delta, the hedge ratio, but *because of the curvature of the option-pricing line the hedge ratio will be out of date whenever there is even the slightest change in the underlying currency's value.* The greater the gamma, the more dangerous it is to sell options and hope to hedge the position with futures.

The solution is to hedge options with options. Obviously, if you sell a particular option in the market and then seek to hedge your position by buying the identical option, you'll usually lose the bid-offer spread. If you want to make money, you must try to sell overpriced options and buy underpriced options. (To tell which is underpriced and which is relatively overpriced, options traders use the *implied volatility,* which is discussed in the section entitled Three Versions of Volatility that follows.)

To properly hedge options with options, traders try to achieve combined positions that are *delta neutral.* Delta neutral means being insulated from price changes in the underlying instrument. The trouble with buying one kind of call and selling a different call is that no two options have the same sensitivity to the underlying currency's value. A 1-cent change in the pound sterling will have a bigger impact on a call with a strike of $1.75 than one with a strike of $1.65, because the former, being more in-the-money, has a greater sensitivity—a higher delta. So if you sell a call with a delta of d_1 and want to hedge them by buying options with a hedge ratio of d_2, you have to hold them in reverse proportion to their hedge ratios: in other words, sell d_2 of the first call and buy d_1 of the second call. Alternatively, if you sell n calls with the d_1 hedge ratio you must buy $n(d_1/d_2)$ calls with the d_2 hedge ratio. I call this "flip-flop delta hedging." One way to remember it is: *use more of the less sensitive option to match less of the more sensitive option.*

Even a delta-neutral position—hedging options with the appropriate number of opposite options—is far from perfect. The reason is gamma. When the price of the underlying changes, the two options' deltas change—but by different amounts! This can help or hurt, depending on which has the greater gamma. In general, being *long gamma*—one that will produce larger gains if there's a big move in the currency—is the safer strategy.

Three Versions of Volatility

We have learned that the term **volatility,** used in an options context, refers to a statistical measure (usually standard deviation) of dispersion or variance. Volatility may be *historical* (backward-looking), *expected* (forward-looking) or *implied* (reflected in an option price). In theory, option valuation should employ expected volatility. Because expected volatility is difficult or impossible to measure directly, historical volatility is often used as an estimate of future volatility or as a starting point for predicting volatility.

Implied volatility is the volatility that is implied by the current market price of an option. Obtaining implied volatility requires the use of an options-pricing model such as the Black model described above. Given the market price of a traded option, and given all the other variables that go into the pricing of an option, only one volatility is consistent with the price at which the option is trading. The technique of finding implied volatility entails, in effect, a trial-and-error method of trying out various levels of volatility until one works.

Figure 8.10 contains data and charts of historical and implied volatilities for two major currencies. The case study in Application 8.3, Rorento Currency Management, offers an analytical application of the concepts of the historical and implied volatility of currency options.

Figure 8.10   *Historical and Implied Volatilities*

HVT 3   Curncy H V T
Hit \<Page> to include Today "as if closed".
14:12   H I S T O R I C A L   P R I C E   V O L A T I L I T Y
Mon 2/22
               J Y H 3   JPN YEN FUT (IMM) Mar93

	PRICE	N= 10-DAY	30	50	100	CALLS	PUTS
		N - D A Y V O L A T I L I T Y of Historical Closing Prices				O P T I O N S Implied Volatility	
2/19/93	84.41	9.91%	8.92%	8.17%	8.81%	13.05%	13.29%
2/18/93	83.94	10.17	8.89	8.14	8.78	12.24	12.24
2/17/93	83.68	10.60	8.91	8.12	8.86	12.26	12.26
2/16/93	83.30	10.68	8.95	8.29	8.84	11.87	11.87
2/12/93	82.89	10.69	8.95	8.27	8.85	11.25	11.24
2/11/93	82.64	11.15	9.09	8.26	9.03	11.52	11.52
2/10/93	82.61	11.95	9.14	8.29	9.69	10.77	10.76
2/ 9/93	82.53	12.02	9.14	8.32	9.75	10.19	10.19
2/ 8/93	80.81	5.66	6.73	6.78	9.14	8.21	8.21
2/ 5/93	80.39	4.65	7.10	6.80	9.11	7.43	7.43
2/ 4/93	80.30	9.94	7.10	6.79	9.13	7.96	7.96
2/ 3/93	80.36	10.00	7.10	6.81	9.13	7.99	7.99

                          260 Annualization Factor   weighted? Y
                                                   Expir 3/ 6/93 @ 3.10%

HVT 3   Curncy H V T
Hit \<Page> to include Today "as if closed".
14:06   H I S T O R I C A L   P R I C E   V O L A T I L I T Y
Mon 2/22
               B P H 3   BP CURCY FUT(IMM) Mar93

	PRICE	N= 10-DAY	30	50	100	CALLS	PUTS
		N - D A Y V O L A T I L I T Y of Historical Closing Prices				O P T I O N S Implied Volatility	
2/19/93	145.10	13.33%	16.23%	17.06%	17.86%	14.95%	14.95%
2/18/93	144.34	13.08	16.11	17.56	18.57	14.78	14.78
2/17/93	144.36	13.51	16.16	17.56	18.66	14.97	15.18
2/16/93	144.16	14.31	16.15	18.59	18.67	14.24	14.35
2/12/93	141.18	8.09	18.37	17.83	18.31	13.31	13.39
2/11/93	141.52	11.45	18.45	18.00	18.39	13.14	13.23
2/10/93	142.24	14.08	18.42	18.00	18.39	13.67	13.67
2/ 9/93	142.76	15.00	18.59	18.79	18.51	13.92	13.92
2/ 8/93	143.26	16.12	18.79	18.83	18.76	13.55	13.65
2/ 5/93	144.04	16.13	19.80	19.03	18.76	13.78	13.78
2/ 4/93	143.76	20.35	19.78	19.05	19.89	15.03	14.97
2/ 3/93	142.78	19.91	19.60	18.97	19.96	15.12	15.48

                          260 Annualization Factor   weighted? Y
                                                   Expir 3/ 6/93 @ 3.10%

Source: From Bloomberg News Service, Feb. 22, 1993.

Trading Volatility: Straddles and Strangles

An investor or speculator who expects a major move in the currency, or who expects the implied volatility to increase, can bet on this prediction without taking a view on the *direction* of the currency by buying a straddle. A *long straddle* is created by purchasing put

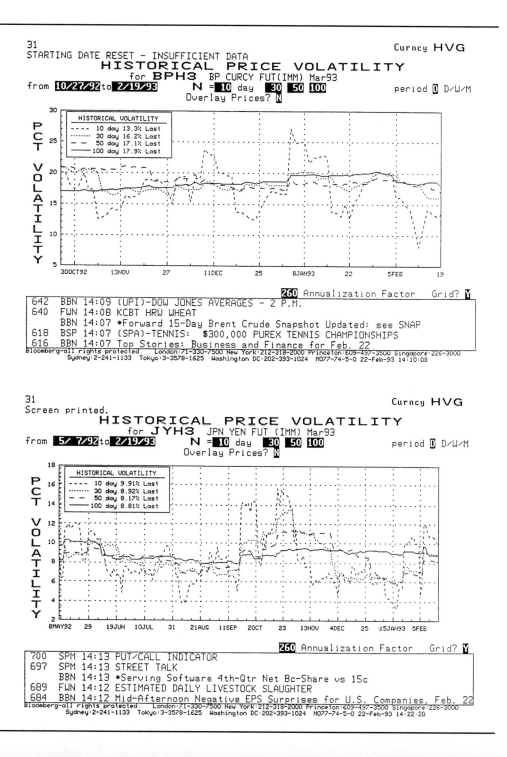

and call options having the same strike price, usually at or near the money.[11] This is shown in Figure 8.11. If a large market move occurs, then either the put or the call is likely to produce enough profit to cover the combined option premium and still leave a profit.

The straddle is costly, even if you are getting your money's worth. Those who wish to bet on a big market move but are reluctant to shell out a great deal of money can construct a *strangle* by purchasing both out-of-the-money put and out-of-the-money calls. Both will be cheap, so the combined price is much lower. As a much larger market move is necessary for this to pay off, a strangle is regarded as a long shot, and most of the time does not pay off. Many people buy straddles, and other out-of-the-money options strategies, because of their ostensibly low price. In my view, this is often a mistake, not only because you get only what you pay for, but also because deep out-of-the-money options are usually very illiquid.

It does not necessarily pay to buy something just because it's cheap. It's much better to buy something that's **underpriced.**

Figure 8.11   *Long Straddle.*   This is used to bet on big moves or an increase in volatility; it is created by buying near-the-money puts and calls.

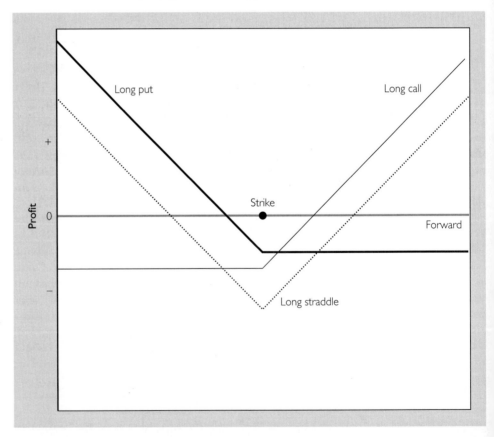

Figure 8.12   ***Long Strangle.***   This strategy is a bet on a really big move. It's created by combining out-of-the-money puts and calls.

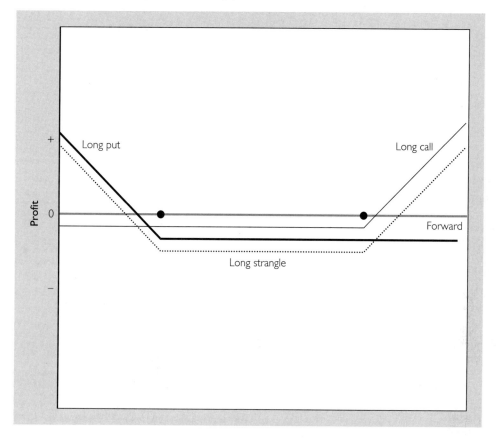

The profit profile of a long strangle is shown in Figure 8.12. A short strangle can be constructed by selling both out-of-the-money puts and out-of-the-money calls. The long-straddle or long-strangle position is frequently referred to as being *long volatility*, because the value of the combined position will increase when implied volatility increases. Similarly, the trader can *sell volatility* when he expects market moves to be smaller than those implied by options prices, by shorting straddles or strangles. Options are unique in that they put a market price on expected volatility.

Currency Collars

A *currency collar* is a way to bet on the direction of a currency, while limiting downside risk, but at a lower cost than purchasing a call alone. Rather than pay the higher price, the trader gives up some of her upside potential. (This is another of the many techniques used by banks to make options seem cheaper than they are. The problem with something that's superficially cheap is that you may not be getting your money's worth. When you buy a collar from a bank, you're in effect buying one call at the offer price and selling another at the bid. Bid-offer spreads can be rather wide in the options market, so this may not be the wisest strategy).

Figure 8.13　　***Currency Collars.***　These are created by buying a call and selling another call with a higher strike to pay part of the price.

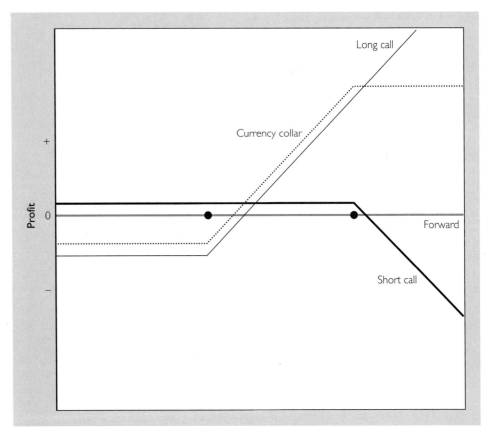

A collar that is bullish is created by buying a call at one strike price and selling a call at a higher strike. (See Fig. 8.13.) The former will be priced higher than the latter because the lower strike implies that the option is more in-the-money. To bet on the market falling, the opposite collar is created: sell a put with a lower strike price, and buy a put with a higher strike price.

Collars are forms of *spreads*. A bullish collar is also called a *bull spread;* a bearish collar, a *bear spread*.

Exotic Options

The types of options listed here by no means exhaust the possibilities for devising option-type instruments designed to serve particular purposes. "Exotic options" encompass myriad techniques devised by banks and securities firms to better serve their customers, often by making the option cheaper than conventional puts and calls. To take a simple example, an **Asian option** is an option on the *average* rather than on the instantaneous spot exchange rate. Because an average is less volatile than the spot itself, the option can be significantly less expensive. Another exotic is the *quanto,* which gives the right to buy or sell an unknown quantity of foreign currency. This option might be needed if, for example, one wishes currency protection on a portfolio of foreign equities, the value of which is subject to stock-price fluctuations. Table 8.3 lists these and some other variants.

Table 8.3   *Exotic Options*

Option	Definition	Remarks
Asian option	Option on the arithmetic or geometric average.	A cheaper option, because volatility is lower.
Barrier option	The payoff is determined by whether the underlying asset price breaches a predetermined barrier level. Can be tailored to appear ("down-and-in" or "up-and-in") or disappear "down-and-out" or "up-and-out") when the barrier is breached.	Usually cheaper than conventional options but can be very difficult to hedge.
As-You-Like-It option	At a certain point before expiration, holder can choose whether it's a put or a call.	
All-or-Nothing option	Pays a fixed sum, or the price of the underlying asset, if the option expires in-the-money.	
Pay-later option	Buyer pays if and only if the option expires in-the-money.	No-fee-unless-you-win feature attractive to some, but its discontinuous nature makes it expensive in the long run.
Rainbow option	Buyer has the right to receive a payoff based on the best performer of a number of different assets.	These options are difficult to hedge and not widely used. Years ago, some bonds allowed the investor to choose, at maturity, the currency of repayment.
Quanto option	The underlying asset and the option payoff are based in different currencies or commodities.	Has many varieties and the strong attractive feature of allowing investors to take a position in a foreign interest rate or stock without facing exchange risk.

Summary

Foreign-exchange options are combined bets on the direction and the volatility of a currency. As a consequence, currency options are not the ideal vehicles for betting on the direction of the currency. Anyone with a view on an exchange rate is better off employing futures, forwards, or a currency mismatch position. Options are for those who understand volatility and who have a view of volatility of rates that differs from the market's view as embodied in market option prices—or for those who require an option's asymmetric risk character to hedge their naturally asymmetric risks, such as an international company whose pricing policy embodies an implicit call option.

Foreign-exchange options are traded both over the counter, where banks are the primary market makers, and in major futures or stock exchanges. The latter are to bank options what futures are to forwards: standardized contracts that largely eliminate default risk. In recent years, long-term foreign-exchange options have been made available to the public in the form of "warrants" or embedded in bonds.

Anyone trading or hedging with currency options must become familiar with the fundamentals of option pricing and of the sensitivity of option prices to key variables. Beginning with put-call parity, which links put and call prices to the forward exchange rate, this chapter described the intuitive thinking behind a widely used version of the Black-Scholes model. By using such a model, we were able to see how changes in the time to expiration, in volatility, and in the price of the underlying currency affect an option's price.

Currency options are frequently bought or sold in conjunction with foreign-currency assets or liabilities, forwards, or futures. The last few sections demonstrated how the user can evaluate such combined positions. The key difference between options positions and the others is that the options price has curvature, or *gamma,* whereas futures and forwards are linear. The degree of curvature is a function of how nearly the option is at-the-money, as well as on the implied volatility and on the time to expiration. Because all these variables can change simultaneously, it is important for professionals in this game to devise ways in which to take a view on one while keeping the others constant. The best known of such techniques is the straddle, which is a way of betting on volatility while remaining insulated from the direction of movement of the currency.

CONCEPTUAL QUESTIONS

1. What are the key distinctions between OTC options and listed options? To what factor or factors do you attribute the rapid growth of the latter type of foreign-currency option?

2. What are the factors that create a market for foreign-currency warrants?

3. Why is liquidity an important consideration in foreign-currency options markets?

4. What are the key differences between options and forwards? When is an option a better hedging tool?

5. In what respect is an American option in futures like a European option?

6. What are the two basic situations in which currency options may be effectively used in corporate exchange-risk management?

7. What are the two ways in which time affects options prices? Which of these is more important?

8. You observe a sudden increase in the price of a traded currency option. To what factors could this be attributed?

9. What is put-call parity? What would you look for if you observed a significant deviation from put-call parity?

10. How would you synthesize a forward contract using options?

11. It has been said that "the value of a call option is the present value of its expected value at expiration." Explain. How does this relate to the intrinsic value of a call?

12. Explain why one would expect an increase in volatility to increase the price of a put option.

13. What are the advantages and disadvantages of buying a strangle rather than a straddle?

PROBLEMS

1. Using the data in Table 8.1, check for arbitrage opportunities in the put and call contracts with a strike price of $0.007 per Japanese yen. The yen futures prices are: March, 66.97; April, 67.15; May, 67.19. You may assume you can borrow short-term money at 8.125% and deposit it at 8.00%.

2. Use profit-profile diagrams to show how you could combine options to create a synthetic short futures position.

3. It is January 15. From Table 8.1, show which contracts you might use to create a synthetic short futures position for March delivery. Assume that you can borrow at 8.125% and lend at 8.00%, and that the futures price is 67.3. What would your net cost be? Would your company be better off or worse off using this in lieu of an actual short futures position?

4. It's still January 15. Using the data in Table 8.1, explain precisely how you would execute a *reversal* in the May 68 contract. Assuming you could borrow at 8.125% and lend at 8.00%, how much money would you gain or lose per contract with this transaction, if the futures price is 67?

5. At what price should the May 65 call trade if the futures price is 67 and the interest rate is 8%?

6. You work for British Telecom, which recently purchased put options on pounds sterling to hedge an amount of US$250,000 that is payable to AT&T. You have calculated the delta of the put to be .37. What kind of, and how many, futures would you use to hedge your position?

7. You are an options trader who has sold 100 December 62 DM puts. Given the following table, which and how many options would you use to achieve a delta-neutral position? Why and how would you expect to profit from this trade?

	December Calls				December Puts			
Stike	Bid	Offer	Implied Volatility	Delta	Bid	Offer	Implied Volatility	Delta
.62	1.37	1.38	12.4%	.85	0.11	0.13	12.4%	.15
.63	0.45	0.46	11.9%	.62	0.27	0.28	11.2%	.38

8. Your boss has asked you to obtain the historical, expected, and implied volatilities of the French franc. Please suggest how you might go about estimating each one.

9. The DM options trader at Bankers Trust has just sold call options on DM10 million for a price of $15,000. How would an increase in volatility from 10% to 11% affect her position?

10. Using the data in Table 8.1, show how you could construct a bear spread using Mar 65 and Mar 68 contracts.

11. As an options trader, you want to bet on an increase in the volatility of the yen. As a result of your previous trading, however, you're short of cash. Using the data in Table 8.1, construct the cheapest available strangle.

Application 8.1	RAYMOND'S NEW ROLE

It is May 28, 1993. You are a professional actor living in New York. In between roles in plays and soaps, you do word processing for the financial sector. One afternoon you are on a job in the trading room of the Empire Financial Group. A phone rings, but everyone's too busy to notice it, so you pick it up.

It's a customer with $2 million invested in a LIBOR-linked floating-rate note that will mature in mid-December 1993. He tells you that yesterday, fearing a further decline in interest rates, he hedged his return with Eurodollar futures contracts priced to lock in a LIBOR rate of 3.51 percent during the final quarterly reset period—that is, September through December.

Now he has called to say he has heard that rates may face upward pressure in forthcoming months, and he wonders whether locking in the FRN rate at its present level was the right thing to do. He is interested in the right to extract himself from the futures contract at roughly the price at which he got into it. Can you pull this one off, Raymond? Specifically, given the data from *The Wall Street Journal* shown in the accompanying tables, can you figure out roughly what prices to quote the customer?

FUTURES PRICES

EURODOLLAR (CME) – $1 million; pts of 100%

	Open	High	Low	Settle	Chg	Yield Settle	Chg	Open Interest
June	96.68	96.70	96.61	96.61	− .06	3.39 +	.06	224,455
Sept	96.49	96.55	96.39	96.40	− .09	3.60 +	.09	272,755
Dec	96.00	96.08	95.86	95.87	− .11	4.13 +	.11	294,062
Mr94	95.91	95.96	95.72	95.74	− .11	4.26 +	.11	193,579
June	95.58	95.61	95.37	95.39	− .11	4.61 +	.11	145,800
Sept	95.20	95.28	95.05	95.07	− .10	4.93 +	.10	126,344
Dec	94.82	94.86	94.65	94.65	− .10	5.35 +	.10	96,520
Mr95	94.75	94.78	94.58	94.59	− .09	5.41 +	.09	91,245
June	94.51	94.55	94.39	94.40	− .07	5.60 +	.07	63,819
Sept	94.33	94.37	94.22	94.23	− .06	5.77 +	.06	49,632
Dec	94.03	94.06	93.92	93.93	− .05	6.07 +	.05	49,155
Mr96	94.01	94.05	93.91	93.93	− .04	6.07 +	.04	44,243
June	93.84	93.87	93.77	93.79	− .01	6.21 +	.01	30,411
Sept	93.71	93.73	93.64	93.65	− .02	6.35 +	.02	27,062
Dec	93.46	93.48	93.39	93.40	− .02	6.60 +	.02	22,564
Mr97	93.45	93.49	93.39	93.41	− .01	6.59 +	.01	18,627
June	93.31	93.33	93.27	93.27	....	6.73	....	14,139
Sept	93.22	93.22	93.16	93.16	....	6.84	....	12,751
Dec	93.46	93.00	92.94	92.94	....	7.06	....	10,277
Mr98	92.98	93.00	92.94	92.94	....	7.06	....	5,899

Est vol 546,739; vol Wed 270,914; open int 1,793,339, −6,861.

EURODOLLAR (LIFFE) – $1 million; pts of 100%

	Open	High	Low	Settle	Change	Lifetime High	Low	Open Interest
June	96.68	96.71	96.68	96.70	+ .04	96.83	91.50	8,259
Sept	96.53	96.54	96.52	96.53	+ .05	96.76	92.50	4,711
Dec	96.06	96.06	96.03	96.06	+ .12	96.70	92.24	4,114
Mr94	95.93	95.93	95.92	95.94	+ .12	96.30	92.20	1,092
June	95.57	95.57	95.57	95.59	+ .13	95.98	93.36	392
Sept	....	....	....	94.83	+ .12	95.30	93.76	126

Est vol 1,506; vol Wed 1,681; open int 18,739, +324.

STERLING (LIFFE) – £500,000; pts of 100%

	Open	High	Low	Settle	Change	Lifetime High	Low	Open Interest
June	94.09	94.09	94.02	94.03	− .02	94.88	87.58	54,914
Sept	94.24	94.25	94.12	94.15	− .05	94.94	87.20	84,592
Dec	94.13	94.18	94.04	94.07	− .04	94.81	88.95	68,307
Mr94	93.85	93.86	93.74	93.76	− .04	94.53	89.87	38,086
June	93.51	93.53	93.43	93.43	− .05	94.23	89.78	29,363
Sept	93.15	93.15	93.05	93.06	− .05	93.91	90.10	17,602
Dec	92.76	92.76	92.71	92.71	− .04	93.55	90.10	11,369
Mr95	92.48	92.49	92.40	92.43	− .03	93.39	90.70	7,793
June	92.24	92.24	92.22	92.22	− .03	92.95	91.73	3,220
Sept	92.08	92.08	92.00	92.00	− .04	92.58	91.65	4,202

Est vol 61,593; vol Wed 43,334; open int 319,448, +5,328.

LONG GILT (LIFFE) – £50,000; 32nds of 100%

	Open	High	Low	Settle	Change	Lifetime High	Low	Open Interest
June	104-30	105-04	104-16	104-25	....	107-18	100-04	34,672
Sept	104-06	104-08	103-20	103-29	− 0-03	106-30	102-16	40,366

Est vol 53,258; vol Wed 117,894; open int 75,107, +2,896.

EUROMARK (LIFFE) – DM 1,000,000; pts of 100%

	Open	High	Low	Settle	Change	Lifetime High	Low	Open Interest
June	92.65	92.66	92.58	92.63	− .02	93.99	90.86	121,537
Sept	93.41	93.46	93.35	93.41	+ .01	94.29	91.12	145,523
Dec	93.91	93.97	93.87	93.94	+ .04	94.62	91.31	123,292
Mr94	94.26	94.33	94.26	94.33	+ .07	94.77	91.53	77,996
June	94.36	94.43	94.36	94.42	+ .06	94.80	91.71	44,782
Sept	94.00	94.41	94.30	94.40	+ .06	94.80	91.81	33,138
Dec	94.15	94.22	94.11	94.18	+ .03	94.61	91.83	23,662
Mr95	94.09	94.15	94.07	94.11	+ .02	94.60	92.45	12,662
June	93.92	93.93	93.90	93.93	+ .05	94.52	93.15	7,597
Sept	93.80	93.80	93.80	93.82	+ .04	94.23	93.62	2,097

Est vol 120,838; vol Wed 86,599; open int 592,286, +11,269.

FUTURES OPTIONS PRICES

EURODOLLAR (CME)
$ million; pts. of 100%

Strike Price	Calls–Settle Jun	Sep	Dec	Puts–Settle Jun	Sep	Dec
9625	0.37	0.27	0.15	0.01	0.12	0.53
9650	0.14	0.13	0.08	0.03	0.23	0.71
9675	0.02	0.04	0.04	0.16	0.39	0.91
9700	0.00	0.01	0.02	0.39	0.61	1.14
9725	0.00	0.00	0.01	0.64	0.85	1.39
9750	0.00	0.00	....	0.89	....	....

Est. vol. 113,745;
Wed vol. 33,669 calls; 60,103 puts
Op. int. Wed 638,929 calls; 747,734 puts

LIBOR – 1 Mo. (CME)
$3 million; pts. of 100%

Strike Price	Calls–Settle Jun	Jly	Aug	Puts–Settle Jun	Jly	Aug
9625	0.49	0.42	0.37	0.00	0.00	0.02
9650	0.24	0.19	0.15	0.00	0.02	0.05
9675	0.04	0.03	0.03	0.05	0.11	0.18
9700	0.00	0.01	0.01	0.26	0.34	0.41
9725	0.00	....	....	....	....	....
9750	....	....	....	....	....	....

Est vol 335   Wed 0 calls 115 puts
Op int Wed   5,698 calls 3,560 puts

TREASURY BILLS (CME)
$1 million; pts. of 100%

Strike Price	Calls–Settle Sep	Dec	Mar	Puts–Settle Sep	Dec	Mar
9625	0.47	0.26	....	0.03	0.16	....
9650	0.25	0.13	....	0.06	0.28	....
9675	0.09	0.06	....	0.15	0.45	....
9700	0.02	....	....	0.33	....	....
9725	0.01	....	....	0.57	....	....
9750	....	....	....	....	....	....

Est vol 45   Wed 0 calls 86 puts
Op int Wed   107 calls 1,195 puts

TREASURY BILLS

Maturity	Days to Mat.	Bid	Asked	Chg.	Ask Yld.
Jun 03 '93	2	2.96	2.86	− 0.04	2.90
Jun 10 '93	9	2.98	2.88	− 0.01	2.92
Jun 17 '93	16	2.98	2.88	+ 0.05	2.92
Jun 24 '93	23	2.93	2.83	+ 0.04	2.87
Jul 01 '93	30	2.94	2.90	+ 0.04	2.95
Jul 08 '93	37	2.96	2.92	+ 0.02	2.97
Jul 15 '93	44	2.96	2.92	+ 0.01	2.97
Jul 22 '93	51	2.97	2.93	+ 0.01	2.98
Jul 29 '93	58	2.98	2.96	+ 0.02	3.02
Aug 05 '93	65	2.99	2.97	....	3.03
Aug 12 '93	72	3.02	3.00	+ 0.01	3.06
Aug 19 '93	79	3.03	3.01	+ 0.01	3.07
Aug 26 '93	86	3.06	3.04	+ 0.01	3.10
Sep 02 '93	93	3.08	3.06	+ 0.01	3.13
Sep 09 '93	100	3.08	3.06	....	3.13
Sep 16 '93	107	3.09	3.07	....	3.14
Sep 23 '93	114	3.13	3.11	+ 0.02	3.18
Sep 30 '93	121	3.11	3.09	+ 0.03	3.17
Oct 07 '93	128	3.13	3.11	+ 0.01	3.19
Oct 14 '93	135	3.14	3.12	+ 0.01	3.20
Oct 21 '93	142	3.15	3.13	+ 0.01	3.21
Oct 28 '93	149	3.15	3.13	+ 0.01	3.22
Nov 04 '93	156	3.17	3.15	+ 0.02	3.24
Nov 12 '93	164	3.17	3.15	+ 0.02	3.24
Nov 18 '93	170	3.20	3.18	+ 0.03	3.27
Nov 26 '93	178	3.22	3.20	+ 0.04	3.30
Dec 16 '93	198	3.22	3.20	+ 0.04	3.30
Jan 13 '94	226	3.25	3.23	+ 0.04	3.33
Feb 10 '94	254	3.32	3.30	+ 0.05	3.41
Mar 10 '94	282	3.35	3.33	+ 0.06	3.45
Apr 07 '94	310	3.39	3.37	+ 0.05	3.49
May 05 '94	338	3.41	3.39	+ 0.06	3.52

Source: *The Wall Street Journal*, May 28, 1993, pp. C12, C13, C15.

Application 8.2

COVER ME

It is 4:00 P.M. Friday in London. Christiana Bank's London branch needs to hedge its pounds-sterling book before the weekend. Suggest how many, and what, futures are required to hedge a position that comprises the following:

- 100 short puts with a delta of 65 percent and an implied volatility of 17 percent
- 100 short futures
- 50 long futures

Using the standard profit-profile diagram, show what your combined positions will look like after you have hedged the position.

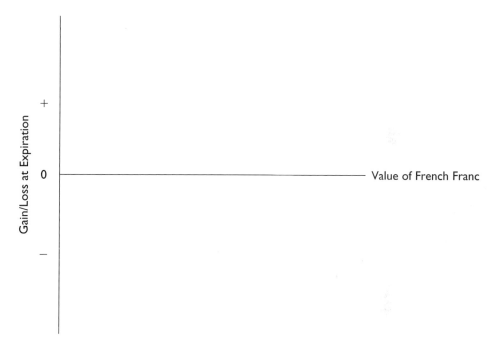

Application 8.3

RORENTO CURRENCY MANAGEMENT

Andre van Rensberg was a South African emigre to the Netherlands who worked in the currency-management department of the Rotterdam-based mutual fund, Rorento. Rorento invested in fixed-income securities denominated in a variety of currencies, including U.S. dollars, and early in 1993 Andre was concerned that the dollar's recent strength could not last. Many of Rorento's investors were German, and they would suffer if the dollar fell significantly. He had been considering purchasing some deutschemark currency options to hedge against the exchange risk, but some in the Rorento currency-management team were concerned that options were, at least at present, "too expensive." "If so," he replied, "perhaps we should be selling options; the premium could be used as a cushion to offset a drop in the dollar."

Andre recalled that he had recently seen a report from Dean Witter, the New York securities firm, that had information about historical and implied volatilities of currency options. He decided to scrutinize the analytics in the report and write a brief memo (in English) justifying his decision to buy, or sell, options on the deutschemark.

Should van Rensberg buy or sell DM options? Which options, or combination of options, should he buy or sell? Write a paragraph justifying your answers.

Exhibit
Volatility Cone Report

Volatility cones

The heart of the report is the volatility cone, which is shown in the middle chart on the left-hand side of the report. The volatility cone is a graphic representation of the maturity structure of volatility and allows a quick visual comparison of implied volatilities in the current lead and first deferred option contracts with ranges of historical volatilities whose horizons correspond to the options' different times remaining to expiration.

The smoothly curved lines represent upper and lower bounds of historical volatilities for trading horizons ranging from one month to one year. These reports show estimates based on two years of data for the period ending on the last trading day of the quarter just completed.

The resulting volatility cones show that short-term historical volatilities are substantially more variable than longer-term historical volatilities. This can be seen in the greater distance between the maximum and minimum 30-day historical volatilities (shown toward the left of the chart entitled Maturity Structure of Volatility) and the maximum and minimum 180-day historical volatilities (shown in the middle of the chart).

Implied volatilities

Overlaid on each cone is the past quarter's history of implied volatilities for what are now the lead and first deferred option contracts. The jagged solid line shows the past quarter's behavior of the current lead option, while the jagged dotted line shows the past quarter's behavior of the current first deferred option. The left-most point of each line is the value of implied volatility for each of the contracts on the last trading day of the quarter just completed. Note that the ends of the two implied volatility plots are separated by 3 months, which is the time between the expirations of the two options.

Cheapness index

We think that the volatility cones provide a useful guide to whether longer-term options are cheap or rich. For that matter, a reasonable measure of an option's richness is the likelihood that realized futures volatility will be less than the option's current implied volatility over its remaining life. An index value in the neighborhood of 50 indicates that the option is more or less neutrally priced. A high index value indicates a high probability that realized volatility would be less than the option's implied volatility and that the option by this standard is expensive. Low index values indicate cheap options.

The past quarter's history of each commodity's cheapness index is also charted in the lower left-hand panel of each individual commodity's report.

VOLATILITY CONE REPORT

- DEUTSCHE MARK -
(CME)

FUTURES VS. IMPLIED VOLATILITY
March 1993 Contract during Fourth Quarter, 1992

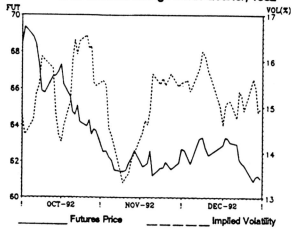

Futures Price — — — — Implied Volatility

MATURITY STRUCTURE OF VOLATILITY

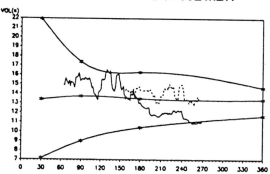

Date (YYMMDD) of Last Implied Volatility : 921231 Period for Historical Cone : Two Years.
Contract Months (YYMM) : Lead = 9303,   Deferred = 9306

CHEAPNESS INDEX
March 1993 Contract during Fourth Quarter, 1992

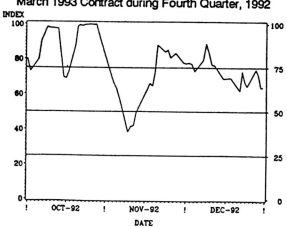

DATE

IMPLIED VOLATILITIES
(JANUARY 1991 THROUGH DECEMBER 1992)

Range of Calendar Days to Expiration	High		Low		Average
	Volatility	Date (yymmdd)	Volatility	Date (yymmdd)	Volatility
15 - 30	17.32	910820	9.27	910214	12.91
31 - 60	20.65	921008	9.28	920430	13.54
61 - 90	18.37	921001	9.99	920624	13.18
91 - 120	15.72	921127	10.39	920521	12.60
121 - 150	16.55	921026	10.07	920429	12.83
151 - 180	14.82	921001	10.47	920622	12.71
181 - 210	14.44	921120	10.73	920528	12.42
211 - 240	15.06	921026	10.70	920430	12.56
241 - 300	14.52	921007	10.85	920617	12.52

LEAD CONTRACT
HISTORICAL VOLATILITIES

	Period Ending*	1-Month	3-Month	6-Month	1-Year	2-Year
	January	14.771				
	February	10.025				
	March	15.944	13.614			
	April	18.454	15.491			
	May	14.899	16.765			
1991	June	11.301	15.135	14.376		
	July	15.646	13.748	14.674		
	August	19.926	16.004	16.202		
	September	9.860	15.762	15.249		
	October	11.648	14.024	14.082		
	November	11.874	11.175	13.647		
	December	11.355	11.643	13.604	14.020	
	January	18.852	14.183	14.276	14.449	
	February	11.864	14.546	12.753	14.591	
	March	8.998	13.933	12.690	14.028	
	April	9.179	10.115	12.432	13.273	
	May	11.274	9.851	12.285	12.991	
1992	June	8.779	9.485	11.951	12.804	
	July	15.447	12.099	11.076	12.777	
	August	10.096	11.797	10.722	11.816	
	September	20.224	15.601	12.996	12.860	
	October	16.497	16.498	14.235	13.256	
	November	14.059	17.132	14.652	13.530	
	December	12.231	14.489	15.119	13.601	13.834
CONE MAXIMUM		21.937	17.397	16.276	14.654	13.835
CONE AVERAGE		13.381	13.712	13.472	13.390	13.824
CONE MINIMUM		7.151	8.998	10.420	11.658	13.795

* *Period ending on last trading day of each month.*

Maturity Structure of JY-DM Volatility

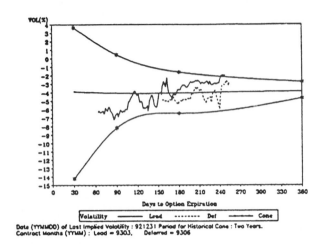

Maturity Structure of DM-BP Volatility

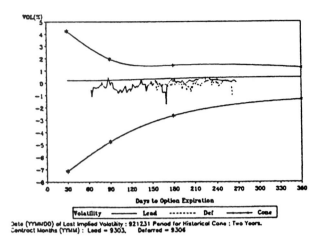

Source: Excerpts taken from *Quarterly Volatility Review*, by Galen Burghardt and Wendell Kapustiak, Dean Witter Institutional Futures, Feb. 2, 1993.

SELECTED REFERENCES

Biger, Nahum, and John Hull. "The Valuation of Currency Options." *Financial Management*, vol. 12 (Spring 1983): 24–28.

Black, Fischer, and Myron Scholes. "The Pricing of Options and Corporate Liabilities." *Journal of Political Economy*, vol. 81 (May–June 1973): 637–659.

Bodurtha, James N., and George R. Courtadon. "Tests of an American Option Pricing Model on the Foreign Currency Options Market." *Journal of Financial and Quantitative Analysis*, vol. 22 (June 1987): 153–167.

Garman, Mark B., and Stephen W. Kohlhagen. "Foreign Currency Option Values." *Journal of International Money and Finance*, vol. 2 (December 1983): 231–237.

Giddy, Ian H. "Foreign Exchange Options." *Journal of Futures Markets*, vol. 3, no. 2 (1983): 143–166.

Hull, John C. *Options, Futures and Other Derivatives*. 2nd Ed. Englewood Cliffs, N.J.: Prentice-Hall, 1993.

Merton, Robert C. "Option Pricing When Underlying Stock Returns are Discontinuous." *Journal of Financial Economics* (January–March 1976): 125–144.

9

International Banking and Credit

International Banking and the Eurocurrency Market

International banking today is intimately bound in with the Eurocurrency markets. Before the existence of the Euromarkets, all international banking involved branch activities within local markets abroad, or traditional foreign lending in which a domestic bank would use domestic funds to make a loan abroad. The key feature of traditional foreign lending and borrowing is that *all transactions are directly subject to the rule and institutional arrangements of the respective national markets*. Most important, these transactions are subject to public policy pertinent to (foreign) transactions in a particular market. To illustrate, when savers purchase securities in a foreign market, they do so according to the rules, market practices, and regulatory precepts that govern such transactions in that particular market. The same applies to those who place their funds with foreign financial intermediaries. Likewise, foreign borrowers who wish to issue securities in a domestic market must follow the rules and regulations of this market—and often these rules simply say "no." And the borrower who approaches a foreign financial institution for a loan borrows at rates and conditions imposed by the financial institutions of that country and is directly affected by the public authorities' policy toward lending to foreign residents.

Enter the Euromarkets. During the past 25 years, market mechanisms have developed that remove international (and even national) borrowing and lending from the jurisdiction and influence of national authorities. This is done simply by locating the market for credit dominated in a particular currency *outside* the country of that currency. The markets for dollar-dominated loans, deposits, and bonds in Europe, for example, are not subject to U.S. banking or securities regulations. We refer to these markets as "Euro," or more properly "external," to indicate that they are distinct from the domestic or national financial systems. Thus the essence of this classification criterion is the absence (or presence), and the nature, of regulation. Differences in interest rates, practices, and terms that exist between domestic and external markets arise primarily from the extent to which regulatory constraints can be avoided.

We can now be more precise about the concept of the "international money market" that forms the focus of this chapter and the next. The core of this market is clearly the Eurocurrency market, where funds are intermediated outside the country of the currency in which the funds are denominated, or outside the immediate regulatory environment governing domestic and foreign transactions. Thus the Eurocurrency market comprises financial institutions that compete for dollar (time) deposits and make dollar loans outside the United States, financial institutions outside Switzerland that bid for Swiss-franc

---

Author's note: Portions of this chapter are excerpted from *The International Money Market,* 2nd Ed., by Gunter Dufey and Ian H. Giddy (Englewood Cliffs, N.J.: Prentice-Hall, 1994).

deposits and make loans in this or another currency (but not the currency of the country in which they operate), and so forth.

The relationship between each Eurocurrency market and its domestic counterpart can be seen as a process of evolution. During the 1960s and 1970s, the major currencies gained enough nonresident convertibility that a Eurocurrency segment was able to arise. The Eurocurrency segment of the money market thrived and grew because domestic money markets were hobbled by outdated regulations such as interest-rate controls and by oligopolistic pricing practices such as lending tied to compensating balances and slow-to-adjust prime rates. The easing of capital controls that followed the move to floating exchange rates in the 1970s allowed depositors and borrowers to shift their business to the external market, which offered more attractive rates and conditions.

By the late 1970s and early 1980s the authorities of the United States, Germany, the United Kingdom, and other countries were forced to acknowledge the success of Eurocurrency-based wholesale banking. They began to ease the more burdensome and unnecessary regulations and to lower reserve requirements and other taxlike burdens. Japan, France, and other countries encouraged the growth of the domestic money market and of innovative banking practices to attract some of the lost banking business back home. Thus the 1980s and 1990s have seen a resurgence of domestic money markets.

Even so, the constraints faced by banks in their domestic markets offer a continuing rationale for the Eurocurrency market (see Box 9.1). For any given country, one can ask (1) how *efficiently* the banking system performs its private economic role of balancing the cash needs of investors and borrowers, and (2) what does the *government* demand of the banking system to serve its public-policy objectives?

BOX 9.1

Why the Eurocurrency Markets Thrive

The Eurocurrency market consists of banks that offer wholesale deposits and loans in favorable jurisdictions and in a variety of currencies, usually other than that of the country in which the banks are located. They are able to do so as long as there is free nonresident transferability and convertibility of clearing balances in the currencies in which the Eurodeposits and loans are denominated.

In such currencies, *international banks have a competitive advantage in financial intermediation resulting from the disadvantage of banks operating in their respective national markets.* The domestic disadvantages are based almost exclusively on governmental rules and regulations, such as

- regulations that influence the credit-allocation decisions of financial intermediaries.
- regulations that burden financial intermediaries with special costs; this factor includes, but is not restricted to, special assessments and taxes.
- rules and regulations that limit interest rates on deposits or assets.
- rules and regulations that force intermediaries to maintain reserves yielding less than the market return for funds of such riskiness.
- all other rules, regulations, and practices that restrict competition among banks in one way or another, or that tolerate the existence of private banking cartels.

In the case of the Eurodollar market, the most important are the regulatory costs referred to in the second category: the cost of non-interest-bearing reserve requirements imposed by the Fed, and deposit insurance fees levied by the FDIC. In fact, in virtually all countries, banks must hold minimum reserve requirements in interest-free accounts with the central bank, or alternatively, invest a substantial proportion of their assets in government securities in order to facilitate the management of the money supply and credit conditions.

In answering these questions, the reader will discover that there are two fundamentally different structures for financial systems around the world. The first, exemplified by the United States, is *securities-market dominated:* most short-term funds are channeled through markets for traded instruments such as Treasury bills and commercial paper. The second is *bank dominated:* the bulk of short-term investments are placed in bank deposits or equivalent instruments such as bankers' acceptances, and most short-term funding is in the form of bank loans. The German system is of this kind, as is demonstrated in Box 9.2, Banking versus Markets: Germany and Japan.

We first examined the Eurocurrency market as a trading phenomenon in Chapter 2. Recall that the term is misleading in two ways:

1. It implies that it is a market for foreign currencies similar or closely related to the foreign-exchange market.
2. The term *Eurocurrency* implies either that the market is located in Europe or that it deals primarily in European currencies.

BOX 9.2

Banking Versus Markets: Germany and Japan

The German, or Continental, system of universal banking contrasts with the Anglo-Saxon market-based systems in several ways. In Germany, corporate financing requirements depend largely on bank loans and much less on stocks and bonds. While American and British companies were abandoning their banks in favor of the money and capital markets in the 1970s and 1980s, German nonfinancial companies used bank loans as the source of 90 percent or more of their net funds raised. The German universal banks, dominated by Deutsche Bank, Dresdner Bank, and Commerzbank, offer a full range of commercial, investment banking, and brokerage services. The importance of these banks derives from their roles as a source of credit and the underwriter of stock and bond issues. Even though they are subject to limits on their own holdings of shares, the universal banks acquire and vote the proxies of shares held for brokerage customers. As a result, they play a major role in company governance.

Company behavior in Germany can be monitored nearly continuously by loan officers. Under normal circumstances, professional bankers are unlikely to intervene in the technical or marketing details of company management, even through they are members of the supervisory boards. They may, however, play a useful role in times of financial crisis, especially if companies must be restructured.

In Japan, individual stockholders own only 30 percent of listed shares. Banks and other financial institutions own 40 percent. For larger companies, a few important city banks will hold shares up to the limit and one of them will serve as the company's main bank. This means the bank maintains close ties to the company in cash-management and credit operations. It will also manage loan syndications. Until recently this was especially important because Japanese companies were financed with large ratios of debt to equity. Although Japanese banks normally do not interfere in company management, if a company is in trouble, the banks step in and, if necessary, replace the existing management, never with outsiders but with incumbent personnel.

The German and Japanese arrangements tend to shield companies both from outside takeover and from bankruptcy. Even though Germany and Japan have laws with provisions similar to Chapter 11 of the U.S. Bankruptcy Act, they are seldom used. Instead, the banks make a private arrangement that typically takes a long time to arrange. During this time, dividends and employment may be cut, but spending on investment and research is often maintained. In contrast to the United States, where management often remains in place during the troubles, in Germany new management usually is brought in. Except where it prolongs a losing battle, the whole process reduces the likelihood of ultimate failure as well as creditors' potential losses.

Neither is true. *The Eurocurrency market is simply a market for bank deposits and loans denominated in a currency other than that of the country in which the bank is located.* The international money market consists of the Eurocurrency market and its linkages to the major domestic money markets. Although the Eurocurrency market is closely tied to the foreign-exchange market (almost all Eurobanks also deal in foreign exchange), it is useful to remind ourselves that the two markets are quite distinct in function. In the foreign-exchange market, one currency is exchanged for another; in the Eurocurrency market, deposits are accepted and loans are granted, usually in the same currency. This chapter deals with the international credit market. In Chapter 10 we will look at the instruments of the international money market, including the deposits that constitute the principal means by which international banks fund themselves.

The fundamental contribution of the Euromarket to international banking goes beyond the separation of the currency of denomination from the country of jurisdiction. Euromarket practices have taken this theme of *separability* a great deal further. A seemingly simple loan has a large number of different features and aspects of risk, and over time international bankers have learned to isolate or "unbundle" these features in order to be able to distribute and to hedge the inherent risks. Financial claims can be unbundled and repackaged to serve clients' needs more efficiently. In the sections that follow we will explore both the mechanics as well as the economics of separating the provision of funds from the assumption of credit risk, liquidity (or "availability") risk, and other features that are involved in a loan.

The Separability of Pricing from Commitment Periods

There was a time when a five-year loan bore a five-year interest rate. The commitment period, the period for which the borrower had the assurance of funds, coincided with the pricing period. This was possible because banks had a stable, almost monopolistic, base of deposit funds in their domestic branches, a base that was not very sensitive to fluctuations in rates. High interest rates and the competitiveness of the Eurodeposit market changed all that. Banks were compelled to pay a market rate of interest for their deposits. Their cost of funds would vary every time they had to roll over their funding—so they took to letting the interest rate on their loans vary in tandem with the cost of deposits.

As lenders, Eurobanks are prepared to extend funds for longish commitment periods—five to twelve years is not unusual—but they are unwilling to carry much of an interest-rate risk. The usual way in which companies borrow short term is under a pre-arranged line of credit. Under such an arrangement, a maximum amount is established that can be borrowed within the commitment period, usually one year, but it is often renewable after a more-or-less thorough review process. Drawdowns carry interest charges based on the current short-term rate, with adjustments typically every one, three, or six months (see Table 9.1 for an example).

Short-term credits are also extended *ad hoc,* normally for periods up to six months at fixed rates. Medium-term lending is more prevalent and is usually done in the form of a revolving loan facility (or *revolver*). In this case, the pricing period rarely exceeds six months. Commitment periods of up to fifteen years and more have been reported, although the majority of loans fall in the three- to seven-year category. If and when the borrower requires a fixed-rate "term" loan, as illustrated in Table 9.1, the bank or banks will hedge their risk by entering into an interest-rate swap—so the rate on the term loan will reflect current fixed-for-floating swap rates.

The base rate is the London interbank offered rate, LIBOR, which is the interest at which a sample of reference banks in the London Euromarket offer funds for deposit in

Table 9.1   ***Pricing of Eurodollar Loan Facility.***   This table compares the features of a revolving credit facility (floating rate) and a term loan (fixed rate).

Menomonee Trading Company Inc.
Credit Facilities Totalling $300,000,000
Summary of Terms

	I. Revolving Credit Facility	II. Term Loan
Amount	Up to $200,000,000	$100,000,000
Purpose	To fund the acquisition of Dan Deming Co. and to refinance certain existing indebtedness	Same
Repayment	Reduction of commitment according to attached schedule	Amortization of loan according to attached schedule
Maturity	July 1, 1997	July 1, 1997
Interest rate	1-, 2-, 3-, or 6-month LIBOR as defined in the loan agreement, plus 1.25%	From closing until maturity, the outstanding principal balance will bear interest at a rate of 11.5% payable quarterly in arrears on the first business day of each quarter.

the interbank market. Loan agreements usually stipulate the banks and the time, typically 11 A.M. London time.[1] The actual interest cost to the borrower is set at a "spread" over the LIBOR rate. This margin reflects (1) general market conditions, and (2) the specific circumstances of the borrower (largely how his creditworthiness is judged competitively by the lending institution). Typically, such spreads, for both corporate and public borrowers, have ranged from ¼ percent, and even slightly less, to 3 percent and above, with the median being somewhere between ½ and 1½ percent. In special circumstances, the contractual spread increases or decreases in specified ways in future interest periods during the life of the loan. These provisions are included to encourage or discourage early repayment of the loan.

In addition to LIBOR-plus pricing, it is a well-established practice in the Euromarket to charge a commitment fee, usually ¼ to 1 percent per annum on the unused portion of the loan, payable at the outset. On the other hand, during times when loan demand is weak and the banks are flush with funds, commitment fees fall victim to competitive pressures. Euroloan agreements invariably specify a drawdown period of, say, up to 18 months, during which time the funds must be used by the borrower; otherwise, the commitment expires or the borrower is charged the stipulated rate just as if he had taken up the funds.

The Syndication Technique in International Lending

Once upon a time, we recall, banks made loans to borrowers: they built a relationship, got to know the company and its business, extended the customer a line of credit. When

---

[1]With the growing importance of Caribbean-based Eurobanking, loan agreements now tend to specify 4 P.M. LIBOR rates. This time is equivalent to 11 A.M. Nassau time and coincides with U.S. trading hours.

funds were needed, the banks loaned those funds, monitored the borrower, and expected to get repaid when the loan matured. When earnings went awry, the banker tried to work things out through pressure and persuasion. In short, there was a close relationship between the lender and the borrower throughout the life of the loan. The banker served the role of originator, provider of funds, manager of interest-rate risk, and nursemaid to the loan.

Nowadays all these functions can be done separately, and some new ones have been borrowed from the securities market. The result has been a dramatic reduction of the tie between bank and borrower. A catalyst has been the distribution method adapted from the securities underwriting business.[2] This is the underwriting and distribution of large, medium-term syndicated credits. A logical consequence is the subsequent trading of certain of these credits among banks and other financial and even nonfinancial institutions. As we shall see, however, underwriting, distribution, and trading have adapted themselves to meet the peculiar requirements of the international-bank lending business.

Loan syndication typically involves a small group of knowledgeable and well-capitalized banks that agree initially to provide the entire loan. These banks then sell portions of their share of the credits to a much wider range of smaller or less knowledgeable banks.[3] Syndication of a large loan serves much the same purpose as syndication of a security such as a bond issue. It provides the borrower with certainty about the amount and price of funds, while allowing wide distribution: if many banks are able to share in small parts of different loans, their risk will be more diversified and they will be more willing to make loans. In the Eurocurrency market, an issuer may come from one country with its own regulations and accounting norms, while lenders are from a dozen or more other nations. *Much of their risk reduction is performed not by credit analysis and monitoring and control but by taking a smaller amount of more diversified assets and by relying on the monitoring role of the lead bank or banks.*

What is a *loan syndicate?* Simply put, it is a highly structured group of financial institutions, formed by a *manager* or a group of co-managers, that lends funds on common conditions to a borrower. To see what distinguishes syndication in the external markets from loan participation and other forms of joint bank lending that are long-standing practices in national markets, we shall look at syndication from the perspective of the borrower and the participating banks, including the lead manager, the co-managers, and the agent bank.

Although members of a direct syndicate have several, rather than joint, agreements with the borrower, it is usual for the members to appoint a manager or an agent to act as a conduit between the syndicate and the borrower. This allows for the dispersion of ownership while retaining some of the benefits of a principal-agent relationship—in particular, the surveillance and negotiation responsibilities of the agent. In practice, the agent may follow a quite different pattern of behavior when legal and fiduciary obligations are guiding choices instead of the fear of losing one's own money, which tends to concentrate one's mind wonderfully.

An international loan-syndication agreement can take one of two forms (or a combination thereof): a *direct-loan syndicate* or a *participation syndicate*. A direct-loan **syndicate** is a multilateral loan agreement in which participant banks, having signed a common loan document, advance funds to the borrower; the obligations of the participant banks are several, rather than joint. A **participation** syndicate, on the other hand, is similar to a principal-agent relationship. A lead bank or banks usually executes a loan agreement with

---

[2]The reader need not concern himself with underwriting techniques at this point. They are covered in some detail in Chapter 12 on the international bond market.

[3]Rarely, one encounters partially underwritten syndicated credits and *best-efforts* syndicated credits.

the borrower and then forms the syndicate by entering into a participation agreement with other banks. The important distinction is that, unlike in the direct syndication case, subparticipants are not co-lenders.

The relationship between a borrower and the syndicate manager is very similar to that between a corporation and its investment-banking house. This relationship is usually one of long standing, because it requires an intimate knowledge of the borrower's requirements, strengths, and weaknesses, as well as of its preferences. Normally, a syndicated loan in the external market is the result of a decision process in which various alternatives, in terms of markets, instruments, and maturities, are considered.

Indeed, it was the traditional U.S. investment-banking houses and U.K. merchant banks that first featured prominently as lead managers of syndicated loans in the external markets. However, as the markets gain maturity, these early pioneers are being more and more displaced by large commercial banks, or rather by their merchant-banking affiliates. The task of a syndicate manager is to obtain the amount of funds required by a borrower at the best conditions currently obtainable in the market. Syndication is usually made on a "best efforts" basis (that is, the syndicate manager obtains a mandate from the borrower to go out and attempt to get the funds via a syndicate but makes no guarantee that the funds will be raised). However, for all practical purposes the borrower expects a commitment, almost equivalent to a firm underwriting. No prospective lead manager can afford to come back to the client and say, "Sorry, we thought we could do it, but . . . ."

Here the major commercial banks have an advantage that cannot easily be duplicated by the traditional investment and merchant bankers: it is the commercial banks that have the funds. This advantage permits them to speak with much more assurance to a borrower, because even though every lead manager intends to place a very large proportion of the total loan with other banks, as a last resort a commercial bank can always increase its own share, should other banks prove less eager to participate than it originally anticipated.

Commercial banks have a second advantage over investment banks that must not be underestimated: other financial institutions will be much more willing to take on a share of a credit if they know that the syndicate manager is confident enough to take more than just a token proportion into its own loan portfolio. And this fact will significantly contribute to the success of the syndicate by increasing the "sell-out rate," the proportion of the total loan placed with other participants.

It is for such services that borrowers are willing to pay somewhere between ¼ and 2 percent "front end" syndication fees, in addition to expenses. For an example of the fee structure in a syndicated loan, see Table 9.2. An edge in distribution or placement power resulting from direct access to deposits has given the investment-banking affiliates of large commercial banks the muscle to partially displace the traditional investment-banking houses. Other skills usually found in investment banks are (1) a view of total corporate finance (as compared to narrow credit evaluation), (2) in-depth knowledge of worldwide financial markets, and (3) the ability to structure a loan or a security into a package that is attractive to the providers of funds while appropriate to the borrower's situation. To some extent, these technical skills can be bought or duplicated by the commercial banks. Within commercial banks, the individuals who possess these capabilities are usually housed in separate merchant-banking affiliates, often based in London. Such organizations lie somewhere on the spectrum between pure, fee-earning financial-service organizations and asset-building organizations whose income comes from the spreads between deposit rates and lending rates.

Whatever the institutional home of the syndicate manager, his ability to persuade other banks to participate in a loan is crucial. The formation of a syndicate is a complex and intricate affair of competition and cooperation: (1) Most syndicates are *ex post;* that is, the syndicate is formed *after* potential lead managers have competed for the mandate from the borrower (and the fees involved); losing competitors often join the syndicate as participating banks. (2) Both reciprocity considerations and correspondence relationship

Table 9.2   *Sample Fee Structure.*   These fees are typical for a syndicated Eurodollar loan.

Menomonee Trading Company Inc.
$300 Million Facility—Fee Structure

Closing fees to initial lenders	1.76% of commitment amount, payable at closing
Closing fees to assignees	Over $50 mm 1.25%
	Up to $50 mm 1.00%
	Up to $25 mm 0.75%
	The closing fee will be based on the assignee's aggregate allocated commitment, payable upon execution of the Assignment.
Commitment fees	½% per annum on the unused portion of the revolving credit facility
Prepayment fees, revolving credit facility	A prepayment fee for payments made other than at the end of a Euroloan period will be calculated in accordance with a formula set out in the Credit Agreement.
Prepayment fees, term loan	Payments made other than as shown in the repayment schedule will be subject to a prepayment fee in accordance with a formula set out in the credit agreement.
Agent's fee	Payable to Agent, First Manhattan Trust, for agency functions in the amount of $100,000 at the closing date and $50,000 per year thereafter unless all facilities are paid in full before these dates

with the lead manager are important factors determining which banks participate. (3) The borrower itself may have a say on who is invited to participate. The borrower will often press for a role of one sort or another for financial institutions that it wants to reward for past service, or with which it wishes to do business in the future. (And vice versa, many banks have found that a useful way to establish a link with a prospective customer is to participate in the target customer's syndicated credit.)

Again following the pattern of securities underwriting, syndicated credits can be made quietly like private placements, or publicly announced in the form of a "tombstone" advertisement that appears in business journals or weeklies that have substantial international circulation.

Why Syndicate Eurocurrency Loans?

Joint lending by a group of banks is common in national markets as well as in the Eurocurrency market. In part this occurs because almost all countries have laws and regulations limiting the amount that can be loaned by any one bank to any one customer. The regulations are designed to

1. protect the customer from undue influence by any one single lender
2. protect the bank from being excessively exposed to the credit of any single customer.

This forces diversification, something that would in any case be called for by the precepts of prudent financial management. Yet even if, by law or by choice, each domestic bank provides only part of the fund needed by particular borrowers, there is no obvious reason for lending to be coordinated by the banks themselves.

One way to understand the rationale for syndication is to ask why the borrower cannot approach a number of banks directly, and obtain from each a portion of the total funds needed.[4] Compared to separate little loans, the syndication method allows lenders to have much better information about (a) the aggregate amount of lending to any one borrower (especially a country) and (b) the terms and conditions of other segments of the loan and of other lending to the same borrower. Hence they will lend a larger amount and at a lower required rate of return than if these features were uncertain. The risk faced by any one lender is related to the ratio of total loans to one borrower to the bank's capital base. And individual lenders face a rising marginal cost of capital. For both reasons, banks will tend to charge a higher margin for a loan from a single bank than for the same loan spread over a number of banks.

Another reason for syndication and trading of loans in the international lending market is that control is minimal and monitoring of less value when the borrower is a sovereign. Lenders cannot easily persuade a country such as Argentina to improve its cash-flow prospects by layoffs the way they might be able to do with, say, an automobile-parts manufacturer. Moreover, the lender does not have recourse to the same legal remedies as with a private borrower.

For sovereign borrowers, therefore, syndication and securitization provides lenders with the ability to diversify. A key aspect of syndicated loans to developing countries, as well as to other borrowers, is that in addition to the diversification feature, syndication agreements go far beyond one-on-one relationships between member lenders and the borrower. They provide for explicit cooperation and have risk-equalizing agreements, such as cross-default and sharing clauses.[5]

Another factor helps explain why syndication first flourished in the Euromarket, and why, in particular, borrowers are willing to pay the fees for syndication. With the multitudes of potential borrowers and financial institutions in the Euromarket, banking relationships rely to only a limited extent on traditionally established links. To illustrate, a corporate borrower whose banking relationships in the national market had grown gradually, beginning with the local bank that first funded the founder's venture, with additional institutions being added as the loan demand grew, is suddenly confronted by a vast choice of lending institutions as it approaches the external markets. Likewise, for the banks, the number of potential customers suddenly multiplies as they begin to operate in the external markets. With the mass of potential customers, familiarity with any individual borrower decreases, too. The result is the lending of relatively small amounts (international lending is risky) to many different customers; smaller and medium-sized banks of necessity rely on the services of a relatively few large banks, which have long international

---

[4]Indeed, this is the usual practice in domestic lending in some countries (including, until recently, the United States) where it is the task of a corporate treasury department to negotiate with various banks; often the result is a common, or at least a coordinated, loan agreement. To put the difference succinctly: in domestic lending, the relationships that count are between the borrower and each individual bank. A managing bank may not be necessary, and it may be rare to find a bank participating in the loan on a "casual," one-shot, basis without direct contact with the borrower. In a syndication, on the other hand, it is the relationship between the lead manager and the participating banks that matters.

[5]A cross-default provision in a loan agreement allows the lender to declare the loan immediately payable and to terminate any further extension of credit if the borrower defaults on any other debt. Sharing clauses provide that losses are shared proportionately by syndicate members.

experience and have shown their confidence in the credit of the borrower by taking a portion of the loan into their own portfolio.

Thus in the relative anonymity and complexity of the international money market, the crucial rationale for syndication is that the managing bank can obtain funds for the borrower faster, in greater amounts, and/or at a lower cost. This form of lending speeds up the process of negotiation with lenders and—most important—it reduces the perceived risk of the institutions that ultimately provide the bulk of the funds.

Of course, the problem of bringing together borrowers and lenders in a fragmented market is nothing new; it is the essence of investment banking, in which the lending underwriter must decide which securities will appeal to investors, and, by adding its prestige to that of the issuer (borrower), places the paper. In many national markets, such as Japan, the United States, and the United Kingdom, investment banking and commercial banking have been strictly separated by law. In the unregulated Euromarket, however, nothing prevents commercial banks from borrowing investment-banking concepts and technique and applying them with great success to the problem of large-scale lending. Many of the formalities of syndicated credits can best be understood by looking at securities underwriting in national or international markets.

To sum up, the prevalence of syndication in the external markets is the result of a lack of restrictions, particularly restrictions that separate investment banking and commercial banking. Syndication permits the application of underwriting techniques to the problem of matching borrowers and lenders without long-established relationships. The facilities available under syndicated credits are the same as those available from individual banks, although very large credits make syndication virtually a necessity. Loan agreements governing syndicated credits are also essentially the same. Agreements between borrowers and individual banks can be tailored to the requirements of the respective financial institution, but agreements documenting syndicated credits—with many participating banks from various countries—are the most representative of the unique lending practices that have evolved in the international money market.

The Transferability and Trading of Loans

In this section we'll take a look at one means by which banks have transformed their business from that of intermediary to that of underwriter and distributor—the loan-sales business.

Loan agreements were originally designed to specify the relationship between lender and borrower. As more and more of these loans are resold to other lenders, however, the agreements have to specify conditions for the *transfer of rights and obligations* and to deal with the relationships between the original lender, the originator, and the new lender, the buyer of the loan.

Today loan agreements are structured to allow sales in one of two typical forms: assignments or participations. Both approaches are intended to pass the right to interest, principal, and credit risk on to another investor, with no recourse to the original lender. Table 9.3 summarizes the differences between the two means of transferring loans, and highlights the major variations on assignments and participations:

1. In an **assignment,** the original lender gets out of the picture altogether by selling all his rights, interest, and obligations in a credit facility or loan to the loan buyer or assignee. The loan agreement and note (claim) is transferred, with the consent of the borrower, to the assignee. (An even stronger divorce and remarriage occurs in an assignment with **novation,** in which the note evidencing the selling bank's claim is canceled, and new notes are issued to the purchaser.)

Table 9.3   ***Means of Transferring Loans.***   Assignment and participation constitute the two basic forms of loan sales.

ASSIGNMENT	PARTICIPATION
FULL ASSIGNMENT The sale of *all* of the originating lender's or *assignor's* rights and interest in a credit facility to a purchaser or assignee. In a full assignment • the borrower usually acknowledges the assignment. • the borrower must consent to release of obligation by the assignor. • the assignee has direct access and enforcement of rights against the borrower. • the loan agreement and note is transferred to assignee at closing.	**PARTICIPATION** An arrangement between a lead bank and one or more lenders or participants. In a participation • the lead bank sells the right to participate in a credit facility or loan. • participants have derivative rights, not direct rights against (or obligations to) the borrower. • counterparty risk exists for the lead bank, which may be responsible for funding participants' shares. • capital rules affect the lead bank.
ASSIGNMENT WITH NOVATION An agreement between the borrower and syndicate that allows the syndicate to add additional (or different) lenders after the initial closing. Novation occurs when (a) the selling bank's note is canceled, and (b) new notes are issued to new and original lenders for adjusted amounts. The added syndicate members • obtain their own notes. • enjoy full rights directly with the borrower.	**LIMITED VOTING PARTICIPATION** The lead bank retains full rights and is only required to obtain consent for changes to the transaction structure, such as repayment dates or releases of collateral. **FULL VOTING PARTICIPATION** The lead bank has the right to veto any waiver or amendment, but must obtain consent before altering the terms of the transaction, such as principal or interest. **FULL PASS-THROUGH PARTICIPATION** The lead bank cannot veto a decision by the majority of lenders, and must • obtain the consent of participants prior to any waivers or amendments. • consult with the participants before taking any affirmative action (such as accelerating or foreclosing on the collateral). • obtain consent before altering the terms of the transaction.

2. More common is the sale of a loan by means of a **participation,** in which the original lender retains a much more centralized role. The lead bank commits to the loan itself, and then sells the right to participate in the loan or facility to other banks. Bits of the loan may be resold and resold again, but *the lead bank's relationship with the borrower remains unaltered because the participation is a contract between the buyer and the lead bank, not the borrower.* Thus participants have derivative rights against or obligations to the borrower, not direct rights. Participation certificates providing evidence of the contract are not negotiable securities and cannot simply be sold; instead, a new contract would have to be drawn up between a buyer and the original lead bank.

Participation is much less cumbersome than assignment or assignment with novation, but can lead to some problems: (1) The original lender no longer bears the credit risk of the borrower, but it does assume a commitment to lend. So if the new buyer backs out, the original lender may have to honor this commitment. (2) The buyer himself has some counterparty risk vis-a-vis the originating bank, because the latter usually continues to administer the collection and distribution of debt-service payments. If there is an interruption of payments, the new lender may find himself trying to collect undistributed funds from the lead bank as well as unpaid interest and principal from the borrower.

We have described the means by which a loan can be sold, but not the rationale for such trading. The answer is comparative advantage. Some banks have the resources to originate, service, and monitor loans, but neither the capital nor the cheap deposits to make holding all of them profitable. Other banks lack the teams of relationship officers and originators to bring in and structure the loan business, but have strong capital and plenty of deposits that they want to put to work. They can afford to take thinner spreads because their overhead is lower and perhaps they are getting cheaper money to boot.

Other banks buy now to sell later. For example, in the good old I'll-scratch-your-back-if-you-scratch-mine tradition, Swiss Bank Corporation may have been invited by the originating bank to be part of a syndicate in a Euroloan. SBC takes its allocation, but does so solely with the intention of selling (**subparticipating**) all or most of the loan to other banks (or, more and more, to nonbank investors such as insurance companies, pension funds, and even cash-rich corporations). For them, a loan is just another instrument to be bought at one price (at origination) and sold at a slightly higher price as quickly as possible.

EXAMPLE 9.1   Most loan sales occur at or soon after the loan or facility is arranged, because that's where the selling banks make their money. Say Paribas, the French bank, joins the syndicate to provide part of the $200 million floating-rate loan facility to Menomonee Trading Corp. (see Tables 9.1 and 9.2). Paribas may commit itself to $30 million; for this it will receive 1 percent up front, ½ percent per annum on the unused portion of the commitment (Table 9.1), and LIBOR plus 1.25 percent per annum on the amount loaned (Table 9.2). Paribas will now try to sell the full $30 million to its friends and acquaintances, such as smaller French, Asian, and African banks. All three forms of compensation will be negotiated as part of the "price" at which Paribas subparticipates the loan. For example, Paribas may offer the loan in $5- and $10-million-dollar lots with a ¼ percent up-front fee, ⅜ percent on the undrawn portion, and LIBOR plus 1 percent on any drawdown. If this is acceptable to a buyer, Paribas will have taken a decent cut of the fee structure. If it is not, Paribas will probably be willing to improve the terms, for it will be eager to get the paper off its books as soon as possible so that capital can be freed to underwrite more loans.

There is much less money to be made from the reselling of loans later in their life, and the aftermarket is therefore thin and illiquid. Loan "distribution" is perhaps a more descriptive term than loan "trading." The exception is the market for LDC debt, where nowadays there is more secondary market trading than new lending.

Apart from LDC debt, the kinds of loan participations that are traded can be divided into three categories: high-quality loans (loans to borrowers who also have access to the Euro- or U.S. commercial paper market), collateralized loans, and leveraged buy-out (LBO) loans.

In the late 1980s, much of the banks' *high-quality loan* business worldwide succumbed to their clients' ability to access the direct markets where they could obtain cheaper financing. The direct markets include Eurocommercial-paper and note-issuance facilities, domestic commercial paper (at least in the United States and the United Kingdom), medium-term notes, and swapped Eurobonds; of these, the most important is commercial paper in its several guises. Top-name borrowers still borrow from banks, but usually opportunistically, when bank borrowing proves cheaper than commercial paper.

Many commercial paper facilities are accompanied by *back-up lines* or *facilities,* and banks can sometimes provide the borrower with loans cheaper than the rate agreed upon in the back-up facility. The borrower will take advantage of this bid-option money as long as it is competitive with commercial paper. Because commercial paper yields are normally below the level that would earn big banks a spread over their cost of funds, the major banks seldom hold onto high-quality loans—they sell them off to other banks or to nonbank investors. The primary and secondary market for such loans is reasonably liquid, because the paper is treated as a commodity. Participations are sold on a name basis with little or no credit analysis accompanying the investment decision. The banks instead concentrate on earning fees from managing and providing these borrowers' back-up facilities (more on this later). Or if they do provide such financing, it is done as a means to support a relationship with the client so as to generate ancillary business.

Note-Issuance Facilities and Euronotes: From Intermediation to Direct Securities Markets

As pointed out previously, syndicated credit has grafted the elements of underwriting and distribution onto traditional bank lending, mainly to distribute risks and create lender solidarity. Additional pressures on the international banking industry have given rise to further innovation. Both bank regulators and bank shareholders in the industrialized countries have had long-simmering concerns about the adequacy of the major banks' capital. By the late 1980s, these groups had discouraged banks from growing any further by taking on low-margin assets and funding them short term in the highly competitive money markets. Yet there remained plenty of opportunities to bring together cash-hungry borrowers and savers that could not employ their burgeoning cash flows.[6]

The banking industry's reply to the divergent needs of the parties involved was to create *facilities*. The mechanics of these Revolving Underwriting Facilities (RUFs) or Note-Issuance Facilities (NIFs) are quite straightforward: Just as in a syndicated credit, a group of banks underwrites a commitment to the client/borrower. Under the facility, the borrower can raise funds for a period of 3–10 years by issuing notes in his own name, typically with a tenor of 1–6 months. The banks sell these at a price to yield less than a **cap** spread, say ⅛, over a reference rate, typically LIBOR. Rarely do the banks put the notes on their books and fund these assets. Indeed, doing so would be considered a failure. Instead, the banks sell the notes to investors, such as financial institutions, often smaller banks with captive deposit bases, or institutional investors in search of short-term paper. (See Box 9.3.)

BOX 9.3 **Note-Issuance Facilities and Eurocommercial Paper**	Note-Issuance Facilities (NIFs), also called Revolving Underwriting Facilities, have become a major source of Euromarket financing since they developed in the early 1970s. NIFs are medium-term arrangements—usually 3–10 years—between a borrower and a group of banks, under which the borrower can issue short-term paper, usually 3–6 months maturity, in its own name. Under this arrangement, underwriting banks are committed either to purchase any notes, known as Euronotes, which the borrower cannot sell or to provide standby credit, in either case at a predetermined spread relative to some reference rate such as LIBOR. Underwriting fees are paid on the full amount of the line of credit, regardless of the amount currently drawn. The

---

[6]These savers were themselves increasingly reluctant to commit all their cash to the banks.

fee may be 5 basis point for top borrowers and may range up to 15 basis points for less creditworthy borrowers. The notes are generally denominated in amounts of $100,000, $500,000, or more. The U.S. dollar is the most common currency of denomination.

High-quality borrowers can issue Euronotes at around LIBID—that is, at about ⅛ below LIBOR. The best-known of these can issue at yields ¹⁄₁₆ or ⅛ below LIBID. This is approximately the same rate as is paid on Eurodollar CDs, which are instruments of comparable liquidity. Euronotes are traded on a secondary market in London. NIFs are arranged on behalf of sovereign issuers, including some LDCs, commercial banks, and corporate borrowers, with the latter constituting the majority of issuers. Only about 20 percent of the amount of NIFs outstanding is actually drawn down at any given time. When funds are needed, the lending bank will arrange to market the Euronotes at the most favorable rate available to the issuer, usually making them available first to a prearranged group of banks called the *Tender Panel*. These banks may keep the notes for themselves, or resell them to other investors. Most of the paper ends up with smaller, nonunderwritten banks, but about a third or more placements are often with nonbank investors, including money-market funds, corporations, insurance companies, central banks, and even some wealthy individuals.

Today, NIFs have been supplanted in importance by facilities without underwriting commitments; these are called *Eurocommercial-paper facilities*, and the Euronotes issued are called *Eurocommercial paper* (ECP). In these arrangements, the issuance of notes is separated from the standby commitment. Eurocommercial paper is often issued at very short notice, in shorter and odder maturities, and the notes can be marketed very quickly through the tender panel. The lead bank is, in this case, simply a marketing agent. In this and other respects Eurocommercial-paper facilities have become more and more like U.S. commercial-paper programs.

Figure 9.1 shows an example of an NIF **tombstone.** The division of the listing of banks into two (overlapping) groups reflects the two-tiered structure of such facilities. The first part is the *underwritten facility,* also called the *committed facility,* which consists of a commitment by a group of banks to provide funds to the borrower if and only if the borrower finds itself unable to raise funds under the second, uncommitted, facility at a rate below LIBOR plus the maximum spread. The underwriting banks receive a fee but do not expect to have their facilities utilized. They will be used only when the borrower is having difficulty funding itself in the public markets—that is, when the borrower is in trouble. The underwriting banks protect themselves against throwing money into a sinking ship by providing that the facility will become void if the borrower suffers a sufficient deterioration of condition that it violates certain ratios or covenants, or if "material adverse conditions" occur.

The second part of the NIF is the *tender panel,* also called the *uncommitted facility,* which is merely an arrangement to auction off notes if and when the borrower wishes to raise funds. The borrower can normally choose to issue notes of, say 1–6 months, and sometimes has a choice of the currency in which the notes are to be denominated. These short-term notes are called **Euronotes.** The tender-panel members promise to show up at the auction but make no commitment to purchase the notes. When they do want the notes (often because they think they can resell them at a small profit), they will bid a certain interest rate relative to LIBOR. For example, a bank may buy Euronotes at a spread of LIBOR − 15bp (basis points), and resell it at LIBOR − 18bp (a lower yield and a higher price). Those who bid the lowest rates get the paper. A bank benefits from

Figure 9.1   ***Example of a Note-Issuance Facility.***   This "tombstone" announcement distinguishes clearly the tender panel members, who provide funds, from the underwriters, who commit to the availability of credit.

The Bigfoot Group

£115,000,000

equivalent

Committed Revolving Facility

Arranged by
Crédit Suisse First Boston Limited

Underwriting Banks

ABN-AMRO N.V. Banque Indosuez Crédit Lyonnais
Deutsche Bank Fuji International Finance Limited Banque Paribas
Samuel Montague & Co. Limited County Bank Kredietbank
Banque Bruxelles Lambert S.A. Citibank Crédit Suisse
Sumitomo Finance International Westdeutsche Landesbank Girozentrale
Finance International Westdeutsche Landesbank

Tender Panel Members

ABN-AMRO N.V. Indosuez Crédit Lyonnais CIBC Limited
Deutsche Bank Fuji International Finance Limited Banque Paribas
LTCB International Limited J.P. Morgan County Bank Kredietbank
Banque Bruxelles Lambert S.A. Citibank Crédit Suisse Commerzbank
Merrill Lynch Capital Markets Sumitomo Finance International
Salomon Brothers International Westdeutsche Landesbank Girozentrale

Tender Panel and Facility Agent
Crédit Suisse First Boston Limited

being on the tender panel in that it has a priority in purchase right—a right of first refusal on the paper. As a member of a tender panel, a bank has no strict obligation to buy notes, except that it is expected to make good-faith bids and may not be invited to future panels if it always chooses to sit on the sidelines.

Apart from the commitment fee that the underwriting banks receive, they have the opportunity to earn a little "turn" (the difference between the price at which a dealer buys and that at which he sells) if they have developed effective distribution capabilities that allow them to ferret out pools of low-cost funds on a global basis. This distribution capability can be further strengthened by making a credible commitment to the investors that the bank will make a secondary market in the instruments, which will enhance the attraction of the notes with a tenor exceeding one month. Such secondary market-making requires the willingness to invest, to hold a "position" in the paper. Thus it demands risk capital and/or hedging capabilities. Relatively few banks are really good at this and there has been a fair concentration of this activity in the hands of about twenty large internationally active banks.[7]

The economics of these facilities is based on the principle of comparative advantage. The underwriting banks, which have the capability of monitoring the bank but are reluctant to book assets at miniscule margins, receive a (small) commitment fee but book no asset. This increase does wonders for their return on equity. On the other hand, cash-rich investors do not have to enter into a medium-term commitment to part with their funds. They receive paper that yields a market return and at maturity can decide whether to reinvest the funds in notes issued by the same borrower or to look for another name if they find the credit inferior to other alternatives.

The primary advantage over the syndicated loan is clearly the *separation of functions* that permits each party to perform only that task that it feels comfortable with: to either sell the availability guarantee or to provide the funds. In theory, the borrower gets more for less. In practice, when a firm comes under pressure, the multiparticipant, arm's-length nature of these facilities can prove less reliable than a traditional syndicated loan. As one market participant remarked:

> *Some borrowers find that a large group of lenders can spell trouble; the larger the number, the tougher it is to secure agreement among them under stress. These borrowers have found that when they negotiated their so-called multiple-option facilities—consolidating all their financings into one cheaply-priced facility—they bought less than meets the eye. When companies are under pressure, these facilities can disintegrate.*

Comparison of a NIF to a Put Option

In the previous section we described the Note Issuance Facility as a commitment on the part of a group of underwriting banks to provide credit to an issuer of short-term Euronotes in the event that the issuer is unable to obtain better than a certain spread relative to LIBOR. This underwritten facility is in effect an option on the *spread,* not the *level* of interest rates. It is a *put option* because the issuer pays a price (the option premium), equal to the up-front fee plus the present value of the ongoing fees, for the right to sell notes at a given spread over LIBOR. This relationship is illustrated in Figure 9.2. When the issuer's notes sell in the market at a rate below LIBOR plus the *cap spread,* the borrower issues Euronotes. When the issuer is unable to attract investors at a rate below LIBOR plus the cap spread, then the borrower draws on the underwritten facility.

In the diagram, the vertical axis shows the gain/loss to the issuer, and the horizontal axis shows the effective spread relative to LIBOR that is available to the issuer. The "hockey stick" profit profile shows the issuer having a limited downside (when its required spread exceeds LIBOR plus the cost of the option). The issuer also has an unlimited gain; when its required spread relative to LIBOR is negative, it benefits from the lower issuance costs. The kink in the profit-profile line occurs at the point at which the issuer's required spread in the Euronote market exactly equals the maximum spread contractually guaranteed in the underwriting facility.

---

[7]The annual "league tables" published in *Euromoney* or the *Institutional Investor* (International ed.) provide a good picture of the dynamics of this competitive market place.

Figure 9.2   *Comparison of a NIF to a Put Option*

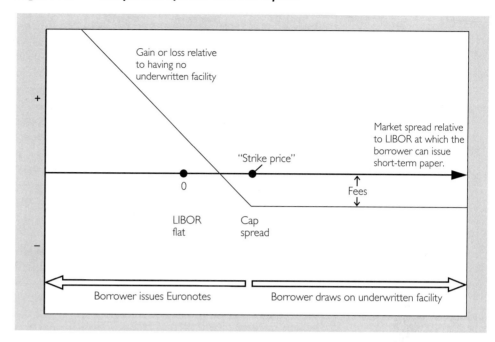

Gain or loss relative
to having no
underwritten facility

Market spread relative
to LIBOR at which the
borrower can issue
short-term paper.

"Strike price"

0   Fees

LIBOR   Cap
flat   spread

Borrower issues Euronotes   Borrower draws on underwritten facility

EXAMPLE 9.2   Western Mining Corp., the Australian natural resources group, finds that it can issue Euronotes in the range of LIBOR − .25% to LIBOR − .125%. With its bankers, it initiates a US$250-million Euronote program. To ensure access to the money market, Western Mining's management decides to pay an additional 15-basis-points fee for an underwritten facility of $150 million. The 0.15% can be regarded as the *option premium*, for the right to *put* or sell its notes to the underwriting banks. The terms of this facility guarantee that, as long as the company meets various solvency criteria, it will have access to short-term bank credit at a rate not to exceed LIBOR + .20. Thus Western's cap spread of 20 basis points, plus its NIF fee of 15 basis points, mean that the most it will have to pay for the underwritten $150 million is LIBOR + .35%. As long as it can raise money in the short-term market at less than LIBOR + .20%, it will do so and its cost will be the Euronote rate plus the cost of the facility. For example, if a particular issue costs LIBOR − .25%, the all-in cost would be LIBOR − .10%.

Eurocommercial Paper

Commercial paper (CP) (short-term unsecured notes issued by corporations) already had a long and successful history in the U.S. domestic market before it was embraced by the Euromarket. In recent years within the United States, the market grew enormously, and by 1990 it reached a volume of almost $400 billion. Corporations and their captive finance companies are the most important issuers. They raise funds in an efficient manner by placing short-term notes with investors, either directly or through a dealer.

Many of the investors in the U.S. commercial-paper market are cash-rich corporations, but there are many other buyers, including money-market mutual funds and more traditional institutional investors. This investor group in the U.S. domestic market tends to be very risk averse, because it represents the investment of short-term funds that is incidental to the firm's real risk-taking activity. So a rating by one of the credit agencies, such as Moody's or Standard & Poor's, is essential. Furthermore, assured availability of funds becomes a problem at times. For example, the market tends to reject the name of an issuer whose credit standing becomes suspicious, and on rare occasions the entire CP market is affected by general concerns about credit. Issuers in the U.S. market may then obtain *committed back-up lines* from banks for a small fee; the banks will make (higher-priced) funds available when the issuer is shut out from the CP market.

In the 1980s, the U.S. CP market received an additional boost by allowing foreign issuers, or domestic issuers with lesser-known names, to sell paper under a letter of credit (L/C) from a reputable financial institution, which effectively transfers the credit risk to the issuer of the L/C.

The rationale for a CP market is that it eliminates the need for the financial intermediary. This simplification makes sense only if the service provided by the intermediary is not worth its cost. Traditionally, the U.S. market has been characterized by a fragmented banking system that had to bear a number of regulatory expenses. At the same time, the nonfinancial sector offered a wide variety of very creditworthy corporate issuers. With the weakening of the large banks as a result of the LDC debt crisis, the banking sector has also lost credit standing and the CP market has flourished accordingly.[8]

Eurocommercial paper (ECP) is somewhat different. (See Figure 9.3 for an example of an ECP tombstone.) Like its U.S. counterpart, it is an unsecured promissory note, but it is issued and placed outside the jurisdiction of the currency of denomination. ECP was introduced in the early 1970s when U.S. capital-transfer restrictions forced U.S. corporate borrowers to raise funds abroad. However, the ECP market confronted a fundamental problem. The major incentive for avoiding intermediation—avoiding the regulatory cost—was absent in the Euromarket. Bank borrowing and Eurodollar deposits provided such effective competition that the ECP market failed to grow very much for many years. This situation changed in 1982, when the credit standing of major banks began to deteriorate, both onshore and offshore. The relative strength of nonbank borrowers, largely well-known multinational corporations and governmental entities, gave them a significant cost advantage over banks, while at the same time investors were willing to accept lower yields in order to avoid perceived bank risks.

A comparison between U.S. CP and ECP illustrates a phenomenon already found in the Eurobond market: various regulations and institutional practices introduce mild barriers to arbitrage, while at the same time investors in each market are driven by somewhat different criteria that lead to cost differentials between the two markets. Specifically, the market characteristics separating the dollar ECP market from the U.S. domestic CP market are:

- Buyers of ECP, coming from a broad range of countries, draw credit distinctions but do not divide issuers consistently by nationality. U.S. investors in CP systematically require foreign issuers to offer higher yields than like-rated U.S. issuers.
- The average rating of U.S. issuers in the ECP market is of significantly lower quality than U.S. issuers in the U.S. CP market. Likewise, foreign issuers in the United States show a distribution of quality significantly better than that of U.S. issuers in the ECP market.
- Central banks, corporations, and banks are important parts of the investor base for particular segments of the ECP market. Banks are said to be the

---

[8]McCauley, Robert N. and Lauren A. Hargraves, "Eurocommercial Paper and U.S. Commercial Paper: Converging Money Markets?" *Federal Reserve Bank of New York Quarterly Review,* Autumn 1987, 24–35.

Figure 9.3   *A Eurocommercial Paper Facility.*   By definition, the facility provides only for the best-effort auction of paper; the borrower has no underwritten assurance of availability of funds.

This announcement appears as a matter of example only.   June 1990

AB Industrikredit

U.S. $300,000,000
Eurocommercial Paper Programme
Rated A-1+/P-1 (Standard & Poor's Corporation and Moody's Investors Service)

Dealers

Daiwa Europe Limited
Skandinaviska Enskilda Banken
Svenska International plc
Swiss Bank Corporation

Issuing and Paying Agent

Manufacturers Hanover Trust Company

Arranger

Svenska International plc

buyers of much of the lower-quality paper issued in the ECP market. The most important U.S. CP holders—money-market funds—are not very important abroad.

- The average maturity of ECP remains about twice as long as that of U.S. CP. Thus ECP is actively traded in the secondary market; in contrast, most U.S. CP is held to maturity by the original investors.
- Issuing, clearance, and payment of ECP are more dispersed geographically and more time consuming than U.S. CP.
- Dealing is highly competitive in the ECP market; in contrast, two firms dominate half of dealer-placed U.S. CP. Dealers in the ECP market estimate that the "turn" averages only 3 basis points a year. For one-month paper that is turned over once, this means earnings of one-quarter of one-hundredth of a percent.
- To date, all ECP has been placed by third parties. Many U.S. CP issuers place paper directly with investors.
- Credit ratings and committed back-up lines associated with them are necessary in the U.S. CP market; in the ECP market, they are common, but not necessary—paper can be sold without such credit enhancement.
- ECP is generally priced in relation to bank-deposit interest rates. Pricing in the United States is based on absolute rates that vary in relation to rates on Treasury bills and bank CDs.

For most U.S. corporations, the U.S. commercial-paper market probably remains a cheaper source of funds than Eurocommercial paper. In fact, most U.S. corporations maintain NIFs chiefly as back-up lines of credit. For some sovereign and state-owned entities and non-U.S. corporations, however, Eurocommercial paper may compare fa-

Figure 9.4   ***Eurocommercial Paper and Medium-Term Notes.***   Beginning in the late 1980s, these securities were frequently used by borrowers in lieu of conventional bank debt.

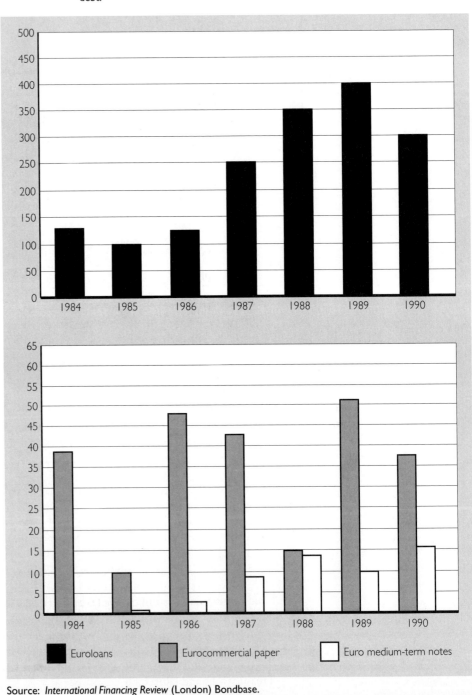

Source: *International Financing Review* (London) Bondbase.

vorably to U.S. commercial paper because of the premium that foreign issuers pay in the U.S. commercial-paper market. (The latter is in part the result of investment restrictions placed on many U.S. institutional investors.) Neither market has what can be called an active secondary market, although Euronotes and Eurocommercial paper probably enjoy somewhat greater liquidity than their U.S. cousins. Most notes are held to maturity after the first few days of active trading following issuance of the notes.

In recent years, banks have tended to offer their clients facilities that give the borrower the option to borrow in any of several different ways. These are called MOFs (**multiple option facilities**) or something equivalent. MOFs typically allow the corporation to access the Euronote market, the U.S. commercial-paper market, or a bank line of credit, including a **swing line** of funds that would be immediately available for temporary purposes. Today, most underwritten facilities are used by those who want a medium-term back-up line on which they do not intend to draw—often to back up a U.S. commercial-paper facility. Both Eurocommercial paper and U.S. commercial paper are used for actually raising funds. Commercial paper is typically quicker, cheaper, and more flexible than underwritten facilities, but it carries the risk of not being able to raise the funds.

As is shown in Figure 9.4, conventional lending has been supplemented to a large extent by Eurocommercial paper as well as its offshoot, the medium-term-note technique, to which we return in the next chapter. Box 9.4, Efim's Funding, offers a glimpse into the variety of ways in which major companies fund themselves in the international credit markets today.

BOX 9.4

Efim's Funding

In August 1992, Efim, an Italian state-owned company, went into voluntary liquidation of its subsidiaries. At that time, Efim had total debts of about 8,500 billion lire. The international syndicated credits and note facilities shown in the accompanying table are the ones which were publicly announced, according to data provided to the *Financial Times* by Euromoney Loanware.

The accompanying table shows the funding sources of a major multinational company and illustrates the variety of currencies, maturities, markets, and techniques employed by such firms. In particular, the table shows the margins at which Efim borrowed (usually quoted as the margin over LIBOR) and the fees paid to banks. *Commitment fees* were those paid by the borrower on the undrawn part of a loan. A *facility fee* is the annual fee paid on the total amount of a committed standby facility, regardless of whether that facility is drawn. A *participation fee* is the amount paid either on signing the loan or upon the first drawdown. A *utilization fee* is paid by the borrower if more than a certain part of the loan is drawn.

Efim and related Companies' Syndicated Loans

Borrower	Loan type	Currency Amount (m)	Sign date	Maturity	All fees	Arranger
Agusta SpA	NPF	$38.218	May 90	1998	MRG: LIBOR 50bp PP:12.5bp	Banca Commerciale italiana SG Warburg Soditic SA
Agusta SpA	REV	$100	Nov 86	1993	MRG: LIBOR 12.5bp CF:8.5bp PP:1-4m 6,25bp, 4-5m 7.5bp 6-9m 8.5bp 10m 10bp	Bankers Trust Int
Agusta SpA	REV	$100	Dec 88	1995	MRG:LIBQR 1-7 yrs 20bp CF: 1-7 yr 10bp PP: 15m 10bp, 5m 5bp	Citicorp Investment Bank Ltd
Agusta SpA	REV	$150	Oct 90	1997	MRG: LIBOR 1-4yr 20bp, 4-7 yr 24bp CF: 12.5bp PP:5-9m 10bp, 10-15m 12.5bp 15m 15bp	Banca Commerciale Italiana
Agusta SpA	NPF	$62.676	Mar 87	1992	MRG: LIBOR 1-5 yr 18.75bp	Bankers Trust Int
Agusta SpA	NPF	$72	Oct 85	1992	MRG: LIBOR 1-5 yr 50bp, 4-7 yr 62.5bp CF: 40bp PP: 2m 10bp, 5m 15bp, 8m 17.5bp	Bankers Trust Int

Borrower	Loan type	Currency Amount (m)	Sign date	Maturity	All fees	Arranger
Agusta SpA		$79.180	Feb 84	1992	MRG: LIBOR 1-8 yr 1.125% CF:50bp	Soditic (Jersey)
Efim	REV	Ecu300	Jly 86	1995	MRG = ECUIBOR 1-4 yr 10bp, 5-9 yr 12.5 bp CF = 10bp PP:2-9m 3.5bp 10-15 5bp, 15m 6.25bp	
Efim	REV	Ecu300	Jan 85	1995	MRG = ECUIBOR 1 yr 25bp, 2-6yr 37.5bp, 7-10 yr 50bp CF = 15bp PP:1-2m 20bp, 3-5m 25bp, 6-9m 30bp, 10m 27.5bp	
NUOVA SAFIM	MOF	Ecu70	Dec 90			Instituto Bancario San Paolo di Torino
NUOVA SAFIM	REV	Ecu180	Oct 90	1995	MRG: LIBOR 1-3 yr 17.5bp 4-5 yr 20bp CF: 10bp PP: 20m 12.5bp, 10m 10bp	Instituto Bancario San Paolo di Torino
NUOVA SAFIM	REV	$150	Jan 89	1994	MRG:LIBOR 1-3 yrs 15bp, 4-5 yr 17.5bp CF:1-5 yr 7bp PP:15m 15bp, 10m 12.5bp, 5m 10bp	Manufacturers Hanover
NUOVA SAFIM	TL	Y5,000	Aug 90	1997		
NUOVA SAFIM	TL	Y2,000	Dec 90	1994	MRG:8.1%	Bank of Tokyo
NUOVA SAFIM	TL	Y2,330	Jly 90	1993		Baring Brothers & Co
NUOVA SAFIM	TL	Y5,000	Jun 90	1993		Lehman Brothers Intl
SAFIM	MOF	£75	Dec 85	1993	MRG: LIBOR 10bp FF:1-5 yr 7.5bp, 6-8 yr 10bp UT:0-33% 2.5bp, 33-66% 5bp,66-100% 7.5bp PP:2.5 7.5bp, 5m 10bp, 10m 15bp, 15m 17.5bp	SG Warburg & Co
SAFIM	MOF	£60	Mar 86	1994	MRG: LIBOR 1-8 yr 10bp FF:1-5 yr 7.5b, 6-8yr 10bp UF:0-33% 2.5bp 33-66% 5bp, 66-100% 7.5bp PP:2.5m 7.5bp, 5m 10bp, 10m 15bp, 15m 17.5bp	SG Warburg & Co
SAFIM	REV	L250,000	Jun 87			Societa Consotile di Co-operazione Bancaria, Fineurop SpA
SAFIM	TL	Y5,000	Nov 82	1992	MRG:JLTP 1-10 yr 20bp	
Breda Construzioni Ferroviarie	REV	L72,000	Feb 91	1994	LIBOR: 27bp CF:17.5bp PP: 18bp	Monte dei Paschi de Siena

MOF = Multiple facility, NPF = Note purchase facility, REV = Revolving Credit, TL = Term loan ECU = European currency unit, US$ = US dollars, LIT = Italian Lira, STG = Sterling, YEN = Japanese yen MRG = Margin, CF = Commitment fee, FF = Facility fee, PP = Participation fee, UT = Utilisation fee

Source: Euromoney Loanware

Source: *Financial Times,* August 28, 1992.

International Banking Risks and Capital Requirements

As the previous sections suggest, commercial banks have operated in increasingly competitive markets for financial services fostered by the process of financial liberalization and innovation. At the same time, the 1980s brought first an escalation of exposure to bad loans in the developing countries, in real estate, and elsewhere, and a prolonged recession. These loans jeopardized profitability and capital, exposing governments to greater risks through their insurance schemes and safety nets for commercial banks. Moreover, differences among major industrial countries in the stringency of capital requirements created competitive inequalities among internationally active banks. A capital requirement, relating the amount of equity and equitylike debt to risky assets, is one means of ensuring that a bank has a sufficient buffer against loan losses and other threats to its solvency.

Against this background, the industrial countries' bank supervisory authorities met in Basle, at the Bank for International Settlements, in 1986 to propose an initial plan to link common minimum-capital requirements for international banks to their credit-risk exposures, including both on-balance-sheet exposures such as loans and off-balance-sheet exposures such as loan commitments. In March 1987, the United States and Great

Britain reached agreement on the common definition of capital adequacy and, in June 1987, Japan joined them. The consensus was subsequently broadened after extensive discussions among the Group of Ten countries, culminating in the *Basle Accord on capital adequacy* in July 1988.

The Accord, sometimes called the *BIS requirements,* called for a minimum 8-percent ratio of capital to risk-weighted credit exposures. At least half of the recognized capital must be in the form of core, or Tier-1, capital, including common stock, noncumulative preferred stock,[9] and disclosed reserves. The remainder—termed supplementary, or Tier-2, capital—includes such components as undisclosed reserves, general loan-loss provisions, asset-revaluation reserves, hybrid-capital instruments, and subordinated debt. The specific items recognized as Tier-2 capital vary; however, subordinated debt is limited by the Accord to 50 percent of Tier-2 capital. General provisions or reserves can qualify as Tier-2 capital only if they do not reflect a known deterioration in the value of assets.

Credit exposures are assigned to five broad categories of relative riskiness. They are given weights ranging from zero to 100 percent. Loans to OECD[10] official borrowers, for example, attract a zero-risk weight, while claims on banks incorporated in OECD countries and interbank claims involving other countries and maturing in under one year have a 20-percent weight. Residential mortgages carry a 50-percent weight, and foreign-currency loans to non-OECD governments and credits to commercial agencies receive a 100-percent weight. (For an application of this weighting system, read Application 9.3, The Saudi Loan.) Off-balance-sheet items such as interest-rate swaps are first converted to balance-sheet equivalents and then subjected to the standard risk weights.

Many banks have found the Accord to be flawed. Particularly troublesome is the differential treatment between OECD and non-OECD borrowers. Other problem areas are associated with the 100-percent weight applied to all commercial loans, some of which have higher credit ratings than banks carrying only a 20-percent risk weight, and the intercountry differences in Tier-2 capital. The closure of the Bank for Credit and Capital International (BCCI) in July 1991 also highlighted some of the shortcomings of the Basle Accord, and exposed gaps in the supervision of banks' foreign establishments.

A June 1991 Price Waterhouse report commissioned by the Bank of England revealed large-scale fraud at BCCI going back several years and illuminated two specific developments that precipitated the bank's problems.[11] (1) The bank's treasury operations from 1977 to 1985 sustained dealing losses totaling an estimated $600 million to $700 million, and (2) the bank had an exposure of more than $700 million to a single borrower with close ties to the bank's management. Neither the market risk undertaken by the bank's treasury nor the large credit exposure was covered by the Basle Accord.[12]

Because the Accord focuses mainly on credit risk, the supervisory authorities have been seeking to broaden its coverage to include various kinds of "market risk"—foreign-exchange risk, interest-rate risk, and position risk in traded-equity securities. The banks'

---

[9]Undeclared dividends on noncumulative preferred stock cannot be accumulated and paid at a later date, as with cumulative preferred stock.

[10]The OECD classification refers to countries either that are full members of the OECD (**Organization for Economic Cooperation and Development**) or that have concluded special lending arrangements with the International Monetary Fund associated with the General Arrangements to Borrow.

[11]A summary of the report's finding appears in Stephen Timewell, "BCCI: Unanswered Questions," *The Banker,* vol. 141 (Sept. 1991), 12–20. For a more in-depth story, see "BCCI: Behind Closed Doors," *Financial Times,* seven-part series, Nov. 9–17, 1991.

[12]Although BCCI was active in 70 countries, the bank's closure had a minimal systemic impact on the international banking system. BCCI's credit rating and general reputation among wholesale banks was such that it was essentially excluded from the interbank market.

exposure to risk has increased in recent years as interest rates and capital controls have been liberalized and permissible banking activities expanded. Of the three types of risk, proposals for dealing with foreign-exchange risk are the most advanced. The aim is to set capital requirements on banks' open foreign-exchange positions. One of the main difficulties in this area is measuring foreign-exchange risk in a portfolio of foreign-exchange positions, because this measurement requires some allowance for correlations among currency movements. Exposure to interest-rate risk raises even more complicated measurement issues that have not been resolved. The supervisors' aim, perhaps futile, is to derive a single-number indicator of interest-rate risk that is simple to calculate. For competitive equality reasons, the measures should be applicable not only across countries but also should be consistent with the regulation of securities firms.

Summary

This chapter has described some of the bread-and-butter activities of international banks in providing global credit, as well as the manner in which their business has evolved during the past decade. The Eurocurrency market permits the separation of the currency of denomination from the country of jurisdiction. International bankers have taken the idea of *separability* a great deal further. A seemingly simple loan has a large number of different features and aspects of risk, and over time international bankers have learned to isolate or "unbundle" these features in order to be able to distribute and to hedge the inherent risks. This chapter looked at loan syndication, loan trading, Euronote underwriting facilities, and other Euromarket techniques as means of separating the provision of funds from the assumption of interest-rate risk, credit risk, liquidity (or availability) risk, and other features of international credit. The chapter concluded with a look at the existing international agreements on bank risk regulation and some of the challenges that face banking authorities in the future if international crises are to be averted.

Conceptual Questions

1. What conditions give Eurocurrency banking an edge over domestic banking?
2. How is the maturity of a Euroloan separated from its pricing period?
3. Identify the key differences between *assignment* and *participation* as a means of achieving transferability for a Eurodollar loan.
4. Define *novation* in the context of loan sales.
5. How can a bank make money by selling a loan that it has bought as part of the originating syndicate?
6. What is a Note Issuance Facility?
7. How does a bank's risk as an underwriter in a loan syndicate differ from its risk as a member of the underwriting group in a RUF?
8. Why does U.S. commercial paper, unlike Eurocommercial paper, require a formal rating and committed back-up lines?

Problems

1. Westdeutsche Landesbank is the sole provider of a four-year, DM100,000,000 term loan to Menomonee GMBH at 6.125 percent. Show by means of a diagram how WestLB could use the swap market to hedge its interest-rate risk if the bank funded 30 percent of the loan by issuing a 4-year MTN (medium-term note) and the remainder by repeatedly issuing three-month Eurocommercial paper.
2. Based on the interest-rate risk to the participants, do you think that the prepayment fee on a revolving facility differs from that on a term loan (see Table 9.2)?

3. You are a loan trader for Bankers Trust. You are about to subparticipate a $20 million, three-year loan to Bangkok Bank for half of the up-front fee of 1¼ percent and all but 25 basis points of the quarterly reset spread over LIBOR. In present-value terms, how much will you earn if LIBOR is 7.5 percent and the three-year rate is 8.00 percent?

Application 9.1	## MONEY IN THE MORNING

It is 11:30 A.M. in Chemical Bank's treasury department, and your boss tells you that you have to figure out a way to fund a $15-million domestic floating-rate loan that the bank has just provided to a customer. The loan is priced at 3-month LIBOR plus ¼ percent per year.

Where will you get the money? Evaluate several different money-market financing alternatives—how they work and their relative costs, drawing on the descriptions of various money-market instruments and funding techniques in the readings.

Among your financing choices are

- federal funds
- repurchase agreements
- time deposits
- certificates of deposit
- Eurodollar deposits

- commercial paper
- Eurocommercial paper
- Note-Issuance Facilities
- floating rate notes
- variable-rate notes

Which make sense, and which don't? The accompanying list of money rates gives indications of some relative interest rates, but you should rank them according to their suitability as well as their cost.

MONEY RATES

Monday, May 10, 1993

The key U.S. and foreign annual interest rates below are a guide to general levels but don't always represent actual transactions.

PRIME RATE: 6%. The base rate on corporate loans posted by at least 75% of the nation's 30 largest banks.

FEDERAL FUNDS: 3% high, 2 15/16% low, 2 15/16% near closing bid, 3% offered. Reserves traded among commercial banks for overnight use in amounts of $1 million or more. Source: Prebon Yamane (U.S.A.) Inc.

DISCOUNT RATE: 3%. The charge on loans to depository institutions by the Federal Reserve Banks.

CALL MONEY: 5%. The charge on loans to brokers on stock exchange collateral. Source: Telerate Systems Inc.

COMMERCIAL PAPER placed directly by General Electric Capital Corp.:3.01% 30 to 59 days; 3.03% 60 to 119 days; 3.05% 120 to 149 days; 3.06% 150 to 179 days; 3.07% 180 to 239 days; 3.12% 240 to 270 days.

COMMERCIAL PAPER: High-grade unsecured notes sold through dealers by major corporations: 3.07% 30 days; 3.08% 60 days; 3.08% 90 days.

CERTIFICATES OF DEPOSIT: 2.58% one month; 2.61% two months; 2.63% three months; 2.70% six months; 2.91% one year. Average of top rates paid by major New York banks on primary new issues of negotiable C.D.s, usually on amounts of $1 million and more. The minimum unit is $100,000. Typical rates in the secondary market: 3.03% one month; 3.06% three months; 3.10% six months.

BANKERS ACCEPTANCES: 2.97% 30 days; 2.97% 60 days; 2.97% 90 days; 2.98% 120 days; 3% 150 days; 3.01% 180 days. Negotiable, bank-backed business credit instruments typically financing an import order.

LONDON LATE EURODOLLARS: 3⅛% - 3% one month; 3⅛% - 3% two months; 3 3/16% - 3 1/16% three months; 3 3/16% - 3 1/16% four months; 3¼% - 3⅛% five months; 3¼% - 3⅛% six months.

LONDON INTERBANK OFFERED RATES (LIBOR): 3⅛% one month; 3 3/16% three months; 3¼% six months; 3 7/16% one year. The average of interbank offered rates for dollar deposits in the London market based on quotations at five major banks. Effective rate for contracts entered into two days from date appearing at top of this column.

FOREIGN PRIME RATES: Canada 6%; Germany 8.50%; Japan 4%; Switzerland 7.50%; Britain 6%. These rate indications aren't directly comparable; lending practices vary widely by location.

TREASURY BILLS: Results of the Monday, May 10, 1993, auction of short-term U.S. government bills, sold at a discount from face value in units of $10,000 to $1 million: 2.89%, 13 weeks; 2.99%, 26 weeks.

FEDERAL HOME LOAN MORTGAGE CORP. (Freddie Mac): Posted yields on 30-year mortgage commitments. Delivery within 30 days 7.11%, 60 days 7.23%, standard conventional fixed-rate mortgages; 4.125%, 2% rate capped one-year adjustable rate mortgages. Source: Telerate Systems Inc.

FEDERAL NATIONAL MORTGAGE ASSOCIATION (Fannie Mae): Posted yields on 30 year mortgage commitments (priced at par) for delivery within 30 days 7.13%, 60 days 7.23%, standard conventional fixed rate-mortgages; 4.95%, 6/2 rate capped one-year adjustable rate mortgages. Source: Telerate Systems Inc.

MERRILL LYNCH READY ASSETS TRUST: 2.68%. Annualized average rate of return after expenses for the past 30 days; not a forecast of future returns.

Source: *The Wall Street Journal,* May 11, 1993.

Application 9.2	RISKY BUSINESS

MEMORANDUM

To: Molly O'Gorman, SVP, Pacific Region HQ
From: Richard Chu, Hong Kong Treasury
Subject: Cost of Funds Index for HIBL

The natives are restless here in Hong Kong and we are finding that this affects our cost of funds for making loans out of here. Justified or not, there seems to be some kind of political-risk premium demanded by depositors placing money in banks here. Therefore, we recommend changing the pricing base for all Asian loans made by Hongkong International Bank Limited. Instead of LIBOR, we recommend using HIBOR (the Hong Kong Interbank Rate) as our pricing index. That way, we on the funding side cannot be blamed for the nonexistent profitability of some of the lending business our relationship managers bring in from places like North Korea.

My gripe begins with the fact that LIBOR, the London Interbank Offered Rate, is the rate at which banks in *London* offer to lend to other banks. The theory is that LIBOR moves up and down with bid rates, but slightly (⅛%) higher than major banks' bid rates, so LIBOR is a conservative estimate of a Eurobank's cost of funds. Our loans here are typically priced off six-month LIBOR, meaning that the rate is reset at the start of every six-month period with the new market rate. So banks in London can fund themselves with new six-month Eurodollar deposits at the beginning of each interest period, thus locking in a spread equal to the contractual lending margin plus the spread between bid and asked rates in the interbank market. The lending margin is the fixed spread that the borrower agrees to pay above LIBOR (or whatever the reference rate is), and supposedly varies with the riskiness of the borrower.

In practice, LIBOR has never really represented the true cost of funds to HIBL or to our parent institution, KIBL. As you know, the guys who set LIBOR never bother to consult with us on our cost of liabilities. On the second business day prior to the beginning of each coupon period, the agent bank collects the offered quotations prevailing at 11:00 A.M. GMT on that day for interbank deposits with the London branches of a group of five leading reference banks. (We're usually asleep at that time.) Actually, KIBL's pooled cost of funds has typically been even lower than LIBID, because with its strong capital, KIBL has been able to raise money in the U.S. commercial-paper market and in the Euronote market. But now, in Hong Kong, through no fault of ours, we risk our cost of U.S.-dollar funds rising significantly higher than LIBOR.

I know it will be hard for your loan officers to explain this to clients, but we in treasury must protect ourselves. Chew on it, as we Chinese say. I'll call you tomorrow at 11:00 A.M. *Hong Kong time.*

London Interbank Fixing (LIBOR)
(11:00 A.M. Jan 3)

3 months U.S. dollars		6 months U.S. dollars	
bid 8¼	offer 8⅜	bid 8⅛	offer 8¼

The fixing rates are the arithmetic means, rounded to the nearest one-sixteenth, of the bid and offered rates for $10 million quoted to the market by five reference banks at 11:00 A.M. each working day. The banks are National Westminster Bank, Bank of Tokyo, Deutsche Bank, Banque National de Paris, and Morgan Guaranty Trust.

Do you agree that the bank should use HIBOR, rather than LIBOR, as a basis for loans made out of Hong Kong? Explain.

Application 9.3 | THE SAUDI LOAN

Kevin Chang had just joined the syndication group at Banque Paribas, the big French bank. He had been asked to summarize his view on whether the bank should respond to invitational telexes concerning two forthcoming syndicated loan deals. The first, from J. P. Morgan in London, was an invitation to participate in a three-year, $3.5 billion financing for the government of Saudi Arabia. The second was from Frankfurt, where Deutsche Bank was seeking participation in a five-year, DM500 million revolving credit for Continental, the German tire group.

Chang decided he should begin with the relative pricing of the two deals. The Saudi loan, for which there were no front-end fees, paid 50 basis points over the London interbank rate. In the Continental deal the return was made up of a facility fee—paid whether or not the loan was drawn down—of ³⁄₁₆ percent and an interest margin of the same level. Returns were supplemented by front-end fees, which ranged down from ⅛ percent for a DM35 million commitment, and utilization fees. If more than one third was drawn, an extra 5 basis points was payable; if more than two thirds, an extra 10 basis points.

As for risk, both issuers were very well known. Deutsche Bank deals usually were well accepted, although Continental was not regarded as in the top rank of European credits. A more serious problem, perhaps, was the 100-percent risk weighting applied to corporate borrowers under the Basle rules, the standards set by the Bank for International Settlements committee on bank supervision. According to the rules, banks had to set aside capital equivalent to 8 percent of the amount lent, and 4 percent on amounts committed but not lent. By contrast, the government of Saudi Arabia was the only one outside the Organization for Economic Cooperation and Development treated as an OECD government for bank-capital purposes. As a result, banks were not required to set aside any capital for their loans to it.

Weighing these factors, which deal do you think would be most attractive to Paribas?

Application 9.4 | LAURA ASHLEY

You have been hired by Banca Espíritu Santo in Lisbon in part to help the bank evaluate the many and varied financing techniques that come its way as Portugal participates more fully in the European Community. Now is your chance to prove yourself. The issue at hand is a proposal from Midland Bank, the British clearing bank, to participate in a new multiple-option facility (MOF), also known as a note-issuance facility, in favor of Laura Ashley Ltd.

Laura Ashley, a prominent clothing, fabrics, and accessories concern based in London, wants to raise £75 million in the form of bank credit chiefly for the purpose of bringing the U.S. bed-linen business, previously licensed to third parties, in house. Laura Ashley's management has chosen to use the two-tier multiple-option facility in preference to a more traditional syndicated bank loan, mainly because Midland has persuaded it that the MOF would be cheaper while providing equivalent access to funds.

Structures such as the MOF involve two facilities, a committed facility and an uncommitted one. Espiritu Santo has received a telex inviting it to be a member of the *underwriting group* of the committed facility, on the theory that the bank could receive a fee for its commitment to provide cash advances to the company under certain unlikely circumstances. The assumption in the syndicate group was that Espiritu Santo had been invited for the first time to join the underwriting group because the bank was also expected to actively participate in the *tender panel* of the uncommitted facility, where short-term notes would be sold at whatever rate the market would bear. Midland has shown confidence that the bank, Portugal's second largest, would be well placed to resell the notes to smaller banks, insurance companies, and corporations in the Iberian peninsula.

Espiritu Santo's management has indicated to you that this confidence is not misplaced. However, before they agree to the invitation to take £20 million of the committed (underwritten) facility, they want to be sure of what their obligations under such a facility would be under various circumstances. Also, as a possible member of the tender panel, they want to know what obligation they would have to provide funds to the borrower, and on what terms. Finally, they want to know how risky the paper sold at the tender-panel auctions is. After all, the bank would have to explain all the risks to potential investors in the Laura Ashley paper. Given that the short-term paper is backed by a long-term committed facility, what, if anything, could go wrong? Listening to their discussions, you have discovered that although they are not necessarily familiar with all the nuances of the MOF, they understand syndicated loans very well. Your task, therefore, is to write a one-page memorandum addressing their concerns by comparing these techniques with more traditional syndicated loan paper.

Apart from the prestige of being a lead manager for such a well-known issuer, the bank would receive a management fee of 0.15 percent upon signature of the facility, an annual underwriting fee, and any profits that could be made from selling the paper at a higher price than that at which it was bought. By way of comparison, a syndicated Eurocurrency loan that Laura Ashley had obtained a few years earlier carried the following fees: 0.175 percent management fee, 0.15 percent annual commitment fee, and 0.20 percent annual margin over LIBOR years 1–5, 0.375 percent margin years 6–10.

This is a summary of the invitation telex received by Espiritu Santo:

LAURA ASHLEY MULTIPLE-OPTION FACILITY

Summary of Terms and Conditions

Issuer:	Laura Ashley Holdings Ltd.
Amount:	GBP 75 million
Term of committed facility:	8 years
Notes:	1-, 2-, 3-, or 6-month bearer notes, ranking pari passu with all other unsecured and unsubordinated indebtedness
Denominations:	GBP 250,000
Coupon on notes:	1-, 2-, 3-, or 6-month LIBOR. Notes will be priced to yield higher or lower amounts depending on tender panel demand.
Cap yield:	LIBOR plus 0.125%
Currency:	GBP, GDM, USD, FFR, or JY, at borrower's option
Utilization fees:	Semiannual fee of 0.05%, calculated in arrears on a per-annum basis on the average amount drawn under the Uncommitted Facility.
Facility and commitment fee:	0.10% p.a. on face amount of borrowings 0.75% on balance of commitments
Front-end management fee:	0.15%
Governing law:	United Kingdom

Application 9.5 | VARD

Examine the accompanying tombstones. How would you contrast the roles each form of financing plays in raising funds for the issuer?

This announcement appears as a matter of record only.

US$ 216,000,000
Back-Stop Revolving Facility

Arranger and Lead Manager
Crédit Lyonnais

Senior Co-Lead Managers
Den Norske Bank A/S   Fokus Bank A/S   NMB Postbank Groep

Co-Lead Managers
Banque Internationale à Luxembourg S.A.
Creditanstalt-Bankverein
DSL Bank Luxembourg S.A.
Girozentrale und Bank der Österreichischen Sparkassen Aktiengesellschaft
Scandinavian Bank Group plc
Société Générale/Société Générale Alsacienne de Banque
Swiss Bank Corporation
Union Bank of Norway Ltd.
Via Banque
Westdeutsche Landesbank Girozentrale

Co-Managers
Banque de l'Union Européenne
Crédit Agricole
Crédit Communal de Belgiqe S.A./Gemeentekrediet van België N.V.
Crédit du Nord
Nordfinanz Bank Zürich
Österreichische Volksbanken Aktiengesellchaft
Skopbank
Westfalenbank Aktiengesellschaft

Participants
Banco di Roma, London Branch
BRED Paris
Compagnie Monégasque de Banque
Kyowa Bank Nederland N.V.

Agent
Crédit Lyonnais

September 1990

This announcement appears as a matter of record only.

V A R D

US$ 230,000,000
Euro-Commercial Paper Programme

Arranger
Crédit Lyonnais

Dealers
Bank of America International Limited
Crédit Lyonnais
Den Norske Bank A/S London Branch

Issuing and Paying Agent
Crédit Lyonnais, Luxembourg Branch

July 1990

SELECTED REFERENCES

Bank for International Settlements. *International Banking and Financial Market Developments*. Basle, various issues.

Dufey, Gunter, and Ian H. Giddy. *The International Money Market*. 2nd ed. Englewood Cliffs, N.J.: Prentice-Hall, 1994.

Gardener, Edward P. M., and Phillip Molyneux. *Changes in Western European Banking*. New York: Harper, 1990.

International Monetary Fund. *International Capital Markets: Developments, Prospects and Policy Issues*. Washington, D.C., various issues.

Price Waterhouse World Regulatory Advisory Practice. *Bank Capital Adequacy and Capital Convergence*. London: Price Waterhouse, July 1991.

Smith, Roy C., and Ingo Walter. *Global Financial Services*. New York: Harper, 1990.

10

Instruments of the International Money Market

The International Money Market

A **money market** is a market for instruments and a means of lending (or investing) and borrowing funds for relatively short periods, typically regarded as from one day to one year. Such means and instruments include short-term bank loans, Treasury bills, bank certificates of deposit, commercial paper, bankers' acceptances and repurchase agreements, and other short-term asset-backed claims.

As a key element of the financial system of a country, the money market plays a crucial economic role: that of reconciling the cash needs of so-called deficit units (such as farmers needing to borrow in anticipation of their later harvest revenues), with the investment needs of surplus units (such as insurance companies wanting to invest cash productively prior to making long-term investment choices). Holding or borrowing liquid claims is more productive than holding cash balances. A smoothly functioning money market can perform these functions very efficiently if borrowing-lending spreads (or bid-offer spreads for traded instruments) are small (**operational efficiency**), and if funds are lent to those who can make the most productive use of them (**allocational efficiency**). Both borrowers and lenders prefer to meet their short-term needs without bearing the liquidity risk or interest-rate risk that characterizes longer-term instruments, and money-market instruments allow this. In addition, money-market investors tend not to want to spend much time analyzing credit risk, so money-market instruments are generally characterized by a high degree of safety of principal. Thus the money market sets a market interest rate that balances cash management needs, and sets different rates for different uses that balance their risks and potential for productive use. Unlike stock or futures markets, the money markets of the major industrial countries have no central location: they operate as a telephone market that is accessible from all parts of the world.

The *international money market* can be regarded as the market for short-term financing and investment instruments that are issued or traded internationally. The core of this market is the Eurocurrency market, where bank deposits are issued and traded outside of the country that issued the currency. Other instruments to be discussed in this chapter, such as Eurocommercial paper and floating-rate notes, serve somewhat different purposes and attract a different investment clientele. However, each is to a degree a substitute for each of the other instruments, and the yield and price of each are sensitive to many of the same influences, so we may feel justified in lumping them together in something called a market. The fact that many of the other instruments of the international money market are priced off LIBOR, the interest rate on Eurodollar deposits, suggests that market participants themselves regard the different instruments as having a common frame of reference.

Author's note: Thanks are due to Steve Fletcher for his contributions to this chapter.

Today, many domestic cash and derivative instruments, such as U.S. Treasury bills and Eurocurrency futures contracts, are traded globally and so are effectively part of the international money market. Euromarket instruments simply represent part of a spectrum of financial claims available in the money market of a particular currency, claims that are distinguished by risk, cost, and liquidity just like domestic money-market instruments. However, domestic money markets are called upon to play public as well as private roles. The latter include the following three functions:

- The money market, along with the bond market, is used to finance the government deficit.
- The transmission of monetary policy (including exchange-rate policy) is typically done through the money market, either through banks or through freely traded money-market instruments.
- The government uses the institutions of the money market to influence credit allocation toward favored uses in the economy.

Hence important differences will persist not only between different domestic markets but also between domestic markets and their external segments.

The purpose of this chapter is to recapitulate and describe key aspects of the instruments of the international money market, many of which the reader has encountered already in other chapters. The viewpoint is deliberately that of the investor. The chapter will also serve as an introduction to the nature and pricing of floating-rate notes.

Returns on Money-Market Instruments

The manager of cash will wish to consider the alternative money-market instruments she has at her disposal by comparing their returns, risks, and other characteristics. In principle, the range includes all the instruments in two dozen or so domestic money-markets open to international investors. Realistically, though, one would normally limit one's attention to a few major currencies and to the more liquid instruments.

For some, the starting point would be U.S. Treasury bills, and some will be constrained to that class of risk. Most international investors will look for a better return than can be had in government Treasury bills, however, so their starting point would be short-term Eurodeposits. In this chapter we look at some of the specifically *international* instruments that might form part of a money-market portfolio: Eurocurrency time deposits and CDs, bankers' acceptances and letters of credit, Euronotes and Eurocommercial paper, and floating-rate notes.

To compare instruments one should be able to express their returns on a comparable basis. Doing so is complicated by the different maturities and payment characteristics of even the limited range of investments considered here, and by the different delivery and accrued-interest calculations adopted by participants in different markets. Let us begin, therefore, by seeking to clarify some of these differences.

The basic idea of a return is that you invest a sum of money today and you get some more back at a later date. The increase, expressed as an annualized percentage of the original investment, is typically how we measure return. Thus if you invest ¥100 today and you receive ¥107 in one year the return is 7 percent. In practice this idea takes three different forms: (1) the bank discount rate, (2) the add-on yield, and (3) the yield to maturity, known in the Euromarkets as the bond-equivalent yield.

1. The *bank-discount-rate method* is a formula devised to make calculations easy to do by hand, but its use persists in these days of financial calculators and computers, for money-market instruments such as Treasury bills, banker's acceptances, and commercial paper.

These carry no coupon but are sold on a discount basis from a face-principal value of 100. The yield quoted on such instruments is calculated as follows:

$$\text{Bank discount rate} = \frac{\text{Discount}}{100} \cdot \frac{360}{\text{Days}}$$

where Discount is the dollar amount of discount from the face value of $100 and Days is the actual number of days to maturity.

For example if the discount on $100 of commercial paper were $1.50 and it had 92 days to maturity, its yield on a discount rate basis would be

$$\frac{1.50}{100} \cdot \frac{360}{92} = 5.87 \text{ percent}$$

Not only is the percentage return based on the maturity value rather than the amount invested, but also the formula assumes 360 rather than 365 days in the year. This convention may be summarized as *discount basis, actual/360.*

2. The *add-on yield* is used in Eurodollar- and Eurocurrency-deposit calculations, because these are typically issued at a price of 100 and the coupon added on at the end. The formula changes to:

$$\text{Add-on yield} = \frac{\text{Interest payment}}{100} \cdot \frac{360}{\text{Days}}$$

where

Interest payment is the dollar amount of payment made at maturity on an investment of $100
Days is the number of days to maturity

For example, if the interest payment on a 90-day Eurodollar deposit is $2.50, then the add-on yield is 10 percent.

The trouble with the add-on yield is that it ignores compounding, which can be important because a one-year Eurodeposit that pays interest semiannually is more desirable than one that pays annually. To take compounding into account we need the yield to maturity or the bond-equivalent yield.

3. The *bond-equivalent yield* or yield to maturity is the rate that equates the present value of all future interest and principal payments with the market price of the instrument. If, as in the Eurobond market, interest is paid annually, we can solve the following equation for *r,* the yield to maturity:

$$P = \frac{C}{1+r} + \frac{C}{(1+r)^2} + \ldots + \frac{C}{(1+r)^n} + \frac{FV}{(1+r)^n}$$

where

P is the present market price of the instrument
C is the annual coupon payment
n is the number of years to maturity
FV is the face value of the instrument (usually 100)

For a portion of a year we use the *30/360 convention,* which assumes that each month has 30 days and each year 360 days.

In the U.S. and Japanese markets, coupons are paid semiannually, and in the Euro-deposit and floating-rate-note markets, interest may be paid semiannually or quarterly.

To find the yield to maturity when interest is paid m times per year, we find r such that:

$$P = \frac{C/m}{1 + r/m} + \frac{C/m}{(1 + r/m)^2} + \ldots + \frac{C/m}{(1 + r/m)^{mn}} + \frac{FV}{(1 + r/m)^{mn}}$$

The first mn terms form a geometric progression, so P can be simplified to

$$P = \frac{C/m[1 - (1 + r/m)^{-mn}]}{r/m} + \frac{FV}{(1 + r/m)^{mn}}$$

which is a more convenient formula because it can be calculated in one cell of a spreadsheet.

EXAMPLE 10.1   What is the yield to maturity on an 18-month Euro–Canadian-dollar CD sold at 99 with a 9 percent annual interest rate paid quarterly?

     To answer this we have to find by iteration the value of r that satisfies the following equation:

$$99 = \frac{9/4[1 - (1 + r/4)^{-4 \cdot 1.5}]}{r/4} + \frac{100}{(1 + r/4)^{4 \cdot 1.5}}$$

After using a spreadsheet program, the answer turns out to be 9.72 percent.

The frequency of payment will make a difference to the effective yield to maturity. The more frequent the payment, the greater the effective yield, because it is always nicer to get money sooner. A common way of comparing apples with apples in the Euromarket is to convert everything to its annual-pay equivalent. The formula for interest conversions of this kind is $(1 + i/m)^m - 1$, where m is the frequency of payments per year. For example, converting a 9 percent rate paid semiannually to its annual equivalent would yield $(1 + .09/2)^2 - 1 = 9.20$ percent.

Table 10.1   *Common Interest Bases*

Major instruments	Interest-rate conventions
U.S. bank deposits	Annual actual/365
Eurocurrency deposits	Annual actual/360
U.S. and Eurocommercial paper	Discount basis actual/360
U.S. banker's acceptances	Discount basis actual/360
U.K. bills of exchange, commercial paper	Discount basis actual/365
U.K. bank deposits	Annual actual/365
U.S. and U.K. Treasury bonds	Semiannual actual/actual
U.S. corporate bonds, Yankee bonds, Federal agencies	Semiannual 30/360
Eurobonds and continental bonds	Annual 30/360
Floating-rate notes	Annual actual/360

Some instruments have interest calculated on the basis of the *actual* number of days to maturity—that is, from settlement (delivery) date to maturity date—the number of days, counting the settlement date but not counting the maturity date—while others make the simplifying assumption that there are only 30 days in every month. And in some cases, the year is assumed to have 360 days, in others 365. Table 10.1 provides a sampling of the interest-rate conventions used in some major money and bond markets.[1]

Eurocurrency Time Deposits and Certificates of Deposit

The overwhelming majority of bank deposits in the Eurocurrency market takes the form of non-negotiable time deposits. An investor puts her money in Credit Suisse, London branch, today; she gets it back, plus interest, in three months' time. Canceling a time deposit is awkward and expensive, so the investor sacrifices liquidity. Those who want greater liquidity invest in shorter maturities. A very high proportion of Eurodollar time deposits, especially in the interbank market, mature in one week or less.

Alternatively, the investor can buy a negotiable Euro certificate of deposit (Euro CD), which is simply a time deposit that is transferable and thus has the elements of a security. Some banks are a little reluctant to issue CDs, because they would prefer not to have their paper traded in a secondary market, especially at times when the bank might be seeking additional short-term funding. The secondary paper might compete with the primary paper being offered. Others will issue CDs readily if investors prefer them, perhaps paying ⅛ percent or more below their equivalent time-deposit rate to reflect the additional liquidity and the somewhat greater documentary inconvenience of CDs.

Other banks (particularly if they wish to have their names better known in the market) might deliberately undertake a funding program using Euro CDs, as exemplified in Figure 10.1. In this circumstance, the CDs are to be distributed like securities, so as to increase awareness of the issuer's name and raise a larger volume of funds for longer maturities than might be possible in the conventional Eurodeposit market.

Banker's Acceptances and Letters of Credit

Banker's acceptances are money-market instruments arising, typically, from international trade transactions that are financed by banks. The banker's acceptance (BA) itself represents an obligation by a specific bank to pay a certain amount on a certain date in the future. To simplify a bit, it is a claim on the bank that differs little from other short-term claims such as CDs. Indeed BAs, when they are traded in a secondary market, trade at a return that seldom deviates much from comparable CDs issued by the same bank. **Letters of credit** (L/C) are documents issued by banks in which the bank promises to pay a certain amount on a certain date, if and only if documents are presented to the bank as specified in the terms of the credit. A letter of credit is generally regarded as a very strong legal commitment on the part of a bank to pay if the conditions of trade documents are fulfilled.

In a typical export transaction, the exporter will want to be paid once the goods arrive (and are what they are supposed to be) in the foreign port. So the exporter asks for *acceptance* by the importer's bank of a *time draft* (essentially an invoice that requests

---

[1]Adapted from Julian Walmsley, *Global Investing: Eurobonds and Alternatives* (London: Macmillan, 1991): 312.

Figure 10.1   ***Negotiable Eurocurrency Certificates of Deposit.***   Although the great majority of Eurodeposits are time deposits, some banks use CDs to fund themselves.

This announcement is neither an offer to sell nor a solicitation of an offer to buy CD's and appears as a matter of record only.

U.S. $100,000,000
Banco Río de la Plata S.A.
New York Agency

360 days US$ Euro CD Issue
due June 1, 1992

under a Euro CD Program
arranged by Citibank, N.A.

The undersigned acted as

Arranger, Issuing & Paying Agent,

Dealer and Distributor on this

Euro CD Issue

June 7, 1991

CITIBAN⟨●⟩

payment on a future date). Upon acceptance by the importer's bank, the innocuous little time draft becomes a valuable document, a banker's acceptance. *Acceptance means that the bank obliges itself to pay the face amount upon the due date.*

The means by which an exporter gets paid is by selling this BA to its own bank, which can hold it as an investment or sell it in the secondary market, when it becomes a money-market instrument. Banker's acceptances are sold at a discount from face value, like Treasury bills and commercial paper, and yields are quoted as discount yields. Why should the bank pay the exporter? The reason is that it has promised the exporter that it will do so upon presentation of documents conveying title to the goods. That promise is what we have described as the letter of credit.

Standby letters of credit are related instruments entailing a commitment to pay on the part of a bank, but they normally do not involve the direct purchase of merchandise or the presentation of title documents. The standby letter of credit says unconditionally that "I'll pay you X dollars on Y date if you show me Z document." That's all you have to do: show him Z document and you receive the money. Standby letters of credit are used to support bid and performance bonds, advance-payment guarantees, and other financial commitments. Nowadays, they are also widely used as a sort of guarante, or more precisely a substitute for someone else's obligation. For example, a relatively unknown Japanese bank, Hokkaido Trust, might wish to issue a CD in the U.S. market. In exchange for a fee and perhaps the pledging of collateral, a prominent Japanese bank such as Sanwa Bank might support the CD with a letter of credit. Sanwa has, in effect, substituted its own liability for that of Hokkaido Trust. Investors prefer an L/C to a guarantee, which obligates the guarantor to pay only if the original obligor fails to do so. The letter of credit, in contrast, is unconditional: it is payable by the issuer of the L/C simply against a draft.

Euronotes and Eurocommercial Paper

Both Euronotes and Eurocommercial paper were introduced and explained in the previous chapter, so we will say little more about them here. As we discussed earlier, these instruments are short-term, unsecured promissory notes issued by corporations and banks. *Euronotes,* the more general term, encompasses note-issuance facilities, those that are underwritten, as well as those that are not underwritten. The term *Eurocommercial paper* is generally taken to mean notes that are issued without being backed by an underwriting facility—that is, without the support of a medium-term commitment by a group of banks to provide funds in the event that the borrower is unable to roll over its Euronotes on acceptable terms. As noted in the previous chapter, most actual issuance in the Euronote market takes the form of nonunderwritten Eurocommercial paper (ECP), so the actual paper that an investor will find available for investment is likely to be ECP.

Like U.S. commercial paper, Euronotes and ECP are traded by convention on a *discount basis,* and interest is calculated as "actual/360," meaning that the price is set as 100 minus the discount interest rate multiplied by the actual number of days to maturity, over 360.

EXAMPLE 10.2   Goldman Sachs sells you Erikssen ECP maturing on December 17 at an agreed rate of 8 percent. If the value date for delivery is October 12, how much do you pay Goldman?

Answer: ECP is priced at a discount from par, and the rate quoted is a discount rate. To get the price as a percentage of the face value, we use the calculation

$$\text{ECP price} = 100 - \text{Discount rate} \cdot \frac{\text{Actual days}}{360}$$

The actual number of days to maturity is 61, so the price is $100 - 8 \cdot 61/360 = 98.64$.

Medium-Term Notes and Deposit Notes

The role of international banks in arranging and managing Eurocommercial-paper facilities in the international credit market has evolved from one of providing loans, to include the underwriting of syndicated facilities and perhaps trading the participations, and finally to being the auctioneer in the distribution of corporate paper. The latter role has carried over into an offshoot of the commercial-paper market, the *medium-term note (MTN)* market. *Deposit notes* are simply MTNs issued by international banks. International institutions such as the World Bank are prominent issuers.

Medium-term notes are in many respects simply fixed-rate corporate bonds but of a generally shorter maturity than Eurobonds or domestic bonds. As an investment vehicle, the MTN is often regarded by institutional investors as a temporary investment that can be designed to suit the particular investor's requirements. The reason is that MTNs, unlike conventional bonds, are offered on a continuous basis in smaller amounts—as little as $2 to $5 million at a time—rather than in single large issues. An investor such as a pension fund might have $7 million to invest for 11 months in a good corporate name. He will call several MTN dealers to see what companies are borrowing, and when he makes his choice the note will be issued *specifically for the investor*. (This specificity explains why MTN financing programs are often described as "investor driven.") In effect, the distribution process in the MTN market resembles a commercial-paper-issuance program, although without the backstop lines of credit that commercial paper programs typically have. Under a comprehensive MTN issuance program, an issuer can raise funds by issuing fixed-rate, floating-rate, or deep-discount paper in any of a number of currencies. Liquidity is provided by either one or a number of "committed" dealers.

The MTN and its offshoots have turned out to be one of the most important developments in longer-term funding in the 1980s and 1990s.[2] The MTN is a commercial-paper–like instrument that has a maturity rivaling that of a corporate bond. Indeed medium-term notes are issued today with maturities ranging from 9 months to as much as 30 years—a lot longer than is available in the Eurobond market. The notes are typically unsecured but need not be. They pay interest on a 30/360-day basis, unlike deposits that pay on actual/360 terms. Some have floating rates based on an index such as LIBOR, just like floating-rate notes. Unlike corporate bonds, few are callable. Like commercial paper, most domestic MTNs are rated, whereas most Euro-MTNs are unrated.[3] As noted, their most significant distinguishing feature is a subtle one—the fact that their issuance and even maturity is largely investor determined, not issuer determined. Corporate bonds are issued infrequently and often entail relatively heavy issuance costs, so the borrower wants to do the issue in large amounts at a known cost and get it distributed as widely as possible. This means that there must be an underwriting syndicate. Not so with MTNs or deposit notes; paper is issued through dealers at the time, in the amount, and for the maturity that the investor wants. MTNs and deposit notes issued by top-name banks have achieved the status of a commodity; very few Eurobonds have.

---

[2]Deposit notes are issued by commercial banks and have the status of deposits; medium-term notes are issued by corporations, including bank holding companies, and are treated like corporate bonds from a legal point of view. In the United States, bank-deposit notes are exempt from SEC registration, as are all MTNs placed privately.

[3]Like the commercial-paper market, the medium-term note market had its origins in the United States. Euro-MTNs are very much like domestic MTNs, with many of the same issuers and the same cast of broker-dealers, although a somewhat different investor base. And of course, there's no Euro-SEC, so some issuers prefer the MTN from a disclosure point of view. As with the commercial-paper market most MTN programs are now global: they offer the issuer access to either market, to spread its sources and tap the cheapest market.

EXAMPLE 10.3 For example, Hoechst A.G., a German pharmaceutical concern, might tell its dealers that the company will accept any money in the 1-to-5-year range at a certain spread relative to the benchmark Treasury yields. The dealers would let their customers know from day to day who was offering notes at what rates and the paper would be sold only on a "best efforts" basis—if and when an investor wanted it. If a Swiss-bank trust department calls the broker (say CSFB) and says, "I'll buy $20 million of 3½ year Hoechst deposit notes at 45 over," the deal would be struck there and then. Hoechst's treasurer would subsequently be contacted to confirm the trade! This process is much easier than waiting for the right Eurobond to be issued. It's cheaper for Hoechst, too,[4] although perhaps a little less predictable than a $250 million underwritten Eurobond. The firm will still get its quarter billion, although in dribs and drabs and at different levels.

In the primary market, MTNs by their nature lack the magnitude of placing power of identical bonds issued in a big corporate bond issue, but they have borrowed so many of the successful features of the commercial paper market—such as broker-sponsored programs, continuous offerings of primary paper, and good market-maker support—that they have replaced underwritten Eurobonds and domestic bonds as the preferred source of longer-term funds for major international banks.

In the secondary market, one potential problem with MTNs from the investor's point of view is that if each note is tailored to a specific investor's needs, then it is somewhat unique and hence is likely to lack liquidity. To be able to price a security and to buy or sell it without difficulty, there should be a reasonable amount of the same or closely comparable securities outstanding in the market. Two approaches have been taken to help improve liquidity, at the expense of some flexibility:

1. *Use multitranche tap notes.* Under this structure, the borrower must issue a minimum amount of paper, such as $50 million, in each tranche. Beyond the minimum the issue can be expanded to satisfy demand; but the minimum ensures that there is always a reasonable quantity of paper outstanding with identical characteristics.

2. *Insist upon standard annual or semiannual coupon dates,* irrespective of the note's issuance and maturity dates. Normally a bond issued on April 1 would have its first annual coupon paid a year later, on March 31. But to standardize things, Air Zenda Capital[5] pays all coupons on its MTN program on June 30. So the first coupon of a Zenda MTN issued on April 1, 1992, would be a *short coupon,* payable two months later on June 30. Assuming this is a 2½ year note, it matures 30 months later, on October 31, 1994. But it paid a coupon on June 31, 1994, so the last coupon (paid at maturity) is also a short coupon. This oddity makes MTN price and yield calculations a bit more challenging.

EXAMPLE 10.4 The date is January 15, 1993. A secondary-market dealer has approached you about buying an Air Zenda 6 percent deutschemark MTN that matures on October 31, 1995. The MTN has a June 30 coupon date. In the view of your boss, the note should yield at least 6.5 percent to be worth buying. What is the maximum price, including accrued interest, that you should be willing to offer for the note?

Answer: The 6 percent coupon is paid annually on June 30. To find the price of the bond that will give a yield of 6.5 percent, we use the conventional present-value formula used in fixed-income securities pricing: the sum of the present values of each of the cash

---

[4]Hoechst may prefer to fund with floating-rate liabilities; so whenever a dealer succeeds in placing some fixed-rate paper, the bank will swap it into floating to achieve a sub-LIBOR, perhaps even sub-LIBID, cost of funds.

[5]The captive finance company of Air Zenda Holdings.

Table 10.2   *Cash Flows for Example 10.4*

Cash flow	Date	No. of days (using 30/360 basis)	No. of years	Amount	Present value
1st coupon	30 Jun 93	165	0.46	6	5.83
2nd coupon	30 Jun 94	525	1.46	6	5.47
3rd coupon	30 Jun 95	885	2.46	6	5.14
Final coupon and principal	31 Oct 95	1005	2.79	102	85.56
Present value of cash flows @ 6.5%					102.00
Accrued interest	15 Jan 93	195	0.54	6	3.25
Present value minus accrued interest					98.75

flows. The interest that has accrued since the last coupon date is part of the total payment to be made.

The computations for medium-term notes are done using the convention of the Eurobond market, namely that interest accrues on a 30-day month, 360-day year basis. Table 10.2 is extracted from a computer sheet, the easiest way to compute unconventional prices and yields.

Thus the maximum you should be willing to pay for the MTN is a *clean price* of 98.75, or a total price of 102.00, including accrued interest. Conventionally, in the international market, the clean price is the one quoted; it is understood that accrued interest will be paid as well.

The *yield* on an MTN is calculated in the same way as a bond yield. That is, it is the internal rate of return that gives the cash flows a present value equal to the total price of the instrument. For example, if you had the opportunity to sell a three-year Eurobond at a yield of 7.20 percent and replace it with the Air Zenda MTN described in Example 10.4 at a clean price of 96.50, how much "yield pickup" could you gain?

Answer: Using the same cash flows as in Table 10.2, the internal rate of return that results in the January 15, 1993, value of 99.75 (96.50 plus accrued interest of 3.25) turns out to be 7.43 percent, so the yield pickup is 23 basis points.

Floating-Rate Notes[6]

The floating-rate note is, as the name implies, an instrument whose interest rate floats with prevailing market rates. Like Eurodollar deposits, it pays a three- or six-month interest rate set above, at, or below LIBOR. Like international loans, this interest rate is reset every three or six months to a new level based on the prevailing LIBOR level at the reset date. More precisely, floating-rate notes issued outside of the country of the currency of denomination are issued in the form of *Eurobonds,* which makes them in some respects as much a capital-market instrument as a money-market instrument. But the framework we use places *pricing* at the center of what defines an instrument, and FRNs are priced in part like money-market instruments and in part like conventional fixed-rate bonds.

---

[6]This section is based in part on "Eurodollar Floating Rate Notes" by Stephen Fletcher, written while he was a member of the international fixed-income research department at Drexel Burnham Lambert.

The floating-rate note has grown up with the Euromarket as a whole. The instrument was introduced in the early 1970s after many investors had gotten their fingers burned by dabbling in the fixed-rate Eurobond market, in which prices fell as inflation drove interest rates up to historically high levels. Investment bankers thought that they would have a ready demand for floating-rate notes among those investors who wanted longer-maturity instruments than bank deposits, ones that would maintain their value in the face of higher interest rates. It turned out that the biggest buyers of floating-rate notes were not banks' customers, but banks themselves. Some saw them as another trading instrument: buy today, sell later at a profit. Most, however, bought them as medium-term substitutes for loans. Some, with a low cost of funds but a dearth of prime borrower customers, were looking for a way to earn a spread with little risk or effort. Other banks preferred them to bank loans because they were treated by the regulators as securities, a treatment that improved the liquidity of the banks' asset portfolios. Whatever the reason, the bulk of FRNs are today held by financial institutions whose cost of funds varies with short-term rates, because an FRN pays a rate that is tied to changes in short-term interest rates.

Figure 10.2 shows a typical "tombstone" announcement of an FRN.

Features of FRNs

All floating-rate notes have a coupon that is reset at fixed intervals in accordance with some preset formula, but there are many variations on this theme. Most FRNs can be characterized by the following features:

- *The reference rate.* The reference rate is the interest rate to which the coupon payment is linked. This is normally a short-term rate, so that some see FRNs as a substitute for money-market instruments. In the Euromarkets, the reference rate is usually LIBOR, although a few FRNs have used other reference rates (such as LIBID, LIMEAN, or the U.S.-Treasury-bill rate). The rate is normally reset at the beginning of each coupon period, and interest is paid in arrears.
- *The margin.* The margin is the spread between the coupon payment and LIBOR. Coupon payments on FRNs are generally LIBOR plus (or minus) some fixed amount. This spread reflects the differential risk at the time of issue between investing in the FRN and investing in a bank deposit paying LIBOR. LIBOR itself is usually about ⅛ percent higher than prime banks' bid rate in the interbank market, reflecting the risk of the bank with which funds would be deposited, and perhaps a discount for illiquidity. An FRN carries the default risk of the issuer over the life of the note and the liquidity risk of a tradable, but not necessarily traded, security.
- *The reference-rate period.* The reference-rate period is the maturity of the security to which the FRN's coupon is linked, such as three- or six-month Eurodollar deposits. An FRN coupon is quoted as the LIBOR-period rate and the margin—for example, six-month LIBOR plus ³⁄₁₆ percent.
- *Frequency of reset.* Reset frequency is the period between coupon-reset dates, and normally coincides with the reference-rate period.
- *Coupon-payment frequency.* This is the interval between coupon payments, and normally coincides with the coupon-reset periods.
- *Maturity.* The date on which the principal on an FRN will be redeemed is the maturity date. Many FRNs have *call* features—that is, the issuer may, at its option, redeem the FRN at certain prespecified dates prior to maturity.

A "plain vanilla" FRN is a fixed-maturity bond whose reference-rate period, frequency of reset, and coupon-payment period are all of the same length. Figure 10.3 illustrates

Figure 10.2   ***Example of a Floating-Rate-Note "Tombstone."***   The interest rate on this FRN has a cap and a floor; together these constitute a "collar." This feature allows the issuer to offer a higher initial coupon than conventional FRNs.

This announcement appears as a matter of record only

New Issue   *March, 1993*

CREDITANSTALT

Creditanstalt-Bankverein
(Incorporated in the Republic of Austria with limited liability)

Issue of
U.S.$200,000,000
Subordinated Collared Floating Rate Notes
Due 2003

Creditanstalt-Bankverein

Kidder, Peabody International   **Lehman Brothers International**
Limited
UBS Phillips & Drew Securities Limited

Credit Suisse First Boston Limited   **Deutsche Bank AG London**
Goldman Sachs International Limited   **Merrill Lynch International Limited**
J.P. Morgan Securities Ltd.   **Morgan Stanley International**
Nomura International   **Salomon Brothers International Limited**
Sanwa International plc   **Swiss Bank Corporation**

Source: *Financial Times*, May 25, 1993, p. 22.

---

the interest-rate behavior of one such FRN. A *mismatch FRN* is one in which the reference-rate period, the frequency of reset, and/or the coupon-payment period are of different lengths. For example, Banque Nationale de Paris has issued a mismatch FRN maturing in April 2005 that pays six-month LIBID "flat," meaning the margin over

Figure 10.3 *Example of a Floating-Rate Note.* The interest rate on an FRN is reset periodically in relation to a reference rate such as LIBOR or LIBID.

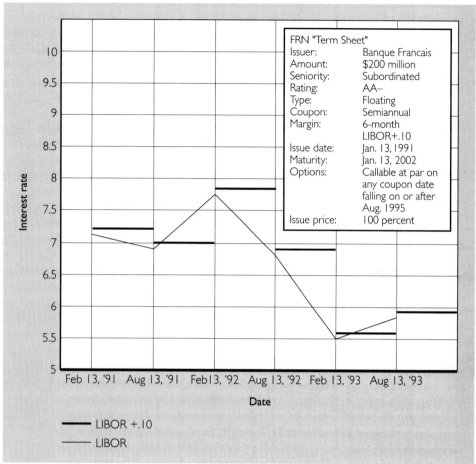

LIBID is zero. The rate is reset monthly but paid semiannually. The coupon is the arithmetic mean of the six one-month interest periods within the six-month coupon period.

Each FRN has a specific method for calculating the LIBOR rate to be used as a reference rate to reset coupons. The method is usually as follows: On the second business day prior to the beginning of each coupon period, the agent bank collects the offered quotations prevailing at 11 A.M. on that day for interbank deposits with the London branches of leading banks from a series of reference banks (listed in the prospectus). The arithmetic mean of these rates, rounded up to the nearest sixteenth, is then taken as LIBOR. Using this rate, the coupon is then calculated on an actual/360-day basis, rounded upwards or downwards to the nearest cent on each note. An agent bank calculates and publishes the coupon rate for each period.

Pricing FRNs

In some respects, an FRN is like a short-term money-market instrument. The rate on the FRN at issue is set high enough that the note is worth 100. At each reset period, the rate is raised or lowered to match the prevailing market rate. So, credit-risk changes aside, its price should return to 100. That means you could buy it today (a reset date) and sell it six months later at par, collecting your six-month coupon—just like a Eurodollar CD.

Even if you made some other assumption about the rollover price (the price at the next reset date), you could use this approach to calculate the money-market return.

We could call this somewhat naive approach the *money-market method*. It is helpful to those who wish to compare the yield on an FRN held as a short-term investment in lieu of another money-market instrument, and the fact that the rate is reset to market offers some comfort to such investors, but not much: FRNs are medium- or long-term bonds, and their prices at reset dates can deviate, and have deviated, far from par, for reasons associated with general FRN market conditions as well as the creditworthiness of the specific issue. Thus we can identify three distinct influences on the price of an FRN:

1. *Credit condition of the issuer.* The price at the reset date will fall below par if the promised margin relative to LIBOR is perceived as insufficient reward for an issuer's deteriorated credit condition. The most direct measure is the issue's *credit rating*. A note issued as a AA may be downgraded to A or worse for reasons specific to the issuer.

2. *Market perceptions of FRNs in general.* Changes in investors' perceptions of the FRN market as a whole or of a particular segment of the market may cause a particular issuer's FRN to trade above or below par on reset dates. In the early days of the market, many issues were seen as generously priced and traded above 100. Then in the late 1980s, the opposite happened. Subordinated bank debt was priced in much the same way as unsubordinated debt until the Bank of England changed its rules concerning the investment by one bank in the debt of another bank. After the change, the market reassessed the relative risk of subordinated to unsubordinated FRNs. This reassessment resulted in a sharp widening of required margins and a fall in bid prices on subordinated debt relative to unsubordinated debt of the same issuers. The most visible and devastating effect was on the price of perpetual FRNs.

3. *Money-market rates.* The FRN price will be affected by changes in short-term rates—specifically, the level of LIBOR between now and the next coupon reset date. A change in this rate will change the FRN's value as if it were a money-market instrument maturing on the reset date.

The method used for pricing and comparing FRNs reflects the fact that they are, in some respects, bond instruments and, in some respects, money-market instruments. When comparing two straight bonds, the standard approach is to consider the yield to maturity of each bond and the liquidity and credit risk of the bonds. The yield is sometimes expressed as a spread over "benchmark" U.S. Treasury yields. But because the FRN's coupon rate fluctuates, the standard yield measures are useless. For this reason, and because so many FRNs are held by those seeking a spread over their short-term cost of funds, the market has developed a measure of an FRN's effective spread over LIBOR: To get the effective spread over the instrument's remaining life, we adjust the quoted margin by amortizing the premium or discount at which the FRN is trading. For example, on November 18, 1991, an Electricidad de Madrid FRN maturing on September 4, 1995, was offered in the London market at 99.64. The stated margin over six-month LIBOR was 0.10 percent over six-month LIBOR, but the effective or discounted margin was 21 basis points. This *discount-margin approach* is the industry standard for comparing FRN spreads.

The Discount Margin and the Neutral Price

The **discount margin** is a measure of the effective spread, relative to LIBOR, that an investor would earn if he bought the FRN at some price today and held it to maturity.

It is the margin relative to LIBOR that is necessary to discount the cash flows from an FRN so that the sum of the present value of the flows is equal to the gross price of the note. It is calculated in a manner similar to the yield to maturity of a fixed-rate bond. Because the coupon stream is uncertain, it is necessary to make some assumption about average LIBOR from the next coupon date until maturity, although, fortunately, the discount margin is not very sensitive to the assumption made.[7] Naturally, nobody can be sure what rates will prevail over the life of the FRN, but one acceptable method is to use the implied forward rate for the remaining life from the yield curve for equivalent fixed-rate instruments. Better still, use the swap yield curve: this is preferable because, as will be seen in the chapter on swaps, an FRN can be converted into the equivalent of a fixed-rate bond using an interest-rate swap.

Before we present the formula, a word about price: FRN prices are conventionally quoted *clean*—that is, not including accrued interest. Accrued interest is calculated on a money market actual/360-day basis by using the formula $A = (\text{LIBOR} + \text{Quoted margin})(\text{Days}/360)$. The variable Days is the actual number of days from, and including, the date of the last coupon up to, but excluding, the settlement date. The gross price is the clean price plus accrued interest—that is, the total price paid.

The *discount margin (DM)* is found by solving, by iteration, the following equation for *DM:*

$$P + A = \frac{(L + QM)/m}{1 + \dfrac{L_s + DM}{100} \cdot \dfrac{D_s}{360}}$$

$$+ \left[\frac{1}{1 + \dfrac{L_s + DM}{100} \cdot \dfrac{D_s}{360}} \right] \left[\sum_{t=1}^{n} \frac{(L_a + QM)/m}{\left(1 + \dfrac{(L_a + DM)/m}{100}\right)^t} \right.$$

$$+ \left. \frac{100}{\left(1 + \dfrac{(L_a + DM)/m}{100}\right)^n} \right]$$

where

P	=	today's price
A	=	Accrued interest, (LIBOR + Quoted margin) (Days since last coupon/360)
QM	=	Quoted margin
DM	=	Discount margin
L	=	Current LIBOR in effect, so that $L + QM$ is the current coupon
L_s	=	LIBOR for time between settlement and next coupon date
L_a	=	Assumed average LIBOR rate over remaining life of FRN (using the swap rate)
D_s	=	Days from settlement to next coupon date
m	=	Number of coupon periods per year[8]
n	=	Number of coupon periods to maturity

---

[7]That's because it appears in both the numerator and the denominator of the valuation formula.

[8]In principle, one should use the number of days between each coupon date over the whole life of the FRN in the formula. A more practical approach is to assume, for all payments except the first, that the payments occur at equal intervals of $1/m$ years.

This formula looks complicated but it's really not. It simply discounts the note's cash flows as in a fixed-rate bond. You can think of the equation as having three parts:

Total price paid equals *present value of next coupon* plus *sum of present values of all subsequent coupons* plus *present value of final principal repayment.*

EXAMPLE 10.5   On June 18, 1992, a Banque Nationale Belgique floating-rate note maturing on July 29, 2004, is priced at 99.26. The stated margin is 12.5 basis points over 6-month LIBOR. The discount-margin approach amortizes the discount of 0.74 over the remaining 12-year life of the note to approximate the effective margin over LIBOR, so the effective margin should be greater than 12.5 basis points. Using the discount-margin formula, what is the discount margin on the BNB floater?

To answer this we need some more information: The current coupon is 7.5 percent. A purchase of the note would settle a week later, on June 25, and the next coupon date is July 29, 1992. The LIBOR rate for this remaining 34 days is 7.0042. The current 12-year rate for interest-rate swaps against 6-month LIBOR is 7.5625, which we shall assume to be the average rate for the remaining life.

Based on this information, a spreadsheet version of the above formula gives a discount margin of 21.7 basis points.

For some investors it is useful to abstract from the money-market aspect of a FRN to gauge the extent to which changes in *risk,* rather than in short-term rates, have affected the note's price. This analysis can be done by waiting until a coupon date to see whether the FRN trades at a discount or a premium when the coupon is reset to a market level. Alternatively, we can determine the price that the FRN would have to trade at on a coupon date to ensure that the investor receives the discounted margin. This price is known as the **neutral price;** it may be considered the price at which a new issue with the same quoted margin as the FRN would be set in order to give a return equal to the discounted margin. Box 10.1 provides a calculation for the neutral price.

Caps, Floors, Calls, and Puts in FRNs

Many floating-rate notes have option features. Most, in fact, have a minimum coupon level; this is called a **floor.** Some have a maximum coupon level, called a **cap.** An FRN that has both a floor and a cap is said to be **collared.**

Recall the floater illustrated in Figure 10.3, paying LIBOR + 10bp. In the past, such an FRN would typically have a floor at 5.25 percent. Thus whenever LIBOR moves below 5⅛ percent on a coupon-reset date, the investor will receive an above-market rate. In effect, the issuer has agreed to pay the investor the difference between the floor rate minus the margin and LIBOR whenever the latter falls below 5.15 percent. From the investor's viewpoint, buying a floored FRN may be regarded as purchasing a plain FRN plus a strip of European call options on LIBOR with strike prices equal to the floor level minus the margin. On each coupon date, the investor receives LIBOR plus the margin, plus the intrinsic value of the option, if any. In the early 1990s, many FRNs were issued with both caps and floors. In effect, the investor sold a cap with sufficient value to pay for the floor.

Some FRNs, though far fewer, have caps on the rates that they will pay. For example, one FRN trading in the market is a Mitsui Trust issue that pays 3-month LIBOR + 0.25%, a generous spread, but which has a ceiling rate of 12.75 percent. This is the equivalent of saying that if LIBOR exceeds 12.50 percent, the investor will pay Mitsui the difference between LIBOR and 12.50 percent. A "cap floater" may be considered as

BOX 10.1

Calculating the Neutral Price

The discounted margin neutral price is the price of the floating-rate note on the next coupon date that gives a return over the period from the settlement to the next coupon equal to the rate plus the discounted margin:

$$\text{Neutral Price} = (P + A) \left[\cfrac{1}{\cfrac{L_s + DM}{100} \cdot \cfrac{D_s}{360}} \right] - \text{coupon}$$

where

P = Today's price
A = Accrued interest
DM = Discounted margin
L_s = LIBOR for the time from settlement to the first coupon
D_s = Days from settlement to first coupon date.

The neutral price will move toward par as the time to maturity decreases.

an uncapped FRN, plus a strip of European puts on LIBOR that the investor has sold, with a strike price equal to the cap level minus the margin. The number of puts equals the number of reset periods in the note's remaining life. The investor is paid in the form of a higher stated margin or a lower price than plain-vanilla FRNs—in other words, with a higher discounted margin.

Credit considerations aside, the neutral price of a capped or floored FRN will depend on the volatility of interest rates, the level of interest rates, and the shape of the yield curve. Box 10.2 discusses the behavior of capped and floored FRNs as the interest-rate environment changes.

BOX 10.2

How Capped and Floored Floaters Behave

How a cap or a floor affects an FRN's price depends on the value of the embedded options: for a floor, the strip of long calls; for a cap, the strip of short puts. The value of both caps and floors depends on the forward rates implied in today's LIBOR yield curve. With an upward-sloping yield curve and steeply rising implied forward rates, the strip of calls embedded in a floor may be much further out-of-the-money than one would guess by simply comparing the floor level with today's LIBOR rate. The reverse is true for a cap: with an upward-sloping yield curve, the high forward rates place the cap further into-the-money (or closer to being in-the-money). As the yield curve moves upward and steepens, caps become relatively expensive, hurting the investor and lowering the capped FRN's neutral price.

This and other effects of caps and floors on FRNs' prices of changing interest rates are summarized below.

		Effect on Neutral Price of Capped FRN	Effect on Neutral Price of Floored FRN
Interest-Rate Volatility	Falling	Increases	Decreases
	Rising	Decreases	Increases
Interest-Rate Level	Falling	Increases	Increases
	Rising	Decreases	Decreases
Shape of Yield Curve	Flattening	Increases	Increases
	Steepening	Decreases	Decreases

Many floating-rate notes are *callable* by the issuer, others are *puttable* by the investor, and some are both. *In all cases the call or put provisions are exercisable only on coupon reset dates. As a result the call or put decision is influenced only by credit-risk considerations and not by interest rates.* This is in sharp contrast to similar provisions in fixed-rate bonds. FRNs tend to be called when the issuer can refinance at a cheaper spread (as indicated by the discount margin) and put when the investor can get a better spread for the same credit risk, irrespective of the level of rates. Investors find that how callable FRNs trade depends on the note's neutral price compared to the call price (which is normally the issue price). Callable FRNs with a neutral price significantly above the call price will tend to trade as if the call date were the redemption date. If a call date is approaching, the discount margin, measured to the call date, will be similar to the spread the borrower pays on its commercial paper. From the borrower's point of view, the call provision in a floating-rate note is similar to that in a note-issuance facility: it is the *right,* but not the *obligation,* to borrow at a preset spread.

SUMMARY

We have devoted a great deal of attention to the Eurocurrency market: it is simply the core of the international money market. The global money market brings together economic units that want to borrow large sums of money for short periods of time with those that want to lend them. This chapter has demonstrated how some of the other instruments of the global money market compete with Eurodeposits for investors' attention.

Instruments discussed in this chapter included banker's acceptances and letters of credit, Euronotes and Eurocommercial paper, and medium-term notes. Each serves somewhat different purposes and attracts a different investment clientele. However, each is to a degree a substitute for each other instrument, and the yield and price of each are sensitive to many of the same influences; these characteristics justify grouping them together. The fact that many of the other instruments of the international money market are priced off LIBOR, the interest rate on Eurodollar deposits, suggests that market participants themselves regard the different instruments as having a common frame of reference.

Floating-rate notes stand to some extent in a category of their own—they are bonds with many of the characteristics of money-market instruments. As far as interest-rate risk is concerned, FRNs are like short-term Eurodeposits. But they are longer-term instruments, so in the credit-risk dimension, they behave like corporate bonds. Methods of pricing and evaluating the return on FRNs reflect this duality: the value of an FRN is a function of the short-term interest rate to the next reset date, the long-term credit risk of the issuer as perceived by the market, and overall liquidity and demand conditions in the market for floating-rate notes. The best way to measure the relative value of FRNs is to use a *spread approach* to their returns: by evaluating their effective margins relative to LIBOR, we are able to evaluate their returns independent of the level of rates.

CONCEPTUAL QUESTIONS

1. In what respect can the different instruments described in this chapter be regarded as belonging to a single money market?
2. Why would an international bank fund itself by the issue of Eurodollar CDs rather than by non-negotiable time deposits?
3. What is the connection between a letter of credit and a banker's acceptance?
4. How does Eurocommercial paper differ from other forms of Euronotes?
5. Under what circumstances might an industrial company like Hoechst prefer to issue a Eurobond rather than a MTN?

6. Why are medium-term notes likely to prove illiquid? What measures have banks taken to remedy this?

7. What market variables influence the price of an FRN? Which of these render the FRN more like a bond-market instrument than a money-market instrument?

8. Why is a flattening of the yield curve likely to increase the neutral price of FRNs with floors *as well as* of those with caps?

PROBLEMS

1. The price of a $1 million Euronote sold on July 4 for settlement on July 10 is $982,000. If the note matures on October 15, what is its yield on a discount-rate basis?

2. Assume you buy in the secondary market a 180-day Eurosterling CD paying an interest rate of 11%. If the £5 million CD has 45 days to run, how many pounds will you receive at maturity?

3. What is the yield to maturity on an eighteen-month Euro-Canadian dollar CD sold at 99 with a 9% annual interest rate paid semiannually?

4. Would you be better off with a CD paying 9% quarterly or one that pays semiannually? Quantify your answer.

5. You are a medium-term note trader at Merrill Lynch. A client has an interest in the 8.5% GMAC MTN that matures on November 10, 1994, as long as it yields 8.3% or better. All GMAC MTNs pay coupons on April 1 and October 1. If the note is to be sold for settlement on December 19, 1993, what price would make your customer happy?

6. You are the manager of Bank Bumiputra's London investment portfolio. On June 18, 1992, you are offered a Bavaria Bank floating-rate note maturing on July 29, 2004, at a price of 100.50. The FRN pays a margin of 12.5 basis points over 6-month LIBOR.

    The LIBOR rate currently in effect is 6.90%, and you also find the prevailing LIBOR rates are: one month, 7.25%; three months, 7.4%; and six months, 7.72%. Assuming LIBOR stays at its current level for the remaining life of the FRN, what is the effective spread Bumiputra could earn over LIBOR by investing in the Bavaria Bank floater?

Application 10.1 | ## EURO-POTPOURRI

Kang Wang-Kie, the newly appointed General Manager of the London branch of the Korea Exchange Bank, has been reading a survey of the international banking markets. As a result, he has asked you, the token American, to help him clarify in his own mind what kind of lending-type assets would be most suitable for the branch. He reminds you that the KEB is flush with funds resulting from Korea's huge export earnings.

As a start, and in order not to lose face in meetings, he would like you to give him clear, one-sentence explanations of the distinguishing features of the following instruments:

- Syndicated term loan
- Note-Issuance Facility
- Eurocommercial paper
- U.S. commercial paper
- Medium-term note
- Eurodollar floating-rate note.

Application 10.2 | ## LAFARGE COPPÉE

Paris, Autumn, 1989. The treasurer of Lafarge Coppée, the French cement group, was considering a proposal from J. P. Morgan, the investment bankers, to issue a FF4-billion perpetual floating-rate note. He knew that Lafarge was in sore need of new long-term financing to refinance at least a portion of its bank borrowings. Acquisitions during the past year in Switzerland, Spain, the United States, Turkey, and France boosted the company to second place in the world cement industry, after Holderbank of Switzerland, but this expansion had entailed accumulating an excessive amount of bank debt. Yet the treasurer was not certain that a "perp" was the right solution. After all, the company had recently been able to issue fifteen-year subordinated French-franc debt at 11 percent.

Perpetual-floating-rate notes had been used extensively for bank financing during the mid-1980s, until a change in bank supervisory regulations had caused the market to crash. (A perpetual FRN is simply a note that pays a floating rate linked to three- or six-month LIBOR, like other floating-rate notes, but with no stated maturity. Because the notes are generally subordinated to other forms of debt, they can be used by banks to meet their regulator-imposed capital requirements. Their demise came when the Bank of England and its counterparts in Japan and elsewhere considered that the perps' subordinated status made them rather risky as *investments* for banks, and decreed that banks would have to have 100 percent capital against any perps they owned. Naturally, many banks tried to unload them, their value plummeted, and issues of them still trade at deep discounts from par.)

As the bankers had explained, this kind of perpetual floater would be different. Morgan would place all FF4 billion of the issue, but Lafarge would receive only FF3 billion in cash. The remaining FF1 billion would be used to purchase a zero-coupon French government bond. The latter would mature in 15 years and the proceeds used to prepay all subsequent interest on the perpetual. The result was that the debt would in effect be extinguished after 15 years. This technique had been pioneered by French state-owned companies such as Rhône-Poulenc to get around the restrictions placed by the government on sales of new shares to the public.

J. P. Morgan had urged Lafarge, a private company, to consider this method as a way to raise long-term subordinated funds without weakening their majority shareholders. The notes would pay six-month PIBOR, the Paris Interbank Offered Rate (now 8.5 percent), plus 45 basis points. Morgan admitted that this was expensive by the standards of conventional floating-rate notes, but a lot cheaper than the 13 percent to 14 percent that was the estimated true cost of raising equity in France at the time. And unlike dividend payments on pure equity, the interest payments on the perpetual notes would be tax deductible. At a marginal corporate tax rate of 42 percent, such considerations were important. The bankers had further pointed out that if Lafarge preferred fixed-rate funds, the floating-rate payments could be swapped into fixed using a French interest-rate swap. Swap rates in France at the time were approximately 10.10 percent for 5 years, 10.25 percent for 10 years, and 10.15 percent for 15 years.

What, the treasurer wondered, were the merits of the proposed issue relative to conventional equity or debt, on an after-tax basis?

Selected References

Credit Suisse First Boston. *Eurodollar Floating Rate Notes Evaluation Techniques*. November 1984.

Euromoney. *The 1992 Guide to European Money Markets*. Supplement to *Euromoney*, September 1992.

Federal Reserve Bank of Richmond. *Instruments of the Money Market*. Revised periodically.

Stigum, Marcia. *The Money Market*, 3rd ed. Homewood: Dow-Jones Irwin, 1990.

Walmsley, Julian. *Global Investing*. London: Macmillan, 1991.

11

The Global Debt Problem

Debt and the International Banks

As of the beginning of the 1990s, the less developed countries (LDCs) had accumulated over a trillion dollars in debt, most of it in the form of bank credits or government loans, and most of it in some kind of trouble: interest, or principal, or both, were in arrears. This resulted in a severe weakening of a number of international banks and a precipitous decline in many countries' creditworthiness. The latter meant curtailed development plans, a drop in living standards in some of the poorest countries, and the forced adoption of unpalatable policies by a number of governments. Despite efforts by the IMF, the World Bank, and developed-country leaders to devise escape routes, the burden of developing-country debt on the world economy has persisted and weakened the global financial system to the point where the term "crisis" is no overstatement.

Developing countries owe debt to three groups: (1) to themselves—that is, to domestic borrowing in their own currencies, much of which has been eroded by inflation;[1] (2) to foreign governments that have given aid in the form of concessional loans, including debt owed to the international organizations such as the World Bank; (3) and to commercial banks.[2] The concern about a debt crisis has focused on about seventeen highly indebted middle-income countries that owe money primarily to international banks. The concern was fueled by a fear of the damage to the international banking system that might result from a failure of creditor banks.

This chapter is about solutions to the global debt problem, from the point of view both of debtor countries and of their creditors, especially the international banks. The chapter will briefly describe the events that led up to what is now known as the "LDC debt crisis." We will then consider a simple framework for understanding which kinds of countries and which kinds of policies have succeeded in avoiding the problem. This approach suggests a gradual way out for those countries mired in international debt. We will see that the abandonment of antimarket policies, the trading of LDC debt, and the conversion of bank debt into equity and other mutually acceptable claims may offer a means to resolve this prolonged crisis. Whatever the outcome, both borrowers and lenders have learned an important lesson from the experience: that there *is* an optimal level and composition of debt, and that this level was far exceeded.

Note: I am in debt to Richard Herring for valuable conversations and materials. I also thank Carol Osler for suggesting the topic of this chapter, and Carlos Abadi for insights into LDC debt trading.

[1]In fact the domestic debt is a cause of high inflation, for debt owed to central banks means the government is paying for its own bonds by printing new money.

[2]Commercial banks are not the only lenders to developing countries, but their lending so far exceeds other sources of private lending such as bond investors that we will focus on them.

Capsule History of the LDC Debt Crisis

What precipitated the global debt crisis? Not debt per se. Less developed countries need financing to grow. This financing can come from domestic sources or from foreign sources. In the history of economic development, some countries, like Japan, have had sufficiently high domestic savings rates to finance their development by means of domestic savings. Others, such as the United States in the nineteenth century, have relied heavily on external financing. Singapore is an example of a country that has supplemented a high domestic savings rate with capital from abroad. Korea incurred a great deal of external debt but managed to repay it. Clearly countries can incur international indebtedness without necessarily encountering substantial difficulty servicing the debt. But when lenders lose confidence to the point where they are loathe to increase their exposure in countries showing debt problems, and when domestic savings are transferred abroad to service the debt, borrowers cannot finance the investment they need to generate growth.

What, then, was different about the recent spate of borrowing that caused things to go awry? There are three basic factors: (1) external circumstances, (2) borrowing and lending by the countries themselves, and (3) the actions of commercial banks.

The debt crisis as we know it started in August 1982, when Mexico declined to continue servicing its debt and technically went into default. Argentina and Brazil soon followed suit, and the proverbial bananas hit the fan.

In part, the crisis was precipitated by *an accumulation of external economic circumstances* in the early 1980s. Tight anti-inflationary monetary policies had been introduced in the industrial countries to counter the excessive inflation of the late 1970s: this led to weak economies in the major industrial countries and a sharp drop in the demand for commodities and in commodity prices. A rise in interest rates increased financing costs, because most of the bank lending had been done on a floating-rate basis.[3] Lower U.S. inflation produced an appreciation of the dollar, which hurt the many LDC borrowers who had contracted debt in dollars but who were reliant on exports denominated in other currencies.

In part, *the countries themselves* were to blame. When an economic boom increased demand, production of commodities was boosted to the point at which commodity prices suffered. Developing countries took as much money as they could get without paying close attention to matching debt-service obligations with debt-service capacity. It could be argued that they relied on the lenders to make a rational evaluation of debt-service capacity and to limit lending accordingly, but the lenders were not being provided with enough economic information to make well-informed decisions that would be in the countries' interests, nor did they have any consolidated picture of how much debt the country was incurring from various sources. (See Table 11.1 and Box 11.1.) To the extent that borrowing countries were doing debt-capacity planning, they were not building in a cash-flow cushion for adverse world events such as those described in the previous paragraph. Nor were they taking advantage of financing structure that would permit risk sharing—giving the private sector, domestic and foreign, some control and potential gain from development growth in exchange for bearing risk. One theory holds that those who influenced country debt policy were aware of the risk, but were personally benefiting from the capital inflow and felt that they were sufficiently influential to resist additional taxes if and when the time came to pay the piper. Whatever the reason, like some com-

---

[3]When a developing country's growth rate exceeds the real interest rate it is paying on its debt, the borrower will eventually pay back its debt. At that stage, the borrower's income should have risen sufficiently for its saving to finance the transfer. In practice, things do not always work out that smoothly. The increase in the real interest rate in the early 1980s forced many developing countries to make net transfers abroad much earlier than they had expected to.

panies and financial institutions in industrial countries, the LDCs had too much debt and too little equity.

But the *commercial banks* are the ones that put billions of dollars at risk. The international banks continued to lend in support of unsound economic policies and risky

Table 11.1   *Debt of the Developing Countries (in US$ millions)*

	1970	1980	1985	1990[a]
GNP	458,877	2,025,358	2,054,541	2,789,927
Total debt stocks	NA	561,754	936,928	1,220,909
Disbursements	13,464	110,076	88,788	106,765
Principal repayments	6,880	45,048	56,090	74,925
Net flows	6,585	65,028	31,740	38,111
Interest payments	NA	45,918	68,482	65,602
Net transfers	NA	19,109	− 36,742	− 27,491
Total debt service	NA	90,967	124,571	140,527

[a]Estimated

Source: World Bank, *World Debt Tables* (Washington, D.C.: IBRD, various annual issues).

BOX 11.1

Country-Debt Concepts

A variety of concepts are used to assess the economic burden of external debt.

Debt stock measures the total liability facing the debtor. The payment obligation arising from this is the *debt service,* comprising interest and principal payments. The debt stock does not necessarily predict the debt service precisely, because currency revaluations, interest-rate fluctuations, and the maturity structure of the debt all affect debt service.

Two concepts describe the net effect of borrowing and repayments on the flow of financial resources. *Net flows* refers to disbursements minus principal repayments. It measures whether new financing exceeds debt being retired. If debt levels remain prudent, net flows should be positive in all but the most advanced developing countries, because domestic investment requires continued external financing. *Net transfers* refers to disbursements minus interest and principal repayments. Negative net transfers imply that total debt-service payments exceed gross inflows, and that net real resources are being transferred out of the economy. This necessitates a trade surplus: the country must send more abroad or buy less from abroad.

Moratoria (the suspension of contractual debt-service payments), *arrears* (overdue service payments), *rescheduling* (changing the time profile of repayments without altering the total debt obligation), and *debt relief* are all ways of altering either the pattern or size of repayment flows. A moratorium or running behind on payments may provide temporary relief but will forestall future investment in the country. Planned, sustainable changes in the debt structure are more likely to create the environment needed for domestic investment and growth.

The debt-crisis countries are primarily those of Latin America and sub-Saharan Africa. The debt stocks of these countries have grown as a share of GNP in the 1980s, to as much as 80 percent for the African group, and private credit flows now represent a diminished share of flows to these developing countries.

Net flows remain positive, except to the middle-income countries of the Pacific; these countries invested their borrowed funds productively and are now repaying debt. But net transfers to the developing world have turned sharply negative: as a whole, the developing world is giving resources to the creditor countries.

borrowing strategies even after the local residents of the borrowing countries had demonstrably lost confidence in their governments' policies. The consequence: a substantial amount of bank lending was used in effect to finance capital flight from the borrowing countries. Guttentag and Herring have suggested three reasons for this odd behavior.[4]

1. Banks suffered from *disaster myopia*—a tendency to neglect low-probability hazards that may produce large losses. This theory, drawn from psychological research on decision making under high uncertainty, is at variance with the economist's conventional assumptions of rational decisions. The latter says that market discipline will force on-average-correct decision-making: those who make systematic errors will incur losses and go out of business. But when the "mistakes" are manifested infrequently, they may be disregarded with impunity for long periods. Country-risk myopia may have been perpetuated by the banks' own incentive systems: evaluations of performance usually cover short periods and use current income that is not adjusted for risk or the front-loading of revenue, as in syndicated loans' up-front fees.

2. Banks underestimated the risks because of *inadequate information and erroneous inferences* from existing information. Information on international reserves, on the balance of payments, and on domestic economic activity is poor, and available only after substantial lags in many developing countries. Many individual banks lending to Mexico, for example, were not aware that the country had borrowed seven billion dollars from various sources in the six months leading up to the August 1982 crisis. As for how the information is interpreted, banks seem to have overestimated the benefits of diversification. After all, it was thought, lending to oil-exporting Mexico would offset the risk of lending to oil-dependent Brazil. Little attention, it appears, was paid to two systematic linkages created by the loan policies of the banks themselves (floating rates and short maturities): all major borrowers were vulnerable to a rise in real interest rates, and all were vulnerable to refunding risk when confidence evaporated.

3. Banks took a calculated *gamble based on the expectation of official support* in the event that things went wrong. By herding—that is, joining one another in large syndicated loans to particular countries—banks may have hoped to ensure that any problem would be a systemwide problem. If all of the major banks got into trouble together, the threat of a banking crisis would induce governments and the IMF to extend more aid to such countries than they would otherwise. In a sense, they were right. When the crisis hit, the OECD governments, the IMF, and the bank regulators all got much more involved in the bank LDC exposure problem than they had been in the past. But the result was not to the banks' benefit: they were pressured to lend more while being asked to write off much of their existing exposure.

Why did the banks' regulators permit international banks to become overexposed? In part the reason was that they themselves had no objective method of assessing the "right" amount of exposure in relation to a bank's capital, so they used the population of banks themselves as the norm, and focused only on those whose exposure was more serious than most others.

Following the crisis, private lending to most of the troubled countries virtually dried up, and many of the world's biggest banks went through a decade of negotiations and balance-sheet adjustment to adjust to the reality of defaults and negotiations with creditor countries. The first phase of this process could be described as the *rescheduling stage*.

---

[4]Guttentag, Jack M., and Richard Herring. "Commercial Bank Lending to Developing Countries: From Overlending to Underlending to Structural Reform," in G. Smith and J. Cuddington, eds., *International Borrowing and Lending: What Have We Learned for Theory and Practice?,* World Bank, 1985, 129–150.

Rescheduling

When the debt crisis first broke, the International Monetary Fund played an important role by altering its priorities, offering large loans to countries such as Mexico in exchange for relief, rescheduling, and new money from the commercial banks. But before long it became clear that most of the banks were reluctant to incur the additional risk associated with refinanced debt that could not be paid. While the IMF and debtor countries were looking for new money, the banks were looking for a way out.

For the first half-decade of the debt crisis (approximately 1982–1987), commercial banks worked with their lawyers, the borrowers, and the bank regulators to try to find a way to reschedule the debt. (Rescheduling refers to arranging to defer and restructure the timing of the interest and/or principal of the loans.) The rescheduling of debt in the 1980s meant deferring payments that were obviously not going to be paid on time, extracting agreements from the borrowers to continue to service the interest on the debt so that the banks could list them as "current" and offer new loans to defer the principal, and the like. Banks neither wanted to concede that the money would never be paid (and write off the loans) nor were they willing to say that the borrowers were "permanent" clients deserving of additional loans.

But years of further deterioration followed. The bank regulators, not to mention shareholders, demanded that the banks own up to what the loans were really worth. The commercial banks began to realize that there might be more merit in admitting what the debt was worth in reality and making more money by trading it.

Since 1986, the banks have developed a number of more constructive approaches to reducing the debt in a voluntary fashion. These included debt buy-backs (in which a debtor buys back part of its foreign debt with either international reserves or new foreign exchange), exit bonds (that exchange existing loans for new, more palatable obligations), and swaps of debt for equity in local companies. The stimuli for many of these were two plans proposed by U.S. Secretaries of the Treasury Baker and Brady.

The Baker Plan and the Brady Plan

The Baker initiative of 1985 stressed the need to *maintain net flows of funds* from official and private lenders. However, the banks never took to the idea of pouring new money after bad in a big way, so the program had limited success. Before 1982, the highly indebted countries received about 2 percent of GNP in resources from abroad; since then they have transferred roughly 3 percent in the opposite direction.

By the end of the 1980s, officials and bankers began to realize that the debt crisis was becoming prolonged to the point that no end was in sight, and a reevaluation of the strategy was undertaken. A turn for the worse had occurred in 1987 when Brazil announced a moratorium on further interest payments to banks, prompting Citibank to announce loan-loss reserves of $3 billion against developing-country exposure. Sentiment in favor of a "menu" of methods to allow banks to put the experience behind them began to gather support. What came to be known as the **Brady plan** of March 1989 was an officially sanctioned effort at *debt reduction conditional upon economic reform*. This reduction would supplement the voluntary debt reduction mentioned above. Debt reduction may now receive official funding from governments, the IMF, and the World Bank, providing it takes place in the context of strong, effective adjustment programs. The strategy treats each individual country separately, and has evolved as particular countries reached agreement with their creditors and official agencies.

Mexico was the Brady plan's first success story, and the way it was done paved the way for other countries. Mexico agreed in February 1990 to offer three options to commercial bank creditors. The banks could (1) get out of their exposure by converting their loans into new, tradable bonds with guarantees attached, but worth 65 percent of the face value of the old paper; (2) convert their debt into new guaranteed bonds whose yield was just 6.5 percent; (3) keep their old loans but with new guarantees, and provide new money worth 25 percent of their exposure's value. Only 10 percent of the banks risked the new-money option, while 41 percent agreed to debt reduction and 49 percent chose a lower interest rate. This saved Mexico $3.8 billion a year in debt-servicing payments.

Venezuela was regarded in a more favorable light by the bankers. In its Brady arrangement, a proposal to encash the country's paper at 45 percent of its face value attracted only 7 percent of the total debt tendered. The other alternatives were (1) the substitution of old debt for new low-interest bonds (attracting 38 percent of the debt tendered); (2) an option for banks to have their old debt guaranteed in return for providing new money worth 20 percent of exposure (31 percent); (3) the right to swap old paper for new bonds whose interest rate rises in steps over six years as (or if) Venezuela's financial position improves; and (4) a choice of exchanging existing loans at a discount of 30 percent for paper paying interest at LIBOR plus about 1 percent.

Uruguay induced banks to provide new money in its Brady deal. Banks holding 28 percent of the debt agreed to make loans equal to 20 percent of their existing exposure. An exchange of old loans for new bonds paying 6.34 percent attracted 33 percent, while another 39 percent sold their debt for 56 percent of face value.

The lesson? Debt reduction can work, *if* banks are offered a range of reasonable choices sufficiently wide that the solution can be made to fit their individual needs and constraints.

While many debtor governments and some creditor governments were asking for *debt forgiveness,* the U.S. resisted this idea as being short sighted (and because the American taxpayer was unwilling to share cost of the banks' errors).[5] The Brady plan was designed to free countries from their debt burden in two linked ways: (1) The country had to carry out structural economic reforms that met the approval of the International Monetary Fund. These reforms were designed to remove government-imposed impediments to productivity and competitiveness and to attract equity capital from abroad. (2) The country had to convert existing debt into something acceptable to the banks but that also reduced the country's debt burden. For example, in the Mexico plan, banks were given the option of converting their loans into so-called "Brady bonds," 30-year bonds whose interest was guaranteed by the Mexican government in conjunction with the IMF, the World Bank, and the Japanese government, and whose principal was collateralized by U.S. Treasury zero-coupon bonds specially issued for the purpose by the U.S. government.

The IMF and World Bank were also asked to help countries engaging in economic reform to repurchase their own debt or to provide incentives for commercial banks to

---

[5]Conditional forgiveness has been used more in those countries whose indebtedness was primarily to other governments, rather than to commercial banks. Most sub-Saharan countries, even populous ones like Nigeria, Ghana, and Zaire, have relatively little bank debt and very little prospect of repaying government-to-government loans.

reduce their claims on debtor countries. In some cases a third element was included in the plan: fresh money from commercial banks.

One problem with previous plans was that even if the debtor government agreed to IMF strictures it was very difficult to get the large number of bank creditors to agree on the recasting of existing loans into something else. One feature of the more successful of the Brady plan restructurings has been that they give the banks some choice as to what their loans are converted into. This is called the *menu approach*. How the Brady-type debt-reduction plans have worked out in three countries is outlined in Box 11.2.

New Policies for the 1990s

While the creative recasting of debt has the potential for significantly relieving countries of the worst of the debt burden, the only long-term solution is to ensure that funds from abroad are used in such a way as to generate more production than the investment cost. In other words, the rate of return must exceed the cost of financing if future overburdening is to be avoided. What steps can the indebted countries take to improve the chances that investments will raise productivity and growth?

As the transformation of Eastern Europe has demonstrated, many countries are embracing more free-market-oriented policies for the decade of the 1990s. Some, like Chile, which were once mired in debt, have chosen their own paths out. Others, like Brazil, are being "lectured to" and are changing policies only reluctantly. But what are the guideposts to the way out?

In the previous section, we concentrated on new financial arrangements to exit the debt crisis. These basically consist of making sure that debt-servicing obligations do not exceed the country's debt-serving capacity. It would be even better if the debt-servicing capacity itself could be improved.

One way in which LDCs could sustain more debt would be if developed countries placed fewer barriers to LDC exports. But the crisis taught that much of the problem lay in ill-advised domestic policies, ones that would not have been sustainable even had exogenous economic events been more favorable. These policies varied from excessively ambitious infrastructure investments and misconceived import substitution strategies to unaffordable subsidies and excessive military expenditures. Today, just as the markets are producing more sustainable financial strategies, many countries are devising more robust domestic economic policies.

One of the major policy reforms that governments in Eastern Europe, Latin America, and elsewhere are initiating is to free markets from excessive control. That is not to say that the government of a developing country has no role to play. It must maintain a stable value, internal as well as external, for its currency. And while many governments have interfered too heavily in the economy and international trade, they have not done enough in areas such as health and education. Research at the World Bank has identified four keys to growth-enhancing policies:

1. *Investment in people.* A necessary condition for development is sufficient spending on primary education, basic health care, nutrition, and family priorities. In many countries, investing in people would require a sharp curbing of wasteful military spending.
2. *Improving the climate for enterprise.* Growth will improve if governments intervene less in industrial and agricultural pricing, deregulate entry to markets, and focus on improving the infrastructure and institutions—such as the legal system—underpinning business.

3. *Open embrace of international trade and investment.* Developing countries should reduce tariffs substantially and impose fewer nontariff barriers to trade. Particularly needed is a move away from discretionary forms of control, allowing a government agency to choose, without constraint, what can be imported or exported.

4. *Firm macroeconomic policies.* Governments need to ensure fiscal deficits are low and that inflation is held in abeyance. Market-based incentives for saving and investment are essential to ensure domestic resources are available to finance development.

Some of the results of the World Bank's research are summarized in Figure 11.1. An analysis of 60 developing countries indicated that countries that have invested heavily in education and removed economic distortions grew at an average rate of 5.5 percent per annum between 1985 and 1987. Countries that embraced only one of these policies grew at just under 4 percent, while countries that adopted neither policy grew at about 3 percent.

The results of a microeconomic analysis of 1200 bank-financed projects over a twenty-year period are summarized in Table 11.2. The return on projects in countries with minimally distorted foreign-exchange markets was about 18 percent, compared with only 8 percent under heavily distorted regimes.

More important than the aid that sometimes provides the incentives for reforms, those countries which reversed antimarket policies have been rewarded by a building of

Figure 11.1   *Both Education and Free-Market Policies Are Required to Stimulate Growth.*

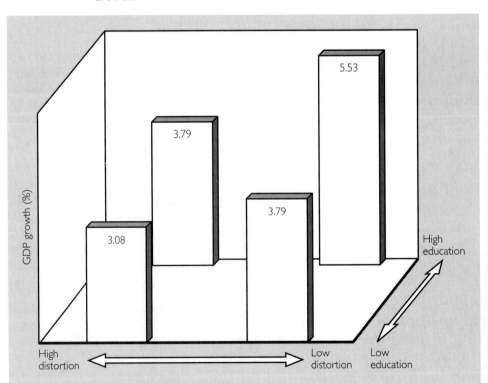

(Based on World Bank research.)

Table 11.2   *World Bank Project Rates of Return Under Different Policies*

Type of Distortion	Degree of Distortion		
	High	Moderate	Low
Trade restrictions	13.4% return	14.9% return	18.5% return
Overvalued exchange rate	7.7% return	14.1% return	17.3% return
Fiscal deficit	13.9% return	14.8% return	17.4% return

Source: World Bank, *World Development Report* (Washington, DC: IBRD, 1991).

confidence by *domestic* business people. In certain countries, such as Mexico and Venezuela, this led to a steady flowback of flight capital, money that had fled the wealth-endangering policies of previous regimes.

Debt-for-Equity Swaps and Privatization

A landmark in the history of the debt crisis occurred in 1985 when Chile negotiated the first debt-for-equity swap (see Box 11.3). A debt-for-equity swap is a simple idea with powerful consequences. We can illustrate the technique with an example: Chile owes Toronto Dominion Bank $220 million. The bank, which has already written down the loan to 70 percent of face value, is seeking a way to reduce its Latin American exposure. Chile now tells its creditors that the government wishes to extinguish a portion of its debt, giving in exchange equity in local companies. Specifically, the Chilean government will give the debt holder 85 percent of the face value of the debt *in local currency;* this money may be used by foreign investors for equity investments in Chile.[6] Toronto Dominion has no wish to hold and manage equity in Chile, but another Canadian company,

BOX 11.3

How Chile Reduced Its Debt

Chile has made extensive use of debt-equity swaps and various other market-based operations in its external debt management. Since the inception of official debt conversion programs in 1985 until early 1990, the cumulative value of conversions of Chile's commercial bank debt exceeded nine billion dollars. Debt conversions in Chile are governed by two chapters of the foreign-exchange regulations. One regulates debt conversions by residents into domestic currency instruments. The other regulates debt-equity conversions by foreign investors in Chile. The terms of conversion are agreed upon by the investor and creditor and must be approved by the Central Bank.

Other major transactions have included Central Bank buybacks arranged with creditor banks. In November 1988, the Central Bank, under the provisions of debt-restructuring agreements, bought $299 million of its external debt to banks using $168 million of its reserves (a discount of 44 percent). A second buy-back operation, carried out in November 1989, enabled the Central Bank to retire $140 million of debt at a total cost of $80 million (or a discount of 43 percent). Informal debt conversions by the private sector are also common in Chile.

---

[6]Depending on the circumstances, these investments may be used to start a new venture, to buy a stake in an existing local company, or to buy equity in a state enterprise that is destined for privatization.

Alcan, has an interest in developing bauxite deposits in northern Chile. So Toronto Dominion sells its debt to Alcan for 75 cents on the dollar. Alcan pays $165 million for $187 million worth of Chilean pesos *and* obtains automatic approval for its investment in Chile.

The last feature is key. Most companies have no interest in the local currency of Latin American countries for its own sake. By giving permission to hold controlling equity stakes in the country (with the consequences for putting ownership and control of employment, expansion and contraction of the business, and eventual repatriation of profits in the hands of foreigners), the government is taking a much more important step than simply buying back its debt with local currency. It not only is initiating an important policy toward foreign investment, but also making the economy more open and perhaps more efficient, if it imports new technology and techniques. At one time it was thought that the bulk of depressed loans might be converted into equity (or similar risk-bearing assets) under official debt-to-equity swap programs and debt buy-backs. But those who take risk want actual or potential control over the issuer, and this has proved unacceptable to the majority of countries that have had debt-servicing difficulties.

From the country's point of view, the debt-for-equity swap idea should both help reduce debt and improve the country's productivity. There may, however, be disadvantages. Local businesses will protest that foreigners are being favored. The country may be getting investors that would have come anyway, and lose the foreign exchange that would otherwise have been brought in. In a perfect world, the debt-for-equity swap would not be necessary: the government would announce its "open" policy and attract investment from abroad; it would then use the foreign exchange to buy back the debt in the secondary market. Some governments have worried that the conversion of external debt into newly minted local money might be inflationary, but such considerations have seldom inhibited some others, particularly because capital inflows can be sterilized by domestic monetary operations.

A twist on the debt-for-equity swap idea is to combine it with **privatization.** When Mexico privatized its banks in the early 1990s, for example, it succeeded in exchanging over a billion dollars of interbank debt for ten-year federal bonds paying LIBOR plus $13/16$ percent. In most developing countries, national utilities and transportation companies have borrowed heavily from abroad and from domestic banks. These countries are now among the borrowers that are unable to service their debts. However, they may not necessarily have overborrowed; rather, they may be simply unable to serve multiple masters. They are expected to help alleviate the unemployment problem. And because they are publicly owned, their products are frequently priced too low to yield an adequate return on their huge investments. If management were free to make its own employment decisions and if prices were set to yield a higher return, retained earnings could provide most of the investment required.

One of the biggest obstacles to economic efficiency, in the eyes of many economists (and consumers), is the fact that much of the economy is owned and run by the government. Government deficits are as high as 10 percent of gross domestic product in some Latin American countries, and roughly a third of those deficits can be attributed to losses by public enterprises. So why not "kill two birds with one stone"—that is, exchange debt for ownership shares in state enterprises? Entrenched interests, the desire to retain control, and a fear of foreign investment have made such plans difficult to get off the ground, but some are now underway.

Of the deals done to date, Argentina's auction of its telephone company stands out as among the most instructive. The company, ENTel, was losing $2 million a day. The government split the telephone company into two parts, selling 60 percent of each through debt-equity swaps. Citibank, supported by Telefónica Española of Spain and the Argentine arm of Italy's Techint, bought the southern part for $114 million in cash plus public-sector debt with a face value of $2.72 billion. Manufacturers Hanover Bank,[7] with the U.S. regional telephone company Bell Atlantic and six Argentine companies, acquired the northern part for $100 million in cash and $2.3 million in debt paper. Of the remaining 40 percent of ENTel, 15 percent went to employees and suppliers and 25 percent was sold to local investors and listed on the Buenos Aires stock exchange.

The U.S. banks may have contributed some of the debt from their own balance sheets, thus easing the burden of write-offs that the banking regulators insist on, but the bulk was almost certainly acquired on the secondary market where defaulted Argentine debt was trading as low as 14 cents on the dollar. Although the figures have not been disclosed, the real purchase cost of the Argentine telephone company could have been less than $1 billion for the two parts combined. Yet Argentina was able to reduce its foreign debt by $5 billion and cut its interest costs by about $500 million a year. The Argentine public felt they were a winner too, because they hoped to get better phone service.

Debt-for-Nature Swaps

One approach to debt forgiveness is to ask for good behavior in return. Thus the industrial countries have sought to structure debt-for-balanced-development, debt-for-education, and other forms of "debt-for" swaps. Among the most prominent is debt-for-nature swaps.

How is bad debt swapped for the good earth? The industrial world is reluctant to forgive debt, even if the debt is widely acknowledged to be unrepayable. At the same time, the world's population as a whole has a strong interest in halting the destruction of irreplaceable rain forests and other natural habitats which, among other things, serve as a sink for greenhouse gases. Many developing countries argue that they simply cannot afford to indulge the rich countries' conservationist ethic at the expense of local poverty. One way to reconcile these problems is the debt-for-nature swap, channeling some LDC debt into conservation. After all, the tropics account for only 6 percent of the earth's land mass but 60 percent of its species.

The mechanism of debt-for-nature swaps is simple: conservation groups, usually using private funds, buy foreign debt owed to banks at a fraction of its face value. The conservation groups then offer to forgive all or part of the debt in exchange for a pledge by the debtor nation to use the windfall gain for environmental purposes.

In the first such swap, in 1987, Conservation International paid $100,000 to Citicorp for an uncollectible $650,000 owed to the bank by Bolivia. Conservation International then agreed to forgive the entire debt in return for Bolivia's promise to protect four million acres of tropical forests. Since then, swaps involving more than $100 million have been carried out with a half-dozen countries. In 1991, Brazil gave the idea a boost when it agreed to devote $100 million each year to saving the Amazon rain forest if banks would discount its debt. The United States and Western European governments are also seeking ways to convert official-aid debt into programs for the conservation of threatened nature.

Table 11.3 gives some examples of debt-for-nature swaps. The technique has received favorable attention. The bank sells some troubled debt. The conservationists get value for the debt in excess of its market price, albeit often in local currency—typically twice as

---

[7]Now part of Chemical Bank.

Table 11.3   *Examples of Debt-for-Nature Swaps*

	Face value of canceled debt (% face value)	Institution	Purpose
Bolivia *1987*	$0.7m (15%)	Conservation International	Set aside 3.7 m acres around Beni biosphere in Amazon Basin
Dominican Republic *1990*	$0.6m (n.a.)	Conservation Trust of Puerto Rico	Protection of hardwood forests, riverbeds and endangered habitats
Madagascar *1990*	$5.0 million (n.a.)	Conservation International	Starting in 1991, $1m a year for 5 years of commercial and trade debt to be converted to finance forest protection and environmental education
Costa Rica *1991*	$0.6 (60%)	Rainforest Alliance	Debt of Central American Bank for Economic Integration bought to protect and acquire forest land in Costa Rica
Mexico *1991*	$4.0m (65%)	Conservation International	Effort to save endangered plants and wildlife, almost half in Selva Lacandona
Ecuador *1989*	$9.0m (12%)	Worldwide Fund for Nature	Protection of rain forest. Funds converted into bonds, which even out stream of local currency payments

Source: World Bank.

much. The country concerned reduces its debt burden and some progress is made toward conservation.

Naturally, as with other forms of debt conversion, there are drawbacks. One is the inflationary consequence of creating the currency for the swap. This can be neutralized, by selling government bonds or by taxation, but not all governments are willing or able to do this. Moreover they are never likely to have much impact on the overall stock of debt. Compare the numbers in Table 11.3 with the following: at the time the table was done, $1,200 billion was owed by the developing world, of which more than $400 billion was owed by the problem debtors of Latin America.

Trading LDC Debt

Chapter 9 dealt with trading in commercial and industrial loans, in which diversification, liquidity, and genuinely differing perceptions of risk and value motivate trading. Trading in LDC debt, in contrast, stemmed from regulatory pressures that in effect forced a large portion of the loans owned by U.S. and other commercial banks to be sold or exchanged. Demand for the debt came from other less-burdened banks, nonbank financial institutions, and opportunistic investors. Trades were often at severely depressed prices. At times this meant that supply and price bore less relation to their "true" value than to regulation-induced supply conditions.

When the market started in the early 1980s, the bulk of secondary-market transactions were *debt exchanges* aimed at rearranging bank portfolios to reduce risk or produce tax benefits. Today transactions include

- *cash sales*—the payment of hard currency by a bank or other investor of debt
- *loan-to-loan swaps*—trades of one loan for another between banks
- *debt buybacks*—debtor countries retire debt at a discount by paying cash to creditors or traders
- *debt conversions*—debt-for-equity swaps or so-called "debt-peso" conversions, in which foreign currency debt is exchanged for obligations in the local currency for some other purpose
- *debt exchanges*—the transformation of bank loans into other types of external debt obligations, usually bonds.

You may notice that some of these are directly related to the menu of choices under the various Brady-plan schemes discussed earlier. Before these existed, pricing in the interbank secondary market had been strongly influenced by the extent to which banks had written down the debt on their books. Indeed, any news about how banks reserve for the loans could influence price more than events in the debtor country. Nobody wanted to sell the loans at an accounting loss, but banks that made severe provisions for loss were sometimes willing to sell them at an economic loss if they could be sold above their book value. Recognizing the potential for sales by well-provisioned banks, market makers tried to pitch their bid prices just below the level of provisions of potential seller banks. The trouble was that book value could be strongly influenced by recent trading and quoted prices. Book-value write-downs could in turn reduce the market makers' prices in a downward cycle that at times totally divorced traded prices from economic fundamentals.

The creation of schemes to exchange debt into new securities more desirable to investors has introduced an underpinning of intrinsic value to the LDC debt market, and, as Figure 11.2 suggests, the improvement in economic policies for the 1990s adopted by many countries has bolstered prices in the market.

Some countries have chosen to repurchase the debt themselves whenever they could scrape together enough money to do so. In 1988, for example, Bolivia bought back 40 percent of its commercial-bank debt at an average discount of 89 percent. Prior to the Brady plan, this offered one of the few ways out of the debt vortex. Of course, using available funds to repurchase debt at far less than face value violates both the spirit and in most cases the letter of the original loan agreement. Most banks, however, recognized the improbability of getting paid back at face value and turned a blind eye.[8] They were happy that at least *someone* was willing to buy the paper so that they could get it off their balance sheets!

Some of the debt is being securitized into fixed- or floating-rate Eurobonds with official international credit enhancement; other portions have been packaged into mutual funds. Another source of end-user demand has been provided by Latin American companies restructuring their own finances or taking over enterprises from the debt-burdened public sector. Restructuring companies can win advantageous terms by converting foreign-currency government debt, purchased in the market at a discount, into local currency.

---

[8]One debt trader described such semilegal buy-back transactions as working in the following manner: the Republic of Andino accumulates some foreign-exchange reserves that have not yet made their way into the official reserve accounting. The funds are placed in a single-purpose offshore company, AnPam, that the government of Panama has set up in, say, Panama. AnPam negotiates with a debt trade to purchase $100 million of bank debt at 23 cents on the dollar. In exchange for $23 million deposited in a U.S. bank, AnPam receives a subparticipation in Andino's bank debt. All debt service paid by Andino on this portion of the debt is paid to a U.S. bank as lender of record, which passes it on to AnPam as subparticipant, which gives it back to the government of Andino. Thus the debt is not actually extinguished but rather *defeased.*

Figure 11.2   ***The Secondary Market for LDC Debt.***   Prices have in the past been influenced as much by regulators' rules on how much banks must reserve against losses as by fundamentals.

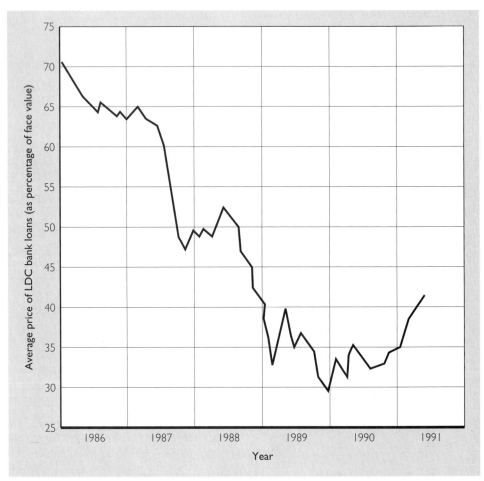

Source: NMB Bank.

Today much of the debt traded in the secondary market is bought either for speculative purposes (by both individual and institutional investors) or to give to the debtor government in exchange for equity or other forms of participation in the local economy. By providing a means by which investors can accumulate debt, this market facilitates its conversion into claims more favorable to the country. (See the earlier discussion on debt-for-equity swaps.)

Some have argued that this is a market in name only. So-called market makers do quote indicative prices, but the amounts they are willing to buy for their own account is limited. Although the market has a nominal annual turnover of several hundred billion dollars, depending on conditions, the average deal size is said to have a **face value** of only $5 million, and trades of this size can move prices unduly. But groups of traders are increasingly seen as desirable adjuncts to the trading floors of major investment and commercial banks; brokers such as Tullett & Tokyo have entered the market; and prices are now quoted on traders' screens. Over-the-counter options are traded by some houses and there is discussion of exchange-traded derivative contracts, too. These are all signs of a maturing market.

Prices are influenced by current supply and demand and by expectations of future performance on the loans. The creditor banks' governments have moved prices by altering the regulations and tax structure faced by banks, and by influencing the policies of international financial institutions. We have mentioned the banks' own write-downs as an influence on prices: for example, following the $3 billion Citicorp provisioning, loan prices dropped because of the perception that the augmented loan-loss provisions signaled a hardening of banks' negotiating stance and would reduce new lending to LDCs. The greatest influence on prices is action by the debtor countries themselves, such as decisions to interrupt debt-service payments. An illustration of these influences is provided by Figure 11.3, which tracks the decline in the value of Brazil's bank debt.

Trading spreads are sometimes very wide, but on the more active debt they are typically about ¼ point or so. Because fluctuations in price often far exceed this, and because liquidity is so poor, the dozen or so market makers listed in Table 11.4 must position themselves, looking to buy and hold undervalued debt, to make a profit commensurate with the risk. The various schemes for transforming debt described in previous sections have greatly widened the range of end-user participants in the market, boosting liquidity.

Figure 11.3   *Secondary-Market Prices of Brazilian Debt, 1986–1990*

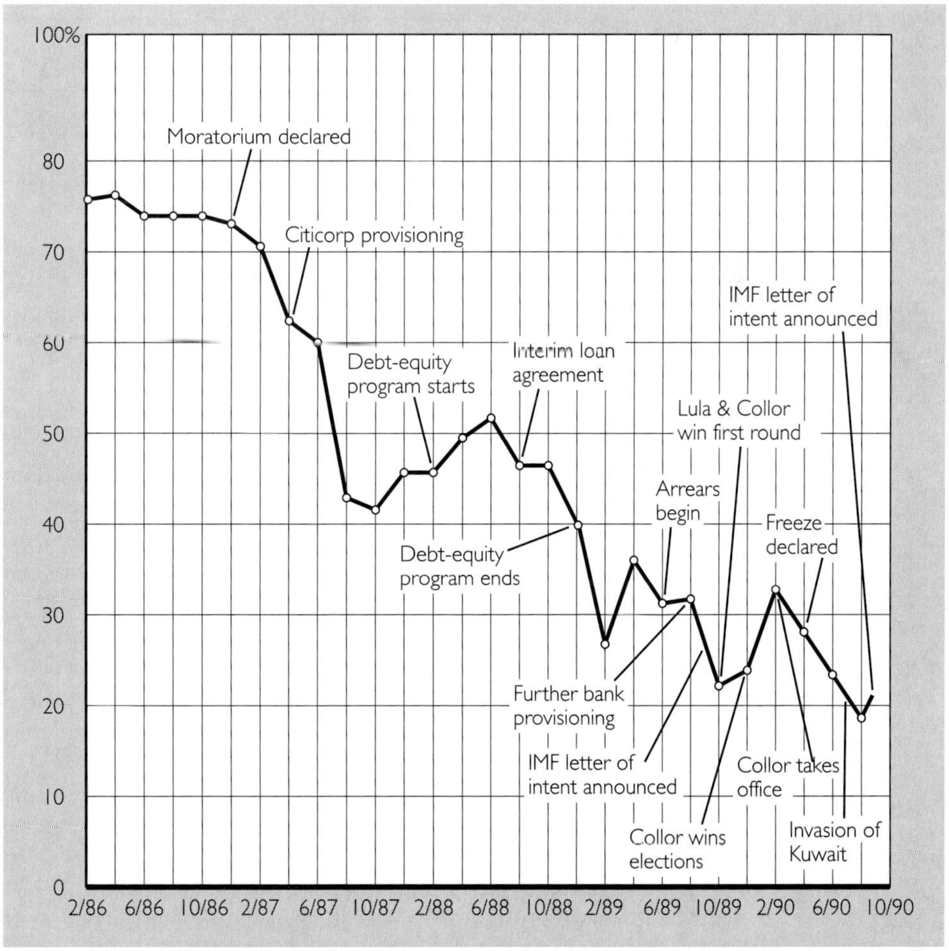

Source: LatinFinance, November 1990.

Table 11.4   *Turnover in the LDC Debt Market and Leading Traders, Ranked by Volume*

Trading House	Rank	Turnover ($ billion)	Number of Traders
JP Morgan	1	16.0	25
Man. Hanover[a]	2	14.5	20
Chase Manhattan	3	14.3	12
NMB	4	12.5	15
Citibank	5	10.5	11
Bankers Trust	6	10.1	16
Chartered WestLB	7	9.4	5
First Chicago	8	9.0	8
Midland Montagu	9	8.8	11
Salomon Bros	10	8.5	12
Banco Santander	11	7.5	6
Chemical Bank[a]	12	7.0	7
Morgan Grenfell[b]	12 =	7.0	6

[a]Manufacturers Hanover, now merged with Chemical Bank.
[b]Took over team from Libra bank in 1990; figures are for last six months of 1990 only.

Source: *Risk Magazine,* as quoted in *Financial Times,* April 5, 1991. Data for 1990.

A Simple Framework: The Right Policies and the Right Financing

In this concluding section of our analysis of the LDC debt problem we will pull together some inferences drawn from the previous discussion to identify the key elements of country financing that works. The basic idea, after all, is to find the right amount and combination of financing to fund productive investment. Let us look at two aspects in turn: (1) the right financing, and (2) the path to making the money sufficiently productive that it can more than pay its own way.

We have learned that the debt problem arose because of the way in which the financing was structured. Briefly, there was too much debt, and it was the wrong kind of debt. Starting with the latter concept, remember that debt is distinguished by the fact that it is contractual. The debtor has to pay a certain interest rate and principal in a specific currency on specified dates. Yet there is no particular reason for the interest rate to be floating or the currency to be dollars or the principal to be payable in a "balloon" amount all on one date. The financing of an investment can and should be tied to the nature of the revenues. If the revenues are stable, then the payments of interest and principal should be stable, too. If the revenues are in some fashion correlated with money-market interest rates, then the loan rate should be floating.

If, as is more likely, the revenues vary with commodity prices or some other identifiable variable, then the debt servicing—interest and principal—should ideally be tied to that variable, too. For example, much of Indonesia's export income is related to prices in the world oil and lumber markets. Its debt could be indexed to benchmark prices of these commodities, just like the oil-linked bonds issued by Mexico or the silver-linked bonds issued by some silver-mining companies. This technique has not been used in the past because the banks making the loans had no way of hedging themselves against these variables; but with the proliferation of futures and swap contracts enabling one to hedge everything from cobalt to carbon-dioxide pollution, this excuse sounds weaker and weaker. A different question is whether the country itself will accept and honor such contracts. In the past, countries were unwilling to index their debt because of a reluctance to share the gains from commodity price increases. But now that banks have discovered that they were expected to share in the losses, they might be much more willing to participate in new financing if they are offered the upside as well as the downside. In other words, no more free call options.

It is still easier for banks to denominate loans in the currency or combination of currencies that best matches the country's export-generated revenue stream. Even if the lender has difficulty funding in a particular currency, forward-exchange contracts can be used to hedge the exchange rate between the currency of lending and the currency of funding. And the interest rate can be fixed, capped, or collared in a variety of ways by means of swap contracts, as described in Chapter 13.

The objective of each of these approaches to flexibility in financing is to share the risk, to increase the probability that the country will be able to continue to service debt despite shocks such as commodity, interest-rate, and exchange-rate changes. In a sense, these hybrids are quasi-equity in character. But equity itself has one big difference: control. Should country financing be done with less debt and more equity? The answer is yes, but the price of doing so is that those who put their capital at risk will want a say over how the capital is employed. Not all countries have proven ready to permit such a transfer of control, especially to foreign investors.

The advantage of equity investment, however, is that it may help solve the other side of the debt equation: increasing the country's capacity to carry debt by improving productivity. Private investors make mistakes; but when your own money is at risk, you tend not to make investments without reasonable prospects of being able to pay all the factors of production, including local labor, as much as or more than their opportunity cost. So equity investors will tend to seek out and manage investments in such a way as to improve the rate of return in the country. To pay a return on foreign investment, moreover, foreign investors must be able to generate (or pay for) sufficient foreign exchange to pay their own way (unless the government offers them foreign exchange at a subsidized exchange rate). In other words, substituting equity investments for debt will tend to raise the country's productivity and growth rate *and* its capacity to service foreign financing. But for this improvement to flourish, property rights must be established to allow profitable and interference-free investment, and a liberal international trading system must be put in place.

Returns on investment and growth rates will tend to be higher in countries whose economic policies provide fertile ground for private investment by being noninterventionist in areas such as international trade and price setting but which provide sufficient investment in human capital and macroeconomic stability.

Figure 11.4 shows some of the conclusions of this chapter in diagram form.[9] Developments in the international debt market, including loan trading (that sets market-determined price signals to lenders and borrowers alike) and more flexible financing techniques (especially equity), produce more appropriate financing, while the right setting for

---

[9]This diagram is adapted from one that appears in Jack Guttentag and Richard Herring, "Financial Innovations to Stabilize Credit Flows to Developing Countries," *Studies in Banking and Finance*, vol. 3 (1986), 263–304.

private-sector productivity raises the overall output and hence the debt capacity of the country as a whole. Both developments benefit both debtor and creditor, whereas debt rescheduling or forgiveness provides relief for the symptoms without necessarily solving the root of the problem.

Figure 11.4   *Solutions to the Debt Crisis.*   Remedies range from short-term, dead-end solutions like rescheduling and forgiveness to permanent, risk-reducing solutions like equity investments and risk-sharing claims.

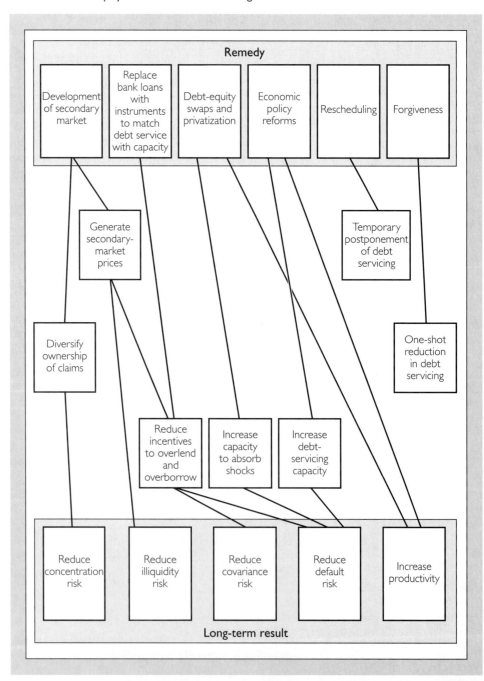

SUMMARY

Countries cannot go bankrupt, but they can default. Unlike the default of a corporate borrower, the lenders cannot call for the liquidation of the delinquent creditor's assets in order to recover some percentage of the money owed. When the LDC debt problem reached crisis proportions in the early 1980s, banks found their home governments unwilling to bail them out and spent years working with the borrowers to reschedule and restructure debt in order to minimize the damage.

But it turned out that the banks had made fundamentally incorrect assumptions both about the inherent risk of overborrowing and about the actions that the industrial countries might take to avert an international banking crisis. The crisis did not cause the banking system to collapse, but it severely weakened some of the world's biggest commercial banks, which were forced to make substantial write-downs of the value of their loans to the developing world. Rescheduling was eventually seen as an exercise in mutual self-deception, so that by the beginning of the 1990s a quite different approach to the LDC debt burden was adopted: market-oriented economic reform coupled with debt reduction. The latter was accomplished by means of a menu of options for commercial banks to sell or convert their claims into something acceptable to themselves, to other investors, or to those who required local currency for direct investment or other purposes. One such purpose was the preservation of the natural environment.

At the conclusion of this chapter, we sought to draw some lessons from the debt crisis. Developments in the international debt market, including loan trading and more-flexible financing techniques, we argued, can yield more appropriate financing, while the right setting for private-sector productivity raises the overall output and hence debt capacity of the country as a whole. Borrowers have learned the merits of sufficient equity to support debt when the business you're in is subject to downturns, and lenders have brought some of the creativity of the international capital market to the country lending business. Creativity in matching borrower with lender manifests itself nowhere more than in the international bond and swap markets, which form the subjects of the next two chapters.

CONCEPTUAL QUESTIONS

1. Identify (a) external economic circumstances, (b) factors in the borrowing countries and (c) factors in the lending countries that contributed to the global debt problem.
2. Define *rescheduling* of country debt. What purpose does it serve? What are its limitations?
3. Contrast the key elements of the Baker plan and the Brady plan.
4. What are the merits of the menu approach to LDC debt reduction?
6. In what way do you conclude that the following factors influence the economic growth of a developing country?

   (a) markets freed from excessive intervention
   (b) investment in human resources

7. Explain a debt-for-equity swap, showing how it can benefit

   (a) the seller of the debt
   (b) the buyer of the equity
   (c) the creditor country

8. What are the possible shortcomings of debt-for-nature swaps?
9. What are possible sources of demand for LDC debt in the secondary market? How would you think this differs from primary-market demand?

10. In what ways would you think that prices in the secondary market are important as signals for each of the following?

    (a) for lender banks

    (b) for borrower countries

11. Examine the table below, which shows indicative secondary-market prices for the bank debt of selected countries. Then answer the following questions:

    (a) If you were an *investor,* suggest a way or ways in which you could have profited had you known, in February 1986, what was going to happen to the prices of these countries' debt.

    (b) If you were a *trader* of country debt in 1986, how do you think your business would have changed between 1986 and 1990?

Secondary-Market Prices of Country Debt

| | Bid-Offer Prices, Percentage of Face Value | | |
	Feb. 1986	Feb. 1987	April 1990
Argentina	62–67	62–65	21.25–21.75
Brazil	74–78	73–75	26.63–27.13
Mexico	65–69	56–58	55.75–56.13
Peru	23–28	16–19	5.50–6.50
Venezuela	78–81	72–74	59.50–60.00

Source: LDC Debt News, *American Banker,* December 19, 1990.

12. Under what circumstances would you think fixed-rate debt would be more suitable for a country than debt the interest on which is indexed to a global commodity price?

Problems

1. Examine Table 11.1, showing the debt of the developing countries. Explain, with numbers, why the entries for net transfers turned negative.

2. Secure a copy of the World Bank's publication *World Debt Tables.* Select a country in Latin America and figure out the country's *stock* of outstanding debt. Also figure out the *net flow* and *net transfers* of funds to the country. Be sure to attach copies of any tables you use to your answer.

3. In 1986, Bolivia repurchased nearly 50 percent face value of its debt in the secondary market. The details were as follows: Prior to the buyback, the face value of Bolivia's debt to banks was $670 million. This was trading at an average price of 6 cents to the dollar on the market. In late 1986, $34 million was donated by an anonymous group of countries to repurchase 46 percent of outstanding debt. When news of this action got out, the traded price of Bolivian debt rose to 11 cents on the dollar. What was the decrease in the value of creditors' claims following the repurchase, assuming the repurchase cost Bolivia 11 percent of face value? Who gained from the transaction?[10]

4. You are the investment manager for Bank Negara 1946 in Jakarta. You have the opportunity to purchase some Philippine U.S.-dollar-denominated bank loans at a discount of 56% from face value. The loans pay LIBOR plus .75% semiannually and would, on the settlement date, have exactly 6 years of remaining life. LIBOR is currently 8.23 percent. You are skeptical about the prospects of the Philippines paying back on time, but the price looks pretty good. Your task is to convince senior management of this assessment, and to do that you intend to calculate the effective spread over LIBOR that would result from buying the paper at a discount. What is the effective spread, using the *discount-margin approach* described in the previous chapter? Be sure to note any assumptions you have to make.

5. How would your answer to the previous question change if your analysts told you that the probability of the Philippines paying back the loan's principal was only 60%?

---

[10]This problem was contributed by Richard Herring.

Application 11.1 | YOUR FRIEND SHINJI

Your old school friend Shinji Horiuchi is an analyst in the Restructuring Department of Sumitomo Bank. He has been asked to assess the alternatives open to the bank with respect to its outstanding $85 million (face value) of loans to Uruguay. The country has continued to pay the interest on its bank debt but not on the debt owed to other governments. However, a series of reschedulings have deferred principal repayments indefinitely and, under pressure from the Bank of Japan, Sumitomo has felt obliged to write off 30% of its exposure to Uruguay. This has reduced the book value of the bank's Uruguay paper to $59.5 million. The debt, which pays an average rate of LIBOR plus 1.25 percent semiannually, is trading in the secondary market at 63 cents on the dollar, largely because some European banks, having even more severe write-downs, have been eager to extricate themselves from Latin America.

Uruguay has recently agreed to an IMF plan by which it would seek to reduce its debt by exchanging bank debt for other claims with a much lower aggregate face value. The country has offered its creditor banks the following alternatives.

- Exchange existing debt at a discount of 35 percent for new debt paying LIBOR plus 1.75 percent.
- Have the principal of existing loans guaranteed by U.S. Treasury bonds maturing in twelve years, in return for providing new loans equal to 25 percent of existing claims.
- Exchange existing debt at a discount of 40 percent for new tradable ten-year bonds whose interest rate of 4 percent is guaranteed by the Uruguayan government and whose principal is guaranteed by the Bank of Japan. Japanese government bonds, denominated in yen, currently yield 7 percent.

Can you help Shinji make his choice?

SELECTED REFERENCES

Corden, William, and Michael Dooley. "Issues in Debt Strategy: An Overview." In J. A. Frenkel, M. P. Dooley and P. Wickham eds. *Analytical Issues in Debt*. International Monetary Fund, 1989, 10–37.

Dooley, Michael P., and Maxwell Watson. "Reinvigorating the Debt Strategy." *Finance and Development,* Sept. 1989.

Fischer, Stanley, and Ishrat Husain. "Managing the Debt Crisis in the 1990s." *The International Finance Reader* (Miami: Kolb Publishing Company, 1991).

Gojdeczka, P., and M. Stone. "The Secondary Market for Developing Country Loans." *Finance and Development* (Dec. 1990): 22–25.

Guttentag, Jack, and Richard Herring. "Accounting for Losses on Sovereign Debt: Implications for New Lending." *Essays in International Finance,* 172. Princeton, N.J.: Princeton University Press, May 1989.

———. "Disaster Myopia and International Banking." *Essays in International Banking,* no. 164. Princeton, N.J.: Princeton University Press, Sept. 1986.

———. "Commercial Bank Lending to Developing Countries: From Overlending to Underlending to Structural Reform," in G. Smith and J. Cuddington, eds. *International Borrowing and Lending: What Have We Learned from Theory and Practice?* World Bank, 1985, 129–150.

James, C. "Heterogeneous Creditors and the Market Value of Bank LDC Loan Portfolios." *Journal of Monetary Economics* (June 1990): 321–346.

12
The International Bond Market

The previous three chapters have centered on different aspects of the international markets for bank credit. We now turn to the organized financial markets for long-term debt (this chapter) and equity (Chapter 13). We will begin this chapter by putting the three major segments of the international bond market into perspective. We will offer some reasons for supposing that the external bond markets, although increasingly integrated with domestic markets, will continue to thrive. The chapter compares Eurobonds and foreign bonds from the perspective of a corporation or government agency as potential issuer, and describes the new-issue process in the Eurobond market. Then, from the viewpoint of international investors, we will look at the nature of the Eurobond secondary market. The chapter concludes with a brief discussion of some special kinds of Eurobonds: equity-linked and asset-backed issues.

The international bond market consists of the Eurobond market, the foreign-bond markets, and those domestic-bond markets (such as the U.S., Japanese, and French markets) in which global bond investors participate actively. The most "international" of these markets is the Eurobond market, which from small beginnings in the control-riddled world of the mid-1960s has grown to the point where (by the early 1990s) it raises over $200 billion per annum in new capital for corporations, financial institutions, and governments.

Domestic Bonds, Eurobonds, and Foreign Bonds

Domestic bonds are usually fixed-interest, fixed-maturity claims with maturities ranging from 1 to 30 years. They are issued by domestic entities, in the domestic currency, and sold largely to domestic residents. They can be public issues, generally subject to registration and disclosure requirements, or private placements. In either case, they are subject to domestic issuance regulations and taxes. They are typically unsecured, general obligations of the issuer, although asset-backed and subordinated corporate bonds are common in some countries, too. They may or may not have a call feature, allowing the issuer to redeem the bond at some price prior to final maturity. In the United States, Canada, and Japan, bonds pay coupons semiannually; in most other countries, annually. They are accompanied by documentation in the form of a prospectus or book containing information about the issuer and stating the rights and obligations of the issuer. They are characterized by an "arm's length" relationship between the investor and the issuer, with little of the flexibility to renegotiate terms in the light of changing conditions, in contrast to the ongoing relationship between borrower and lender in traditional bank lending. The bondholder's chief recourse, in the event of a default or dispute, is to the courts.

In many ways Eurobonds are no different. Anyone acquainted with the domestic markets for corporate bonds in the United States or the United Kingdom will find much about the Eurobond market familiar. Like domestic corporate bonds, the bulk of the market consists of medium-term, fixed-rate, coupon-paying bonds issued by reasonably well-known and creditworthy corporate and sovereign borrowers. The publicly issued bonds are traded in secondary markets of varying liquidity. What differentiates the Eurobond market is that *the bonds are issued and sold in a jurisdiction outside the country of the currency of denomination.* Thus the market is freer of certain constraints than the domestic market is, constraints such as registration requirements and withholding taxes.

Foreign bonds, unlike Eurobonds, are issued *within* the domestic market of the currency of denomination, but they are issued by nonresident borrowers. A bond issued within the United Kingdom by a nonresident issuer such as the Asian Development Bank, for instance, is a foreign bond.

The *international bond market* is a loose term encompassing both the market for Eurobonds and for foreign bonds, and perhaps also the global market for certain domestic bonds such as the benchmark U.S. Treasury bonds and their equivalents in other major countries. The Eurobond market, though, is the core of the international bond market.

The Importance and Diversity of the Market

The Eurobond market has expanded to the point where it is one of the world's biggest and freest sources of long-term public funds. Figure 12.1 shows that, as of the beginning of the 1990s, the market was capable of raising over $200 billion in new funds per annum. Its new-issue volume today far exceeds that of corporate bonds issued in traditional national markets, and in terms of trading turnover, only the bond markets of major countries yield a higher volume. The increase in the volume of bonds has been in part stimulated

Figure 12.1   *Volume of New Issues in the Eurobond Markets, 1985–1990*

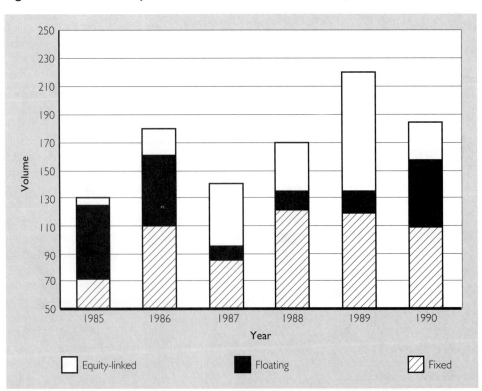

Figure 12.2 *Currency Breakdown of New Issues in the International Bond Market.* The chart shows the dominance of the dollar but growing importance of the ECU.

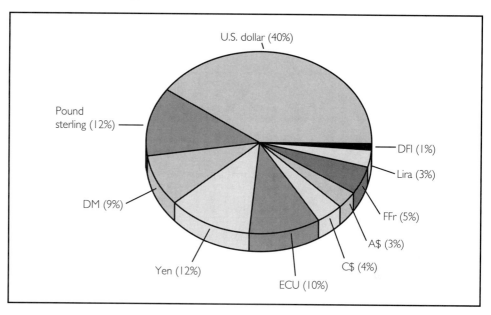

Source: Based on percent of Eurobond new issue volume in 1990.

and paralleled by the growth in secondary-market trading.[1] Although the majority of Eurobonds are fixed-rate "straight" issues, about a quarter of the issues are floating-rate notes and anywhere from 10 percent to 25 percent are equity linked.

Figure 12.2 indicates the dominance of the major currencies—U.S. dollars, pounds sterling, German marks, and Japanese yen—in the denomination of Eurobond issues. Not far behind them, however, is the ECU, the European Currency Unit.

Fundamentally, the Eurobond market performs the same function as is performed by the external money market: funds are gathered internationally, denominated in a variety of currencies, and made available to borrowers from various countries largely without being influenced by national authorities.[2] These features set it apart from both domestic-bond markets and traditional foreign-bond markets.

The Structure of the International Bond Market

Figure 12.3 provides a sketch of the linkages among the principal markets constituting the international bond market, using the U.S. dollar and the Japanese yen markets as examples. For each currency, the bond markets can be divided into two parts: the markets *within* the country of the currency, namely the domestic- and foreign-bond markets, and the markets *outside* of direct jurisdiction of the country of the currency—that is, the

---

[1]For details see Gunter Dufey and Ian H. Giddy, *The Evolution of Instruments and Techniques in International Financial Markets* (Tilburg: S.U.E.R.F., 1981), 17–22.

[2]Some governments, such as Switzerland and Japan, exert informal pressure on international issuing houses and banks to refrain from using their currencies to denominate Eurobond issues without explicit permission.

Figure 12.3   ***Linkages Among International Bond Markets.***   Issuers and investors compare terms in the domestic and Eurobond markets, which are linked across currencies via currency swaps and long-dated forward contracts.

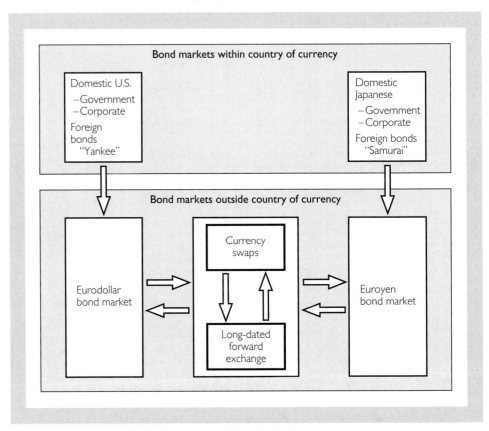

Eurobond markets. As we have seen, Eurobonds can be denominated in any one of several dozen different currencies. These different markets are linked to one another through the currency-swap market, which provides contracts for future exchange of interest and principal in two different currencies, or alternatively through the long-dated forward-exchange market.

The fact that each segment of the Eurobond market operates outside the direct jurisdiction of its "home" authorities means that the government has the means of segmenting the domestic market from its Euro counterpart—for example, through capital controls, taxes, or issuance or trading restrictions. When segmentation occurs, the cost of issuance and the yield to investors differs between the domestic and offshore markets.

Factors Segmenting Domestic and Eurobond Markets

In most countries the domestic-bond market is a prime means by which long-term savings are channeled to investment purposes, both private and governmental. Concerned with husbanding scarce long-term savings, the authorities have been loath to allow a free-for-all approach to issuance of bonds in their domestic markets. Their concern may be to prevent capital from flowing abroad, to maintain control over the allocation of resources within the domestic economy, or to avert disruptions to the domestic capital market that would occur from time to time if investors were free to make their own mistakes. All these considerations give rise to domestic constraints on bond issuance, constraints that, in some cases, have persuaded issuers and investors that the Eurobond market is a better place to meet than is the domestic market.

It was restrictions on domestic issuance by foreign borrowers in the U.S. market that first led to the development of the Eurobond technique in 1964. The previous year, the United States, concerned about the balance-of-payments effects of free outflows of long-term capital, imposed the so-called Interest Equalization Tax (IET). The IET, levied on U.S. investors in foreign bonds, lowered the effective return on such bonds to the point at which it was uneconomical for foreign issuers to borrow money in the U.S. market. This prompted the development of issuing techniques that allowed fixed-interest securities to be placed with international investors *outside* of the country of the currency, effectively circumventing restrictions in the national markets. In other words, the Eurobond was invented. While the IET was rescinded in 1974, the domestic U.S. market and the dollar sector of the Eurobond market remained segmented until, in 1984, the United States removed the *withholding tax* on foreign holders of domestic bonds.[3] (A withholding tax is imposed on the issuer, and reduces the interest paid to the investor. For example, the 30 percent U.S. withholding tax, before it was eliminated, reduced a coupon of 10 percent to an effective 7 percent.) Subsequent to 1984, yields in the domestic U.S. market and the Eurodollar bond market, as it is sometimes called, converged to near-equality. More on the effect of withholding taxes below.

Gradually, other countries have followed suit. The domestic- and offshore-bond markets of Britain, France, Canada, the Netherlands, and Australia are now open to both domestic and nonresident issuers and investors. Nevertheless, the shape of regulation and of domestic cartels in bond issuance continues to favor domestic issuers, plus a limited range of foreign issuers—international organizations such as the World Bank and prominent international corporations. Segmentation prevails, although the degree to which it does varies considerably from country to country.

Although one might suppose that the more restrictive the domestic market, the greater the incentive for issues to be done in the Euromarket, this is only partially true. The reason is that governments can, to a large extent, control their currency's segment of the Eurobond market. Thus the Euroyen market began in the early 1980s when and only when the Japanese Ministry of Finance allowed it to open, and even then, the government permitted only an orderly progression of issuers. The Swiss government *still* does not sanction the issuance of Eurobonds denominated in Swiss francs, so none are done—all Swiss-franc bonds are issued in Switzerland itself, in a fashion made orderly by the dominance of the three biggest Swiss banks. A government is able to influence the corresponding Euromarket in a number of ways. All clearing of a currency normally goes through the country of the currency, so it would be difficult to transfer Swiss francs if the Swiss National Bank did not permit a transaction to occur. This prohibiting tool is disruptive and seldom used; instead, the authorities can hold sway over a market by persuading the country's major commercial and investment banks that it would not be in their interests to participate in the issue, effectively scotching any attempt to place the bond broadly. Even if all the underwriters were from countries other than the country of the currency, the government could twist their arms by restricting their ability to do business in the country. For example, Portugal exercises very tight control over the volume and timing of escudo-denominated Eurobonds and over which issuers are permitted access to the market.

---

[3]In the United States, as elsewhere, *foreign bonds* were not subject to any withholding tax.

Sometimes a sector of the Eurobond market may be closed entirely. For several years during the late 1970s and early 1980s, for example, the Euro French-franc bond market was closed: no franc-denominated Eurobonds were issued, and none were permitted.

We have mentioned capital-outflow controls, withholding taxes, and moral suasion by governments as factors segmenting the national and Eurobond markets. Other factors include registration requirements on investors, disclosure requirements imposed on issuers, and trading and sales restrictions imposed on securities firms and their clients.

In most countries, including the United States, the owner of a bond or stock must have his or her name listed, or **registered,** in the records of the issuer. Bond registration may be a convenience: it means that ownership is evidenced by book entry, which now entails flipping a few electrons on a computer disk. This kind of registration allows for easier transfer of ownership and payment of interest and principal. In the Eurobond market, as well as in certain European countries, bonds are issued in bearer form; that means that the bearer of the physical certificates is presumed to be its legal owner. **Bearer instruments** provide ease of transfer of wealth when one has to cross national boundaries in a hurry, as many Europeans remember their families having to do at various times of conflict on the continent. Bearer bonds also allow confidentiality of ownership, which is important to some investors, especially those whose relations with the fiscal authorities are strained.

Bearer bonds are anathema to the taxman, and this is nowhere more true than in the United States. For this reason and because of the desire to protect individual investors from being sold something about which they do not have full information, the U.S. authorities have taken pains to discourage the sale of Eurobonds to U.S. individual investors. Under the Securities Act of 1933, all public issues of new securities must be registered with the **SEC (Securities and Exchange Commission)**. In principle, therefore, Eurobonds cannot be sold to U.S. citizens. However there is no law that says U.S. citizens cannot, on their own initiative, purchase Eurobonds or other unregistered securities, for that matter. Especially because Eurobonds are bearer bonds, the U.S. authorities have no direct or indirect way of knowing exactly who owns what.

The SEC has instituted two obstacles, neither insurmountable, to U.S. purchases of newly issued Eurobonds. (1) U.S. investment banks leading or participating in the initial issue of a Eurobond are constrained by the requirement that the issue "is made under circumstances reasonably designed to preclude distribution or redistribution of the securities within, or to the nationals of, the United States." (2) After issue, the securities firms are required to comply with a *seasoning requirement:* sales of Eurobonds to U.S. citizens can take place only after 90 days from the issue date, after they have been "seasoned" in the secondary market.

To avoid running afoul of the SEC requirements, the underwriting houses for Eurobonds have adopted three standard practices:

1. All dollar-denominated Eurobonds, as well as many others, carry the following bold-type warning: "These securities have not been registered under the United States Securities Act of 1933 and may not be offered, sold or delivered, directly or indirectly, in the United States or to U.S. persons as part of the distribution of the securities."
2. The lead managers require members of the selling group to swear they'll sell no bonds to U.S. nationals, "cross my heart and hope to die."
3. The bonds are distributed in two stages. Initially the borrower issues one great big bond, called a **global bond,** a certificate representing the whole issue. Bond purchasers have registered ownership shares in the global bond instead of the individual bearer bonds. After a 90-day waiting period, investors have the option of exchanging these ownership shares from any of the designated paying agents, for individual bearer-bond certificates

typically in denominations of $1000 or $5000. Even then, the investor is supposed to sign a statement saying that he is not a U.S. citizen nor is he acting on behalf of a U.S. citizen, and the paying agent is required to keep a file of these statements.

Private Placements and Rule 144A

The prohibition on sales to U.S. nationals is waived for so-called private placement Eurobonds. In the United States, bonds do not have to be registered if they are privately placed rather than publicly distributed. A U.S. private placement is a note purchased by one, or only a few, investors. The SEC does not feel it has to protect the interests of, say, a large insurance company that has its own team of sophisticated analysts. The private-placement exemption from registration and disclosure is extended to Eurobonds as long as the U.S. investors meet the following requirements:

- They are large and sophisticated.
- There are only a few investors.
- They have access to information and analysis similar to that which would ordinarily be contained in a registered offering prospectus.
- They are capable of sustaining the risk of losses.
- They intend to purchase the bonds for their own investment portfolios rather than for resale.

This last requirement has put a crimp on the sale and trading of Eurobonds in the United States, and many institutional investors grumble that the limitation on trading has undermined the liquidity of their bonds. As a result, the SEC introduced *Rule 144A,* which allowed the sale and subsequent trading of Eurobonds among those investors who met the private-placement criteria.

Constraints in Other Domestic-Bond Markets

Outside the United States and Great Britain, bond markets simply have not been a major source of corporate financing in the past. The Eurobond market has set an example of the way in which bonds can be quickly issued and placed in a variety of currencies, and so is encouraging the growth of domestic corporate-bond markets in countries such as Japan, Germany, and France. Even so, much reform must occur before some of these markets rival the efficiency of the U.S. and U.K. domestic-bond markets. Until that happens, the Euromarkets will provide the bulk of fixed-interest bond financing for companies in many countries. For example, Japan's domestic-bond market remains hampered by the following constraints (enforced by the Ministry of Finance in conjunction with the banks themselves):

- *A queueing system.* It takes up to three months to launch an issue. (In the Euroyen market, issues can be launched on a few days' notice.)
- *Fixed underwriting fees and a fixed (noncompetitive) pricing system.* This system fails to accommodate market movements between the time the deal is priced and the time it is launched.
- *The commission-bank system.* Every issue has a commission bank, acting both as a consultant to the issue, and as a trustee representing investors. The bank gets a fee for the obligatory service. The system gives commercial

banks control of the corporate-bond market, even though securities houses actually launch the issues. Because banks can look at every deal before it comes to market, they get to keep the best credits for themselves by lending out money directly—providing funds in the form of a loan in lieu of a bond issue.

- *Strict limits on who may issue what.* Only companies with a single-A credit rating or better can issue straight bonds in Japan. This rule, together with other limits, cuts out more than two-thirds of the companies listed on the Tokyo stock exchange.

Dismantling a set of constraints like this means a loss of power or profitability for those public officials and private financial institutions who would be charged with designing reforms. This does not happen easily.

Regulation and Taxation

It is a myth that the Eurobond market is "unregulated." Every issue takes place in some country, and every bond is sold to the resident of some country, a resident who is subject to the laws and taxes of that jurisdiction. True, the issuance procedure of Eurobonds generally operates outside the jurisdiction of the national governments in whose currencies the bonds are denominated. However, the domestic authorities (typically the central bank) of many countries have often exercised significant influence on the new-issue market. The home authorities have, usually in cooperation with the dominant local banks, established guidelines concerning issuing calendars, underwriting syndicates, types of issues, and so on. The U.S. Federal Reserve System and securities authorities do not have any such guidelines concerning U.S.-dollar issues.

In contrast to the primary markets, the secondary markets are completely free from government regulation. However, both the primary and the secondary markets are *self-regulated,* with regulation carried out by professional trade associations that seek to ensure efficient and open markets. The secondary market is regulated by the International Securities Market Association (ISMA), and the primary market is regulated by the International Primary Markets Association (IPMA). In the event of legal problems, the governing law is stated in the issuing prospectus and is generally either English law or that of the issuer's country.

Eurobonds are debt securities issued in a way so as to escape restrictions prevailing in national bond markets. Eurobonds are quite distinct from Eurodollars, because bond markets enable final borrowers to issue securities to investors directly, whereas financial intermediation in the Eurodollar market allows investors to hold short-term claims on Eurobanks, which "transform" deposits into (often longer-term, riskier) loans to final borrowers. In the Eurobond market, no intermediaries intervene between borrower and lender (except during the underwriting and distribution process). Eurobonds represent direct claims on corporations, governments, or governmental entities, and therefore are, in most respects, very much like domestic bonds.

Traditional foreign bonds are issued in a particular country by a foreign borrower, in the currency of that country. The Eurobond market, in contrast, is "external": like the Eurodollar market, it is not tied to any particular location and thereby, to a certain extent, escapes the norms and regulations that restrict the access of foreign issuers to individual national markets.

Even countries with the most liberal regulatory philosophy limit the access of foreign borrowers who wish to raise funds by issuing securities. Such restrictions, which are easily enforced, are usually rationalized on the grounds that they

- protect the balance of payments from excessive capital outflows.
- preserve scarce capital resources for domestic borrowers.
- protect domestic investors from risky securities.

On the other hand, most countries find it difficult, for political or simply practical reasons, to prevent individual investors from taking their funds outside their country of residence in order to purchase securities abroad.

Internationally operating investment banks have exploited this discrepancy in regulation by developing issuing techniques that, in effect, circumvent restrictions on foreign issuers in national markets. These techniques usually involve some or all of the following:

- Eurobond issues are given the form of private placements rather than broadly advertised in public markets.
- Eurobonds are placed through syndicates made up of issuing houses and banks in many countries that sell the bonds, often to nonresident investors.[4]
- Eurobonds are sold principally in countries other than that of the currency in which they are denominated.
- The bond issues are structured in such a way that interest is not subject to withholding taxes.

Conceptually, Eurobonds are in fact a little difficult to pin down and are less amenable to clear-cut definition than Eurodollar deposits and loans. For example, most, but not all, Eurobonds are issued by entities domiciled outside of the country of the currency; but this is a feature shared with traditional foreign bonds, and is by no means universal. The important aspect is the combination of issue and placement techniques that free the bonds of withholding taxes and other restrictions that would reduce their attraction to internationally mobile investors. This will cause the price and yield of such a bond to follow other Eurobonds rather than domestic bonds, or traditional foreign bonds issued in a (protected) national market.

Most countries tax their domestic residents on income earned from dividends and interest through income tax. And most countries fail to see why foreigners receiving the same kind of income should be exempt from such tax. So they impose a *withholding tax* on interest paid to nonresidents. This means that the net income to the investor is reduced substantially: for example, a 20 percent withholding tax reduces a coupon of 10 percent to an effective 8 percent. Worse still, many international investors have to pay income tax to their own governments on income, including interest, earned abroad. So one is taxed twice on the same income.[5] To remedy this double taxation, many countries have concluded *tax treaties* that provide for the investor to reclaim all or part for foreign withholding taxes paid, but this is an awkward process and at best involves a delay in receipt of the tax credit. Many investors do not have the patience for it. So they prefer Eurobonds, where no tax is withheld.

Many Eurobond investors have a further incentive to steer clear of bonds subject to a withholding tax: investors are not subject to taxation, either because their country of residence does not tax foreign income until repatriated, or because they simply choose not to declare interest income, or because as institutional investors (pension funds of international institutions and corporations, offshore insurance companies, international

---

[4]Nonresident accounts are held by, say, French investors in Switzerland, Belgian and Dutch investors in Luxembourg, and African investors in the United Kingdom. These nonresident accounts are exempt from exchange and capital controls imposed by the host country on its own residents.

[5]For this reason, and because withholding taxes have never proved to be much of a revenue source (because footloose investors have the Eurobond alternative), withholding taxes are gradually being abandoned in the major industrial countries. This change is in part responsible for the boundaries between the domestic and Euro markets becoming fuzzier.

BOX 12.1

The Netherlands Antilles and Withholding Tax

On June 29, 1987, the U.S. Treasury announced a decision to terminate a tax treaty with the Netherlands Antilles, which was to become effective on January 1, 1988. Without the tax treaty, approximately $35 billion of U.S.-dollar Eurobonds were liable for withholding tax. Thus the Treasury's announcement brought the tax-call clause (see the discussion on the withholding tax in the Regulation and Taxation section) into operation, making many bonds callable. Because a large number of the bonds were trading above their call value at the time, the Treasury's actions would have resulted in large losses for many investors. The consequent uproar led the Treasury to retract its earlier statement and announce that Eurobonds would remain exempt from withholding tax.

The precise withholding tax status of U.S.-dollar Eurobonds depends upon their date of issuance:

- *Bonds Issued Before July 19, 1984:* All interest paid on U.S.-dollar bonds to foreign investors was subject to a 30 percent withholding tax. However, the U.S. tax treaty with the Netherlands Antilles resulted in bonds that were issued through subsidiaries in the Antilles being exempt from the withholding tax.
- *Bonds Issued After July 19, 1984:* Legislation was passed (effective July 19, 1984) that exempted interest payments to overseas investors from withholding tax on the condition that the so-called TEFRA requirements were met. These requirements were designed to ensure that a record of the investors' nationality was kept. Because of the tax treaty, bonds issued through the Antilles continued to be exempt from withholding tax and did not need to meet the TEFRA requirements. However, because the TEFRA requirements were easily met, most U.S. Eurobonds issued after July 19 were issued outside of the United States.

The Netherlands Antilles affair was concerned exclusively with those bonds issued before July 19, 1984, and with the handful of bonds issued after that date through the Antilles without the TEFRA requirements being met.

mutual funds, central banks) they have tax-free status in their respective jurisdiction. Tax-exempt investors have no way of recovering the tax withheld, so they are outright losers of this money. For them, therefore, it is essential to invest in bonds that are free of withholding tax. Thus, *Eurobonds must be issued free of withholding tax to be competitive.* Although government issuers and their entities typically exempt themselves from their national withholding tax on interest paid to nonresidents, private corporate issuers must form a special finance subsidiary in one of the few jurisdictions that do not levy a withholding tax. The Netherlands Antilles have served as the preferred jurisdiction in which such captive finance companies, Naamloze Vennootschap (or NVs, for short) are incorporated.[6] Not only does the government in the capital of Curaçao refrain from imposing a withholding tax, it also maintains an extensive network of bilateral tax treaties. One of those is in force with the United States, stipulating a zero withholding-tax rate on interest paid from a U.S. source to an NV—provided certain conditions are met. The treaty permits corporations to use the funds raised via a Eurobond issue in the United States, without being subject to the withholding tax when interest is paid to the NV. Today,

---

[6]Other locations include Luxembourg and suitable U.S. states, primarily Delaware, that register so-called 80/20 corporations, a designation derived from an Internal Revenue Service rule that if more than 80 percent of such a corporation's income comes from abroad, no U.S. withholding tax is due.

most U.S. corporations have no need to use the Netherlands Antilles, because they can set up financing companies that are the equivalent of NVs within the United States. As experienced investors know, however, tax rules and treaties can change, as the event described in the accompanying Box 12.1 on the Netherlands Antilles illustrates.

New-Issue Procedures

Companies might need medium- and long-term funds for internal growth, for new investments, or for an acquisition. Banks need longer-term money to fund their loan portfolios or to boost their capital, as defined by the regulatory authorities. Governments and international organizations seem to need financing, too. For many of the world's big borrowers, the obvious place to issue a bond is the Eurobond market, because the domestic market in most countries is too narrow to support much bond issuance. For a select few companies, governments, and international organizations, the Eurobond market is chosen if and when it proves the cheapest place to raise funds. Because of the diversity of investors in the market and the variety of forms in which the bonds appear, the market is by no means perfect and issuers often choose to use the market simply because their investment bankers have identified an anomaly that allows the issuer to obtain unusually low-cost funds, often as a result of combining the bond with a swap.

Whatever the reason, the process of issuing a Eurobond begins with a discussion between the borrower and its bankers. (See Figure 12.4 for a diagram of the key dates in the issuance of a Eurobond.) The issuer specifies the desired currency of denomination, the amount, and a target rate, meaning an interest rate at which the issuer would be willing to borrow. If the bank obtains a mandate to arrange the issue, this bank becomes the **lead manager** of the Eurobond.[7] On instruction of the issuer, or if the deal is large or complex, the lead manager may invite several other banks to be **comanagers**. Together they form the management group, who negotiate the interest rate and other terms of the deal in such a way as to be acceptable to the target-investor population. (For a description of the other roles of the lead manager, see Box 12.2.) If a currency or interest-rate swap is an integral part of the financing, the swap counterparty will be lined up. The lead managers and their lawyers also prepare the documentation and obtain necessary clearances, legal and informal. The bond will normally be listed in Luxembourg or in a similar location where **listing** is cheap and there is no prospect of present or future withholding tax. The listing is a formality, designed to satisfy those institutional investors who are permitted to invest only in listed securities. Few of the bonds will ever be actually traded on the Luxembourg exchange.

A key role of the management group is to form an *underwriting group* of 25, 50, or up to several hundred banks, investment banks, and securities houses from different countries. The managers will share the task of sending out an *invitation telex* to many banks, inviting their participation in the deal. The underwriters, which include the management group, are selected on the basis of their ability to place the bonds in different submarkets of the Eurobond investor universe. They demonstrate their confidence in their own ability by committing themselves to purchasing a share of the bond issue at a set price from the issuer. When a bank underwrites a bond at issue, it is in effect giving the issuer a *put option*. It is committing to purchase a given amount of the bonds at a certain price on an agreed date. After the commitment is made, if the bond's price falls, or if the underwriter is unable to place the paper, the bank loses.

A third level of participation in the issue is the **selling group** of banks and dealers who actually sell the bonds to end investors. The selling group consists of the managers,

---

[7]There can be more than one lead manager.

Figure 12.4   ***Key Dates in the Issuance of a Eurobond.***   After the issue's terms have been announced but before the formal offering, Eurobonds trade in an informal "gray market" at prices that often deviate from the official offering price.

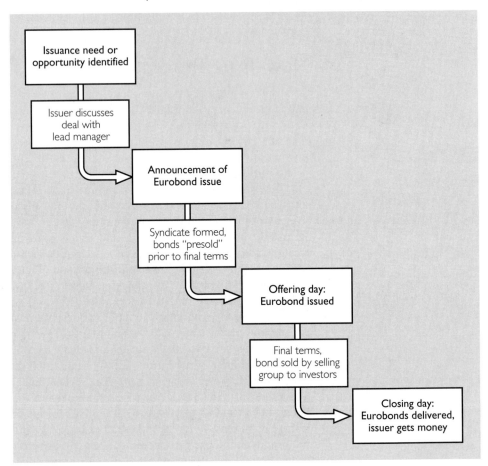

the underwriters, and other banks or dealers who will try to sell the bonds but are not committed to purchasing them if they cannot be sold to the public. Figure 12.5 shows a diagram of the organization of a Eurobond syndicate.

The difference between the management group and the selling group corresponds to the difference between commitment and allotment. Managers actually pay the issuer, and each manager is responsible for the amount of its *commitment,* as stated in the invitation telex. Members of the selling group, on the other hand, receive an *allotment* of bonds to sell. A manager's commitment is a proportional responsibility: if one of the selling group fails to come up with its allotted amount on the closing date, all managers are responsible for paying that amount to the issuer on a pro-rata basis.

In sum, the typical Eurobond issuance syndicate consists of three overlapping parts (Figure 12.5): the managers, the underwriters, and the selling group. Although this is a typical arrangement, it is not uncommon for a small group of banks with strong placement power to keep the whole deal for themselves, acting as managers, underwriters, and sellers all by themselves.

At this point the bond can be announced along with its features and tentative terms. By this time, a preliminary version of the *prospectus,* called a "red herring," will have been prepared. Members of the selling group will now actively canvass the investing public for

BOX 12.2

Roles of the Lead Manager in the Issuance of a Eurobond

The lead manager plays a key role in the success of a Eurobond before, during, and after issuance.

Before issuance, the lead manager's role is

- to understand the borrower's requirements and supply the borrower with timely information about the market's receptivity to certain currencies, amounts, and swap-market conditions.
- to identify the cheapest financing method for the issuer, using hybrid bonds or swaps. The lead manager may serve as swap counterparty as well as lead manager; or the lead manager may invite a bank that has given a good swap quotation to serve as swap counterparty and give that bank a co–lead manager position. In the latter case, the co-lead manager's compensation will act in part as compensation for the swap.
- to advise on timing and to hit any market window.

During issuance, the lead manager's role is

- to act on behalf of other managers in performing a "due diligence" investigation of the borrower's condition, in order to protect investors.
- to establish a good reputation for the issuer. Stingy pricing may produce the cheapest cost for the particular issue but may discourage participation in future deals of the issuer as well as damage the lead manager's reputation.
- to actively stabilize the bond's price in the gray market.
- to arrange all closing formalities and payments, including payment of the net proceeds to the issuer and allocation of fees to the managers, underwriters, and selling group.

After issuance, the lead manager

- plays a role as market maker.

Author's note: Thanks to Takeo Kusunose for suggesting these points.

interest in the deal. The red herring will be perused by the salespeople who are calling their clients to solicit interest in the bond.

Although the precise terms of the bond remain provisional until the official offering date, the bonds may actually begin trading before this date in a sort of "when issued" market called the **gray market**. Certain Eurobond houses will trade the unissued bonds for forward delivery at prices that are even advertised on Reuters screens. The gray market is a short-term forward market, enabling investors to assure themselves of a certain investment at a known price, for bonds to be issued. It also allows members of an underwriting syndicate to verify their placement of the bonds to be issued, thus reducing the inherent uncertainty in a bond issue and ultimately reducing the spread paid by the issuer. Because the final issue of the bond has not yet been set, gray-market prices are expressed as a discount (or, more rarely, a premium) from the price when it is set. A gray-market dealer making a market in a World Bank bond may quote a price of *less ⅜,* which means that he is offering to sell the bonds at ⅜ percentage points below the final offering price. If the final offering price is 101, the gray-market dealer will deliver them at 100⅝. A gray market can only work for bonds whose issuer is well known and whose nonprice features are established.

After a few days or weeks of this preplacement, or gray-market, period the selling-group members will give feedback to the lead managers. After a few days of "premarketing" the bonds, they will gain sufficient confidence to return to the issuer with a

Figure 12.5   ***The Three Groups in a Eurobond Syndicate.***   In some deals a small group of banks assumes all three roles, acting as managers, underwriters, and sellers.

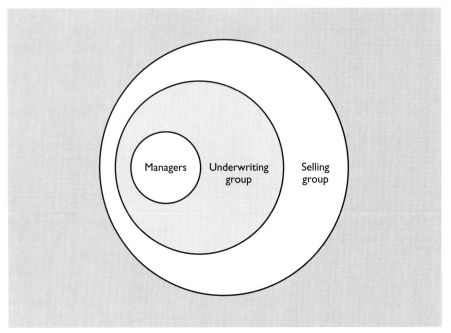

commitment to the final terms. The key feature will be the *coupon;* if necessary, the amount and even the maturity of the Eurobond will be adjusted to meet investor preferences. If the bond carries any "sweeteners" such as warrants or a convertible feature, the terms of these may be altered. When agreement is reached with the issuer, the documents are formally signed on the **offering day.** At this point, the syndicate commits itself to purchasing the entire issue at the offering price minus the fees. A final version of the prospectus is printed and distributed and the bonds are publicly offered.

Members of the issuing syndicate will try to sell the bonds at the offer price printed on the front of the prospectus (or higher, if they can). In practice, however, there is little uniformity in the price at which the bonds are sold to different investors and, in contrast to the control exercised in the United States, syndicate discipline is poor. Bonds are often placed at a price below the offer price. Selling-group members buy the securities at the issue price, minus the dealer's discount (selling commission), and may pass along the majority of that discount to other dealers or even to institutional investors. In sum, competition prevails, and the net spreads earned by many participants in Eurobond syndicates have been razor-thin.

An important responsibility of the lead manager is **stabilization**, which is achieved by intervening in the market to support the price of the new issue in order to sustain the appearance of a well-selling issue and provide some reward to the syndicate members. The lead manager is permitted to undertake stabilization in the primary market by both direct participation and by adjusting the amount allotted to various members of the selling group. Current norms permit the lead manager to use the total fee—management fees plus underwriting fees—for stabilization.[8] Although stabilization activities are totally at

---

[8]When we talk of rules and norms in the new-issue market, we mean the rules of the nongovernmental club of international underwriters, the International Primary Market Association.

the discretion of the lead manager, supporting an issue in this manner is often critical to the manager's reputation in the Eurobond community.

Two weeks after signing, on the **closing day**, the securities are delivered to the buyers in exchange for cash, and the borrower receives his funds. The game is over, except for the 19th-hole stories. These are told in the pages of the *Financial Times, International Financing Review,* and *Euromoney,* which are also the places where lead managers who wish to advertise their prowess publish the "tombstone" announcements of deals done. Figure 12.6 contains an example of such a tombstone. Notice that the bond was issued in the name of a finance subsidiary, with a guarantee from the parent.

Figure 12.6   *A "Tombstone" Announcement of a Newly Issued Eurobond.*   Such tombstones list the lead managers first and then, in lower groups, the other groups of banks that underwrite and distribute the securities.

Redland International Funding PLC

A$150,000,000

15³/₈% Guaranteed Notes due 1996

unconditionally and irrevocably guaranteed by

Redland PLC

J. P. MORGAN SECURITIES LTD.	SANWA INTERNATIONAL LIMITED
ALGEMENE BANK NEDERLAND N.V.	BANK OF TOKYO CAPITAL MARKETS GROUP
BARING BROTHERS & CO., LIMITED	BAYERISCHE VEREINSBANK AKTIENGESELLSCHAFT
HESSISCHE LANDESBANK – GIROZENTRALE	IBJ INTERNATIONAL LIMITED
SWISS BANK CORPORATION Investment Banking	UBS PHILLIPS & DREW SECURITIES LIMITED

S.G. WARBURG SECURITIES

5th November 1989   *All of these Securities have been sold. This announcement appears as a matter of record only.*

Table 12.1   *Fees and Net Price for Each $100 Bond Price*

	Fees (as a percentage)	Fees (as an amount)	Net price
Price paid by investor (in theory)			101.50
Price paid by member of selling group	60%	0.90	100.60
Price paid by member of underwriting group	60% + 20%	0.90 + 0.30	100.30
Price paid by managers (plus praecipium paid to lead manager)	60% + 20% + 20%	0.90 + 0.30 + 0.30	100.00

Fees

The typical fee structure in a Eurobond underwriting can be divided into three components: the total fees, or "spread," consist of a *management fee,* an *underwriting fee,* and a *selling concession.* The size of each component and of the total fees differs according to the service provided and the risks taken. The total spread ranges from less than ½ percent for very easy deals to as much as 2½ percent for more complex deals, such as those involving equity linkages. Some writers have observed that fees in the Eurobond market are greater than those in the United States and some other countries for comparable issues. That observation is only superficially true. Fees in Eurobond underwriting, or in any underwriting for that matter, are not really fees at all. What they represent is the extent to which the managers, the underwriters, and the selling group obtain a discount on the stated offering price of the bonds.

Assume, for example, that an issue is done with total fees of 1½ percent. A typical breakdown of the three components of the spread might be: management fee 20 percent, underwriting fee 20 percent, and sales concession 60 percent. The lead manager gets an additional bonus: it can subtract a "praecipium" from the management fee, the balance being allocated to each manager based on its commitment amount. Managers are invariably underwriters, and all underwriters are part of the selling group, because their objective is to sell the bonds. Assume also that the offer price of the bond is 101½ percent.[9] Table 12.1 shows the amounts paid by the various parties for each $100 of par value. Thus the advantage of being a lead manager or an underwriter is not that you obtain any guaranteed fees, but rather that you are able to obtain the bonds at a lower price. Because there is no assurance that you will be able to sell them to the end investor at 101.50, there is really no knowing how much of the fee you will actually be able to keep.

Fixed–Price Reoffer

The standard method of distribution of Eurobonds is a two–tier structure: the bookrunner, or lead manager, who officially launches the deal for the borrower, and a group of underwriting banks who, in exchange for part of the underwriting fees, help to syndicate it. But the high degree of competition in the 1980s for underwriting business, especially among those who cared more about their rankings in the league tables than

---

[9]This is done so that the issuer can obtain 100 percent of the face value.

about the short-run profitability of the deal, led the banks to price the deals more and more tightly. In effect, much of the fee income was given to borrowers, investors, or both. Although this was in part done by reducing the fees on the deals, a more insidious reduction in profitability occurred through the practice of selling all or a large proportion of the bonds to investors at a price below the official issue price. In other words, the stated coupon was set at a level slightly below that which would ensure sale of all of the bonds, and the market clearing price was often below par. This meant that some of the apparent fees were not kept by the underwriters. For example, a book-runner technically earning a one-time fee of, say, 2 percent of the issue for five-year debt, would, to win the business from competing investment banks, let the borrower issue the bonds at 9.75 percent when the yield that investors expected was 10 percent. The resulting loss to the bank when it sold the bonds to end-investors was covered *in part* by the fee.

This practice left the fee structure intact while effectively reducing returns to the point at which many participants in the market barely broke even, and eventually many pulled out of the business, reducing liquidity to investor and issuer alone. Why did so many participate in this game? Moving up in the league tables supposedly burnished a bank's image and helped it bring in business of other kinds. Some banks, such as U.S. and Japanese commercial banks, saw this as the ideal means of building up their capabilities in the investment-banking and underwriting business that they were prohibited from doing at home. Some issuers have actually said, in effect, "We cannot make any money on the issuance of the bonds themselves; the only way we can cover our operating losses on the underwriting of Eurobonds is to trade the bonds, playing an interest-rate speculation game. Or, having participated in an underwriting syndicate, we just sit on bonds that were supposedly bought for redistribution so that losses will not have to be booked immediately, and, if interest rates go down, the bonds can be sold at a profit eventually."

The *fixed-price-reoffer* method of distribution broke the mold of Eurobond issuance. This technique, standard in U.S. public bond offerings, attempts to guarantee underwriters a return on a transaction. Participants in the deal agree not to sell the bond at below the offer price until such time as the syndicate has formally "broken." The advantage from the borrower's point of view is that the fee can be lower. However, the deals are no longer overpriced, so it is not evident that the issuer's effective cost of funds is any lower. The book-runners and comanagers have a contractual obligation not to discount fees by selling bonds cheaply to investors even before the distribution of the bonds has been completed. This agreement makes underwriters much more willing to participate in an issue that otherwise could easily result in a loss, but it requires a cartel-like discipline on the part of the underwriters. Thus it works as long as the more-or-less oligopolistic leaders of the industry, houses such as Nomura, Deutsche Bank, and Morgan Stanley, agree not to undercut one another. Interestingly, the introduction of this method to the Eurobond market was pioneered by the most prominent of Eurobond issuers, the World Bank, because it wanted to see a more orderly market in which it could be assured of support for large issues. Sensibly, other borrowers were reluctant to do deals without the participation of the biggest underwriting houses for fear of needing their support at other times. But as with any cartel, abuse of the cartel's power may eventually lead disaffected members to underprice the others if cartel prices are too distant from what the issuers and investors will bear.

A Week in the Life of the Eurobond Market

Every Monday, the London *Financial Times* publishes a roundup of the previous week's new deals in the Eurobond market. An example is shown in Table 12.2. Reading one of these can provide a fascinating walk through the many variations of the "plain vanilla" straight bond. During the week shown, for example, there were deals in 13 different

Table 12.2   *A Week's New Issues in the Eurobond Market.* The footnotes are often the most interesting aspect of these listings, because they identify any maior special feature of the bond being issued.

NEW INTERNATIONAL BOND ISSUES

Borrower	Amount m.	Maturity	Coupon %	Price	Yield %	Launch spread bp	Book runner
US DOLLARS							
Best Denki(a)Φ	160	May.1997	1.375	100	-	-	Daiwa Europe
Kingdom of Belgium	500	Jun.1998	5.375	99.42R	5.511	+21 (5⅛%-98)	JP Morgan Securities
Toyota Motor Finance(Neths)	250	Jun.1996	4.75	99.79R	4.827	+33 (4¼%-96)	CSFB
Chugai Pharmaceutical Co.(g)Φ	220	Jun.1997	1.125	100	-	-	Nomura International
National Bank of Hungary	150	Jun.1998	8	99.5R	8.126	+275(5⅛%-98)	Bankers Trust Intl.
Credito Italiano, Hong Kong‡	100	Jun.2003	(h)	99.75R	-	-	Credito Italiano, Milan
Nissho Iwai Europe	75	Jun.1998	6	100R	6.000	-	IBJ International
Petrobras‡	300	Jun.1998	(q)	99.5R	-	-	Chase Investment Bank
Grace 1 International(r)	100	Mar.2000	8.18#	100	-	-	Daiwa Europe
Petroleos Mexicanos	150	Jun.1996	6.25	99.49R	6.442	+183 (4¼%-96)	Deutsche Bank London
IBM Brasil(u)	90	Dec.1995	8.5#	99.911R	8.540	-	Citibank Intl.
IBM Brasil(v)‡	30	Dec.1995	(v)	100R	-	-	Citibank Intl.
YEN							
Sanyo Electric Co.	20bn	Sep.1999	5.1	100.1R	-	-	Daiwa Europe
Sanyo Electric Co.‡	10bn	May.1998	(d)	101.85	-	-	Sumitomo Finance Intl.
D-MARKS							
Nichii Co.(b)Φ	400	May.1997	2.75	100	-	-	Deutsche Bank
Republic of Venezuela(l)	100	May.1998	10.25	102	9.708	-	Commerzbank
FRENCH FRANCS							
CCF, Luxembourg‡	500	Jun.1998	(m)	99.9R	-	-	CCF
STERLING							
Allied-Lyons Fin.Services(n)§	200	Jul.2008	6.75#	100R	-	-	CSFB
CARS No.2(o)‡	100	Dec.1997	(o)	100R	-	-	Goldman Sachs Intl.
European Bank Inv.Tst.‡	116	Mar.2001	(s)	99.65R	-	-	Goldman Sachs Intl.
Alliance & Leicester B/S‡	150	Jun.1997	(t)	99.61R	-	-	Kleinwort Benson
CANADIAN DOLLARS							
Bayerische Hypobank	100	Jul.1998	7.375	98.6R	7.723	+40 (6½%-98)	Hambros Bank
GECC(p)	100	Nov.1998	7.25	98.975R	7.50	+30 (6½%-98)	Wood Gundy
ITALIAN LIRA							
GECC	150bn	Jun.2000	10.375	101.837	9.998	-	Deutsche Bank London
European Investment Bank(i)‡	100bn	Mar.1996	(i)	100.05	-	-	San Paolo, Turin

Source: *Financial Times*, May 24, 1993, p. 18.

currencies. Some were convertible, some carried warrants, and two had their principal redemption linked to the Japanese Nikkei stock index. One dollar-denominated issue gave the investor the right to choose redemption in dollars or in ECU at $1.15 per ECU. So it goes.

Borrower	Amount m.	Maturity	Coupon %	Price	Yield %	Launch spread bp	Book runner
Helaba	500bn	Jun.2003	zero	37.64	10.264	-	IMI Bank Luxembourg
Rabobank	150bn	Jun.2000	10.375	101.80	10.005	-	BCA

ECUS

Borrower	Amount m.	Maturity	Coupon %	Price	Yield %	Launch spread bp	Book runner
Kingdom of Denmark	250	Jun.1996	6.75	100.056R	6.729	-	Morgan Stanley Intl.

PESETAS

Borrower	Amount m.	Maturity	Coupon %	Price	Yield %	Launch spread bp	Book runner
KfW Intl. Finance(j)	10bn	Jun.1998	10.35	101.4	9.98	-	Banco Central Hispano.

AUSTRIAN SCHILLINGS

Borrower	Amount m.	Maturity	Coupon %	Price	Yield %	Launch spread bp	Book runner
Petroleos Mexicanos	700	May.1998	8.375	100.5	8.249	-	Creditanstalt-Bankverein

ESCUDOS

Borrower	Amount m.	Maturity	Coupon %	Price	Yield %	Launch spread bp	Book runner
European Investment Bank	10bn	Jun.1998	12	101.7	11.534	-	BPI

SWISS FRANCS

Borrower	Amount m.	Maturity	Coupon %	Price	Yield %	Launch spread bp	Book runner
Nichii Co.(c)★φ	300	May.1997	1.125	100	-	-	UBS
Commerzbank(e)★φ	110	Jul.1998	2.5	100	-	-	Swiss Bank Corp.
Gastec Service(f)★§	50	Nov.1997	2#	100	-	-	Nomura Bank (Switz.)
Sagami Chain Co.(k)★φ	40	Jun.1997	1	100	-	-	Nomura Bank (Switz.)

LUXEMBOURG FRANCS

Borrower	Amount m.	Maturity	Coupon %	Price	Yield %	Launch spread bp	Book runner
Goldman Sachs Group	1bn	Jun.2000	7.75	101.875	7.397	-	BGL

Final terms and non-callable unless stated. The yield spread (over relevant government bond) at launch is supplied by the lead manager. ★Private placement. §Convertible. φWith equity warrants. ‡Floating rate note. #Semi-annual coupon. R: fixed re-offer price. a) Denom.: $5000 + 1 warrant. Exercise price: Y1517. FX: 112.20Y/SFr. b) Denom.: DM5000 + 5 warrants. Exercise price: Y1538. FX: 69.65Y/DM. c) Denom.: SFr50,000 + 50 warrants. Exercise price: Y1538. FX: 76.84Y/SFr. d) Coupon pays 3-month Libor + 0.25%. e) Denom.: SFr50,000 + 50 warrants; 10 warrants entitle holder to one share in each of Veba, RWE and Preussag at a strike price of DM1185. f) Conversion price: Y892. FX: 76.79Y/SFr. Callable on 20/11/95 at 102% declining by 0.5% semi-annually. Acceleration clause effective from 20/5/94 subject to 150% rule. g) Final terms fixed on 25/5/93. h) Coupon pays 6-month Libor - 0.125%; minimum 6%, maximum 10%. i) Coupon pays 3-month Libor - 0.25%. Fungible with the outstanding L400bn. j) Matador bond. k) Final terms fixed on 24/5/93. Callable on 3/6/95 at 102% declining by 0.5% semi-annually. l) Fungible with the DM150m launched on 1/4/93. Plus 34 days accrued interest. m) Coupon pays 8.25% fixed annual in the first year and 18.75% - 2 x 6-month Pibor thereafter. n) Conversion price: £6.22. Callable at par from 21/7/98 or earlier if 85% of bonds are converted. o) Fungible with the outstanding £185m launched in Nov.1992. Average life years: 3.42 years. Coupon pays 3-month Libor + 0.45%. p) Issue launched on 29/4/93 was increased to C$250m. q) Coupon pays 6-month Libor + 4.4%. r) Extendable at bondholders option for a further 2 years. s) Coupon pays 3-month Libor + 0.2%. t) Coupon pays 3-month Libor + 0.1875%. u) Tranche A of $120m issue. v) Tranche B of $120m issue. Coupon pays 400bp + 6-month Libor. Note: Yields are calculated on ISMA basis.

Repurchasing Eurobonds

If a company can issue a Eurobond, it can also buy back the bond from the market. Why might an issuer wish to do so? One common reason is that the borrower is flush with funds and no longer needs the debt. It makes no sense to have a large cache of cash sitting in the bank earning LIBOR minus ¼ percent while paying a coupon of Treasury plus 1 percent to bondholders. But having cash is not a necessary precondition; the borrower may simply wish to refinance on different or better terms.

One possible reason for a debt-repurchase plan might be to retire debt of one kind (say, a Swiss-franc debt) and replace it with another (say, an ECU bond) that better suits the company's needs and outlook. Yet repurchasing a bond is a costly and time-consum-

Figure 12.7   *A Eurobond Buy-Back Program*

Commonwealth of Australia

Sterling Repurchase Offers

The Commonwealth of Australia repurchased £117,546,700 of its four outstanding sterling bond issues during the Repurchase Offers completed in August, 1990. A total of £109,843,290 bonds now remains outstanding, representing 27.5 per cent. of the original issue amounts.

S.G. Warburg Securities
Repurchase Agent

ing process, especially if the bonds are widely distributed in a lot of different countries. It has been estimated that a borrower has to pay a price representing 30 basis points, more or less, over the current market price to persuade a significant number of bondholders to sell their bonds. With the high degree of development of the currency and interest-rate swap market, it is far more efficient to alter the currency or rate characteristics of one's debt by means of an offsetting swap than it is to buy back and reissue a bond.

In the late 1980s and early 1990s, a number of British companies undertook buybacks and exchange programs for their debt denominated in U.S. dollars and in ECUs because of certain tax benefits resulting from buying back debt that was trading at a discount. Some who tried to do the same thing in the sterling market, however, found a poor response on the part of investors, because of the lack of substitutes. Thanks in part to the surplus run by the British government, there was a dearth of long-term sterling debt. For a buy-back to work, investors must be able to substitute something comparable that they see as a better value.

One of the biggest buy-back programs was undertaken in 1990 by the Australian government, which by running a budget surplus was able to reduce its foreign debt by several billion dollars (see Figure 12.7). As with all such programs, not all investors were willing to cash in. When this happened, the Australian Treasury constructed an "immunization portfolio," buying matching assets that funded the interest payments and redemption of the remaining debt.

The Secondary Market

Although most Eurobonds are privately placed or traded briefly following initial issuance and then closely held by individual or institutional investors, some, particularly those issued in large amounts by well-known borrowers, trade actively in a secondary market. For these bonds, two-way prices are quoted by a coterie of market-makers—banks in London, Zurich, Hong Kong, and elsewhere.

Issuers whose bonds trade actively include sovereign borrowers, such as the Republic of Finland, supranational institutions such as the European Investment Bank, major banks such as Dai-Ichi Kangyo, and prominent corporations such as General Electric. Some of these bonds, such as certain World Bank issues, will become "benchmark" Eurobonds used as key indicators for the pricing of other, comparable, bonds.

Most dollar-denominated Eurobonds are today quoted in relation to the "Treasury curve," meaning their yields are seen as a spread over the benchmark U.S. Treasury bond in the same sector—that is, of comparable maturity. Prices are quoted and transactions are executed on a "net" basis, free of commissions. The market-maker quotes a bid price and an offer price. If you buy from him at his offer price, you'll pay that price, plus accrued interest, and no more.

Yields in the Eurobond market are conventionally quoted in terms of yield to final maturity assuming annual pay, because Eurobond coupons are paid once a year. To compare them with Treasuries, therefore, one has to convert the yield to a semiannual basis. A potentially more serious problem arises from the fact that many Eurobonds have call features.[10] Many dealers and investors handle this by substituting a quotation based on yield to first call in place of yield to maturity, but of course this in no

Table 12.3 *Eurobond Secondary Market Turnover*

Euromarket Turnover ($m)			
Primary Market			
	Straights	Conv	FRN	Other
US$	620.3	0.0	60.0	16,899.0
Prev	1,015.4	0.0	0.0	12,036.9
Other	1,805.7	0.0	113.2	8,235.0
Prev	461.2	5.5	728.1	4,901.9
Secondary Market			
US$	16,048.7	622.3	5,557.3	7,591.8
Prev	17,974.1	675.6	7,044.2	8,765.2
Other	20,623.5	1,015.9	4,672.8	41,356.7
Prev	16,869.6	961.4	6,149.1	30,625.2
	Cedel	Euroclear	Total
US$	15,690.5	31,706.9	47,399.4
Prev	18,066.2	29,445.2	47,511.4
Other	30,877.0	46,945.8	77,822.8
Prev	25,063.6	35,638.4	60,702.0

Week to November 15, 1990

Source: *Financial Times*, Nov. 16, 1990.

---

[10]As do some Treasuries, exacerbating the problem!

BOX 12.3

A Typical Secondary-Market Straight-U.S.-Dollar Eurobond Issue

Amount: $50 to $500 million

For some AAA borrowers, however, issues of up to $1 billion are possible, and many issues exceed $250 million.

Maturity: 10 years or less

It is estimated that 80 percent of outstanding issues have a maturity of less than ten years, 40 percent of which are in the four- to six-year range. The maturity of new issues depends upon market conditions.

Coupon: Annual (payable in arrears)

Seventy percent of outstanding Eurobond issues have coupons in the 7- to 13-percent range. New issues are priced close to par to yield a spread over Treasuries, and the range is similar to that in the U.S. market.

Yield: 30 to 120 basis points over Treasuries

Sovereign AA issues trade in a range of from 30 to 40 basis points over Treasuries. Corporate AA issues trade 60–90 basis points over Treasuries; BBB range around 120 basis points or more over.

Amortization: Bullet

A bullet is a single payment of all principal at maturity or on the call date. Sinking funds, which specify or permit early amortization of principal, are rare on new issues, although some older issues do have them.

Call Option: None

For maturities of less than seven years, call options are unusual. For maturities of seven to ten years, calls may be attached at a premium declining to par.

Listing: London or Luxembourg

Although the bonds are traded over the counter, they are usually listed on a European exchange.

Denominations: $1,000, $5,000, or $10,000

Security: Senior unsecured debt

Guarantees, letters of credit, and collateralization are acceptable.

Rating: AAA or AA

Ratings traditionally have not been used in the Euromarkets, but as the issuer and investor base has grown, ratings have become more necessary. Just over 50 percent of outstanding issues are rated. Of these, 47 percent are AAA and 36 percent are AA.

way properly accounts for the value of the call option in the bond. (Some details of a typical U.S. dollar Eurobond issue are given in Box 12.3.)

Table 12.3 gives an indication of a particular week's turnover in the secondary market, while Table 12.4 provides a peek into one day's trading prices in the Eurobond secondary market. The prices are indicative only, being a composite of quotations from a number of market-makers, but they are suggestive of the variety of issuers and currencies and types of bonds—straights, floaters, and convertible bonds, not to mention hybrids such as dual-currency bonds—found in this market. Bid-offer spreads, even for these most liquid of Eurobonds, are frequently as much as ½ percent to ¾ percent apart, in contrast to U.S. Treasuries where a basis point spread of 10 is common.

Table 12.4 ***Price Quotations from the Eurobond Secondary Market.*** Each quotation shows the issuer, the coupon, and the year of maturity. The yield to maturity, computed from the dealers' bid price, is below the coupon whenever the bid price exceeds 100.

FT/ISMA INTERNATIONAL BOND SERVICE

Listed are the latest international bonds for which there is an adequate secondary market. Closing prices on May 17

U.S. DOLLAR STRAIGHTS	Issued	Bid	Offer	Chg. day	Yield
ABN 9⅛ 94	200	105¾	106¼	+⅛	4.11
AlbertaProvince 9⅜ 95	600	110⅜	110¾	–¼	4.75
Austria 8½ 00	400	113¼	113⅝	–⅛	6.03
Bank of Tokyo 8⅜ 96	100	108⅛	108¾	+⅛	5.25
Belgium 9⅝ 98	250	116⅞	117⅜	–⅛	5.74
BFCE 7¾ 97	150	108¼	109	–⅛	5.29
BNP 8⅝ 94	300	105⅜	105⅞	–⅛	3.97
British Gas 0 21	1500	10½	10⅞	–⅛	8.24
Canada 9 96	1000	111	111⅜	–⅛	4.67
CCCE 9¼ 95	300	108½	108⅞	–⅛	4.20
Cia Naviera Perez 9 96	100	99⅛	99⅞	+⅛	9.50
Council Europe 8 96	100	108⅜	109⅛	–⅛	5.10
Credit Foncier 9½ 99	300	117⅜	117¾	+¾	5.85
Denmark 9¼ 95	1571	108⅝	109	–⅛	4.27
ECSC 8¼ 96	193	109¼	109⅞	–⅛	5.30
EEC 8¼ 96	100	108⅞	109½	+⅛	5.07
EIB 7¾ 96	250	107⅞	108½	–⅛	4.97
EIB 9¼ 97	1000	114¾	115⅛	–⅛	5.45
Elec de France 9 98	200	113¾	114⅜	+¼	5.66
Euro Cred Card TST 9 94	325	105⅜	105⅞	–⅛	4.92
Eurofima 9¼ 96	100	111⅛	111⅞	–⅛	4.92
Export Dev Corp 9½ 98	150	116⅛	116⅝	+⅜	5.79
Finland 7⅞ 97	200	106⅝	107½	–⅛	5.82
Finnish Export 9⅜ 95	200	110⅛	110⅝	–⅛	4.85
Ford Motor Credit 6¼ 98	1500	101¼	101⅝	–⅛	6.03
Gen Elec Capital 9⅜ 96	300	111⅞	112⅜	+⅛	5.08
GMAC 9⅛ 96	200	108	108¾	–⅛	5.95
Ind Bk Japan Fin 7⅞ 97	200	107¼	107¾	+¼	5.75
Inter Amer Dev 7⅝ 96	200	107⅞	108¼	–⅛	4.98
Italy 8½ 94	1500	105⅞	106¼		4.18
Kansai Elec Pwr 10 96	350	113⅛	113⅝	–⅛	4.97
LTCB Fin 8 97	200	106⅜	106⅞	–⅛	5.99
Matsushita Elec 7¼ 02	1000	104	104⅜		6.77
New Zealand 9 94	850	106⅛	106½	+⅛	3.99
Nippon Cred Bk 10⅜ 95	150	110⅜	111⅛	–¼	5.12
Nippon Tel Tel 9⅜ 95	200	108⅜	108⅞	+⅛	4.40
Ontario 7⅜ 03	3000	104⅜	104⅝	–⅛	6.86
Oster Kontrollbank 8½ 01	200	113	113⅜	–⅛	6.33
Petro-Canada 7¼ 96	200	105¾	106½	–⅛	5.13
Quebec Hydro 9¾ 98	150	115⅛	115¾	–⅜	6.32
Quebec Prov 9 98	200	111½	112¼	–½	6.20
Sainsbury 9⅛ 96	150	110⅝	111¼	–¼	5.57
SAS 10 99	200	111⅞	112⅝	–⅛	7.39
SBAB 9½ 95	500	109¼	109¾	–⅛	4.63
SNCF 9½ 98	150	116⅜	116⅞	–⅛	5.74
Spain 6½ 99	1500	102⅝	102⅞	–⅛	5.98
State Bk NSW 8½ 96	200	108⅞	109¾	–⅛	5.33
Sweden 5½ 95	2000	101⅞	102⅛	–⅛	4.69
Swedish Export 8⅜ 96	700	108⅞	109¼	–⅛	5.00
Tokyo Elec Power 8¾ 96	300	110⅝	111⅛	–⅛	5.12
Tokyo Metropolis 8¼ 96	200	110	110⅜	+⅛	5.02
Toyota Motor 5⅝ 98	1500	99⅞	100⅛	–⅛	5.65
United Kingdom 7¼ 02	3000	105⅞	106	–⅛	6.40
World Bank 8⅜ 99	1500	113⅜	113⅝	–⅛	5.91
World Bank 8¾ 97	1500	112¾	113	–⅛	5.07
Xerox Corpn 8⅜ 96	100	107¾	108⅜	–¼	5.75

DEUTSCHE MARK STRAIGHTS	Issued	Bid	Offer	Chg. day	Yield
Austria 5⅞ 97	500	97⅞	98⅜		6.51
Belgium 7¾ 02	500	104¼	105⅛	–⅛	7.08
Credit Foncier 7¼ 03	2000	101⅞	102	–⅛	6.97
Deutsche Finance 7½ 95	1000	101½	101¾	–⅛	6.50
ECSC 8⅝ 96	700	106½	106½	+¼	6.51
EEC 6½ 00	2900	99¾	99¾	–⅛	6.54
EIB 7½ 99	400	104¼	104¾	–⅜	6.67
Finland 7½ 00	3000	102¼	102⅜	–⅛	7.06
Ireland 7¾ 02	500	104	104½	+⅛	7.14
Italy 7¼ 98	5000	101¼	101⅜	–⅛	6.92
KfW Intl Finance 7¼ 97	1500	103¼	103⅝	–⅛	6.39
Spain 7¼ 03	4000	101¼	101¼	–⅛	7.06
Sweden 8 97	2500	104⅞	105⅛	+⅛	6.68
Tokyo Elec Power 7⅝ 02	1000	103⅞	104¼	–⅛	7.04
United Kingdom 7⅛ 97	5500	102¾	102⅞	–⅛	6.38
Volkswagen Com 8⅝ 97	400	105½			7.06
World Bank 0 15	2000	22¾	23⅛	–⅜	6.77
World Bank 5¾ 96	300	100	100½	–⅛	5.74
World Bank 8¾ 00	1250	111⅞	112⅜	–¼	6.56

SWISS FRANC STRAIGHTS	Issued	Bid	Offer	Chg. day	Yield
Asian Dev Bank 6 10	100	105⅜	105½		5.51
Council Europe 4¾ 98	250	100½	100⅞		4.63
EIB 6¾ 04	300	110¼	111	–¼	5.51
Elec de France 7¼ 06	100	112¾	113½	+¼	5.79
Finland 7¼ 99	300	109½	109¾		5.44
General Motors 7½ 95	100	103	104		5.76
Hyundai Motor Fin 8½ 97	100	106½	107½		6.70

OTHER STRAIGHTS	Issued	Bid	Offer	Chg. day	Yield
Arbed 7½ 95 LFr	600	99	100	+½	8.00
ECSC 7¾ 94 LFr	1000	100	101		7.72
World Bank 8 96 LFr	1000	101	102	–¾	7.60
Bank Voor Ned Gem 7⅝ 02 Fl	1000	105	105½	–⅛	6.89
Energie Beheer 8¾ 98 Fl	500	110⅛	110⅝		6.48
AlbertaProvince 10⅝ 96 C$	500	107⅛	107⅝	–⅛	7.62
Bell Canada 10⅝ 99 C$	150	109⅜	110⅛	–⅛	8.59
British Columbia 10 96 C$	500	106⅛	106½	–⅛	7.66
EIB 10⅛ 98 C$	130	108⅝	109½	–¼	7.89
Elec de France 9¾ 99 C$	275	107⅜	107⅞	–¼	8.19
Ford Credit Canada 10 94 C$	100	102⅝	103⅛	–⅛	7.63
Gen Elec Capital 10 96 C$	300	105¾	106⅜	–¼	7.81
KfW Int Fin 10 01 C$	400	108⅛	108¾	–⅛	8.52
Nippon Tel Tel 10¼ 99 C$	200	108¾	109¼	–¼	8.41
Ontario Hydro 10⅞ 99 C$	500	110⅝	110⅞		8.49
Oster Kontrollbank 10¼ 99 C$	150	109½	110	–⅛	8.22
Quebec Prov 10½ 98 C$	200	108½	109	–⅛	8.49
Belgium 9⅛ 96 Ecu	1250	104⅞	105⅛	–⅛	7.15
Credit Lyonnais 9 96 Ecu	125	103⅝	104½	+⅛	7.59
Denmark 7⅝ 96 Ecu	250	100⅜	100⅞	+⅜	7.47
EIB 10 97 Ecu	1125	108⅞	109⅛	+⅛	7.19
Ferro del Stat 10⅛ 98 Ecu	500	108⅜	108⅞	+⅛	7.88
Italy 10¾ 00 Ecu	1000	113¼	113⅝	+⅛	8.16
Spain 9 96 Ecu	1000	104¾	105	+⅛	7.19
United Kingdom 9⅛ 01 Ecu	2750	108⅞	109⅛	+¼	7.56
AIDC 10 99 A$	100	111½	112	–⅛	7.57
BP America 12¼ 96 A$	100	113⅛	113⅝	+¼	6.91
Comm Bk Australia 13¾ 99 A$	100	129⅞	130⅜	–⅛	7.62
Eksportfinans 12⅜ 95 A$	75	111⅛	111¾	–⅛	6.38
McDonalds Canada 15 95 A$	100	116¼	116¾	–⅛	6.50
NSW Treasury Zero 0 20 A$	1000	10¾	11⅛	–⅛	8.44
R & I Bank 7¾ 03 A$	125	98	98⅛	–⅛	8.05
Sth Aust Govt Fin 9 02 A$	150	104⅞	105⅜	–⅛	8.22
Unilever Australia 12 98 A$	150	118½	119	–⅛	7.35
Abbey Natl Treas 13⅜ 95 £	100	110⅝	111⅛	–¼	6.78
Alliance Leics 11⅜ 97 £	100	111	111⅜	–⅛	8.03
British Gas 12¾ 95 £	300	109½	109⅞	–⅛	6.73
British Land 12½ 16 £	150	114	114⅝	+¼	11.12
EIB 10 97 £	637	107¾	108	+⅛	7.51
Halifax 10⅜ 97 £	100	108⅛	108½	+⅛	7.80
Hanson 10⅜ 97 £	500	107	107¼	–⅛	8.35
HSBC Holdings 11.69 02 £	153	112⅛	112½	+⅛	9.63
Italy 10½ 14 £	400	106	106⅜	–⅛	9.81
Land Secs 9½ 07 £	200	98	98½		9.77
Ontario 11⅛ 01 £	100	112⅞	113¼	–⅛	8.75
Powergen 8⅞ 03 £	250	100⅛	100⅜	–¼	8.84
Severn Trent 11½ 99 £	150	112⅞	113¼	–⅛	8.70
Tokyo Elec Power 11 01 £	150	113¾	114	+⅛	8.56
World Bank 11¼ 95 £	100	108⅛	108⅝	+⅛	6.76
Abbey National 0 96 NZ$	100	77⅜	79⅜		7.88
TCNZ Fin 9¼ 02 NZ$	75	110½	111½		7.61
CEPME 10 95 FFr	2000	106⅛	106½		6.78
Elec de France 8¾ 22 FFr	3000	107¾	108¼	+¼	8.05
SNCF 9¼ 97 FFr	4000	107⅝	108		6.95

FLOATING RATE NOTES	Issued	Bid	Offer	C.cpn
Alliance Leics 0.08 94 £	300	99.82	99.91	6.2675
Banco Roma 0 99	200	99.31	99.54	3.2812
Belgium 1/16 97 DM	500	100.00	100.11	8.0000
BFCE –0.02 96	350	99.78	99.88	3.7300
Britannia 0.10 96 £	150	99.35	99.49	6.2250
CCCE 0 06 Ecu	200	98.85	99.24	9.5469
Citizens Fed 0.15 96	100	99.58	99.95	5.0000
Credit Foncier –1/16 98	200	100.42	100.78	5.0000
Denmark –⅛ 96	1000	99.34	99.45	3.0625
Dresdner Finance 1/32 98 DM	1000	99.83	99.94	7.8438
Elec de France ⅛ 99	400	102.10	102.81	5.2500
Ferro del Stat 1/16 97	420	99.04	99.28	3.2250
Finland 0 97	1000	99.22	99.39	3.4375
Halifax BS 1/16 95 £	350	99.85	99.95	6.1250
Ireland 0 98	300	99.52	99.66	3.6700
Italy 0 00	500	100.10	100.43	3.6250
Leeds Permanent ⅛ 96 £	200	99.75	99.87	6.2500
Lloyds Bank Perp S 0.10	600	78.50	79.52	3.3710
Malaysia 1/16 05	650	99.51	99.93	5.2500
Nationwide 0.08 96 £	300	99.25	99.40	6.1113
New Zealand ⅛ 96	250	100.05	100.17	3.8750
Renfe 0 98	500	99.07	99.25	3.1250
Societe Generale 0 96	300	99.33	99.50	3.2500
State Bk NSW 3/16 98	250	99.80	100.03	3.5938
State Bk Victoria 0.05 99	125	99.03	99.29	3.7219
United Kingdom –⅛ 96	4000	99.77	99.83	3.0625

STRAIGHT BONDS: The yield is the yield to redemption of the bid-price; the amount issued is in millions of currency units. Chg. day=Change on day.
FLOATING RATE NOTES: Denominated in dollars unless otherwise indicated. Coupon shown is minimum. Spread=Margin above six-month offered rate (‡ ‡three-month §above mean rate) for US dollars. C.cpn=The current coupon.
CONVERTIBLE BONDS: Denominated in dollars unless otherwise indicated. Cnv. price=Nominal amount of bond per share expressed in currency of share at conversion rate fixed at issue. Prem=Percentage premium of the current effective price of acquiring shares via the bond over the most recent price of the shares.

Data supplied by International Securities Market Association.

Source: Excerpted from the *Financial Times*, May 18, 1993, p. 22.

Secondary–Market Linkages Between the Domestic and the Eurobond Markets

As is the case in the Eurodeposit market, each currency sector of the Eurobond market is linked to its corresponding domestic market through arbitrage both by borrowers and by investors.

The U.S. withholding tax discussed earlier in this chapter is one factor that inhibits arbitrage between the U.S. domestic market and the Eurobond market on the part of foreign private investors. (Foreign central monetary institutions are exempt from the U.S. withholding tax.) When the U.S. withholding tax on both new corporate and government bonds was reduced to zero in July 1984, it became apparent that this was not the only barrier keeping foreign investors away from U.S. domestic securities. The provisions of the Tax Equity and Fiscal Responsibility Act (TEFRA) of 1982 do not permit the issuance of securities in bearer form. Because most money (private) investors either do not declare interest income and/or hold foreign securities in contravention to (existing or anticipated) exchange-control laws, they object to having their identity revealed abroad, especially if the country in question has little regard for the investors' desire or privacy. Thus it is possible for Eurobonds (denominated in U.S. dollars) to yield less than domestic bonds, simply because investors outside the United States who wish to hold dollar-denominated paper from U.S.-based issuers find domestic bonds unattractive.

The degree to which foreign issuers themselves can arbitrage yield differences is also limited. Compliance with SEC registration and disclosure requirements is not only cumbersome and expensive, but may compel non-U.S. corporations to reveal information that is politically sensitive in their home country. The restriction imposed by state laws on U.S. institutional investors, such as bank trust funds, insurance companies, and pension funds, against including foreign securities in their portfolios represents another obstacle to inward arbitrage. And because institutional investors dominate the demand for taxable fixed-interest securities in the U.S. market, discrimination against foreign paper effectively has limited access to the U.S. market by foreign issuers.

Not only are there barriers to arbitrage between the U.S. domestic and the Eurobond market (similar barriers segment other major bond markets from their offshore parallel markets),[11] but it appears that the institutional investors that tend to dominate the U.S. market are influenced by somewhat different factors than the private individuals who play a significant role in the demand for Eurobonds. In particular, private Eurobond investors who take up on average in excess of 50 percent of all issues seem to be less influenced by formal credit ratings but tend to look more to name recognition. Thus companies that are "household names" sell particularly well. Private investors also have a much stronger aversion to long-term maturities, and they seem to be more sensitive to currency expectations, when compared to professional U.S. portfolio managers, whose fiduciary obligations are measured in nominal returns. It is not surprising, therefore, to find periods when U.S. issuers can raise medium-term funds for up to 2 percentage points less than in the domestic market (although higher issuing costs, necessary because of the "retail distribution," reduce the net yield advantage).

More and more, the Eurobond market is regarded not as a distinct entity but rather as an extension of the domestic market in the particular currency. The interest rate at issue and the price in the secondary market is set at a level that makes the Eurobond yield

---

[11]For details on controls see: Organization for Economic Co-operation and Development, *Experience with Controls on International Portfolio Operations in Shares and Bonds* (Paris: OECD, 1980).

comparable to yields in the domestic market. In the case of dollar-denominated Eurobonds, the "benchmark" for a comparison of yields is a similar-maturity U.S. Treasury
bond.

U.S. Treasury bonds are taken as the reference point for other U.S. dollar-denominated bonds for two reasons:

- U.S. Treasury bonds have the lowest default (credit) risk of all the U.S.-
  dollar bonds.
- The U.S. Treasury market is the most liquid U.S.-dollar bond market.

Figure 12.8 illustrates the price structure of the straight sector of the U.S.-dollar Eurobond
market relative to the U.S. Treasury market, and relative to U.S. domestic corporate
bonds. The spreads to U.S. Treasuries will typically be determined by the issuer's sovereign states or corporate creditworthiness and by the particular issue's liquidity. Eurobonds are like U.S. corporate bonds, and their yields can be adjusted to make them
comparable to the U.S. domestic market, as is illustrated in Figure 12.9. The Eurobond
market bore lower yields for many years as Eurobonds attracted many international investors who avoided U.S. domestic bonds for fear of registration and withholding taxes.
Now, however, the dominance of institutional investors has made the two fungible. The
close links between the U.S. Treasury market, the domestic corporate bond market, and
the Eurobond market are generally broken for only two reasons. (1) The reputation of

Figure 12.8   ***Eurobond Versus U.S. Treasury Bond Yields.***   U.S.-Treasury-bond yields are
used as a reference point for dollar-denominated Eurobond yields, because Treasuries
have the lowest default risk and the highest liquidity of all dollar-denominated bonds.

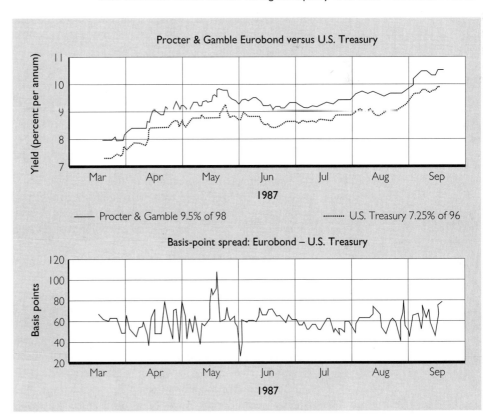

Figure 12.9   *Eurobond Versus Domestic Bond Yields, Expressed as a Spread over Comparable U.S. Treasury Yields.*   Eurobonds pay coupons annually, whereas U.S. domestic bonds pay semiannually. Hence Eurobond yields must be adjusted to make them comparable to U.S. Treasury and corporate bonds.

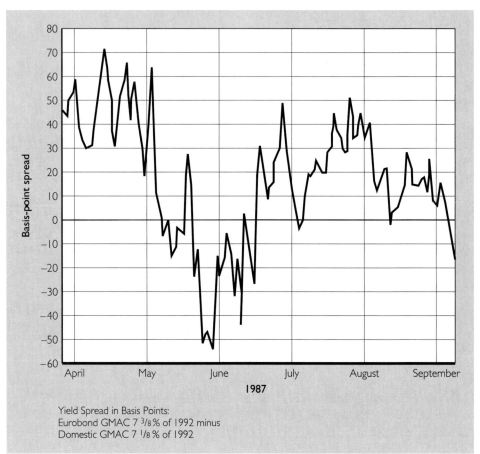

Yield Spread in Basis Points:
Eurobond GMAC 7 ³/₈% of 1992 minus
Domestic GMAC 7 ¹/₈% of 1992

the issuer affects the perception of the credit risk. Thus household names such as Walt Disney or Chrysler often trade at spreads narrower than would be expected from their credit rating because they are well known to retail investors. (2) Conversely, less well-known names, such as some Korean companies, trade at spreads wider than their credit ratings would suggest.

The trading patterns of the market primarily result from the large proportion of the investor base whose returns are measured in currencies other than the U.S. dollar, and from the relationship between the U.S.-dollar Eurobond market and the U.S. Treasury market. In times of uncertainty surrounding the U.S. dollar and U.S. interest rates, non-dollar-based investors tend to move out of U.S.-dollar instruments, and dollar-based investors who continue to maintain U.S.-dollar investments tend to move to the more liquid U.S. Treasury market.

These two influences can increase the volatility of the spread between Eurobonds and Treasury bonds and can result in its widening. The increase in volatility is evident when we consider the April–May and August–September periods compared to the June–

July period of 1987. A widening of spreads followed the October sell-off in world equity markets and the move into bonds, particularly the move into high-quality paper such as U.S. Treasury bonds.

Liquidity

A bond's liquidity depends both upon the size of the trade and the external conditions in which that trade is to take place. The world's most liquid bond market is the U.S. Treasury market. It is able to handle trades of large size, in many market environments, and to absorb severe external shocks across the whole range of outstanding issues. This breadth and robustness is unique even among government bond markets. In the Japanese government bond market, for instance, the benchmark issue is the most widely traded bond, and other issues are relatively illiquid.

The same "selective" liquidity is seen in the Eurobond market. In July 1987, the straight-U.S.-dollar sector had an annual turnover of US$928 billion, approximately 4.3 times total outstandings, and the sector traded on an average bid/offer spread of half a point. However, the Government of Canada 9-percent bond due 1996 had an annual turnover of approximately US$24 billion, or 24 times its total outstandings, and traded on a bid/offer spread of 15 basis points. Furthermore, trade sizes of US$10 million are common and have no effect on the price of the Canadian issue. In the less liquid issues, the maximum trade size can be anywhere from US$1 million to US$5 million, with prices trading on a half-point bid/offer spread or on an indication-only basis.

The key to investing in the Euromarkets is to understand the trading behavior of individual issues, which is based on

1. the size of the issue and the proportion of the issue locked away in accounts holding to maturity or as asset swaps.
2. the location of the paper not being held to maturity and the behavior of the investors holding that paper.

Credit Risk

Compared to the domestic U.S. corporate-bond market, the straight sector of the U.S.-dollar Eurobond market has, on average, lower credit risk. This statement is based not only on the minimal history of default in the Eurobond market but also on a comparison of the ratings accorded bonds in the two markets by the professional rating agencies (see Table 12.5). Standard & Poor's (S&P) and Moody's, the U.S. rating agencies, provide

Table 12.5 *Distribution of S&P Bond Ratings*

Ratings	Share of Eurobond Market	Share of U.S. Domestic Market
AAA	47%	2%
AA	36	8
A	10	19
BBB	4	15
Below BBB	3	56
	100%	100%

the majority of Euromarket credit ratings. S&P alone accounts for 51 percent of the ratings on outstanding U.S.-dollar issues. The dominance of these two agencies grew out of their strong positions in the domestic U.S. market. They had the advantage of both their experience in rating U.S. corporations and their appeal to those familiar with the domestic U.S. corporate market.

The widespread use of credit ratings is new to the Euromarket. These ratings were unnecessary until recently, for two reasons: (1) initial investors in the Euromarket were unfamiliar with credit ratings, and (2) borrowers were large and sufficiently well known to have unquestionable creditworthiness. But as the market developed, it expanded to include both less-well-known issuers and investors who desired credit ratings.

Euroratings, a specialist in the Euromarket, has recently begun to publish ratings on both short- and long-term U.S.-dollar paper with particular emphasis on non-U.S. issuers. Because their domestic markets and reputation have made it unnecessary, most non-U.S. issuers are unrated. When considering unrated issuers, such as the Kingdom of Belgium, Honda, or Deutsche Bank, two important considerations should be borne in mind: (1) individual countries have different tax and accounting regimes that prevent financial statements from being directly comparable, and (2) different work ethics and working environments make management and employee behavior fully understandable only within the context of their own culture.

Indirect appraisal of a borrower's credit standing can be obtained using a number of sources:

- *Domestic bond-rating agencies.* Japan and the United States (which together account for 52 percent of outstanding U.S.-dollar issues) have a well-developed system of ratings. In addition to Standard and Poor's and Moody's, Fitch provides ratings for the domestic U.S. market. In Japan there are four main agencies: Mikuni's, Nippon Investors Service, Japan Bond Research Institute, and Japan Credit Rating Agency. Australia has Australian Ratings, and Canada has the Canadian Bond Rating Service and Dominion Bond Rating Service.
- *Commercial paper ratings.* A company may have a U.S. commercial paper rating but not a Eurobond rating. In general, the commercial paper rating will provide an upper bound for a firm's long-term debt rating.
- *International Bank Credit Rating Agency (IBCA).* IBCA provides both commercial and country risk assessment of all the major banks. Thus Deutsche Bank can be compared with Citibank, and the Kingdom of Belgium can be compared with the United States using these ratings.

The predominance of high-grade debt in the Eurodollar market contrasts sharply with the high proportion of high-yield, high-risk debt in the domestic market.

From the investor's standpoint, the many AAA-, AA-, and A-rated companies and the distribution of issuers throughout countries and industries in the Eurobond market offer the U.S. investor a unique opportunity to diversify and balance his portfolio by including the world's investment-grade issuers. It is only through the straight sector of the U.S.-dollar Eurobond market that the investor has access to a variety of high-quality banks or industrial companies or to dollar-denominated debt from OECD government and supranational borrowers. Furthermore, many unrated issues from borrowers whose creditworthiness is accepted by non-U.S. investors without reference to ratings can result in attractive spreads to Treasuries on certain issues.

Evaluating the credit risk of sovereign borrowers involves some special considerations. When a rating agency grants a credit rating, it determines the relative probability of default by assessing the issuer's ability to service its outstanding debt. The relative credit standing of the 7⅜ percent of 1996 Treasury bond and the Canadian 9 percent of 1996 depends on the relative ability of the United States and Canada to generate U.S. dollars to service outstanding government debt. In general, the ability of either a government or a corporation to generate U.S. dollars depends upon either the ability of that body to produce goods and services or the existence of assets that may be sold for U.S. dollars. There is, however, an important difference between Treasury bonds and sovereign Eurobonds: U.S. Treasury bonds are denominated in the domestic currency of the U.S. government; U.S. dollar-denominated sovereign issues are *not* in the domestic currency of the issuer. Thus the United States has the (almost) unique advantage of being able to print U.S. dollars to service its debt.

In terms of management abilities, the policies and prospects of the present government and opposition parties can be assessed to determine the anticipated course of events in the light of the financial strength of the country. However, a sovereign issuer has three distinct advantages over a corporate issuer:

1. If the bond is denominated in its own currency, it can print money.
2. It can raise taxes.
3. It can expropriate all the assets within its borders.

Sovereign issues and corporate issues can be directly compared for financial strength and management abilities. In terms of financial strength, we can consider the natural-resource profile, industry structure, foreign trade, budget balance, and the size and maturity structure of outstanding government debt to construct a country balance sheet and profit-and-loss account. These financial statements can then be subjected to a ratio analysis in the same way that corporate financial statements are. Ratios such as external debt to GNP, public sector borrowing requirement to GNP, and net debt to trade balance are then used in place of the more familiar current ratio, debt-equity ratio, and so forth.

Bond's the Name, Equity's the Game

A large proportion of new issues of Eurobonds are called bonds but behave like equity, because they incorporate equity options of one sort or another. In other words, the investor obtains some sort of equity participation along with the bond itself. This feature is much more prevalent in the international bond market than in domestic markets, because it offers one way in which investors can reap the benefits of an equity play along with the tax and other conveniences offered by Euromarket instruments.

Equity linkages take three forms:

- Convertible bonds, where the investor has the right to convert his bond into shares. For example, in April 1993 the Compañía de Teléfonos de Chile issued a ten-year U.S.-dollar Eurobond paying 4.5%. Straight 10-year bonds at the time paid around 6.75%.
- Eurobonds with equity warrants. Such bonds are accompanied by a separable warrant, which is a long-term call option, to buy the issuer's shares at a certain price. An example is the four-year, 1.5% Eurobond issued by Yamanouchi Pharmaceuticals in April 1993, at a time when similar straight bonds bore coupons of about 6.0%. The low coupon reflects the fact that each $10,000 bond carried two warrants to buy a share of Yamanouchi stock at ¥2,563 (at an exchange rate of 113.70¥/$), at a time when the company's shares were trading at ¥2,500 in Tokyo. Figure 12.10 shows an example of a Eurobond with warrants.

• Bonds in which the principal is linked to a stock-market index, notably the Nikkei index of Japanese stocks. Many such bonds were issued in the late 1980s. These are often complex structures tailored to particular groups of investors' needs and constraints, as is described in Chapter 17.

Figure 12.10   ***An Equity-Linked Eurobond.***   Eurobonds with features such as equity warrants typically pay a much lower coupon than straight bonds do. The lower yield is the price paid by the investor for the warrant. Warrants are simply long-term call options issued by a company on its own stock.

This announcement appears as a matter of record only.

New Issue   *7th September 1990*

KOBE STEEL, LTD.

U.S. $340,000,000
4⅞ per cent. Bonds 1994
with
Warrants
to subscribe for shares of common stock of Kobe Steel, Ltd.

Issue Price 100 per cent.

Yamaichi International (Europe) Limited

Daiwa Europe Limited	*DKB International Limited*
IBJ International Limited	*The Nikko Securities Co., (Europe) Ltd.*
Nomura International	*Sanwa International plc*
Barclays de Zoete Wedd Limited	*Credit Suisse First Boston Limited*
Kleinwort Benson Limited	*Merrill Lynch International Limited*
Bank of Tokyo Capital Markets Group	*Baring Brothers & Co., Limited*
Chase Investment Bank	*Dresdner Bank Aktiengesellschaft*
Lehman Brothers International	*Mitsui Taiyo Kobe International Limited*
Morgan Stanley International	*NatWest Capital Markets Limited*
New Japan Securities Europe Limited	*Nippon Kangyo Kakumaru (Europe) Limited*
Salomon Brothers International Limited	*S.G. Warburg Securities*
Yasuda Trust Europe Limited	*Amsterdam-Rotterdam Bank N.V.*
Banque Indosuez	*BNP Capital Markets Limited*
Citicorp Investment Bank Limited	*Commerzbank Aktiengesellschaft*
Cosmo Securities (Europe) Limited	*Credit Lyonnaise Securities*
Robert Fleming & Co. Limited	*Goldman Sachs International Limited*
Kidder, Peabody International Limited	*KOKUSAI Europe Limited*
LTCB International Limited	*Manufacturers Hanover Limited*
Marusan Europe Limited	*Mitsubishi Finance International plc*
Mitsubishi Trust International Limited	*J.P. Morgan Securities Ltd.*
Nippon Credit International Limited	*Paribas Capital Markets Group*
J. Henry Schroder Wagg & Co. Limited	*The Shinyei Ishino Securities Company Limited*
Société Générale	*Swiss Bank Corporation* *Investment Banking*
Taiheiyo Europe Limited	*Tokyo Securities Co., (Europe) Ltd.*
Towa International Limited	*Toyo Securities Europe Ltd.*
Toyo Trust International Limited	*Universal (U.K.) Limited*

Wako International (Europe) Limited

Because equity-linked bonds are more difficult to explain and more costly to distribute, the issuance fees are normally greater than for straightforward Eurobonds, as may be confirmed by reference to Table 12.2. We will return to hybrid bonds of this kind in the chapters on international equity markets and financial innovations.

Asset-Backed Eurobonds

At one time, Eurobonds traded principally on the "name" of the borrower, in contrast to the U.S. market. There, the overwhelming dominance of institutional investors produced greater sophistication in analyzing the underlying credits, and the rating agencies' evaluation counted heavily, in part because of the fiduciary responsibilities of many institutional investors. Today Eurobond investors are prepared to look at a much wider range of issues, the primary attraction of many of which is that they carry a high rating from Moody's or Standard and Poor's. *Asset-backed Eurobonds* are among the most interesting of the ratings-driven type of Eurobonds. The concept of an issue collateralized by otherwise unattractive assets has attracted a substantial portion of investors' funds in the Eurobond market. This concept follows the model of the securitization of mortgages in the United States, in which a pool of government-guaranteed mortgages then forms a new security.

Figure 12.11 offers an example of one such Eurobond. This one shows a fixed-interest Eurobond that is designed to raise money to finance what are, in effect, short-term loans to the customers of Sears Roebuck, the U.S. department-store chain. Note that the bond is guaranteed neither by Sears Roebuck itself, nor by Sears' financing subsidiary, Sears Receivables Financing Group. Yet the bond carried a triple-A rating. How was this possible?

The way a bond such as this is able to qualify for the agencies' top rating despite the maturity-mismatched and default-risky assets backing it is through *overcollateralization*. In brief, Sears puts up (say) $135 worth of receivables for every $100 of the Eurobond. Thus the value of the collateral can fall by 35 percent before the bondholder is hurt. Moreover Sears might promise to "top up" the collateral if its value falls below a certain multiple, say, 130 percent, of the value of the bond. Finally, a third-party guarantee for a fraction of the collateral may also be provided to give an additional measure of assurance to the bond investor. These cushions are provided for two reasons: (1) The rating agencies set out criteria for providing an AAA rating, including the degree of overcollateralization (also called "haircut") required for different kinds of collateral. Junk bonds require a higher level of overcollateralization than mortgage-backed securities, for example. (2) The community of investors in the Eurobond market may require even more—that a well-known insurance company's imprimatur is provided in the form of a contingent guarantee, for instance. For all this, the Eurobond investor must give up some yield.

Despite their high rating, AAA asset-backed Eurobonds still provide significantly higher spreads to Treasuries than do direct issues of top borrowers carrying the same AAA rating. The reason is not the default risk but the prepayment risk. Each transaction typically is engineered to pay down early, in the event that the excess spread created by the cash flow falls below certain levels, as decided by the rating agencies. The spread is defined as the excess of the cash flow from the assets, expressed as an interest rate, over the bond's coupon. Many deals have a "spread trigger" that is, say, 450 basis points above the coupon. If the spread falls below that level for three months in a row, the bonds start to pay down principal. In a recession, rising defaults could trigger these protective mechanisms in asset-backed bonds, causing the bonds to repay principal early and exposing investors to reinvestment risk.

Figure 12.11 **An Asset-Backed Eurobond.** Asset-backed bonds are designed to obtain a high rating from the credit-rating agencies, allowing a company such as Sears to pay a lower interest rate than it would on general-obligation bonds.

NEW ISSUE   APRIL 1990

The Investor Certificates have not been registered under the United States Securities Act of 1933 and may not be offered, sold or delivered, directly or indirectly, in the United States or to U.S. Persons as part of the distribution of the Investor Certificates. The Investor Certificates have been sold and this announcement appears as a matter of record only.

U.S. $500,000,000

Sears Roebuck Euro Accounts Receivable Select Trust 1990-1

$9\frac{3}{4}$% Credit Account Pass-Through Certificates

Sears, Roebuck and Co.
Servicer

Sears Receivables Financing Group, Inc.
Seller

Each Investor Certificate represents an undivided interest in the Sears Roebuck Euro Accounts Receivable Select Trust 1990-1 formed pursuant to a Pooling and Services Agreement among Sears, Roebuck and Co., Sears Receivables Financing Group, Inc., and the First National Bank of Chicago as trustees. The property of the Trust includes a portfolio of Sears Credit Account Receivables purchased or to be purchased by or through Sears, Roebuck or its affiliates in the ordinary course of business and all amounts received in payment of such receivables. Sears, Roebuck will continue to service such receivables, and its wholly owned subsidiary, Sears Receivables Financing Group, Inc., owns the remaining undivided interest in the Trust not represented by the Investor Certificates, subject to subordination of a portion of its interest to certain interests of such holders of such Investor Certificates.

Price 101.35%

Credit Suisse First Boston Limited	**Goldman Sachs International Limited**
J.P. Morgan Securities Ltd.	**Salomon Brothers International Limited**
Citicorp Investment Bank Limited	**Deutsche Bank Capital Markets** Limited
Morgan Stanley International	**Nomura International**
Société Générale	**Swiss Bank Corporation** Investment Banking

UBS Phillips & Drew Securities Limited

SUMMARY

In conclusion the external bond market, like the external money market, exists to avoid the regulation, control, and allocational influence of national authorities. As with the Eurocurrency deposit market, however, its existence depends on the willingness of governments to enable investors and borrowers to move across borders. As long as these conditions remain, and as long as governments continue to direct credit allocation and interest rates in domestic money and capital markets, it is reasonable to expect that the Euromarkets will retain their important role in financing the growth of the world economy through the sophisticated institutional framework that both markets have developed.

CONCEPTUAL QUESTIONS

1. Carefully explain the key differences between domestic corporate bonds, Eurobonds, and "foreign bonds." Where would an Australian-dollar bond issued in the United States by Sallie Mae, the U.S. Student Loan Market Association, fit into the picture?
2. What features differentiate Eurobonds from domestic bonds from the *investor's* point of view?
3. What features differentiate Eurodollar bonds from U.S. domestic bonds from the *issuer's* point of view?
4. Briefly explain how yields in the Eurodollar and Euroyen secondary markets might be linked through the currency swap market.
5. How can the Swiss authorities restrain the issuance of Swiss-franc Eurobonds?
6. Identify the ways in which the U.S. authorities inhibit the free trading of Eurobonds in the United States.
7. Explain the SEC's "seasoning requirement" for Eurobonds sold in the United States.
8. List and briefly explain the stages in the issuance of a Eurobond.
9. What is the *gray market* for Eurobonds?
10. The total fees in a Eurobond underwriting are typically broken up into a management fee, an underwriting fee, and a selling concession. Explain the role of each.
11. Why are many Eurobonds issued through offshore subsidiaries?
12. How can a Eurobond backed by risky LBO (leveraged buy-out) loans acquire a AAA rating?

PROBLEMS

1. Examine the bond announced in Figure 12.6. Assume that you had bought A$50,000 of the bond in the gray market at "less ¼." How much would you actually pay for it? And when would you actually have to pay the money?
2. Assume you bought the bond described in Figure 12.6 but then sold it 15 months later when the yield had fallen to 14%. How much money would you receive?
3. Look at the equity-linked bond of Figure 12.10. If similar bonds without equity features yield 8.5%, what is the investor in effect paying for the option she is receiving?
4. Assume that a five-year General Electric Credit dollar-denominated Eurobond is trading at 35 basis points above a five-year GECC domestic bond. What might account for the difference? What might cause this spread to change?
5. Identify the key features associated with the risk of investing in the bond described in Figure 12.6. Contrast them with the risks associated with the asset-backed bond of Figure 12.11.

| Application 12.1 | A DAY IN THE LIFE OF THE EUROBOND MARKET |

Life goes on in the Eurobond market, according to the accompanying example of the daily report on the primary market from the London *Financial Times*. But how many of the bonds that were brought to market on May 27 were ordinary folk? Examine each of the issues, taking into account any associated commentary and footnotes, and try to identify in each case (1) what the investor is getting, (2) what the underwriting banks are getting, and (3) the effective cost to the issuer. Pay particular attention to reasons for the differences in coupons between different issues.

Eurobond Market Buoyed by Asset-Backed and Targeted Deals

LONDON. THE PRIMARY MARKET was busy yesterday as several specially structured issues were placed and a quarter-billion deal backed by cellular phone receivables met a warm reception.

The latter was a $250 million issue brought by Credit Suisse for **Celnet Trust 1990-1,** a special purpose vehicle of the securitization of receivables for cellular telephones serviced by Cellular Network Inc. The issue had been extensively marketed by a large syndicate of banks in Europe and in Asia.

Demand was heavy, with traders reporting strong speculative interest from investors who believed the deal would see even stronger interest in Japan. As a result the spread tightened to Treasuries. Credit Suisse set the offer price at 99.80, giving a spread over US Treasuries of 75 basis points. (At launch time the benchmark 7-year Treasury note was yielding 8.45%.)

Having been fully placed, the issue was quickly freed to trade and rose to 99.85 bid. The issuer was said to have swapped half the proceeds into floating rate US dollars to achieve an attractive sub-Libor funding rate.

The Eurobond market also managed to absorb a $500m Japanese warrant deal, one of the largest of its kind since the plunge of the Tokyo stock market. Nomura, the lead manager, reportedly placed the bulk of the deal back in Japan.

Credit Suisse First Boston was the lead manager of a $150m three-year bond for **Holderbank Inc.,** the Swiss cement concern. The bonds offered a 9 3/4 percent coupon, and were snapped up by eager Swiss investors.

CSFB was quoting the paper at 100 1/8 bid before the Treasury market backed off, when the price moved to 99 7/8 bid, still very comfortably inside the 1 3/8 per cent full underwriting fees. Traders opined that the terms were very generous, and speculated that Holderbank might even have been able to borrow the funds more cheaply by going direct to the banks for a loan. "It's a gift," said one official.

Merrill Lynch brought a $100 million convertible deal for **Battle Mountaingold** to a lukewarm reception given today's weakness in the price of gold. The borrower is a US gold producer with interests in Australia and Papua New Guinea.

The par-priced bonds were trading at 99 1/8 bid among fair demand from Swiss institutions and gold funds based in France. A Merrill official said that the paper was one of the few gold instruments that carried a good yield in addition to upside potential.

In the French franc sector, Credit Commercial de France was the lead manager of a fungible FFr750m deal for **SNCF,** the state railway authority. Combined with the already outstanding FFr2bn of bonds, the deal produced the largest French franc issue on the Eurobond market.

The new paper gave little away to investors, with pricing at 37 basis points over OATs, putting it in line with the trading level of the outstanding bonds. CCF said that the issue was trading slightly outside fees, at less 1 7/8 bid.

A L100bn deal for **Viennische Stadtsbank** traded around full fees, and was in demand from German as well as Italian funds. Proceeds were swapped into floating-rate US dollars.

A ¥15bn four-year issue for **Irish Building Society** was launched by IBJ International. The lead manager said the bonds were aimed at specific accounts and would not trade actively. The same was said to be true of the **Bank of Montreal** issue led by Nippon Credit International. The yen-denominated issue's principal was linked to the performance of the Japanese stock market.

Deutsche Bank brought a Pta10bn five-year Matador deal for **Eurofima** to a slow reception as European investors' infatuation with the Spanish currency seems to be wearing thin.

Fuqua Industries, a US consumer products group, announced in Switzerland a partial buy-back offer on its Sfr100m 6 per cent deal issued by Warburg Soditec in 1989. The borrower said it is willing to buy up to Sfr30m of the deal at 82 per cent plus accrued interest. Before the offer, which is open until tomorrow, the paper was trading at around 76 points.

New International Bond Issues

Borrower	Amount m.	Coupon %	Price	Maturity	Fees	Book runner
Celnet Trust 1990-1¶ (b)	US$250	9¼	99.80	1998	1⅞–1⅝	Credit Suisse
Marui Corp*	US$500	(4⅜)	100	1995	2¼–1½	Nomura
Holderbank (a)	US$150	9¾	101	1994	1⅜–1	CSFB
Battle Mountaingold••	US$100	7½	100	2006	2½–1½	Merrill Lynch
SNCF	FFr750	9¼	98.55	1997	1⅞–1¼	CCF
Viennische Stadtsbank (a)	L100bn	13	101⅜	1994	1⅜–⅞	BNL
Eurofima (a)	Pta10bn	12⅝	101⅛	1996	1⅝–1	Deutsche Bank
Irish Bldg Soc.• (a)	¥15bn	7.4	101⅝	1995	1⅝–1⅛	IBJ
Bank of Montreal• (c)	¥2.8bn	7¼	101⅛	1993	1⅛–⅝	Nippon Credit

¶Final terms. *With equity warrants. •Private placement. ••Convertible. (a) Non-callable. (b) Callable at par after 5 years. If call not exercised, bond pays 50bp over Libor in last year. (c) Redemption linked to Nikkei stock index.

Application 12.2 | # HOLD THOSE TAXES!

You are an international portfolio advisor working at Deutsche Bank in Stockholm. A client has called leaving a message that he would like you to explain why his portfolio suddenly contains 50 million marks worth of 10-year German-government bonds instead of the Euro-DM bonds he typically holds. On the basis of the accompanying articles provided by your research department, can you draft a telex summarizing your reasoning for the purchase of these "Bunds"?

Hint: If you're not familiar with the way swaps work, you may wish to leave this example until you have read Chapter 13.

EUROMARKET UPDATE

Gören Engberg
Stockholm

After the October 9 announcement that the German government intends to place a 10% withholding tax on the interest paid by German-domiciled bond issuers, the spread between AAA-rated Euro-Deutsche mark issues and Bunds drastically reversed. Prior to the announcement, the World Bank 6-1/4 of 7/97 was trading at an average spread of 22 basis points over the 6-3/8 of 8/97 Bund. As the graph below illustrates, this spread inverted and the World Bank issue is currently yielding 31 basis points below the 8/97 Bund.

Has the market overreacted? To answer this, several points must be made:

- The tax is still not law. If enacted, it will not take effect until next year.
- As long as an investor can claim the tax withheld in Germany as a tax credit against his or her domestic tax liability, the impact of the proposed tax will be minimal. The investor will suffer the opportunity cost of the interest lost (between the coupon payment date and the date the tax credit is taken) on the amount withheld (calculated to be one to four basis points).
- Many countries (see list below) have double-taxation agreements with Germany which specify a 0% withholding tax rate on interest income. Investors who are tax entities in those countries will be able to claim a tax refund from the German Ministry of Finance. The opportunity cost in this case will be determined by the processing expediency on these claims.

Thus, the spread reversal is due mainly to administrative and psychological factors rather than economic considerations. Given

World Bank 6¼ of 1997–Bundesrepublik 6⅜ of 1997 Basis-Point Spread

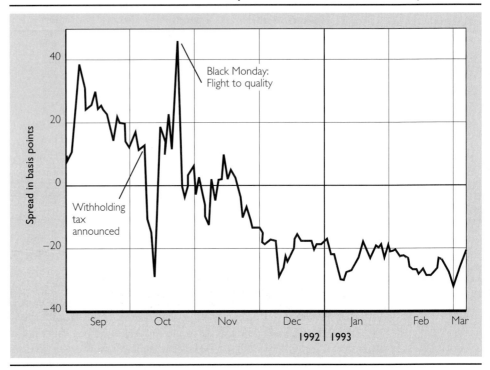

the relative size of the two markets, even after the implementation of any withholding tax, the higher standing of government paper and the liquidity premium associated with it should translate into a positive spread between AAA Euro-Deutsche marks and Bunds.

Countries with Double-Taxation Agreements with Germany Specifying 0% Withholding on Interest

Austria	Switzerland	The Netherlands
Finland	U.S.	Sweden
Ireland	Denmark	U.K.
Luxembourg	France	
Norway	Italy	

USING CURRENCY SWAPS IN A BUND SPREAD TRADE

Gören Engberg
Stockholm

A unique opportunity may now exist to benefit from the spread between Bundesrepublik bonds (Bunds) and the swap market, using a currency swap as a means of going short the German market.

In the last issue of *International Investment Opportunities Biweekly* we spotlighted the anomalous fact that AAA-rated Euro-Dm bonds were trading at yields below Bunds. This, of course, is a reversal of the normal relationship that prevailed before the October 9 announcement of a withholding tax on interest. We argued that the impact of the tax had been exaggerated and that the spread should narrow or return to being positive (Euro-Dm yields above Bund yields).

Investors agreeing with this view would like to short the Euro-Dm issue and buy the Bund; yet one cannot short even the most liquid Euro-DM bonds, for more than a few days. But an alternative way to play the Bund-Euro-DM spread exists: Use a Deutsche mark currency swap as a proxy for a Eurobond.

The principle is simple. A typical DM/dollar currency swap involves a fixed Deutsche mark coupon and principal payment (or receipt) against a floating U.S. dollar LIBOR receipt or payment. The fixed Deutsche mark side is linked to the German corporate bond market; hence entering into a currency swap to pay fixed marks (and receive 6-month dollar LIBOR) is equivalent to selling (shorting)

Currency Swap Rates Versus Euro-DM and Bund Basis-Point Spread

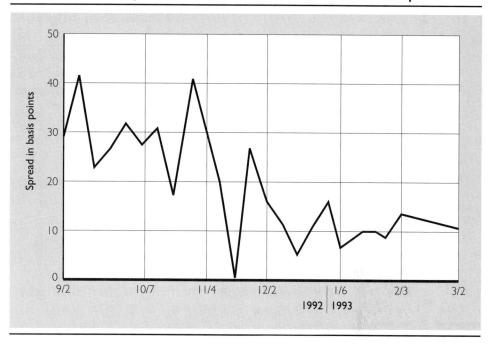

a Deutsche mark Eurobond. Since a currency swap is readily reversible, this is a short position that is relatively easy to unwind. The trade we advocate is for the dollar-funded investor to purchase the 10-year Bund and simultaneously enter into a currency swap to pay fixed marks and receive 6-month dollar LIBOR. Specifically:

(a) Buy 6¼% June '98 Bund, funded with 6-month LIBOR.
(b) Enter into a 10-year swap to pay fixed DM, receive 6-month U.S. dollar LIBOR.

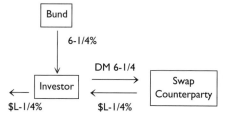

These are rough rates. Assuming the investor can fund at dollar LIBOR minus ¼%, he does the trade at zero spread; otherwise there may be a small positive or negative carry.

The figure shows the swap rate to be trading at a very low spread over Bunds. If the spread widens by an amount greater than the cost of reversing the trade (this be-

ing about 10 basis points in yield), the investor profits regardless of the direction of Bund rates. When the spread widens:

(a) Sell the Bund.
(b) Unwind the swap.

- If yields have risen: Profit in swap exceeds Bund loss.
- If yields have fallen: Profit on Bund exceeds swap loss.

In this trade, the investor is explicitly assuming the spread risk between swap and Bund yields. The risk is only that of the swap-Bund spread narrowing even further. Deutsche Bank's swap desk recommends putting on this trade if and when the spread temporarily narrows further, as it does on occasion.

German Withholding Tax Update

In confirming the tax reforms, the German cabinet clarified the interest withholding issue. The 10% tax on interest will apply only to coupon payments, not to accrued interest. Market participants had feared that a net interest rule would damage the liquidity of the secondary market. This announcement improves the prospects for a Bund-swap spread trade working out.

| **APPENDIX 12.1** | **Yield and Proceeds Computations in the International Bond Market** |

This appendix provides some basic formulas for the computation of yields, prices, and money proceeds from the trading of Eurobonds. The formulas are based on conventions established in the market and adopted by the industry self-regulatory body, the International Securities Marketing Association (ISMA).

The value date of Eurobonds is normally five business days after the trade date, although moves are afoot to change this to three days. An adjustment is made if the value date is a public holiday in the country in which payment or delivery is to take place. A month is usually counted as 30 days and a year as 360 days. Interest accrues on a straight Eurobond from and including the day following the most recent coupon (or, for a new issue, the day from which interest is to accrue), up to but excluding the value date of the transaction.

Once a trade has been agreed upon, a sum called the *net proceeds* changes hands on the value date. This net proceeds is calculated as follows:

$$\text{Net proceeds} = \text{Face value of bond}\left[\text{Trade price} + \frac{(\text{Coupon})(\text{Days accrued})}{360}\right]100$$

Straight Eurobonds are normally issued at par, but some may be issued at a small discount to par or at par plus the fees. The price is expressed as a percentage of the face value of the bond. Interest is normally paid annually, occasionally semiannually or quarterly.

We normally compare the merits of similar bonds by reference to their yields. The most straightforward measure is to calculate the **current yield,** expressed as a percentage:

$$\text{Current yield} = \left(\frac{\text{Interest payment}}{\text{Market price}}\right)100$$

The current yield does not take into account any capital gain or loss associated with the bond and is of use only for measuring the yield for bonds with long maturities. Current yield cannot be used for comparing bonds of different maturities or for those that trade at a premium or discount. A simple improvement takes into account the difference between the face value and the market price, spread over the number of years to maturity. This is called the *simple yield:*

$$\text{Simple yield} = \left(\frac{\text{Coupon rate} + \dfrac{\text{Principal} - \text{Market price}}{\text{Years until maturity}}}{\text{Market price}}\right)100$$

In Japan, bond yields have traditionally been quoted on a simple-yield basis. The main problem with this measure is that it ignores the fact that money now is worth more than money later. To take into account the time value of money, a better method is to find the **yield to maturity** or *redemption yield.* This is the internal rate of return, the discount rate that equates the price to the future cash flows on the bond.

One may find the internal rate of return by hand, by iteration: assume a yield, and find the present value of the cash flows. If that number equals the market price, the assumed yield is the internal rate of return. If not, try another yield, and repeat the process until you're close. This tedious process is performed in a flash by computer spreadsheets and business calculators. Eurobond market traders often use dedicated calculators (such as the Monroe) to make sure that their numbers comply with the market conventions. The ISMA calculation is as follows:

$$P + CPN(1 - f) = \frac{FACE}{\left(1 + \dfrac{i}{100}\right)^{n+f}} + \frac{CPN}{i\left(1 + \dfrac{i}{100}\right)^{1-f}}\left[1 - \frac{1}{\left(1 + \dfrac{i}{100}\right)^{n+1}}\right]$$

Where

P	= Market price of the bond, relative to 100
CPN	= Coupon rate corresponding to the time interval implied by the coupon frequency; for example, 10 percent per annum paid semiannually means $CPN = 5$.
$FACE$	= Price at redemption; normally 100
i	= Internal rate of return, or yield to maturity
$n+f$	= Remaining life of the bond in coupon periods; n is an integer, and f the fractional part.

Normally one knows the market price, so it is the task of the calculator or computer to solve for i, the internal rate of return (or redemption yield, in market parlance). The higher the price, the lower the yield, and vice versa. The sensitivity of the price to changes in the yield is known as **duration**,[1] or sometimes in the bond trader's jargon as volatility. The current yield, the simple yield, and the redemption yield will all be the same only when the bonds are priced at par.

Eurobonds, as mentioned, normally pay coupons annually, in contrast to the bonds in the U.S. market, where semiannual coupons are the norm. Conversion of annual to semiannual yields and vice versa is important to Euromarket participants because Eurobond yields are often expressed as a spread over U.S. Treasury yields for purposes of comparison. An annual coupon will always give a greater coupon than a semiannual coupon of the same rate. The formulas that follow convert from semiannual and quarterly yields to an annual yield, and vice versa.

$$\text{Annual yield} = 100\left[\left(1 + \frac{\text{Quarterly yield}}{400}\right)^{4} - 1\right]$$

To convert from an annual yield to semiannual or quarterly yields:

$$\text{Semiannual yield} = 200\left[\left(1 + \frac{\text{Annual yield}}{100}\right)^{1/2} - 1\right]$$

$$\text{Quarterly yield} = 400\left[\left(1 + \frac{\text{Annual yield}}{100}\right)^{1/4} - 1\right]$$

By convention, periods in Eurobond computations are determined on an "actual/360" basis, that is,

$$\frac{\text{Actual number of days}}{360}$$

---

[1] Duration computations may be found in any finance textbook, or (in the context of swaps) at the back of Chapter 13.

Interest is accrued as though each month had 30 days. The number of days between two dates Day1/Month1/Year1 and Day2/Month2/Year2 is found as follows:

$$\text{Number of days} = (\text{Year2} - \text{Year1})360 \\ + (\text{Month2} - \text{Month1})12 + (\text{Day2} - \text{Day1})$$

If either Day1 or Day2 is 31, then for the purposes of the calculation, use 30 instead of 31. For example, there are 29 Eurobond days between July 1 and July 30, and also 29 days between July 1 and July 31. The ISMA method, although widely used, does not apply to all domestic markets. The number of days used to define a year and to define a month varies, so care must be taken to ensure that the correct conventions are employed in each calculation.

SELECTED REFERENCES

Bowe, Michael, *Eurobonds*, 2nd ed. (Kent, UK: Square Mile Books, 1993).

Kim, Yong Cheol, and Rene M. Stulz. "The Eurobond Market and Corporate Financial Policy: A Test of the Clientele Hypothesis." *Journal of Financial Economics,* vol. 45, no. 3 (1990): 817–834.

Walmsley, Julian. *Global Investing: Eurobonds and Alternatives* (London: Macmillan, 1991): ch. 9–13.

13

Currency and Interest-Rate Swaps

The swap market constitutes the most important development in the international capital markets of the past decade. It has fundamentally transformed the way in which today's corporate financier or his banker look at funding choices. For example, if Brilliance China Motor Company plans to raise floating-rate, U.S.-dollar funds for an investment in Guangzhou, it might find investors, such as Japanese life-insurance companies, more attracted to a yen-denominated bond at a fixed rate. The company would issue the yen bond and simultaneously enter into a *currency swap* with a bank, agreeing to swap yen fixed payments and principal for dollar floating payments and principal. The net result would be to give Brilliance China, in effect, the floating-rate dollar funding it sought, and at advantageous terms.

Other applications can be found on the investment side. European financial institutions such as ING Bank, for example, have frequently bought fixed-coupon Eurobonds and entered into *interest-rate swaps* to convert the interest payments into floating-rate, LIBOR-based payments. (The latter are more suited to a commercial bank's portfolio.) Currency and interest-rate swaps are also widely used by banks, corporations, investors, and government agencies to hedge against adverse interest-rate and currency movements. British Airways, for instance, concerned that its North American revenues may be vulnerable to weakness of the U.S. dollar, could enter into a currency swap to make fixed-rate dollar payments for three years in exchange for receiving fixed-rate sterling. This chapter will explain these techniques and their rationale, and explore applications such as those mentioned.

What Are Interest-Rate Swaps and Currency Swaps?

A swap is an agreement to exchange payments of two different kinds in the future. **Swaps** exist because different companies have different access to financial markets, and because they have different needs. Some have better access to the Japanese market than others; some need floating-rate funds, whereas others need fixed. It is often more advantageous to "swap" payments with another party, thus transforming one's liability, rather than borrowing directly in the market of choice. Currency and interest-rate swaps are techniques that transform the currency and interest-rate characteristics of a liability (or an asset) from one form to another. Coupled with a currency swap, Swiss-franc debt resembles dollar debt; or teamed up with an interest-rate swap, a fixed-rate bond assumes the character of a floating-rate note.

An **interest-rate swap** is a contract between two parties who agree to exchange interest payments of two different kinds, in the same currency, over a number of future

Authors note: Thanks to George Hongchoy and Craig Bamsley for comments.

The term *swap* means exchange, and is somewhat overused in international finance. Most important is to distinguish between the short-term foreign-exchange swaps that traders use, and the longer-term exchanges of coupon and principal that are the subject of this chapter.

- *Short-term foreign-exchange swaps* are agreements to buy a currency at one date and to sell the currency at another date in the future.
- *Interest-rate and currency swaps* (or *coupon-exchange agreements*) are long-term exchanges:

  Interest-rate swap: An agreement to exchange one type of coupon for another over a specified period. Typically, it will exchange a fixed coupon for a floating coupon, such as six-month LIBOR.

  Currency swap: An agreement to exchange coupons and principal amount in one currency for coupons and principal in another currency. Typically, it will exchange a fixed nondollar coupon (and principal) for a floating (six-month LIBOR) U.S.-dollar coupon (and principal).

successive interest-contract periods. (Another term for interest-rate swaps is *coupon swaps*.) The interest payments are expressed as a percentage of some principal amount, called the *notional principal*. By convention, the floating side of the payments is usually the six-month Eurodollar rate, LIBOR. Interest-rate swaps are used to convert variable-rate debt or assets into fixed-rate, or vice versa.

In a variation of the basic interest-rate swap, both sides are floating—for example, six-month LIBOR against an index of Eurocommercial paper rates. A swap in which both sides are floating is called a *floating-floating swap* or a **basis-rate swap.**

Different borrowing needs and access in the *international* markets has given rise to the **currency swap**. To transform an asset or liability from one currency to another, we must change not only the coupons but also the final principal. (The latter conversion is not necessary in an interest-rate swap because both are the same amounts in the same currency.) So a currency swap is a contract between two parties who agree to exchange interest and principal payments in one currency for interest and principal payments in another currency. The typical currency swap involves the exchange of floating-rate U.S.-dollar coupons (six-month LIBOR) for a fixed rate in another currency, and an exchange of the principal amounts at maturity. (For a recap of the key definitions, see Box 13.1.)

Example of a Basic Currency Swap

The technique of currency swapping is best explained by means of an example. We shall see how Flower Power and Light, a U.S. utility based in Berkeley, California, engages in a Swiss-franc–U.S.-dollar currency swap with Novo Nordisk, a Danish biotechnology firm. Both parties come out ahead. To begin, we must consider what each might have done in the absence of a swap market.

Flower Power has no interest in the international markets except as a means to an end, and in the normal course of events might have obtained the U.S.-dollar funding it needs by means of a bank loan, on which it could obtain five-year funds at a rate of LIBOR plus ¼ percent, adjustable every six months. Novo, on the other hand, wants to open a plant in Switzerland, and to finance it with fixed-rate Swiss-franc debt. To do so directly would cost it 5¾ percent per annum.

Without a Swap

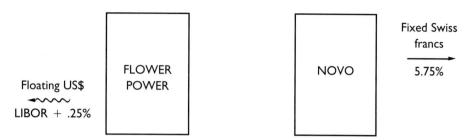

Now Flower Power and Novo Nordisk meet, having been introduced by a bank acting as a broker. Flower has been advised that it can issue a Swiss-franc bond, and at the favorable rate of 5 percent per annum, for there is an appetite for well-run U.S. utilities in Switzerland. Novo's experience is that it can borrow cheaply in the Eurodollar market, namely at LIBOR flat. They agree to an exchange of coupons and principal that will allow each of them to obtain funds more cheaply than in the absence of a swap.

Briefly, what they will do is this: Flower Power and Novo will each issue debt in the market in which they have their greatest advantage. Then they will exchange the proceeds, and subsequently exchange debt-servicing payments, each in effect paying the other's coupons. At the end they will reexchange the initial principal amounts, enabling each to repay the debt it has issued.

As a prelude to the swap itself, therefore, Flower Power will issue a five-year Swiss-franc bond, receiving (say) 150 million Swiss francs. At today's spot-exchange rate of SF1.50/US$, this is equivalent to 100 million U.S. dollars. Simultaneously, therefore, Novo will borrow US$100 million for five years.

Prelude to a Swap: Each Borrows in Advantageous Market

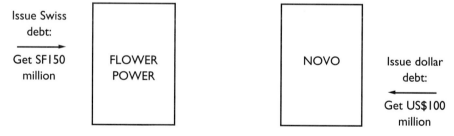

Under the terms of the currency swap, Flower Power and Novo agree that, on a principal amount of US$100 million and its Swiss-franc equivalent at the time of the swap, Flower will pay to Novo U.S.-dollar LIBOR flat every six months, in exchange for which Novo will pay to Flower SF 5 percent every year. At the end of five years, Flower will pay Novo US$100 million in exchange for SF150 million.

But now Flower Power has 150 million Swiss francs, for which it has no need, and Novo Nordisk has 100 million dollars, which are not suitable for its Swiss investment. So the initial stage of the swap *may* provide for Novo to give Flower US$100 million in exchange for SF150 million. This step is a convenient, but not a necessary, part of the currency swap, for each could simply have sold its debt proceeds in the spot market with the same result. (Remember that the spot exchange rate is US$1.00 = SF1.50 at the time the swap is done.) The next diagram depicts the principal exchange.

The Currency Swap: Initial Exchange of Principal

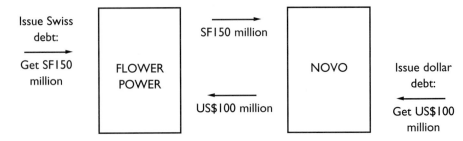

The swap has been carefully constructed so that every year when Flower Power's Swiss-franc interest payments come due, Novo will pay Flower 5 percent in Swiss francs, and similarly Flower will pay Novo the U.S.-dollar LIBOR rate when Novo needs to make its own interest payments.

The Currency Swap: Periodic Coupon Exchanges

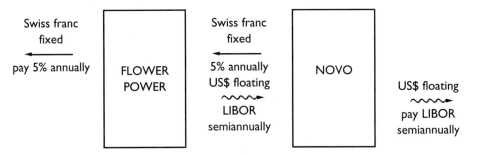

You'll see that Flower's Swiss interest receipts and payments are a wash, leaving it with only the U.S.-dollar LIBOR payments on a net basis. Equally, Novo is left with only a net Swiss-franc payment. That's the way they wanted it. The coupon exchange happens every year, including the last year. Also in the final year of the swap, the principal amounts are reexchanged, enabling each to repay the debt it has borrowed.

The Currency Swap: Final Reexchange of Principal

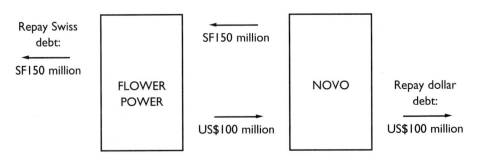

Boxes and arrows like these are widely used to summarize the terms of a currency or interest-rate swap. Following market practice, we will henceforth omit all but the boxes showing the interest flows. The issuance of debt is important but not part of the swap itself, and the initial exchange of principal need not necessarily take place. The final reexchange of principal is understood to be part of every currency swap unless specifically excluded. So the crucial negotiating terms of the swap are the coupon exchanges.

We can now recap the results of the currency-swap example:

Flower Power's situation after the swap:
    Debt: Paying five-year Swiss francs, 5%
     Swap: Paying LIBOR
           Receiving five-year Swiss francs, 5%
Net costs: LIBOR flat, floating

Novo Nordisk's situation after the swap:
    Debt: Paying LIBOR
     Swap: Paying five-year Swiss francs, 5%
           Receiving LIBOR
Net costs: Swiss francs, 5%, fixed

The swap has enabled *both* sides to reduce their borrowing costs. Flower Power ends up paying a floating rate whose cost will drop if interest rates fall. Its net cost is the Eurodollar offer-rate flat, 25 basis points cheaper than it otherwise would have been able to get directly. It borrowed in Switzerland but has no Swiss-franc exposure—all Swiss-franc outpayments are precisely matched by Swiss-franc inpayments. Novo effectively gets Swiss-franc debt at a fixed rate of only 5 percent per annum, lower by ¾ percent than they estimated the all-in cost of raising Swiss money directly.

From each according to his ability, and to each according to his need—that's the principle of swapping. Indeed we can borrow from the theory of international trade, and the principles of comparative advantage, to understand why swaps are now such an important part of the world capital market.

The essence of the swap technique is that it permits a *separation*[1] between (a) the contracts (securities) that specify the obligations of a borrower (or rights of an investor), and (b) the ultimate cash-flow characteristics that borrowers and investors face. Thus a firm such as Flower Power can sell Swiss-franc-denominated bonds to investors who want Swiss-franc paper but change the Swiss-franc obligations into a dollar liability through a currency swap. This separation, then, permits access to the markets in which the firm obtains the best conditions, without being constrained by the nature of its funding requirements. By this device, conflicts between the preferences of investors and requirements of borrowers can be avoided; neither side must compromise. The swap tool, then, buys flexibility to exploit any discrepancies in markets that manifest themselves in different interest and/or exchange rates in different segments of the same market. In this sense, it is an **arbitrage** technique.

The following section will look at the fundamental principle behind choosing in which markets to issue or invest—namely, those in which the firm has a **comparative,** not an absolute, **advantage.** We will then highlight some of the market imperfections that help identify where one's comparative advantages lie. Finally, we argue that the swap market has now developed to the point at which the tail is wagging the dog: far from being an adjunct to the bond market, the swap market is now in many ways more important than the bond market itself. The international swap market is the focal marketplace for nongovernmental credit-market conditions.

---

[1]The principal tool of financial innovation is the "unbundling," or separating of different financial claims and the repackaging, or "bundling" into combinations that better fit the counterparties' needs. On this point see Gunter Dufey and Ian H. Giddy, "The Evolution of Instruments and Techniques in International Financial Markets," Societe Universitaire Europeene de Recherches Financieres, Series 35A, 1981.

Comparative Advantage

The theory of comparative advantage says that we can all benefit from specializing in those activities in which we have a relative advantage, "export" the results, and import those things in which we have a relative disadvantage. Even though you may be better at virtually everything than I am, it does not pay for you to try to do it all yourself. There are bound to be some things that you are *relatively* better at than other things, and the same holds for me.[2]

This is as true of financing and investment activities as it is of other things in life. Company A may have a better credit rating than Company B, and hence may be able to get credit cheaper in all markets. But it still pays for A to specialize in borrowing in the market in which it has its greatest advantage, relatively speaking, and to engage in a swap with B that will tap only that market in which *it* has a comparative advantage. Consider the following example. Banzai Bank can borrow cheaply in both the fixed- and the floating-rate markets, while it costs Gaijin Jeans more to borrow in both markets, as shown in Table 13.1.

Banzai is better at selling both types of securities, but its advantage is greater in the fixed-rate market than in the floating-rate market. If all Banzai wants is fixed-rate funds, that's fine. But, typically, an international bank will have a great need for floating-rate funds, and Banzai is no exception. It could borrow at LIBOR − .25%, but its advantage is 75 basis points in the fixed-rate market and only 35 basis points in the floating-rate market. Banzai has a comparative advantage in selling fixed-rate debt; it follows that Gaijin has a comparative, but not an absolute, advantage in the floating-rate market. The net difference between Banzai's two advantages is 40 basis points: this is the amount by which the two credit markets price the two companies' debt differently, and so this amount represents the potential gains from trade.[3] By trade, of course, we mean swapping. Let us see how a swap might produce these gains and how they might be distributed.

Let each party borrow in the market in which it has a comparative advantage, and then enter into a fixed-floating swap of this kind:

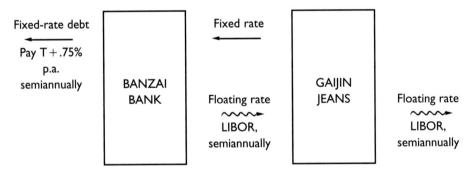

We have not yet specified *what* fixed rate Gaijin pays Banzai. What swap rate do you think would work? To answer that, look at Table 13.2 which shows the borrowing actually done in boldface type and adds the swap flows.

From the borrowing done and the payments on the swap, Banzai ends up with an *effective cost of funds* of (Treasury + .75%) − (Treasury + 1.25%) + LIBOR, which equals LIBOR − .50%, a net savings of 25 basis points. Similarly, Gaijin's net cost is

---

[2]You make money. I'll make words. Then we trade.

[3]We are measuring the *static* gains from trade, as though this 40-basis-point advantage will stay in place irrespective of how much each borrows in a particular market. Obviously, there is a limit to which one can sell debt of a particular kind without driving the price down, and the yield up, and eroding the relative advantage.

Table 13.1   *Swap Economics Based on Comparative Advantage*

	Fixed-Rate Market	Floating-Rate Market
Banzai Bank	Treasury + .75%	LIBOR − .25%
Gaijin Jeans	Treasury + 1.50%	LIBOR + .10%
Difference	0.75%	0.35%
	Net Difference = 0.40%	

Table 13.2   *Swap Economics Based on Comparative Advantage: The Outcome*

	Fixed-Rate Market	Floating-Rate Market	THE SWAP Pay	Receive	Saving
Banzai Bank	**Treasury + .75%**	LIBOR − .25%	LIBOR	T + 1.25%	0.25%
Gaijin Jeans	Treasury + 1.50%	**LIBOR + .10%**	T + 1.25%	LIBOR	0.15%
Difference	0.75%	0.35%			
	Net difference = 0.40%			Total Saving = 0.40%	

Treasury + 1.35%, a 15-basis-point savings. Other combinations are possible: the fixed rate could be different, and there's no law that says the floating side has to be LIBOR flat—it often isn't. But the total net savings, however distributed, must add up to 40 basis points, and, for the swap to be worthwhile, each party must gain something. How much each gains from the swap depends, among other things, on the relative market power of the counterparties.

The Economics of Swaps

What is the economic rationale for swaps? And under what circumstances is it beneficial for a company to employ a swap—in other words, to contract to change the currency or other characteristics of an asset or liability?

The swap is the technology for transforming the characteristics of financial claims. Swaps are needed as long as it is profitable to transform them. Put differently: if the world had a complete set of claims with all possible combinations of characteristics—if all firms could issue securities in all markets at identical terms—then swaps and other hedges might not be necessary, as long as one condition were fulfilled. That condition is that each type of claim could be bought or sold at a price at least as good as the cost of replicating that claim by means of another claim plus a swap. These conditions are obviously not always fulfilled (see Box 13.2 for an illustration). Thus *incomplete markets* and *market inefficiencies* are what provide the economic rationale for swaps.[4] When swaps are seen this way, it is not saying too much to conclude that they have gained a permanent place in financing and investing techniques, or as permanent as anything is in the world of finance!

---

[4]The reader who seeks a more considered treatment of the economic explanations of swaps may consult Larry D. Wall and John J. Pringle, "Alternative Explanations of Interest Rate Swaps: A Theoretical and Empirical Analysis," *Financial Management,* Summer 1989, 59–70, and other references listed at the back of the chapter.

BOX 13.2

Are Swaps Unnecessary?

Consider a company that has, in the past, issued fixed-rate Australian dollar debt and now wishes instead to have yen debt on its balance sheet. This could be achieved by means of an Aussie-yen currency swap. But is it necessary? Two answers are possible:

- *No*. The same result can be achieved by repurchasing the outstanding Aussie debt and reissuing a bond denominated in yen.
- *Yes*. Although the bond-market alternative is certainly feasible, it entails a costly and time-consuming herding-in of widely distributed securities in the secondary market, and the fee-ridden issuance of a new bond in Japan. Why bother, when a single currency swap can achieve almost exactly the same effect rapidly and cheaply?

Conclusion: Swaps are necessary and will continue to thrive as a means by which borrowers and investors can transform the characteristics of their liabilities or assets. Although it is often possible to do the same in the bond market, it is more cumbersome and expensive.

Credit-Market Imperfections[5]

We've shown that comparative advantage is the principle governing whether, and by how much, swaps benefit borrowers with differential access to markets. But we've said nothing about *why* they have such differential advantages in different markets. If all markets treated a given company alike in a godlike objective fashion, swaps would produce slim pickings. The fact that they can offer substantial savings means that there are market imperfections, although sometimes only temporary ones. The swap market is of course a very competitive one, with few barriers to entry, so the profits available from swapping have been reduced, but they are still significant enough to outweigh the costs and credit risks involved. The following identifies some of the more egregious imperfections between markets that can be exploited by swaps.

Home-Market and Familiarity Effect

The most attractive market in which to borrow may well be a company's home market. Investors tend to perceive domestic companies as less risky than foreign companies of equal credit quality. This may be because investors are more familiar with the company's name or business or that there is just more information available to the investor about the domestic company. There may also be statutory restrictions on institutional investors that forbid them from holding more than a small amount of foreign-currency bonds. This will make the domestic companies appear more attractive by default.

There may also be effects resulting from cultural and language differences between the foreign company and the domestic investors, as well as a certain amount of patriotism. For example, an Iranian company bond issue may not have been well received in the United States during the hostage crisis in 1979, while it may have been accepted by agnostic investors in Europe.

Investors prefer companies they are familiar with. These companies usually have a track record that investors can evaluate to determine credibility. The amount of infor-

---

[5]This section is adapted from "Interest Rate and Currency Swaps: Theory, Mechanics and Risks" by Gunter Dufey, University of Michigan, unpublished working paper.

mation available on familiar companies makes it easier and less costly for investors to monitor financial performance. Therefore, a proven or frequent borrower may get financing on better terms than an issuer new to the market. Familiarity doesn't always coincide with domesticity. In many cases, a foreign issuer, like the World Bank in Japan, may be more familiar to the market because it has entered the market more often than a domestic counterpart, thus developing a reputation with the investors.

Differing Risk Perceptions Between Markets

The public-capital (bond) market and the bank-credit market appear to evaluate companies' credit risk differently. Because credit assessment is subjective, this fact isn't too surprising. A company can issue in the market in which it receives the better evaluation and lower rates (thereby lowering funding costs) and then swap into the desired type of instrument.

Banks also tend to more readily accept the additional risk that a lower-quality borrower entails. This may be because banks hold a more diversified portfolio of loans, or because they may be in a better position to monitor borrower behavior and reduce their actual losses on "bad" accounts by working with a borrower. Partially offsetting this tendency may be the lower risk premium required on liquid, tradable securities versus illiquid bank loans; but few issues of low-quality borrowers can be described as liquid.

Therefore, banks tend to charge a lower risk premium relative to the bond market. As shown in the preceding example for an interest-rate swap, this will give the BBB-rated borrower the comparative advantage in the floating-rate credit market over the AAA-rated borrower because it pays a smaller risk premium. The net interest-rate differential can then be arbitraged and split between the counterparties.

Different currency markets may also have divergent risk perceptions because of factors such as familiarity of issuer, different credit-evaluation mechanisms and benchmarks, and various cultural attitudes toward risk.

Regulation of Issuers and Investors

In most markets, there is government regulation that seeks to limit the amount of debt issued by foreign companies, to protect domestic investors from increased risk and to preserve market borrowing capacity for domestic companies. The authorities of some countries, such as the Netherlands, use a queuing system that forces foreign companies to sign up on a "wait list" until they can determine whether the market can handle the issue.

Another common regulation is that certain types of domestic investors are limited to holding only a small percentage of their total portfolio in foreign-company debt instruments. In Japan, for example, large institutional investors such as pension funds, trust funds, and life-insurance companies have foreign-investment limits intended to ensure that the investors will act prudently and buy lower-risk domestic securities, thus guaranteeing that the money will be there when the retirees and widows need it. There may also be regulations restricting foreign investors on how much they can invest in domestic security issues. Commercial banks typically face restraints on the extent of their lending to certain industry categories or corporate groups.

Politics may exclude certain borrowers from particular markets. In the late 1980s, for example, South African companies were not permitted to issue bonds in the United States; instead, they undertook private placements in Switzerland, which could then be swapped into the currency of choice.

All this government regulation makes certain markets more attractive to particular companies (usually domestic) than they are to others. In many instances, access to the market may be impossible. A bond swap can get around all this by allowing a company to enter directly through a counterparty who has favorable standing in the market.

Subsidized Financing

A currency swap may allow a company to take advantage of favorable export financing and other government programs that may only be available in a currency not desirable to a company. The company could then swap the exchange risk out of the subsidized borrowing. To illustrate, Western Mining of Australia may finance the purchase of extraction equipment from Mitsubishi Heavy Industries with a low-interest, yen-denominated loan from the Export-Import Bank of Japan. Because mineral revenues are, as a rule, denominated in U.S. dollars, Western Mining would want to do a currency swap to effectively convert the yen payments into dollars.

Availability of Funds in Different Markets

Temporary supply/demand imbalances often arise in particular money and capital markets. This may be because two countries are in different stages of an economic cycle or because reserve requirements for banks are lowered, releasing a large amount of funds into the bank-credit market. Excess demand in a market will drive rates up, whereas excess supply will force rates down. Borrowers will want to enter markets in which there is excess supply. The excess-supply market may not have the desirable interest-rate or currency features, so a swap can be used to arbitrage the differing economic conditions between markets and provide the desired traits to the borrower.

Nature of Counterparties

Balance-sheet management is one of the most important benefits that swapping provides. The nature of each counterparty will determine the type of assets and liabilities it will carry. The most common contrast is that between a commercial bank and an industrial company. The bank's assets are the loans issued to customers. These are typically short term and on a floating-rate basis. Therefore, the bank will want liabilities to match and can usually obtain this from the floating rates offered on deposits held with the bank. However, because banks that have a high credit standing can normally generate funds from customer deposits, they do not tap the bond markets available to them. Their bond issues will have a rarity value that allows them to issue at lower rates. Lloyds Bank, for example, might be able to issue a sterling bond at a relatively narrow spread over U.K. government-bond yields. It can issue a fixed-rate bond and then swap the fixed-rate debt payments for floating-rate payments to match its assets, thus exploiting its comparative advantage in the bond market.

An industrial company like Sandoz, on the other hand, will hold most of its assets in the form of fixed assets and inventory. These assets support operations that typically generate a relatively stable return from year to year. To offset this, Sandoz will want fixed-rated bonds to finance its assets. Sometimes the company's investment needs will be so high that the bond market can get overwhelmed with the borrower's bonds, forcing the company to pay a premium. To avoid the premium, Sandoz will employ floating-rate financing in the form of bank credits or commercial paper. As a result, the bank and the industrial company will be in opposite positions. By swapping, the bank can obtain the floating-rate debt it needs and the industrial company will receive the fixed-rate debt it desires while taking advantage of lower rates in different markets.

Intertemporal Rate Differences

Changes over time can also affect the difference between markets. Relative changes can create arbitrage opportunities between debt issued before the change occurred and new debt issued currently. For example, in Great Britain in the early 1990s, interest rates dropped sharply and the yield curve flattened, making fixed-rate funding much more attractive than it had been in the past. Hence many companies undertook currency swaps to fix their variable cost of funds.

Excessive Use of a Market

An issuer may desire to stay in a particular market, but that market may not have the debt capacity needed. Investors may get saturated with the issuer's financial instruments and charge a premium on any additional borrowings. For example, at one point Philips Petroleum found the Dutch-guilder market saturated with its bonds, while demand for Philips paper was still strong in Switzerland. So it borrowed in Swiss francs and swapped the issue into Dutch guilders.

You can recognize that none of these market imperfections is static. Although the descriptions have been general in nature, market imperfections tend to be quite situational, often appearing only as temporary "windows of opportunity." By their very nature, swap transactions destroy the imperfections that give rise to their use. This is the essence of an arbitrage transaction. The savings available from currency and interest-rate swaps have fallen dramatically since the market's early days, indicating that imperfections are diminishing.

Bond–Market Redundancy

The swap market, we have seen, has become a widely employed means of arbitraging various bond-market imperfections. Indeed, many corporate treasurers regard swaps as an essential adjunct to bonds and other credit instruments as financing techniques. Even institutional investors, such as banks and money managers, employ swaps to transform the characteristics of their assets (we'll encounter examples of this later). Markets are actively made by a community of banks, some of which offer almost unlimited variations on the basic currency and interest-rate swaps described in this chapter. The "plain vanilla" swap has become a commodity.

Knowing that it can find a swap to transform its "advantageous" debt into almost any kind it desires, the corporate or governmental borrower is no longer at the mercy of the bond market when it wants to tailor its debt to suit the nature of the business. Naturally, where there is an advantage to be gained it will issue debt of the kind in which it has a comparative advantage, and swap into something else. But swaps are frequently used by borrowers and investors alike even when there is no glaring imperfection to exploit. *Swaps are simply more convenient and logical to use than fussing with the buying and selling of bonds.* At the extreme, a corporate issuer need tap only one market—perhaps the deepest, most liquid market, such as the U.S. bond market or the medium-term note market at the long end, or the commercial paper market at the short end. All the rest can be done with swaps. General Electric need never borrow Japanese yen or Australian dollars or issue floating-rate notes. It can accomplish all its "nonvanilla" needs with swaps. Nippon Life need not sell any U.S. bonds when it wishes to reduce its exposure to the dollar or to rising U.S. interest rates; it can do the same at probably lower cost by putting on a currency swap, or "unwinding" one that was previously put on. Many individual Eurobonds and domestic bonds are quite illiquid, while swaps, being much more standardized and more readily hedged, are liquid and flexible (and becoming more so every day).[6] Hence, it is not implausible to say that *far from being a mere adjunct to the bond markets, the swap has made much bond-market activity redundant.*

Swap Around the Clock

Enough theory. It's time to look at how firms use the swap market. We'll sketch four different applications, each illustrating one of the four major types of swap: an interest-rate swap, a basis swap, a standard fixed-floating currency swap, and a fixed-fixed currency swap.

An Interest-Rate Swap

Interest-rate swaps involve the exchange of fixed for floating interest rates in a single currency. Although the example we use is a U.S.-dollar interest-rate swap, active interest-rate swap markets exist in most of the major currencies. Apart from the timing of coupon payments and other market-specific conventions, the example could just as easily have been in, say, Japanese yen.[7]

Swaps are not used only in conjunction with new issues. Interest-rate swaps in particular are used to alter a borrower's interest-rate risk profile in lieu of repaying and reissuing debt. Such is the case with Toyo Trust, which has five-year fixed-rate debt on which it is paying 1 percent above today's five-year Treasury note (which it wants to convert into floating), and with Sammi Steel, which has floating-rate debt on which it is paying six-month LIBOR plus .25 percent (the cost of which it wants to fix). Toyo's alternative would be to borrow floating-rate funds at LIBOR, whereas Sammi's best alternative would be to issue fixed-rate debt at Treasury plus 1.75 percent. Thus before the swap,

> Toyo's situation: Paying five-year Treasury + 1%
> *Alternative cost:* LIBOR flat, floating
>
> Sammi's situation: Paying LIBOR + .25%
> *Alternative cost:* T + 1.5%, fixed

---

[6]An example: In the late 1980s, the U.K. government all but ceased to issue new long-term government bonds ("gilts"). This halt led to a scarcity of liquid, "benchmark" instruments for traders to use for hedging and to adjust their positions. By the early 1990s, the gap had been filled by the sterling fixed-floating swap market: interest-rate swaps were traded as commodity-like substitutes for gilts.

[7]One difference: U.S. interest-rate swap rates are quoted as a spread over the similar-maturity U.S. Treasury "benchmark" bond or note yield. Some countries do not have suitable benchmark bonds, so swap rates are simply quoted as an absolute level rather than as a spread over the benchmark.

Toyo Trust is an active "swapper," and has solicited Sammi's business. They reach an accord on terms. Toyo promises to pay LIBOR minus .25 percent to Sammi every six months. In exchange, Sammi agrees to pay today's Treasury note rate, plus 1 percent per annum to Toyo every six months. So after the swap,

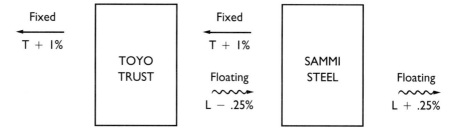

Toyo's new situation:
    Debt: Paying five-year Treasury + 1%
    Swap: Paying LIBOR − .25%
           Receiving five-year Treasury + 1%
Net cost: LIBOR − .25%, floating

Sammi's new situation:
    Debt: Paying LIBOR + .25%
    Swap: Paying five-year Treasury + 1%
           Receiving LIBOR − .25%
Net cost: T + 150%, fixed

Both have done better than they would have done using the appropriate bond-market alternatives. Toyo ends up paying a floating rate whose cost will drop if interest rates fall. His net cost is ¼ percent below the Eurodollar offer rate, 25 basis points cheaper than he otherwise would have been able to get directly. Sammi ends up paying a fixed rate at only 1.5 percent per annum above the U.S. Treasury rate, lower by ¼ percent than he estimates the all-in cost of raising fixed-rate money in, say, the Eurobond market.

Variation: A Basis Swap

A basis swap is one in which two floating rates are exchanged. These floating rates are linked to two different market indexes, such as LIBOR, the U.S. Treasury bill rate, the U.S. prime rate, the Federal Reserve's index of commercial paper rates, or the Bank of England Composite Index of Eurocommercial paper rates (BOECI). Basis swaps are also done between different reset periods of the same index; for example, one-month LIBOR against three-month LIBOR. Basis swaps are offered as a matter of course by the major players who trade swaps, and are typically quoted against six-month U.S.-dollar LIBOR, although other combinations are common, too. For example, the swap desk of Swiss Bank Corporation may offer to pay/receive three-month BOECI plus 75/78 basis points in exchange for six-month LIBOR.

    To illustrate the technique, we shall assume that Credit Lyonnais' New York branch has made an LBO loan to Ralph's, a grocery chain, in which Ralph's has the option of paying LIBOR plus 2.50 percent or U.S. prime plus 1.25 percent. Ralph's now informs its lenders that it will opt for the prime-based pricing. But Credit Lyonnais' funding is in the Eurodollar market, so it faces "basic risk." Prime moves in intermittent jumps, whereas LIBOR changes daily in response to credit conditions. Credit Lyonnais calls a few swap-market-makers, and finally agrees to a basis swap with Bankers Trust. The

terms are three-month LIBOR against Prime minus 1.20 percent, payable quarterly.[8]
Schematically, the result is as follows:

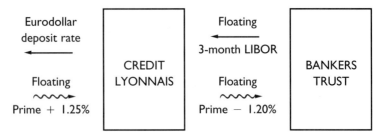

Taking deposits in the three-month Eurodollar market, a prominent bank like Credit
Lyonnais can probably fund itself at around ¼ percent below LIBOR. If so, the bank is
earning a margin of 2.70 percent over its cost of funds. The basis swap has enabled it to
"match-fund" the leveraged-buy-out loan. We do not need to know how Bankers Trust
is hedging its basis swap; as we'll see in a later section, it's likely to be assumed into an
overall "portfolio" of swaps.

A Currency Swap

The first example in this chapter was a currency swap, but that one was slightly atypical
in one respect: it involved two corporations. Most swaps have a bank as at least one of
the two parties to it. The reason is *counterparty risk,* the possibility that one party to the
swap will walk away from it, leaving the other with a mismatched and possibly losing
position. Corporations do not want to devote resources to evaluating and bearing credit
risk, so they tend to stick to large banks as counterparties. This fact helps explain why
the usual currency swap involves both a transformation of currency and of interest rate—
from fixed to floating (see Box 13.3 on swap quotations). Loans by commercial banks
are normally priced on a floating-rate basis, while such banks have substantial borrowing
power in the fixed-rate market in various currencies. So banks want to transform fixed
foreign currency into floating-rate dollars. Corporate borrowers, on the other hand, often
have easy access to short-term or floating-rate funds, but sometimes want to fix their cost
of funds, especially in the more constrained nondollar markets. So they want to transform
floating-rate dollars into fixed foreign currency. *Thus fixed foreign currency against floating
U.S. dollars is the standard currency swap.*

Here's an example: Procter & Gamble has easy access to the short-term markets in
the United States, but wants to borrow fixed-rate deutschemarks for its new DM300-
million facility in Leipzig. Dresdner Bank has plenty of fixed-rate DM funding, and would
gladly transform some of it into LIBOR-based U.S.-dollar funding. P&G accordingly
finds Dresdner's swap terms to be the most attractive in the market, and agrees to swap
six-month LIBOR against fixed DM for seven years on a principal amount of DM350
million. P&G's local currency revenues will be used to service the DM swap payments.

---

[8]Although there is no fixed relationship between the U.S. bank Prime Rate and LIBOR, Prime is usually
between 1 percent and 2 percent above LIBOR. Thus the Prime-based rate that is equivalent to LIBOR is,
say, Prime minus 1.5 percent. In the example in the text, three-month LIBOR is echanged for Prime minus
1.20 percent. Another way of interpreting a floating-floating swap quote is to see that the two sides of such a
swap must roughly represent the equivalent borrowing cost for the same borrower in two different markets.

Omitting the details, a "box and arrows" diagram of the swap and related cash flows would look something like this:

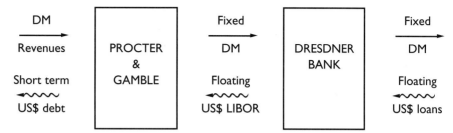

BOX 13.3

Interpreting Swap Quotations

The key to interpreting quotations of interest-rate and currency swaps is to know that fixed rates are conventionally exchanged for *six-month LIBOR*. This makes it necessary only to quote the fixed-rate side of the swap; the floating-rate side is taken as given. Swaps are usually quoted on a **bid** and **offer** basis; the bid, the lower of the two, is what the quoting bank, the market-maker, would be willing to *pay* in exchange for six-month LIBOR, whereas the higher rate is what the quoting bank would be willing to *receive* in exchange for six-month LIBOR.

When U.S.-dollar interest-rate swaps are quoted, they are generally quoted as a *spread over Treasury,* because U.S. Treasury note and bond yields form the base for most market-driven longer-term rates in the United States. Based on the accompanying quote sheet, a U.S.-dollar two-year interest-rate swap would look like this:

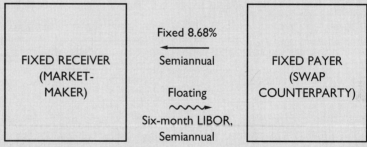

U.S. swaps usually involve semiannual pay on the fixed side, and foreign currency and Eurobond-related swaps normally involve annual pay. The 8.68 percent in the diagram (8.02 + .66) is what the quoting bank, the market-maker, would be willing to receive, assuming that the swap counterparty's credit risk was acceptable.

As a fixed payer, the market-maker would be willing to pay the lower of the two fixed rates against six-month LIBOR, as the following example of a yen/dollar swap illustrates:

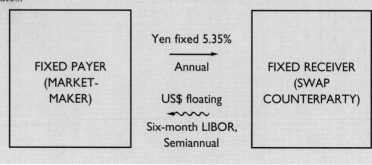

The principal amount of the swap is DM350 million, so the payments will be the specified percentages of those amounts, typically payable semiannually to match the twice-a-year LIBOR payments. The dollar payments will be six-month LIBOR, also divided by two because they are paid semiannually, multiplied by the dollar-principal amount. The latter will be DM350 million divided by the mark/dollar spot rate at the time of the swap—for example, about US$184 million at a spot rate of DM1.90 per dollar. At the end of seven years, Procter & Gamble will pay Dresdner DM350 million and receive US$184 million from Dresdner.

Variation: A Fixed-Fixed Currency Swap

So your eyes are going to glaze over if you see yet another swap diagram? We'll skip them just this once, even though there are *two* sets of swaps, for we are going to construct

Table 13.3 **A Swap-Quotation Sheet.** The quotations are given as fixed rates (or, in the U.S. case, as a spread over Treasury yields) payable or receivable against six-month U.S.-dollar LIBOR.

U.S. interest-rate swaps quoted as benchmark Treasury bond yield plus a spread

Fixed US$ vs. floating US$

Bid 8.64, Offer 8.68

Fixed foreign currency vs. floating US$

FICTIONBANK SWAP-INDICATION SHEET

Years	US$ interest-rate swaps			Currency swaps	
	Treasury curve benchmark yields S.A.	Spread (BP)		DM/$ ann.	¥/$ ann.
2	8.02	62-66		7.00-7.10	5.35-5.45
3	8.01	70-75		7.00-7.10	5.35-5.45
4	8.01	72-76		7.00-7.10	5.35-5.45
5	8.02	78-81		7.00-7.10	5.35-5.45
7	8.13	77-81		7.02-7.12	5.40-5.50
10	8.14	78-81		7.02-7.12	5.45-5.53

	Currency swaps			
Years	SFR/$ ann.	£/$ ann.	ECU/$ ann.	A$/US$ ann.
2	6.60-6.70	12.80-12.90	9.20-9.30	15.65-15.80
3	6.20-6.30	12.35-12.45	9.15-9.25	15.25-15.40
4	6.05-6.15	11.90-12.00	9.10-9.20	15.15-15.30
5	6.00-6.10	11.75-11.85	9.05-9.15	14.78-15.13
7	5.95-6.05	11.50-11.60	9.05-9.15	NA
10	5.95-6.05	11.26-11.36	9.05-9.15	NA

Currency swaps quoted against six-month US$ LIBOR. Quoting bank would pay £11.26% annual vs. US$ six-month LIBOR, or receive £11.36%.

a fixed-fixed currency swap out of two normal, fixed-for-floating currency swaps. Suppose that Kangaroo Brewing has five-year, fixed-rate Australian-dollar debt, but wishes to change it into low-interest Japanese-yen debt. Kangaroo can easily obtain quotes on conventional currency swaps (fixed against six-month U.S. dollar LIBOR) such as those in the sample swap quotation sheet in Table 13.3. The bank is willing to pay a fixed 14.78 percent Australian-dollar rate in exchange for six-month LIBOR, or receive 15.13 percent. The bank's swap quotes for Japanese yen are pay 5.35 percent, or receive 5.45 percent, against six-month LIBOR.

Kangaroo Brewing can take these quotations at face value and achieve its goal by engaging in *two* currency swaps against six-month LIBOR:

First swap: Pay floating six-month US$ LIBOR, receive fixed 14.78% Australian dollars.

Second swap: Pay fixed yen 5.45%, receive floating six-month US$ LIBOR.

Clearly the floating payments cancel out, leaving Kangaroo with a net swap that pays fixed 5.45 percent yen and receives fixed 14.87 percent "Aussie" in exchange. Of course, the bank will not force Kangaroo to go through the facade of engaging in two swaps, and instead will quote yen against Australian-dollar swap rates upon request. The quote will not differ very much from that worked out of the "synthetic" fixed-fixed currency swap worked out in the previous section.

This example illustrates the general condition that swap quotations are only a starting point for constructing and pricing the swap actually implemented in most cases.

How Swap Rates Are Determined

How do banks come up with their particular swap-rate quotations, such as those given in Table 13.3? The answer is that swap rates are determined to a large extent by yields in the corporate bond market.[9] To see why swap rates cannot differ much from corporate-bond yields, consider the choices open to each of the two parties—a corporation[10] and a bank—to a typical fixed-floating swap. The considerations are the same for currency and interest-rate swaps.

The *corporation* pays a fixed medium- to long-term rate (in exchange for LIBOR) instead of issuing a bond in the market of choice directly. If LIBOR represents the corporation's short-term cost of funds, the fixed side can be compared directly with the rate at which it can issue a bond. The swap rate cannot exceed the comparable bond rate. The more issuers arbitrage between markets using swaps, the more swap rates will be driven toward the point of indifference between bond yields and swap rates for a particular class of corporations. Of course, this will apply only to corporations that have ready access to the swap market, which means well-regarded credits.

On the *bank* side, the swapping bank must hedge the fixed payments being received by issuing fixed-rate debt itself, or by doing another swap with a corporation or bank, so that somewhere in the chain, the original swap is offset by a sale of fixed-rate debt. Hence the general level of swap rates cannot be below the rate that such issuers would have to pay in the fixed-rate market. With a few exceptions, the most active banks are rated approximately AA credits. In a competitive, well-developed market, therefore, the swap rate roughly represents the rate at which AA banks or corporations can borrow.

---

[9]Indeed, the swap rate for a particular maturity is a very good indicative yield for good-quality corporate bonds.

[10]Many swaps are interbank. That is not important for our purposes, because the prices in the interbank market must ultimately be constrained by "customer" swaps—those done with corporations or governmental entities.

Within these parameters, the market swap rate may deviate from this generality. Some banks and even corporations use swaps not for financing purposes but for selective positioning and hedging. Hence swap rates can be influenced by strong interest-rate or currency expectations. When changed expectations exert a forceful influence on swap rates, a temporary "window" may be created, giving ready borrowers a chance to obtain cheaper swapped financing. Any particular bank may quote slightly off-market rates for particular transactions when the swapper's "book" is imbalanced; she'll try to attract the swap she needs by quoting an attractive rate. A large-scale financing and swap program, such as those done from time to time by the World Bank, can also create a temporary imbalance in the market. And as in all these markets, banks will tend to quote less advantageous rates for odd-sized, especially smaller, transactions.

EXAMPLE 13.1   **Marimekko Negotiates a Swap to Obtain Cheaper Funding**

The Problem. Pentti Hakkonen is the treasurer of the international division of the Finnish clothing and accessories company Marimekko Oy. The company has recently undertaken a major expansion of its sales to Japan and is seeking ways to obtain fixed-rate yen financing. On a recent visit to London, Hakkonen has held discussions with a number of banks about Marimekko's financing options. He found that Marimekko could obtain a syndicated bank loan facility at LIBOR plus ⅛ percent, adjustable quarterly. One Japanese bank had suggested a Euroyen bond. Taking fees into account, the all-in cost of a four-year yen deal would be 6.55 percent. A third possibility was to rely on fixed-rate U.S.-dollar financing at the subsidized rate of 8.00 percent from the Finnish government's export credit agency. Upon his return, Hakkonen had obtained quotations for four-year swaps from several banks. The best rates he had been able to obtain were:

> *Interest-rate swap:* U.S. Treasury + 75–80 basis points, semiannual
>
> *Basis swap:* Six-month LIBOR against three-month LIBOR + 5–8 basis points
>
> *Currency swap:* yen/US$, 6.70–6.80%, annual

The four-year U.S. Treasury yield at the time was 7.70 percent. Hakkonen's task was to couple the swaps with the financing alternatives in such a way as to express them on a comparable basis, and then to find the cheapest way to get fixed-rate yen funds. How should he do this?

A Solution. The first step is to lay out the three different ways of achieving fixed-yen debt, as shown in Table 13.4.

Next, Hakkonen can obtain *approximate* costs of each of the second two alternatives by summing the coupon flows and exchanges, taking care to select the appropriate side of the pay/receive spread in the swap quotations, as shown in Table 13.5.

Thus a first pass at costing out the financing choices favors the Finnish government loan—hardly a surprise. To get a more precise comparison, Hakkonen must now take account of the fact that basis points cannot simply be added or subtracted without regard to the *timing* of the payments or their *currency of denomination*. Basis points received earlier (every three months rather than semiannually, or semiannually rather than annually) are more valuable than those received later. And basis points denominated in the stronger, lower-interest currency (such as the yen) are more valuable than those received in the weaker currency. Hakkonen will also want a swap that eliminates currency risk to the company. As it stands, the currency swaps would leave Marimekko with basic yen interest but some net U.S.-dollar flows. Finally, in the second and third alternatives, the two separate swaps will, in practice, be combined into one, and Marimekko might be able to

Table 13.4   *Marimekko's Financing Alternatives*

Method 1	Method 2	Method 3
• Borrow fixed-rate yen at 6.55%	• Borrow floating-rate dollars at three-month LIBOR + ⅛% • Convert three-month LIBOR into six-month LIBOR via a basis swap • Convert six-month US$ LIBOR into four-year fixed yen via a ¥/$ currency swap	• Borrow fixed-rate dollars from the government at 8% • Convert these into floating six-month LIBOR via an interest-rate swap • Convert six-month US$ LIBOR into four-year fixed-yen via a ¥/$ currency swap

Table 13.5   *Marimekko's Financing Alternatives* (cont.)

	Method 2 (borrow floating dollars and swap)		Method 3 (borrow fixed dollars and swap)	
	Pay	Receive	Pay	Receive
Borrowing	3-mo $LIBOR + .125%		4-yr $8.00%	
Swap to convert to 6-month US$ LIBOR	6-mo $LIBOR	3-mo $LIBOR + .05%	6-mo $LIBOR	4-yr $8.45%
Swap to convert to 4-year yen	4-yr ¥6.80%	6-mo $LIBOR	4-yr ¥6.80%	6-mo $LIBOR
Net cost (approx.)	4-yr ¥6.875%		4-yr ¥6.35%	

obtain better terms on the combined quotation. What Pentti Hakkonen will now do, therefore, is request quotations for a swap in which Marimekko receives fixed U.S.-dollars, 8 percent annually, and pays fixed yen annually, for four years. The lowest quote on the fixed-yen side will be his final cost of funds.

Basis-Point Equivalents: The Theory and an Easy Method

Swap deals are seldom done at precisely the rates quoted on a standard quote sheet such as shown in Table 13.3. Almost every swap deal entails making adjustments to the fixed side, the floating side, or both. Understanding how this is done is essential to calculating gains from swap financing in practice.

In most swaps, one side (usually the market-making bank) accommodates the other by adjusting the level or timing or currency of payments to suit the other's peculiar financing or investment requirements. For example, Chase Manhattan Bank's standard 10-year sterling/dollar swap quotation may be sterling 12.10–12.20 annual against six-month US$ LIBOR flat, whereas ICI, the British chemical company, may need to receive six-month LIBOR − ¼% and to pay semiannual sterling coupons. Chase might then come back and say, "Okay, you pay sterling 11.91 semi; we pay six-month LIBOR less 25." Chase has lowered its swap rate from 12.20 to 11.91 because ICI is giving up 25 basis points on the dollar side. Chase's concession is more than 25 basis points because dollars for future delivery are worth more than pounds sterling and because Chase is getting half of the annual sterling interest six months earlier.

The principle of converting basis points from annual to semiannual is, of course, the time value of money. Yields quoted semiannually are lower than annual yields because they can be compounded more frequently. Based on equal terminal values,

$$\left(1 + \frac{I_X}{X}\right)^X = \left(1 + \frac{I_Y}{Y}\right)^Y$$

where X is the number of interest periods per year for the one rate, I_X, and Y is the number of interest periods per year for the other rate, I_Y. Rearrange to solve for one rate given the other:

$$I_X = \left[\left(1 + \frac{I_Y}{Y}\right)^{Y/X} - 1\right]X$$

For example, the semiannual equivalent of an annual rate of 12.20 percent is 11.85 percent.

The theory behind converting basis points to be paid in the future from one currency to another is based on the assumption that they can be converted through the forward market. In principle, therefore, the method is to convert each basis-point payment or receipt into monetary units, translate at the appropriate forward rate for each date in the future that the payment is made, and reconvert into percentage points.

That's a bit cumbersome. Here's an alternative method that has stronger intuitive appeal for many. Basis points are simply fractions of a percentage point, and so are independent of currency units. They are paid periodically just like an annuity. So we can find the *present value* of a series of basis points by using the usual present-value formula for a series of equal payments, taking into account the frequency of payments. The equivalent basis points in the other currency is that present value, expressed as an annuity (using the other currency's interest rate and payment frequency). The swap rates serve as an approximation for the annuity interest rates in the respective currencies. This method is not perfect, but it's good enough for most purposes. In the Chase example above, if the 10-year U.S.-dollar swap rate is 9 percent, then 25 basis points in dollars would be equivalent to 28.7 basis points in pounds sterling.

To see how we get this, first find the present value of 25 U.S.-dollar basis points $(BP_{US\$})$, paid semiannually, at 9 percent:

$$PV(25BP_{US\$}) = \sum_{t=1}^{20} \frac{12.5}{(1 + .045)^t} = 162.6$$

Next, find the sterling annuity equivalent of this present value, at the sterling swap rate of 11.9 percent paid annually:

Annuity value of 162.6 @ 11.91% (Annual) = $28.67BP_{UK\pounds}$

A general formula for finding BP_A, the basis points equivalent in currency A of BP_B, a certain number of basis points in currency B, is

$$BP_A = BP_B \left[\frac{\left(1 + \dfrac{r_B}{m_B}\right)^{nm_B} - 1}{r_B \left(1 + \dfrac{r_B}{m_B}\right)^{nm_B}} \right] \left[\frac{r_A \left(1 + \dfrac{r_A}{m_A}\right)^{nm_A}}{\left(1 + \dfrac{r_A}{m_A}\right)^{nm_A} - 1} \right]$$

where

r is the annuity interest rate (or swap rate)
n is the number of years of the swap
m is the number of times per year the interest is paid.

This calculation may look complicated, but it's easy enough to program in a spreadsheet. If you plan to use this method in practice, be sure to adjust the interest rate to a realistic rate of return that could be obtained on an annuity investment, or that would have to be paid on an annuity borrowing.

EXAMPLE 13.2   **Turning a Swap Quotation into a Cost-of-Funds Estimate**

The Problem. Ardath Deming, Ford's International treasurer, woke up one morning with the urge to concoct some German-mark debt before dinner. Ford's Eurocommercial paper was costing it about LIBOR − ⅜%. Deming figured this level could be maintained for the next two years. She wondered what the all-in cost would be if she swapped some of this short-term debt into two-year fixed-rate DM funding. The Reuters screen showed the following indicative swap quotations:

Years	Treasury Yields	U.S. Swap Spreads (Semiannual)	DM/$ Swaps (Annual)
2	9.20	55–59 bp	6.70–6.76
5	9.45	57–62 bp	7.05–7.09
7	9.77	70–75 bp	7 18–7 26
10	9.80	70–75 bp	7.30–7.34

A Solution. Like me, Ardath Deming finds it helpful to draw diagrams. She'll assume that Ford will issue 180-day ECP for the next two years at LIBOR − ⅜, and that she'll have to pay the offer side of the two-year swap market. (In practice, she hopes to negotiate a better rate with a swap dealer.)

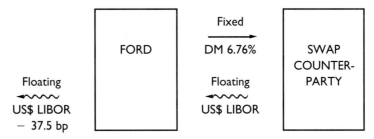

The swap Ford really needs is to receive floating LIBOR − 37.5 basis points, not LIBOR flat. What rate would that translate to in DM terms? Using the formula given in the previous section, 37.5 U.S. basis points translates into 36.6 DM basis points. So Ford's all-in cost will be about 6.39 percent.

Swap Valuation

In this section we will show that the cash flows in swaps are so like those in conventional fixed-income securities that a swap can be valued using bond-valuation techniques. (Alternative methods, such as decomposing swaps into a series of forward interest-rate contracts[11] or the "zero-coupon method" described in the Box 13.4, are merely refinements of the bond-valuation approach.) Swaps are like bonds or money-market instruments in that they are no more or less than a series of contractual cash flows; hence they rise and fall in value just as fixed-income corporate obligations do when interest rates fluctuate. The "duration" of a swap, like that of a bond, measures its price sensitivity to interest-rate fluctuations (see Appendix 13.1). Currency swaps change value as exchange rates change. Understanding swap valuation helps determine the appropriate compensatory payments when swaps are sold or unwound, and how they should be treated when a trading position is marked to market, and who loses what in the event of a default.[12]

BOX 13.4

The Zero-Coupon Method of Swap Valuation

Swaps are now big business, and the major players constantly seek small arbitrage opportunities. One such opportunity sometimes arises from the shortcomings of the conventional net-present-value formula: because all cash flows are discounted at the same rate, inaccurate valuation can result. So most of the major players now use the zero-coupon method of swap valuation rather than the bond method described in the text. Under the zero-coupon method, all coupons and the principal to be paid or received are valued individually by discounting at a zero-coupon rate for the corresponding maturity; the totals in each currency are summed and the net value, at the prevailing spot rate, is the swap's value.

Zero-coupon Treasury yields are computed using the so-called bootstrap method, which is increasingly used in the United States to value fixed-income securities. The method entails using the six-month and twelve-month Treasury-bill yields and the 1.5-year Treasury-note yield to solve for the 1.5-year zero yield, then using all three zero yields to find the 2-year zero yield, and so forth, for a whole spectrum of maturities. Swap rates are expressed as a spread over the Treasury zeroes.

Similarly, forward-exchange rates are computed using the ratio of zero-coupon-bond prices, because the latter represent the cumulative interest rate in each currency, so the forward rate becomes the spot rate, adjusted for the cumulative, compounded interest-rate differential. The computation is simply

$$\text{Forward-exchange rate} = \frac{(1 + R_t^{US})^t}{(1 + R_t^{UK})^t}$$

where R_t^{US} and R_t^{UK} are the zero-coupon bond yields in dollars and sterling, respectively.

Using the zero-coupon method for bonds, forward contracts, and swaps ensures that the three markets are closer to equilibrium—that is, that fewer arbitrage opportunities arise.

---

[11]An explanation of an interest-rate swap as a portfolio of forward contracts may be found in Clifford W. Smith, Charles W. Smithson, and Lee M. Wakeman, "The Market for Interest Rate Swaps," *Financial Management,* Winter 1988, 34–44.

[12]The reader should note that this section is written for expositional purposes rather than for precision in swap valuation. When swaps must be valued in practice, it is often found that the market is illiquid and that imperfections prevent one swap being readily replaced with another. The balance-sheet approach to swap valuation is a good starting point; but the only precise value of a swap is *the price at which it can be replicated in the market with a replacement counterparty*.

Swaps Viewed as Bonds on a Balance Sheet

A typical interest-rate swap consists of fixed cash flows on one side and floating-rate flows on the other. The fixed side can be treated for valuation purposes like a bond, whereas the floating side is like a money market instrument (or, more accurately, like a floating-rate note). A bank or corporation engaging in a swap is long one, short the other. (For example, it may "own" the bond side and have "issued" the money-market-instrument side.) Let us illustrate this with an example, deferring consideration of credit risk until later so that we can concentrate on market risk alone at this point. In our first example of an interest-rate swap, Toyo Trust entered into the following U.S.-dollar fixed-floating swap with Sammi Steel:[13]

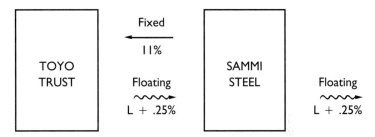

This is a five-year swap. Let's look at Toyo's side in a balance-sheet framework. Toyo is receiving fixed, which is like owning a five-year Treasury bond. It is paying six-month LIBOR, which is like having issued a six-month CD, and rolling it over until maturity; in other words, it's more like issuing a floating-rate note (FRN). In either case, the value of the floating side is like that of a six-month U.S. Treasury bill; it fluctuates with money market rates in between reset dates, but is worth par at each interest reset date because the interest is reset to a market level. We can illustrate Toyo's swap as follows:

Toyo's interest-rate swap:
receive fixed, pay floating

"ASSETS"	"LIABILITIES"
Receiving fixed US$ 11% semiannual for 5 years	Paying floating 6-mo US$ LIBOR + .25% semiannual for 5 years
Like a 5-year bond	*Like a 5-year FRN*

The value of the swap is the value of the net worth of this stylized balance sheet. Of course, the notional principal in a swap is the same on the asset side as on the liability side, so the principal payments at maturity in the balance sheet cancel one another out and have no effect.

Changes in the value of Toyo's interest-rate swap arise purely from changes in interest rates. For example, if five-year rates fall by 1 percent, the bond price increases and the swap's value rises by the amount, minus any rise in the liability side that might result from a fall in the short-term rate. (The latter depends on the amount of time before the

---

[13]In the original example the fixed side of the swap was "Treasury plus 1 percent." Here we assume the U.S. Treasury yield at the time the swap was done was 10 percent.

next reset date. On each reset date the floating side returns to par, so all that matters is the change in value of the fixed side.) Because the swap is symmetrical, whatever we've said about Toyo's swap is equal and opposite for Sammi's swap. What Toyo gains, Sammi loses, and vice versa.

As for currency swaps, the method is identical. The "receive" payments are expressed as an asset, and the "pay" flows as a liability. Take Procter & Gamble's DM/dollar currency swap described earlier. Fixed 6 percent deutschemarks, paid annually, are exchanged for floating U.S.-dollar LIBOR, paid semiannually; and at the end the principal amounts are reexchanged.

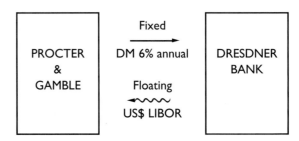

From P&G's point of view, the swap is like a seven-year U.S.-dollar floating-rate note paying six-month LIBOR funded with a seven-year DM bond. The swap principal was DM350 million, and the dollar equivalent was US$184 million. We can treat P&G's swap using a swap balance sheet:

P&G's currency swap:
receive floating US$, pay fixed DM

"ASSETS"	"LIABILITIES"
Receiving floating 6-mo US$ LIBOR semiannual for 7 years	Paying fixed DM 6% annual for 7 years
Principal US$184 million	Principal DM350 million
Like a 7-year US$ FRN	*Like a 7-year DM bond*

Again, the value of P&G's swap equals the "net worth" of this balance sheet. Interest-rate changes can affect this net worth; for example, a rise in German rates will decrease the value of the liability side, thus increasing the value of the swap. But the major influence on a currency swap is a change in the exchange rate between the dollar and the deutschemark. In part, the reason is that currencies are more volatile than interest rates, but a more important factor is that, unlike interest rate swaps, the final principal exchange matters a great deal because the amounts are in two different currencies. At the initiation of Procter's swap, the dollar is worth 1.90 marks. If the dollar falls below DM1.90, P&G's swap drops in value; if it rises, the swap's value rises, too.

The Net Worth of a Swap Is Zero at First

When an interest rate or a currency swap is initiated, it has neither positive nor negative value. Until rates change, the asset side equals the liability side of the swap, be it a currency swap or an interest-rate swap. Toyo's bond-like asset and its FRN-like liability are both worth 100; P&G's $184 million FRN "asset" is equal in value to its DM350 bond "debt" until the exchange rate (or an interest rate) changes. So the "net worth" of any swap seen as a balance sheet is zero at first. Of course, if the swap's value were to be nonzero, then one side would have to compensate the other side for engaging in the swap, and such compensation is unusual.[14]

Valuation as Rates and Currencies Change

We have said that a swap has a "value" after initiation equal to the net worth of the balance sheet representing the cash inflows and outflows of the swap. One measure of the sensitivity of an interest-rate swap's value to changes in interest rates is **duration**; how this applies to swaps is described in Appendix 13.1. As the section on swap unwinds that follows will demonstrate, a company can actually realize the value of a swap's gains (or its losses) before maturity if it wishes. If the interest rates or exchange rate at which the swap was contracted have changed, we can discover what it's worth by calculating its net worth; here's how:

Assume it is exactly two years into P&G's swap, and that German rates have risen to 7 percent while the dollar/mark exchange rate is now 1.75 marks per dollar. What has happened to the value of P&G's swap? Does it have a positive net worth ("in the money") or a negative net worth ("out of the money")? To answer that, all we have to do is value each side of the swap balance sheet as it now stands.

P&G's currency swap two years later:
receive floating US$, pay fixed DM

"ASSETS"	"LIABILITIES"
Receiving floating 6-mo US$ LIBOR semiannual for 5 years	Paying fixed DM 6% annual for 5 years
Principal US$184 million	Principal DM350 million
Like a 5-year US$ FRN	*Like a 5-year DM bond*
VALUE TODAY: US$184 mm (unchanged because we are at an interest reset date)	DM VALUE TODAY: PV @ 7% = DM335.65mm = US$191.8mm (@ DM1.75/$)

Net Worth = −$7.8mm

The net effect is that Procter & Gamble's currency swap is out of the money. Although the DM value of the swap's "liability" side dropped in DM terms thanks to higher German rates, the DM's rise against the dollar increased the dollar value of the contractual outpayments to $191.8 million, $7.8 million higher than the value of the inpayments. (The latter remains at $184 million because we are at a reset date.)

---

[14]But not unheard-of; see the section in this chapter entitled Off-Market Swaps.

The general valuation formula for a receive-fixed, pay-floating-interest rate swap is:

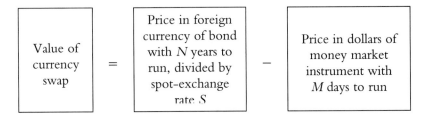

where N is the remaining life of the swap, and M is the time to the next interest-reset date. The sign is reversed for a receive-floating, pay-fixed swap.

The equivalent calculation for a received-fixed-nondollar, pay-floating-dollars currency swap is:

$$\boxed{\begin{array}{c}\text{Value of}\\\text{currency}\\\text{swap}\end{array}} = \boxed{\begin{array}{c}\text{Price in foreign}\\\text{currency of bond}\\\text{with } N \text{ years to}\\\text{run, divided by}\\\text{spot-exchange}\\\text{rate } S\end{array}} - \boxed{\begin{array}{c}\text{Price in dollars of}\\\text{money market}\\\text{instrument with}\\M \text{ days to run}\end{array}}$$

where today's spot exchange rate S is in foreign currency units per U.S. dollars.

To summarize, the three elements that change the value of a currency swap are

- exchange-rate change.
- interest-rate change on the "fixed" side.
- interest-rate change on the "floating" side.

The two elements that affect the value of an interest-rate swap are

- interest-rate change on the "fixed" side.
- interest-rate change on the "floating" side.

These are listed in rough order of importance. Indeed, the last factor, the interest rate on the floating side, becomes negligible if the swap is valued on an interest-reset date.

Off-Market Swaps

We have seen how a swap can have a positive or negative value when changing market conditions cause the swap's contractual interest rates or exchange rate to be out of line with current market rates. Some swaps are designed that way from the beginning. The parties will agree, perhaps, that the fixed-rate side of the swap should be set at a rate quite different from prevailing swap rates. Such swaps are called *off-market swaps*.

Suppose that the prevailing swap rate for a three-year French-franc–U.S.-dollar currency swap is 9.50 percent annual against six-month US$ LIBOR. I ask you to do such a swap with me but I want you to pay me 10.50 percent instead. According to our method of swap valuation, my side of this swap will be *in the money* right from the start. By how much? The present value of a FF100 million three-year bond paying 10.50 percent discounted at the market yield of 9.50 percent is FF102.5 million, so this swap is worth 2.5 percent of its notional principal. From your point of view, the swap is out of the money by an equal amount. Hence, to induce you to enter into the swap with me, I will have to pay you FF2.50 for every FF100 of notional principal.

Why do people want to do off-market swaps? A common use is to create an equal and opposite swap to offset an older swap whose rates are out of line with current interest rates and exchange rates. Or I may wish to convert an existing fixed-interest borrowing that was done earlier at rates different from today's. Yet another purpose, illustrated in Example 13.3, is in the context of *asset swaps*—the transformation of the currency and/or interest-rate characteristics of an *investment* rather than a liability. The application exemplifies a common use of asset swaps: a financial institution, seeking floating-rate U.S.-dollar investments, finds a mispriced Eurobond. He buys the cheap bond and combines it with a fixed-floating currency swap to create a synthetic U.S.-dollar floating-rate asset. Other varieties of asset swaps are of course also possible.

EXAMPLE 13.3 Application: An Asset Swap for ABN-AMRO

Swaps are used to transform assets as well as liabilities. Such was the purpose of Dirk Woudhuys' call to the swap desk of Citibank London one morning for a quote on a three-year ECU/US$ swap. (Citi's reply: 8.55–8.60, annual.) As investments manager for the London branch of the Dutch bank ABN-AMRO, Dirk was on the constant lookout for floating-rate assets that would earn his bank a spread over LIBOR without taking excessive risk. Woudhuys' intention was to create a *synthetic floating-rate note* by purchasing a fixed-rate nondollar bond and coupling it with a currency swap.

First, ABN-AMRO would take advantage of an opportunity to buy ECU20 million face value of the European Investment Bank 7.50 percent European Currency Unit bonds maturing in three years' time from Banque Bruxelles Lambert. These triple-A-rated bonds were priced at 96.70 to yield 8.80 percent annual, about 25 basis points above the yield on comparable AAA Eurobonds at the time. Then Woudhuys would arrange an ECU20 million, three-year currency swap: ABN-AMRO would pay fixed ECU 7.5 percent to Citibank (or another counterparty) and receive floating US$ LIBOR plus a spread in exchange. Because the counterparty would be receiving a below-market fixed ECU rate and paying above LIBOR, ABN-AMRO would have to pay an up-front sum for this off-market swap.

Woudhuys wanted to negotiate the swap such that ABN-AMRO would pay exactly 3.30 points—that is, 3.30 percent of ECU20 million—for the swap. Then his total cost would be 100 points (96.70 for the bond and 3.30 for the swap)—that is, the full ECU20 million. At the current spot rate of $1.25 per ECU, ABN-AMRO's investment in the synthetic U.S. dollar "floater" would be $24 million.

At a yield of 8.60 percent (Citi's swap quote), Dirk worked out that a swap of ECU 7.5 percent against six-month LIBOR flat would cost ECU 2.80 percent of par, leaving 0.50 percent. Dirk used the current U.S.-dollar three-year swap rate of 9.15 percent to compute the annuity equivalent of 50 basis points up front. He estimated 9.5 basis points every six months for three years—that is, 19 basis points per annum. LIBOR plus 19 for a triple-A credit? "Better than we can earn by lending," he thought, "but I had better draw the little boxes before calling Citi for a firm quote on this off-market swap. At the start we'll pay 96.7 to Bruxelles for the EIB bond and 3.3 to Citi for the swap, for a total outlay of $24 million":

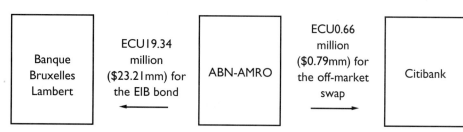

"Then during the life of the bond, with the swap in place, we'll pass our EIB coupons onto Citi and receive LIBOR plus 19 basis points in exchange.":

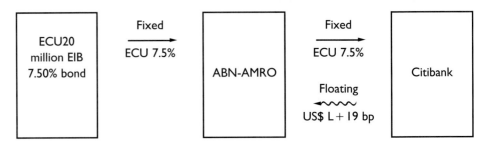

"At the end we'll give the ECU20 million principal from the bond to Citi and they'll give us $24 million in exchange. *Geen moeilijkheid* (No problem)!"

Trading Swaps

In the early days of the swap market, banks served as matchmakers or almost passive intermediaries between two counterparties, matching a swap on one side with an identical swap on the other side. But it was time-consuming to find two or more companies with equal and opposite requirements for each and every transaction, and the swap market only really got off the ground when commercial banks adopted a different approach. They found that by warehousing, or "positioning" swaps, they were able to supply liquidity to the market and customers were willing to give their custom to swap desks that could provide a variety of swaps rapidly. Just as in other trading operations, once volume reached a certain level, the net exposure of the intermediary could be held to quite a low level. In addition, the more sophisticated banks soon recognized that their swap book could be integrated with their "natural" asset/liability structure in terms of both interest-rate risk and foreign-exchange positions.[15] Although a few "structured" swaps are still done, especially in fringe currencies, most swaps are standard, commoditylike transactions nowadays; banks stand ready to take standard swap commitments on the assumption that they will be able to "lay off" the market risk in the interbank swap market or elsewhere.

One way to think of this is to characterize swaps as being in the "mature" stage of their product life cycle. They are standardized and liquid, and high competition has driven trading margins down to a minimum. The spreads at which interest-rate swaps trade fell from about 75 basis points in 1982 to 5 basis points by the early 1990s.

The Interbank Market: Banks and Brokers

The bulk of the swap market today is made up of interbank swaps. Some industrial corporations, like Intel, Rhone-Poulenc, and several of the cash-rich Japanese concerns, trade swaps aggressively as part of their treasury operations. Some investment banks like Morgan Stanley and insurance companies like AIG run swaps trading groups, typically through specially capitalized subsidiaries. However, the need to evaluate the credit risk of counterparties and the capital required to bear swap risk dictate that the bulk of swaps is done by commercial banks. Moreover, because so much of swap trading is designed

---

[15]Not all banks have been able to overcome the organizational and information-management problems. Thus, one can still find a swap group trying to accommodate customers, and quite another group of swappers who work for the bank's treasury to support the institution's own asset/liability management.

for position taking and adjustment, swap traders do much of their swap business with other swap traders.

A bank seeking to put on or take off a swap position will usually scan the swap quotation pages on Reuters and Telerate to see whose prices seem to be the most competitive, although screen prices are at best indicative. Better still is to call the traders to get a feel for their positions and requirements. For a wider range of choices, a swapper will contact one of the FX/money market *brokers* that serve as a clearing house for swap traders. A broker such as Tullett & Tokyo has swap pages on Reuters and will be able to quickly get in touch with potential swap counterparties for both interest-rate and currency swaps.

Running a Swap Book

These days only a small proportion of the swaps done by the major banks is directly tied to a financing. Rather, banks actively swap with one another to offset positions taken with customers, or to manage an asset/liability position that arises from their asset and liability mismatches, or to take a view on interest rates, or to take advantage of a temporary arbitrage opportunity in the swap market.

The swaps market is dominated by **market-makers** who run a book or warehouse of swaps, caps, and other derivatives. Market makers such as J.P. Morgan Bank are willing to give two-way quotations on standard swaps; they stand ready to "receive fixed" interest in exchange for a floating rate, or to "pay fixed." They typically have an actively managed portfolio of swaps of different kinds on their books. They manage the market risks of the overall portfolio rather than those of any one swap. Because they do not rely on matching one swap with an equal and opposite one, they are able to assume more complex swaps. Their quotations on standard swaps are published on Reuters screens and elsewhere, and they may be willing to give tailor-made quotations on nonstandard swaps. More complex swaps are more difficult to hedge, particularly if they involve optionlike features, so quotations on these are scarcer and less competitively priced.

In effect, such banks are running a swap portfolio or "book," with fixed-receive swaps on the one side and fixed-pay swaps on the other side. Every fixed-receive, floating-pay swap is analogous to what banks call a "positive mismatch," because it is like funding short term and lending long term. Put differently, it is like being "long" in the bond market. So a bank that wants to run an interest-rate swap-trading book in a particular currency (and there are many) has only to draw on its interest-rate risk traders for the skills required to manage swap-trading positions.

Swaps are also employed to run so-called gapping positions, in which long positions at some maturities are offset by short positions at slightly different maturities to take advantage of perceived yield-curve anomalies. In fact, this is the typical business of interest-rate traders, as they can take bigger absolute positions in this market with less risk than betting on movements of the whole yield curve.

Running a currency swap book is a little more difficult, of course, because it involves long-term currency positions as well as interest-rate positions. A bank that engages in a currency swap will want, as its first order of business, to eliminate the bulk of the currency risk by taking a short position in the foreign-exchange market to offset its long position arising from the swap. That risk reduction can be done as simply as it is done in short-term foreign-exchange trading. For example, if you have just agreed to a currency swap in which your bank is receiving fixed Italian lira and paying floating dollars, you are long on the lira—exposed to any fall in the lira against the dollar. Unless you are doing this to balance an existing short position in the lira, or unless you are able to do a profitable countervailing swap immediately (unlikely), it might be advisable to sell lira spot. The spot market, with two-day delivery, is the quickest and most efficient way to take a temporary long or short position in a currency. Later you can look for opportunities to put on a "short" lira currency swap, one that offers a more appropriate match for your lira/dollar swap, but until that time you can manage your currency-rate risk in the short-term foreign-exchange market and your interest-rate risk with interest-rate swaps, futures, future-rate agreements (FRAs), and of course short-term assets and liabilities.

Analogously, a bank that agrees to an interest-rate swap is concerned about changes in the general level of rates, so its first action would be to offset the swap, temporarily, with a long or short position in the government-bond market or in government-bond futures. Later, the cash or futures position can be replaced with a duration-matched swap position.

Swap Unwinds

Corporations use swaps not only to lower their borrowing costs but also as a flexible instrument to manage interest-rate and currency exposure in a flexible fashion. For this purpose, the ability to "unwind" a swap is helpful. To *unwind a swap* means to terminate it before the date of final exchange of payments.

For example, recall Toyo's interest-rate swap with Sammi Steel. Six months after the swap took place, rates may have fallen. Toyo now decides to fix its cost of funds again, human nature being what it is. Naturally, Toyo's swap manager cannot simply walk away from his commitment. What can he do? One option is to enter into an equal and opposite new swap, with a different counterparty, that defeases (cancels out) all the cash flows on the original one. Toyo could telephone a swaps trader, such as Bankers Trust, who is willing to enter into a second, offsetting swap with Toyo. An alternative is that Bankers Trust will assume the remaining swap exchanges with Sammi, but this only works if Sammi is judged by Bankers Trust to be an acceptable counterparty. In effect, the swap has been "reversed" (or traded), and doing so will produce a gain or loss that equals the "value" of the original swap.[16] The way in which this value is realized is through the up-front payment that is necessary to compensate one or other party to the new swap for agreeing to do an off-market swap.

Had Toyo done its original swap with a professional swap market-maker such as Chemical Bank, a third alternative might be possible: Chemical might be willing to cancel the swap altogether, again with a payment changing hands that approximately equals the swap's value. For an example of this, see Application 13.2, The Aussie Unswap, at the end of this chapter.

Swaps Versus Long-Dated Forwards

Anything that can be done with swaps can also be done with forward contracts, although with somewhat different results in terms of the timing of cash flows. A currency swap converts a long-term debt from one currency into another, which is what a short-term forward-exchange contract does for money-market instruments. It's easy to use a forward contract when the instrument is in effect a zero-coupon security, such as a three-month CD. But to hedge a bond, you would have to sell each of the annual or semiannual

---

[16]As Appendix 13.2 explains, swap agreements these days allow for the assignment of a swap to a new counterparty, as long as both original counterparties agree.

Figure 13.1   ***Equivalence of Long-Dated Forward and Currency Swap.***   Swap pays interest-rate differential over time; forward contract incorporates compounded interest differential into single final payment.

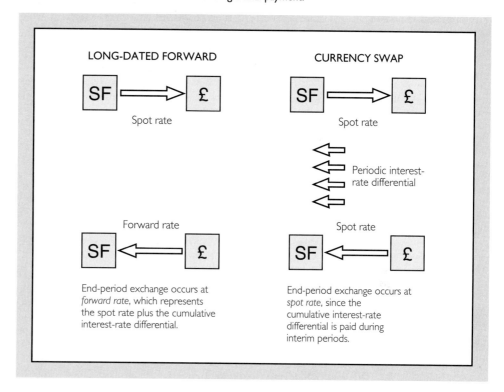

coupons as well as the final principal with a string of forward contracts. Professional arbitrage between the two markets ensures that the result will be about the same, but corporate borrowers and institutional investors dislike the uneven cash flows that result from converting a claim via a series of forward contracts.[17]

Another way of looking at the relationship between currency swaps and long-dated forward contracts is illustrated in Figure 13.1. From interest-rate parity, the forward price in Swiss francs of one pound sterling equals the spot price plus the compounded interest-rate differential. In a currency swap, an equivalent exchange takes place; however, the interest-rate differential is paid over time, leaving only the spot rate to be paid at the end.[18]

Interest-rate swaps can be replicated directly with futures contracts, or their over-the-counter cousins, future-rate agreements (FRAs). The latter entail a cash payment that is the difference between some fixed-in-advance rate and whatever the market rate (usually LIBOR) turns out to be. A strip of FRAs produces much the same effect as an interest-rate swap, and traders use one to hedge the other. (A "strip" is a series of FRAs done back to back, covering the maturity of the swap.)

---

[17]Some of the biggest corporate borrowers say they don't care—a bond, a swapped bond, or one hedged with forwards are all just a string of cash flows. They'll take whatever produces the lowest internal rate of return.

[18]This representation was suggested by George Hongchoy.

The Credit Risk of Swaps

In the Procter & Gamble currency swap whose value we estimated, P&G had lost and Dresdner had gained from the change in German rates and in the German mark. P&G would have to pay the value of the swap, and Dresdner would have to be compensated for canceling the contract. This also means that Dresdner would incur an equivalent loss if Procter should default on the swap at this point. Had the DM headed south instead of north during the first two years of the swap, P&G would be the one worrying. More generally, each party to a swap faces mutual potential credit risk (or "counterparty risk") arising from the possibility of default after interest rates have moved.

Market Risk and Credit Risk

Our "balance sheet" approach to swap valuation demonstrated that every change in interest rates or exchange rates affects each party to a swap, in equal and opposite ways. Every change in interest rates or exchange rates, therefore, changes the exposure of one party to the other. At first the value of the swap is zero. As soon as market rates change, however, the swap becomes "in the money" for one party and "out of the money" for the counterparty. *Every in-the-money swap entails credit exposure, because the value of the swap is an amount owed by the counterparty, just like a loan.* The greater the movements of market interest rates and exchange rates, the greater the likely exposure of one party or the other. *Thus credit risk is intimately tied to market risk.*

Estimating Exposure[19]

To estimate the magnitude of exposure that a counterparty faces when engaging in a currency swap, we return to the "balance sheet" approach introduced earlier. For example, in an interest-rate swap, the fixed-rate *payer* in a fixed/floating intermediary swap can be viewed as an *issuer* of a fixed-rate security and the *purchaser* of a floating-rate note.[20] In turn, the floating-rate *payer* can be viewed as the issuer of a floater and the buyer of a fixed-rate security. Consider, then, the credit risks faced by the intermediary (Sakura Bank) that has undertaken equal offsetting U.S.-dollar interest-rate swaps vis-a-vis two different counterparties in the following box diagram:

| TNT Australia | → Fixed US$ 9.60% / ~ Floating US$ LIBOR | SAKURA BANK | → Fixed US$ 9.50% / ~ Floating US$ LIBOR | Keppel Shipping |

---

[19]This section borrows from "Interest Rate and Currency Swaps: Theory, Mechanics, and Risks" by Gunter Dufey, University of Michigan, unpublished working paper.

[20]See James Bicksler and Andrew H. Chen, "An Economic Analysis of Interest Rate Swaps," *Journal of Finance,* July 1986, 652.

If interest rates rise,[21] Sakura's swap vis-a-vis TNT Australia loses value,[22] the swap vis-a-vis Keppel gains value. Sakura now has an exposure to Keppel Shipping in Singapore. If Keppel defaults, Sakura incurs a loss equal to the value of the swap. The swap vis-a-vis TNT Australia is unaffected, because Sakura must continue to make floating payments to TNT and receive the below-market fixed payments of 9.60 percent. (A swap to replace Keppel's would provide a lower fixed payment.) If TNT Australia goes bankrupt, on the other hand, Sakura loses nothing and may even gain if TNT's creditors don't notice that TNT has an in-the-money swap (fat chance of that). From the perspective of the intermediary, then, for a loss to occur, two events must coincide: the counterparty must (a) default *and* (b) the market must have changed in such a way as to cause its financial condition to have deteriorated. Although there is definitely a positive correlation between these events, their movement together is by no means perfectly correlated.[23]

How can this help a swapper measure credit exposure? It's easy enough to calculate the exposure at the time of the default—that is, the *ex post* loss. However, when making credit decisions, this risk has to be judged *ex ante*. Because the magnitude of loss depends on *future* interest-rate movements, which are, by definition, unknown, such judgments are difficult to make. Historical data are of limited use, because changes in the political/economic environment can affect the volatility of interest-rate movements.

Conceptually, the risk of currency swaps is the same, the magnitude of risk being determined by the volatility of exchange rates during the life of the swap. However, there is one important difference: in a currency swap, exchange-rate changes also affect the values of the respective principal amounts and the interest payments, and this also increases the risk exposure. The value of the swap will be affected by both exchange-rate and interest-rate changes, and of course these are linked in fairly complex ways. Over long periods of time, a weak (depreciating) currency is associated with high (nominal) interest rates. Over shorter periods of time, however, high (real) interest rates are associated with a strong (appreciating) currency, substantially increasing the burden of the floating-rate payer.

From the above discussion it emerges that the intermediary must price the cost of its services by relying on

(a) the expected volatility of the relevant rates over the life of the swap (not unlike in option pricing).
(b) the creditworthiness of the borrower.
(c) the interaction of (a) and (b).

The last point refers to the fact that engaging in a swap itself may influence the credit risk of the counterparty. Swaps can be used to reduce a firm's exposure to currency or rate fluctuations, or to deliberately take a view. Perhaps, therefore, a swap transaction that *increases* the sensitivity of the counterparty's net cash flow to unexpected changes in interest and/or exchange rates (a "speculative" swap) should be priced *higher* than a swap

---

[21]Possible twists in the yield curve are neglected for ease of exposition.

[22]We assume that the general default of the party that gains (here, Keppel) is not relevant, as the administrator of the defaulting firm will be able to protect the positive value of the swap for the benefit of other creditors. However, the legal situation is not clear, especially when contract language suggests cancellation of swap obligations.

[23]To the extent that corporations tend to be net payers of fixed-rate funds, rising rates improve their position, *reducing* the risk of default. Conversely, when the economy is weak and interest rates are lower, the credit risk of corporate fixed-rate payers may increase.

that reduces it (a "hedge").[24] Of course, for a company that does a lot of borrowing and swapping, there is no way to know whether any particular swap, in combination with other swaps and debt-market instruments, is a hedge or a speculative position.

Collateralized Swaps

The potential credit exposure on a swap equals the amount by which the swap's value can change as a result of interest-rate and exchange-rate changes. Because this exposure can be high, most swap business is limited to counterparties with respectable credit standings. One way to allow lower-credit companies and financial institutions to participate in the swap market is to request them to provide collateral against the possibility of default. This collateral, or margin, can be debited if the swap loses value, and then topped up to an acceptable level—in effect, the credit risk can be marked to market from time to time, according to some agreed-upon valuation formula. Many banks do this on a small scale and are seeking ways in which the technique could be expanded.

Netting of Swaps

When two counterparties do a lot of swaps with one another, that gross amount can be huge and can entail great credit risk. Hence many swap agreements between active banks and other organizations specify that payments due should be *netted*. Netting in the context of swaps means that payments due on the same date in the same currency as a result of two or more swaps will be netted—that is, only one net payment is due and payable, and of course only in one direction. Netting of swaps has become an important legal issue because of questions concerning its enforceability by courts and jurisdictions. At present, netting agreements are unequivocally enforceable in only a limited number of jurisdictions, of which the United States is one.

Defaults and the Law

A swap agreement done in accordance with the master agreement of the International Swaps and Derivatives Association (ISDA) is now a well-established legal contract in most jurisdictions. Still, uncertainties remain about the "right of offset" under various jurisdictions, and the so-called "settlement" risk (the risk that one party loses effective control of one payment without receiving countervalue) remains unsettled in the courts. Swap contracts, however, are now very specific on how the "value" of the swap is to be calculated in the event of a default, triggering cancellation of the swap. Some details are provided in Box 13.5 and in Appendix 13.2, which summarizes the key terms of the widely used ISDA master agreement for swaps.

A 1990 amendment to the federal Bankruptcy Code of the United States added a new provision that preserves a swap party's contractual right to terminate a swap agreement and offset any amounts owed under it if the counterparty files bankruptcy or becomes insolvent or if a trustee is appointed for the party.

The biggest legal dispute to date in the arena of swaps is the *Hammersmith* case. Approximately 600 million pounds sterling may have been lost by international banks as a result of their swaps with British local authorities being validated by the British House

---

[24]This point has been made in Clifford W. Smith, Jr., et al., "The Evolving Market for Swaps," *Midland Corporate Finance Journal,* v. 3 no. 4, Winter 1986, 20–32.

BOX 13.5

Swap Termination, Replacement, and Compensation

Because of the absence of a true secondary market, many swap-market participants have developed sophisticated conventions for the termination and replacement of swaps.

Many swaps and other OTC contracts are terminated prior to maturity. This happens for one of three reasons:

1. *Voluntary termination.* Such termination is similar to secondary-market trading in the conventional sense.
2. *Events of termination.* Some examples are the institution of a withholding tax on swap payments, changed regulation that prevents one party from fulfilling its obligations, or a merger that affects the tax or credit condition of one of the parties.
3. *Events of default.* Some events (short of bankruptcy) that cause default are misrepresentation, breach of covenant, cross default, credit-support default, or simply missing a payment.

A counterparty to a swap who finds that a swap no longer serves the purpose can "sell" the swap in one of four ways:

1. Negotiate a cancellation directly with the other counterparty (the most common method).
2. Enter into an equal and opposite swap with another counterparty (but this doubles the credit exposure).
3. Assign the swap to a third party. In other words, arrange with a new counterparty to assume all the rights and obligations of the old swap. Because permissive assignments are not allowed under most swap agreements, this approach requires the consent of both counterparties; hence it is seldom used. Where it is done, it usually entails novation, both terminating the old swap and arranging the origination of a new one.
4. Novation is the only method of achieving a true transfer of obligations and rights under a derivative contract. This method requires the consent of all parties, because there must be a new agreement between the original contract parties and the transferee that the transferee will be substituted for all purposes in the position of the original counterparty. Certain swap contracts provide that the bank counterparty may freely novate its rights and obligations to an affiliate. More rarely, transfer provisions allow a bank to freely novate its rights and obligations to one of a class of financial institutions on a short list.

Whichever way the swap is "sold" there must be a mechanism for determining the cancellation payment. Such a mechanism is also necessary for determining how much is owed when a swap is terminated prematurely because of an event of default on the part of one of the parties.

ISDA, the International Swaps and Derivatives Association, has developed swap protocols that are now widely accepted. ISDA master agreements provide for three basic methods for measuring and assessing payments for early termination or default. These are:

1. the *agreement-valuation method,* based on market quotations.
2. the *indemnification method,* based on the cost of making the nondefaulting party whole.
3. the *formula method,* by which the amount of compensation is calculated from a pricing formula that is incorporated into the swap agreement.

In recent years, the agreement-valuation method has become nearly universal. Under this method, the contract's value at the termination date is obtained from market quotations solicited by the nondefaulting party. In practice, this means asking market-makers for quotations on how much they would pay, or expect to be paid, to replace the defaulting party to the swap. The market-maker's valuation would be based on the present value of the swap's remaining cash flows, or option valuation if option-type features are incorporated. (Calculating the size of the monetary inducement required to obtain a replacement swap on the same terms is called *marking to market*.)

The party that is out of the money then makes a close-out or termination payment to the other party. Although most swap agreements say that only the defaulting party is obliged to pay, few parties to the swap are sure that this one-sided clause would withstand court scrutiny if put to the test.

of Lords. About 130 municipal bodies had entered into interest-rate swaps with the banks in the 1980s. One of them was Hammersmith and Fulham, the London borough's local council. The council engaged in interest-rate swaps worth hundreds of millions of dollars as part of a massive bet on the direction of U.K. interest rates—a bet that it lost. Huge losses were incurred, and the council owed 55 banks about GBP300 million. The council suspended payment on the swaps, resulting in a lawsuit that ended, after two years in lower courts, in the House of Lords, Britain's highest court. The Law Lords ruled that all swap contracts entered into by local authorities are null and void.

The ruling in the *Hammersmith* case was that local councils did not have the legal authority to enter into interest-rate hedging contracts. It brought home to all participants the need for banks to assess the legal risk—the authority—and the credit risk of their counterparties in swap transactions. It has also made banks much more wary of doing business with counterparties, especially governmental authorities, whose activities in derivatives seem out of proportion to their normal business.[25]

Accounting and Taxation of Swaps

There are three possible ways for the accounting profession and the tax authorities to look at interest-rate and currency swaps:

1. They can be "melded" with the debt or assets that they are designed to hedge, so that only the *net* interest paid or received counts. This is the way most swap practitioners prefer it.
2. One can say that swaps, whatever their purpose, are merely forward contracts for exchanges in certain ratios, and their treatment should therefore follow that of currency forwards or interest-rate futures. The trouble with this method is that it could mean marking the hedge to market, while the underlying debt is kept on the company's accounts at book value, producing strange and unrealistic paper gains and losses.
3. One can treat swap cash flows as though they were actually interest payments—the "coupons" paid and received would be interest for tax and accounting purposes, and so would be taxable and tax deductible, accord-

---

[25]At one stage, Hammersmith and Fulham's swap dealings reportedly accounted for ½ percent of the entire worldwide swap market. "Cleaning Up the Town Hall Mess," *Euromoney,* April 1991, p. 31.

ingly. However, this method is anathema to most practitioners; most swap contracts go to lengths to refer only to "payments" and "amounts," avoiding the term "interest" like the plague so as to steer clear of any withholding-tax liability.

Swaptions

Like so many other things these days, some swaps are designed with embedded options. A **swaption** is an option on a swap. Swaptions take several forms. One kind is a swap that can be terminated or extended without penalty. A callable bond is a fixed-income instrument on which the issuer (the "fixed payer" in swap jargon) has the right to terminate early without paying a penalty. A right-to-terminate swaption is the same idea. The purchaser of a swaption, the fixed payer, has the right to "call" (terminate) the swap without a penalty. For this, he or she has to pay the writer an up-front fee—in effect, an option premium. A mirror-image swaption is one that the fixed receiver has the right to cancel; again, the party who has the right pays the up-front premium to the counterparty who provides the right. This latter kind of swaption resembles a put option, and is priced accordingly.

Another form of swaption is the extendable swap. In effect, it is the same as the put-like and call-like swap described above; the right to terminate a swap is equivalent to the right to continue with the swap beyond the right-to-termination date.

Some swaptions give a party the right to enter into a swap in the future. Under such a swaption agreement, no swap takes place at first. For a fee or premium, one party gives the other party the right to enter into the swap on specified terms, including the rate, at some future date or dates. One way to think of the difference is that a swaption is a hedge against the risk of *not* having a swap when it is needed, whereas a callable swap hedges the risk of having a swap that is not wanted.[26] Because swaptions are like callable or puttable bonds, giving the right to pay fixed or to receive fixed coupon payments at a certain date in the future, their valuation is based on bond-option valuation.

Trigger swaps are closely related to swaptions; under this arrangement, the swap is triggered if and only if LIBOR or some other market rate reaches a certain level. When triggered, the swap remains in place until a preset termination date.

A *forward swap* is similar but, as the name implies, it is a forward contract to engage in a swap on a particular date in the future. Both parties commit themselves to enter into the swap agreement under specified terms, unlike a swaption in which one party commits while the other party has the choice. Combinations of conventional and forward swaps can be tailored to clients' cash-flow requirements. Thus the amount of a swap can increase in a prearranged fashion, or decrease (the amortizing swaps); the coupon can be stepped up or stepped down; the swap can have only one exchange of payments (a zero swap— in effect, a forward contract), and so on.

A *differential swap* (diff swap) pays the difference between a floating rate in one currency and a floating rate in another currency, minus (or plus) a spread, with all payments denominated in a single currency and no exchange of principal. For example, a U.S. money manager, Steinhardt Partners, which is receiving three-month U.S.-dollar LIBOR from a portfolio of money market instruments, would, in a diff swap, pay that dollar

---

[26]A caveat: Some players use the term *swaptions* loosely, to incorporate all kinds of swaps that have optionlike features, including puttable and callable swaps.

LIBOR on an agreed notional principal amount to the arranging bank, say, CSFP,[27] in exchange for deutschemark LIBOR minus a spread that reflects the interest differential between the two currencies. The diff swap works by exploiting the difference between the relative shapes of two yield curves and the interest-rate expectations of the buyer of the diff. The transaction is settled entirely in dollars, so no exchange of principal is necessary. CSFP creates the diff swap using two interest-rate swaps, one in dollars and one in deutschemarks. Because Steinhardt bears no exchange risk, the bank is faced with a complex option-type hedging task, known as *quanto risk*. This is but one example of a plethora of "exotic" swaps that appeared in the early to mid-1990s.[28]

Other kinds of swaps are common—commodity swaps, zero swaps, and debt-for-equity swaps, as described in other chapters. Some, like gold swaps, are little more than simultaneous spot and forward contracts; others, such as third-world debt-for-equity swaps, are simply exchanges that have none of the forward-exchange characteristics of interest-rate and currency swaps; and still others, such as step-up coupon swaps, are hybrids of conventional swaps and can be priced accordingly. All this proves is that the term *swap* is widely and glibly used.

Caps and Floors

Deutsche Bank has made a five-year revolving Eurodollar loan to Swedish Match (SM) to fund the latter's export receivables. The interest rate is three-month LIBOR flat. The client, however, wants protection against rising rates for the first two years of the loan. Deutsche has offered to lock in the rate for that period by means of an interest-rate swap, but Swedish Match is reluctant to fix its funding at a higher cost when short-term rates might well stay low. So Deutsche has instead arranged to sell its client a *cap* that will ensure that SM's cost of funds will never exceed, say, 12.5 percent. Had Deutsche's client been an investor, wanting protection against rates falling *below* a certain level, the bank would have sold a *floor* to the client.

Caps and floors, which limit the rise or fall of a specified floating interest rate to a certain level, are in effect a "strip" of put or call options, respectively. A **cap** is an agreement by the seller of the cap to compensate the buyer, usually a borrower, whenever the hedged reference rate (usually LIBOR) exceeds a specified ceiling rate. For this protection against rising rates, the borrower pays a premium, usually up front.

For example, assume Hyundai, borrowing money for three years at six-month LIBOR, wishes to prevent its semiannual borrowing cost from ever exceeding 9 percent. LIBOR is now 7 percent. Korea Exchange Bank sells a cap to Hyundai for a front-end price of 4 percent of the principal amount being hedged. Then, for the next three years, if LIBOR exceeds 9 percent at any of the five subsequent semiannual rate-fixing dates, KEB will pay Hyundai the difference between LIBOR and 9 percent. If LIBOR turned out to be 10 percent, for example, then KEB would pay Hyundai 10 percent minus 9 percent on a semiannual basis—that is, ½ percent of the amount being hedged. If LIBOR then fell to 8 percent at the next six-month period, no payment would be made because LIBOR is below the ceiling rate. This concept is illustrated in Figure 13.2

A Eurodollar *put option* pays the difference between three-month LIBOR and a fixed rate or strike price, if LIBOR actually exceeds the fixed rate at the start of a single three-month period. A cap does the same, but for a series of periods. Hence a cap on U.S.-dollar interest rates can be regarded as a strip of Eurodollar put options. Caps are now so

---

[27]Credit Suisse Financial Products, a subsidiary of the Swiss bank Credit Suisse.

[28]See for example Simon Brady, "Derivatives Sprout Bells and Whistles," *Euromoney,* August 1992, 29–48, and *Risk* magazine, various issues.

Figure 13.2   ***Example of a Cap.***   A cap pays the amount by which LIBOR exceeds the cap rate—in this case, 9 percent. A swap, in contrast, would fix the rate at a certain level, such as 8 percent.

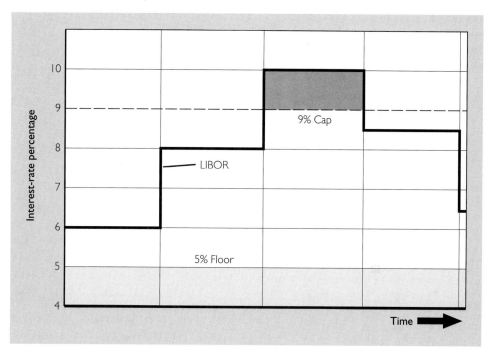

common that there is a reasonable active secondary market for them. Because a cap is a one-sided commitment, it is easier to assign than is a swap.

A **floor** is merely the downside equivalent of a cap. It is an agreement by the seller to pay the buyer any amount by which LIBOR, or another reference rate, falls below the preset "floor" during a series of future interest-fixing periods. If LIBOR is 7 percent and the floor or minimum rate is set at 5 percent, for example, the seller would pay the buyer 5 percent minus LIBOR whenever LIBOR falls below 5 percent on any future interest-fixing date (such as every quarter) for, say, the next seven years. Because the floor agreement hedges against rates falling below a fixed (strike) rate for a sequence of future periods, it is the equivalent of a strip of Eurodollar call options.

A *collar* is the simultaneous purchase of a cap and sale of a floor. The net cost is the value of the cap less the value of the floor. Borrowers often prefer to purchase a collar rather than a cap because the out-of-pocket cost is lower. The effect of purchasing a collar, of course, is that while the borrower's periodic interest cost cannot exceed a certain maximum rate, neither can his cost fall below a (different) minimum level. (When the collar's band is zero—that is, when the cap level is the same as the floor level—then the collar becomes a swap, because it fixes the rate under all circumstances. From this fact one can derive various relationships between caps, floors, and swaps, but this is not the place to do so.[29]

Take Hyundai, which earlier bought a cap from Korea Exchange Bank for 4 percent. Suppose Hyundai bought a collar instead, one that incorporated a ceiling (as before) of 9 percent but also a floor of 5 percent. Then, if LIBOR exceeds 9 percent, KEB pays

---

[29]For details, see John Hull, *Options, Futures and Other Derivatives,* 2nd ed. (Englewood Cliffs, N.J.: Prentice-Hall, 1993).

Hyundai, but if LIBOR goes below 5 percent, Hyundai pays KEB. If the floor that Hyundai provides to KEB is worth (say) 3 percent, then the net cost to Hyundai of the collar is only 1 percent. As illustrated, Hyundai's reference borrowing rate can only fluctuate between the ceiling rate of 9 percent and the floor rate of 5 percent.

Caps, floors, and collars, in short, are the options market's answer to interest-rate swaps.[30]

Summary

Currency and interest-rate swaps have dramatically increased the range of choices open to global financiers and investors. Interest-rate swaps in a given currency enable participants to alter the coupon characteristics of debt claims—from fixed to floating, for example, or from one floating index to another. Currency swaps enable borrowers and investors to transform the currency of denomination as well as the interest-rate characteristics of financial claims. Although standard, liquid swaps involving the exchange of fixed-dollar or nondollar payments for semiannual U.S.-dollar LIBOR are routine, "designer swaps" can readily be created using modern financial engineering technology. Swaps with optionlike characteristics, for instance, are now common.

The economic rationale for swaps lies in market imperfections that inhibit arbitrage between capital markets. These imperfections allow firms to benefit from any comparative advantage in financing or investing in one market relative to another. The widespread use of swap-linked financing in lieu of direct borrowing suggests that the gains from arbitraging such imperfections outweigh the credit risks arising form the possibility of counterparty default.

The existence of counterparty risk helps explain why the swap market is today dominated by commercial banks. Swap-dealing groups at banks trade them in the context of other money and bond-market instruments. Swap contracts resemble such instruments in that they consist of contractual cash flows, the value of which rises or falls with changing market conditions. The swap market, in conclusion, has earned itself a permanent place in the global capital market.

Conceptual Questions

1. Foreign-exchange traders used short-term foreign-exchange swaps for decades before currency swaps came into being. Is there any difference between the two techniques, apart from the fact that one is short term and the other long term?
2. In a currency swap, both the final principal and the periodic coupons are exchanged. Why is this unnecessary in an interest-rate swap?
3. It has been said that currency swaps represent an arbitrage technique. If that's so, and if "there's a whole lot of swapping going on," why are there opportunities still remaining for companies to engage in currency swaps?
4. In what sense has the swap market made some bond markets redundant?
5. Why, in the standard currency swap, is a fixed rate exchanged for a floating rate? Isn't that making things more complicated by combining an interest-rate risk with a currency risk?
6. Are interest-rate swap rates more influenced by (a) U.S. Treasury bond yields, (b) corporate bond yields or (c) interbank lending rates? Why?

---

[30]Giddy's Law: Whenever someone thinks of a variation, someone else will think of a variation on the variation. There are now forward caps and captions—options on caps. I've never heard of floortions or collartions, but that doesn't mean they don't exist. It doesn't pay to get too enamored of the jargon, for someone always has a new name for a new twist.

7. What is meant by the "value" of a swap? Why is a currency swap's value at initiation normally zero? Under what circumstances is the initial value not zero?
8. What purpose is served by putting a value on a swap?
9. Why might a company want to do an off-market swap?
10. How can a company reverse a swap previously undertaken?
11. If Company A undertakes a currency swap with Company B, what circumstances might give rise to credit-risk exposure to A?
12. How does a callable swap differ from a swaption?

PROBLEMS

1. Three companies, Harpo, Groucho, and Chico, each have borrowing needs in both the fixed and the floating markets in Canadian dollars. The following are the rates at which they can borrow:

	Fixed Rate	Floating Rate
Harpo	11%	C$LIBOR + 1%
Groucho	10%	C$LIBOR + 0.5%
Chico	12%	C$LIBOR + 2%

What swap opportunities exist?

2. You are a newly hired assistant manager with Royal Bank of Canada in Quebec. A customer calls for a quotation on swapping his fixed-rate, seven-year U.S.-dollar debt into floating-rate debt. What swap rate would you quote her? (Use the sample swap quotation sheet in Table 13.3.)

3. Now the same customer tells you that she's paying 8.5% on her fixed-rate debt. Would your quotation change?

4. You are Royal Bank's newly promoted relationship manager covering Hydro Quebec. Your client calls for a quote on swapping five-year fixed-rate pounds sterling into fixed-rate ECU. What would you quote him? (Again, use the sample swap quotation sheet in Table 13.3.)

5. Norway's Christiana Bank can issue a four-year Dutch-guilder Eurobond at 7.35% annually with 1% up-front issuance costs. If the guilder/dollar swap rate is 7.50%, what LIBOR-based floating cost of funds can Christiana attain? (Use the sample swap quotation sheet in Table 13.3 if necessary.)

6. Sammi Steel engages in a five-year interest-rate swap paying 11 percent annually, receiving six-month LIBOR + 0.25% semiannually. Three years later, the two-year swap rate has fallen to 9%. Is Sammi's swap "in the money" (positive value) or "out of the money" (negative value)? By how much?

7. If the duration of the "liability" side of Sammi's swap three years after initiation is 1.8, what is the duration of the swap? Based on the swap's duration, how much will Sammi gain if the swap rate rises from 9% to 9.20%?

8. You are a swaps trader at Royal Bank of Canada. You have just arranged a three-year swap to transform Hydro Quebec's floating Canadian-dollar debt into fixed-rate U.S. dollars. What steps might you take to hedge your risk?

9. The World Bank has three choices: (a) issue a three-year Swiss-franc foreign bond at 5% with 0.75% fees; (b) sell a three-year floating-rate medium-term note at US$ LIBOR − .25% and swap into Swiss francs; or (c) sell a three-year fixed-rate U.S. dollar MTN at 8.00% annually and convert to Swiss francs via the forward-exchange market. Which is cheapest?

	US$ Swaps vs. 6-month LIBOR	SF Swaps vs. 6-month US$ LIBOR	Exchange Rates, SF/US$
Spot	—	—	1.620
1 year	7.82–7.86	4.80–4.86	1.578
2 years	7.90–7.95	4.83–4.89	1.525
3 years	7.86–7.92	5.10–5.14	1.490

Application 13.1

KIWI MAGIC

Fay, Richwhite, the New Zealand merchant bankers, recently organized a U.S.-dollar-denominated syndicated three-year loan facility for Lion Brewing, the Auckland-based beverage concern. Lion's purpose in borrowing the money was to purchase a small hotel-cum-pub chain in Australia; hence they really wanted fixed-rate Australian dollar funds. At Fay, Richwhite's urging, however, Lion had borrowed floating-rate U.S. dollars and engaged in a swap with the Singapore subsidiary of Australian National Bank, who was seeking to fund their Eurodollar loan with LIBOR-linked dollar money. ANB (Singapore), meanwhile, had issued a three-year, A$-denominated Eurobond, the entire issue being placed with a Japanese insurance company. The bond, but not the swap, was guaranteed by ANB's parent bank in Sydney.

In summary, Lion had borrowed floating-rate dollars but engaged in a swap to exchange fixed "Aussies" for floating U.S. dollars, effectively creating fixed-rate Australian-dollar financing for itself.

1. Show, using the accompanying diagrams, the initial, annual, and final cash flows arising from this currency swap.
2. What flows (if any) would have occurred if Lion has engaged in a swap to obtain fixed-rate U.S. dollars rather than Australian dollars?
3. What circumstances would persuade Lion to engage in such a currency swap?
4. Consider what would happen if ANB (Singapore) reneged on the swap.

Assume that at the time of the deal, U.S. and Australian dollar three-year corporate bond rates were 12 percent and 14 percent respectively, and that the A$/US$ exchange rate was A$1.30. Assume also that two years later, the Aussie has fallen by 2 percent and Australian rates for one- to three-year issues are 13 percent. Is Lion a winner, a loser, or indifferent as a result of the termination of the swap?

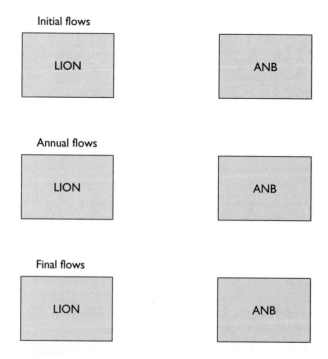

Initial flows

LION   ANB

Annual flows

LION   ANB

Final flows

LION   ANB

| **Application 13.2** | THE AUSSIE UNSWAP |

You are the rookie in the Swaps Group at Ozzibank in Sydney. Your new boss, assigned to head the group as a result of a reorganization, thinks you are an expert in currency swaps. Rather than disillusion him, you agree to answer an inquiry from Wilmington Integrated Chemicals, a major customer of the bank.

It seems that WIC may be interested in "unwinding" a currency swap undertaken with Ozzibank a year ago. At that time WIC wanted to finance its Australian subsidiary in local currency, but found access to the Australian bond market difficult. Instead, therefore, WIC had "swapped" US$20 million of its LIBOR-based dollar financing into Australian dollars. The terms of the swap were five-year Australian-dollar 14 percent annual against six-month U.S.-dollar LIBOR, paid semiannually. The exchange rate at the time was A$1.15 per US$. The Australian dollar has now fallen to A$1.25, and LIBOR is 8.9375 percent.

Because the value of their liability has dropped, WIC wants to cancel the A$ swap and cash in on their gain. WIC's treasurer has discussed replacing it with a U.S.-dollar fixed-floating swap. WIC wants to know how much the company would recieve from Ozzibank if the swap were terminated. Your new boss wants you to explain the following:

1. How would termination affect Ozzibank's exposure? What could the bank do about it?
2. How much, if anything, should Ozzibank be willing to pay WIC to cancel the swap? (Refer to the accompanying swap quote sheet.)
3. If Ozzibank declined to pay WIC anything to unwind the swap, what could the company do?
4. Assume that, for tax reasons, WIC did not want to receive a lump-sum payment but wanted the payment rolled into a more favorable quote on the interest-rate swap mentioned above. What rate would you quote?

Ozzibank Sydney Swap-Indication Sheet

	US$ Interest-Rate Swaps		Currency Swaps	
YEARS	Treasury Curve Benchmark Yields (s.a.)	Spread (B.P.)	DM/$ (ANN.)	¥/$ (ANN.)
2	8.02	62–66	7.00–7.10	5.35–5.45
3	8.01	70–75	7.00–7.10	5.35–5.45
4	8.01	72–76	7.00–7.10	5.35–5.45
5	8.02	78–81	7.00–7.10	5.35–5.45
7	8.13	77–81	7.02–7.12	5.40–5.50
10	8.14	78–81	7.02–7.12	5.45–5.53

	Currency Swaps			
YEARS	SFR/$ (ANN.)	£/$ (ANN.)	ECU/$ (ANN.)	A$/US$ (ANN.)
2	6.60–6.70	12.80–12.90	9.20–9.30	15.65–15.80
3	6.20–6.30	12.35–12.45	9.15–9.25	15.25–15.40
4	6.05–6.15	11.90–12.00	9.10–9.20	15.15–15.30
5	6.00–6.10	11.75–11.85	9.05–9.15	14.78–15.13
7	5.95–6.05	11.50–11.60	9.05–9.15	NA
10	5.95–6.05	11.26–11.36	9.05–9.15	NA

Application 13.3 | PAI HO

Anthony Cheung is an enterprising young capital markets specialist working for The Hongkong Bank in the powerful bank's headquarters in Central Hong Kong. Today he is seeking to arrange a deal that would reap a fee while entailing no counterparty risk for the bank. On a recent visit to Taipei he found that Pai Ho Company, a low-rated Taiwanese firm, could borrow U.S. dollars from their house bank, ICBC, at LIBOR plus 1.5 percent under a five-year revolving loan commitment. Pai Ho needed fixed-rate money to finance exports to Japan, but Hongkong Bank Tokyo reported that Pai Ho would have to pay 13 percent for fixed-rate yen via a private placement in Japan.

At the Jockey Club last Saturday, Anthony ran into a friend whose family owned Foo Ton Bank of Hong Kong. He found that Foo Ton could issue a fixed-rate Euroyen bond at an 11 percent all-in cost or arrange a five-year underwritten Note Issuance Facility at a maximum cost of LIBOR plus .5 percent.

Suppose Anthony was able to arrange a direct currency swap between the two parties, in such a way that the savings were split evenly. How much would the resulting fixed-rate money cost Pai Ho?

PAI HO	FOO TON

Application 13.4 | WHOSE ZOO?

You are the treasurer of the Kalamazoo Zoo. To supplement donations from the zoo's Who's Who, the zoo breeds and exports emus to Peru. Following the advice of Prof. Hugh Hu of Utah U., you insist that Peru pay in ECU. Prof. Hu also suggested you fund this program by issuing a Eurobond denominated in ECU (to match revenues), but you have found that this is not feasible—Eurobond investors' reactions are, predictably, "Who's Zoo?"

Still, there is hope. You *can* borrow five-year money locally at semiannual LIBOR plus ¾ percent, and Dresdner Bank has agreed to enter into a currency swap with you. LIBOR is currently 8.9375 percent, the five-year U.S.-dollar swap rate is 10 percent, and Dresdner's swap quotations are shown in the accompanying chart.

1. Diagram the swap with arrow-and-box diagrams.
2. What will your cost of capital be if you do the swap?
3. How will a 1 percent rise in ECU short-term interest rates affect the value of your swap? (Assume long-term rates remain unchanged.)
4. How will a 1 percent rise in ECU long-term interest rates affect the value of your swap? (Assume short-term rates unchanged.)

Dresdner Bank Swap Quotations

Years	Swap Rates, ECU Fixed (ann.) vs. U.S.-Dollar LIBOR (s.a.)
2	8.00–8.10
3	8.00–8.10
4	8.20 8.30
5	8.20 8.35
7	8.25–8.35
10	8.40–8.50

Application 13.5 | KANG WANG-KIE AND THE SYNTHETIC FRN

Your name is Kang Wang-Kie, and you are the General Manager of the London branch of Korea Exchange Bank. You now understand Eurodollar floating-rate notes, but what are *synthetic* U.S.-dollar floating-rate notes? Your assistant has given you the following memo to read over the Queen's Birthday holiday. The memo lists the characteristics of synthetic FRNs and explains how they work, using an example. Your assistant says that if there's anything you don't understand he'll explain it on Wednesday. He proposes that KEB invest $15 million in the J. P. Morgan Eurobond to achieve an effective spread of 15 basis points over LIBOR. What questions do you plan to ask him on Wednesday?

KOREA EXCHANGE BANK

MEMORANDUM

TO: Mr. Kang

FROM: Vicki Lester, AVP-Investment

DATE: November 28, 1989

SUBJECT: Synthetic U.S.-Dollar Securities

Synthetic dollar securities consist of two components: (1) a bond denominated in a foreign currency, and (2) a cross-currency interest-rate swap ("currency swap") that converts the bond principal and interest into U.S. dollars. In a typical transaction, an investment bank sells, say, a deutschemark bond to an investor, and simultaneously arranges a currency swap between the investor and a swap counterparty (usually a major financial institution). The currency swap fully hedges the investor against any foreign-exchange-rate risk on all interest and principal payments, and gives the investor a floating- or fixed-rate yield in U.S. dollars.

The main benefit of a synthetic security to an investor is that the yield received is significantly higher than yields available on comparable securities in the U.S. market.

PRODUCT CHARACTERISTICS

- Minimum principal amount is $5 million.
- Bonds are of investment-grade quality.
- Bonds are noncallable with bullet maturities.
- Maturities range from two to seven years.

LIQUIDITY

Synthetic securities are relatively illiquid investments. The bonds can usually be sold at any time but may be subject to wide bid-offer spreads. The cost of reversing the concomitant currency swap will be equal to the bid-offer spread, which can be as much as 1½ points. In addition, the investor incurs the swap-spread risk between the foreign currency and U.S. Treasury markets.

CREDIT RISK

Because the currency swap is legally a separate agreement from the bonds, the investor assumes the credit risk of the swap counterparty (and vice versa). In the event of default by the counterparty, the investor will incur any gain or loss associated with replacing or terminating the swap agreement.

RECENT OPPORTUNITIES

Name	S&P Rating	Issue	U.S. $ LIBOR (s.a.)
J. P. Morgan	AAA	ECU 6¾% due '91	+15
EIB	AAA	ECU 9¼% due '95	+20
Texas Eastern Corp.	BBB−	SFR 5⅜% due '96	+90

EXAMPLE OF SYNTHETIC U.S.-DOLLAR FRN

1. Investor buys DM10 million of Company A 6¼ percent bonds due 1992 at 102. Annual YTM—6.01 percent.
2. Investor swaps DM principal and interest for U.S. dollars at floating rate of LIBOR + 30bp DM10 million × $1/DM1.79, spot rate = $5.6 million.

SWAP MECHANICS

(A) *Initial Principal Exchange* **(settlement date)**

    *Depending on the swap structure, this amount may be either the par value or the market of the bonds.

(B) *Periodic Interest Exchanges* **(coupon dates)**

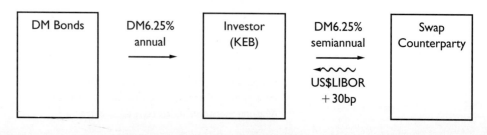

(C) *Final Principal Exchange* (maturity date)

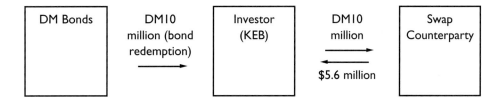

| **Applicaton 13.6** | MR. KANG VISITS CAROLINA |

You have been appointed the swaps trading manager for Carolina Bank, the London subsidiary of NCNB, a U.S. bank. Your first job is to prepare for a visit by a Mr. Kang of the Korea Exchange Bank, which is interested in doing a swap with Carolina Bank. KEB has been offered a "special price" of 101⅝ on the Canadian Pacific 10¾ maturing in 1993 and yielding 10.13 percent. (See the accompanying excerpts from FT/ISMA International Bond Service.) Mr. Kang has no interest in the bonds per se, but is considering an investment in a "synthetic floating-rate note" that will, he hopes, pay a spread of 120–150 basis points over his cost of funds. He estimates the latter to be LIBOR minus ⅛ percent.

You know that NCNB has recently been able to issue medium-term (fixed-rate) notes (MTNs) at an all-in cost of about 8.60 percent. You also know that NCNB is looking to swap these for medium-term floating-rate funds at a cost no higher than LIBOR − ¼ percent. (NCNB claims it can issue Eurocommercial paper at LIBOR − ¼.)

1. Show, by means of a diagram, how you would explain to Mr. Kang the cash flows that would have to take place to create his synthetic FRN.
2. What swap terms would you quote to KEB? (You should initially give them a quote that would be most advantageous to Carolina Bank.)
3. What is the spread on the proposed synthetic FRN above which Carolina would be unwilling to provide the swap?

Excerpts from FT/ISMA International Bond Service

U.S.-Dollar Straights	Issue size	Bid price	Yield
BNP 8 ¼ 93	125	99 ½	8.88
BNP 8 ⅛ 94	300	100 ⅜	8.49
BP AMERICA 9 ⅛ 99	250	105 ⅛	8.91
BP CAPITAL 9⅛ 93	150	102 ⅛	8.77
BR.COL.HYDRO 11 ⅛ 92	200	109 ⅜	8.78
CAMPBELL SOUP 10 ½ 95	100	104 ⅛	9.53
CANADA 9 96	1BN	104	8.14
CANADA 11 ½ 90	500	100 ⅝	9.11
CANADIAN PACIFIC 7 ½ 96	100	92 ⅜	9.02
CANADIAN PACIFIC 10 ¾ 93	100	101 ⅝	10.13
CEPME 7 ⅛ 92	125	97 ½	8.41
CHEVRON CORP 8 ¼ 96	300	96 ⅜	8.89

Application 13.7 | VODKA AND TULIPS

Ethnic unrest in Russia was giving Moscow a headache once again. In Amsterdam, however, Frits Dambrink saw this as a possible investment opportunity for his bank, Noordse Nederlandse Bank. Yesterday, Russia's Bank for Foreign Economic Affairs braved both investor worries about ethnic unrest in the country and a weak German government-bond market to bring to market a deutschemark-denominated Eurobond issue. The five-year, DM500 million issue carried an

TERM SHEET
ISSUER: Russia's Bank for Foreign Economic Affairs
GUARANTOR: Russia
TENURE: 5 years
AMOUNT: DM500 million
COUPON: 8⅞ annual
ISSUE PRICE: 100
FEES: 2% total, 1.25% selling concession
BOOK RUNNER: WestLB
CALL PROVISIONS: Noncallable, except for usual tax call provisions

8⅞ percent coupon and was issued at par (see the accompanying term sheet). But Deutsche Landesbank, the lead manager, was having a hard time placing the full amount, and indeed was having to provide some "stabilization" support for the bonds by bidding for them in the secondary market. Even so, the issue was rumored to be trading "below fees." Because the total underwriting fees for the issue were 2 percent of par, Frits knew that this meant that the bonds were priced at below 98.

Frits played with the keys on his Reuters monitor. One member of the underwriting syndicate, he saw, was willing to unload the Russian paper at a discount of 2½ percent, which he calculated would yield 9.53 percent, or 183 basis points above the yield on the benchmark 10-year Bund (the German government bond).

At present NNB was seeking high-yielding investments at a floating rate in U.S. dollars. If I could get these at 97½ percent, Frits thought, I would bet that this issue would provide us with the 100 basis points over six-month LIBOR that we've been looking for. To do this, I would have to combine the bond with a currency swap. Later, if the bonds trade closer to par, we might be able to get out at a profit.

1. Can you explain, by means of a diagram, the transactions that would have to occur to enable NNB to achieve its desired investment?
2. Frits wants to call up a swap trader at Commerzbank to obtain a quotation for the swap he would require. What swap quotation would be necessary to achieve the target spread of LIBOR plus 100 basis points?
3. What transactions would be involved if NNB were to get out at a profit one year later?

SELECTED REFERENCES

Arak, M., A. Estrella, L. Goodman, and A. Silver. "Interest Rate Swaps: An Alternative Explanation." *Financial Management* (Summer 1988): 12–18.

Beidleman, Carl R., ed. *Cross Currency Swaps.* Homewood, Illinois: Business One-Irwin, 1992.

———. *Interest Rate Swaps.* Homewood, Illinois: Business One-Irwin, 1990.

Bicksler, J., and A. H. Chen. "An Economic Analysis of Interest Rate Swaps." *Journal of Finance* (July 1986).

Bierwag, G. O., et al, "Duration: Its Development and Use in Bond Portfolio Management." *Financial Analysts Journal* (July–August 1983): 15–35.

Dufey, Gunter, and Ian H. Giddy. "The Evolution of Instruments and Techniques in International Financial Markets." Societe Universitaire Europeene de Recherches Financieres, Series 35A, 1981.

Euromoney Publications. *Swap Finance.* three volumes, updated periodically.

Henderson, S. K., and L. B. Klein. "Glossary of Terms Used in Connection with Rate Risk Management." New York Institute of Finance, 1990.

Marshall, John F., and Kenneth R. Kapner. *The Swaps Market.* Miami: Kolb Publishing, 1993.

Schwartz, Robert, and Clifford Smith, eds. *The Handbook of Currency and Interest Rate Risk Management.* New York Institute of Finance, 1990.

Smith Clifford W., Jr. et al. "The Evolving Market for Swaps." *Midland Corporate Finance Journal,* vol. 3, no. 4 (Winter 1986): 20–32.

Turnbull, Stuart M. "Swap: A Zero Sum Game?" *Financial Management* (Spring 1987): 15–21.

Wunnicke, Diane B., David R. Wilson, and Brooke Wunnicke. *Corporate Financial Risk Management.* New York: Wiley, 1992.

APPENDIX 13.1 Duration of a Swap

The duration of an interest-rate swap is the change in its value, expressed as a percentage of the notional principal, resulting from a 1 percent change in market yields. This measure of the interest-rate sensitivity of a fixed-income instrument is widely used in the bond market, and both the computation and the concept apply with little modification to swaps. As a rule, bonds and swaps with longer maturity are more vulnerable to interest-rate changes; however, duration measures this vulnerability more precisely because it takes into account the size and timing of coupon payments.

The duration of an interest-rate swap is simply the duration of the asset side minus the duration of the liability side. For example, at the start of the five-year Toyo-Sammi swap above, the duration of the fixed side was 4.1 and that of the floating side 0.5. The net duration of the swap was therefore 3.6. This means that if interest rates rise by 1 percent, the swap will lose 3.6 percent of its notional principal.

The Macauley duration of a bond is measured as a weighted-average term to maturity of each payment in which the weights are the present values of the cash flows from the bond, divided by the bond's price:

$$\text{Duration} = \sum_{t=1}^{n} t \left[\frac{\dfrac{CF_t}{(1+r)^t}}{\text{Price}} \right]$$

$$\text{Price} = \sum_{t=1}^{n} \frac{CF_t}{(1+r)^t}$$

where

CF_t = interest and/or principal payment in period t
t = time in years to the interest and/or principal payment
n = number of years to final maturity
r = yield to maturity

Strictly speaking, it is the *modified duration* that measures the price sensitivity of a bond to changes in interest rates:

$$\text{Modified duration} = \frac{\text{Duration}}{1 - \dfrac{\text{Market yield}}{m}}$$

where m = number of coupon interest payments per year.

The modified duration measures the percentage change in the price of an instrument for a 1 percent change in the yield. So, to obtain the percentage change in an instrument's price, multiply its modified duration by the market yield's change. Knowing the duration of each of two instruments, such as swaps, allows one to determine how many of one will hedge the other—in other words, relative duration provides the hedge ratio.

Duration should not be used where precision is required, for the Macaulay measure of duration, shown in the first equation, assumes a flat yield curve and parallel shifts in the curve. Also, a bond's duration changes slightly as the market yield changes. For practical purposes, these effects are small as long as rates have not changed a great deal. When yields change substantially, however, one should take into account the bond's *convexity*. Convexity measures how much duration changes for a given change in yield. Most fixed-receive swaps have positive convexity, meaning that as yields rise, the price sensitivity (duration) falls; and as yields fall, the duration increases. From the point of view of a swap trader, positive convexity is a desirable characteristic.

APPENDIX 13.2   Summary of Key Clauses in the ISDA Master Agreement

The International Swaps and Derivatives Association has published a series of documents that have been accepted as the basis for standardizing the terms and conditions of swap agreements. Two types of master agreements, introduced in 1987 and supplemented in subsequent years, provide a set of standard terms applicable to interest rate or currency swaps, together with an accompanying schedule that allows the parties to tailor their agreement by listing terms specific to swaps between the two parties.

The two versions of the standard form agreements (that is, the code-based U.S.-dollar version and the multicurrency version) employ the same basic ordering of provisions and, for the most part, the same numbering of their sections. The first section provides for the identification of the parties to the swap. This is followed by sections dealing with payments, representations, agreements, events of default and termination events, early termination, transfer, multibranch provisions, notices, tax matters, credit support documentation, governing law and jursidiction, definitions, and confirmations.

Payments

Most payment terms are specific to the swap and, therefore, are specified in the accompanying schedule. The standard terms provide for the netting of payments on a given swap when payments between the parties are to be made on the same date and in the same currency. As an extension, the agreement provides that the parties net payments on all swaps governed by the same master agreement when those payments are to be made on the same date and in the same currency.

Representations

This section contains representations and warranties that each party to the swap makes to the other. The representations and warranties are deemed to be repeated with each new swap that is governed by the master agreement. The *basic representations* concern corporate authority to enter into the swap agreement and the validity of the agreement. Other representations include the *absence of certain events,* such as the occurrence of an event of default or a termination event; the *absence of litigation* that might threaten the legality, validity, or enforceability of the contract; the *accuracy of financial information;* and the *accuracy of specific information* that is furnished in writing by one party to the other.

Agreements

This section provides for supplemental agreements to furnish documents, excluding tax covenants in the code-based form, as detailed by the parties in the schedule accompanying the master agreement. These might include such things as the periodic furnishing of financial statements or legal opinions, the provision of credit-support documentation, or other documents.

Events of Default and Termination Events

Events of default indicate that a credit problem has arisen and entitle the nondefaulting party to terminate all swaps governed by the master agreement. Termination events result from occurrences other than credit problems and allow for the termination of those swaps directly affected by the termination event.

The agreements provide for seven specific events of default, but the parties may specify others if they like. The specific events of default, most of which apply to both parties, are failure to pay, breach of covenant, credit-support default, misrepresentation, default under specified swaps, cross default, and bankruptcy. *Failure to pay* refers to any failure by either party to pay an amount that is required under the agreement. A *breach of covenant,* as an event of default, refers to a failure by either party to pay an amount that is required under the agreement. A *breach of contract,* as an event of default, refers to a failure to comply with any convenant of the swap agreement other than the making of a required payment, a tax-related matter, or a failure to give notice that a termination event has occurred. *Credit-support default* refers to any default under applicable credit-support documents. It only applies to a party if a credit-support document is required by that party or on behalf of that party. *Misrepresentation* refers to a breach of any representation (other than a tax representation) made in the swap agreement or credit-support documentaion. *Default under specified swaps* refers to a default that results in the designation or occurrence of a termination event under another swap. *Cross default* refers to a default on some other indebtedness. This event of default can be applied to both parties, only one party, or excluded entirely from the swap agreement by so indicating in the accompanying schedule. The *bankruptcy* event of default is broadly defined to allow for significant variations in the bankruptcy and insolvency laws of the countries covered by the swap agreement.

The agreement specifies certain termination events. These are illegality, a tax event, a tax event upon merger, and a credit event upon merger. An *illegality* is deemed to have occurred if a change in law or regulation makes it impossible for either party to perform its obligations. A *tax event* occurs if a withholding tax is imposed on a swap transaction. In this event, the party required to pay the tax may opt to terminate the swap. A *tax event upon merger* occurs if a merger results in a deterioration of the creditworthiness of one of the parties. In such an event, the other party may elect to terminate all swaps governed by the master agreement.

Early Termination

Upon the occurrence of an event of default, the nondefaulting party has the right to designate an *early termination date*. In the case of the bankruptcy, the termination is automatic. With the exception of bankruptcy, the nondefaulting party must provide notice to the defaulting party as to the early termination date.

In the case of the occurrence of a terminating event, the party that is entitled to designate an early termination date varies with the nature of the terminating event. As previously mentioned, in the case of an event of default, all swaps governed by the same master agreement are terminated. In the case of a termination event, only the affected swaps are terminated.

Once a notice of early termination has become effective, each party to a terminated swap is released from its obligation to make its required payments under the swap. The parties must then calculate *termination payments*.

Transfer

This section of the agreements provides a general prohibition against the *transfer* of rights and obligations under the agreement to other parties. Allowance is made for specifying exceptions to this general prohibition. These exceptions must be detailed in the accompanying schedule. This is the general prohibition against permissive assignment discussed earlier in this section.

Multibranch Provisions

This section of the agreements allows institutions with multiple branches that operate from several locations to govern all swaps with a single master agreement.

Notices

This section requires that addresses and telex numbers for purposes of providing required *notices* be specified in the accompanying schedule. All notices provided must be in writing and sent to the required address or telex.

Tax Matters

The tax section of the agreements deals with three tax issues: gross up, tax representation, and tax convenants. As a general rule, counterparties are required to make their payments without any withholding or deductions for taxes. However, if a party making a payment is legally required to withhold taxes from the payment, that party is required to gross up the amount of the payment for any amount withheld on account of "indemnifiable taxes." The party is, however, released from its *tax-gross-up* obligation if the withholding is the result of a breach of a tax-related representation or covenant made by the other party. The parties must specify all applicable tax representations in the accompanying schedule and must agree to give notice of breaches of tax representation (tax covenants).

Credit-Support Documentation

The parties should identify in the accompanying schedule all required *credit-support documents*. These include guarantees, security agreements, and letters of credit.

Governing Law and Jurisdiction

This section of the agreements defines a number of important terms that are used in the swap documentation.

Definitions

This section defines a number of important terms that are used in the swap documents.

Confirmations

The agreements require the exchange of *confirmations* that detail the terms of each new swap entered under the master agreement. In the code-based form, intended for U.S.-dollar interest-rate swaps only, these confirmations must specify the notional amount, the trade date, the effective date, the termination date, the fixed-rate payer, the fixed-rate payment dates, the fixed amount of each payment, the floating-rate payer, the floating-rate payment dates, the floating rate for the initial calculation period, the floating-rate option, the designated maturity, the spread (plus or minus), the floating-rate day-count fractions, the reset dates, compounding (if applicable), and certain other terms, as appropriate.

In the multicurrency form, all of this same information must be provided, but other information is required as well. This includes the relevant currencies, initial exchange, final exchange, and so forth.

14
International Equity Markets and Portfolio Diversification

The benefits and costs of international portfolio diversification must be considered by anyone holding an equity portfolio. Similarly, the firm considering raising new equity must address the requirements of the global, not just the domestic, marketplace. This chapter discusses the merits of international equity investment and the means by which this may be done.

Although investors may contemplate an international portfolio and issuers may target their issues to global investors, the practical reality is that each ends up employing national stock markets. These markets vary in some important respects. Accordingly, the chapter begins with a brief comparative survey of the principal stock markets.

The World's Major Stock Markets

The U.S. market has long been the world's biggest, but it has a strong challenger in Japan, whose market is presently larger than all those of Europe combined. Determining which country takes the leading position in market size depends on how well each country's stock market and currency happens to be doing at the time, so it is not of great significance. Table 14.1 contains a listing of the world's major stock markets, along with their size, as measured by capitalization—the sum of all the values of the companies whose stocks were traded in the exchanges as of September, 1990. Here we discuss three major markets, that of the United States, the United Kingdom, and Japan.

1. The *U.S. market,* dominated by the New York Stock Exchange, has long held the leading position by virtue of the depth and diversity of its trading, its liquidity, and the degree of protection afforded investors through regulation by the SEC (Securities and Exchange Commission). Part of the reason for the importance of the U.S. market is that the United States, like Great Britain, has a financial system dominated by public issues and exchangeable securities, whereas financing in certain other countries, such as Germany and Japan, has traditionally been dominated by bank lending. The stock exchanges in the United States are private and characterized by avid competition. Rivals to the NYSE include the American Stock Exchange and the National Association of Securities Dealers Automated Quote System (NASDAQ), an electronic over-the-counter market, and several regional exchanges.

2. The *U.K. market* has the longest history of the major markets, having its origin in a coffee house dating back to 1773 (although Amsterdam can claim a still older vintage). Yet today it is among the most modern, with innovations continuously introduced in order to attract trading in continental European shares as well as Japanese and North shares. Like most of the bigger markets, Britain, in a "Big Bang" of reform, has removed restrictions on who can trade, how trading is done, and how commissions are set. A side effect of these sweeping reforms, introduced in the mid-1980s, was the abandonment of

Table 14.1   *Capitalization of the World's Major Stock Markets*

FT-ACTUARIES WORLD INDICES QUARTERLY VALUATION

The market capitalisation of the national and regional markets of the FT-Actuaries World indices as at JUNE 30, 1993 are expressed below in millions of US dollars and as a percentage of the World Index. Similar figures are provided for the preceding quarter.
The percentage change for each Dollar index value since the end of the calendar year is also provided.

NATIONAL AND REGIONAL MARKETS Figures in parentheses show number of lines of stock	Market capitalisation as at JUNE 30, 1993 (US$m)	% of World Index	Market capitalisation as at MARCH 31, 1993 (US$m)	% of World Index	% change in $ index since DECEMBER 31, 1992
Australia (68)	103395.7	1.25	107176.6	1.37	+5.27
Austria (18)	10354.4	0.12	9861.5	0.13	+4.79
Belgium (42)	54451.8	0.66	56425.1	0.72	+10.13
Canada (108)	141914.2	1.71	136258.3	1.74	+10.55
Denmark (33)	26551.3	0.32	24917.5	0.32	+17.26
Finland (23)	11782.7	0.14	9464.2	0.12	+34.13
France (97)	252093.3	3.04	270100.3	3.45	+4.18
Germany (62)	252256.8	3.04	264841.2	3.38	+4.54
Hong Kong (55)	140999.5	1.70	124357.7	1.59	+29.61
Ireland (15)	10354.1	0.12	10159.8	0.13	+19.38
Italy (72)	95556.4	1.15	77188.3	0.98	+23.22
Japan (470)	2555926.9	30.81	2167381.8	27.65	+39.73
Malaysia (69)	51205.9	0.62	44007.0	0.56	+24.65
Mexico (18)	42058.0	0.51	45162.7	0.58	−6.63
Netherland (24)	123710.0	1.49	124364.7	1.59	+10.10
New Zealand (13)	12141.3	0.15	11454.1	0.15	+16.14
Norway (22)	6736.1	0.08	6853.1	0.09	+11.09
Singapore (38)	28671.6	0.35	25408.8	0.32	+17.05
South Africa (60)	79274.5	0.96	70124.0	0.89	+34.30
Spain (46)	69793.4	0.84	72207.3	0.92	+7.48
Sweden (36)	62477.3	0.75	58120.0	0.74	+1.90
Switzerland (52)	166713.1	2.01	152253.0	1.94	+12.48
United Kingdom (219)	786153.9	9.48	772938.1	9.86	+2.09
USA (519)	3210116.9	38.70	3196720.3	40.79	+3.47
Europe (761)	1928994.5	23.26	1909694.2	24.37	+5.78
Nordic (114)	107547.4	1.30	99354.8	1.27	+8.77
Pacific Basin (713)	2892341.0	34.87	2479786.1	31.64	+36.96
Euro–Pacific (1474)	4821325.5	58.13	4389480.3	56.00	+22.58
North America (627)	3352031.0	40.41	3332978.5	42.52	+3.76
Europe Ex. UK (542)	1142830.6	13.78	1136756.1	14.50	+8.47
Pacific Ex. Japan (243)	336414.1	4.06	312404.3	3.99	+18.86
World Ex. US (1660)	5084572.1	61.30	4641025.3	59.21	+22.05
World Ex. UK (1960)	7508535.1	90.52	7064807.4	90.14	+15.54
World Ex. So. Af. (2119)	8215414.5	99.04	7767621.5	99.11	+13.96
World Ex. Japan (1709)	5738762.1	69.19	5670363.8	72.35	+5.46
The World Index (2179)	8294689.0	100.00	7837745.5	100.00	+14.13

© The Financial Times Limited, Goldman, Sachs & Co, and NatWest Securities Limited. 1987

the trading floor in favor of telephones and computer screens, the latter linked through a network called SEAQ. London appeals to many investors because the Exchange has a very efficient market structure, tailored to trade in large issues with dispersed ownership, in contrast to the New York Stock Exchange, which retains many outdated elements, notably the specialist system, geared to the individual investor.

3. The *Japanese market,* despite its size, has features that reflect its relatively recent vintage; most of its growth is associated with Japan's extraordinary postwar growth. Even with Japan's rise to the top position, as measured by capitalization, Japan's stock exchanges retain many features that have been abandoned by reforms in other countries. Entry by new securities firms is strictly restricted, and fixed commissions still prevail. More worrisome to many international investors is the peculiar, perhaps manipulated, valuation of Japanese stocks: price/earnings ratios of 60 are not unusual for companies that in Western markets might be valued at a P/E of 10 to 20. (Admittedly one cannot take this comparison at face value, as earnings are measured differently.) Buying and selling, and hence price setting, tends to be dominated by the "big four" Japanese securities firms: Nomura, Daiwa, Nikko, and Yamaichi. Cross-holdings are prevalent, especially between banks and industrial companies, and the market has been shaken by a series of scandals, such as the

Recruit Cosmos affair of 1989 (bribery of government officials), and the revelation in 1991 that the large securities firms were compensating certain customers for stock-market losses that the clients had incurred.

A number of other markets are prominent in global equity trading, such as Germany, France, Switzerland, Canada, and Australia. Some characteristics of these markets are listed in Table 14.2.[1] Also gaining prominence are the markets of several newly industrializing countries such as Malaysia and Mexico, to be discussed in a later section. Rather than describe any more markets, let us note some of the key differentiating features of the principal stock markets. Solnik[2] has identified some ways in which stock markets differ:

- *Public versus private bourses.* In some countries, such as France, the stock exchange or "bourse" was established by the government and remains under its strong influence, whereas other countries have private bourses set up by the members themselves for the purpose of trading with one another. As may be seen from Table 14.2, in countries such as Japan and the United States, several private exchanges may compete with one another. Yet other countries' stock markets are "bankers' bourses"; in Germany, for example, banks have a legislative monopoly on brokerage.

- *Cash versus forward markets.* Almost nowhere are stocks, once traded, delivered on the same day. A typical "spot" or cash settlement in the equity business is five business days. In certain countries (notably France and Brazil), however, forward delivery is common. In the Paris Bourse all major stocks are traded on a forward market: delivery takes place at the end of the month, although the price is fixed at the time the trade is done. In Switzerland delivery often takes place several months after the trade date. Naturally the price for forward delivery differs from the spot price by the **cost of carry**, the principal component of which is the interest rate.

- *Fixed versus continuous quotation.* Most of the major markets today offer *continuous* pricing of stocks, at least the major stocks: the price is whatever the market will bear at any given time. In the United States, continuous quoting and reasonable liquidity is aided by *specialists* who have an assigned right and obligation to make a market in particular stocks; in other countries, *dealers* or *jobbers* are market-makers who compete with one another. But in Frankfurt and many small markets, for the majority of stocks in which trading is thin, the price is determined by auction, and a single consensus price applies to all transactions.

- *Computerization versus floor trading.* The enormous amount of subtle information on supply and demand that can be assimilated when all traders are physically present on a trading floor has allowed such trading to persist long beyond the availability of technology to conduct computerized trading. As markets have become national and international markets, however, the computer screen has increasingly become the forum for trading. Present systems allow automated matching of trades, with large trades being conducted over the telephone rather than left to the computer. To be effective for all trading, computer-based trading systems will have to retain many of the human-interaction features of face-to-face trading.

---

[1] Most of the information in this table was derived from Chapter 16 of *Global Investing* by Julian Walmsley (London: Macmillan, 1991). For more details on the markets see the selected references at the end of this chapter.

[2] Bruno Solnik, *International Investments* (Reading, Mass.: Addison-Wesley, 1991), 106–112.

Table 14.2   *Characteristics of Major Stock Markets*

	Exchanges (volume)	Execution	Settlement	Regulation
United States	New York (80%), American (15%), Boston, Cincinnati, Midwest, Pacific, Philadelphia, NASDAQ (over-the-counter, screen-based).	Open outcry on exchanges; telephone for OTC. All share in registered form. Commissions negotiable.	Fifth business day after trade date. NYSE trades clear through National Stock Clearing Corporation. Depository Trust Company holds securities for its members.	SEC
United Kingdom	International Stock Exchange (London: includes Birmingham, Manchester, Liverpool, Glasgow, Dublin); Unlisted Securities Market.	Telephone/screen market (SEAQ). Must be through Stock Exchange member. Commissions negotiable. Most shares in registered form; physical delivery is normal.	2–3-week account period. Central clearing system, Talisman, operated by Stock Exchange.	Dept. of Trade
Japan	Tokyo (83%), Osaka, Nagoya, five others. Exchange has three sections: first is large shares (96% of capitalization); second is new or unlisted shares; third is unlisted shares trading over the counter.	By the Zareba (open outcry) method. Must be through member of Japan Securities Dealers Association. All equity is in registered form. Fixed commissions.	Fourth business day after trade. Clearing through Japan Securities Co., subsidiary of Tokyo Stock Exchange.	Ministry of Finance
Germany	Frankfurt (60%), Dusseldorf (20%), Munich, Hamburg, Stuttgart, Hanover, Berlin, Bremen. Official market supplemented by semiofficial market with less stringent listing rules. Also OTC market.	Large stocks trade continuously. Smaller stocks dealt at a price set daily.	Two business days (five days by arrangement). Delivery through German banks. Settlement via regional clearing agencies (Wertpapiersammelbanken) or the Auslandskassenverein for foreign securities.	Stock Exchange Board

	Exchanges (volume)	Execution	Settlement	Regulation
France	Paris (95%), Lyons (4%), Bordeaux, Lille, Marseilles, Nancy, Nantes. Three markets: Cote Officielle: large and foreign companies; Second Marche: small and medium-size; Marche Hors-Cote: over-the-counter market.	Forward market, some trades cash. Automated execution system replacing system of placing orders in pigeonholes. Price movement restrictions: 5% cash, 8% forward.	Forward: last working day of month. Cash: immediately after trading session.	COB
Switzerland	Zurich (60%), Geneva (20%), Basle (10%), Bern, St. Gallen, Lausanne, Neuchatel. Three markets: Official: on floor of exchanges between members; Semiofficial: on floor, in unlisted companies; Unofficial: telephone, interbank trading in unlisted companies and new issues. Registered, bearer, and participation certificates exist.	Open outcry for official/semiofficial markets. 70% of trades are for spot settlement, but forward trades up to nine months possible.	Spot: within three days. Forward: last day of month. Stocks deposited in SEGA (centralized clearing house) and book-entry transfers made.	Swiss National Bank
Canada	Toronto (75%), Montreal (20%), Vancouver (5%), Alberta, Winnipeg. Over-the-counter market trades unlisted shares.	On the floor of the exchanges, through member firms. Automated execution for certain trades. Negotiable commissions. Equity is in registered form.	Five business days. Canadian Depository for Securities provides automated clearing and custody services.	Provincial Securities Commission
Australia	Australian Stock Exchange (includes Sydney, Melbourne, Adelaide, Brisbane, Hobart, and Perth). Main Board Market handles large and foreign shares; Second Board, small and unlisted companies.	Between brokers at trading posts on exchanges. Automated trading system in Sydney and Melbourne for actively traded shares. Commissions negotiable. Equity is in registered form. Physical delivery.	Five business days, normally. No official settlement period.	AASE

Emerging Stock Markets

The 1980s saw a new phenomenon in international investing: the coming to prominence of the emerging stock markets of newly industrialized countries such as Korea, Taiwan, and other rapidly growing economies with opening stock markets such as Mexico and Turkey. Table 14.3 gives some indication of the relative size of 20 emerging markets.

These markets have made some investors rich. Yet some find that entering a thin, narrow market driven much more by "the herd"—poorly informed individuals seeking a gambler's gain—than by fundamentals requires nerves of steel and a long purse. *Two examples:* South Korea's bourse rose fourfold between October 1986 and its peak in March 1989, but by the end of 1990 it had fallen 40 percent. Taiwan's market was even more exciting. Between the beginning of 1987 and its peak in February 1990, Taiwan's stock market rose more than tenfold; by October of that same year, it had fallen by more than 80 percent. Ironically, part of the excess demand was the result of misguided regulation supposedly designed to protect Taiwan's numerous individual investors. During the boom many companies sought to satisfy some of the demand by issuing new shares. They were inhibited from doing so by stiff regulatory controls on primary issues. It reportedly took a minimum of a year to get listed and often as long as three years before the company's

Table 14.3   Overview of Emerging Stock Markets
Third Quarter, 1990

	Market Capitalization (US$ Millions)	Number of Listed Companies	Average Daily Value Traded for Quarter (US$ Millions)	Price/ Earnings Ratio
Latin America				
Argentina	3.438	174	3.16	−4.35
Brazil	24,907	584	17.56	7.18
Chile	11,216	216	2.82	6.17
Colombia	1,335	80	0.25	11.06
Mexico	27,998	205	52.65	10.27
Venezuela	5,219	66	2.70	19.33
East Asia				
Korea	93,886	669	233.53	19.12
Philippines	6,634	151	4.59	24.32
Taiwan, China	64,958	193	2,834.79	21.96
South Asia				
India[a]	46,412	2,471	86.36	27.04
Indonesia	7,109	116	17.97	30.48
Malaysia	38,143	266	49.56	19.93
Pakistan	2,832	473	1.03	10.35
Thailand	22,582	204	101.77	12.24
Europe/Mideast/Africa				
Greece	16,475	129	18.08	26.69
Jordan	2,009	105	2.67	7.76
Nigeria	1,400	126	0.04	5.96
Portugal	8,875	181	7.14	15.54
Turkey	26,342	100	21.74	40.10
Zimbabwe	1,853	56	0.19	10.09

[a]Bombay only.

books were in a shape satisfactory to the authorities. Companies already listed faced rigid timetables if they wanted to issue more equity, and were required to issue the shares at a discount of up to 50 percent of their market price, again supposedly to protect small investors. The result was that, as of 1991, there were only 200 listed companies in Taiwan, but about 580 traded on the unregulated gray market.

That is not to say that *as a whole* the emerging markets listed in Table 14.3 are more risky than those of developed countries, given their expected return. Rather, the international investor might be well advised to resist the temptation to concentrate investments in a particular emerging market that is currently "hot." The International Finance Corporation, which helps countries to develop their stock markets, has established regulatory criteria for the 20 markets. At the time of writing only a handful of nations—Brazil, Chile, Mexico, India, South Korea, and the Philippines—had accounting standards that, according to the IFC, were acceptable internationally. Even if a country's structure and rules seem to provide the framework for adequate investor protection, in reality the markets may not work that way. Insider trading is unavoidable in countries with concentrated family holdings and cross-ownership between banks and corporations.

International Equity Trading

All the major stock exchanges are primarily *local* markets, deriving the great bulk of their turnover from intra-country trading. As markets grow and barriers fall, however, the national markets are gradually being integrated into a fledging *global stock market*. As the magnitudes of flows between the four major stock-trading regions of the world demonstrate (see Figure 14.1), there certainly is sufficient cross-border buying and selling to warrant calling this an international market for stocks. For the most part, however, international trading goes on in the same manner as domestic trading. For example, a Dutch mutual fund buys and sells General Motors stock on the New York Stock Exchange just as an American fund would do. For convenience of clearing transactions and to avoid currency-exchange costs and time-zone inconveniences, it would be more desirable to have a single market for all the world's actively traded stock. London's International Stock Exchange (ISE) is presently the closest thing to such a market (see the turnover figures for foreign equities in Table 14.4). By the end of 1990 the French Bourse had reportedly lost a third of its business in French shares to SEAQ International, the computer-based foreign-equity market run by the ISE.[3]

An alternative to the internationalization of domestic stocks is the vehicle of **multiple listing**. Shares of Sony, Nestlé, and IBM, for example, are listed and traded in New York, Tokyo, London, Paris, and several other exchanges. In the United States and certain other countries, this multiple listing is done through *depository receipts,* which are claims on foreign stocks; these are explained in a later section. Such listing does make it easier for domestic residents to buy foreign stocks on their home exchanges, but it suffers from two disadvantages:

1. *It is costly.* A Japanese firm wishing to list in the United States, for example, must satisfy the requirements of the SEC as well as those of the exchange on which the stock is listed. Such requirements include recalculating all the published accounts according to the generally accepted U.S. accounting principles (GAAP) and translating them into English.

Table 14.4   *Turnover in Major Equity Markets*[a]

	Total turnover (in £ million)	Of which, foreign equities
Amsterdam	5,924	43
Australia	5,882	0
Frankfurt	48,703	1,896
Hong Kong	6,225	18
London ISE	79,709	39,444
NASDAQ	74,725	4,228
NYSE	194,523	n/a
Paris	19,541	641
Tokyo	210,302	2,036
Toronto	7,778	46

[a]Data for second quarter 1990.

Source: *Financial Times,* Nov. 28, 1990.

---

[3]Reported in *The Economist,* Dec. 8, 1990, p. 86.

Figure 14.1   *The International Equity Market.*   Gross cross-border equity flows, 1989, in billions of dollars.

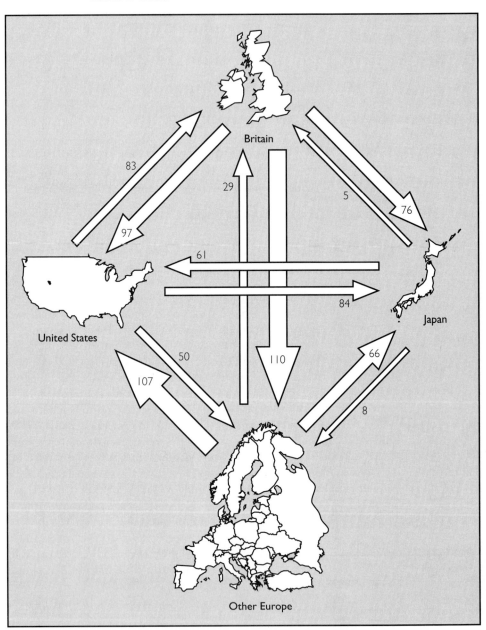

2. *Some multiple listings have turned out to be cosmetic*: the bulk of trading in a particular stock is likely to be concentrated in one or two markets, for the obvious reason that buyers and sellers gravitate to the market with good liquidity. Some argue that the value of multiple listings is negligible.

What of *Euroequities?* This term refers to shares that are in part *issued outside their home country,* and which resemble Eurobonds in that they are distributed worldwide through a multinational syndicate of banks to better achieve worldwide distribution. Figure 14.2 contains an announcement of such an issue. The international portion would not be

Figure 14.2 **Multimarket Issue of Stock.** Such issues contain a portion to be distributed internationally (sometimes known as Euroequity) but they lack a Euro secondary market.

All of these securities having been sold, this announcement appears as a matter of record only.

elf aquitaine

Société Nationale Elf Aquitaine

Global Offering
8,000,000 Ordinary Shares

2,600,000 Ordinary Shares

This portion of the offering was offered in France by the undersigned.

Banque Nationale de Paris   Banque Paribas

Banque Indosuez   Crédit Lyonnais   Société Générale

Caisse des Dépôts et Consignations   Caisse Centrale des Banques Populaires

Caisse Nationale de Crédit Agricole   Crédit Commercial de France

Banque de Neuflize, Schlumberger, Mallet   Banque Worms   J. P. Morgan et Cie SA

Banque du Phenix   Banque Française du Commerce Extérieur

Banque pour l'Industrie Française   Crédit du Nord   Banque Eurofin

Banque OBC-Odier Bungener Courvoisier   Banque Pallas France

Banque Stern   Compagnie Financière de CIC et de l'Union Européenne

L'Européenne de Banque   Sofabanque

1,800,000 Ordinary Shares

This portion of the offering was offered outside France and the United States by the undersigned

Paribas Capital Markets Group   Goldman Sachs International Limited

Banque Indosuez

Barclays de Zoete Wedd Limited   BNP Capital Markets Limited

Credit Suisse First Boston France S.A.   ABN AMRO

County NatWest Limited   Daiwa Europe Limited

Deutsche Bank Aktiengesellschaft   Dresdner Bank Aktiengesellschaft

Enskilda Securities Skandinaviska Enskilda Limited   Kleinwort Benson Limited

Lehman Brothers International   Merrill Lynch International Limited

Morgan Stanley International   Nomura International

RBC Dominion Securities International   Salomon Brothers International Limited

Swiss Bank Corporation   UBS Phillips & Drew Securities Limited

S.G. Warburg Securities   Yamaichi International (Europe) Limited

7,200,000 American Depositary Shares
Representing 3,600,000 Ordinary Shares

This portion of the offering was offered in the United States by the undersigned.

Goldman, Sachs & Co.

Merrill Lynch & Co.

Salomon Brothers Inc.

Alex. Brown & Sons Incorporated   The First Boston Corporation   Bear, Stearns & Co. Inc.

Crédit Lyonnais Securities (USA) Inc.   Dillon, Read & Co. Inc.

Donaldson, Lufkin & Jenrette Securities Corporation   A. G. Edwards & Sons, Inc.

Kemper Securities Group, Inc.   Kidder, Peabody & Co. Incorporated   Lazard Frères & Co.

Lehman Brothers   Montgomery Securities   J. P. Morgan Securities Inc.

Morgan Stanley & Co. Incorporated   Oppenheimer & Co., Inc.   PaineWebber Incorporated

Paribas Corporation   Prudential Securities Incorporated

Smith Barney, Harris Upham & Co. Incorporated   Société Générale Securities Corporation

S.G. Warburg Securities   Wertheim Schroder & Co. Incorporated

Dean Witter Reynolds Inc.   Howard, Weil, Labouisse, Friedrichs Incorporated

Advest, Inc.   Arnhold and S. Bleichroeder, Inc.   William Blair & Company

J. C. Bradford & Co.   Piper, Jaffray & Hopwood Incorporated   Rauscher Pierce Refsnes, Inc.

Sutro & Co. Incorporated   Wheat First Butcher & Singer Capital Markets

First Southwest Company   Furman Selz Incorporated   Interstate/Johnson Lane Corporation

Janney Montgomery Scott Inc.   Johnston, Lemon & Co. Incorporated   The Ohio Company

---

Joint Global Coordinators

June, 1991   Paribas Capital Markets Group   Goldman Sachs International Limited

subject to regulation by the SEC or any other national body, except the International Securities Dealers Association, a self-regulatory organization. However, almost all such issues have a domestic as well as an international tranche, so the issuing company saves little in the way of disclosure requirements or regulatory constraints. Beyond the initial issue, the stocks tend to find their way back to their home market. This result is not surprising, because to be true equity they must carry the same rights as domestic stock, and to ensure liquidity they must be fungible with domestic stock. Effectively, therefore, Euroequities cannot be distinguished from domestic shares, and there is no distinct Euro secondary market for equities. They trade over the counter or on the issuing companies' domestic stock exchanges.

Obstacles to International Investment

This chapter will make the case for international investment. Yet there is no doubt that many investors in large countries such as Japan and the United States balk at the difficulties of international investing. Even when not subject to restrictions on the proportion of foreign stocks that can be held in a portfolio, international funds managers in the United States feel obliged to warn prospective U.S. investors of the special risks for foreign investment.[4]

A list of perceived obstacles to international investment might include:

- *Information barriers.* Language differences, different accounting standards and methods, and the high cost of sources of information on companies in some markets all act as information barriers to investment.
- *Political and capital control risks.* When you invest in a foreign stock market, your money is under another jurisdiction, and you are a foreign investor, who might be treated differently from domestic investors (for better or for worse). Although many think of nationalization and expropriation as a major manifestation of political risk, these acts are rare; instead, governments exert their sovereignty by restricting companies' activities, by taxing them in one form or another, and, when under pressure, perhaps by restricting the outflow of capital that has been invested.
- *Foreign-exchange risks.* The revenue stream that constitutes the value of a foreign stock is likely to be denominated in a foreign currency, so currency fluctuations can have an effect on the value of the international portion of a portfolio.
- *Restrictions on foreign investment and control.* Some countries, fearing that flows of foreign-portfolio investment could distort values in a small domestic market and cause inflation, restrict foreign purchases of domestic stock. Others,

---

[4]"There is the possibility of expropriation, nationalization or confiscatory taxation, foreign exchange controls (which may include suspension of the ability to transfer currency from a given country), default in foreign government securities, political or social instability or diplomatic developments which could affect investments in securities of issuers in those nations. In addition, in many countries there is less publicly available information about issuers than is available in reports about companies in the United States. Foreign companies are not generally subject to uniform accounting, auditing and financial reporting standards, and auditing practices and requirements may not be comparable to those applicable to United States companies. In many foreign countries, there is less government supervision and regulation of business and industry practices, stock exchanges, brokers and listed companies than in the United States. Foreign securities transactions may be subject to higher brokerage costs than domestic securities transactions. In addition, the foreign securities markets of many of the countries in which the fund may invest may also be smaller, less liquid, and subject to greater price volatility than those in the United States." (Templeton World Fund Prospectus, Jan. 1, 1990, p. 3.)

Table 14.5   ***National Stock-Market Indexes***
(April 1988–March 1991)

	Mean	Standard Deviation (Annualized)
Australia	5.88	18.51
Canada	4.20	9.97
France	18.67	18.22
Germany	12.19	22.11
Hong Kong	15.37	24.85
Italy	1.15	18.55
Japan	−5.14	23.53
South Africa	18.75	30.29
Switzerland	5.66	19.45
United Kingdom	8.62	16.30
United States	12.27	14.37

for nationalistic reasons, restrict the proportion of foreign investment in domestic companies or insist the shares owned by foreigners have limited rights of control.

- *Taxation.* Many countries impose, or retain the right to impose, a special tax on dividends and interest paid to foreigners—a withholding tax. Tax treaties may permit reduction of this tax, and one may get a credit at home for taxes paid abroad, but the latter is cumbersome.
- *Higher costs.* Financial reform, competition, and the existence of low-cost avenues to equity investment have sharply lowered the costs of domestic investment in certain developed countries. In most countries, the costs are much higher. In addition, the cross-border investor faces additional management fees, custodial costs, and communications charges.

Many investors' biggest fear in going into foreign stocks, particularly those in emerging stock markets, is manipulation of prices and distorted values as a result of distorted information in closely controlled companies. To quote from a newspaper article referring to investment in Taiwan:

The rules governing financial transactions are scarcely rigorous, and the state of the accounting profession is such that obtaining a reliable picture of even a large listed company's true liabilities is by no means easy. Moreover many of the largest companies are still actively controlled by an aging generation of family founder-shareholders.[5]

In addition, volatility is systematically higher in some national equity markets than others. Table 14.5 expresses the findings of one study[6] in U.S. dollars.

These returns are expressed in a common currency, so that part of the reason for some of the volatility shown is the effect of exchange rates. Part is attributable to the way in which indexes are constructed, and part to the fact that nations vary in their industrial structure, some having industries that are inherently more volatile. Because of this array of concerns, the prospective international investor may be forgiven for "fear of foreign." Yet a properly diversified portfolio can far outperform a portfolio limited to domestic securities. The next few sections show why and how.

The Diversification Benefits of International Investment

Harry Markowitz won a Nobel prize for providing the mathematical basis for measurement of the gains from the diversification of investment portfolios. The next few sections discuss what portfolio theory and its extensions have established and show why the theory's conclusions might not apply without qualification in the international context. We conclude that, given academics' failure to come up with a clear-cut theory of international portfolio diversification, the benefits of international investment must be established by looking at the evidence. In short, the benefits of diversification globally (and domestically, for that matter) should be looked at as empirical issues.

---

[5]Peter Wickenden, "Why Taiwan Is Not Another Japan," *Financial Times,* Sept. 12, 1990.

[6]Richard Roll, "Industrial Structure and the Comparative Behavior of International Stock Market Indices," *Journal of Finance,* vol. 67, no. 1 (March 1992), 3–41.

The empirical approach to international diversification has two components: (1) It establishes the riskiness of foreign investment and the extent to which combining a foreign with a domestic portfolio reduces risk. (2) If foreign investment reduces risk, how does it affect expected return? If you can reduce risk *and* increase expected return via international diversification, the case for international diversification is established. Then we have to make sure we understand *how* international diversification is best achieved.

Portfolio theory begins with the theory of efficient markets, discussed earlier in the context of foreign-exchange forecasting. If the market for stocks is efficient, then any available information that is relevant to the value of a stock is already taken into account in pricing it, so only new information can change its price. If there was a significant delay before the stock reacted to new information, then professional investors could make systematic profits—and they would do so more and more until the point at which their actions would produce an almost instantaneous reaction in the stock's price to newly available information. The result of all this is that stocks in general are priced fairly, in the sense that one cannot get an abnormal return by selecting individual stocks. This means that the *expected return is commensurate with the risk of the stock.*

The International Capital-Asset Pricing Model

The **capital-asset pricing model** (CAPM) is an offshoot of the theory that says diversification pays when stock returns are imperfectly correlated. If risk can be reduced through diversification, then a fully diversified portfolio is less risky than an individual stock, given its return. Therefore, people will take advantage of this potential to reduce risk without sacrificing return—in other words, the bulk of rational investors will hold a well-diversified portfolio roughly equivalent to the "market portfolio." The **market portfolio** consists of all the stocks in the economy, weighted by their market capitalization (share price times number of shares outstanding). Stocks that help diversify, that reduce the risk of the market portfolio, will be in demand; their prices will be bid up and they will therefore carry a lower return. Stocks bearing *nondiversifiable risk,* whose inclusion adds to the risk of the market portfolio, will be disdained until their price falls to a level commensurate with that nondiversifiable risk. Thus the expected return and price of financial assets will be a function of the extent to which their returns are correlated with the aggregate market's returns. A proxy for the aggregate market is a market index, such as the S&P 500 index in the United States or the FT–SE index in Britain.

In its simple form, the CAPM starts with a simple regression equation showing the relationship between the return on a particular asset R_J and the market return R_M:

$$R_J = \alpha_J + \beta_J R_M + \varepsilon_J$$

where α_J and β_J are constants. Because ε_J is a random error term it disappears when we take expectations:

$$E(R_J) = \alpha_J + \beta_J E(R_M)$$

that is, an individual stock's expected return is equal to a constant (the alpha) plus some fraction (the beta) of the market return. The model also predicts that the stock's price will be bid up or down to the point where $\alpha_J = (1 - \beta_J)\Gamma$, where Γ (gamma) is a constant *common* to all companies. Substituting for α in the equation we get

$$E(R_J) = \Gamma + \beta_J E(R_M - \Gamma)$$

Intuitively, if Γ is thought of as the risk-free rate—a return factor unaffected by different states of the world—then the theory states that an asset's expected return equals the risk-free rate plus some coefficient (beta) times the excess of the whole market's return over the risk-free interest rate.

The capital-asset pricing model has been developed and refined in the context of the U.S. and other major stock markets, each of which has been treated as relatively self-contained. Indeed, within each of the major stock markets, such as those in New York, London, Paris, and Tokyo, stock prices behave as if the market is efficient and intramarket arbitrage ensures that returns are no higher than is warranted by their non-diversifiable risk in the domestic context.

But the world is now much more open to capital flows that it was when the CAPM was first developed, so it is natural to wonder whether the correct arena for diversification and the theories that follow from it is not the *global* stock market. If it were, then inter-market arbitrage would make stock returns conform to a global CAPM—that is, each domestic stock's return would be a function of the risk-free rate and the global portfolio return.

However, in the international context, an important assumption of the CAPM is violated. That assumption is that all the world's stocks are traded by a band of professionals who buy and sell stocks in response to new information—who sell those stocks whose return is low relative to the nondiversifiable risk and buy those whose return is unusually high. As the section Obstacles to International Investment showed, there are many barriers to cross-border investment that inhibit such rapid arbitrage, and in some cases outright prevent it. Moreover, unless we were to assume that real expected returns are equal everywhere because of purchasing power parity, it is implausible to suppose that there is one risk-free rate that satisfies all the world's investors, irrespective of their home currencies. And if purchasing-power parity does not hold, investors in different countries will never agree upon a common *numéraire*.

The empirical evidence is mixed, confirming the theoretical doubt about a global CAPM.[7] A number of studies over the past two decades have failed to identify the single global "market portfolio" to which the world's stock prices should be related. Instead, there seem to be some stocks whose return is relatively isolated from the theoretical influences, and many others who conform at best to a "multifactor" model reminiscent of the **arbitrage-pricing theory** (see Box 14.1). On the other hand, it may be that some of the evidence is illusory: return volatility across countries may reflect nothing more than the fact that some indexes are more diversified and less concentrated than others. And the lack of correlation among markets may be attributable to different industrial structures: some countries, like South Africa, are industry specialists and their stock-market behavior perhaps reflects international perturbations of the industries in question.[8]

BOX 14.1

The Arbitrage Pricing Theory

The arbitrage pricing theory (APT) says that the capital-asset pricing model is OK as far as it goes, but that in focusing on the individual asset's contribution to the market portfolio's fluctuations, it ignores the fact that the market's fluctuations are themselves a hodge-podge of different influences, or *factors*. Roughly, the APT argues that a company's share-price performance is linked to the company's sensitivity to changes in key variables in the economy, such as energy prices, exchange rates, or interest rates. If a company is, say, particularly vulnerable to an unexpected rise in the dollar-yen exchange rate, then investors will require some extra return for holding the stock to compensate for this risk.

---

[7]See, for example, Simon Wheatley, "Some Tests of International Equity Integration," *Journal of Financial Economics,* vol. 21, no. 2 (1988), 177–212.

[8]For details see Roll, "Industrial Structure and the Comparative Behavior of International Stock Market Indices," *Journal of Finance,* vol. 67, no. 1 (March, 1992), 3–41.

International versions of asset-pricing models have presented the argument that prices and returns of individual stocks in, say, the United States are influenced not only by their contribution to diversification in the domestic stock market but also by their contribution to some globally diversified portfolio. Yet this intercorrelation of markets is surprisingly low, given the increasing integration of world financial markets.[9] What we can conclude from the current state of evidence on asset pricing in the international context is that the world's stock markets do not behave as if they were integrated with one another.[10]

The Best Domestic Portfolio Is a Capitalization-Weighted One

One of the great insights yielded by the capital-asset pricing model is that the **market portfolio**—that is, all the stocks traded in the market, or an appropriately weighted subset of it—is also the *best portfolio* for investors to hold. Efficiency ensures that is the case: if it were not the best one, the community of investors would quickly discover that a different proportion would produce a more optimal risk-return trade-off and the desired stocks would be bid up in price, and the unwanted ones down, to the point at which the aggregate weightings equaled the desired optimal weightings.

But wait—what if some people wanted a different portfolio? The *separation theorem of asset pricing* says that it does not matter. People's differing risk preferences can be satisfied by means of different mixes of the optimal market portfolio and the risk-free asset. So everyone is best off picking a portfolio weighted like the market—in other words, in picking an *index portfolio*—and mixing in a bit of Treasury bills if the market portfolio's mix is too strong for one's taste.

The strongest argument in favor of holding the market portfolio or an index fund is that if you don't, you or your fund managers must believe that they can outperform the market, that you must have superior information or forecasting ability. Moreover, you are prepared to pay the additional brokerage costs that an "active" as opposed to a "passive" approach entails.

Can One Extend the Logic to a Global Portfolio?

Domestically, especially in the United States, index-targeting portfolios have become a major business. Why not save money if the fund's performance is likely to be, on average, at least as good as an active portfolio? The same question is now being asked about international portfolios. Good indexes of world stock-market performance are now available. One kind is exemplified by the Financial Times-Actuaries (FT-A) set of country, region, and world indexes, which are computed and published daily (see Table 14.6). The purpose of these indexes is to be as representative as possible: hence they contain a large number of stocks, as shown in the table. These indexes are among the best ways to

---

[9]Gerald P. Dwyer and R. W. Hafer, "Are National Stock Markets Linked?" *Federal Reserve Bank of St. Louis Review* (Nov./Dec. 1988), 3–14.

[10]It is only fair to acknowledge that the evidence is mixed. Recent work by Harvey finds a "price" of world covariance risk, which puts more econometric substance into the international CAPM than the above statement indicates. See Campbell R. Harvey, "The World Price of Covariance Risk," *Journal of Finance,* vol. 46, no. 1 (1991), 111–158.

Table 14.6   *Indices of World Stock-Market Performance*

FT-ACTUARIES WORLD INDICES

Jointly compiled by The Financial Times Limited, Goldman, Sachs & Co. and NatWest Securities Limited in conjunction with the Institute of Actuaries and the Faculty of Actuaries

NATIONAL AND REGIONAL MARKETS	THURSDAY MAY 20 1993								WEDNESDAY MAY 19 1993					DOLLAR INDEX		
Figures in parentheses show number of lines of stock	US Dollar Index	Day's Change %	Pound Sterling Index	Yen Index	DM Index	Local Currency Index	Local % chg on day	Gross Div. Yield	US Dollar Index	Pound Sterling Index	Yen Index	DM Index	Local Currency Index	1993 High	1993 Low	Year ago (approx)
Australia (68).....................	134.72	+1.3	128.36	94.10	113.01	127.91	+0.2	3.87	133.05	127.97	92.93	112.30	127.65	144.19	117.39	152.52
Austria (18).........................	144.03	+0.4	137.23	100.61	120.82	120.71	+0.0	1.70	143.49	138.01	100.23	121.12	120.71	150.96	131.16	168.24
Belgium (42)........................	147.42	+0.8	140.47	102.96	123.66	120.52	+0.0	4.70	146.32	140.73	102.19	123.50	120.52	156.76	131.19	142.27
Canada (109).......................	128.19	+0.5	122.14	89.53	107.52	117.70	+0.5	2.81	127.57	122.69	89.10	107.67	117.08	128.19	111.41	126.45
Denmark (33).......................	221.72	+0.6	211.26	154.87	185.99	186.59	+0.0	1.21	220.30	211.88	153.88	185.94	186.59	225.64	185.11	235.92
Finland (23).........................	97.90	+0.0	93.28	68.38	82.12	113.05	+0.0	1.09	97.90	94.16	68.38	82.63	113.05	100.43	65.50	79.36
France (98)...........................	151.92	+0.6	144.75	106.11	127.43	129.64	+0.0	3.46	150.95	145.18	105.43	127.40	129.64	167.36	142.72	164.37
Germany (62)........................	110.78	+0.6	105.55	77.39	92.92	92.92	+0.0	2.27	110.09	105.89	76.91	92.92	92.92	123.56	108.91	123.56
Hong Kong (55)..................	289.04	+0.4	275.40	201.89	242.47	286.79	+0.4	3.25	287.78	276.79	201.01	242.91	285.53	289.45	218.82	244.43
Ireland (15)..........................	159.67	+1.3	152.13	111.53	133.94	148.70	+0.4	3.56	157.68	151.65	110.14	133.09	148.07	170.40	129.28	161.05
Italy (73)...............................	72.82	+0.6	69.38	50.86	61.08	79.81	+0.3	2.42	72.38	69.62	50.56	61.09	79.59	72.82	53.78	71.18
Japan (470)..........................	142.87	-0.2	136.13	99.79	119.86	99.79	-0.2	0.84	143.17	137.70	100.00	120.86	100.00	146.85	100.75	104.93
Malaysia (69).......................	343.04	+1.5	326.85	239.60	287.75	339.14	+1.5	1.99	337.93	325.01	236.03	285.22	334.28	343.04	251.66	236.59
Mexico (18).........................	1514.71	+0.4	1443.24	1058.01	1270.62	5153.79	+0.3	1.31	1508.24	1450.60	1053.49	1273.04	5137.56	1725.81	1410.30	1615.69
Netherland (24)...................	164.34	+0.6	156.58	114.79	137.86	135.76	+0.0	4.07	163.30	157.06	114.06	137.84	135.76	172.75	150.30	158.13
New Zealand (13)..............	49.00	+1.4	46.69	34.23	41.11	48.05	+1.1	4.76	48.34	46.49	33.77	40.80	47.55	49.32	40.56	46.82
Norway (22)..........................	159.00	+0.7	151.50	111.06	133.38	147.29	+0.0	1.79	157.90	151.87	110.29	133.28	147.29	166.21	137.71	185.06
Singapore (38)....................	254.29	-0.1	242.30	177.62	213.31	189.08	-0.1	1.82	254.49	244.77	177.76	214.80	189.34	254.49	207.04	216.78
South Africa (60)...............	200.98	+1.0	191.50	140.38	168.59	200.97	+0.0	2.51	199.02	191.42	139.01	167.98	200.97	208.08	144.72	246.32
Spain (46).............................	129.21	+0.4	123.11	90.25	108.39	120.74	-0.1	4.94	128.66	123.74	89.87	108.59	120.86	132.82	115.23	159.18
Sweden (36).........................	177.17	+0.7	168.81	123.75	148.62	191.66	+0.0	1.76	175.96	169.24	122.91	148.52	191.66	178.35	149.70	198.36
Switzerland (55)..................	123.14	+0.6	117.33	86.02	103.31	111.84	+0.0	1.94	122.35	117.67	85.46	103.28	111.84	123.58	108.91	105.11
United Kingdom (218).......	178.10	+0.9	169.70	124.39	149.39	169.70	+0.0	4.05	176.51	169.77	123.28	148.97	169.77	181.99	162.00	197.99
USA (519)..............................	184.19	+0.7	175.50	128.66	154.51	184.19	+0.7	2.77	182.94	175.95	127.79	154.42	182.94	186.27	175.38	168.39
Europe (765).......................	145.28	+0.7	138.43	101.48	121.87	131.97	+0.0	3.38	144.22	138.71	100.74	121.73	131.97	149.02	133.92	155.16
Nordic (114).........................	167.90	+0.6	159.97	117.27	140.84	160.22	+0.0	1.56	166.90	160.52	116.58	140.87	160.22	169.44	142.13	181.21
Pacific Basin (713).............	147.06	-0.1	140.13	102.73	123.37	106.33	-0.1	1.12	147.18	141.56	102.81	124.23	106.46	150.03	105.89	111.09
Euro–Pacific (1478)............	146.21	+0.2	139.32	102.12	122.65	117.33	-0.1	2.04	145.85	140.28	101.87	123.10	117.42	148.94	117.26	128.94
North America (628)...........	180.70	+0.7	172.17	126.23	151.60	179.66	+0.7	2.78	179.49	172.63	125.39	151.53	178.46	182.38	171.51	165.76
Europe Ex. UK (547)..........	125.09	+0.6	119.19	87.39	104.96	110.66	+0.0	2.91	124.31	119.56	86.85	104.95	110.64	128.65	112.51	129.79
Pacific Ex. Japan (243).....	188.51	+0.8	179.62	131.69	158.15	172.32	+0.5	3.17	186.93	179.79	130.59	157.80	171.47	188.51	152.70	171.82
World Ex. US (1665)...........	147.00	+0.3	140.07	102.69	123.32	119.50	-0.1	2.06	146.61	141.01	102.41	123.75	119.56	149.39	118.51	131.12
World Ex. UK (1966)..........	156.58	+0.4	149.19	109.38	131.36	136.34	+0.3	2.15	155.99	150.03	108.96	131.68	135.99	157.19	134.22	137.49
World Ex. So. Af. (2124)....	158.29	+0.4	150.82	110.57	132.79	138.92	+0.2	2.34	157.62	151.60	110.11	133.05	138.59	158.98	137.29	142.01
World Ex. Japan (1714).....	168.56	+0.7	160.61	117.75	141.42	161.54	+0.4	2.99	167.38	160.98	116.92	141.30	160.86	168.56	157.47	163.94
The World Index (2184)......	158.48	+0.4	151.00	110.70	132.95	139.44	+0.2	2.34	157.80	151.77	110.23	133.20	139.12	159.07	137.32	142.70

Markets closed May 20: Austria, Belgium, Denmark, Finland, France, Germany, Netherlands, Norway, South Africa, Sweden and Switzerland.

Source: *Financial Times*, May 21, 1993.

evaluate the performance of different countries' or regions' equity markets. An alternative approach to indexing is exemplified by an index compiled by Morgan Stanley Capital International, known as EAFE (Europe, Australia, and the Far East). This widely cited index does not claim to be as comprehensive or representative as the FT-A indexes; rather, it combines *replicability* with being reasonably representative.[11] The index is replicable in an actual portfolio because it includes only the major, liquid stocks in countries whose markets are fully accessible to foreign investors. Many other international funds use EAFE as a benchmark for performance comparison. Also, one could mimic the EAFE index by buying the same stocks in proportion to their weighting in the index.

The approach has been followed by a few funds in the United States and elsewhere. Because they can be managed on "automatic pilot" at low cost, their fees and expense

---

[11]The same company, a subsidiary of the investment bank Morgan Stanley, produces other indices including a comprehensive one, the MSCIP World Index.

ratios are low. Table 14.7 compares the fees and operating expenses of two international mutual funds offered in the United States, one (Vanguard) an index fund and the other (Fidelity) a managed portfolio.

Table 14.7   An Index-Matching International Mutual Fund

	Sales Load[a]	Annual Expenses[b]	Five-year[c] Performance
Vanguard International Equity Index Fund	0%[d]	0.32%	n.a.
Fidelity Overseas Fund	3%	2.0%	18.10
EAFE Index			18.04

[a]Fees including sales redemption and exchange fees.
[b]Expenses including management fees, advisory fees, accounting costs, and other expenses.
[c]At end 1990.
[d]Shareholders are charged 1% upon purchase, paid to the fund, not to Vanguard.

Source: Fund prospectuses.

Figure 14.3   *The Global Efficient Frontier—Passive Versus Active Portfolios*

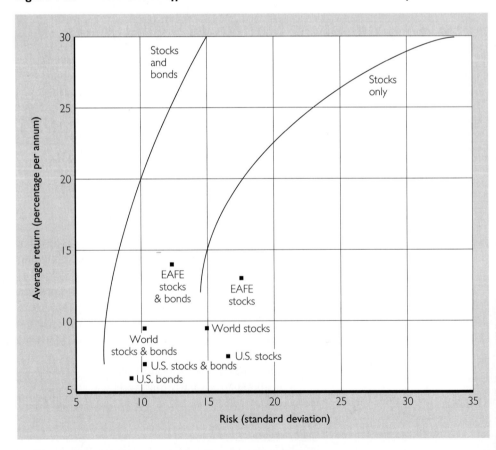

Source: Solnik and Noetzlin, "Optimal International Asset Allocation," *Journal of Portfolio Management*, Fall 1982.

For the international investor, however, the capitalization-weighted portfolio may not be the optimal one. The reason lies in market segmentation. The evidence suggests that the world stock market is not yet efficient, at least not in the sense of "mean-variance efficiency" required by the CAPM. In particular, because of real exchange risk (deviations from purchasing-power parity), the optimal portfolio for an investor in one country may not be the optimal portfolio for an investor in another, even if there were a single risk-free asset acceptable to both. Hence in the international context one may be able to make a stronger case for an active approach to portfolio management than in the domestic context, in which the evidence in favor of market efficiency is fairly strong.[12] Solnik and Noetzlin[13] find that an indexlike global portfolio, weighted according to market capitalization, is *not* on the efficient frontier.

The location of the efficient frontier in one of their key charts, reproduced here as Figure 14.3, shows that optimal asset allocation makes it feasible to double or even triple the returns of a passive index portfolio for the same level of risk.

In the next section we will explore this idea of optimal asset allocation a little further, providing the reader with the basic tools needed to choose the composition of an international portfolio.

International Portfolio Diversification: Practical Applications

In this section we will explore, using empirical evidence, the proposition that international diversification can increase returns, reduce risks, or both. In doing so we will introduce four techniques for portfolio evaluation:

1. the measurement of portfolio returns
2. the measurement of portfolio risks
3. finding the minimum variance portfolio
4. finding the locus of optimal portfolios

These exercises are for expositional purposes only. Historical returns and risks are in no way a forecast of what will happen in the future, and the portfolio conclusions will change with new data.

Let us begin with the measurement of portfolio return. By return we mean the *total return,* including reinvested dividends or interest, on a given investment. If I put $100 into a stock today and with reinvested dividends as well as capital gains I have $115 a year later, then the *ex post* return is 15 percent per annum. The return on any portfolio, including an internationally diversified one, is simply the weighted average of the returns on the assets that comprise the portfolio. Let an American stock A have an expected return $E(R_A)$ and a Belgian stock B have an expected return $E(R_B)$. For consistency we measure both in U.S.-dollar terms. My $1 portfolio consists of weight w_A of A and w_B of B. Because my whole portfolio is invested in the two securities, $w_A + w_B = 1$. The expected return on the portfolio, $E(R_P)$, is

$$E(R_P) = w_A E(R_A) + w_B E(R_B)$$

---

[12]As Peter Bossaerts has pointed out, active portfolio management might be necessary even in 100 percent efficient markets, if, for instance, markets are never static, and become complete only as traders dynamically seek to act on new information.

[13]B. Solnik and B. Noetzlin, "Optimal International Asset Allocation" *Journal of Portfolio Management,* Fall 1982.

EXAMPLE 14.1   During the period 1970–1989, the total return in the U.S. stock market was 11.26 percent per annum, while that in France was 13.96 percent, measured in U.S. dollars. From the formula for a portfolio's return, an investor who had 60 percent in the American market and 40 percent in the French market in 1970 would have achieved a total return of:

$$R_P = .6(.1126) + .4(.1396) = .1234$$

The principle can be applied to a multiasset portfolio. In the same period, Canada's equity return was 12.67 percent, Germany's 14.02 percent, Japan's 20.76 percent, and the United Kingdom's 17.81 percent. Assume a U.S. pension fund had 70 percent invested in the U.S. stock market and the remainder in equal proportions in the five other countries. The total return is again the weighted average of the individual returns:

$$
\begin{aligned}
R_P &= .70(.1126) + .06(.1396) + .06(.1267) + .06(.1402) + .06(.2076) \\
&\quad + .06(.1781) \\
&= .1264
\end{aligned}
$$

Historical returns cannot be generalized to equal expected returns; nevertheless, the example suggests that over a 20-year period there would have been a distinct benefit to the U.S. investor to holding part of her portfolio in foreign markets. Yet two additional questions suggest themselves: (1) Did these higher returns come at the expense of higher risk, and if so, was the higher return worth the additional risk? (2) Why did the pension-fund manager pick 70 percent domestic and 30 percent foreign funds? Are these the optimal proportions, and if not, can we identify the best weights?

Risk to an investor means the volatility of total return on her investment. The risk of an individual asset is its contribution to the volatility of the total portfolio. We often use standard deviation or variance to measure portfolio risk. Markowitz showed the ease with which one can reduce the risk of investing without sacrificing expected return.

Take two assets, A and B, with the same expected return and also the same variance ($\sigma_A^2 = \sigma_B^2$). Investing \$1 in either A or in B will give the same expected return and the same variance. Also investing \$0.50 in A and \$0.50 in B will give the same return as investing in either alone. But investing \$0.50 in A and \$0.50 in B will produce less variance as long as the two assets' returns are imperfectly correlated—that is, as long as the correlation coefficient $\rho_{AB} < 1$. This result follows directly from the formula for σ_P^2, the variance of a two-asset portfolio:

$$\sigma_P^2 = w_A^2\sigma_A^2 + w_B^2\sigma_B^2 + 2w_Aw_B\rho_{AB}\sigma_A\sigma_B$$

where w_A and w_B are the weights of A and B in the portfolio respectively. If the correlation of A's return with B's return were perfect, as it would be if they were both the same asset, then $\rho_{AB} = 1$ and the total variance equals σ_A^2. But if $\rho_{AB} < 1$, then the total variance is less than σ_A^2.

Let us look at some historical data. Table 14.8 lists the standard deviation and correlation coefficients of the dollar returns for the equity markets of six industrial countries for the period 1961–1989. From these we can calculate the standard deviation of a hypothetical portfolio.

This table, simple though it is, provides some insights into the international equity market. The Canadian and British markets are quite highly correlated with the U.S. market, and the French and German markets are correlated with one another. The U.S. investor, one might suppose, would benefit most from diversifying into those areas that correlate least with the domestic market, namely the markets of France and Japan. But when we look at the standard deviations we are reminded that, as *measured in U.S.-dollar terms,* all the other markets look risky. The reason is exchange risk: currency fluctuations

Table 14.8   *Standard Deviation and Correlation Estimates, Equity Markets, 1961–1989*

		Canada	France	Germany	Japan	United Kingdom	United States
	Standard Deviations	.1715	.2893	.3082	.3278	.3410	.1606
Correlation Coefficients	Canada	1					
	France	.4368	1				
	Germany	.1659	.7238	1			
	Japan	.2239	.4231	.2447	1		
	United Kingdom	.3496	.1169	.1312	.0346	1	
	United States	.6844	.2876	.4318	.2274	.6327	1

Source: Data provided by James Bodurtha, The University of Michigan.

add risk to all foreign markets. (The same would be true for a German national looking at investments in the United States; in general, currency volatility makes foreign investments, taken in isolation, seem riskier.)

So, for international diversification to reduce risk, the imperfect correlations must offset the greater variances. The example that follows suggests that they do.

EXAMPLE 14.2   The manager of a mutual fund based in San Francisco has observed the higher returns that his counterparts at other funds have been making on their Japanese investments. He is considering placing 15 percent of a new, flexible fund in a diversified portfolio of Japanese stocks. But can he convince his Board that doing so would reduce risk?

Based on historical data, the standard deviations in the preceding table indicate that Japanese stocks are riskier than the U.S. market—twice as risky. But to find the combined risk, we must take account of the imperfect correlation between the two markets by using the formula for portfolio variance:

$$\sigma_P^2 = .85^2(.1606^2) + .15^2(.3278^2) + 2(.85)(.15)(.2274)(.1606)(.3278)$$
$$= 0.02411$$

and

$$\sigma_P = 0.1553$$

Thus risk can be reduced from the U.S.-only standard deviation of 16 percent to 15.5 percent. And, based on the expected-return numbers given earlier, the weighted-average return increases to 12.68 percent. This kind of analysis can provide a persuasive demonstration of the risk-reducing powers of international diversification.

Let us take this reasoning a little further, still using the data for the United States and Japan given in Example 14.2. The formulas for the return and risk of a two-asset portfolio allow one to derive and plot a table of returns and standard deviations for various proportions of domestic and foreign assets, ranging from 100 percent U.S. to 100 percent Japanese stocks. The use of a computer spreadsheet makes this a relatively simple matter. Such a plot is reproduced in Figure 14.4. This graph of risk and return is the so-called *efficient frontier,* which allows the investor to select a desired level of risk and to discover what return can be achieved by holding a specific combination of two assets. The bottom

Figure 14.4   ***Two-Asset International Diversification.***   Mixing a portfolio of U.S. stocks with a portfolio of Japanese stocks can reduce risk, improve return, or both.

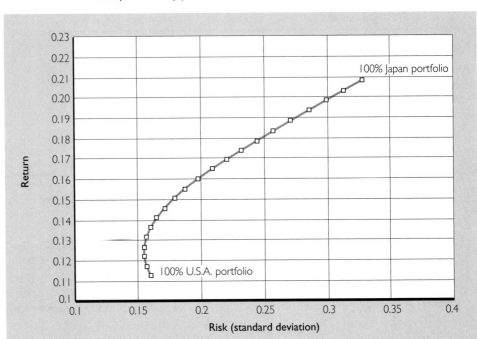

part of the curve shows how, even if one already holds a broad portfolio of U.S. stocks, diversifying internationally *can improve return while also reducing risk.* Moving rightward along the upper part of the graph, the reader can also see that a higher return can be achieved for the same risk level. Specifically, if one wishes to hold risk at the same level as that of the 100 percent U.S. portfolio (standard deviation = 16.06 percent), the return rises from 11.26 percent to 13.6 percent if one places 24 percent of one's funds in the Japanese market.

What if the investor's goal is to minimize risk? The leftmost point in Figure 14.4 shows the *minimum-risk* portfolio. Using the data at hand one can find that this combination is achieved when the investor holds 83.4 percent of his portfolio in the United States and the remainder in Japan. There are two ways of finding the minimum-risk portfolio: (1) by iteration—keep changing the proportions in the portfolio until the lowest standard deviation is achieved, or (2) by means of a relatively straightforward formula as follows:

$$\text{Minimum variance weight} = w_A^{\min} = \frac{\sigma_A^2 - \sigma_A \sigma_B \rho_{AB}}{\sigma_A^2 + \sigma_B^2 - 2\sigma_A \sigma_B \rho_{AB}}$$

The notation used here is the same as that described earlier. The minimum variance portfolio is achieved when $w_A^{\min}$ is invested in asset A and $1 - w_A^{\min}$ is invested in asset B.

The next step is to remove the constraint of only being allowed to hold two assets. When three or more assets are included in a diversified portfolio, the equations for return and risk generalize to the following:

$$\text{Portfolio return} = E(R_P) = \sum_{i=1}^{n} w_i E(R_i)$$

where w_1 are the weights of each asset in the portfolio. Again, expected return is simply the weighted sum of the individual asset returns. The formula for the standard deviation of a portfolio is a little more involved:

$$\text{Portfolio variance} = \sigma_P^2 = \sum_{i=1}^{n}\sum_{j=1}^{n}w_iw_j\sigma_i\sigma_j\rho_{ij}$$

When $i=j$, the term $w_iw_j\sigma_i\sigma_j\rho_{ij}$ becomes $w_i^2\sigma_i^2$. The portfolio standard deviation is the square root of the portfolio variance.

The general portfolio return and variance formulas are extremely powerful tools in portfolio management because they allow the investor to find a range of asset weightings that are superior to other combinations. Indeed, the formulas are the basis for *portfolio-optimization* techniques, which we will discuss next.

The data requirements for finding efficient portfolios are not severe; the table of standard deviations and correlations, along with expected returns, are all one needs. We shall use those data to derive two sets of portfolios. Each investor will be permitted to invest in the United States and five other countries—Canada, France, Germany, Japan, and the United Kingdom. The perspective, as before, is that of the dollar-based investor who can invest in non-U.S. as well as U.S. assets. The two sets of portfolios are selected to be (1) *capitalization weighted* and (2) based on *portfolio optimization*. We shall see which works better. To find the best capitalization-weighted portfolios, we take the value of all shares traded in the stock market of the non-U.S. countries being considered, and weight them accordingly. The weights are

Canada	3%
France	4%
Germany	5%
Japan	35%
United Kingdom	13%
United States	40%

Using the portfolio return-and-risk formulas given above, we find that

Capitalization-weighted portfolio return:	15.72%
Capitalization-weighted portfolio standard deviation:	17.88%

In combination these measures are superior not only to the single-country U.S. portfolio but also to the combined U.S.-plus-Japan portfolios, *if* combined with a risk-free asset such as Treasury bills.

To achieve *portfolio optimization,* we take this idea one step further. Why not let the proportions of all possible assets vary until the *optimal* proportions are found? Nowadays even personal computer spreadsheets allow one to solve for optimal solutions such as this one. The results of letting the computer find the best proportions for various levels of return in our six-asset portfolio are reprinted in Figure 14.5 and plotted in Table 14.9.

As before, the lowest-return portfolio is a purely domestic one. The investor can increase return *and* reduce risk by adding foreign stocks in some proportion. The minimum-risk point is reached when the portfolio includes 47 percent of its stocks from the United States, 38 percent from Canada, 6 percent from Germany, and 9 percent from Japan. (The proportions are all positive because of a self-imposed restriction on short sales.) Adding more Japanese exposure increases return and adds risk; that's where the trade-off comes in and where the investor's preferences play a role. The investor seeking the maximum return will hold 100 percent of the portfolio in Japan; but this seems

Figure 14.5   *International Portfolio Diversification.*   The benefits are evident from this plot of the "efficient frontier" based on 30 years of data from six countries.

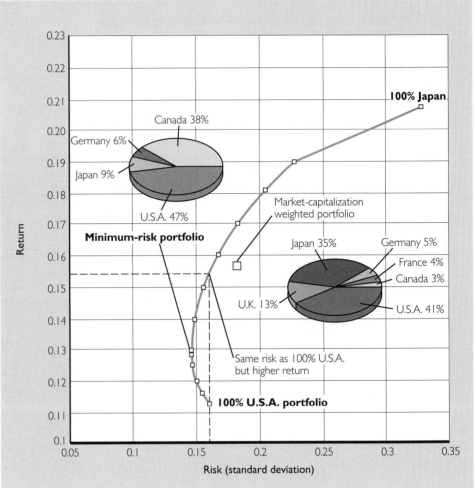

foolhardy or courageous, for the evident leveling-off of the efficient-frontier curve means a small additional return is being obtained at the cost of a great deal of added risk.

Two additional points: (1) The market-capitalization portfolio shown in Figure 14.5 is inside, and therefore dominated by, the efficient frontier derived from historical standard deviations and correlations. This is consistent with our earlier remarks about not trusting the market-weighting approach in the international context; also, the weightings can change sharply with exchange-rate fluctuations. (2) The dotted line shows how one can find a point on the efficient frontier directly above the 100 percent U.S. portfolio, demonstrating vividly how much additional return for the same risk can be obtained by diversifying internationally. More carefully constructed studies, such as that by Grauer and Hakansson, have reached similar conclusions.[14]

[14]Robert R. Grauer and Nils Hakansson, "Gains from International Diversification: 1968–85 Returns on Portfolios of Stocks and Bonds," *Journal of Finance,* vol. 42, no. 3 (1987), 721–739.

Table 14.9   *Spreadsheet Calculations for Optimal Portfolio Analysis*

INTERNATIONAL PORTFOLIO DIVERSIFICATION

PORTFOLIO EXPECTED RETURN				PORTFOLIO VARIANCE						
					CORRELATION MATRIX					
ASSET	RETURN	WEIGHT	PRODUCT	STD DEV	CAN	FR	GER	JAP	UK	USA
1 CANADA	0.1267	37.86%	0.04796	0.1715	1					
2 FRANCE	0.1396	0.00%	0	0.2893	0.44	1				
3 GERMANY	0.1402	6.41%	0.00899	0.3082	0.17	0.6	1			
4 JAPAN	0.2075	9.01%	0.01869	0.3278	0.22	0.4	0.24	1		
5 UK	0.1781	0.00%	0	0.341	0.35	0.2	0.13	0.03	1	
6 USA	0.1126	46.72%	0.05261	0.1606	0.68	0.4	0.43	0.23	0.63	1
		1								
				Portfolio Variance						0.02163
	Portfolio return		**12.83%**	**Portfolio Std Deviation**						**14.71%**

OPTIMAL PORTFOLIOS	Given	Best		Composition					
	Return	Std. Dev.		CAN	FR	GER	JAP	UK	USA
ALL US	0.1126	0.1606		0%	0%	0%	0%	0%	100%
	0.115	0.1548		17%	0%	0%	0%	0%	83%
	0.12	0.1494		33%	0%	5%	2%	0%	60%
	0.125	0.1475		36%	0%	6%	6%	0%	52%
MIN RISK	0.1283	0.1471		38%	0%	6%	9%	0%	47%
	0.13	0.1472		39%	0%	7%	11%	0%	44%
	0.14	0.1509		44%	0%	9%	16%	5%	25%
	0.15	0.1572		50%	0%	12%	20%	11%	7%
	0.16	0.168		43%	0%	11%	28%	18%	0%
	0.17	0.184		30%	0%	9%	37%	24%	0%
	0.18	0.2045		17%	0%	7%	46%	30%	0%
	0.19	0.2282		4%	0%	5%	55%	36%	0%
MAX RETURN	0.2075	0.3278		0%	0%	0%	100%	0%	0%

This concludes our discussion of optimal portfolio allocation. In the real world, international portfolio managers use these principles explicitly or implicitly, although tempered with a strong dose of country selection based on their peculiar views on each market's prospects. Box 14.2 provides an example of how practicing international-fund managers differ in the composition of their portfolios at a particular point in time. Many fund managers' goal is to "beat the bogey" (outperform a stock-market index), so they allocate more to some markets, and less to others, than the index-weightings suggest. For example, in Box 14.2, fund F allocated 40 percent to the United States and only 12 percent to Japan—in retrospect, a canny move!

BOX 14.2

How Portfolio
Managers Allocate
Their Funds

Practicing portfolio managers differ substantially in their allocations from the "market" portfolio and from one another. Here is one survey of how funds managers' portfolios deviated at one point in time from the "neutral" weightings of the Morgan Stanley Capital International index.

Global Equity Holdings by Area, Percentage

Country	MSCI Index	A	B	C	D	E	F
United States	33.7	30	30	28	28	30	40
Canada	2.6	3.5	—	—	2	2	—
Britain	9	9.5	5	7.5	10	11	6
West Germany	4.2	7.5	10	3	5	4.5	11
France	3.6	7	5	5	5	4.5	8
Switzerland	2	4	3	3	3	4	4
Italy	1.8	7	5	3	2.5	2.5	4
Holland	1.6	3	2	2	2.5	2	4
Scandinavia	2.2	2	5	3	2.5	1.5	2
Other Europe	2.1	4.5	5	1.5	2.5	—	3
Japan	34	18	14	35	24	36	12
Australia	1.4	2	3	2	6	1	1
Hong Kong	0.8	0.5	7	2	3	0.5	2
Singapore	0.7	0.5	3	4	2	0.5	3
Other Pacific	0.3	1	3	1	2	—	—

Source: *The Economist,* July 14, 1990.

How to Invest Internationally

Many investors do not have to be persuaded of the merits of international investments; it is the implementation that poses a problem. This section provides a brief comparison of several different ways in which an individual or institutional investor can diversify into a foreign or global portfolio:

1. One can buy foreign stocks on a domestic exchange if they are listed directly or if *depository receipts* (claims on the underlying foreign stocks) are traded.
2. If depository receipts are not available, one can *purchase the stocks on their own exchanges,* often by going through a foreign broker and perhaps by having a funds manager select the portfolio.
3. There is now a proliferation of *international mutual funds* that provide a low-cost means of international or regional equity diversification.
4. For a growing number of countries, the easiest means of access may be through *closed-end country funds.*
5. Another approach, widely used in Europe, is through *equity-linked Eurobonds,* in particular, convertible bonds and bonds with warrants.
6. A degree of international exposure can be achieved by *purchasing shares of companies whose business is global.*

Let us look more closely at each in turn.

Depository Receipts

One of the easiest ways to invest abroad is to do so at home. Americans and Europeans can buy, in their own stock exchanges, certain individual company shares that are traded in exchanges other than their own. Some companies have deliberately sought to diversify their sources of equity capital and perhaps lower their cost of capital by listing their shares in several stock exchanges, even though this is a fairly expensive process. Even if the stock itself is not listed for direct trading, one may still be able to buy it through *claims* on the stock, called *depository receipts*. Hundreds of Japanese, Australian, and European firms, for example, are traded in U.S. exchanges (and over the counter) in the form of ADRs—*American Depository Receipts*.

An ADR is a document evidencing ownership of a share or shares held on the investor's behalf by a U.S. bank in a foreign country. Chase Manhattan Bank, for example, might have its branch in Singapore take custody of a number of shares of the Straights Shipping Company. Chase New York will then issue a receipt stating that x shares of Straights Shipping are held in Chase Singapore and will continue to be so held as long as the ADR exists. Chase will then arrange for the Straights Shipping ADR to be listed for trading on, say, the American Exchange. The SEC requires issuers of ADRs to comply with U.S. regulations regarding disclosure of corporate information unless the ADR has strictly limited distribution in the United States.

The U.S. bank holding the underlying stock takes care of many of the administrative chores associated with owning stocks abroad, such as keeping track of rights and exchange offers, receiving dividends, and paying withholding taxes. The dividends are converted into U.S. dollars and paid to the investor in dollars, minus taxes and custodial and other fees.

Depository-receipt programs exist in other countries such as the Netherlands and the United Kingdom. The non-U.S. equivalents of ADRs are called *international depository receipts*.

The investor who buys foreign shares at home still has to understand the individual stock in its home context. This means doing research on each company, or at least knowing enough about them to have confidence that they are worth buying. Of course, some shares are widely known and traded and, in certain cases, may be a good and low-cost proxy for the local market—for example, Deutsche Bank (Germany), PT Danareksa (Indonesia), and Philippine Long Distance.

Direct Purchase and Managed Portfolios

Many institutional investors avoid trading depository receipts, finding the stock more liquid when traded in its own home market. One can buy individual stocks directly. To buy them, you may have to open an account with a local brokerage firm; alternatively, some domestic firms may have a relationship with a local firm, so you can open it through your own broker. In the latter arrangement, you will probably be charged a commission by both brokers. In each case, the investor will have to learn about delivery and clearing, foreign exchange, restrictions (if any) on foreign buying and selling, market-makers and the price-setting process, commissions, taxes, and other transactions costs and reporting requirements.

An alternative, realistic only for institutional investors or for wealthy individuals, is to have a money-management firm undertake to allocate and trade your funds on your behalf, drawing on the experience and economies of scale of a professional portfolio manager while enabling you to set constraints and guidelines tailored to your particular objectives.

Table 14.10   *Global Equity Funds*

Global Equity Funds	% Change in Net Asset Value ∎					Total Net	Telephone
	12 Months 1990	2 Years 1989-90	3 Years 1988-90	5 Years 1986-90	10 Years 1981-90	Assets#	Number
b—American Fds New Perspective (b)	− 2.0	22.9	35.5	92.4	282.5	1567.0	(800) 421-0180
First Investors Global Fund (b)...........	− 12.2	20.9	40.0	156.4	NA	245.7	(800) 423-4026
Freedom Global Fund†	− 19.5	6.0	15.6	NA	NA	30.8	(800) 225-6258
John Hancock Global Trust	− 13.1	1.3	11.8	47.3	NA	79.3	(800) 375-1610
Lexington Global†	− 19.0	1.3	17.8	NA	NA	51.3	(800) 526-0056
Merrill Lynch Intl Holdings	− 8.9	11.6	22.2	71.5	NA	174.9	(609) 282-2800
b—MFS Lifetime Global Equity† (b) (r)	− 4.7	21.5	18.9	NA	NA	78.5	(800) 225-2606
b—Oppenheimer Global	− 0.8	33.7	64.3	135.5	253.0	790.7	(800) 525-7048
P Webber Classic Atlas	− 8.7	10.9	28.9	85.4	NA	207.5	(800) 647-1568
Pru-Bache Global Fund† (b) (r)	− 16.5	− 6.5	− 2.1	53.8	NA	244.1	(800) 225-1852
Putnam Global Growth	− 9.3	12.9	23.1	78.6	291.4	574.2	(800) 225-1581
Scudder Global Fund†	− 6.3	28.7	53.2	NA	NA	245.8	(800) 225-5163
Shearson Global Opportunities	− 12.6	3.9	13.3	39.6	NA	62.4	(800) 451-2010
Templeton Growth	− 9.0	11.5	37.6	71.5	219.5	2329.9	(800) 237-0738
b—Templeton Small Co Growth.............	13.6	34.0	72.4	80.6	NA	685.0	(800) 237-0738
Templeton World	− 16.0	3.2	23.4	50.5	246.2	3667.0	(800) 237-0738
Thomson McKinnon Global Fund† (b) (r) ..	− 15.4	8.5	20.0	NA	NA	9.3	(800) 426-0107
Transamerica Global Growth† (b) (r)	− 17.8	− 4.4	− 6.4	NA	NA	6.8	(800) 999-3863
Tyndall-T V EuroPacific	− 18.1	− 9.4	− 2.6	NA	NA	10.2	(800) 527-9500
Van Eck World Trends	− 7.8	4.4	10.8	66.3	NA	49.1	(800) 221-2220
MSCIP World Index	− 18.7						
Morgan Stanley Capital Int'l Perspective							
E.A.F.E. Index	− 24.7						
Europe, Australia, Far East							

∎ Dividends and capital gains included but not reinvested. NA not applicable, not available, or not meaningful. (b) 12b-1 plan; % of fund's assets may be used for marketing purposes. (r) Redemption fee or contingent deferred sales charge may be imposed. b—, s— Recent *Selector* buy/sell recommendation. † No-Loads. # $Millions.

Source: United Mutual Fund Service

International Mutual Funds

Probably the logical choice for most individual investors is to invest globally by purchasing shares of an internationally diversified mutual fund. There are many open-end mutual funds that will take care of the difficulties of getting information and trading on foreign stock exchanges on your behalf, and provide good diversification to boot. Such funds tend to emphasize the more liquid stock in the biggest stock exchanges, seeking in some cases to allocate the portfolio in rough proportion to the market capitalization of the developed countries' stock exchanges.

Some charge up-front fees, but many in the United States are no-load funds. Most U.S. funds are *international,* meaning that they invest in foreign stocks (or bonds); a few are *global,* investing in the United States as well as abroad. Listings of international mutual funds are published in financial newspapers and several services provide comparative analysis such as the one reproduced as Table 14.10.

Closed-End Country Funds

Some investors refrain from individual stock-picking within foreign countries but like the idea of being able to choose specific countries in which to invest, so they purchase country-specific mutual funds, including funds that are themselves traded in the investor's home market: *closed-end mutual funds*.

To compare: open-end mutual funds are open-ended in the sense that they only invest as much as people have put into the fund, and if more people want to invest in the fund, then they use the money to buy more shares. Closed-end unit trusts, on the other hand, initially invest a fixed amount in the stocks of a particular country and issue shares against the portfolio, and no new shares are issued. Thus they avoid the problem of having to buy more shares every time someone puts a little more into the trust, and, more significantly, they avoid having to sell shares if people want to pull out of the fund. To invest in the fund, you have to buy the shares from someone else in the open market; to exit, you have to sell the shares to someone else at whatever price they'll pay. As a result, the shares may not trade at precisely the price at which the underlying portfolio is valued (the *net asset value*, or NAV). Some trade at a discount to NAV, and some trade at a premium.

Investing in closed-end country funds has been described as being like a nineteenth-century adventure to far-off places. With names like the Siam Fund, the Shanghai Fund, the Malacca Fund, and the Genesis Malay Maju, these funds can take the unwary investor to places from which few return unscathed. The reason is that their market prices so often seem to bear only minimal relation to their underlying portfolio net asset value. In the late 1980s, many of the funds traded at a big premium to their net asset values but in a most erratic fashion. For example, no fewer than 11 funds were set up by 1990 to invest in Indonesia, and these raised funds totalling $200 million *more* than could be invested in Indonesia's tiny, illiquid stock market, whose total capitalization (of freely traded shares) barely exceeded $1.5 billion. So much of the money has a hard time finding its way in—and once in, a harder time still finding a way out!

International closed-end funds took off in the early 1980s with the creation of the Korea Fund. They were based in part on the fact that some countries, like Korea, did not permit foreigners to buy shares directly. The other rationale was that most global fund managers sitting in London, Boston, or Zurich had neither the time nor the local knowledge to carefully select which stocks to buy and sell in the smaller, more constrained capital markets like those of Malaysia, the Philippines, Mexico, and Turkey, even if foreigners could buy them freely. The markets are sometimes intricate and the business dealings of the companies obscure. The dominant business role of certain families in some countries, and overseas Chinese in others, makes it difficult for the outsider to know when to sell. Specialist experts, with ultimate knowledge of the markets, would be paid a fee to advise on the investment and management of the portfolios. In all these countries the funds had to be closed-end funds, because liquidation of open-end funds would have to be done at net asset value. In a highly illiquid portfolio, this liquidation might bring severe losses that would then be shared by *all* shareholders, not just those exiting. In a country fund, liquidity is instead ensured by having at least one securities house acting as market-maker, standing ready to buy and sell the shares in the market. Then the funds' liquidity is likely to be much greater than that of the underlying shares.

Table 14.11 lists some country funds. Note that the percentage difference between market price and net asset value varies between a premium of 26.9 percent and a discount of 19.4 percent. Although closed-end funds have been extensively studied in the United States, researchers are only beginning to understand what affects the premium or discount on country funds. One explanation might be that although most closed-end funds trade at a discount, some country funds might provide the only means of access to a restricted market, so they would be priced at a premium to their underlying value—except where the premium is offset by political risk. Thus Korea Fund trades at a premium, but Brazil, despite restrictions on foreigners' access, trades at a slight discount. However, the market prices of country funds can be volatile and the portfolio valuations of illiquid stocks are

Table 14.11   Closed-End Country Funds

	Price	NAVa	% Difference
Brazil Fund	8.62	8.76	− 1.6
First Australia	7.63	8.61	− 12.8
Germany Fund	11.50	11.16	3.0
Italy Fund	10.00	11.37	− 13.7
Korea Fund	12.25	10.04	18.0
Malaysia Fund	12.37	12.42	− 0.4
Mexico Fund	14.00	15.37	− 9.8
Spain Fund	10.87	11.20	− 3.0
Taiwan Fund	21.37	15.63	26.9
Thai Fund	15.88	14.74	7.2
U.K. Fund	9.25	11.04	− 19.4

aNAV = Net asset value of shares in the portfolio.

Source: United Mutual Fund Selector, Feb. 15, 1991.

suspect, so we must not be too categorical about the determinants of country-fund prices.[15]

Equity-Linked Eurobonds

In a sense, the Eurobond market has become a global equity market—not directly, but through bonds whose value is influenced far more by changes in equity values than by changes in interest rates. The principal forms that these equitylike Eurobonds take are bonds with warrants, convertible bonds, and equity index-linked bonds. The last, which generally are private placements with limited trading, will be discussed in Chapter 17.

1. *Eurobonds with warrants* provide the investor with a vehicle for buying a bond with a *separable* option on the issuer's stock. Some investors like the idea of buying the protection of the bond and the potential for gain, the "play," of the warrant. In most cases, however, the warrants are separated from the bond and each is sold to a different investment clientele. The *ex-warrant bonds* may be sold to bond investors who like the capital-gain component of a discount bond, or a group of such bonds may be consolidated and sold together with an interest-rate swap to convert them into synthetic floating-rate notes. The *warrants* often gravitate back to the issuer's home market, acting as a substitute for equity options, where such options are prohibited or restricted. Such has been the case with much of the huge volume of Eurobonds with warrants that have been issued by Japanese companies.

2. *Convertible Eurobonds* serve a similar purpose for many investors. The investor has a bond but also an option on the stock. The investor may be unable to buy options on the stock directly because they are traded only in the issuer's home country, where disclosure and taxes may discourage foreign participation. Some institutional investors who are not permitted to buy equities directly but can buy bonds of various kinds use convertibles as a "back door" way of participating in the equity market.

---

[15]The Thai Fund and the Thai Capital Fund are closed-end funds managed by the same firm in Bangkok; yet the former, better-known fund has consistently traded at a premium, whereas the latter trades at a discount.

3. Many third world companies have issued convertible bonds, taking advantage of growing interest in emerging markets. These are often bought for different reasons than buying convertibles of, say, an American company. In markets like Korea, largely closed to the outside world, a convertible (or a country fund) may be the only way for foreigners to buy into the market. Even in countries like Indonesia, where the markets are open to foreigners, a convertible avoids the settlement problems that plague underdeveloped markets. The convertibles are cleared through the Eurobond clearing houses, Cedel and Euroclear. Liquidity may also be better than the underlying stock. And because convertibles are denominated in dollars, there is some protection against the devaluation of the local currency. However, if the devaluation goes too far, that protection may be illusory, because the company may have difficulty servicing its foreign-currency debt.

Global Firms

Finally, there is an *indirect* way to participate in the global economy—that is, to buy the domestic shares of companies whose business is global. Companies such as IBM, Coca-Cola, and Procter & Gamble in the United States, ICI in the United Kingdom, and Nestlé in Switzerland derive such a large proportion of their income from nondomestic operations that some analysts regard these as proxies for a global portfolio. The disadvantage of this indirect approach is that these firms' culture, character, management, and home-country regulation are all domestic, so one may lose the dynamics of diversifying into competing countries. Also the country and industry characteristics of your "global" portfolio may end up being somewhat skewed.

Another dimension to consider is currency exposure. Multinational companies can provide some hedge against a fall of the investor's domestic currency; for example, a weak dollar may mean that companies with extensive overseas holding such as IBM may provide currency gains. Yet it is not easy to make precise judgments about the impact of currency changes on the reported or actual earnings of multinational companies. Many companies employ sophisticated hedging programs to mitigate the effects of currency gyrations. Another problem is that few companies disclose the extent to which currency gains or losses affect per-share earnings. The geographic configuration of a particular company's overseas production and marketing activities can have a major influence on its ability to benefit from a drop in the U.S. dollar. A 20 percent fall in the value of the dollar, for example, would tend to benefit profits of Eastman Kodak and Polaroid considerably more than those of Xerox or Minnesota Mining and Manufacturing. The latter two do a large part of their worldwide manufacturing outside the United States, whereas Kodak and Polaroid export more heavily from U.S. factories.

Should One Diversify a Bond Portfolio Globally?

Does the diversification argument apply without qualification to global investments in bonds, such as government bonds? Not necessarily.

The arguments *pro* are based on the same notion of diversification as for a global-equity portfolio—interest rates and currencies in different countries do not move together, so one can reap the benefits of imperfect correlation that reduce the risk of a portfolio below that of any individual asset. In the context of a risky portfolio, therefore, it may benefit the investor to diversify a bond portfolio: it is purely an empirical issue.

The argument *con* says that many individual and institutional investors in a bond portfolio are trying to reduce risk by avoiding equities and risky corporate liabilities and by roughly matching the duration and currency of denomination of their assets with that of anticipated future cash flows. Adding foreign-currency-denominated bonds to the portfolio would add a totally new element of risk: obviously, currency fluctuations are not a part of the risk for a single-currency bond portfolio. Hence the only justification for taking on this additional element of risk would be to improve return above what could be earned from a purely home-currency portfolio of bonds. However, the international Fisher effect says that the interest-rate differential between countries approximately equals the expected rate of change of the exchange rate. If this is the case, the prices of bonds worldwide will be bid up or down to the point at which their yields are roughly the same, taking into account currency rises and falls. Evidence of this tendency may be found, ironically, in the marketing materials of one fund manager who runs both equity and bonds funds that are diversified internationally. Both the equity and the bond index returns are reproduced in Table 14.12. It is perhaps not surprising that globalization of an equity portfolio produces a superior performance overall to that of a purely domestic index. Of course, the equity numbers tell very little about risk. But the story is very different for a bond portfolio! Although the U.S. portfolio (or any one market, for that matter) can show a far better performance in a given year than other markets, *for the 10-year period, the annualized return was very similar for the United States and for an average of other countries' bond markets.* On the basis of this limited evidence, then, there is not much to be said for global diversification of a government-bond portfolio.

This is only one set of numbers, and other samples or periods can produce different results. But we should emphasize that the argument does not rely on the particular data or on the international Fisher effect. If a bond portfolio is free of interest-rate risk, *given the investor's liability structure,* then adding exchange risk is most unlikely to benefit the portfolio even if somewhat higher expected returns are attainable.

Table 14.12   *Equity- and Bond-Market Returns*

ANNUALIZED EQUITY-MARKET RETURNS
PERIODS ENDED DEC. 31, 1989

	1 Year	3 Years	5 Years	10 Years
EAFE Index[a]	11.0%	21.5%	36.8%	22.9%
S&P 500	31.6%	17.3%	20.3%	17.5%

[a]Index is from Morgan Stanley International Europe, Australia, Far East Index; Frank Russell International.

ANNUALIZED BOND-MARKET RETURNS
PERIODS ENDED DEC. 31, 1989

	1 Year	3 Years	5 Years	10 Years
Salomon Brothers Non-U.S. Dollar World Government Bond Index[a]	−4.5%	8.8%	19.7%	11.8%
U.S. Government Bond Index	17.4%	6.3%	14.2%	12.2%

[a]Index is from Salomon Brothers International.

Hedging the Currency Risk of International Portfolios

Although one may contest the merits of international diversification in a government-bond portfolio, there should be little argument over the benefits or hazards of hedging away the currency risk of foreign-currency-denominated bonds. Except when there are imperfections that give rise to temporary covered-interest arbitrage opportunities, the fully hedged return on a foreign-currency bond should be the same as on a domestic bond. Hence one would not normally expect to gain from hedging a foreign-currency bond portfolio.[16] Indeed, the additional counterparty risk from swaps or long-dated forward-exchange contracts could *add* risk.

With international equity portfolios, the debate becomes fuzzier. The reason is that equities, unlike bonds, do not promise contractual cash flows denominated in any one currency. Even if the shares of a company like Western Mining are nominally denominated in, say, Australian dollars and traded on the Australian Stock Exchange in Sydney, the reality is that its revenues are denominated in U.S. dollars and so Western Mining's shares are *effectively* U.S.-dollar denominated. With many other firms, the effective mix of currencies determining the firm's performance is less clear-cut. In short, because equity carries no currency label, one cannot easily determine *in principle* what and how much to hedge; see the accompanying box.

On the other hand, one cannot simply ignore the currency factor, for many companies have revenue streams in foreign currencies, so the currency element *is* present in an international portfolio. It does not necessarily add risk. For instance, if stock prices and exchange rates are negatively correlated, variance may actually be reduced. There are several methods of hedging foreign equities:

1. One approach is to hedge the anticipated cash flows, chiefly dividends, as precisely as possible. But this is simply not practical and could lead to gross over- or under-hedging as dividends are cut or increased by unexpected amounts, and as holdings are liquidated.
2. A second method is to hedge the current market value of the portfolio, by selling the foreign currency forward (or in the futures market) in an amount equal to the foreign-currency price times the number of shares held. The amount of the hedge would be adjusted periodically as the market value of the foreign shares fluctuated, in a continual-rebalancing fashion akin to the delta hedging of an options position.
3. A third method is to treat foreign exchange as an asset itself, one that can be included in the portfolio. From the historical variance-covariance matrix one can determine how much of the foreign-exchange asset (or short position) should optimally be included in the portfolio. Again, one should be wary of the notorious instability of such covariances.

---

[16]When an arbitrage opportunity does exist, one can exploit it by means of an *asset swap*—purchasing a bond and entering into a currency swap to fully hedge all the cash flows into fixed-rate or floating-rate domestic currency, as described in Chapter 13.

4. Finally, one can use one of the modern "quanto" style options designed specifically to hedge an unknown quantity.[17] Investors in foreign equities or bonds can combine the equity investments with one-sided protection against: (1) adverse movements in exchange rates alone, (2) adverse moves in equity prices alone, or (3) combinations of both.

SUMMARY

This chapter has discussed the many barriers to international investment that remain despite the extraordinary growth and increased efficiency of many individual stock markets around the world. The evidence suggests that there is still no single, world equity market in which all stocks can be priced according to a unified relation between expected return and risk, although this conclusion may be modified as barriers to capital flows erode and as studies refine techniques for testing equity-market integration. In the major domestic markets, efficiency ensures that stock prices behave more or less in line with the predictions of the capital-asset pricing model. This model states that the expected return will be a linear function of the risk-free rate and the excess return on the market portfolio. But segmentation of individual markets means that no such single model has yet been found that explains the expected return of stocks in different countries.

On the other hand, consistent with domestic conclusions, diversification unequivocally pays. Combining a domestic with an international portfolio of stocks can reduce risk significantly, and can also increase return for a given level of risk. The improvement continues if bonds from different countries are included. But the evidence also suggests that it is not optimal to passively hold a capitalization-weighted passive portfolio of international assets, as the CAPM would prescribe.

Whether the portfolio is active or passive, the conclusion is that the investor is probably forgoing a significant improvement in his portfolio if he does not include a substantial proportion of foreign stocks in his portfolio. The chapter described a number of ways in which investors can invest in a global portfolio. Bonds offer diversification benefits, too, although for match-funded domestic institutions, the inclusion of foreign-currency bonds may add currency risk without improving return.

CONCEPTUAL QUESTIONS

1. What does the capital-asset pricing model say about the expected return of a stock in the domestic context?
2. If the world's stock markets were efficient and integrated, what could you conclude about the pricing of stocks?
3. If the CAPM applied in the global, rather than individual national, context, what could one conclude about the composition of the optimal portfolio for someone who is unusually risk averse?
4. If the CAPM does *not* hold in the global context, does it pay to diversify internationally? Why or why not?
5. What is the argument for including bonds in a globally diversified portfolio that up to now only holds stocks?
6. Do foreign-exchange fluctuations add to, or reduce, the diversification potential of an international portfolio?
7. Why should a country fund be closed-ended rather than open-ended?
8. Carefully explain the reasons why an international investor might include Korean convertible bonds in her portfolio.

---

[17]*Risk,* vol. 5, no. 3 (March 1992), 59.

PROBLEMS

1. If the expected return for equity investments in the United States is 11.26% per annum and that in Germany is 14.02%, what is the expected return on a portfolio that includes 25% U.S. and the remainder German equity?
2. How risky is the portfolio in problem 1, compared to a purely American one? To answer this, you may use the standard deviation and correlation estimates provided in the chapter.
3. Trace the efficient frontier for portfolios that can contain U.S. and German assets.
4. For an investor who can hold U.S. and German assets in his portfolio, what proportion of German assets minimizes his risk, as measured by the portfolio's standard deviation?

The following are more advanced problems:

5. Compute the expected return and standard deviation of a portfolio that is diversified *domestically* in equal weights of the following asset categories: cash, government bonds, corporate bonds, and equity. Use the following data:

	Cash	Govt. bonds	Corp. bonds	Equity
Expected return	6.511%	6.655%	7.379%	11.256%
Standard deviation	0%	10.755%	8.957%	16.055%
Correlations				
Cash	1			
Govt. bonds	0	1		
Corp. bonds	0	.9034	1	
Equity	0	.3378	.5219	1

6. Using the information in the previous problem, compute and trace the efficient frontier of portfolios that include various proportions of the four U.S. asset classes. Does this compare favorably to the efficient frontier for the international equity portfolio computed in the chapter (see Figure 14.5 and Table 14.9)?

Application 14.1 | ASSET Al

Your uncle Al Al-Akbar from Alaska has asked you to help him manage his personal portfolio, worth about $2 million. If you do well he will leave half of it to you in his will. Most of it is presently in cash. He has sent you a clipping from a newspaper article that he recently read. Would you advise him to allocate his assets differently than is suggested in the following article? Use the information in this chapter to evaluate the method described and compare it with alternative approaches.

Asset Allocation

In times like these, investors worry that they can't digest all the conflicting reports and make the right investment decisions. Should they move to stocks? to bonds?

The truth is, you would probably be better off if you ignored upheavals and forgot about the investment of the month. Instead, research suggests, you should set up a portfolio that is broadly diversified over several different asset classes—such as domestic and international bonds, stocks, and cash—and then resist the urge to tinker with it at every announcement of world, or domestic, events.

According to Brinson Partners, a guideline might be the breakdown of investments on all world markets, excluding tax-free U.S. bonds and non-U.S. real estate, given in the following table:

Cash equivalents	6.3%
Dollar bonds	2.3%
Nondollar bonds	22.7%
U.S. bonds	18.7%
U.S. equity	14.5%
Non-U.S. equity	29.0%
Venture capital	0.1%
Real estate	6.8%
Total value	$24.5 trillion

Application 14.2 | CRIES AND WHISPERS

The meeting was getting rowdy, and the professor was despairing. Clas Wihlborg, a professor of finance at the University of Gothenberg, was attending a meeting of the board of the Pension Benefit Fund of the Swedish company, Stora. Prior to his joining the board, the fund had traditionally held 30 percent of its assets in shares of the company itself. Wihlborg had succeeded in persuading his fellow board members to reduce this significantly, on the basis that holding shares in Stora subjected the fund's beneficiaries, the employees, to double risk. This fact was brought home dramatically when the recession in Europe of the early 1990s caused Stora to cut back sharply on staff and also knocked Stora's share price on the Stockholm Exchange down by over 25 percent. The PBF's holdings of Stora shares was now less than 10 percent. Wihlborg's new goal was to increase the international component of the pension fund's portfolio of stocks and bonds.

The other board members were engaged in an animated discussion about "the Professor's proposal" to reduce the share of Swedish equity in the portfolio to 20 percent, from its present 80 percent. Some, notably those who had resisted the sale of Stora stock, regarded the proposal as unpatriotic. Others feared the foreign-exchange risk that would result from putting Swedish workers' money abroad. The Swedish economy had experienced a mini-boom in recent months, following a long-delayed devaluation of the krona against the ECU. Some thought the market was on a rising trend, and were loathe to risk underperforming other Swedish companies' pension plans. Yet with weakening demand for Swedish products in Germany (Sweden's biggest market), the stock-exchange euphoria could easily be punctured, argued others.

"Hold everything," cried Wihlborg, raising his voice above the hubbub of discussion at the board meeting. "I want to show you some numbers! Our first obligation is to the pension-fund beneficiaries, and I have some data that demonstrate unequivocally that they would be better off with a pension fund that holds at least half of its portfolio in foreign stocks! If these numbers do not persuade you, I will have failed in my duty and I will resign from this board!"

The din abated to muted whispers. Heads turned toward the flip chart, where Wihlborg was copying some numbers from a sheet he held in his hand.

The Professor's Flip Chart

Scenario	Return from a Home Portfolio (Sweden)	Return from a Foreign Portfolio (Rest of the World)	Probability of Scenario
No. 1	15%	20%	50%
No. 2	−7%	10%	35%
No. 3	20%	−15%	15%

"The most probable scenario for the next three years," said the professor, "is a strong recovery in the world economy and a slowdown in Sweden, providing a 20 percent return from abroad and a 15 percent return at home. I assign a 50 percent probability to this scenario."

"Less likely is a return to exchange-rate stability in the European Community, with Sweden being obliged to refix the krona to the ECU to maintain credibility as a prospective member of the EC. The probability of this is 35 percent, and I have estimated that it would cause a 7 percent drop in the domestic market and a 10 percent return on an international portfolio."

"Finally, I would assign a 15 percent probability to a breakdown of international trade negotiations, especially in Europe. This would result in a loss of 15 percent in an international portfolio while returning 20 percent in Swedish stocks because of reduced foreign competition. All these figures are in terms of Swedish krona returns."

"Hah!" cried a rival on the board. "All you have shown is that foreign investments can show bigger losses than domestic ones. Better we take our chances with the devil we know. Maybe we'd be safest putting the money into risk-free government bonds at 9 percent!"

"On the contrary," responded Wihlborg. "These numbers show that foreign returns are imperfectly correlated with domestic returns, thus reducing risk. Moreover, the expected return on an international portfolio is higher, so we can increase return *and* reduce risk for Stora employees."

The murmuring around the table grew louder as the Swedes looked at Wihlborg's table with puzzlement.

"One moment," Wihlborg said to the group. He turned to his assistant and whispered: "Take your laptop computer into the next room, and calculate what the returns and risks would be for different proportions of foreign investment, ranging from 20 percent to 80 percent. Draw a picture of risk and return so everyone can see the tradeoff. If you can, calculate the minimum return portfolio. But hurry! The mood here is getting ugly!"

SELECTED REFERENCES

Directory of World Stock Exchanges. London: Economist Publications, 1991.

Levy, Haim, and Marshall Sarnat. *Portfolio and Investment Selection: Theory and Practice.* Englewood Cliffs, N.J.: Prentice-Hall, 1984.

Solnik, Bruno. *International Investments.* 2nd ed. Reading, Mass.: Addison-Wesley, 1991.

Tapley, M., ed. *International Portfolio Management.* London: Euromoney Publications, 1986.

Walmsley, Julian. *Global Investing.* London: Macmillan, 1991.

15
Global Commodity Markets

Commodities are increasingly traded like financial instruments. Indeed, the derivative markets for financial instruments, like Treasury-bill futures, originated in the agricultural-commodities exchanges. Now the tables have turned: commodity-trading techniques and instruments are adopting the innovations of the financial world such as swaps.

This chapter is devoted to a look at the instruments of global commodity markets, and at how prices are set, especially as they are linked to currency and interest-rate instruments.

Globally Traded Commodities

Commodities, like stocks, are traded both in organized exchanges and over the counter. In the actively traded commodities, most trading gravitates to the commodities exchanges: London, Chicago, New York, and Tokyo, as well as many smaller, specialized exchanges from Jakarta to Johannesburg. Table 15.1 provides a list of some of the commodities traded on these exchanges. At the risk of over-simplification, traded commodities may be divided into two broad categories: hard commodities such as silver and soft commodities such as wheat. The importance of such a distinction is that commodities that are perishable are priced somewhat differently from those that can be stored indefinitely in a mine or vault. Practitioners employ other breakdowns such as between oil, metals, foods, fibers, grains, and oilseeds. Gradually, other categories are emerging, as manufactured products such as semiconductor chips and services such as freight become so uniform that they can be traded like pork bellies.

Commodities are traded globally in *spot, forward, futures,* and *options* markets, and are increasingly being incorporated into more complex investment and financing techniques such as commodity swaps and commodity-linked bonds.

Commodity-Price Indicators

Commodity prices are quoted daily in the financial newspaper. For many who seek to understand how the general trend of commodity prices affects variables such as inflation, interest rates, and bond prices, it is more helpful to have an *index* of commodity prices or subindexes such as for metals prices. For example, the commodity indexes shown in Table 15.2 appear daily in the *Financial Times*.

Each week *The Economist* publishes a set of commodity-price indicators in its statistical section (see Application 5.1, The Deviant Economist). The indexes are denominated in dollars, sterling, and SDRs (the IMF-sponsored composite currency unit). Based on 1985 = 100, the indexes are weighted by the value of imports into OECD countries in 1984–1986 (net of intra-European Community trade in farm products covered by EC subsidies). The weights in the index are listed in Table 15.3. These weights also show the relative importance of different commodity groups in the world economy.

Table 15.1   *Commodities and Commodity Markets*

Markets	Commodities
Spot markets	
London, over the counter	Oil ($), oil products, such as naphtha ($); gold ($), silver ($), platinum ($), palladium ($), copper ($), lead ($), tin (£, $, Malaysian ringgit), zinc ($); cattle (£), sheep (£), pigs (£), sugar ($, £), barley (£), maize (£), wheat (£), rubber (£, Malaysian ringgit), soybeans (£), cotton ($).
London Metal Exchange	Aluminum ($), copper (£), lead (£), nickel ($), tin ($), zinc ($).
London Bullion Market	Gold ($, £), silver (£, $).
U.S., over the counter	Crude oil, fuel oil, gasoline (all $); aluminum, antimony, copper, gold, silver, lead, pig iron, platinum, mercury, steel scrap, tin, zinc (all $); butter, broilers, eggs, flour, coffee, cocoa, sugar, hogs, cattle, pork bellies, corn, soybeans, wheat, coconut oil, corn oil, soybean oil, cotton, wool, rubber, steer hides (all $).
Futures markets	
London IPE	Crude oil ($), gas oil ($).
London FOX	Sugar ($), cocoa (£), coffee (£), potatoes (£), soymeal (£), wheat (£), barley (£), pigs (£), freight ($).
New York	Crude oil, heating oil, gasoline (all $).
COMEX, NYM	Gold, platinum, palladium, silver, copper (all $); cocoa, coffee, sugar, cotton, orange juice (all $).
Chicago CME, CBT	Gold, silver; corn, oats, soybeans, maize, wheat, cattle, hogs, pork bellies (all $).
Options markets	
London	Crude oil, aluminum, copper, coffee, cocoa (all $).
Chicago	Crude oil, heating oil; gold, silver, copper; sugar, cotton, corn, soybeans (all $).

Table 15.2   *Commodity Indices (as reported daily in the* Financial Times*)*

INDICES			
REUTERS (Base:September 18 1931 = 100)			
May 18	May 17	mnth ago	yr ago
1676.3	1681.7	1650.2	1592.4
DOW JONES (Base: Dec. 31 1974 = 100)			
May 17	May 14	mnth ago	yr ago
Spot 119.16	119.92	124.91	118.58
Futures 121.69	121.52	121.94	119.47

Source: *Financial Times*, May 19, 1993.

Table 15.3   ***Weights Used in* The Economist *Indexes of Commodity Prices***

Metals	Weight[a] (%)	Nonfood Agriculturals	Weight[a] (%)	Foods	Weight[a] (%)
Copper	28.4	Wool 64s	10.5	Beef	6.7
Lead	4.4	Wool 48s	10.5	Lamb	2.1
Zinc	9.9	Cotton	20.2	Wheat	4.9
Tin	6.3	Jute	0.2	Maize	8.5
Aluminum	41.8	Sisal	0.3	Coffee	33.3
Nickel	9.2	Hides	11.2	Cocoa	10.7
	100%	Rubber	14.2	Tea	3.0
		Timber	26.8	Sugar	8.1
		Soybeans	4.4	Soybean meal	7.6
		Soybean oil	0.4	Soybeans	10.3
		Coconut oil	0.6	Soybean oil	1.1
		Palm oil	0.7	Groundnut oil	0.7
			100%	Coconut oil	1.4
				Palm oil	1.6
					100%

Of the total:

| | Metals 29.3% | | NFAs 20.9% | | Foods 49.8% |

[a]These weights are based on the value of OECD commodity imports.

Source: *The Economist,* January 5, 1991, p. 56.

Supply, Demand, and Expectations in Price Determination

Despite OPEC, the overwhelming determinant of prices of globally traded commodities is market supply and demand. If there is a freeze in Brazil, the price of coffee goes up because *expected supply* is lower, not because the international coffee exporters' organization seeks to raise the price. If fewer cars are sold the *demand* for chromium goes down, and so does its price. But the supply factor is influenced by an important feature of some commodities: *stockpiles*. If the Dutch suddenly announce that they are going to sell from their strategic reserves of coffee, the price need not rise.

The drop in the price of platinum in the early 1990s serves as an illustration of these three factors: demand, supply, and stockpiles. In trying to explain the price of platinum falling below that of gold, observers noted a supply factor: strike settlements in South Africa would restore the platinum mines to normal production. Others took note of demand factors: the sluggish U.S. economy and the development of automobile catalytic convertors that might substitute other metals for platinum. But one of the major influences was surely the stockpile factor: rumors that the Soviet Union might have to sell large amounts for hard currency, and proposals that the United States sell some of its strategic metal reserves.

As in the financial markets, *anticipations of future supply and demand* are the principal influences on current prices. It is the cost of storage that produces this effect. If I make cars, I need platinum now. But as a producer or holder of the metal I have the choice of selling it now or in the future. If I anticipate increased future demand or constraints on future supply, I will store it until the price has risen, as long as I can recover the cost of storage. An important component of the cost of storage is the cost of financing the stored goods, and that's where the link between the commodity markets and the financial markets comes in.

Agricultural products are typically seasonal. You would expect the price to be low when the commodity is harvested, and you would be correct. But people like their cereal and orange juice in winter, too, so the excess of demand over supply pushes prices up. Noticing that they can make more money by satisfying out-of-season demand, agricultural firms build storage elevators and freezers. As long as they can get a higher price later in the year, it is worth the cost of storage.

But what if, for some reason, the price of grain is expected to be *lower* later? Then producers and stockpilers will sell now, driving the price down to the point at which the spot price is below the anticipated future price by the cost of storage. Figure 15.1 illustrates the seasonal pattern of a perishable commodity. The price rises until the harvest, to reward those who store all year and sell when nothing is being produced; then it falls; then it rises again.

The existence of futures markets means that the stockpiler does not have to *guess* whether the price will be high enough to compensate him for incurring the cost of storage. By selling the goods forward at a higher price he can ensure that his costs are covered. As Figure 15.2 demonstrates, the sequence of certain foods' futures prices sort of matches the predicted zig-zag pattern.

Theory tells us that there is a very specific relationship between the spot price and the futures price of a commodity: *the futures price will exceed the spot price by the cost of storage, including the cost of financing.* This is known as the **cost-of-carry theory** of commodity futures. The sections that follow lay out this cost-of-carry theory more specifically, as well as its corollary, the "backwardation" effect, which occurs when market participants give up some nominal return in exchange for the convenience and security of physical possession of a commodity.

Figure 15.1   *Stylized Pattern of Agricultural Futures Prices.*   Each year, prices rise to cover the cost of storage.

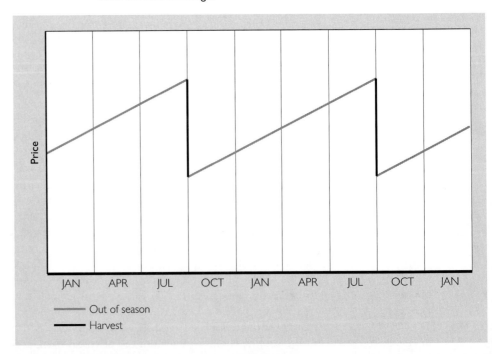

Figure 15.2   ***Actual Pattern of Wheat Futures.***   Like most other perishable commodities, wheat shows an interrupted cost-of-storage rise.

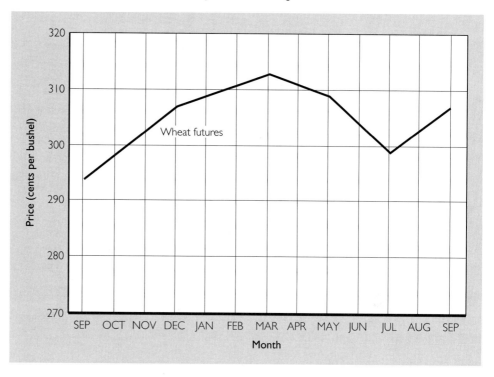

Futures Prices and the Cost-of-Carry Theory

The market for metals, especially the market for precious metals, provides further insights into the link between commodities and financial markets. The reason is that the noninterest costs of storage are low relative to the financing costs. Rats don't eat palladium, and one doesn't have to freeze silver; apart from financing, the chief costs of storing precious metals are custodial and insurance.

We can now write a simple model of a commodity futures price based on the cost of carry:

$$F_t = S_0(1 + R_t + C_t)^t$$

where

F_t = Futures price for delivery t years from today
S_0 = Spot price today
R_t = Interest rate for t years
C_t = Noninterest costs of carry, expressed as an annual rate.

Actually, for some commodities such as gold and platinum, the cost of physical storage and insurance is so small relative to the cost of financing the holding that we can neglect it. The equation then becomes

$$F_t = S_0(1 + R_t)^t$$

This is the fundamental relationship between spot and futures prices in the commodity markets.

Let's take an example using gold to show why this equation makes sense. Assume that the spot price of gold is $450 per ounce, and that the one-year interest rate is 6 percent. (The Eurodollar rate is usually the best rate to use for these calculations.) From the equation, the one-year futures price should be $450(1 + .06) = $477. What if it is not? If the 12-month futures is $500, I can borrow $45,000 at 6 percent, buy 100 ounces of gold, and sell one gold futures contract. The latter is an agreement to deliver 100 troy ounces of gold in one year's time at a price of $50,000. The financing cost is $2,700, so my total cost is $47,700. Profit: $2,300.

Conversely, if the futures price of gold is *below* the theoretical price, it pays anyone who owns gold (such as a central bank) to sell it today, and then to buy gold futures and invest the proceeds at 6 percent.

Realistically, of course, one cannot borrow and lend at the same rate, so there is a small range within which the gold futures price is in equilibrium.

EXAMPLE 15.1

On August 8, 1991, the spot price of silver was 392.5 cents per ounce. The February 1992 futures price on the Chicago Board of Trade exchange was 405.0 cents. If six-month Eurodollar deposits were quoted at $5\frac{11}{16}$ percent bid, $5\frac{13}{16}$ percent ask in the interbank market, was there an opportunity for a bank's gold-trading department to make a profit?

From the cost-of-financing formula, the six month futures price should lie between

$$F_{.5} = 392.5(1 + .058125)^{.5} = 403.75$$

and

$$F_{.5} = 392.5(1 + .056875)^{.5} = 403.51$$

Hence the actual price lies outside the theoretical bounds, and it would pay to buy spot, hold the silver, and sell it for February delivery. The potential profit is 1.25 cents per ounce of silver.

The example suggests that, in practice, the theory may not predict futures prices perfectly. If we test this idea by using prices quoted in newspapers, there are deviations from the theoretical futures prices. These newspaper quotations represent transactions done at different times, not prices that would actually be encountered by someone seeking to do arbitrage.

Table 15.4 reproduces a range of metals and oil spot and futures prices found in *The Wall Street Journal* on a particular day. The reader is invited to test the proposition that spot and futures prices are roughly linked by the cost of carry, as measured by the Eurodollar interest rate. For those commodities for which no comparable cash-market quotation is provided, the nearby futures price may serve as a proxy for the spot price.

Fear and Backwardation

Sometimes the model breaks down, and the naïve cost-of-carry equation gives radically incorrect predictions. An example will show why. Suppose the actual platinum futures price were *below* the theoretical price of $360 per ounce—for example, only $350. Then it would not pay to store the metal; instead owners of platinum would sell spot, invest the proceeds, and buy futures. But what if those same owners were reluctant to give up the physical possession of platinum? By holding a commodity despite its inadequate return they are demonstrating their willingness to pay a premium for ownership, or for what is

Table 15.4 *Spot and Futures Commodity Prices, Linked by the Eurocurrency Interest Rate*

EURODOLLAR INTEREST RATES

One month	Three months	Six months	One year
5 11/16-5 9/16	5 11/16-5 9/16	5 13/16-5 11/16	6 1/8-6

Thursday, August 8, 1991.

Open Interest Reflects Previous Trading Day.

—METALS & PETROLEUM—

COPPER-HIGH (CMX) – 25,000 lbs.; cents per lb.

	Open	High	Low	Settle	Change	Lifetime High	Lifetime Low	Open Interest
Aug	102.40	102.40	102.15	102.30	....	109.00	96.10	477
Sept	102.30	102.70	102.00	102.35	– .20	110.50	95.40	14,296
Oct	101.50	101.50	101.50	101.75	– .10	106.90	95.30	914
Nov	101.10	101.10	101.10	101.40	– .15	105.00	95.10	403
Dec	11.00	101.20	100.80	101.00	– .20	108.50	94.50	8,872
Jan	....	....	....	100.40	– .20	104.50	95.00	357
Feb	....	....	....	99.95	– .20	105.10	95.00	150
Mar	99.40	99.40	99.40	99.45	– .20	106.80	93.90	2,271
Apr	....	....	....	98.80	– .20	99.10	93.50	170
May	....	....	....	98.20	– .20	106.20	93.30	1,473
July	....	....	....	97.05	– .20	103.80	92.80	1,193
Sept	....	....	....	96.05	– .20	103.45	92.80	889
Dec	....	....	....	95.35	– .20	100.50	91.60	715
Mr93	....	....	....	94.65	– .20	96.65	92.80	265

Est vol 4,200; vol Wd 8,203; open Int 32,780, + 247.

GOLD (CMX) – 100 troy oz.; $ per troy oz.

	Open	High	Low	Settle	Change	Lifetime High	Lifetime Low	Open Interest
Aug	358.00	358.00	356.40	357.20	+ .60	468.00	354.00	881
Oct	360.00	360.70	359.10	360.00	+ .50	476.00	356.90	8,333
Dec	363.40	364.10	362.50	363.30	+ .50	483.00	360.20	60,752
Fb92	366.50	367.20	366.00	366.50	+ .40	456.50	363.70	7,972
Apr	370.00	370.50	369.20	369.60	+ .40	446.00	367.30	6,296
June	372.40	373.30	372.40	372.80	+ .40	467.00	370.80	5,741
Aug	....	....	....	376.10	+ .40	426.50	376.50	2,543
Oct	....	....	....	379.40	+ .40	410.80	379.00	1,065
Dec	....	....	....	382.90	+ .40	431.00	381.80	2,345
Fb93	....	....	....	386.60	+ .40	404.20	404.20	554
Apr	....	....	....	390.20	+ .40	410.00	388.50	373
June	....	....	....	394.00	+ .30	418.50	392.20	2,002

Est vol 14,000; vol Wed 12,885; open Int 98,895, + 1,506.

PLATINUM (NYM) – 50 troy oz.; $ per troy oz.

	Open	High	Low	Settle	Change	Lifetime High	Lifetime Low	Open Interest
Aug	....	....	....	347.40	– 7.50	355.50	355.50	136
Oct	356.00	357.50	350.00	350.90	– 7.50	513.00	355.50	13,452
Ja92	361.00	362.50	355.00	355.60	– 7.50	451.50	350.50	3,551
Apr	366.00	366.00	363.00	359.60	– 7.50	438.50	361.00	1,061
Jly	....	....	....	363.60	– 7.50	427.50	376.50	559
Oct	....	....	....	371.60	– 7.50	404.00	375.00	304

Est vol 2,295; vol Wed 1,798; open Int 19,063, – 158.

PALLADIUM (NYM) 100 troy oz; $ per troy oz.

	Open	High	Low	Settle	Change	Lifetime High	Lifetime Low	Open Interest
Sept	86.50	86.50	83.10	83.50	– 3.00	119.40	80.75	2,091
Dec	87.10	87.50	85.10	84.75	– 3.05	114.30	82.50	1,393
Mr92	87.50	87.50	87.50	85.60	– 3.00	103.50	86.75	715

Est vol 214; vol Wed 199; open Int 4,231, – 94.

SILVER (CMX) – 5,000 troy oz.; cents per troy oz.

	Open	High	Low	Settle	Change	Lifetime High	Lifetime Low	Open Interest
Aug	....	....	....	391.1	– 4.3	446.0	388.0	21
Sept	397.0	398.5	392.0	392.7	– 4.3	654.0	367.5	41,874
Dec	404.0	405.0	398.5	399.2	– 4.4	623.5	374.0	32,001
Mr92	412.0	412.0	405.5	406.1	– 4.5	613.0	382.0	6,821
May	415.0	415.0	415.0	410.8	– 4.5	589.0	385.0	5,951
July	421.0	421.0	417.0	415.5	– 4.6	557.0	395.0	4,562
Sept	425.5	425.5	421.0	420.4	– 4.7	483.0	412.0	956
Dec	433.5	433.5	431.5	428.3	– 4.9	507.0	408.0	4,996
Mr93	442.0	442.0	441.0	436.8	– 5.1	513.0	437.5	1,228
May	445.0	445.0	445.0	442.6	– 5.3	473.0	443.0	563

Est vol 10,000; vol Wed 4,521; open Int 99,000, + 126

EXCHANGE ABBREVIATIONS
(for commodity futures and futures options)

CBT-Chicago Board of Trade; CME-Chicago Mercantile Exchange; CMX-Commodity Exchange, New York; CRCE-Chicago Rice & Cotton Exchange; CTN-New York Cotton Exchange; CSCE-Coffee, Sugar & Cocoa Exchange, New York; FOX-London Futures and Options Exchange; IPE-International Petroleum Exchange; KC-Kansas City Board of Trade; MCE-MidAmerica Commodity Exchange; MPLS-Minneapolis Grain Exchange; NYM-New York Mercantile Exchange; PBOT-Philadelphia Board of Trade; WPG-Winnipeg Commodity Exchange.

SILVER (CBT) – 1,000 troy oz.; cents per troy oz.

	Open	High	Low	Settle	Change	Lifetime High	Lifetime Low	Open Interest
Aug	....	....	....	392.5	– 2.5	541.0	363.0	5
Oct	398.5	398.5	395.0	395.0	– 3.0	537.0	380.0	180
Dec	403.0	405.0	398.5	399.5	– 3.5	575.0	374.0	4,604
Ap92	....	....	....	410.0	– 4.0	485.0	385.0	85
June	420.5	420.5	415.0	415.0	– 4.5	494.0	414.0	647

Est vol 100; vol Wed 68; open Int 5,629 + 2

CRUDE OIL, Light Sweet (NYM) 1,000 bbls.; $ per bbl.

	Open	High	Low	Settle	Change	Lifetime High	Lifetime Low	Open Interest
Sept	21.48	21.72	21.46	21.58	+ .22	28.72	16.90	52,278
Oct	21.40	21.60	21.37	21.48	+ .18	28.40	17.04	48,733
Nov	21.33	21.47	21.28	21.35	+ .12	28.10	17.20	22,972
Dec	21.18	21.30	21.12	21.20	+ .07	27.70	17.10	36,137
Ja92	21.13	21.17	21.07	21.06	+ .05	27.60	17.25	20,319
Feb	20.95	21.00	20.89	20.92	+ .04	27.00	17.50	13,576
Mar	20.68	20.80	20.74	20.77	+ .02	26.75	17.25	10,440
Apr	20.68	20.70	20.62	20.64	....	26.50	17.50	16,336
May	20.60	20.63	20.60	20.54	– .01	24.60	17.30	3,331
June	20.51	20.53	20.51	20.48	– .01	24.50	17.70	6,453
July	20.42	20.48	20.42	20.44	– .02	23.59	17.90	6,658
Aug	....	....	....	20.43	– .03	21.33	17.75	2,704
Sept	....	....	....	20.44	– .03	24.00	17.78	2,031
Oct	....	....	....	20.46	– .03	21.40	18.85	2,294
Nov	....	....	....	20.48	– .03	21.45	19.70	1,089
Dec	....	....	....	20.51	– .03	24.00	18.25	3,429
Ja93	....	....	....	20.53	– .03	20.91	20.10	1,098
Feb	....	....	....	20.55	– .03	20.83	20.50	130
Mar	....	....	....	20.58	– .03	21.25	18.64	1,865
June	....	....	....	20.67	– .03	23.00	18.60	7,316
Dec	....	....	....	20.87	– .03	23.00	18.70	4,444
Ju94	....	....	....	21.08	– .03	21.00	20.60	3,642

Est vol 92,068; vol Wed 107,334; open Int 272,275, + 2,602.

HEATING OIL NO. 2 (NYM) 42,000 gal.; $ per gal.

	Open	High	Low	Settle	Change	Lifetime High	Lifetime Low	Open Interest
Sept	.5920	.5990	.5920	.5953	+.0054	.8428	.5025	27,934
Oct	.6035	.6100	.6035	.6063	+.0047	.8500	.5130	14,274
Nov	.6130	.6205	.6130	.6178	+.0052	.7800	.5230	10,829
Dec	.6240	.6300	.6240	.6278	+.0054	.8262	.5330	26,946
Ja92	.6250	.6320	.6250	.6304	+.0061	.8200	.5340	15,619
Feb	.6135	.6135	.6135	.6169	+.0051	.6240	.5225	7,575
Mar	.5890	.5940	.5890	.5909	+.0051	.5975	.5415	3,635
Apr	.5720	.5720	.5720	.5689	+.0051	.5765	.5000	5,722
May	.5550	.5550	.5550	.5524	+.0051	.5600	.4875	2,680
June	.5475	.5475	.5475	.5424	+.0051	.5520	.4800	1,120
July	.5420	.5420	.5420	.5384	+.0051	.5620	.5160	2,226
Aug	....	....	....	.5444	+.0051	.5800	.5070	385

Est vol 16,368; vol Wed 28,645; open Int 119,040, + 905.

CASH PRICES

Thursday, August 8, 1991.
(Closing Market Quotations)

METALS

Aluminum			
Ingot lb. del. Midwest	q.58-.59	.58-.59	.79½
Copper			
Cathodes lb.	p1.05-.08	1.05-.08	1.35½
Copper Scrap, No 2 wire NY lb	k.84	.84	1.01
Lead, lb.	p.33	.33	.51
Mercury 76 lb. flask NY	q100-111	100.-111.	260.00
Steel Scrap 1 hvy mlt Chgo ton	94.00	94.00	118.00
Tin composite lb.	q3.6888	3.6809	3.8960
Zinc Special High grade lb	q.48422	.48422	.87¼

PRECIOUS METALS

Gold troy oz			
Engelhard Indust bullion	358.86	358.06	384.50
Engelhard fabric prods	376.80	375.96	404.15
Handy & Harman base price	357.60	356.80	383.60
London fixing AM 357.00 PM	357.60	356.80	383.60
Krugerrand, whol	a357.75	358.00	384.00
Maple Leaf, troy oz.	a368.75	368.00	396.50
American Eagle, troy oz.	a369.75	369.00	396.50
Platinum, (Free Mkt.)	349.00	356.00	482.75
Platinum, Indust (Engelhard)	355.00	357.25	481.00
Platinum, fabric prd (Engelhard)	455.00	457.25	581.00
Palladium, Indust (Engelhard)	87.00	87.00	116.00
Palladium, fabrc prd (Englhard)	102.00	102.00	131.00
Silver, troy ounce			
Engelhard Indust bullion	3.970	3.988	4.890
Engelhard fabric prods	4.248	4.267	5.232
Handy & Harman base price	3.950	3.955	4.860
London Fixing (in pounds)			
Spof (U.S. equiv. $3.9725)	2.3164	2.3205	2.6090
3 months	2.3795	2.3805	2.7060
6 months	2.4385	2.4445	2.8030
1 year	2.5585	2.5655	2.9910
Coins, whol $1,000 face val	a2.889	2.919	3.490

a-Asked. b-Bld. bp-Country elevator bids to producers. c-Corrected. d-Dealer market. e-Estimated. f-Dow Jones international Petroleum Report. g-Main crop, ex-dock, warehouses. Eastern Seaboard north of Hatteras. l.–f.o.b. warehouse. K-Dealer selling prices in lots of 40.000 pounds or more, f.o.b. buyer's works. n-Nominal. p-Producer price. q-Metals Week. r-all bids. s-Thread count 78×54. x-Less than truckloads. z-Not quoted. xx-f.o.b. tankcars.

OIL PRICES

Thursday, August 8, 1991.

CRUDE GRADES OFFSHORE-d	Thur	Wed	Yr.Ago
European "spot" or free market prices			
Arab lt.	hn16.95	16.55	23.85
Arab hvy.	hn13.95	13.55	22.20
Iran, lt.	hn17.15	16.75	24.95
Forties	h19.80	19.40	23.70
Brent	hn19.70	19.30	24.90
Bonny lt.	hn20.15	19.75	26.90
Urals-Medit.	hn18.55	18.15	26.50
DOMESTIC-f			
Spot market			
W. Tex. Int Cush (2025–2030) (Sep)	h21.60	21.35	25.65
W. Tx.sour, Midl (1775–1865)	h19.80	19.50	24.85
La. sw. St.Ja (2050–2055)	h21.95	21.70	26.10
No. Slope del USGULF	hn18.50	18.25	24.60

Open-market crude oil values in Northwest Europe around 17:50 GMT in dlrs per barrel, for main loading ports in country of origin for prompt loading, except as indicated.

REFINED PRODUCTS			
Fuel Oil, No. 2 NY gal.	g.5845	.5790	.6900
Gasoline unlded, premium NY gal.	g.78.45	.7490	.8630
Gasoline, unlded, reg. NY gal.	g.7305	.7015	.8030
Propane, Mont Belvleu, Texas, gal.	g.2910	.2875	.3600
Butane, normal, Mont Belvieu, Texas, gal.	g.3835	.3810	.3850

a-Asked. b-Bld. c-Corrected. d-as of 11 a.m. EST in Northwest Europe. f-As of 4 p.m. EST. Refiner's posted buying prices are in parentheses. g-Provided by Telerate Systems. H-Dow Jones International Petroleum Report. n.a.-Not availabel. z-Not quoted. n-Nominal. r-Revised.

Source: *The Wall Street Journal,* Aug. 9, 1991, p. C12.

known as **convenience yield**. Convenience yield can be thought of as a net dividend accruing to the owner of the physical commodity at the margin.

What factors motivate convenience yield in a commodity such as platinum? It is not that owners like to gloat over possessions but rather that they fear not being able to get the metal when they need it in six months or a year's time. A resurgence in auto demand may mean a sudden imbalance in the market as demand exceeds available supply and car companies without platinum face a loss of sales. Similary, some people regard gold as a passport to political freedom in an emergency. It is in the pricing of oil contracts, however, that the convenience-yield theory has found its most useful applications. Users of oil and other raw materials hold inventories because they permit production to proceed smoothly without interruptions caused by shortages of the raw material. The owners of oil inventories will sometimes continue to hold them even if the spot price is expected to decline; the decline in the value of the inventory is offset by the convenience of having the inventory on hand.

Let us therefore modify the equation to incorporate CY, the intangible factor that makes people want to hold goods and that therefore reduces their perceived cost of carry.

$$F_t = S_0(1 + R_t + C_t - CY)^t$$

where CY is the convenience yield, in percent per annum.

One way to use this equation is to observe a situation in which the actual futures price falls significantly below that suggested by the cost-of-carry model and to then solve for the convenience yield. We call such a situation **normal backwardation**. The oil prices in Table 15.4 provide an example.

EXAMPLE 15.2   Following the 1991 Gulf war, uncertainty prevailed for some time in the oil market. Owners of oil seemed unwilling to give up possession of the liquid despite the fact that they could get better prices in the spot market than those offered in the futures and forward contracts. They were reluctant in part because prices had escalated but were expected to drop with a resumption of supply when the war was over. Buyers would have been better off postponing purchases and hedging the future cost by buying oil futures, but many chose to stockpile. The reason was fear, and the result was a persistent normal backwardation in the oil futures markets: futures exhibited a downward trend rather than an upward trend.

For example, on Thursday, August 9, 1991, spot oil was priced at $21.58 per barrel, while August 1992 futures were trading at $20.43 (see data from Table 15.4). How much convenience yield were owners implicitly obtaining from owning rather than hedging?

The answer is obtained by solving for CY in the previous equation relating CY, F_t, R_t, and C_t:

$$CY = 1 + R_t + C_t - \left[\frac{F_t}{S_0}\right]^{-t}$$

and substituting the oil numbers:

$$CY = 1 + .06125 + 0 - \left[\frac{20.43}{21.58}\right]^{-1} = 11.45\%$$

It seems that the convenience, or fear, factor in the oil market was substantial.

We have discussed the convenience yield in an intuitive fashion, but in fact it has been the subject of formal research and empirical testing in oil and other commodities.[1] The convenience yield has been shown to be related to the value of inventories held, and to follow a stochastic process. We have also seen the link between spot futures oil prices and the interest rate. A similar relationship holds, again in the precious metals, between two *futures commodity prices* and *interest-rate futures*.

Link Between Commodity Futures and Interest-Rate Futures

The futures price of gold on one date is tied to the futures price on another date by the cost of carry between those two dates. The cost of carry between two futures dates is the forward interest rate, which can be found from the interest-rate futures market.

For example, the Eurodollar interest-rate futures quotations on the same day as the data in Table 15.4 are listed in Table 15.5. From Table 15.4, the December and June gold futures prices are $363.3 and $372.8, respectively, whereas the interest rate that can be locked in for that same period is $(6.12 + 6.21)/2 = 6.165$, the average of the December and March three-month Eurodollar futures rates.

The yield from holding gold for the six-month period is $(372.8/363.3) - 1 = 2.61$, or 5.23% per annum. This value is below the Eurodollar futures rate, indicating some backwardation in the gold market, too.

The theoretical cost-of-carry relationship between commodity futures and interest-rate futures can be summarized in the following equation:

$$F_{t+n} = F_t(1 + R^F_{t,t+n})^t$$

where

F_i = Commodity futures for delivery at i

$R^F_{t,t+n}$ = Interest-rate futures for period t to $t + n$

Table 15.5   *Eurodollar Futures*

EURODOLLAR (IMM) — $1 million; pts of 100%							
					Yield		Open
	Open	High	Low	Settle	Chg	Settle	Chg	Interest
Sept	94.24	94.26	94.22	94.23	+ .02	5.77	− .02	220,418
Dec	93.93	93.95	93.86	93.88	....	6.12	....	212,623
Mr92	93.82	93.87	93.78	93.79	....	6.21	....	148,768
June	93.42	93.48	93.39	93.41	+ .02	6.59	− .02	71,465
Sept	92.90	92.99	92.90	92.92	+ .04	7.08	− .04	50,847
Dec	92.35	92.47	92.35	92.39	+ .06	7.61	− .06	34,148
Mr93	92.29	92.39	92.28	92.31	+ .04	7.69	− .04	31,154
June	92.09	92.18	92.07	92.09	+ .02	7.91	− .02	29,377
Sept	91.88	91.94	91.84	91.86	....	8.14	....	17,362
Dec	91.59	91.63	91.55	91.56	− .01	8.44	+ .01	13,066
Mr94	91.62	91.65	91.57	91.58	− .02	8.42	+ .02	10,447
June	91.52	91.55	91.48	91.48	− .02	8.52	+ .02	8,258
Sept	91.39	91.43	91.36	91.37	− .01	8.63	+ .01	6,285
Dec	91.22	91.23	91.17	91.18	− .02	8.82	+ .02	6,840
Mr95	91.24	91.25	91.20	91.21	− .02	8.79	+ .02	4,580
June	91.19	91.20	91.14	91.14	− .03	8.86	+ .03	3,052
Est vol 176,833; vol Wed 200,882; open int 868,875, +6,836.								

Source: *The Wall Street Journal*, Aug. 9, 1991.

Commodities and the Currency Market

Today most of the world's commodities are traded in dollars. Some, however, were shown in Table 15.1 as being traded primarily in sterling, or in both sterling and dollars, or in some other currency. And many currencies are traded in local markets in the local currency.

When a commodity is priced in more than one currency, arbitrage will normally ensure that the law of one price (LOOP) governs the link between the two prices.[2] That

---

[1]See, for example, Rajna Gibson and Eduardo Schwartz, "Stochastic Convenience Yield and the Pricing of Oil Contingent Claims," *Journal of Finance*, vol. 45, no. 3 (July 1990), 959–976, or E. Fama and K. French, "Commodities Futures Prices: Some Evidence on Forecast Power, Premiums, and the Theory of Storage," *Journal of Business*, vol. 60 (1987), 55–74.

[2]For more on the Law of One Price and purchasing power parity, see Chapter 5.

is, the price of good X priced in currency A will be the same as the price of the identical good priced in currency B, translated at the current spot-exchange rate between A and B. For example, if aluminum is priced in New York at $0.58 and the dollar/sterling exchange rate is $1.70, then the aluminum price on the London Metals Exchange should be £0.34.

In practice, only time-zone differences and other minor factors interfere with the LOOP as applied to traded commodities, and dealers accept the relationship as fact, with some exceptions. The exceptions occur, as one might expect, where perfect arbitrage is not possible. An example occurs in South Africa. Strangely enough, the price of gold in South African rands, translated at the current exchange rate, can *exceed* the world market price, because South Africans are presently not permitted to import and export gold freely. As a haven against roaring local inflation and political risk, therefore, the yellow metal commands a premium in a land in which potential supply far exceeds local requirements.

Note that if the LOOP holds for the spot market, it almost certainly holds for the forward and futures markets, too. The futures price of copper denominated in French francs should equal the futures price for copper in dollars, translated at the forward- or futures-exchange rate between the French franc and the dollar. In practice, this is of little importance in the organized exchanges because most commodity futures are denominated in dollars in the first place, but the "future LOOP" relationship can be important in over-the-counter forward-delivery contracts denominated in the buyer's or seller's local currency.

Commodities in a Portfolio

Do commodities deserve a place in a prudent investor's portfolio? Although commodities and commodity futures can certainly be among the riskiest investments when taken on their own, there is a simple reason to suppose that commodities could improve the risk-return profile of a diversified portfolio.

The first consideration is the return component of the risk-return profile. If the cost-of-carry theory is valid, the price of commodities should rise at a rate roughly equal to the interest rate, plus any other storage costs. This expectation follows directly from the cost-of-carry formula. Substituting $E(S_t)$ for F_t, we can find the *gross* rate of return from holding a commodity as

$$\text{Expected gross return} = \left[\frac{E(S_t)}{S_0} \right]^{-t} - 1 = R_t + C_t$$

So unless we are talking about a commodity with normal backwardation, the expected rate of change of a commodity price should be higher than a typical financing rate such as LIBOR.

The second consideration is the risk component of the risk-return profile. Commodities are subject to many influences independent of those affecting equities and so should have low correlations with returns on standard equity portfolios, thus offering diversification potential. It is well known, for example, that gold has an extremely low to negative correlation with conventional equities. Would gold therefore enhance a portfolio?

To test this, look at the following return, standard deviation, and correlation values for gold and the major equity markets:[3]

---

[3]The measures provided are based on data for the same period, 1961–1989, as those used to test for the value of international diversification in Chapter 14.

Figure 15.3 *Can Commodities Improve Portfolios?* Evidence suggests combining gold with domestic or global portfolios offers better risk-return tradeoffs.

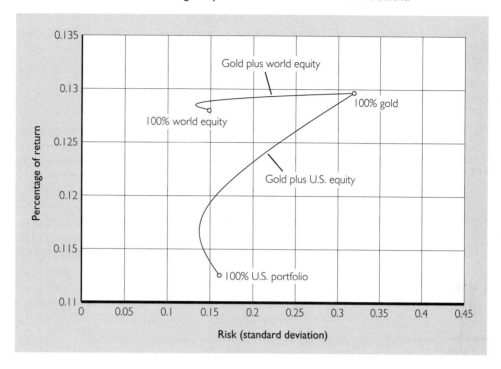

Gold Return	Gold Std. Dev.	Correlations of Gold with the Equity Markets of					
		Canada	France	Germany	Japan	U.K.	U.S.
12.97%	0.3200	0.0375	−0.0621	−0.1934	0.0677	0.1278	−10.35

A reasonable return and low-to–negative correlations suggests diversification potential despite the high standard deviation. Using the formulas for portfolio returns and standard deviations given in Chapter 14, we can now trace the locus of risks and returns of portfolios that include gold. This is done in Figure 15.3.

First, we combined gold in various proportions with a portfolio containing only U.S. equities. Adding gold offered significant improvements, lowering risk and raising potential return. On the same graph we plotted another set of portfolios, this time combining gold with the minimum-variance *world* portfolio as computed in Chapter 14. Here the gain is less dramatic, but it is still an improvement, especially in reducing risk. In short, the data suggest that combining gold with a domestic *or* a global portfolio can reduce risk and/or improve expected return. On the other hand, gold's behavior has undergone several radical transitions, and as a general principle one should be *extremely* skeptical of extrapolations of a particular period's rate-of-return results into the future.

Commodity Swaps

A commodity swap involves the exchange of fixed and floating cash flows pegged to the price of a commodity, just as an interest-rate swap involves the exchange of fixed and floating interest-rate flows. Indeed, the commodity swaps market began its growth in the late 1980s, when dealers in swaps and options applied their technology to commodities.

Variations include options (which give buyers the right to buy or sell a notional commodity at some future date), caps and floors on commodity prices, and swaps linked to the provision of loans or the issuance of bonds. In many respects, the commodity swap is little more than a long-dated, over-the-counter forward contract in a commodity, with settlement in cash rather than physical delivery of the commodity itself. The following example shows how the technique works.

EXAMPLE 15.3   Gail Forster, procurement manager for the Australian airline Qantas, was afraid that the price of jet fuel, currently about $20 per gallon, might take yet another hike. The best deal that she was able to get with her suppliers was to fix the price for the next three months; but she felt that in the light of present unsettled conditions in the Middle East, a hedge for at least a year and a half was necessary. Neither in Sydney nor in Chicago did the futures market provide sufficient liquidity in the sort of maturity that she was seeking; nor could they precisely hedge the cost of the refined fuel used by modern jets.

Through a colleague at Singapore Air she got in touch with the commodity swaps group at Banque Paribas, and after some negotiation she was able to sign an 18-month contract to exchange payments as follows.

Qantas had $30 million of U.S.-dollar floating-rate debt on which it was paying LIBOR plus ¼ percent semiannually. Paribas would swap floating-rate payments equal to this amount for an amount that would vary *inversely* with the price of fuel oil as quoted in the industry journal, *Aviation Weekly* (AW). The exchanges are illustrated in the accompanying diagram.

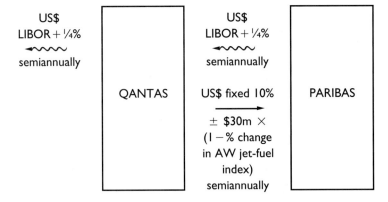

As in the conventional interest-rate swap, no exchanges of principal are made either at the beginning or at the end. In the past, the airline had done floating-for-fixed swaps, where the fixed rate roughly matched Qantas' borrowing cost in the bond market. In this deal, if the price of jet fuel remains unchanged, the swap resembles a "plain vanilla" swap: Qantas receives floating LIBOR plus ¼ percent and pays fixed 10 percent semiannually, on a principal amount of $30 million. But if the cost of fuel rises, as measured by the index of jet fuel prices published in *Aviation Weekly*, then Qantas pays less, by the percentage rise multiplied by $30 million. ($30 million equals Forster's anticipated fuel cost for two quarters.) For example, if the fuel price rises from $20 to $21 per gallon, a 5 percent increase, then Qantas would pay Paribas 10 percent minus 5 percent—that is, 5 percent on $30 million. Conversely, if the jet-fuel price falls, Qantas must pay more than 10 percent.

Oil accounts for the bulk of the commodity swap market, the remainder being largely made up of industrial metals like copper, aluminum, zinc, and platinum. A few commodity swaps are done on soft commodities such as pulp, paper, and orange-juice concentrate. Commodity swaps tend to flourish in those markets in which there is already an exchange-traded contract, because the market-makers require a place to hedge their exposure. Yet the greater bulk of the commodity swap market is in the oil business, where there is liquidity in only two or three oil instruments. For example, the Electricity Supply Board of Ireland frequently seeks a hedge against price fluctuations in its blended fuel oil, as illustrated in the accompanying block diagram. Banks do give it quotes on swaps on the basis of a similar blend whose price is quoted in the weekly oil publication, *Platts*. The bank providing such a hedge might protect itself using the short-term futures contracts in crude oil. There can be substantial basis risk between the short-term price of crude and the longer-term price of a blend, so such a hedge must be actively managed and properly priced. Even so, some banks offer commodity swaps out as long as 10 years.

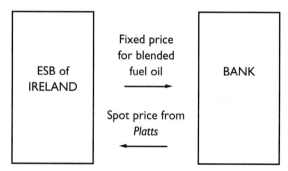

Where hedging is more difficult or risky, the margins in the over-the-counter market are higher.[4] Margins also reflect the relative immaturity of the market. Commodity swaps are said to be two to three times as profitable as interest-rate and currency swaps.

Option-Based Commodity Hedges

Even though many commodity hedges are of the forward or swap variety, the rise in banks' sophistication in the management of option-type risk has allowed them to offer a number of contingent hedges to companies in the commodities business. As in other fields, such companies are reluctant to pay the kinds of option prices that a bank would necessarily charge for conventional options, so many variants seek to lower the option buyer's out-of-pocket costs. One way of achieving this is with a *barrier option*, in which the option is activated or inactivated if, at any time during the life of the option, a price barrier is breached.

A variant is the *digital option*, which alternates between two discontinuous levels of protection and can be structured so as to involve no up-front fee. Its use is illustrated in Figure 15.4.[5] China Light uses significant amounts of natural gas in its manufacturing

---

[4]Cross-hedging can be perilous. In 1990, for example, some banks hedged jet-fuel swaps by shorting heating-oil futures. It seemed a safe bet, because prices for heating oil and jet fuel had always moved in tandem. When the 1991 Gulf war struck, however, the spread between the two commodities widened, from 2–3 cents to about 26 cents.

[5]The description of this technique is adapted from "Mundane Problems, Exotic Solutions," *Euromoney*, August 1992, 42–48.

Figure 15.4   *An Option-Based Commodity Swap.* This swap is designed to hedge China Light's cost of natural gas.

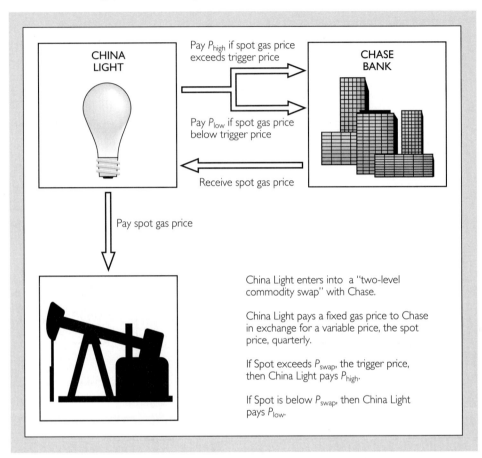

CHINA
LIGHT

Pay P_{high} if spot gas price exceeds trigger price

Pay P_{low} if spot gas price below trigger price

Receive spot gas price

CHASE
BANK

Pay spot gas price

China Light enters into a "two-level commodity swap" with Chase.

China Light pays a fixed gas price to Chase in exchange for a variable price, the spot price, quarterly.

If Spot exceeds P_{swap}, the trigger price, then China Light pays P_{high}.

If Spot is below P_{swap}, then China Light pays P_{low}.

process, and is able to pass on cost increases only after a significant move in gas prices. One way to fix the cost is by a conventional commodity swap that would pay the spot price periodically in exchange for a fixed swap price. As an alternative to fixing its cost by means of a commodity swap at a price P_{SWAP}, Chase Manhattan Bank offers the company a *two-level swap* at P_{LOW} or P_{HIGH}, depending on whether the spot gas price has breached a trigger price equal to the original fixed swap price, P_{SWAP}. The initial fixed price under the two-level swap is set at P_{LOW}, below the current swap price. China Light continues to pay this price unless the spot price of gas exceeds the trigger price P_{SWAP}, at which point China Light moves to the higher fixed rate with such a move large enough to be passed on through a government-approved price increase. To the extent that the spot prices fall below the trigger, China Light would revert to the lower price. This structure gives China Light protection with a lower initial fixed price than the swap price, and capitalizes on the utility industry's discontinuous price elasticity to cost increases.

Commodity-Linked Bonds

Commodities are playing an increasingly important role in the international capital market. As the international financial community grows more comfortable with the notion that commodities can be used in many of the same hedging and arbitrage transactions as financial instruments, so commodities or commodity indexes are being incorporated into bonds[6] and other financial instruments. Today there are even bank deposits whose value is linked to gold.

In the Eurobond market, issues whose interest or principal or both are linked to a commodity such as gold, silver, or oil are becoming common. Companies have two very different motivations for issuing bonds of this kind: (1) to provide a hedge for their natural business, and (2) to meet investors' requirements.

1. The first motivation is exemplified by PEMEX, the Mexican state oil company, which issued oil-linked bonds starting as early as April 1973. In issuing its Petrobonos, PEMEX sought to hedge the mismatch between its debt-servicing costs and its revenues. This kind of commodity-linked bond, because it is issued by companies for which the commodity linkage provides a hedge for their natural business, will have the linkage tailored to the issuer's needs. Another example is the bond issued by Sunshine Mining, a silver mining company. Unlike the PEMEX Petrobonos, Sunshine Mining's silver-linked bond offers the investor a more complex option-based play on the price of silver. (The tombstone and excerpts from the prospectus are shown in Application 15.3 at the end of this chapter.) Yet another example is provided by the $210 million of copper interest-indexed senior subordinated notes issued by the Magna Copper Company in November, 1988. This issue, which matures in November, 1998, pays interest each quarter that is tied to the average price of copper in accordance with the following schedule:

Average Copper Price ($)	Indexed Interest Rate (%)
2.00 or above	21
1.80–1.99	20
1.60–1.79	19
1.40–1.59	18
1.30–1.39	17
1.20–1.29	16
1.10–1.19	15
1.00–1.09	14
0.90 0.99	13
0.80 or below	12

The investor is given a floor and a ceiling on the interest rate paid each quarter for the 10-year life of the bond. In other words, the note incorporates 40 long-call options with a strike of $0.80 and 40 short-call options with a strike of $2.00.[7]

2. The second motivation is based on a kind of arbitrage. Some companies and financial institutions issue commodity-linked bonds even though they may have no business in that commodity. These are typically *tailored to investors' requirements*. The commodity linkage is completely offset by a commodity swap or forward contract, as a rule provided by the same bank or banks that arranged the bond issue. The banks offer the issuer a package designed to provide cheaper funding costs. This arrangement is possible because investors are, in effect, willing to accept a lower return for the

---

[6]A further look at commodity-linked bonds may be found in the discussion of hybrid bonds in Chapter 17.

[7]Note that because the payoff on the options is a nonuniform step function of the price of copper, Black-type option-valuation models will provide only a rough approximation of the value of these options.

Figure 15.5   ***Commodity-Linked Bonds.***   These bonds may be used to hedge the issuer's natural business risk, or, as in this example, to obtain cheap funding through arbitrage.

> ### Notice
>
> ### U.S. $100,000,000
> # Union Bank of Finland Ltd
> #### Oil Indexed Notes due 1992
> #### of which U.S. $50,000,000 in principal amount is being issued as the initial Tranche
>
> Notice is hereby given by J. Aron & Co. as Calculation Agent for the Oil Indexed Notes due 1992 of Union Bank of Finland Ltd that the fourth Interest Payment Date (as defined in such Notes) shall be June 19, 1991 and the Rate of Interest for the fourth Interest Period (each as defined in such Notes) shall be 17.505%. This results in an interest payment of U.S. $875.25 for each U.S. $10,000 principal amount of Notes.
>
> *December 24, 1990*

---

combination of a bond and a long-dated commodity contract (forward, swap, or option) that the investor could not readily obtain elsewhere.

Such is evidently the motivation for the Union Bank of Finland oil-indexed notes, whose interest rate is advertised in Figure 15.5. UBF itself has no interest in a liability tied to the oil price beyond the fact that stripping off and selling the index feature will produce a low all-in cost of funds.

Summary

Global commodity markets are becoming integrated with the global financial markets. Commodities are traded for spot, futures, and optional delivery in many of the same markets around the world where foreign-exchange, Eurocurrency, and interest-rate derivatives are traded. Commodities can play a role in investors' portfolios in three ways:

1. Holding a commodity and selling it forward can be a profitable investment, as long as the forward premium exceeds the cost of financing and storing the commodity. In equilibrium, the difference between the spot price and the forward or futures price will equal the "cost of carry." In precious metals, the dominant component of the cost of carry is the interest rate, which creates a strong linkage between the commodity futures markets, the money markets, and even the interest-rate futures markets. The simple cost-of-carry theory is modified by noninterest costs and by the possibility of a premium being placed on physical ownership, producing normal backwardation in futures prices.
2. Commodities have a low or negative correlation with other assets, such as equities, that typically comprise a diversified portfolio, and so can provide important risk-return improvements, even to a globally diversified portfolio.

3. Many investors manifestly prefer their commodities wrapped up in bonds. The reason for this preference may lie either in institutional constraints on direct participation in the commodities markets or because the credit risk inherent in long-dated forward contracts precludes investors from participating in their preferred markets. Issuers are nowadays meeting this need by issuing commodity-linked bonds, either to hedge their natural exposure or because, coupled with a commodity swap, they can offer advantageous financing terms.

CONCEPTUAL QUESTIONS

1. Briefly explain the role of stockpiling in determining the price of a commodity like aluminum.
2. List the considerations that would determine whether the Australian Wheat Board would hoard grain after an unusually good harvest.
3. Explain how the cost-of-carry theory differs between perishable agricultural commodities and "hard" commodities such as zinc.
4. Suppose that the Chicago Mercantile Exchange decided to initiate a futures contract on one-megabyte semiconductor chips. Would the cost-of-carry theory explain the relationship between spot and futures prices? Pay special attention to the convenience-yield factor, and to the possibility of product substitution.
5. What is *normal backwardation*? Would you expect this phenomenon to exist in the market for diamonds?
6. Comment on the following newspaper reports appearing in different sections of the same paper on the same day:

   Sterling's weakness continued to support copper prices yesterday and on the London Metal Exchange the cash position closed £14.50 higher at £1,324.50 a tonne. But dealers described business as "routine," with the dollar price of the metal little changed.

   Sterling lost ground to the dollar and the D-mark, influenced by the general improvement of the U.S. currency as traders covered short positions, and by expectations that next week's meeting of the Bundesbank council will result in higher German interest rates. Against this background, the belief that there is still some room to cut U.K. interest rates had a depressing effect on the pound.

7. Silver is used in the photography business. Why might the Fuji Film Company choose to issue a bond linked to the price of silver rather than hedging its risk with futures or with a commodity swap?
8. Referring to Figure 15.5, explain how Union Bank of Finland might have used a commodity swap in conjunction with its bond issue.

PROBLEMS

1. At the end of 1990, *The Economist* commodity price index stood at 126.1. If the price of aluminum fell 20%, what would happen to the index?
2. The spot price of live hogs is 52 cents per pound. If the Eurodollar interest rate is quoted at $5\frac{1}{2}\%$–$5\frac{5}{8}\%$, and it costs 3¢/lb to pen and feed a hog for a year, what would you expect the six-month futures price to be?
3. Based on the February 1992 closing gold-futures price in Table 15.4 and the spot price and the interest rates on August 8, 1991, would you advise your uncle Al to sell his gold or buy more? Be specific, showing how much profit or loss each strategy would entail.
4. Refer to the copper-futures prices in Table 15.4. Does copper seem to have a convenience yield? If so, how much?
5. Implicit in the palladium-futures contract in Table 15.3 are two Eurodollar-futures interest rates. What are they? How do they compare with the actual Eurodollar-futures prices quoted in the chapter? What arbitrage might one do to take advantage of any discrepancy?

| **Application 15.1** | MARTA |

In May, 1990, the Metropolitan Atlanta Rapid Transportation Authority (MARTA) faced a problem in budgeting and controlling the cost of keeping its 700 buses on the road. The vehicles require about 9 million gallons of diesel fuel per year. The budget has to be approved before the fiscal year begins, even though the volatility of fuel prices makes it impossible to predict how much the fuel will actually cost. In the previous year the price of diesel had risen from under 50 cents to over 90 cents per gallon.

This year MARTA solved the problem by entering into a one-year, fixed-for-floating diesel price swap with Paribas. The swap started on July 1, 1990, and payments were made quarterly.

Show, by means of the diagram below, how the commodity swap worked. What do you think happened when the price of diesel fuel rose from 53 cents in June, 1990, to 71 cents at the end of the year?

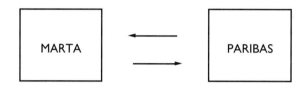

| **Application 15.2** | TDC OF NEW ORLEANS |

The Trade Development Corporation of New Orleans has the opportunity to buy some valuable capped offshore wells in the Gulf of Mexico. However, TDC lacks the credit-worthiness to access the capital market to finance the purchase.

Credit Francaise has approached the agency with a proposal for a natural-gas indexed loan that would provide an up-front lump-sum capital infusion for TDC. In return, the producer would be obligated to make monthly payments equal to a fixed volume of gas multiplied by the spot price for that month.

Your bank has been invited to join the lending syndicate for the loan. Credit Francaise has said that the loan is attractive because, in their words, "the repayment terms will be set in relation to a fixed volume of gas rather than in dollars, the producer's ability to repay is assured regardless of movements in the price of natural gas during the life of the loan. It eliminates both interest-rate risk and price-volatility risk for TDC, and allows TDC to finance the acquisition of the reserves on favorable terms."

Do you agree? What are the risks to your bank? How would your bank hedge the interest-rate and commodity-price risks, and how would this affect the pricing of the loan?

| **Application 15.3** | SUNSHINE MINING |

The accompanying tombstone and excerpt from the prospectus allude to a commodity-linked bond issued by Sunshine Mining Company. Can you think of reasons why Sunshine chose to do this particular form of financing, and what the investor's cash flows would be under various scenarios?

PROSPECTUS SUPPLEMENT
(To Prospectus dated January 14, 1985)

$40,000,000

Sunshine Mining Company

9¾% Silver Indexed Bonds Due April 15, 2004

(Interest payable April 15 and October 15)

Each $1,000 Face Amount Bond shall be payable at maturity or redemption at the greater of $1,000 or a specified average Market Price of 58 Ounces of Silver ("Indexed Principal Amount"). If the Indexed Principal Amount is greater than $1,000, the Company may at its option deliver Silver to holders electing to accept such delivery in satisfaction of the Indexed Principal Amount. As of the close of trading on April 10, 1985, the Spot Settlement Price of Silver on the Commodity Exchange, Inc. in New York was $6.608 per Ounce and, accordingly, at such price 58 Ounces of Silver would be valued at $383.26.

The Bonds will be redeemable in whole on or after April 15, 1990, at the option of the Company, at the Indexed Principal Amount together with accrued interest, if the Indexed Principal Amount equals or exceeds $2,000 for a period of 30 consecutive calendar days. On each interest payment date commencing April 15, 1988, the Company will call for redemption through operation of the sinking fund, 7½% of the Adjusted Original Issue (original issue less Bonds retired by the Company, other than through operation of the sinking fund, as provided in the Indenture). Each holder whose Bonds have been called for redemption through operation of the sinking fund shall have the right to elect not to have his Bonds redeemed.

The Bonds are secured by a specified percentage of the Annual Mining Production at the Sunshine Mine.

The Company will apply to list the Bonds on the New York Stock Exchange. Listing will be subject to meeting the requirements of the Exchange including those relating to distribution.

THESE SECURITIES HAVE NOT BEEN APPROVED OR DISAPPROVED BY THE SECURITIES AND EXCHANGE COMMISSION NOR HAS THE COMMISSION PASSED UPON THE ACCURACY OR ADEQUACY OF THIS PROSPECTUS. A REPRESENTATION TO THE CONTRARY IS A CRIMINAL OFFENSE.

Drexel Burnham Lambert Incorporated has agreed to purchase the Bonds from the Company at 86.5% of the principal amount. The Bonds are being issued at an original issue discount.

The Bonds may be sold by Drexel Burnham Lambert Incorporated, directly or through dealers or agents, to the public from time to time in one or more transactions at varying prices determined at the time of sale or at negotiated prices.

The Bonds are offered by Drexel Burnham Lambert Incorporated, subject to prior sale, when, as and if delivered to and accepted by Drexel Burnham Lambert Incorporated and subject to certain further conditions. It is expected that delivery of the Bonds will be made against payment therefor on or about April 18, 1985.

Drexel Burnham Lambert
INCORPORATED

April 11, 1985

All of these securities having been sold, this announcement appears as a matter of record only.

$40,000,000

Sunshine Mining Company

9¾% Silver Indexed Bonds due April 15, 2004
(Interest payable April 15 and October 15)

This represents the fourth issue of Silver Indexed Bonds since the first was issued on April 10, 1980.

Drexel Burnham Lambert
INCORPORATED

April 19, 1985

SELECTED REFERENCES

Black, Fisher. "The Pricing of Commodity Contracts." *Journal of Financial Economics*, vol. 3 (1976): 167–178.

Brennan, Michael, and Eduardo Schwartz. "A New Approach to Evaluating Natural Resource Investments." *Midland Corporate Finance Journal*, vol. 3, no. 1 (Spring 1985): 37–47.

Duffie, D. *Futures Markets*. Englewood Cliffs: Prentice-Hall, 1989.

Working, Holbrook. "The Theory of the Price of Storage." *American Economic Review*, vol. 39 (1948): 1254–1262.

International Financing

16
International Financing Decisions

Corporate Financing Decisions in Theory and Practice

This chapter offers the financial manager's view of the international capital and money markets: how should the markets be used, and what guides the best *mix* of financing sources?

Neither in theory nor in practice are there simple norms of corporate financial structure. In this chapter we will review some common-sense approaches to choosing the appropriate mix of debt and equity, and within the category of debt, the composition of debt: fixed versus floating, short term versus long term, secured versus unsecured, and, most importantly in the global marketplace, the best mix of currencies. Indeed, one of the most crucial and difficult issues in corporate international financing decisions is, In which currency should the company denominate its debt? To answer this and other questions, we begin with the principles of corporate finance as well as several topics covered earlier, notable the parity relationships (Chapter 5), the international bond and equity markets (Chapters 12 and 14), and swap financing techniques (Chapter 13).

The place to begin is with the classic choice between debt and equity. A seminal article by Modigliani and Miller in 1958 demonstrated that in a world with perfect capital markets, a corporation's debt-to-equity ratio is irrelevant to the firm's market value. In such a world, the value of the firm is determined only by its investment decisions, which can therefore be entirely separated from financing decisions.

Fortunately for the corporate financial manager, subsequent and more realistic theories suggest that financing decisions are not irrelevant. By relaxing the key assumptions of the MM theory—no taxes, no transactions costs, and investment decisions independent of financing decisions—these theories take into account the costs of taxation, information, and more important, monitoring and control. They point to a variety of ways in which adapting financing techniques to the character of the business can increase the value of the firm to shareholders.

The double taxation of corporate income and the worldwide practice of tax deductibility of interest payments provide an incentive for debt finance. This incentive, however, is weakened by the direct and indirect costs of financial distress and bankruptcy, which are more likely to be encountered in a highly leveraged company. Information flows are not perfect, and this has an important influence on financing decisions. In particular, managers have better information on firm performance and prospects than outside creditors and shareholders do. By maintaining stable dividends, firms help to signal their confidence about future prospects. This may explain why firms continue to pay dividends even if they need additional external finance or if taxes on capital gains are lower than those on dividend income.

Furthermore, because the interests of managers may differ from those of creditors and shareholders, the latter must incur costs in trying to monitor and affect the way the company is run. Decisions on capital structure (as well as on the use of internal or external finance, short- or long-term finance, bond issues or bank debt, domestic or foreign currency, and so on) will be influenced by the ability of creditors and shareholders to get the information they need in order to exercise control over managers. Recent theories have provided some plausible explanations for the differences in corporate financing patterns between the bank-based systems of Germany and Japan on one side and the market-based systems of the United States and the United Kingdom on the other. The two bank-based systems involve greater corporate indebtedness (although the difference is not as great as suggested by reported accounting data). This may be explained by the closer relationships between banks and industry—that is, by the ability of bankers to influence the decisions of managers. In short, the costs of financial distress depend on the relationship between creditors and the firm, a relationship that differs between countries depending on banking norms and laws as well as bankruptcy laws.

What kinds of firms should borrow rather than use equity finance? Taxation provides one answer: the greater the "tax shield," the more should a company reduce its tax burden by financing with tax-deductible debt. But the costs of financial distress limit this, so we have to look at the probability of high financial leverage causing a firm to get into trouble. The more earnings fluctuate, the riskier higher leveraging becomes. As Figure 16.1 illustrates, the optimal debt ratio involves a tradeoff between the tax shield provided by additional debt and the higher expected costs of financial distress. The firms that can best afford to be highly leveraged are large, capital-intensive firms with highly predictable earnings patterns, such as utilities. In fact, modern finance got its start with infrastructure projects such as canals, railways, and, later, public utilities. Today much of the capital for investments by public utilities in industrial countries is provided by retained earnings because the basic infrastructure investments have already been made. Thanks to the sta-

Figure 16.1   *The Effect of Borrowing on a Firm's Value.* A firm's value can be increased with leverage, thanks to the interest tax shield; but too much leverage increases the expected costs of financial distress.

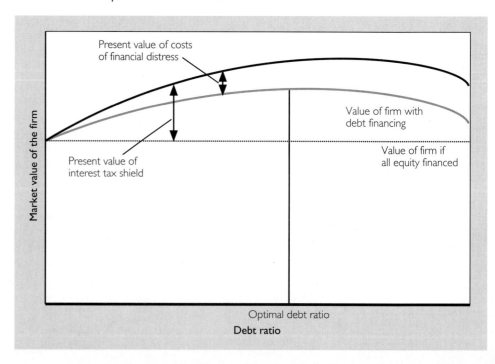

bility of their income and the long life of their assets, they are usually able to raise the external finance they need by issuing bonds or other long-term debt.

Some large, capital-intensive firms have less capacity for debt. Steel, cement, and oil and petrochemical firms have less predictable income streams. These should rely more on equity financing, much of which can come from retained earnings if the firms are profitable. On the other hand, if they are private and sufficiently well known to the public, these firms can obtain funding by issuing equities or by finding foreign partners. For firms such as these in developing countries, they might seek equity funding in the international markets where the appetite for greater risk (and greater expected return) may be higher.

In theory, if the costs of bankruptcy were zero, a firm could go in and out of bankruptcy with barely a ripple and a tax-minimizing 99.9 percent leverage ratio might be optimal. In bankruptcy situations, ownership would be transferred from shareholders to creditors but the firm's true value would be unaffected. Of course, in practice this is far from the truth. A good deal of value can be lost when a firm is in or even threatened by bankruptcy. The longer the bankruptcy process is stretched out, the more value can be lost. In this respect, there are significant differences among countries arising from differences in bankruptcy laws and practices. The law in some European countries comes closer to the theoretical notion of "debtholders taking possession of the firm" than in the United States, where firms can be protected from debtholders' claims by Chapter 11 of the Bankruptcy Act.[1]

Although research suggests that the out-of-pocket costs of bankruptcy are not necessarily huge, the firm may suffer irrecoverable losses in other ways. Management time is diverted, key employees leave, and customer and supplier confidence may be shaken. This is particularly true of firms with *intangible assets* such as reputation, patents, and human capital. For example, drug companies and computer-software developers might suffer such enormous losses of people and other intangible assets that for them the costs of financial distress are prohibitive. For such companies, the tax-shield benefits of high leverage are not worth the risks. Other firms with tangible assets, assets that are less likely to be dissipated by financial distress, tend to have a more leveraged, tax-efficient capital structure.

So leverage is not all bad. Indeed, a further rationale for leverage is sometimes advocated: it can improve the operating earnings of the firm by imposing discipline and giving managers equity incentives. This is what happens in a leveraged buy-out which can reap efficiencies not easily achieved in conventional firms (see Box 16.1).

BOX 16.1

Can High Leverage Produce Operating Benefits?

Some argue that the extreme, albeit temporary, leverage of defensive recapitalizations, or leveraged buyouts, can improve the real operations of the firm by

- shifting management's focus from growth to efficiency.
- forcing outsider scrutiny.
- reducing corporate overhead and eliminating layers of management.
- rewarding not the building of staff but the downsizing and improving of operating cash flow.
- converting operating cash flow into earnings as debt is paid down and the firm recapitalized.

---

[1]See also the comparison of bank-company relationships in Germany, Japan, and the United States in Chapter 9.

The **leveraged buy-out** is for the most part a response to the lethargy and bureaucracy that afflict large, diversified firms. The LBO or MBO (management buy-out) typically involves management purchasing their own firm, seeking to force realization of realizable value by taking control. Bureaucratic firms often perform badly because they are difficult for outsiders to penetrate and because they limit management responsibility. Management suddenly becomes very focused on what costs and businesses really are needed when it is their own money on the line. Managers are seldom billionaires, so they cannot achieve this without help. Equity partners and high-leverage financing of the purchase permits "democracy" in purchase of ownership and control. But the high leverage is only a means to an end; it is a temporary structure pending asset sales, operating efficiencies, and other means of recapitalizing the firm and restoring a normal capital structure.[2]

From "How Much Debt?" to "What Kind of Debt?"

Given that a portion of the firm's capital structure will be debt, the question turns from the *proportion* of debt to the *composition* of that debt. The debt can be fixed or floating rate; domestic or foreign currency denominated; short term or long term. It can be asset-based financing, or subordinated, or quasi-equity in character such as convertible bonds. It can be coupled with currency or interest-rate swaps.

Whatever it is, the basic considerations are the same. The nature of financing should normally be driven by the nature of the business, in such a way as to make debt-service payments match the character and timing of operating earnings. *Because this reduces the*

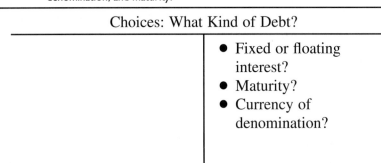

**Figure 16.2   *The Composition of Debt.*   Choices include interest rate set, currency of denomination, and maturity.

Choices: What Kind of Debt?
• Fixed or floating interest?   • Maturity?   • Currency of denomination?

Debt-service payments should be structured to match the timing and character of operating earnings, unless the firm has justification for taking a view that differs from that of the market

---

[2]As Peter Bossearts has pointed out, the success of leveraged buy-outs often depends on the ability of managers to hedge marketwide risks such as interest rate and currency risks. This leaves them exposed merely to company-specific risk over which they should have much more control. The failure of some LBOs can in fact be attributed to the failure to hedge away unnecessary risk.

probability of financial distress, it allows the firm to have greater leverage and therefore a greater tax shield. Deviation from this principle should occur only in the presence of privileged information or some other market imperfection. Market imperfections that provide cheaper financing exist in practice in a wide range of circumstances.

We may begin by considering three fundamental choices that firms face in considering the composition of their debt: the length of time for which the interest rate is set, the currency in which the debt is denominated, and the maturity or "availability period" of the debt (Figure 16.2).

Fixed Versus Floating Debt

The debt of many companies is mostly short term, so that the interest rate changes frequently. Other companies seek to gain certainty by obtaining as high as possible a proportion of long-term, fixed-rate debt. Which of these strategies make sense under what circumstances?

We can answer this and subsequent questions by reference to two fundamental principles which can be stated as follows:

> *Principle 1: Other things being equal, it pays firms to choose the composition of debt that minimizes the probability of financial distress.*

The essence of the first principle is that debt should suit the character of the revenues. Companies that have relatively fixed revenues, such as utilities, should have fixed-rate debt. Companies whose revenues are directly linked to the level of interest rates, such as financial institutions which hold floating-rate home loans, should have floating-rate debt. Manufacturing or retailing companies that have a large proportion of short-term accounts receivable are in part just financial intermediaries, and part of their liabilities should accordingly be floating. To the extent that short-term rates are correlated with inflation, companies whose revenues are linked to the general level of prices might also be best advised to have floating-rate debt.

The Dreyfus Group is a company that manages money-market mutual funds in North America. Its revenues are largely in the form of management fees, which are proportional to the volume of assets under management. When interest rates decline sharply, investors tend to move out of money-market funds and into bond or other investments that offer higher returns, so the company's revenues suffer. Thus the sensible way to finance Dreyfus's operations would be with floating-rate debt.

> *Principle 2: It pays a company to deviate from the minimum-risk debt composition if and only if the firm can "beat the market" when the firm's predictions differ from forecasts implied by market prices.*

The assumption underlying the second principle is that companies as a rule do *not* have privileged information or the ability to forecast interest rates and other variables better than the market, so it does not pay to use the company's financing as a vehicle for speculation. The term structure of interest rates contains information about the market's rate expectations, in the form of implied forward interest rates. The firm that seeks to manipulate the mix of short- and long-term debt in anticipation of beneficial interest-rate changes is betting against the market professional whose buy/sell decisions determine, on the margin, the level of long-term relative to short-term rates.

Hoffman-LaRoche is a drug company with relatively stable revenues. Its sales are largely recession-proof and unaffected by the level of interest rates. Fixed-rate debt would appear to be the logical choice. Yet on occasion the company has borrowed substantial amounts of short-term, variable-rate money. Why? When the yield curve slopes steeply upward, short-term debt would *seem* to be cheaper than long-term debt—but this could be an illusion. According to the expectations theory of the term structure, the expected cost of compounded short-term rates equals the long-term rate. So implicitly Hoffman-LaRoche is betting that future short-term rates will be lower than the market's forward rates suggest.

Having chosen whether to have fixed or floating debt, the firm must identify the most effective and cost-efficient way of implementing its choice. Floating-rate U.S.-dollar debt, for example, can be obtained by issuing a floating-rate note, by issuing a U.S. corporate bond and doing an interest-rate swap to achieve a lower floating rate, or even by issuing an ECU Eurobond and entering into a currency swap to obtain a cheaper floating-rate cost.

Maturity and Availability

The maturity decision differs from the decision on fixed- versus floating-rate debt. Long-term debt can be issued with a floating interest rate, and short-term debt can be given a fixed rate by means of an interest-rate swap. Choosing the maturity of debt means choosing the length of time for which funds are committed or *available* on specified terms. These terms include the spread over a benchmark rate, repayment options, and covenants. Beyond the availability period, the terms on which funds are borrowed have to be renegotiated.

Following the first principle mentioned in the previous section, the repayment schedule of debt should match the expected payment flow from the company's assets. Thus an electric utility building a nuclear power plant should postpone debt repayment for decades, whereas a finance company that purchases corporate receivables can match these with 60-day funding. Often a company will have a mix of several kinds of revenues and can construct a financing mix accordingly. As one corporate treasurer has put it, "We seek to lower our cost of capital but also give weight to the fact that some capital markets dry up from time to time. We need the ability to be flexible in finance."

Once a company has chosen a certain availability period, it must choose the most effective and cost-efficient way of implementing its choice. In general, there are two ways of securing longer-term access to funds. One is simply by borrowing long term. The other is by borrowing short term but also purchasing "access insurance" from banks—in other words, negotiating and paying for a committed revolving bank facility. When this is done in conjunction with a Euronote program it is called a Revolving Underwriting Facility or the equivalent. In either case, up front and annual commitment fees are paid. Because we have previously described such facilities as providing a series of options on the *spread*, the fees can be regarded as the price of such options.

The second principle dictates that a company should deviate from the "matching" rule if its forecast differs from that of the market. In the context of the maturity decision, this means that the additional cost of long-term access is less than, or greater than, its expectations of the cost of repeatedly tapping the short-term markets.

Not infrequently a company will use the short-term market to fund long-term operations, on the grounds that its credit is excellent *and expected to remain excellent* so that it is not worth paying the additional cost of long-term debt or of a bank revolver. In a sense, the firm's forecast of its expected *spread* relative to a benchmark rate differs from the market's forecast as reflected in the bond rate (swapped into floating) or the fees for a committed facility. Because the latter constitutes an option on the spread, the firm is in effect taking a view on the future volatility of the spread it will have to pay in the short-term market.

EXAMPLE 16.1   ## SmithKline's Switch

Until 1992, SmithKline Beecham, the pharmaceuticals and personal-care company, had relied almost entirely on commercial paper and other forms of short-term financing. SKB made active use of its $1.5 billion U.S.-commercial-paper program. The company's good credit standing, however, gave it access to the long-term market on favorable terms. Hence in March 1992 the firm tapped the Eurobond market for the first time, issuing a five-year, 9½ percent bond denominated in Canadian dollars. The purpose was to diversify SKB's sources of funds and to extend the maturity of its debt, thus reducing uncertainty about *availability*. However, the issue did nothing to reduce *interest-rate uncertainty*, because the entire deal was swapped into floating-rate U.S. dollars at a level below the London interbank offered rate.

Financing, Debt Denomination, and the Exchange-Risk Factor

One of the central questions of corporate international finance is, In which currency should a company's debt be denominated?

For example, the Australian subsidiary of Glaxo, the British drug company, exports to Japan and gets paid in yen. Should the subsidiary's debt be denominated in pounds, Australian dollars, or Japanese yen? And would the answer be different if the exports were invoiced in U.S. dollars?

To answer this kind of question, we must first recognize that *the choice of currency for debt is an exchange-risk hedging decision*, just as is the decision to buy or sell currency forward. The principle of interest-rate parity ensures that the two are equivalent: because the forward premium equals the interest-rate differential, borrowing in currency A normally costs precisely the same as borrowing in currency B and simultaneously buying currency B in the forward-exchange market.

Hence to be able to answer the "which currency" question it behooves us to review the concept of a company's currency exposure. If we knew what Glaxo Australia's currency exposure was, we would be able to more easily focus on the issue of the right currency in which to denominate the firm's debt.

Sometimes it's easy to tell what a firm's currency exposure is. Take a leasing company. Its assets—lease payments—are contractually denominated in dollars or a particular currency, and it will be exposed to currency fluctuations unless its liabilities are similarly denominated. But for most nonfinancial firms it's not so clear cut. What is the currency exposure, for example, of Intel's subsidiary in Ireland? One cannot answer that without knowing something of the company's business and the competition.

Manufacturing firms typically have three kinds of exposure.

- **Transactions exposure**, as the name suggests, results from particular transactions, such as an export for which a known cash flow in a given currency will take place on a certain date. If Intel invoices a German company in deutschemarks for a semiconductor shipment, then the firm has German-mark exposure and can hedge this by borrowing marks. This kind of exposure is readily hedgeable using forwards, futures, or debt (but *not* normally options).

- **Translation exposure** (or accounting or balance-sheet exposure) results from the way accounting conventions dictate that Intel's operations in Ireland should be translated into U.S dollars. If the U.S. firm's assets in Ireland are regarded as denominated in Irish punts, then the subsidiary's accounting value is exposed to the punt, and the firm may wish to hedge this exposure by financing in punts.

- Most companies, however, recognize that the accountants' valuation may mislead and that what counts is **economic exposure**, or cash-flow exposure. The essence of economic exposure is how the firm's revenues and costs will respond to exchange-rate changes. Even though Intel invoices German customers in marks, its future revenues may be unaffected by fluctuations in the mark if the currency of *determination* of prices in the semiconductor business is the dollar or even the yen. The currency of determination is the currency in which most of the competition prices similar products.

EXAMPLE 16.2 **Paper Losses, Paper Gains**

Assume that St. Ives, the pulp and paper company, is planning to set up a distribution facility in Singapore for storage and sale of Canadian pulp to Japan and Australia. What is the company's exposure? In what currency should this expansion be financed?

Transactions exposure arises from specific, contractual transactions such as an accounts receivable or payable. Assuming St. Ives, a Canadian company, will invoice pulp redistributors in Japan and Australia in local currency, for those transactions it would be advised to match-fund the accounts receivable in Japanese yen and Australian dollars.

Translation exposure arises from the accounting treatment of foreign subsidiaries and profits. The location of the distribution subsidiary in Singapore might mean that St. Ives has a Singapore-dollar-denominated asset that, to be hedged and to avoid accounting-value fluctuations, should be financed in Singapore dollars. However, the particular location of the distribution warehouse has little to do with the economics of costs and revenues, so hedging the accounting exposure probably would not be appropriate.

Economic exposure is the extent to which the cash flows and the value of the firm are affected by the exchange-rate changes. Economically, because bulk pulp is a U.S.-dollar-denominated commodity, the U.S. unit is the currency of determination. So perhaps a subsidiary producing pulp revenues should be financed in U.S. dollars.

The issue of currency exposure is fundamental to the debt-denomination decision.[3] It is no exaggeration to say that *an understanding of currency exposure precedes any decision of the right currency in which to denominate a firm's debt.*

Matched-Currency Financing as a Hedge: Is It Justified?

Should firms strive to match the currency of financing to the currency of revenues? In the spirit of Modigliani-Miller, if investment decisions are fixed, and there are no taxes or transaction costs (including bankruptcy costs), investors can replicate any foreign-exchange matching or hedging that the corporation can do. They do not need the company to perform risk management on their behalf. Even if one introduces transactions

---

[3]Currency exposure issues are pursued in greater depth in books on corporate international finance such as those by Eiteman, Stonehill, and Moffett; Levi; and Shapiro, listed under Selected References at the end of the chapter.

costs to hedging activities, institutional investors can plausibly reduce costs through diversification and by using forward contracts and the like to hedge only the residual exchange risk in a portfolio. In short, the market does not reward the corporation (in the form of a lower required return on equity) for devoting resources to the elimination of diversifiable or hedgable risk.

Indeed, the corporate treasurer may actually damage the interests of the shareholder if he undertakes unwanted hedging. Although dividends are paid in a particular currency, shareholders do not necessarily want the firm's management to hedge with respect to that currency. Equity, after all, does not bear a currency sign. Its value reflects the complex mix of economic and firm variables, many of which the investor is deliberately seeking when he invests in the company's stock. If I buy shares in Ciba-Geigy, the Swiss chemicals firm, it is not because I want a Swiss-franc-denominated security. Whether or not I am a Swiss investor, I am seeking the mix of business and currency cash flows that Ciba represents, and very little of this is of Swiss-franc origin. So it would be wrong for Ciba to hedge all its dollar and yen exposure into Swiss francs, even if it could identify what the true exposure was. The investor would just have to unhedge what the corporate treasurer had misguidedly hedged.

A related reason to beware of hedging nominal cash flows by matched-currency financing is that different investors may want a different currency mix in their portfolios, perhaps because their consumption baskets are denominated in different currencies or because capital market barriers constrain their portfolio choices in different ways. A study by McCauley and Zimmer, for example, offers support for this notion: there appear to be systematic differences in the cost of equity between countries, differences that may in part be explained by real exchange risk.[4] If the corporate treasurer cannot guess what the investor's "base currency" is, he cannot know which cash flows to hedge and which to leave alone.

Finally, investors may penalize firms that hedge if the hedging is discretionary rather than consistent. Anecdotal evidence supports the view that the more sophisticated the financial management of a company, the greater the role played by their own views on direction and volatility in selecting the kind and timing of exchange-risk management. Whether or not this adds volatility to the firm's reported earnings, it creates an uncertainty for investors who may be perfectly capable of doing their own consistent hedging.

Despite the arguments offered above, there is ample evidence that the majority of large, international firms do hedge exchange risk, and that they do so selectively rather than fully. The rationale may be found by relaxing the MM assumptions of no transactions costs or taxes. Consider first the effect of costs of financial distress on the return required by the firm's creditors. Exchange-rate volatility may make earnings volatile and thus increase the probability of financial distress. If hedging reduces the nominal volatility of the firm's earnings, it will in turn reduce the expected value of the costs of financial distress (including bankruptcy), as is shown in Figure 16.3. Some of these costs are borne by creditors ("Costs of bankruptcy to creditors" in the figure), in which case a reduction in expected distress costs will reduce lenders' required rate of return. In addition, for a given level of debt, lower earnings volatility will entail a lower probability of a negative net worth.

In Figure 16.3, the probability distribution of the value of the firm is mapped against the return to creditors. In this context, creditors are regarded as writers of a put option on the value of the firm, an option that is in the money for negative values of the firm's

---

[4]Robert N. McCauley and Steven A. Zimmer, "Exchange Rates and International Comparisons in the Cost of Capital," in Yakov Amihud and Richard Levich, eds, *Exchange Rate Effects on Corporate Financial Performance and Strategies*, forthcoming.

Figure 16.3 ***Probability Distribution of the Value of the Firm, Mapped Against the Return to Creditors.*** Creditors incur bankruptcy costs if exchange-rate variations drive the firm's net worth below zero, so they will charge a lower risk premium if hedging reduces the probability of this happening.

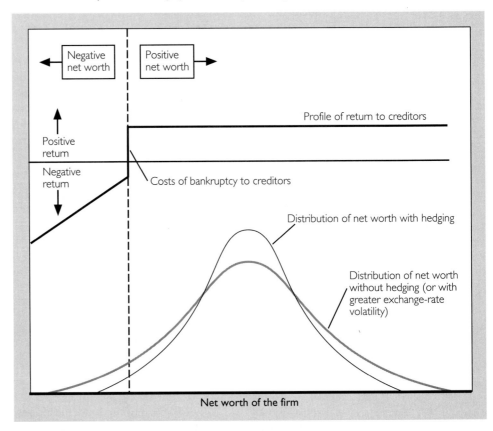

net worth (to the left of the dotted line). At this point, creditors face a one-shot bankruptcy cost, reducing their returns. As the firm's net worth turns out to be even more negative, creditors' losses increase. Lower inherent volatility of exchange rates or effective hedging lowers the probability of bankruptcy, so a lower option premium (margin for risk) could be charged.

Matched currency funding may also improve after tax earnings, thanks to the tax-shield benefit of leverage in double-taxation countries. Consider the following simple framework:

$$
\begin{array}{c}
\text{value of firm} \\
\text{to shareholders}
\end{array}
=
\begin{array}{c}
\text{value} \\
\text{of assets}
\end{array}
-
\begin{array}{c}
\text{value} \\
\text{of debt}
\end{array}
+
\begin{array}{c}
\text{present} \\
\text{value of} \\
\text{tax shield}
\end{array}
-
\begin{array}{c}
\text{present value of} \\
\text{expected costs of} \\
\text{financial distress}
\end{array}
$$

The last two are a function of leverage, among other things. The double taxation of corporate income and the worldwide practice of tax deductibility of interest payments provide an incentive for debt finance. This incentive, however, is weakened by the direct and indirect costs of financial distress and bankruptcy; the greater the volatility of earnings, the greater the costs. More leverage means more volatile earnings, so the tax-shield gains from leverage are, at some point, offset by the deadweight costs of financial distress.

The greater the probability of distress, the lower the leverage level that is optimal for the firm and the lower the tax shield. *Because currency matching reduces the probability of financial distress, it allows the firm to have greater leverage and therefore a greater tax shield.* Thus the greater the degree of bankruptcy-cost-reducing hedging, the greater the value of the firm and the lower the cost of capital.

The Currency Denomination of Debt: Two Principles

The reasoning just discussed allows us to establish two principles that should govern the currency-denomination decision:

1. The firm should use its debt to hedge against currency risk as far as possible. The risk of financial distress will be minimized if the currency of debt is the same as the "natural" exposure of the firm. So if prices in the wholesale-chemicals market are determined in dollars, then Glaxo's Australian subsidiary might best finance its contractual exposure (yen receivables) in yen and the remainder of its operations in U.S. dollars.
2. If the firm has a strong opinion that the international Fisher effect does not hold—that is, that the interest-rate differential is *not* an unbiased, efficient predictor of future exchange-rate changes—then it may choose to deviate from the "matching" strategy. If Glaxo's financial managers are convinced that, say, the dollar/sterling interest differential underestimates the prospective depreciation of the pound sterling, then borrowing may be switched to pounds.

Once management has decided, based on exposure analysis and on its view of the future relative to those reflected in market rates, on the appropriate currency denomination for its debt, it must choose how best to implement that decision. The choice normally boils down to cost. Is it cheaper, for example, for Phillips to borrow in Dutch guilders or to borrow in Swiss francs and do a currency swap to effectively convert the debt-service payments into guilders?

EXAMPLE 16.3 **Financing Jaguar in Japan**

Jaguar, the prestigious British automobile company, does all of its manufacturing in Great Britain. The bulk of its revenues come from exports. In the early 1990s its principal export market, the United States, was gradually ceding rank to Japan. In the latter market, Jaguar was competing head-on with the local Lexus and Infiniti lines as well as with European companies such as Rolls-Royce, Porsche, and Mercedes-Benz. How would you advise Jaguar to finance its expansion into Japan?

The answer begins with an understanding of the currency of determination of sales in Japan. While in the past the bulk of Jaguar's export revenues were dollar determined, in Japan the dominant competitors are the Japanese companies themselves, so the yen is the currency of determination. The fact that production takes place in Britain has little to do with the determination of Jaguar's revenue stream; what counts is where the cars are sold, and who the competition is. So to finance further penetration of the Japanese market, Jaguar should reduce its dollar debt and increase its yen debt. In all probability the easiest way to do this would be by means of yen-dollar currency swaps.

The Use of Swaps, Caps, and Hybrids in Financing

Today many firms use derivatives such as swaps, caps, and collars in their financing, and many others finance with hybrid bonds that tie the interest or principal to some variable like an interest rate, a currency, a commodity, or a stock index.[5] What is the explanation for these techniques, and when is it advisable for a company to use them? We will show that both derivatives and hybrids can be used to *hedge* a natural exposure that the company has, or to take a *position* on the direction or volatility of some market variable. When derivates are used to "unwind" a hybrid feature, their use is as an *arbitrage* to exploit a market imperfection. These ideas are summarized in Box 16.2.

Let us begin with the use of derivatives in financing. Swaps, caps, and the like are used for one of three purposes: (1) to hedge an existing exposure that the company is subject to, (2) to take advantage of an imperfection in the capital market, or (3) to position the company to take advantage of a favorable movement in some market variable such as interest rates. As we have seen in the chapter on that subject, interest-rate and currency swaps are widely used in conjunction with financing to transform the payment characteristics of debt into that which the company desires. A swap transforms fixed- into floating-rate funding or yen debt into dollar financing, or both. They are used in conjunction with debt issues when they allow the company to exploit market imperfections and market segmentation in the capital market. They give the firm cheaper funding than it could have obtained by borrowing directly in the market or currency that it desires.

Used in this way, swaps are instruments of arbitrage: they merely transform or "unwind" certain characteristics of debt that were included only to attract investors. Their goal is to secure cheaper funds than could be obtained with "straight" financing. Sometimes swaps are used as pure positioning instruments. Because a company's management thinks interest rates are coming down, it will swap fixed-rate debt for floating-rate debt, perhaps reversing the swap later. Caps, floors, collars, and other *option-type* derivatives are frequently positioning rather than hedging instruments. Firms do not normally have a

---

BOX 16.2

Derivatives and Hybrids in Financing

Derivatives and hybrids can be used alone for hedging or positioning purposes, or in conjunction to arbitrage a market imperfection.

	Derivatives	Hybrids
Hedging	Used alone to offset an existing exposure; e.g., S&L purchases swaption to hedge mortgage portfolio	Commodity linkage or other feature embedded in debt to hedge issuer's natural business; e.g., Pemex issues oil-linked bond
Positioning	Used alone or in conjunction with debt but not precisely matching features of the debt; e.g., firm buys cap to accompany floating-rate debt	Option or other feature embedded in debt but not "stripped out"; e.g., Turkey's issuance of bonds with put features
Arbitrage	Used together in such a way that the derivative offsets the bond's hybrid feature	

---

[5]A number of hybrid financing techniques will be explained in the next chapter.

cap feature in their bond issues that they are trying to reverse; rather, they use the interest-rate cap to implement a combined view on the direction and volatility of interest rates, a view that differs from that of the market.

A parallel argument may be made regarding **hybrid bonds as financing vehicles**. On occasion, hybrid bonds are issued to hedge an existing exposure of the issuer, as in the case of the commodity-linked financing techniques employed by some issuers and alluded to in Chapter 15. Firms in developing countries may gain special benefits from issuing debt instruments with a quasi-equity component, such as payments linked to the price of the commodity whose fluctuations are the cause of earnings variability. Creditors have proved willing to bear the risk of price fluctuations in this manner. Mexico, for example, has issued bonds indexed to the price of oil.

More often bonds with unusual features are sometimes used to exploit a market imperfection and get cheaper financing. They will normally be tailored to investor preferences or constraints rather than to the issuer's needs. We return to this technique in the next chapter. The hallmark of this use of hybrid financing is that the special features are stripped off the bond by means of a tailored-derivative hedge, thus insulating the issuer from either favorable or adverse effects of the hybrid feature. The following example illustrates this principle.

EXAMPLE 16.4   **Sallie Mae**

A currency-linked hybrid bond was issued in the late 1980s by Sallie Mae, the U.S. student-loan financing agency. The U.S.-dollar-denominated bond had a principal that increased with the value of the U.S. dollar value of the Japanese yen. This bond was sold to retail investors in the United States as a means of taking a view on the dollar/yen exchange rate. Sallie Mae, however, bore no currency risk, because the issuer precisely reversed the currency feature via a long-dated currency forward contract with a bank. The U.S. agency's sole purpose was to lower the cost of its long-term dollar financing. The application was arbitrage.

In certain cases the issuer does *not* unwind the hybrid feature even though the feature is not a natural hedge for the firm's business. Some companies issue bonds with call features or put features, and the company benefits or loses depending on where interest rates or the company's creditworthiness goes. Used in this way, hybrid bonds constitute a vehicle for taking a speculative view on rates or some other variable. The most common manner in which hybrids are issued "naked"—that is, without an unwinding hedge—is in the case in which the hybrid feature offers an option on the company's stock. We consider these in the next section.

Quasi-Equity Financing

A vast amount of international financing in the past decade has been quasi equity in character. The majority has taken one of two forms: (1) bonds issued with a detachable long-term option on the issuer's stock, called warrants, or (2) bonds that are convertible into the issuer's stock. When should warrants or convertibles be used? Unfortunately, there is no neat answer, or rather no satisfactory answer that can explain why, for example, so many Japanese companies have issued Eurobonds with detachable warrants. Because we will return to these instruments in the next chapter, we restrict the remarks here to some normative guidelines on the use of warrants, convertibles, and other quasi-equity financing in the context of constructing the overall financing plan.

With double taxation of corporate income, debt saves the company money, but it carries the risks and costs of financial distress. The best of both worlds can be had by having debt with tax-deductible interest but with equitylike subordination features or risk-reduction features. Example: bonds with principal linked to the company's profitability or a proxy for it, such as a commodity price.

Yet a great deal of equity-linked debt does not seem designed to take advantage of this lacuna. Let us begin with **warrant bonds**. Because such bonds are accompanied by a valuable long-term option on the company's stock, they bear a very low coupon. So the debt increases the issuer's income and provides very little tax shelter relative to straight debt. As for the warrant itself, the company has decided to sell options on its own stock. By taking a short position in options on its stock the firm is in effect speculating that volatility and the stock price itself will be lower than the prices implied by the warrant's effective price—in other words, that it can be sold for a higher price than its true value. Why might the warrant be overpriced in this way? One answer might be that investors regard this as a leveraged, unconstrained way to go long on the company's stock, and because of regulations and creditworthiness constraints they can find no other way of taking such a position.

Companies issuing **convertible bonds** are taking a similar view, albeit a more complex one, particularly when the convertible bond is denominated in a foreign currency. (Many Japanese convertibles have been issued in Swiss francs or U.S. dollars.) A convertible bond offers the investor the right to exchange the bond for a certain amount of equity; in exchange, the issuer pays a lower-than-normal coupon. Here the option is inseparable from the bond and is not a pure equity option but a call option on the relative price of the bond component and the company's stock. Valuation is complicated by the fact that convertible bonds normally also have a call feature, allowing the company to force conversion when the stock rises above its conversion price.

Because they bear a lower-than-normal coupon, convertible bonds are not highly tax efficient. They involve a risk for the company because if the stock rises, it will be given away cheap, but if it falls, the firm will have to repay debt. If the debt is in a foreign currency the risk could be substantial, as many Japanese companies discovered when their stock fell and the yen fell against the Swiss franc. The circumstances in which they should be issued are therefore those in which the firm has a complex view on its own stock, on interest rates and perhaps on currencies.

Convertibles and other forms of equity-linked debt are often issued by companies at the riskier end of the spectrum. Stable companies issue straight public debt, whereas the nature of the debt that is used for more speculative ventures, including leveraged buyouts, tends to be custom made. Equity kickers are common and all aspects are negotiable. Often the providers of equity are also the providers of some of the debt.

Asset Securitization and Nonrecourse Project Financing

A special category of financing is one in which certain of the company's assets are segmented, often into a special subsidiary company, for the purpose of backing up debt.[6] The purpose is typically to obtain financing more easily and cheaply and to prevent or

---

[6]See also the discussion under Asset-Backed Eurobonds in Chapter 12.

limit creditors' recourse to the company itself. The assets range from credit-card receivables to a whole project such as a coal mine.

Asset securitization happens when a company or financial institution dedicates the cash flows from selected assets to securing certain liabilities and then creates securities from those liabilities. More than a collateral technique, it is a cash-flow technique. In theory this is a technique that has wide applicability, because every firm has some kind of assets that are, at least in principle, amenable to segmentation for financing purposes. Many companies and banks have done so, arguing that asset-backed financing offers them lower interest rates and better balance-sheet ratios. So the question becomes, Can a company really save money by linking liabilities to certain assets? And if so, when and how should it be done?

Let us begin by reiterating the statement with which we began this chapter: a company's value comes from its real business: you cannot normally increase its value by rearranging its liabilities. Put differently, you can't fool smart investors. If you tie up your best assets, the unsecured debt will fall in value, and your overall cost of capital will stay the same. The counter argument is that you *can* fool people, especially the government. Even if you siphon off the best assets, the cost of the remainder of your debt will be unaffected. But what might be the reasons for this? Three possibilities present themselves: investor ignorance, investor constraints, and liability insurance.

The investor-ignorance argument says that if you give investors clarity about the assets backing their securities, and remove those assets from the invidious control of the company's management, they will be satisfied with a much lower rate of return. Fair enough. But it must follow that the existing and future creditors of the parent company are not aware that the company's credit condition has deteriorated, so that they do not raise *their* required rate of return by an offsetting amount. One company says: "Even though [our off-balance-sheet financing] was disclosed we felt it was giving us extra flexibility because it was being ignored by the market. We felt we could use $50 to $100 million with no effect on our ratings"[7]

This argument surely does not bear scrutiny. Even if some investors concentrate on balance-sheet ratios, there is overwhelming evidence that accounting numbers are a veil that is pierced by the marginal (smart) investor. So simply removing your prize assets from the company and securitizing them will not always work. The investor-constraints line of reasoning is more plausible: many institutional investors are constrained to purchase only "investment grade" securities, and some are limited to AAA paper. Achieving a triple-A rating by segregating good assets to back part of a firm's financing can open up a market that was otherwise closed to the firm. But even this argument relies on the absence of arbitrage between assets of different ratings.

In actuality, the imperfection that drives much of the asset-backed securities market today is government support for the debt of certain borrowers, especially financial institutions such as banks and thrifts. If deposit insurance leaves the creditors of the parent bank unimpaired when the best assets are sold, then these institutions have a strong incentive to strip them off and securitize them. The bank will raise funds more easily and cheaply if it can package high-quality liquid assets into a special unit in such a way as to obtain a top rating from the rating agencies. A further incentive is provided by regulatory capital requirements that focus on the relationship between capital and the size of assets.

To work, asset-backed finance must satisfy certain criteria. Obviously the cost of funds must be lowered, and this usually means working with the rating agencies to satisfy them that the assets and the legal structure protect investors. The issuer may be required

---

[7]Harry Winn, Treasurer of American Hospital Supply, in "A Discussion of Corporate Capital Structure," *Midland Corporate Finance Journal.*

to "top up" the pool of assets backing the securities, but in other respects there must be no recourse to the parent, because the disposal of the assets must be treated as a "sale" to obtain favorable accounting and regulatory treatment. The legal structure must be one that avoids double taxation, and this has proved a stumbling block in some countries. A skeleton of the technique follows.

1. The firm sells or assigns certain assets, such as consumer receivables, to a special-purpose vehicle (SPV).
2. The assets are chosen and the legal structure designed to get an investment-grade rating. This is done in one or more of the following ways:
   - The SPV's debt is "overcollateralized."
   - A guarantee or letter of credit is purchased from a third party.
   - The parent agrees to replenish the asset pool if its value falls.
   - The SPV has a subordinated debt tranche.
   - Some residual risk is assumed by the parent.
3. The SPV issues high-rated debt.

In summary: you may be able to make a chicken worth more than the sum of its parts by repackaging its parts. So asset securitization may be a valid component of a firm's financial plan, *if*

   - the right conditions of market imperfections are present, else the cost of other debt will rise to offset the savings on the securitized assets. This would typically be the case where investors are severely constrained or when the government provides explicit or implicit backing for the issuer's debt.
   - the right tax and legal framework exists.

If no market imperfections are present, firms should beware of the securitization siren. You can't make money by cutting up a dog.

Nonrecourse project financing is a technique that predates but is closely related to asset securitization. Project financing to develop a coal field, for example, entails segmenting discrete, readily identifiable cash flows. The firm takes those cash flows and builds debt instruments around them. The flows are packaged and sold as private placements to investors that are best suited to take particular risks.

Project financing is not suitable for the normal operations of a corporation, especially for operations that have a high degree of synergy and internal transfer-pricing linkages with the rest of the firm. To qualify for project financing, a project must be capable of standing alone as a completely independent entity, and it must have a definable conclusion. Such an enterprise is the aluminum smelter to be constructed in Dunkerque, France, the financing of which is shown in Figure 16.4. From the corporate sponsor's point of view, the advantage is that creditors of the project have no recourse to the corporate owner or owners. From the creditors' point of view there is a reciprocal benefit: the cash flows are dedicated to the creditors with management having no option to divert them. Upon completion, the capital is returned to investors, removing management's discretion on how it should be reinvested. As one study puts it, "By returning such decisions to the marketplace, project financing has the potential to accomplish a fundamental reform and, in the process, create considerable value for stockholders."[8]

Creditors are also protected by detailed legal contracts that spell out the relationships among the participants. The ability to understand, write, and enforce such contracts is thus crucial to the success of nonrecourse project financing. Among the most important of such contracts are long-term agreements to sell the output. A hydro-power plant in

---

[8]Kensinger and Martin, "Project Finance: Raising Money the Old-Fashioned Way," *Midland Corporate Finance Journal,* p. 70.

Maine, for example, raised most of its funding through nonrecourse debt supported by a contract to sell electricity to Central Maine Power for almost half of its expected useful life of 50 years. Project financing can be highly leveraged despite the riskiness of the underlying commodity price, partly because of long-term purchase contracts but also because identifiable, tangible assets and few obligations to long-term employees and other corporate stakeholders make the assets readily redeployable under liquidation. In other words, the "costs of bankruptcy" are minimal compared to the situation in which the project was part of a large corporation.

Project financing is complex and can only be handled by sophisticated financial institutions. Yet far from being an aberration it may represent a major force in corporate financing. It offers tax advantages, reduces costs, and improves managerial incentives, allocates risks to those best able to bear them and allows *external* investor scrutiny of a project before it is undertaken. None of management's "pet projects" could ever qualify for leveraged nonrecourse financing. Perhaps in the future, when business activities are stand-alone and project-oriented rather than process-oriented in nature, investors will see themselves as better served by finite-lived contractual arrangements than by amorphous corporations.

Figure 16.4   *Announcement of the Financing of a Self-Contained Project*

PECHINEY

ALUMINIUM DUNKERQUE

CONSTRUCTION OF AN ALUMINIUM SMELTER IN DUNKERQUE, FRANCE

Ordinary Shares and Participating Subordinated Notes

FF 1,700,000,000

Placement Agents

Lead Placement Agent

BANQUE NATIONALE DE PARIS

Placement Agent	Placement Agent
BANQUE INDOSUEZ	GOLDMAN SACHS INTERNATIONAL

Financial Investors Equity Participants

Banque Nationale de Paris   GE Capital   Norwich Union Life
AGF Vie   Crédit National   Banque Indosuez
Citibank S.A.   Caisse Centrale des Banques   Crédit Agricole
Groupe CIC   Populaires   Legal & General Venture

Financial Advisors

BANQUE INDOSUEZ   GOLDMAN SACHS INTERNATIONAL

July, 1990

Limited Recourse Project Financing

U.S. $680,000,000

Lead Managers

CHASE INVESTMENT BANK LIMITED   CREDIT LYONNAIS

Co-Lead Managers Equity Participants

BANQUE NATIONALE DE PARIS   BANQUE INDOSUEZ   CREDIT AGRICOLE
CAISSE CENTRALE DES BANQUES POPULAIRES   CREDIT NATIONAL
COMPAGNIE FINANCIERE DE CIC

Co-Lead Managers

CREDIT SUISSE   SOCIETE GENERALE   COMMERZBANK AG
BANK OF AMERICA NATIONAL TRUST AND SAVINGS ASSOCIATION
BARCLAYS BANK SA   THE FUJI BANK LTD   NOMURA BANK INTERNATIONAL PLC
THE ROYAL BANK OF CANADA GROUP   THE SANWA BANK LTD
AMSTERDAM-ROTTERDAM BANK NV   BANCO DI NAPOLI   BANK OF MONTREAL
THE BANK OF TOKYO LTD   BANQUE PARIBAS   BAYERISCHE VEREINSBANK SA
CITIBANK N.A.   CREDIT DU NORD   DEUTSCHE BANK AG
MORGAN GUARANTY TRUST COMPANY OF NEW YORK   MELLON BANK N.A.
THE MITSUI TAIKO KOBE BANK LTD   NMB BANK (France)   THE SUMITOMO BANK LTD
UNION BANK OF SWITZERLAND

Managers

BANQUE FRANÇAISE DU COMMERCE EXTERIEUR   BANQUE WORMS
BANQUE BRUXELLES LAMBERT SA   ALGEMENE BANK NEDERLAND NV
BAYERISCHE LANDESBANK GIROZENTRALE   THE DAI-ICHI-KANGYO LTD
DRESDNER BANK LUXEMBOURG SA   THE LONG TERM CREDIT BANK OF JAPAN LTD
MIDLAND BANK SA   NATIONAL WESTMINSTER BANK PLC
SWISS BANK CORPORATION

Agent

CREDIT LYONNAIS

June, 1990

This announcement appears as a matter of record only

A Roadmap for Financing Choices

Figure 16.5 offers a framework for considering financing choices. The first issue is, How much debt and how much equity? We have argued that the key determinants of that decision are tax reduction from deducting interest, the constraint put on the amount of debt by the risks and costs of bankruptcy, and the managerial incentive effect of debt.

Based on these considerations, Heineken, the Dutch beverages company, might choose 65 percent as the appropriate proportion of debt in its capital structure. Once the

Figure 16.5   ***Financing Choices.***   How much debt and what kind of debt? This charts a course of choices including fixed versus floating, short term versus long term, which currency, and the use of hybrids.

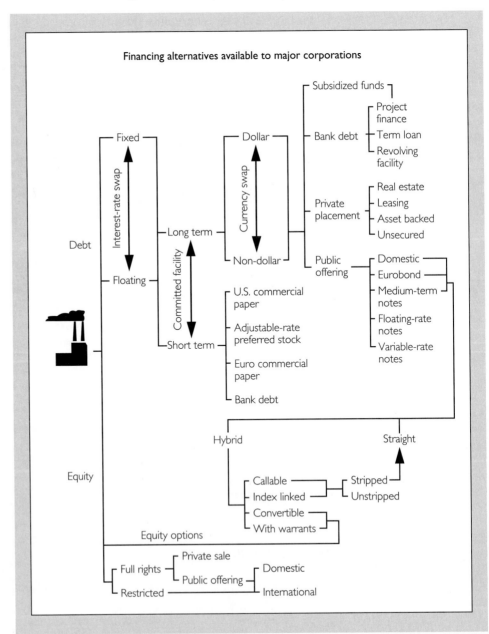

proportion of debt and equity has been chosen, the firm can go about selecting the best *kind* of debt (and equity). The first issue is the debt's payment characteristics: should it be fixed or floating, short term or long term, and in which currency should it be denominated? The vertical arrows signify that fixed can be converted to floating and vice versa using interest-rate swaps; short term can be made long term with a committed facility like a RUF,[9] and the currency of debt can be transformed via currency swaps.

Should Heineken's debt be fixed or floating? Because much of its cash flow is insensitive to interest rates, a large proportion should probably be fixed. Heineken can issue fixed-rate debt or, if it has access to cheap floating-rate funds, borrow the latter and fix the rate by means of an interest-rate swap. Following the diagram, floating-rate funds can be long term (a syndicated loan or a floating-rate note, for example) or short term. If Heineken selects short-term funding, this can be coupled with a committed bank facility to add long-term availability to the short-term funding source.

Having selected the nature of the debt, Heineken's management can seek the cheapest source. At the short end, common sources are commercial paper and adjustable-rate preferred stock (ARP)[10] in the U.S. domestic market, or Eurocommercial paper[11] and short-term Eurocurrency loans in the offshore markets.

In either case the currency-swap technique can be used to transform the denomination of Heineken's debt. For example, the company might find it advantageous to borrow in Dutch guilders and then use a guilder-dollar currency swap to create effective dollar financing for its North American sales.

Long-term sources include subsidized credit from national or international agencies, bank loans including nonrecourse project loans, term loans and revolving-credit facilities, various forms of secured and unsecured private placements, and public issues. When individual assets or a self-contained project can be segregated from those of the company, as in the construction of an independent gas-turbine facility by the construction company Komatsu, off–balance-sheet financing without recourse may prove more attractive to lenders than general-obligation debt.

Prominent companies like Heineken often occupy a preferred place in institutional investors' portfolios. Public bond issues can be done in certain domestic markets as well as the Eurobond market,[12] and the latter include medium-term notes (MTNs),[13] floating-rate notes and variable-rate notes (VRNs) on which the spread as well as the benchmark rate adjusts to accommodate market conditions. Although the straight bond, or MTN, is the most common, many companies choose to issue *hybrids* such as callable, index linked and quasi-equity debt. Some hybrid bonds are merely devices for exploiting a market imperfection to get cheaper money; these are "stripped" by means of derivatives. For example, Heineken could issue a floating-rate note with a "collar"—a cap and a floor on the interest rate—and sell the collar's cash flows to an investment bank in exchange for a subsidy to the company's financing cost. Others remain naked, giving the issuer a hedge for existing exposure (as is often the case in a commodity-linked bond) or a desired position, such as the right to call debt.

This brings us to the equity portion of the diagram. Convertibles or warrant bonds are normally complex positions taken by the company. Some companies, such as high-technology ventures, have to add a "sweetener," like the right of conversion, to their

---

[9]Revolving Underwriting Facility; see Chapter 9.

[10]This technique is discussed in Chapter 17.

[11]See Chapters 9 and 10.

[12]See Chapter 12.

[13]See Chapter 10.

debt to persuade investors to hold something with a great deal of downside risk; others attach warrants to obtain ostensibly low-cost funding. Equity financing itself is more straightforward and normally the preferred choice for a company like Heineken. Common-stock issues carry full voting rights and can be private or public issues. Public issues, whether sold domestically or internationally, are fungible—equity is equity—so little price advantage can be gained from foreign listings. Where foreign access to domestic common stock is restricted, as in Switzerland or South Korea, firms may give limited-rights stock to international investors or raise quasi-equity finance through convertible bonds.

Summary

Does the manner in which a company finances itself affect shareholder value? The answer is yes. The choice of capital structure, of financing instruments, and of the use of derivatives can lower corporate or investor taxes (up to a point), reduce transaction costs, and preserve company incentives to undertake the right investments.

The choice of capital structure is only the starting point of financing decisions. The chapter considered three dimensions of the What kind of debt? question: the issues of currency, maturity, and interest-reset period. Two principles governed these choices: (1) It pays firms to match the composition of debt to the payment characteristics of assets, for doing so minimizes the probability of financial distress and allows more tax-reducing debt. (2) It pays a company to deviate from the minimum-risk debt composition if and only if the firm can "beat the market" when the firm's predictions differ from forecasts implied by market prices. In this respect and in others, financing decisions are inseparable from hedging decisions.

Swaps, caps, and other derivatives play a role in financing in three different ways: (1) to hedge an existing exposure that the company is subject to, (2) to take advantage of an imperfection in the capital market, or (3) to position the company to gain from a favorable movement in some market variable such as interest rates. Hybrid bonds, when used in conjunction with options or other derivatives, can be an effective way of obtaining cheaper funds by exploiting a market imperfection. But some hybrids, notably warrant and convertible bonds, are not hedged and so must be regarded as positioning instruments.

Many companies today employ one or another form of asset-backed finance. These work if the right market imperfections are present, else the cost of other debt will rise to offset the savings on the securitized assets. This would typically be the case where investors are severely constrained or when the government provides explicit or implicit backing for the issuer's debt.

The chapter concluded with a framework that offered some guidelines for the sequence of financing choices. The principles behind them may be summarized as follows:

- Choose the *proportion* of debt on the basis of reducing taxes up to the point at which the tax-shield benefit is offset by the costs of financial distress. Then choose the best *kind* of debt.
- Liabilities should be designed to match assets in such a way as to minimize the probability of (costly) financial distress.
- Companies should deviate from the "matching" principle if and only if their view is persuasively better than the forecasts implied in market rates and prices.
- Once the form of financing is chosen, the company may employ the financing and hedging techniques (using swaps and other derivatives) that achieve the goal at the lowest cost.

CONCEPTUAL QUESTIONS

1. How can Modigliani and Miller argue that capital structure does not matter? What are the assumptions of the MM proposition?
2. Show how relaxing each of the key assumptions of the MM theory can demonstrate that particular capital structures can increase shareholder value.
3. "Because of the international Fisher effect, it is irrelevant which currency a company uses to finance its operations." Write down the arguments for and against this proposition.
4. Qantas is trying to develop a strategy for the currency, maturity, and interest-rate reset period of its debt. What principles should it use to identify the right financing mix?
5. Provide examples, backed by reasoning, of hedging, positioning, and arbitrage uses of a bond whose principal is tied to the price of natural gas.
6. The French publishing company Hachette has recently had some trouble raising equity capital. Some in the firm have argued in favor of securitizing Hachette's accounts receivable. Under what conditions should such a firm use asset securitization as a source of funding?
7. Do you think the production of beverage cans would qualify as the sort of project suited to non-recourse leveraged financing? Explain.

PROBLEMS

1. Dole, the fruit company, is planning to set up a distribution facility in Belgium for storage and sale of Honduran bananas to France and Germany. In what currency should this expansion be financed? Explain with reference to the three kinds of currency exposure.
2. Hutchinson Whampoa has traditionally relied upon commercial paper issued in the Hong Kong market to finance itself in local currency. In that market the firm pays approximately HIBOR $-$ 30bp. After an internal review management has concluded that the debt should be long-term fixed-rate yen liabilities. Show, by means of diagrams, how the firm can achieve its goal while continuing to use the CP market in Hong Kong.
3. BASF, the German chemicals company, has just issued a 5-year hybrid EuroDM bond that gives the investor a put option after 2 years at par. Some within the company argue that since BASF has in effect written a put, the interest-rate risk should be hedged by buying a swaption from a German bank. Others say that this would be too expensive. Show how this would work. What are the arguments for and against hedging the put?

Application 16.1 | THE POLAR ELECTRIC APPLIANCE COMPANY

In late 1990 the Polar Electric Appliance Company, a wholly owned Mexican subsidiary of Empresas Polar de Venezuela, was considering several alternative financing sources to obtain $35 million (or equivalent). The money would be used both to expand production and to develop marketing and distribution in its Monterey, Mexico, facilities.

The company manufactured plug-in kettles and other small household appliances. While the focus had originally been the Southwestern U.S. market, the plug-in kettle had never really caught on in the United States. Now the major market for electric kettles was in English-speaking Canada. By keeping costs down, Polar Electric had gained a major share in the Canadian market. Its only serious competitor was a Canadian company located in Ontario.

Until now, the company had always financed itself internally, with funds from the parent company in Caracas. Working-capital financing had been in U.S.-dollar-denominated bank loans. One of its bankers was now advising the company to consider financing the expansion in Canadian dollars. The bank pointed out that the inverted yield curve in Canada made this an excellent time to lock in long-term funding.

Apart from continuing to obtain funds from the parent, the following options were possible methods of funding:

1. Finance by discounting its three-month receivables from exports to Canada, which were invoiced in U.S. dollars. The cost would be US$ LIBOR + 40bp. US$ LIBOR was 7.35%.
2. Switch invoicing to Canadian dollars and finance through the Canadian Bankers Acceptance Market, at approximately C$ LIBOR + 30bp. C$ LIBOR was currently 10.97%.
3. Obtain a six-year US$ revolving facility, under which the company could borrow at LIBOR + 25bp with an annual commitment fee of ¼%.
4. Issue a six-year Eurodollar bond. The firm had been advised that it could raise funds at the prevailing AA swap rate, which was U.S. Treasury bonds plus 75bp. The six-year benchmark Treasury yield was currently 8.2%.
5. Issue a six-year EuroCanadian dollar bond at the AA rate of 9.5%.
6. Obtain a regional development loan at 7% in Mexican pesos from the Monterey Development Authority. This would require conforming to the employment requirements of the authority, but the company felt that this would not be a problem, given the expanded production that was anticipated. The only catch was that the repayment of interest and principal would be indexed to the U.S.–dollar/Mexican-peso exchange rate.

Which choice of funding should Polar Electric use? Be sure to consider the interest rate, the maturity, the currency, and the availability of funds.

Application 16.2 | FINANCING CIBA

Ciba-Geigy is a Swiss-based worldwide producer of pharmaceutical, agricultural, and chemical products. It operates in 60 countries employing 90,000 people, and in 1992 it had group sales in excess of $15 billion equivalent. Its expenditures on research and development are heavy, reaching approximately $1.7 billion equivalent in 1992. Capital expenditures exceeded $1.3 billion.

Assume that you have been invited to a meeting with Ciba-Geigy's top financial managers to discuss their debt strategy. Look at the attached information about Ciba-Geigy. Based on the nature of its business and the characteristics of its assets, what do you think is the optimal way in which the company should be financed? Consider the following:

- How much debt should Ciba-Geigy have in relation to equity? What is its actual debt-equity ratio, and what would you advise the company?
- Should the debt be fixed or floating? How much of the debt is fixed? What would you advise the company to do?
- How much of the company's debt should be long term?
- Based on the distribution of Ciba's sales and assets, what should be the currency composition of its debt? In fact, what is it? And what would you advise the company to do?

Exhibit I. Ciba's Business Portfolio

HEALTHCARE	AGRICULTURE	INDUSTRY
PHARMA • SELF-MEDICATION • DIAGNOSTICS CIBA VISION	**PLANT PROTECTION • ANIMAL HEALTH • SEEDS**	**TEXTILE DYES • CHEMICALS • ADDITIVES PIGMENTS • POLYMERS • COMPOSITES METTLER TOLEDO**
PRODUCTS Medicines to treat — Heart/circulatory diseases — Diseases of the central nervous system — Illnesses of bones and the locomotor system — Allergies and respiratory illnesses — Cancer, immunological, infectious, and other diseases Over-the-counter medicines, for example for colds and flu, pain, and skin care • Diagnostic instruments and reagents Contact lenses — Lens care products — Ophthalmic medicines	**PRODUCTS** Herbicides — particularly for maize • Insecticides — particularly for cotton • Fungicides — mainly for cereals and vegetables • Parasiticides and medicines for farm and domestic animals • Seeds — maize, soya, wheat	**PRODUCTS** Dyestuffs and chemicals for textiles, paper, and leather Antimicrobials • Fluorescent whitening agents • Additives for plastics, elastomers, synthetic fibres, dyestuffs, photography, lubricants, PVC stabilisers • Pigments for paints, protection of surfaces, printing inks, plastics, fibres, ceramics, glass Adhesives • Synthetic resins • Formulated systems • Photo resists for the printed circuit board industry • Lightweight components for the aerospace industry • Precision balances and scales from laboratory to heavy industrial use • Analytical instruments
CUSTOMERS Patients • Doctors • Hospitals • Pharmacies • Institutions Laboratories • Opticians	**CUSTOMERS** Farmers • Gardeners • Wholesalers • Cooperatives Public and private institutions • Veterinary surgeons Animal owners	**CUSTOMERS** Textile industry • Leather industry • Paper industry Manufacturers of cosmetics and detergents • Plastics processors • Oil industry • Photographic industry Automobile industry • Aerospace industry • Electronics industry • Construction industry • Ceramics and glass industry Paint industry • Printing ink manufacturers • Laboratories, industry, retail
MARKET POSITION Pharma: among the 5 leading companies worldwide in a highly fragmented market Self-Medication: international presence, strong position in Europe Diagnostics: growth business Ciba Vision: No. 2 worldwide	**MARKET POSITION** Plant Protection: No. 1 worldwide • Animal Health: among the leaders in animal parasiticides Seeds: growth business in maize; in some countries among the leaders	**MARKET POSITION** Textile Dyes: No. 1 worldwide • Chemicals: No. 1 worldwide in fluorescent whitening agents • Additives: No. 1 worldwide Pigments: among the 3 leading companies • Polymers: fragmented market, leading position in some segments Composites: No. 1 among the integrated manufacturers Mettler Toledo: worldwide No. 1 scales and balances
Healthcare 1992 Sales: SFr. 8662 million	**Agriculture 1992 Sales: SFr. 4817 million**	**Industry 1992 Sales: SFr. 8725 million**
SALES BY DIVISION	**SALES BY DIVISION**	**SALES BY DIVISION**

Source: Ciba Annual Report, 1992.

Exhibit II. Excerpts from Ciba's Annual Report
Source: Ciba Annual Report 1992, pp. 43, 46, 47, 52, 54–56.

Consolidated current value Profit and Loss statement

IN MILLIONS OF SWISS FRANCS

	1992	1991	Change, %
Revenue			
Group sales to third parties	22,204	21.077	+5
Interest, royalties, and revenue from minority holdings	484	392	+23
	22,688	21.469	+6
Expenditure			
Raw materials, intermediates and finished products (variable product costs, including inward freight and duties)	6,197	6.003	+3
Wages, salaries, bonuses and welfare benefits	6,783	6.598	+3
Interest payable	490	486	+1
Depreciation on fixed assets[1]	1,251	1.201	+4
Other expenditure[2], including taxes	6,447	5.901	+9
	21,168	20.189	+5
Group operating profit	1,520	1,280	+19
as a percentage of sales	6.8	6.1	
Group operating cash flow	2,771	2,481	+12
as a percentage of sales	12.5	11.8	

[1] Current value basis (see explanatory note on page 39). Book depreciation (historical-cost basis) on fixed assets was 1992: SFr. 1,095m., 1991: SFr. 1,054m.
[2] Includes minority profit attributions: 1992: SFr. 2m. loss, 1991: SFr. 3m. profit.

Consolidated Balance Sheet

Assets   Of the Group's total assets at 31 December 1992, 15,621 million Swiss francs, or 51 per cent, are long term assets and 14,979 million Swiss francs current assets. The proportion of long term assets decreased by 1 percentage point in 1992 after having increased continuously since 1987.

Liquid funds   The greater part of the 5,267 million Swiss francs in liquid funds is held by the Parent company. 2,035 million Swiss francs, or 39 per cent, are invested in marketable securities.

Liabilities   Total liabilities increased by 409 million Swiss francs to 12,526 million Swiss francs. This figure includes 5,340 million Swiss francs in interest-bearing debt (principally bank debt, debenture loans, private placements and employee savings deposits), making up 43 per cent of total liabilities; 3,181 million Swiss francs of this are short term, including the commercial paper issued in the USA, the United Kingdom, and the Euromarket, plus 95 million Swiss francs in money market debt in Switzerland. Apart from these 95 million Swiss francs, all bank debt was incurred by Group companies in their local currencies. The debenture loans and private placements were denominated in the following currencies: US dollars, 75 per cent; Swiss francs, 21 per cent; pounds sterling, 4 per cent.

Equity   Equity represents 59 per cent of the Balance Sheet total (1991: 57 per cent).

Key ratios   The principal ratios have changed as follows during the year:

Debt/equity ratio (liabilities and equity respectively, as percentages of the balance sheet total): 41:59 (1991: 43:57).

Assets protection ratio (ratio of equity to long term assets plus one half of inventories): 1.02 (1991, 0.97). The entire long term assets plus 59 per cent of inventories are covered by equity

Current ratio (ratio of current assets to current liabilities): 1.98 (1991, 1.79).

Quick ratio (ratio of liquid funds plus receivables to total current liabilities): 1.24 (1991, 1.05).

Consolidated Balance Sheet

IN MILLIONS OF SWISS FRANCS

	31 DECEMBER 1992	31 DECEMBER 1991
Current assets	**14,979**	13,759
Liquid funds[1]	**5,267**	4,268
Customer receivables	**4,064**	3,821
Various current assets	**1,468**	1,520
Stocks	**4,180**	4,150
Long term assets	**15,621**	14,679
Fixed assets[2]	**13,920**	12,935
Other long term assets (investments, loans and other assets of a long term character)	**1,701**	1,744
BALANCE SHEET TOTAL	**30,600**	28,438
Current liabilities	**7,549**	7,692
Suppliers	**1,117**	1,198
Banks	**2,163**	2,337
Other current liabilities	**4,269**	4,157
Long term liabilities	**4,753**	4,200
Debenture loans and private placements	**1,710**	1,507
Other loans and long term liabilities	**3,043**	2,693
Minority interests	**224**	225
Group equity	**18,074**	16,321
BALANCE SHEET TOTAL	**30,600**	28,438

[1]Of which:	Cash/P.O. Giro/Bank	3,232	2,609
	Securities	2,035	1,659
[2]Of which:	Land and buildings	6,289	5,961
	Plant	7,631	6,974
	Use of historical cost less appropriate depreciation would give a valuation of	8,849	8,283
	Insurance value of fixed assets	26,855	24,875

Sales by business sector

IN MILLIONS OF SWISS FRANCS

	1992	1991	Change, % 1	Change, % 2
Healthcare	8,662	7,824	+11	+12
Agriculture	4,817	4,798	0	+1
Industry	8,725	8,455	+3	+3
GROUP TOTAL	**22,204**	21,077	+5	+6

Business sector operating profit

IN MILLIONS OF SWISS FRANCS

	1992	1991	1992 as % of 1991
Healthcare	1,285	1,253	103
Agriculture	493	507	97
Industry	527	349	151
TOTAL OPERATING PROFIT	**2,305**	2,109	109
± Financial profit/(expenditure)	(41)	(141)	29
Remaining corporate overhead including income taxes	(744)	(688)	108
GROUP OPERATING PROFIT AFTER TAXATION	**1,520**	1,280	119

[1]Calculated on the Group sales figures expressed in Swiss francs
[2]Local currency basis

Group sales by geographical area[1]

IN PER CENT

Region	1992	1991
Europe	43	44
of which EC	36	36
North America	32	32
Latin America	7	7
Asia	13	13
Africa, Australia, Oceania	5	4

Sales in the principal local currencies[2]

IN MILLIONS

Country	Currency unit	1992	1991	Change, %	Average inflation-rate[3] %
USA	US $	4,651	4,247	+10	3
Germany	DM	2,409	2,492	−3	4
UK	£	428	410	+4	4
France	Franc	6,553	6,465	+1	3
Italy	Lira	1,023,641	979,489	+5	5
Japan	Yen	122,699	119,766	+2	2
Spain	Peseta	43,177	42,084	+3	6
Canada	C$	476	447	+6	2
Brazil	US $[4]	406	399	+2	–
Switzerland	Franc	435	386	+13	4
Mexico	Peso	759,829	639,580	+19	16
Australia	A $	320	235	+36	1
Netherlands	Guilder	538	497	+8	4
Belgium/Luxembourg	Franc	7,266	6,766	+7	3

[1]Calculated on the sales figures in Swiss francs

[2]Sales by or on behalf of local companies (excluding inter-company shipments)

[3]Movement of retail price index, 1992. Source: O.E.C.D., *Main Economic Indicators*, February 1993 (Mexican and Australian percentages estimated)

[4]Special reporting in US dollars for countries with hyperinflation

Number of employees by geographical area

	31 DECEMBER 1992	Propor-tion, %	Propor-tion, %	31 DECEMBER 1991	Propor-tion, %	Propor-tion, %
Europe	47,078		52	48,345		53
of which Switzerland .	22,133	24		22,639	25	
of which EC	23,636	26		24,434	27	
North America	23,231		26	22,980		25
Latin America	7,946		9	8,096		9
Asia	9,412		10	9,165		10
Africa, Australia, Oceania .	2,887		3	3,079		3
GROUP TOTAL	90,554		100	91,665		100

Capital expenditure by geographical area

IN MILLIONS OF SWISS FRANCS

	1992	Propor-tion, %	Propor-tion, %	1991	Propor-tion, %	Propor-tion, %
Europe	1,234		66	1,285		66
of which Switzerland .	569	31		668	34	
of which EC	645	35		608	31	
North America	470		25	499		25
Latin America	71		4	68		3
Asia	69		4	91		5
Africa, Australia, Oceania .	13		1	14		1
GROUP TOTAL	1,857		100	1,957		100

Fixed assets by geographical area

IN MILLIONS OF SWISS FRANCS

	31 DECEMBER 1992	Propor-tion, %	Propor-tion, %	31 DECEMBER 1991	Propor-tion, %	Propor-tion, %
Europe	9,533		68	9,117		70
of which Switzerland .	5,769	41		5,328	41	
of which EC	3,788	27		3,731	29	
North America	3,200		23	2,746		21
Latin America	537		4	476		4
Asia	538		4	479		4
Africa, Australia, Oceania .	112		1	117		1
GROUP TOTAL	13,920		100	12,935		100

The Group in figures, 1982-1992

		1982	1983	1984	1985	1986	1987	1988	1989	1990	1991	1992
Group sales	SFr.m.	13,808	14,741	17,474	18,221	15,955	15,764	17,647	20,608	19,703	21,077	**22,204**
Change in relation to preceding year	%	+1	+7	+19	+4	−12	−1	+12	+17	−4	+7	**+5**
Group operating profit after taxation	SFr.m.	622	776	1,187	1,472	1,161	1,100	1,325	1,557	1,033	1,280	**1,520**
Change in relation to preceding year	%	+19	+25	+53	+24	−21	−5	+20	+18	−34	+24	**+19**
As % of Sales		4.5	5.3	6.8	8.1	7.3	7.0	7.5	7.6	5.2	6.1	**6.8**
Depreciation of fixed assets	SFr.m.	836	804	863	897	844	858	943	1,078	1,087	1,201	**1,251**
As % of Sales		6.1	5.4	4.9	4.9	5.3	5.4	5.3	5.2	5.5	5.7	**5.6**
Group operating cash flow	SFr.m.	1,458	1,580	2,050	2,369	2,005	1,958	2,268	2,635	2,120	2,481	**2,771**
Change in relation to preceding year	%	+9	+8	+30	+16	−15	−2	+16	+16	−20	+17	**+12**
As % of Sales		10.6	10.7	11.7	13.0	12.6	12.4	12.9	12.8	10.8	11.8	**12.5**
Current assets	SFr.m.	9,105	9,695	11,766	12,053	12,127	12,223	13,293	13,665	12,835	13,759	**14,979**
Change in relation to preceding year	%	+10	+6	+21	+2	+1	+1	+9	+3	−6	+7	**+9**
Long term assets	SFr.m.	9,737	10,035	10,709	10,514	10,171	9,935	11,418	12,418	13,315	14,679	**15,621**
Change in relation to preceding year	%	+5	+3	+7	−2	−3	−2	+15	+9	+7	+10	**+6**
Current liabilities	SFr.m.	3,943	4,216	4,919	4,954	4,826	5,153	6,059	6,408	7,170	7,692	**7,549**
Change in relation to preceding year	%	+11	+7	+17	+1	−3	+7	+18	+6	+12	+7	**−2**
Long term liabilities	SFr.m.	3,220	3,289	3,469	3,462	2,888	2,635	3,094	3,195	3,273	4,200	**4,753**
Change in relation to preceding year	%	+7	+2	+5	0	−17	−9	+17	+3	+2	+28	**+13**
Equity	SFr.m.	11,537	12,071	13,921	13,978	14,401	14,188	15,370	16,237	15,454	16,321	**18,074**
Change in relation to preceding year	%	+6	+5	+15	0	+3	−1	+8	+6	−5	+6	**+11**
Research and development expenditure	SFr.m.	1,175	1,248	1,456	1,674	1,627	1,673	1,797	2,075	2,051	2,185	**2,350**
As % of Sales		8.5	8.5	8.3	9.2	10.2	10.6	10.2	10.1	10.4	10.4	**10.6**
Capital expenditure	SFr.m.	868	830	1,007	1,213	1,232	1,368	1,616	1,987	2,058	1,957	**1,857**
Change in relation to preceding year	%	−1	−4	+21	+20	+2	+11	+18	+23	+4	−5	**−5**
As % of Sales		6	6	6	7	8	9	9	10	10	9	**8**
Personnel costs incl. welfare	SFr.m.	4,206	4,390	4,893	5,184	4,924	4,842	5,402	6,132	6,275	6,598	**6,783**
Change in relation to preceding year	%	+3	+4	+11	+6	−5	−2	+11	+14	+2	+5	**+3**
Number of employees		79,413	79,173	81,423	81,012	82,231	86,109	88,757	92,553	94,141	91,665	**90,554**
Change in relation to preceding year	%	−1	0	+3	−1	+2	+5	+3	+4	+2	−3	**−1**

| Application 16.3 | THE MORNING AFTER AT OLYMPIA & YORK |

In the late 1980s Olympia & York, the Canadian property group, built up a commercial paper program of about C$800 million, in part to finance investments in the ambitious Canary Wharf financial services center in London's docklands. By 1991, however, troubles with that venture and with other O&Y property investments made investors less and less willing to hold Olympia & York's short-term paper, and the company reduced the program to C$400. In early 1992 Canada's Dominion Bond Rating Service placed the O&Y commercial paper rations on "alert" status, and the company reluctantly terminated its two remaining commercial-paper programs.

In a press statement, the rating services said, "There is basically nothing fundamentally wrong on a long-term basis with Olympia & York or these two commercial-paper programs, but a combination of continuing rumors and negative press is making it increasingly difficult for the company to roll over commercial paper." Or as one banker put it, "It's fine to own a piece of real estate, but it's not cash."* At the time, a large proportion of the London project and of the company's New York office buildings remained vacant. The family-owned concern had declined to disclose details of the unquoted company's financial condition, so analysts could not be sure of O&Y's actual level of debt. Estimates put it as high as C$20 billion.

The company then had to hastily arrange additional bank lines of credit at higher costs and with more severe constraints to replace the commercial paper, and was forced to sell some of its assets to raise funds. These events preceded and perhaps precipitated a cumulative bankruptcy of the Olympia and York subsidiaries in 1992 and 1993.

With the benefit of hindsight, what can you say about possibly preferable ways in which Olympia & York could have financed themselves in the late 1980s? Justify your choice or choices.

SELECTED REFERENCES

Eiteman, David, Art Stonehill, and Michael Moffett, *Multinational Business Finance*. 6th ed. Reading, Mass.: Addison-Wesley, 1991.

Froot, Kenneth A., David Scharfstein, and Jeremy Stein, "Risk Management: Coordinating Corporate Investment and Financing Policies," NBER Working Paper No. 4084 (1992),

Kensinger, John, and John D. Martin, "Project Finance: Raising Money the Old-Fashioned Way," *Journal of Applied Corporate Finance* (1989), pp. 69–81.

Lessard, Donald, "Global Competition and Corporate Finance in the 1990s," *Continental Bank Journal of Applied Corporate Finance* (1990), 19–28.

Levi, Maurice, *International Finance*, 2nd ed. New York: McGraw-Hill 1990.

Shapiro, Alan C., *Multinational Financial Management*. 3rd ed. Boston: Allyn and Bacon, 1989.

Smith, Clifford W., and Rene M. Stulz, "The Determinants of Firms' Hedging Policies," *Journal of Financial and Quantitative Analysis*, 20 (December 1985), 391–405.

Smith, Clifford W., Charles W. Smithson, and D. Sykes Wilford, "Five Reasons Why Companies Should Manage Risk." In Robert J. Schwartz and Clifford W. Smith, *The Handbook of Currency and Interest Rate Risk Management* (New York Institute of Finance, 1990), 19.3–19.14.

---

*Financial Times, March 21, 1992, p. 1.

Smith, Roy C., and Ingo Walter, *Global Financial Services.* New York: Harper Business, 1992.

Stern, Joel, and Donald H. Chew, Jr., *The Revolution in Corporate Finance.* 2d ed. Cambridge, England: Blackwell Publishers, 1992.

Stulz, Rene M., "Optimal Hedging Policies," *Journal of Financial and Quantitative Analysis*, 19 (June 1984), 127–140.

17

The Future: Understanding and Using New Instruments

Constructing the Edifice

The international financial market has altered dramatically in the last decade, and is likely to continue to do so. As we have seen in previous chapters, the Eurobond market has proved fertile ground for the introduction of many experimental techniques, and the recent opening up of domestic capital markets may augur a burgeoning of instruments designed to meet the requirements of investors and issuers in the home markets. Today's potential investor or issuer is confronted with dual-currency bonds and reverse-dual-currency bonds; with swaps and options and swaptions and captions; and with "bunny bonds" and "bull and bear" bonds and TIGRS and Lyons, not to mention flip-flops and retractables and perpetuals and Heaven-and-Hell bonds; and bonds linked to the Nikkei index or German Bund futures contracts or the price of oil. What's it all about, one has to wonder. Who buys these things? Who issues them, and why?

This chapter introduces a practical approach to the analysis and construction of innovative instruments in international finance. Many instruments of the international capital market, new or old, can be broken down into simpler securities. These elementary securities include zero-coupon bonds, pure equity, spot and forward contracts, and options. Later in this chapter, for example, we will analyze the breakdown of a dual-currency bond into a conventional coupon-bearing bond and a long-dated forward-exchange contract. The combination or modification of basic contracts gives us many of the innovations we see today, and if we understand the pricing of bonds, forward contracts, and the like, in many cases we can estimate the price of complex-sounding instruments. When one encounters a new technique, one seeks to understand its *component elements*. We call this the *building-block approach*. We'll see numerous examples in the pages that follow.

The building-block method also enables us to go a step further: to understand the role of such securities in a portfolio of assets or liabilities. An extension of the building-block approach is one that teaches us the behavior of innovative securities, alone or in combination. Simply stated, this *functional method* regards every such instrument or contract as bearing a price, or value, which in turn bears a unique relationship to some set of variables such as interest rates or currency values. The more one can break the instrument down into its component parts or building blocks, the easier it is to specify how the instrument's value will change as the independent variables change.

Once we know how the instrument is constructed and hence how its value behaves, we can readily compare it with existing instruments which, alone or in combination, have the same behavior. For example, some instruments' value varies with market interest rates, so that they are bondlike; others are affected by the condition of the issuing company, so that they are more equitylike. Many instruments combine elements of both. Each should be priced in accordance with the price of comparable instruments; if they are not, there may be a mispricing. The functional approach can be of great practical value to investors and issuers who wish to better understand the risks of instruments offered to them by banks. The approach can also be used to identify arbitrage opportunities between instruments, and to hedge one instrument with another.

We begin by seeking to explain why it is that new instruments are introduced and which ones are likely to succeed.

Economics of Financial Innovation

No financial innovation can be regarded as useful, nor will it survive, unless it creates benefits to at least one of the parties involved in the contract. These benefits could involve lower costs of capital for the issuer or higher returns for the investor. The benefit could be lower taxes paid, or a reduction in risk, such as foreign-exchange exposure of a corporation or government. More generally, the contribution of any financial innovation lies in the extent to which it helps complete the set of financial contracts available for financing or investing, positioning or hedging. They are introduced in response to some market imperfection.

EXAMPLE 17.1   In the early 1980s, certain German banks introduced investment instruments whose return was equal to the change in the German stock-market index, the DAX, including reinvested dividends. This enabled individual German investors to overcome the absence of an equity-index futures contract in Germany and to avoid the high fees charged by investment trusts.

But even if both the investor and the issuer are better off, there will only be a net gain if these benefits more than offset the costs of creating the innovation. These costs include research and development, marketing, and distribution costs. Moreover, the firm providing the innovation must be able to capture or appropriate some of the benefits generated.

One fundamental factor inhibiting investors' demand for new instruments is that something new and different tends to be inherently illiquid. If an instrument is one of a kind, traders cannot easily put it into a category that allows it to be traded at a predictable price and in a positioning book along with similar instruments. And to the extent that the new instrument is difficult to understand, the costs of overcoming information barriers may inhibit secondary-market development.

Some innovations may actually destroy value, because they are misunderstood by one party to the contract. The instrument does not behave in the way it is described as behaving. Or one aspect of the risk of the instrument (such as the credit risk of swaps) is not fully appreciated by one party. The excessive investment by U.S. savings-and-loan institutions in high-yield "junk" bonds in the 1980s can be seen in this light. These securities were described as bonds with disproportionately high yields. Yet a functional analysis of their behavior reveals that they were much more akin to equity than to bonds, and so should have borne a return like the equity return of the issuing company. Superficial analysis can lead to completely inappropriate investment or financing.

In many instances the investor or issuer may not be aware that he could have done the same thing in a cheaper way via another combination of instruments. This is not an indictment of the banker promoting the instrument. In principle, one can always find some way in which the issuer (for example) could have done better had her investment banker more fully informed her of all the alternatives. Bond salespeople and corporate finance specialists do not have an obligation to fully inform the client about all the alternatives (including competitors' products), unless the client explicitly pays for that information. There are many situations in which the investor or issuer could have found a cheaper solution elsewhere but faced transactions costs, regulations, or high costs of information-gathering that prevented ready access to the ostensibly cheaper alternative.

One way to interpret this situation is to describe financial product innovations as "experience goods." They must be consumed before their qualities become evident.

For innovations to be produced they must provide an above-average return. Innovation of any kind involves the production of an information-intensive intangible good whose value is uncertain. Although often costly to produce, new information can be used by any number of people without additional cost; it is a common good. The socially optimal price of a public good is zero. Indeed, the ease of dissemination of new information makes it likely that its price will quickly fall to zero. However, if this new information, once produced, bears a zero price, there is little or no private incentive for the production of innovations. There is no effective patent protection for financial instruments.

Yet a few firms seem to have been leaders in the production of innovations. Because financial products are experience goods, it may be that customers will tend to purchase new instruments and services chiefly from firms that have a reputation for initiating techniques of sound legality and predictable risk. Whenever the true risks, returns, or other attributes of the new instrument are difficult to ascertain, there will be fixed information costs that serve as a barrier to acceptance of that instrument. The imprimatur of a reputable firm can allay investors' or issuers' fears. This reassurance is particularly effective in cases in which the issue must be done quickly to take advantage of a "window" in the market, as Example 17.2 shows.

Hence, despite the absence of legal proprietary rights, reputable banks and other financial institutions will have a temporary monopolistic advantage that enables them to appropriate returns from investment in the development of financial innovations. Other, perhaps more inventive, firms and individuals will tend to be absorbed by those who command a temporary monopoly.

EXAMPLE 17.2 In the autumn of 1992, Britain dropped out of the European Exchange-Rate Mechanism, freeing its domestic monetary policy from the constraints of a tie to the deutschemark. On Tuesday, January 26, 1993, the Bank of England lowered the base rate, Britain's key short-term rate, from 7 percent to 6 percent. On Thursday of that week, Salomon Brothers in London led the first issue of collared floating-rate notes in sterling. The bond was a £100 million 10-year issue for the Leeds Permanent Building Society.

The deal offered investors LIBOR flat, with a minimum interest rate of 7 percent, ⅞ point higher than the current six-month London interbank offered rate, and a maximum of 11 percent. This is typical of the collared FRN structure, of which over $8 billion had been done in dollar-denominated form at the time. Collared FRNs incorporate a floor and a cap on the floating rate, with the floor being *above* current money-market rates to attract coupon-hungry investors. The steep yield curve in the United States in the early 1990s made it possible for issuers to sell caps and buy floors in the over-the-counter derivatives market, and to use them to subsidize the cost of the issue while offering the investor an above-market yield, at least initially.

Salomon Brothers had arranged a number of deals of this kind in the dollar Eurobond market, and had done preparatory work for a sterling version. It was not until the base-rate cut made the British yield curve steepen that it became viable, however, and Salomon was quick to exploit the window. The opportunity to reduce funding costs, and confidence that Salomon had the experience and credibility to get it right, are factors that gave Leeds Permanent the confidence to pioneer the structure in sterling. Similar collared FRNs were soon issued by other U.K. building societies and banks.

Competition and the Product Cycle in Financial Innovations

The advantage certain firms have in new instruments is, before long, eroded as uncertainty is reduced and clients can more confidently turn to lower-cost imitators. The high initial returns are eroded by competition from other banks as well as by the market forces that tend to eliminate those imperfections that gave rise to the innovation in the first place. The product may become a "commodity." For example, when interest-rate caps were first introduced, corporate acceptance was long and difficult and only a few firms with high credibility were able to profit from them, and this only because the margins were substantial. As familiarity and acceptance increased, the field was invaded by many banks and securities houses with the ability to trade and broker these interest-rate options, and the prices of caps were driven down to a level resembling that of the underlying options. At this point, the low-cost producers assumed a large market share.[1]

This sequence can be illustrated by means of the product life-cycle diagram familiar to many readers (Figure 17.1). Financial innovations behave like other new products but with a faster dissemination rate. Some financial innovations, however, set in motion a different process, one which leads to their demise. That process is not related to the market but rather to the political/regulatory process. Many innovations, after all, are

Figure 17.1   *The Product Life Cycle in International Financial Innovations.*   Contrast those that mature and endure with those that evoke a regulatory response that eliminates their rationale.

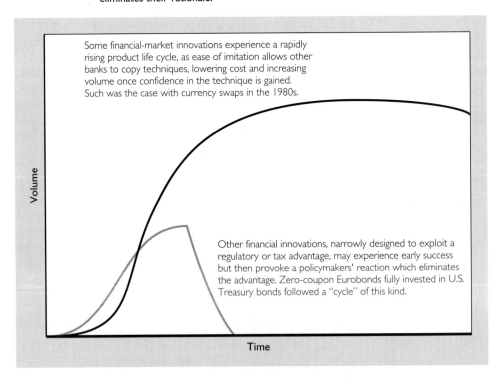

Some financial-market innovations experience a rapidly rising product life cycle, as ease of imitation allows other banks to copy techniques, lowering cost and increasing volume once confidence in the technique is gained. Such was the case with currency swaps in the 1980s.

Other financial innovations, narrowly designed to exploit a regulatory or tax advantage, may experience early success but then provoke a policymakers' reaction which eliminates the advantage. Zero-coupon Eurobonds fully invested in U.S. Treasury bonds followed a "cycle" of this kind.

[1]In this instance, another important factor is credit risk. A corporation buying a cap from a bank has to concern itself with the potential for default on the cap writer's obligations, so creditworthy banks will retain a disproportionate share.

designed to circumvent regulations, restrictions, and taxes. The regulatory authorities, seeing that the technique has an erosive effect on their jurisdiction, react by closing loopholes or by eliminating the barrier that motivated the innovation in the first place.

Sources of Innovations

Most financial innovations just provide different ways of bundling or unbundling more basic instruments such as bonds, equities, and currencies. Of course, there are many, many different ways of rearranging the basic financial products. So two questions arise: (1) Why do particular innovations seem to emerge and thrive? (2) Why do investors or issuers need the innovation in the first place? What's to stop them from putting together the structure from the basic instruments themselves, rather than paying investment bankers to do so? The answer lies in imperfections—market imperfections that make *the whole worth more than the sum of the parts* and that constrain investors, issuers, or both from constructing equivalent positions out of elemental instruments. Many of these imperfections arise from barriers to international arbitrage, from currency preferences, and from the different conditions investors and issuers face in different countries.

The example of convertible Eurobonds illustrates this concept.

EXAMPLE 17.3 In 1992, a British company, Carlton, issued a £64.25 million convertible, bearer-form Eurobond. The subordinated issue had a 15-year life and paid a coupon of 7.5 percent, at least 2 percent lower than comparable straight Eurobonds issued at the time.

The late 1980s and early 1990s saw a huge volume of Eurobonds with equity features issued by U.S., Japanese, and European corporations. A convertible bond pays a lower-than-normal coupon but gives the investor the right to exchange each bond for a certain number of shares in the issuing company. Once the issuer's share price rises by more than the conversion "premium," the investor has more to gain from conversion than from holding the bond to maturity. As in the Carlton case, the company often has a call option, giving it the ability to compel the investor to choose between redemption and conversion when the shares exceed the conversion price by a comfortable margin. This option has the effect of forcing conversion. The question then becomes, Why would one choose to buy this hybrid instrument rather than a bond alone, or an option on the stock alone, or—if the investor wants the benefit of both—to buy a combination of the two? Three answers are possible:

1. One might say that perhaps there is no *domestic* equity-option market available to the investor, possibly because regulations do not permit it, giving rise to the need for an *international* proxy. This situation has occurred in Japan and helps to explain why so many Japanese companies have issued Eurobonds with warrants.[2] The latter, being separable, provide a better solution to the incomplete markets argument than convertibles. And there are active equity-option markets in other countries, such as the United States and Britain.

---

[2] A uniquely international dimension of some of these warrants is that they are denominated in *Swiss francs*. A Swiss-franc-denominated warrant on a yen-denominated share is a form of the *quanto option* described in Chapter 8. It is difficult to hedge; indeed, as far as I can ascertain, none of the Japanese companies issuing such warrants sought to hedge them in a scientific fashion. Hence the contingent liability inherent in any issue of warrants was made more complicated by the currency factor.

2. Another explanation for the existence of hybrid international securities lies in the freedom of certain offshore instruments from domestic taxes. Eurobonds are issued in locations free of withholding taxes and in bearer form, a practice that helps preserve investor anonymity. But all shares are issued by the parent company directly and are listed and registered in the home country. Registration means that the issuer, and therefore the fiscal authorities, are told the shareowner's identity. So individual investors seeking to avoid paying taxes on their equity portfolios find that convertible Eurobonds offer the "play" of equity without undue tax risk. When it comes time to convert, the bonds are sold to equity investors in the country of the issuer who are not concerned with the fact that the shares are registered.

3. Many convertible bonds are also bought by institutional investors that do not have a tax-avoidance motivation. These buyers are getting around a regulatory or self-imposed rule restricting equity investments. Some pension funds, for example, are not permitted to buy equity. Convertible bonds give them participation in the upside gain on the shares while guaranteeing interest and repayment of the bonds should the shares fall. Sound conservative? The problem is that the market price of a convertible bond rises *and* falls like the shares when the embedded option is in the money or near the money. So the institutional investor may be violating the spirit, if not the letter, of the restriction.

At least five kinds of market imperfection, alone or together, seem to make the whole worth more than the sum of the parts in hybrid international securities. Thus we can identify

1. innovation that results from transactions costs or costs of monitoring performance
2. regulation-driven innovation
3. tax-driven innovation
4. constraint-driven innovation
5. segmentation-driven innovation

We will illustrate some of these by reproducing "tombstone" announcements, which serve no purpose except to proclaim the bankers' prowess: a sort of investment banker's graffiti.

Transactions and Monitoring Costs

These costs play a role in many of the instruments in today's capital market. Most mutual funds offer individual and medium-sized investors economies of scale to overcome the erosive effect of brokerage, custody, and other costs associated with buying, holding, and selling securities—costs which can be particularly high for international investors. For example, ECU-denominated bonds and other currency-cocktail bonds offer built-in currency diversification. The costs of assessing and monitoring performance on contracts can also deter many from employing simple techniques like forwards, debt, and options. Where monitoring costs are high, credit risk must be eliminated, usually by means of one or both of two techniques: collateral and marking to market with cash compensation. Thus the futures contract enables poor-credit companies to hedge future currency, interest-rate, and commodity-price movements without monitoring costs.

For investors who wish to take a position in a currency, equity, or commodity, credit-risk considerations often preclude them from doing forwards or swaps directly. They can, however, buy bonds whose interest or principal varies with the market price of interest.

Their "counterparty," the issuer, has no credit risk, because instead of the investor making a payment if he loses, the issuer simply reduces the interest or principal to be paid to the investor. A callable bond falls into this category.

Regulation-Driven Innovations

Laws and government regulations restrict national capital markets in many ways. Banks, issuers, investors, and other market players are prevented from doing certain kinds of financing or entering into certain kinds of contracts. For example, banks are told that a certain proportion of their liabilities must be in a form that qualifies as "capital" for regulatory purposes, a requirement that stems from the international agreement known as the *Basle Accord*. Hence the financial papers are filled with announcements of "convertible exchangeable floating-rate preferred stock" and the like, fashioned purely to meet the capital requirements. Issuers may not be permitted to issue public bonds without intrusive disclosure. Insurance companies may not be allowed to invest more than, say, 20 percent of their assets abroad despite a paucity of domestic investment opportunities. These laws and regulations may be well intentioned but may have unanticipated side effects or become redundant as markets and institutions mature and economic conditions change. Yet entrenched interests develop around certain rules, making them difficult to change. Sometimes, as when interest rates or taxes reach unusual levels, or when competition threatens, financial-market participants find it worthwhile to devise ways to overcome the restrictive effect of outdated or misguided regulations.

For example, in the 1980s, foreign investment in Korean equities was severely restricted. One way to get around this was for prominent Korean companies to issue Eurobonds that were convertible into common stock. Because the bonds behaved like equity, they served the international investor's purpose, to a degree.

Circumvention of regulation is the source of many innovations that are not what they seem at first glance. An example is the yen-linked Eurobond issued by Japan Air Lines in the mid-1980s and illustrated in Figure 17.2 This deal was done when the Japanese capital market was more protected than it is now. Foreign borrowers were not allowed into the domestic bond market, and all domestic yen bonds were subject to a withholding tax of 15 percent. Japanese firms were not permitted to issue yen-denominated Eurobonds, although they were, with Ministry of Finance approval, allowed to issue Eurobonds denominated in other currencies.

JAL wished to save money by issuing a Eurobond free of withholding tax, on which it would pay a lower rate than one subject to the tax. But it wanted yen, not dollar financing. The currency swap market did not yet exist. So JAL issued a *dollar-denominated* Eurobond that repaid a dollar amount equivalent to ¥2.8 billion. In effect, the principal redemption was yen-denominated. But the interest was also yen linked, for, as the tombstone suggests, the bond paid a fixed percentage, 7⅞ percent, of the yen redemption amount. So, in effect, it was a yen bond; but it satisfied the letter of the law in Japan, and did so with the approval of officials at the Ministry of Finance, who gave selected Japanese companies a back-door feet-wetting in the Euroyen bond market. (The fact that the JAL deal was officially sanctioned is evident from the name of the guarantor, and from the veritable who's-who of international investment banking listed as underwriters.) Later, the front door was opened, and eventually the withholding tax was removed. This example illustrates the reality that many regulation-defying innovations are undertaken with the explicit collusion of the regulatory authorities who may be unable or unwilling to remove the regulations themselves.

Figure 17.2   *Japan Air Lines Yen-Linked Eurobond.* Here we have an example of a regulation-induced innovation. The bond was nominally denominated in U.S. dollars because it was issued at a time when the Japanese government prohibited the issuance of yen-denominated Eurobonds by Japanese companies.

February 1982   *These bonds having already been sold this announcement appears as a matter of record only*

Japan Air Lines Company, Ltd.

(incorporated with limited liability under the laws of Japan)

U.S. $ Denominated 7⅞% Yen-Linked Guaranteed Notes 1987
of a principal amount equivalent to
Yen 8,600,000,000

Unconditionally and irrevocably guaranteed by

Japan

DAIWA SECURITIES CO. LTD   MORGAN GUARANTY LTD

BANK OF TOKYO INTL LTD   BANQUE DE PARIS ET DES PAYS-BAS
CREDIT SUISSE FIRST BOSTON LTD   DEVELOPMENT BANK OF SINGAPORE
IBJ INTERNATIONAL LTD   KUWAIT INVESTMENT COMPANY (S.A.K.)
NIKKO SECURITIES CO. (EUROPE) LTD   SALOMON BROTHERS INTL
SWISS BANK CORPORATION INTL LTD   S.G. WARBURG & CO. LTD

ALGEMENE BANK NEDERLAND N.V.   AMRO INTL   BANCO DEL GOTTARDO
BANK OF AMERICA INTL LTD   BANK OF TOKYO (HOLLAND) N.V.
BANQUE DE L'INDOCHINE ET DE SUEZ   BANQUE DE NEUFLIZE, SCHLUMBERGER, MALLET
BANQUE NATIONALE DE PARIS   BARCLAYS BANK   BARING BROTHERS & CO. LTD
CAISSE DES DEPOTS ET CONSIGNATIONS   CHASE MANHATTAN LTD   CHEMICAL BANK INTL GROUP
CITICORP INTL GROUP   COMMERZBANK AKTIENGESELLSCHAFT   CONTINENTAL ILLINOIS LTD
COUNTY BANK LTD   CREDIT COMMERCIAL DE FRANCE   CREDIT INDUSTRIEL ET COMMERCIAL
CREDIT LYONNAIS   CREDITANSTALT-BANKVEREIN   DAI-ICHI KANGYO INTL LTD
DBS-DAIWA SECURITIES INTL LTD   DG BANK DEUTSCHE GENOSSENSCHAFTSBANK
DILLON, READ OVERSEAS CORPORATION   FUJI INTERNATIONAL FINANCE LTD
GOLDMAN SACHS INTL CORP.   HILL, SAMUEL & CO. LTD
THE HONGKONG BANK GROUP   INDUSTRIELBANK VON JAPAN (DEUTSCHLAND) AKTIENGESELLSCHAFT
KUWAIT FOREIGN TRADING CONTRACTING AND INVESTMENT CO.   KIDDER, PEABODY INTL LTD
KLEINWORT, BENSON LTD   LLOYDS BANK INTL LTD   LTCB INTERNATIONAL LTD
MANUFACTURERS HANOVER LTD   MERRILL LYNCH INTL & CO.   MITSUBISHI BANK (EUROPE) S.A.
MITSUI FINANCE EUROPE LTD   SAMUEL MONTAGE & CO. LTD   MORGAN GRENFELL & CO. LTD
MORGAN GUARANTY PACIFIC LTD   MORGAN STANLEY INTL   NEW JAPAN SECURITIES EUROPE LTD
NIPPON CREDIT BANK INTL (HK) LTD   NIPPON KANGYO KAKUMARU (EUROPE) S.A.
NOMURA INTL LTD   ORION ROYAL BANK LTD   SANWA BANK (UNDERWRITERS) LTD
J. HENRY SCHRODER WAGG & CO. LTD   SOCIETE GENERALE   SOCIETE GENERALE DE BANQUE S.A.
SUMITOMO FINANCE INTERNATIONAL   TAIYO KOBE BANK (LUXEMBOURG) S.A.   TOKAI BANK NEDERLAND N.V.
UNION BANK OF SWITZERLAND (SECURITIES) LTD   WAKO INTERNATIONAL (EUROPE) LTD
WESTDEUTSCHE LANDESBANK GIROZENTRALE WOOD GUNDY LTD   YAMAICHI INTL (EUROPE) LTD

Tax-Driven Innovations

The tax authorities are usually much less willing to give in than the regulatory authorities, so innovators must stay one step ahead of the game for the innovation to survive. (Sometimes, however, the tax authorities will not fight to close a loophole because they recognize that the loss of firms' competitive position will mean minimal tax gathered relative to the cost of more vigilant enforcement. Such was the case with the U.S. withholding tax on corporate bonds issued in the United States and sold to nonresidents. American companies found that they could avoid the withholding tax by issuing Eurobonds offshore and channeling the funds back home via Netherlands Antilles subsidiaries, and the Internal Revenue Service did not close that loophole because it was unlikely that foreigners would otherwise have bought the domestic bonds and paid the 30 percent withholding tax.)

All Eurobonds are designed to be free of withholding tax, and many have additional features that offer tax advantages to issuers as well as investors. For example, certain breeds of the perpetual floating-rate note gave issuers an approved form of capital (in effect, preferred stock), but with the interest (and in rare cases even the principal) being tax deductible.

Another technique that has enjoyed many years of success is money-market preferred stock, also called auction-rate preferred. Preferred stock pays a fixed dividend in lieu of interest, and investors get preference over common shareholders, but the dividend can be reduced or skipped if earnings are insufficient. Under the tax laws of most countries, interest is tax deductible while dividends are not. But in some countries, notably the United States and Great Britain, corporations owning shares in other corporations are only partially taxed on dividends received. So if one U.S. company (A) issues preferred stock to another company (B), B is taxed at a reduced rate on the dividends paid on the preferred, but A cannot deduct the payments from taxes owed. So companies with zero tax liabilities often issue preferred stock instead of straight bonds.

A mutation of conventional preferred stock is money-market preferred stock, issued with short effective maturities of (typically) seven weeks. The investor is told what the expected dividend will be, but of course has no guarantee that it will be paid at all, given that he is buying shares. So the investment banker arranging the deal holds an auction at the end of every seven weeks, replacing the existing investors with new buyers. The new dividend to be paid is raised or lowered in the auction process such that the money-market preferred is priced at par, at 100 cents on the dollar. Typical language in the prospectus might be: "At an initial dividend rate of 4.50% per annum with future dividend rates to be determined by Auction every seven weeks commencing on [date]." So the investor gets all his principal and interest, just as though he had purchased commercial paper or some other money-market instrument. Although the rate paid is lower than comparable money-market instruments, the effective after-tax return is higher. For the borrower who does not need the tax deduction that conventional interest offers, this has proved to be a low-cost way of financing.

Constraint-Driven Innovations

Not all market imperfections stem from government regulations and taxes; some are self-imposed, taking the form of trustee rules or standards set by self-regulatory organizations. For example, many institutional investors promise to invest only in instruments below a certain maturity or only in "investment grade" bonds, meaning those rated BBB (or equivalent) and above.

One common constraint is the institutional investor's ability to buy and/or sell options, swaps, or other derivatives. When an important category of investor desires the revenues that option writing provides or the protection plus opportunity that options buying offers, there is an opportunity for an investment banker to devise a specially tailored security that incorporates the sought-after strategy. The embedded option or other derivative is often then "stripped out" of the instrument by the same (or a collaborating) bank. Such was the case with Nikkei-linked Eurobonds, which were issued in droves in the 1980s and 1990s. Example 17.4 describes how they worked.

EXAMPLE 17.4   Figure 17.3 reproduces the announcement of a Nikkei-linked Eurobond issued by Kredietbank, one of Belgium's largest commercial banks. Why would a bank whose principal business is in Europe borrow three billion yen, and why is it linked to the performance of the Japanese stock market, as measured by the Nikkei index?

The answer is arbitrage. Kredietbank, together with its advisors Bankers Trust and New Japan Securities, is taking advantage of a constraint on certain Japanese institutional investors, namely their inability to sell options directly. Japanese institutional investors have frequently sought higher coupons than are available in conventional Japanese bonds and have been willing to take certain risks to achieve this goal. For many years one risk deemed acceptable by Japanese investors was the risk that the Japanese stock market would plummet. The market had achieved gain after gain and it looked as if there was no turning back. Some institutions were therefore willing to bet that the market would not fall more than, say, 20 percent from its then current level. At the time the Kredietbank deal was done, in 1990, the Nikkei index had soared to 38,000. Given these conditions, a typical structure for a deal like this one was as follows:

First, as is sketched out in the following paragraphs, a Japanese securities firm like New Japan Securities identifies investors, such as Japanese life-insurance companies, who are interested in a high-coupon investment in exchange for taking a tolerable risk on the Japanese stock market. The risk they are willing to take is equivalent to a put option: they will invest in a note whose principal will be reduced if, and only if, the Nikkei index declines below 30,400.

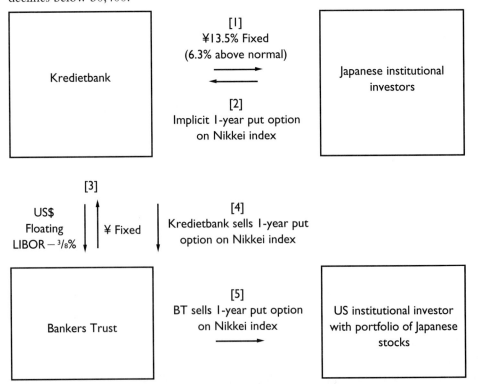

Simultaneously, capital-market specialists at the London subsidiary of Bankers Trust identify a bank who is willing to consider a hybrid financing structure as long as the exchange risk and equity risk are removed and the financing produces unusually cheap

Figure 17.3   ***Example of a Constraint-Driven Innovation.***   The Nikkei-linked Eurobond ties the principal redemption to the performance of the Japanese stock market.

This announcement appears as a matter of record only

NEW ISSUE   **FEBRUARY 1990**

KREDIETBANK INTERNATIONAL FINANCE N.V.

(Incorporated with limited liability in the Netherlands Antilles)

¥3,000,000,000

13.5 per cent. Guaranteed Nikkei Linked Notes due 1991

unconditionally and irrevocably guaranteed by

KREDIETBANK N.V.

(Incorporated with limited liability in the Kingdom of Belgium)

Issue Price 101.125 per cent.

New Japan Securities Europe Ltd   Bankers Trust International Ltd

Daewoo Securities Co., Ltd.   IBJ International Ltd
Kredietbank N.V.   Mitsui Trust International Ltd

financing. This bank is Kredietbank, whose goal is to achieve sub-LIBOR funding. Bankers Trust will provide a swap that will hedge Kredietbank against any movements of the yen or the Nikkei index. Specifically, Japanese institutional investors such as life-insurance companies will pay Kredietbank ¥3 billion for a one-year note paying 13.5 percent annually ([1] in the diagram). This is 6.3 percent better than the current one-year yen rate of 7.2 percent. At maturity the note will repay the face value in yen unless the Nikkei falls below 30,400, in which case the principal will be reduced according to a formula such as the following:

$$\text{Redemption amount} = MIN \left[1, X \times \frac{(30,400 - \text{Nikkei})}{30,400} \right] \times 3,000,000,000$$

where X is the number of options sold by the Japanese life insurance companies to Kredietbank in exchange for the coupon subsidy [2]. The higher the number for X, the greater the subsidy that can be paid.

Kredietbank first changes the yen received into dollars. It then enters into a yen-dollar currency swap with Bankers Trust in which Kredietbank will pay (say) LIBOR minus ⅜ percent semiannually, and, at the end, the dollar equivalent of the initial yen principal [3]. For example, if the spot rate is ¥135 per dollar, then Kredietbank receives the sum of $22,222,222 (equal to ¥3,000,000,000/(¥135 per dollar)) at the outset, pays half of LIBOR minus ⅜ percent of this sum each six months, and pays the same sum at the end.

In return, Bankers Trust pays Kredietbank the precise yen amounts needed to service the debt, namely 13.5% of ¥3,000,000,000 at the end of each year and the principal amount as defined by the formula above, at maturity [4]. If the Nikkei happens to fall below the "strike" level of 30,400, then Bankers Trust, not Kredietbank, reaps the benefit.

Bankers Trust sells the potential benefit to a third party, such as a U.S. money manager seeking insurance against a major drop in the value of its portfolio of Japanese stocks [5]. The U.S. buyer of the Nikkei put pays Bankers a premium that exceeds the "price" of the Japanese investor received by a comfortable margin, leaving enough to subsidize Kredietbank's cost of funds and still leave something on the table for the investment bankers.

Although Bankers Trust and New Japan Securities might normally earn some fees from comanaging a ¥3 billion private placement such as this one, the real "juice" in the deal comes from the pricing of the option (the put option on the Nikkei index) that is embedded in the note. A key factor in making deals like this work is adjusting the interest rate and the principal redemption formula so as to leave everybody satisfied.

Segmentation-Driven Innovations

Academics have long debated whether securities tailored to particular investment groups can actually save issuers money, or whether supposed advantages are eventually arbitraged out. The huge volume of CMOs (collateralized mortgage obligations) in the United States seems to favor those who argue that splitting up cash flows to meet particular groups of investors' needs and views does provide added value. These instruments, some of which take the form of Eurobonds, divide the cash flows from mortgage pools into tranches based on timing of principal redemption (for investors with different maturity needs) and, in some cases, segregate the interest from the principal.

Distinct market segments of several kinds seem to exist in the international financial markets. Many investors, of course, have a strong currency preference. Credit-risk problems prevent the majority of these from doing swaps and forwards themselves to arbitrage out differences. Some view a currency as risky in the short term but stable in the long term; it is for these investors that dual-currency bonds were invented. The example that follows shows how these bonds work.

EXAMPLE 17.5 Dual-currency bonds pay interest in one currency and principal in another. The interest rate that they pay lies somewhere between the prevailing rates in the two currencies.

For example, the Sperry Corporation, through a Delaware financing subsidiary, issued a US$56 million dual-currency bond in February 1985. The interest rate, payable annually in dollars, was 63¾ percent. The principal, however, was equal to 100 million Swiss francs. The final maturity was February 1995.

The spot-exchange rate at the time was SF1.7857 per U.S. dollar, making SF100 million equivalent to $56 million. The 10-year U.S.-dollar and Swiss-franc interest rates at the time were 9.1 percent and 6.2 percent, respectively, for comparable single-currency bonds.

How was the interest rate on the Sperry bond set? One can estimate the "correct" rate as follows: Recognizing that Sperry probably hedged the principal to be repaid in 10 years, we need the Swiss-franc/U.S.-dollar 10-year forward-exchange rate to see what the repayment really cost Sperry. From interest-rate parity, the forward rate can be calculated as follows:

$$
\begin{aligned}
\text{10-Year Forward} &= \text{Spot} \times \left[\frac{(1 + \text{Swiss rate})}{(1 + \text{U.S. rate})} \right]^{10} \\
&= 1.7857 \times \left[\frac{(1 + .062)}{(1 + .091)} \right]^{10} \\
&= 1.3640
\end{aligned}
$$

From this, Sperry's dollar repayment amount is SF100,000,000/1.3640 = $73,315,169. So Sperry repays $17,315,169 more than it borrowed, or $1,134,258 expressed as an annual annuity. This is 2.03 percent of $56 million, so the theoretical rate should be 7.07 percent (9.10 percent minus 2.03 percent). The difference between the actual rate paid and the theoretical rate is Sperry's savings, assuming our calculations are correct. In point of fact, the forward rate is unlikely to conform precisely to interest parity and there are additional costs to a deal like this, so Sperry's savings would be smaller.

Nevertheless, it is clear that in this deal, as in many of this kind, the investor is receiving less than the theoretical rate. Why? For the issuer to tailor a bond to investors' needs and views, there must be some cost savings. And the investor cannot replicate such structures directly, because small investors would never be able to enter into a 10-year forward contract.

Securitization of mortgages, car loans, credit-card receivables, and other assets with predictable cash flows represents a whole category of segmentation-driven innovation that is becoming more prevalent outside the United States—for example, in Britain and in the Euromarket, and even in developing countries such as Mexico. Box 17.1 describes the use of the technique in Turkey.

BOX 17.1

**Asset-Backed
Securities in Turkey**

The Turkish Capital Markets Board has aggressively sought to modernize the country's capital market, and in 1992 it pushed through a decree that enabled Turkish banks to securitize certain assets.

The first such deal was done by a privately owned bank, Interbank, which issued TL4.25 billion in securities backed by its leasing receivables. The issue had maturities of from one to 10 months and bore an interest rate of 72.36 percent. At the time, one-year bank deposits paid about 70 percent and three-month deposits about 62 percent. Other institutions, such as Pamukbank and Yapi ve Kredi, followed with issues backed by consumer credits, mortgages, export receivables, and other assets.

In these deals and others like them, the assets are sold to a special-purpose company that finances the purchase with a cushion of equity (provided by the sponsor) and a public-debt issue or issues. Conditions required for them to work include protection of the issuer from additional taxes, accounting and regulatory treatment that allows the sponsor to take the assets off its balance sheet, and protection for the investor, including proper isolation of the assets' cash flows from the condition of the sponsor. The debt being issued typically has sufficient "overcollateralization" by the assets to achieve an investment-grade rating.

Understanding New Instruments: The Building-Block Approach

In this section and the next we offer two related approaches to the analysis of hybrid instruments such as the ones we have been discussing.

A number of attempts have been made to categorize new financial instruments. Some class them by interest-rate characteristics—fixed, floating, or floating capped, for example. Others seek to divide them by rating, maturity, equity-linkage, or tax status. In a classic study, the Bank for International Settlements categorized innovations according to their role: risk-transferring, liquidity-enhancing, credit-generating, or equity-generating.

The best way to group instruments depends in large part on the purpose for which the grouping is being made. The building-block approach is used to learn how to construct or reverse-engineer existing or new instruments. The idea is not so much that the reader will necessarily learn much new about instruments that exist now, but rather to develop a method that can be applied to new instruments as they appear.

The premise of the building-block approach is that hybrid instruments can be dissected into simpler instruments that are easier to understand and to price. Many, although by no means all, hybrid securities can be broken down into components consisting of

- bonds—creditor (long) or debtor (short) positions in zero-coupon bonds
- forward contracts—long or short forward positions in a currency, bond, equity, or commodity
- options—long or short positions in calls or puts on a currency, bond, equity, or commodity

The building-block approach combines two or more bonds, forwards, or options to create the same *cash flows* as some more complex instrument. A simple example: a coupon-paying bond is simply a series of zero-coupon bonds equal to the interest and a larger zero at the end equal to the principal. Arbitrage should ensure that the price of the coupon bond equals the sum of the prices of all the little zeroes. Another example: a zero-coupon

Figure 17.4 *Callable Bond Yields Can Be Misleading.* Neither the yield to maturity nor the yield to the call date tells one what return will be obtained for a given holding period. A superior approach is to estimate the value of the embedded call option.

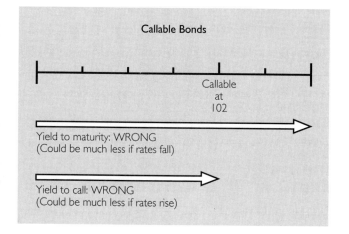

Callable Bonds

Callable at 102

Yield to maturity: WRONG
(Could be much less if rates fall)

Yield to call: WRONG
(Could be much less if rates rise)

bond in one currency plus a forward contract to exchange that currency for another is the same as a zero–coupon bond in the second currency.

We have already encountered a number of applications of the building-block approach without calling it by name. Chapter 7 showed how a futures contract can be broken into a series of repriced forward contracts. In Chapter 13 we learned that a currency swap is equivalent to a fixed-rate bond in one currency and a short position in a floating-rate note in another currency. And in Chapter 15 we constructed commodity-price-linked instruments from conventional bonds and forwards or contracts on commodities.

Let us illustrate how the building-block method lets one better judge the value and pricing of a hybrid instrument than more ad hoc approaches by decomposing a callable bond into its components. Discussions by brokers with their investor clients often focus on the *yield to maturity* versus the *yield to call* of a callable bond. They like to point out when a callable bond appears superior to a noncallable bond when judged by either criterion. As Figure 17.4 illustrates, however, the investor cannot judge a callable bond by either, or even both, measures of return. Whichever way rates move, the investor gets the worst of both worlds and should be compensated fairly for this risk. The way to judge the fairness of the bond's pricing is not by looking at yield but rather at the value of the components, and then comparing them with the investor's practical alternatives, given his or her needs, constraints, and views.

So to better evaluate and compare different callable (and noncallable) bonds, decompose the bond into (1) noncallable bond (bought by the investor) and (2) call option (sold to the issuer by the investor). Find the value of each component, to discover whether the composite bond is overpriced or underpriced relative to the investor's realistic alternatives. One method for doing so is as follows:

1. Use the market yield on similar noncallable bonds to find the value of the straight bond.
2. Subtract the price of the callable bond from the value of the noncallable bond to find the price received for the call option.
3. Compare that with the value the investor could have received from selling call options in the market (may use option-pricing model), or compare it with the implicit value of call options embedded in other callable bonds from comparable issuers currently available in the market.

Another practical application of the building-block method is in the decomposition of so-called inverse-floating-rate notes, also known as reverse floaters or yield-curve notes.[3] These instruments have been issued in large numbers in the United States, Germany, and elsewhere during the past decade.

---

[3]See Donald J. Smith, "The Pricing of Bull and Bear Floating Notes: An Application of Financial Engineering," *Financial Management*, vol. 17, no. 4 (Winter 1988), 72–81.

EXAMPLE 17.6   In February 1986, Citicorp issued a $100,000,000, five-year Eurobond that it termed "adjustable-rate notes." The deal had the following features, as described in the preamble to the prospectus:

> *Interest on the Notes is payable semiannually on February 27 and August 27 beginning August 27, 1986. The interest rate on the Notes for the initial semiannual interest period ending August 27, 1986, will be 9.25% per annum. The Notes will mature on February 27, 1991, and will not be subject to redemption by Citicorp prior to maturity.*

So far so good. It's a five-year noncallable note with a generous first coupon (six-month rates at the time were in the region of 8⅛%). The preamble went on to say:

> *The interest rate for each semiannual interest period thereafter, determined in advance of the interest period as set forth herein, will be the excess, if any, of (a) 17⅜% over (b) the arithmetic mean of the per annum London interbank offered rates for United States dollar deposits for six months prevailing on the second business day prior to the commencement of such interest period.*

This is a lawyer's way of saying that the notes pay 17⅜% minus LIBOR but never less than zero.

Let's reverse-engineer this. Seeing an instrument paying the difference between two rates reminds one of a swap. Indeed, part of this instrument is like an interest-rate swap and part is a bond (after all, the investor is lending money). To replicate the cash flows of the Citicorp note,

1. buy a five-year fixed-rate bond paying 8.6875 percent (17.375/2).
2. enter into a five-year swap where you *receive* fixed 8.6875 percent and *pay* LIBOR.

You'll now receive 17.375 percent minus LIBOR every six months. But one more thing: you'll never have a negative payment under the Citicorp deal, so to mimic it you should also

3. Buy an interest-rate cap at 17.375 percent. This pays the difference between LIBOR and 17.375 percent should LIBOR exceed that level. It's deep out-of-the-money, so it's cheap.

Now you are in a position to evaluate this hybrid against other investments. If the five-year bond yield (and by implication the swap rate) exceeds 8.6875 percent by a sufficient amount (as it did in February 1986), it may be worthwhile replicating the instrument rather than buying it. In reality, most individuals and money-market investors who might purchase a reverse floater do not have access to the swap market and/or may not be permitted to hold fixed-rate bonds, so this deal may look better even if its pricing gives Citicorp cheap financing. Even so, the autopsy can serve a purpose: one realizes that the effective duration of this instrument is more akin to that of a 10-year bond (or two five-year bonds) minus a six-month instrument than to that of other floating-rate notes (which typically have a duration of .5 or less). So it has a high degree of price risk.

The price risk factor cited in the previous example may be more important than knowing how to duplicate the instrument. Moreover, many new financial instruments, such as those with prepayment options that are contingent on corporate events rather than on interest-rate conditions, are not easily broken down. For these, one may need complex option-based models. Both considerations suggest that sometimes a price-based analytic approach may be more useful.

Hedging and Managing New Instruments: The Functional Method

This section describes the *functional method,* a second approach to the analysis of hybrid or complex securities. The method's aim is not dissection, for one cannot always break instruments down for practical purposes, but rather to describe the *price behavior* of any hybrid bond or other instrument. The method helps to show which instrument serves precisely what purpose for particular investors or issuers. The method can also be used to create optimal hedges or arbitrages for one instrument against another.

The premise of the functional approach is that, for practical purposes, the only thing that matters about an international bond or other instrument is changes in its value—in its market price, if it is tradable. Although one does not always think of a bond this way, in the final analysis one seldom cares more about a bond's beauty or soul than about its market value.

The key idea of the functional approach is that the value of every financial instrument can be characterized as a *function of a set of economic variables.* These variables might be ones such as the three-month U.S. Treasury-bill rate or the dollar-sterling spot-exchange rate, or the Financial Times' subindex of consumer electronics stocks, or the price of an individual company's stock. The presumption is that each instrument's payouts are contractually linked to the values or outcomes of a set of variables or events. If it is true that we can, in principle, express the value of every financial instrument as a function of a set of known variables like those listed above, then it seems that in order to understand what an instrument does, what it's good for, and how its price behaves under different scenarios, we have to know three things:

- the *precise variables* or factors that have the most effect on the instrument's price
- the *functional relationship* that shows how a given movement in each variable's value translates into changes in the instrument's value
- the *relationship between the factors*—whether, in particular, specific factors are positively, negatively, or not at all correlated with each of the other significant factors

EXAMPLE 17.7 Consider an example, a two-year Euroyen bond. Our task is to describe, as fully as possible, its price behavior in U.S. dollars. We will attempt to do so in three stages:

1. *Identify the variables:*
   - yen–dollar exchange rate (because we are interested in the dollar price of the bond).
   - two-year Japanese interest rate on an equivalent bond.
   - one-year Japanese investor rate. (Because coupons are paid annually in the Euroyen market, the bond's value will be affected by the present value of the first year's coupon.)
2. *Describe the functional relationship* between the bond's price and the set of key variables. Here's where the building-block approach can be helpful: the valuation of the components of the security may yield the valuation of the hybrid instrument as a whole. In the case of a Euroyen bond, we can say the U.S.-dollar value is the present value of the cash flows in yen, all translated into dollars at today's spot-exchange rate:

$$P_{\$¥} = \text{Spot} \left[\frac{¥ \text{ coupon}}{(1 + R_1^¥)} + \frac{¥ \text{ coupon } + \text{ principal}}{(1 + R_2^¥)^2} \right]$$

3. *Estimate the correlation among the variables.* We cannot fully understand the influence of any one variable on the bond unless we know whether that variable is independent of the others. Japanese interest rates of different maturities are highly correlated, and probably inversely related to the yen-dollar spot-exchange rate (yen per dollar). In real life we have to make approximations. For most purposes it would probably suffice to ignore the interest-rate–exchange-rate relationship (a poorly understood one at best), and assume that the one-year and two-year Japanese interest rates move perfectly in tandem.

This sequence of steps allows us to simplify the relationship and to use the duration concept to show the sensitivity of Euroyen bond prices to two-year Japanese interest rates. We then simply translate the price change into the U.S.-dollar value at the spot-exchange rate, giving the dollar-price change in the Euroyen bond.

On its own, the function or formula helps price the instrument and can be used for sensitivity analysis in, say, portfolio management. But its chief value is in combination with similar analysis applied to other instruments. As long as there is some overlap in the functional variables, we can perform comparative analysis to show the price behavior of a *combination* of instruments—for hedging or arbitrage purposes, or to identify the most effective way of positioning in a particular market. Box 17.2 gives an example.

BOX 17.2

The Valuation of an Oil-Linked Bond

The functional method requires a model for valuation of the instrument. This is not always easy to devise with precision. Here we describe an effort to value a bond with embedded long-term options on the price of oil. The oil-linked bond was issued by Standard Oil of Ohio Company at the end of June 1986. The bond represented $37,500,000 face value of zero-coupon notes maturing on March 15, 1992. The holder of each $1000 note was promised par at maturity *plus* an amount equal to the excess, if any, of the crude-oil price (West Texas Intermediate) over $25, multiplied by 200 barrels. The limit for the WTI price was $40, so that the maximum the investor could receive at maturity was ($40 − $25) × 200 = $3000, plus the par value of $1000. In addition, each holder could redeem his or her note before maturity on the above terms on the first and fifteenth of each month beginning April 1, 1991.

For the purpose of calculating the settlement amount, the oil price was defined as the average of the closing prices of the New York Mercantile Exchange light-sweet crude-oil futures contract for the closest traded month during a "trading period," defined as one month ending 22 days before the relevant redemption or maturity date.

Let us decompose the Standard Oil issue. Each note can be regarded as a portfolio consisting of (a) a zero-coupon corporate bond, plus (b) one "quasi-American" call option with an exercise price of $25, plus (c) a short position in one quasi-American call option with a $40 exercise price. The "quasi-American" feature results from the intermittent early-exercise right in the last year of the bond's life.

Making some simplifying assumptions, Gibson and Schwartz have been able to develop a valuation model for this bond and to test it by using actual trading prices for the issue. The model was based on arbitrage-free option-pricing principles; the data were actual (but infrequent) transaction prices of the bond over the period August 1, 1986, to October 14, 1988. Transaction prices were used in preference to bid and ask quotations because the spread was too wide, averaging 10 percent of the bid price. Gibson and Schwartz found that the key variables in the valuation of oil and similar commodity-linked bonds were the volatility and the convenience yield.

Hybrids in Corporate Financing

Hybrid instruments, we have seen, are widely used by corporations and banks in financing. Among the most versatile of instruments for the design and issuance of hybrid claims is the medium-term note, because the distribution technique of MTNs lends itself to being tailored to one or a few specific investors. This section will describe the design and use of a hybrid instrument that was used by a major European bank as part of its funding. The names have been disguised, but the sequence of events and the technique itself are close to the original.

The story begins in Munich, where Bavaria Bank has its headquarters. To help meet its ongoing funding requirements, the bank recently set up a medium-term note program of the kind described in Chapter 10. The program was managed by EuroCredit, an investment bank in London.

EuroCredit, the *intermediary*, is a well-established and experienced bank in the Euromarkets. Its staff has the technical and legal background needed to arrange structured financing, and has trading and positioning capabilities in swaps and options—a "warehouse." Its underwriting and placement capabilities lie not so much in the capital it has to invest in a deal but rather in its relationships with investors and with corporations, banks, and government agencies that use over-the-counter derivatives. Indeed, with recent economic conditions portending a rise in interest rates, EuroCredit has perceived mounting interest in caps, swaptions, and other forms of interest-rate protection. EuroCredit has a high credit rating, making it an acceptable counterparty for long-term derivative transactions. These capabilities equip it to create hybrid structures for financing.

An official of EuroCredit described the background to the deal:

> The issuer, Bavaria, has excellent access to the short-term interbank market, but was seeking to extend the maturity of its financing. It was looking for large amounts of floating-rate U.S.-dollar and German-mark funding for its floating-rate loan portfolio. It had set a target for its cost of funds of CP less 10 (the Eurocommercial paper rate minus .10%). Because its funding needs were ongoing and any new borrowing would replace short-term interbank funding, it was not overly concerned with the specific timing of issues or the amount of maturity. This flexibility made a medium-term note program the ideal framework for funding. Best of all, Bavaria was willing to consider complex, hybrid structures as long as the bank was fully hedged.
>
> We have a standard sequence of steps that we follow for borrowers of this kind [see Box 17.3]. What we now needed was to identify an investor or investors for whom we could tailor a Bavaria note.

BOX 17.3 **Structured Financing: A Sequence of Steps**	1. Initiate medium-term note program for the borrower, allowing for a variety of currencies, maturities, and special structures. 2. Structure an MTN to meet the investor's needs and constraints. 3. Line up all potential counterparties and negotiate numbers acceptable to all sides. 4. Upon issuer's and investor's approval, place the securities. 5. Swap and strip the issue into the form of funding that the issuer requires. 6. Sell the stripped-off derivative to a corporate or investor client that requires a hedge. 7. Offer a degree of liquidity to the issuer by standing willing to buy back the securities at a later date.

> *An institutional investor client of ours, Scottish Life, has a distinct preference for high-grade investments, so Bavaria's triple-A rating brought them to mind. They have been on the lookout for investments that would improve their portfolio returns relative to various indexes and to their competition. An initial discussion with them revealed that they invest in both floating-rate and fixed-rate sterling and U.S.-dollar securities. Like other U.K. life-insurance companies, they are constrained in certain ways; in particular, they can buy futures and options to hedge their portfolio, but they cannot sell options.*

The stage was now set for EuroCredit to arrange a note within its medium-term-note program, one designed to meet Scottish Life's needs and constraints, and to negotiate the terms and conditions with the various parties.

The deal that emerged was a U.S.-dollar hybrid floating/fixed-rate note, paying an above-market yield, on which Bavaria had the right to extend the maturity from 3 years to 8 years. "Although it was a really private placement," said the EuroCredit official, "we wrote it in the form of a Eurobond with a listing in Luxembourg. This was to meet Scottish Life's requirement that it buy only listed securities."

The following "term sheet" summarizes the main features of the note:

AMOUNT:	US$40 MILLION
COUPON:	First three years: semiannual LIBOR + ⅜% per annum, paid semiannually
	Last five years: 8.35%
PRICE:	100
MATURITY:	February 10, 2000
CALL:	Issuer may redeem the notes in full at par on February 10, 1995
FEES:	30 basis points
ARRANGER:	EuroCredit Limited

The crucial elements are the coupon and call clauses. First, to appeal to the investor, the issuer has agreed to pay an *above-market rate* on both the floating-rate note and the fixed-rate bond segments of the issue:

FRN portion: .75% above normal cost

Fixed portion: .50% above normal cost

But, by having the right either to extend the issue or terminate it after three years, the issuer has in effect purchased the right to pay a fixed rate of 8.35 percent on a five-year bond to be issued in three years' time. *Through its investment bank, the issuer will sell this right for more than it cost him, and so lower his funding cost below normal levels.* This effect is illustrated in the diagram on page 525.

One could argue that Scottish Life would have been better off selling the swaption directly to EuroCredit or even to EuroCredit's client. This is not realistic; the institutional investor is not permitted to write options directly, although, as is typical, it is permitted to buy callable bonds and other securities with options embedded. Moreover, the investor may not have a sufficient credit rating to enable it to sell stand-alone long-term derivatives at a competitive price.

Investor constraints such as these are necessary, but not sufficient, conditions for a hybrid bond such as the one described to become reality. The characteristics of the

```
┌─────────────────┐   Bavaria sells 3-year floating      ┌─────────────────┐
│                 │         rate note paying             │                 │
│                 │          LIBOR − ³⁄₈%                │                 │
│                 │            ─────────▶                │                 │
│  BAVARIA BANK   │                                      │  SCOTTISH LIFE  │
│                 │   For an additional ³⁄₄% per         │                 │
│                 │   annum, Bavaria buys right          │                 │
│                 │   to sell 5-year fixed-rate          │                 │
│                 │   8.35% note to SL in 3 years        │                 │
│                 │            ◀─────────                │                 │
└─────────────────┘                                      └─────────────────┘

   │  For 1% per annum,
   │  Bavaria sells
   │  EuroCredit a
   │  swaption (the right to
   ▼  pay fixed 8.35% for 5
      years in 3 years)

┌─────────────────┐    EuroCredit sells the
│                 │    swaption to a corporate
│                 │    client seeking to hedge its
│   EUROCREDIT    │    funding costs against
│                 │    a rate rise
│                 │
└─────────────────┘
```

intermediary are often underestimated. Not only must it have the "rocket scientists" who can devise and price complex options, but it must also be able to trade and position them so as to be able to offer a deal quickly rather than having to wait to find a buyer of the derivative before the deal can be consummated. It must have excellent institutional investor relationships, preferably in places where the money is, such as the United States, Germany, and Japan. Insight into institutional and corporate needs and constraints is a scarcer commodity than a Ph.D. in physics from Moscow State University. The financial institution must have experience, credit, and people that can be trusted. Few banks qualify.

Global Financial Markets in the Next Decade

Nobody knows for sure what the future holds. Even so, an observer of global financial markets can be confident that innovation and adaptation of instruments will continue. This and some of the conclusions reached in earlier chapters allow us to venture a few predictions:

1. The structure of individual economies, and of the world economy, is in a state of change. As a result, there is a great challenge for creativity in international financial techniques to deal with problems that include: the

changing demographic composition of the industrial countries, the emerging capital markets, developing economies that lack adequate domestic financial markets *and* banking systems, and the once-socialist economies in transition.

2. As new countries compete more vigorously with the old, the existing order will break down. This means that any financial institution resting on its laurels will come under great competitive threat, and to survive and thrive it must change in response to whatever the new order is.

3. Global and regional monetary arrangements such as the European monetary system will continue to be in flux for some years to come. Few believe that unfettered freely floating exchange rates will eliminate adjustment problems. Multiyear deviations from purchasing-power parity will persist. Yet countries seeking the discipline of fixed exchange-rate arrangements will have to contend with the strains in money and currency markets that accompany any attempt to fix exchange rates before economic policies are unified.

4. In the light of these economic changes and pressures, investors, banks, and broker-dealers must vastly upgrade their understanding of, and ability to manage, complex financial instruments, particularly option-based instruments such as those described in this and preceding chapters.

5. With the erosion of barriers to international competition in goods, services, and financial markets, there is an increasingly strong interrelationship among money, bond, currency, commodity, and equity markets, and between the derivative markets in each of these categories.

6. Despite the preceding statement, academic and practical understanding of exchange-rate determination, and of the determination of equity prices in an international context, is still in a state of flux. For some years to come, the jury will be out on some of the theories propounded in this book, as well as on those that will inevitably replace them.

7. Policymakers will face severe demands at both the micro and macro levels. Bank and securities-market regulators have much work ahead of them to develop credible standards for credit-risk and market-risk control, as well as for disclosure requirements. On the other hand, with banks losing their privileged positions, any increase in regulatory costs inserts a wedge between investors and borrowers, driving companies and individuals to foreign or offshore markets.

In short, neither regulators nor practicing bankers nor academic scholars can afford to be complacent about the global financial markets in the decade to come.

SUMMARY

Financial innovations are challenging and fun. Most of the time they do not work. When they do, it is because they successfully overcome some market imperfection. This chapter has sought to help the reader understand the conditions that are necessary for hybrid securities to succeed as well as to learn their use as investment and financing vehicles.

Imperfections that drive innovations include transactions costs and the costs of monitoring performance, government regulations, taxes, constraints, and market segmentation.

Most instruments of the international capital market can be broken down into simpler securities. These elementary securities or *building blocks* include zero-coupon bonds, pure equity, spot and forward contracts, and options. Reverse financial engineering can be done to determine how a hybrid instrument could be replicated using simpler instruments.

For many purposes it is sufficient to know how the instrument will behave, given changes in certain market variables. The *functional method* regards every such instrument or contract as bearing a price or value, which in turn bears a unique relationship to some set of variables, such as interest rates or currency values. This relationship can be complex, but the idea is simple and can be illustrated in the matrix below. To fill in the blank cells for a particular security, ask whether the instrument's value bears a forward-type (linear) or an option-type (kinked) relationship to the market variable, and what that relationship is.

A Hybrid-Bond Matrix

	FORWARD-TYPE LINKAGE	OPTION-TYPE LINKAGE
INTEREST RATE		
CURRENCY		
COMMODITY		
EQUITY INDEX		
EQUITY OF COMPANY		

As numerous examples in the chapter demonstrated, an analytical approach, even one that makes simplifications for practical reasons, can be of great value to investors and issuers who wish to better understand the risks of instruments offered to them by banks. The approach can also be used to identify arbitrage opportunities between instruments, and to hedge one instrument with another.

Dissecting new financial instruments offers great challenges and encourages a way of thinking that may help equip us to adapt to the significant changes in the world economy that are inevitable in the next decade.

CONCEPTUAL QUESTIONS

1. In choosing an investment bank to arrange an innovative, tax-driven lease-financing bond issue, what strengths would you look for to minimize the chances of the deal going wrong?

2. Using current financial newspapers such as the *Financial Times* or the *Wall Street Journal*, or magazines such as *Euromoney* or *Risk*, identify two kinds of financial innovations: one that has lasted but has become more competitive, and one that has been relegated to disuse by a change in regulations or taxes. Explain how the product-innovation cycle has worked for each of them.

3. Many Eurobonds have been issued with equity warrants. A warrant is nothing but a long-term, over-the-counter call option on the issuing company's shares. The warrant is separable from the bond, and tradable independently. What possible advantage might the issuer and/or investor obtain from packaging the two together?

4. Use the building-block approach to dissect the Ford Motor Credit bond described in the following announcement:

Ford Motor Credit Maximum Rate Notes
$100,000,000

10¾% Maximum Rate Notes due December 3, 1992

Interest on the Notes is payable semi-annually at a rate equal to 10.75% per annum; *provided, however* that if the arithmetic average mean of the London interbank offered quotations for six-month U.S. dollar deposits prevailing two business days before the beginning of any Interest Period exceeds 10.50%, then the rate for such Interest Period will be reduced from 10.75% by the amount of such excess.

5. In 1987, Sallie Mae issued currency-linked bonds that were sold to US. individual investors. These bonds had the characteristic that the principal amount would rise if the U.S.-dollar value of the Japanese yen fell, and vice versa. Explain why Sallie Mae, a federal agency, would issue such bonds and why investors would buy them.

6. Many hybrid financing techniques take the form of an option embedded in a bond that is bought by an investor and that is "stripped off" by the issuer. List the conditions necessary for such deals to work.

7. In Chapter 15 we learned about a copper-linked bond issued by the Magma Corporation. Use the *functional approach* to describe the price behavior of that bond. In other words, show how the value of the bond would be expected to change as interest rates, the price of copper, and the equity price of Magma change.

8. Example 17.2 described a collared sterling floating-rate note issued by the Leeds Permanent Building Society. Show, by means of a diagram, what transactions would have to take place between Leeds and Salomon Brothers to allow this structure to give Leeds a below-market cost of funds. Also explain why this structure might work in a currency with a steep yield curve, but not in a currency where the yield curve is flat.

PROBLEMS

1. The EBRD (European Bank for Reconstruction and Development), as part of its funding in the Far East, has announced the issue of a 10-year, dual-currency ECU/Japanese yen bond. The coupon will be paid in yen at a semiannual floating rate equal to the Euroyen interbank offered rate plus 2 percent, expressed as a percentage of 18 billion yen. The final principal amount of ECU100 million will be repaid in ECU. The spot yen/ECU cross rate is ¥180 per ECU, and the 10-year swap rates are ECU: 10.10%, yen: 5.3%. If you worked for a Japanese leasing company whose cost of funding was yen LIBOR + 0.35%, would you buy this bond? What is its theoretical value?

2. What is the minimum price that Bankers Trust could charge its U.S. clients for the option or options embedded in the Nikkei-linked bond issued by Kredietbank described in the chapter?

3. In 1981, Exxon Capital Corporation N.V. (Netherlands Antilles) issued a 20-year U.S.-dollar-denominated zero-coupon Eurobond with a face value of $1.8 billion. The issue was priced to yield 10.7%, free of withholding tax, and issuance costs were 1.5%. At the same time, 20-year U.S.-Treasury zero-coupon bonds, subject to a 30% withholding tax, were traded at a yield of 11.6%. By taking advantage of the tax treaty between the United States and the Netherlands, Exxon Capital Corporation could invest in U.S. Treasuries without paying withholding tax. How much could Exxon earn on this arbitrage-based deal?

4. The Republic of Turkey issued a five-year puttable bond in 1990. The bond paid 9.70%, only 45 basis points over the comparable U.S. Treasury yield, and was puttable at 99 after 4 years. If the yield curve was flat and the volatility of one-year Treasury-bill prices is estimated at 7%, what is Turkey's effective cost of funds?

5. The European Investment Bank, an official European Community institution, issued DM300,000,000 of floating-rate notes in 1993, as described in the accompanying "tombstone." Explain how the notes work, and what the components, or building blocks, of the deal are. Also show, by means of a diagram, how the EIB could have hedged this to obtain fixed-rate deutschemark financing.

New Issue
Closing
February 10, 1993

All these Notes having been sold, this advertisement appears as a matter of record only.

European Investment Bank

DM 300,000,000
Floating Rate Notes of 1993/2003

Issue Price:	100 %
Interest Rate:	9 % p.a., payable in arrears on February 10, 1994, thereafter 13 % p.a. less Six-Months-DM-LIBOR, payable semi-annually in arrears on February 10 and August 10 of each year. The deduction shall not exceed 13 % p.a.
Repayment:	February 10, 2003, at par
Listing:	Düsseldorf and Frankfurt/Main

Trinkaus & Burkhardt
Kommanditgesellschaft auf Aktien

ABN AMRO Bank (Deutschland) AG   **Bank Austria**
Z-Länderbank Bank Austria AG   **Bank Brussel Lambert N.V.**

Bayerische Hypotheken- und Wechsel-Bank
Aktiengesellschaft   **Bayerische Vereinsbank**
Aktiengesellschaft   **BHF-BANK**

Creditanstalt-Bankverein   **Daiwa Europe (Deutschland) GmbH**

Deutsche Apotheker- und Ärztebank eG   **Deutsche Bau- und Bodenbank**
Aktiengesellschaft

DSL Bank
Deutsche Siedlungs- und Landesrentenbank   **Hamburgische Landesbank**
- Girozentrale -

Landeskreditbank Baden-Württemberg   **Samuel Montagu & Co. Limited**

J. P. Morgan GmbH   **Morgan Stanley GmbH**   **NOMURA BANK (Deutschland) GmbH**

Raiffeisenbank Kleinwalsertal   **Salomon Brothers AG**

Schweizerische Bankgesellschaft (Deutschland) AG   **SGZ Bank AG**

Stadtsparkasse Köln   **WGZ-BANK**
Westdeutsche Genossenschafts-Zentralbank eG

EIB FRN tombstone. Source: *Financial Times*, March 4, 1993, p. 18.

Application 17.1

COMMONWEALTH OF PUERTO RICO
VARIABLE-RATE, TAX-EXEMPT DEBT

Puerto Rico, although not one of the 50 United States of America, enjoys Commonwealth status. As a result, its general-obligation bonds are exempt from federal, state, and local taxes in the United States. In August 1992, the island took advantage of this exemption to sell $538.7 million worth of fixed-rate and variable-rate securities.

Of this total, $343.2 million worth were conventional fixed-rate bonds. Their maturities and yields were: 1994, 3.90 percent; 1997, 4.90 percent; 2002, 5.75 percent; 2006, 6.05 percent; 2009, 5.90 percent; and 2014, 6.25 percent.

The variable-rate notes made up the remainder of the financing and comprised equal amounts of auction-rate notes and yield-curve notes. The auction-rate notes, which were privately placed, were short-term investments that would be repriced every fifth Thursday through a Dutch auction. If the results of these auctions produced a rate lower than a certain fixed rate, the differences was given to investors of the yield-curve notes, increasing their return. But if the Dutch auction produced a higher rate than the fixed rate, the difference reduced the yield on the yield-curve notes. In extreme cases the yield could be zero. The notes were insured by Financial Security Assurance, earning them a triple-A rating.

The yield-curve notes, which matured in 2008, were sold out immediately, perhaps because their initial coupon was a generous 9.01 percent in a market starved for yield (see the accompanying table of key rates).

Key Rates
in percent per annum

Prime rate	6.00
Discount rate	3.00
Federal funds	3.25
3-mo. Treas. bills	3.06
6-mo. Treas. bills	3.12
7-yr. Treas. notes	5.94
30-yr. Treas. bonds	7.31
Telephone bonds	8.35
Municipal bonds	6.25

Sources: *The New York Times*, Aug. 20, 1992, p. D15; and bond dealers.

1. Explain, with a diagram, how the auction-rate and yield-curve notes work.
2. What incentives would investors have to buy Puerto Rico's yield-curve notes?
3. What hedge, if any, would Puerto Rico need to protect itself against interest-rate risk in conjunction with the issuance of these notes? Explain your answer precisely.

Application 17.2

A CALL TO GUERNSEY

You are the assistant manager of the international bond syndicate desk of Crédit Suisse in Zurich. The manager of a trust in the Channel Islands telephones you. He is interested in investing in a U.S.-dollar-denominated Eurobond, and wants to get a good yield. You tell him about some new issues that are available but note that some of them are callable. He says that's okay, as long as he's getting good value for his money. He asks you to fax him a list of bonds currently available.

An hour later he calls you. He has studied the fax and has identified three bonds that are satisfactory credits for his trust and seem to offer decent yields. But he would like your advice in deciding which of the three offers the best value for the money.

The three bonds, all priced at par, are

1. a five-year Sony Eurodollar bond paying 9.1 percent, callable at 102 in three years
2. a five-year BASF Eurodollar bond paying 9.3 percent, callable at 101 in four years
3. a five-year SNCF noncallable Eurodollar bond, paying 8.7 percent

Explain the method you would use to compare the value of the three bonds from the investor's point of view. To help you, some information about conditions in the bond market and in the Treasury bond options market is given:

March 24, 1991	U.S. Treasury yield curve	AA corporate yields	U.S. Treasury Bond Futures 8% $100,000—32nds of 100	
			Jun Close	Sep Close
			94-26	94-03
3 months	5.97	6.30		
1 year	6.28	7.40		
2 years	7.09	7.67		
3 years	7.32	8.04		
4 years	7.55	8.44		
5 years	7.76	8.72		
10 years	8.07			
30 years	8.26			

U.S. Treasury futures options—64ths of 100

Strike	Calls Jun	Calls Sep	Puts Jun	Puts Sep
93	2–27	2–55	0–39	1–49
94	1–47	2–21	0–59	2–15
95	1–10	1–55	1–22	2–49

Application 17.3

BIG

MEMORANDUM

TO: Andy Hubert,
           SVP, U.S. Capital International
FROM: Jack Levant
DATE: September 1, 1987
SUBJECT: Brand International Gold

As discussed with you last week, we propose to raise a $100 million for Brand International Gold (a subsidiary of Brand Holdings), in the Eurobond market. U.S.C.I. would be co–lead manager with Soditec of Switzerland of a U.S.-dollar denominated bullet bond plus gold call-warrant package. London would run the books.

Kindly evaluate the proposed structure (Exhibits I and II). Do you think Brand would bite? What is your judgment on potential investor appetite, based on similar deals that have been placed (Exhibits III and IV)? Can you suggest any changes to the terms and conditions that would make the deal more palatable to issuer or investors?

EXHIBIT I. PROPOSED BIG EUROBOND WITH GOLD WARRANTS

The Bond

Guarantee:	Guaranteed by parent company (Brand Holdings)
Size:	U.S. $100 million
Maturity:	10 years
Coupon:	6.5% (annual)
Price:	100
Call Features:	None
Ranking:	Senior unsubordinated
Rating:	Single-A rating will be sought.
Collateral:	Partially collateralized with U.S. gold mines (St. Joe Gold)

Each U.S. $1,000 bond will have two warrants attached. The warrants will be detachable after issue.

The Warrants

Commodity: 1 troy oz. gold
Strike: U.S. $500
Expiration: 3-year American

Advantages to the issuer:

- The issuer is paying a coupon substantially below that which would otherwise be available in the Euromarkets; he does this by forgoing some of his gain if gold rises.

Advantages to the investor:

- The investor is receiving warrants that have a strike price sufficiently close to the spot price for it to appear probable that the warrants will be in-the-money at expiration.
- Actually, when compared to the estimated forward price of gold, the warrants are about $186 in the money (see Exhibit II)!
- The terms of the warrants are similar to those which have been launched recently in the Euromarkets (see Exhibit III).
- Gold warrants have predominantly been purchases by retail investors either seeking a ''bet'' on gold or an inflation hedge. In the Euromarkets, such investors prefer to invest in corporations with a high credit rating. The guarantee is necessary to achieve an acceptable rating.

- By estimating the value of the warrants (see Exhibit IV) and subtracting that value from the $1,000 face value of each bond, we can calculate the effective return on the naked 6½ percent bond. With 10-year treasuries at 9 percent, the effective bond return gives a spread of 400 b.p., a return that is in line (perhaps a little tight) with other AAA-guaranteed bonds.

Valuation of the Warrants and Alternative Structures

Exhibit II shows our valuation of the package using a European option-valuation model for the warrants and a cost-of-carry model for the price of the forward contract. The standard deviation is the volatility of the price of gold. The interest rate is that of three-year Treasuries. The "effective bond cost" is the cost of the bond to the investor if the warrants could be sold immediately after issue for the "gold call value." The "effective bond return" is the yield to maturity of a bond priced at the "effective bond cost." The "issuer's initial cost" is the yield to maturity of the issuer's cash flows, including the cost of the guarantee. This calculation ignores the potential costs of warrant exercise.

If this structure is deemed unsuitable, alternative structures could be devised by altering one or more of the following:

1. coupon
2. guarantee
3. time to expiration of the warrants
4. strike price of the warrants
5. number of warrants per U.S. $1,000

The effect of each of the variables on the issuer's cost, the effective bond return, and the gold call value are detailed as follows:

Coupon:	Changing the coupon has no effect on the gold call value. Increasing the coupon both increases the issuer's cost and the effective bond return.
Guarantee:	The guarantee has no effect on the gold call value or the effective bond return. The guarantee would have an implicit cost to the parent company in the form of an additional contingent liability. (Alternatively, BIG could seek a Letter of Credit from one of its banks. We estimate that an LOC from Australian National Bank would cost about 70 basis points. The balance between coupon and the guarantee is important if the bonds are to be seen as tradable ex-warrant.)
Time to Expiration:	As the time to expiration increases, the gold call value increases, increasing the bond return. However, there is no effect on the issuer's initial cost, because (1) the time value has increased, and (2) the forward price increases have made the option more in-the-money. Because investors often do not fully value these elements, it is perhaps advisable to keep the time to expiration relatively short.
Strike Price:	As the strike price increases, the gold call value falls, decreasing the effective bond return. However, there is no effect on the issuer's initial cost. Although the option is valued off the *forward* price, investors often consider the spot price. Thus the balance between the strike and the spot, and the strike and the forward is important.
Number of Warrants:	As the number of warrants increases, the effective bond return increases. The gold call value and the issuer's initial cost are unchanged. However, the effect of warrant exercise upon the issuer's cost is increased.

Exhibit II. BIG Bond and Warrant Valuation

BRAND GOLD WARRANT
30-August-87
(ASSUMING TEN-YEAR ISSUE)

→ BOND COUPON	6.50%
→ SPOT GOLD PRICE	456
→ FORWARD PRICE	586
→ STRIKE PRICE	500
→ TIME IN YEARS	3
→ INTEREST RATE	8.25
→ STD DEVIATION	17
INTRINSIC VALUE (PV)	$68.18 PER OZ.
GOLD CALL VALUE	$91.32 PER OZ.
ISSUER'S COST	6.56%
NUMBER OF OZ. GOLD PER BOND	2.00
TOTAL VALUE PER $1,000 BOND	$182.65
EFFECTIVE BOND COST	$817.35
EFFECTIVE BOND RETURN	9.40%

Note: Assumed cost of the letter of credit: 40 basis points up front.

EXHIBIT III. BIG BOND: COMPARABLE GOLD CALL WARRANTS IN THE MARKET

Naked and Detached Gold Call Warrants
SwFr/grammes warrants

Issuer	SwFr strike per 1000 grammes	Warrant expiry date	Gold content per warrant	SwFr offered price	Premium per year of warrant life*	Implied volatility
Roche	25,100.00	30/09/90	10g	60	12.61%	38.55%
Bank Leu	27,000.00	01/03/89	100g	365	23%	42.12%
Belgium I	24,500.00	30/04/90	50g	320	14.12%	43.72%
Belgium II	25,200.00	30/04/90	50g	310	14.91%	43.86%
CSFB	23,350.00	30/03/90	10g	67	13.17%	43.97%
Credit Suisse	23,150.00	20/03/90	10g	69	13.3%	45.28%
UBS	25,750.00	15/06/90	10g	70	16.33%	49.41%
EDF	23,500.00	04/04/90	50g	430	16.42%	58.77%
					Average	45.71%

US$/oz warrants

Issuer	US$ strike per oz	Warrant expiry date	Gold content per warrant	SwFr offered price	Premium per year of warrant life*	Implied volatility
Morgan Guaranty	425.00	31/07/91	5oz	1180	6.58%	11.96%
Indosuez	410.00	16/04/89	10oz	1595	6.88%	14.85%
Standard Oil	565.20	06/11/91	3.3oz	530	10.59%	19.68%
Echo Bay Mines	560.00	30/09/91	6oz	1050	11.07%	22.92%
Citibank I	430.00	16/03/89	10oz	1645	10.09%	27.50%
Citibank III	440.00	12/01/89	5oz	740	11.03%	28.01%
Citibank II	420.00	03/10/88	10oz	1500	10.26%	28.32%
GM Canada	510.00	22/11/88	5oz	585**	19.44%	35.91%
Aegon	500.00	16/06/89	5oz	869**	17.07%	40.57%
					Average	25.52%

*The premium an investor would pay if he purchased the warrant at its offered price and used the warrant to purchase gold at the strike price, rather than purchasing gold direct. This premium is then divided by the remaining life of the warrant in years.

**No prices for the detached warrant are quoted in the market. These prices were calculated by discounting 2.5% Aegon of 1992 and 2.75% GM Canada of 1992 at 4.6% p.a. to give theoretical prices for the notes ex-warrants of 90.81 and 91.90 respectively. These were subtracted from the offered prices of the notes cum-warrants, and the result then divided by the number of warrants per note to give the theoretical warrant prices of SwFr869 and SwFr585 quoted here.

Source: Morgan Guaranty (Switzerland) Ltd

Source: *International Financing Review* (London), June 13, 1987

EXHIBIT IV. EXCERPTS FROM SAINT-GOBAIN PROSPECTUS

ECU 75,000,000

Saint-Gobain Nederland B.V.

**4¹/₂ per cent. Guaranteed Notes Due 1992 with
Call Warrants on Gold exercisable at U.S. $490 per troy ounce**

Unconditionally and irrevocably Guaranteed by

Compagnie de Saint-Gobain

Interest on the ECU 75,000,000 4¹/₂ per cent. Guaranteed Notes Due 1992 (the "Notes") will be payable annually in arrear on May 6 in each year, and will be at a rate of 4¹/₂ per cent. per annum. See "Terms and Conditions of the Notes — Interest"

The Notes will be issued with 75,000 warrants (the "Warrants" and together with the Notes, the "Securities"). Each warrant entitles the holder thereof to a U.S. Dollar cash amount being the amount by which the price of gold .995 fine (London P.M. fixing) exceeds U.S. $490. The Warrants are exercisable at any time from May 6, 1987 up to and including May 4, 1990. See "Terms and Conditions of the Warrants".

The Notes, unless previously redeemed or purchased and cancelled, will be redeemed on May 6, 1992. Saint-Gobain, Nederland B.V. may redeem all the Notes in the event of the imposition of certain withholding taxes. See "Terms and Conditions of the Notes — Redemption".

The Offering Price of the Securities is 100 per cent. of the principal amount of the Notes

---

Application has been made to list the Securities on the Luxembourg Stock Exchange.

A temporary Global Certificate in respect of the Notes is expected to be deposited with a common depositary (the "Common Depositary") on behalf of the Euro-clear Clearance System and Cedel S.A. on or about May 6, 1987. Definitive Notes will be available on or after the date which is the earlier of November 6, 1987 and 90 days following completion of the distribution of the Notes, as determined by Salomon Brothers International Limited.

A Global Warrant representing the Warrants is expected to be deposited with the Common Depositary on or about May 6, 1987. No definitive warrants will be issued.

TERMS AND CONDITIONS OF THE WARRANTS

The terms and conditions of the Warrants will (subject to completion and amendment) be as follows.

The issue of 75,000 warrants (the "Warrants") entitling the holders thereof to a U.S. Dollar cash amount being the difference between (a) the price (London P.M. fixing) on the Exercise Date (as defined below) of one troy ounce of gold .995 fine and (b) U.S.$490, at any time up to and including May 4, 1990 of Saint-Gobain Nederland B.V. (the "Issuer") was duly authorised on April 10, 1987 by a resolution of the Board of Directors of the Issuer and the giving of the guarantee (the "Guarantee") in respect of the Warrants was duly authorised on April 16, 1987 by a resolution of the Board of Directors of Compagnie de Saint-Gobain (the "Guarantor").

The Warrants will be issued subject to and with the benefit of a Warrant Agreement dated May 6, 1987 (the "Warrant Agreement") between the Issuer, the Guarantor and Morgan Guaranty Trust Company of New York as warrant agent (the "Warrant Agent"). The Warrantholders (as defined below) are entitled to the benefit of, are bound by and are deemed to have notice of all the provisions of the Warrant Agreement (which includes the form of the Global Warrant), copies of which are available for inspection at the specified office of the Warrant Agent.

1. *Form and Title*

The Warrants will at all times be represented by a global warrant (the "Global Warrant") which will be deposited with Morgan Guaranty Trust Company of New York, Brussels Office, as common depositary on behalf of the Euro-clear system ("Euro-clear") and Cedel S.A. ("Cedel"). The persons for the time being appearing in the book of Euro-clear and Cedel as being entitled to Warrants shall be the "Warrantholders". Transfer of the Warrants may only be effected through Euro-clear or Cedel and title to the Warrants will pass upon registration of the transfer in the books of Euro-clear or Cedel.

2. *Status*

The Warrants constitute general unsecured contractual obligations of the Issuer. The Issuer is under no obligation to purchase or hold gold.

3. *Guarantee*

Under a deed of guarantee dated May 6, 1987 the Guarantor irrevocably guarantees as caution solidaire (jointly and severally) to the holders of the Warrants the payment as provided in the terms and conditions of the Warrants of all amounts which may be due by the Issuer in respect of the Warrants, when and as the same shall become due and payable. The Guarantor undertakes to make all such payments without any withholding or deduction for or on account of any French taxes, duties, costs or other charges.

Such guarantee is hereinafter referred to as the "Guarantee" and will be endorsed on the Warrants. An executed copy of the Guarantee will be deposited with the Warrant Agent.

4. *Exercise Rights and Exercise Price*

Each Warrant may be exercised on any Business Day (as defined below) at any time from May 6, 1987 and up to and including May 4, 1990 and entitles the holder thereof to receive a Cash Payment (as defined in Condition 5 below) in accordance with Condition 5 below. Any Warrant which has not been duly exercised in the manner set out below under Condition 5 on or before May 4, 1990 shall become void.

5. ***Exercise Procedure***

(a) ***Exercise Notice***

Warrants may be exercised by delivery by tested telex of a duly completed Warrant Exercise Notice (the ''Exercise Notice'') in the form set out in the Warrant Agreement, copies of which may be obtained from Euro-clear, Cedel or the Warrant Agent, to Euro-clear or Cedel, as the case may be, not later than 10.00 a.m. (Brussels or Luxembourg time respectively) on any Business Day (the ''Exercise Date'') (i) specifying the number of Warrants being exercised, (ii) irrevocably instructing Euro-clear or Cedel to debit the Warrantholder's account with, and transfer to the Warrant Agent, entitlement of the Warrants being exercised, (iii) specifying the numbers of the Warrantholder's accounts at Euro-clear or Cedel to be debited with the Warrants being exercised and specifying the numbers of the Warrantholder's account at Euro-clear or Cedel to be credited with the Cash Payment and (iv) certifying that the beneficial owner of such Warrants is not a U.S. Person.

SELECTED REFERENCES

Dufey, G., and Ian H. Giddy. "Innovation in the International Financial Markets." *Journal of International Business Studies* (Fall 1981):33–52.

Finnerty Joseph D. "Financial Engineering in Corporate Finance: An Overview." *Financial Management,* vol. 17, no. 4 (Winter 1988):14–33.

Journal of Financial Engineering, various issues.

Risk Magazine, various issues.

Smith, Clifford W., Charles Smithson, and D. Sykes Wilford. *Managing Financial Risk.* Cambridge, Mass.: Ballinger, 1990.

Walmsley, Julian. *The New Financial Instruments.* New York: John Wiley & Sons, 1988.

18
A Recap of This Book

International finance is concerned with the global dimensions of financial markets, institutions, instruments, and techniques, and with the public-policy issues arising from these markets and methods. This final chapter seeks to recap, in a nontechnical fashion, the key ideas in this book.

One goal of the book has been to show the reader that while much of modern international finance revolves around foreign exchange, the field today goes beyond the financing and hedging of export-import transactions. A rich array of techniques employed by private market participants entails cross-border use of one another's national money and capital markets, as well of the specifically international markets, such as the Eurocurrency and Eurobond markets. Banks can no longer simply take deposits and make loans; to succeed they must be arrangers and underwriters of financing, supporting access to a range of markets and techniques to suit changing borrower and lender requirements. Currency and interest-rate swaps have dramatically widened the scope for use of foreign currency instruments by borrowers and investors. Other risk-management tools such as forwards, futures, and options are used with little regard to geographical location and blur the distinction between domestic and international finance. Commodities and equities are now part of the repertoire of those who arrange financing for governments, banks and multinational companies. As international and domestic restrictions erode, new instruments and techniques evolve. The international financial markets are having a profound influence on domestic markets. The removal of regulatory restrictions in Europe, Asia, and elsewhere has allowed for the expansion of the international bond and equity markets, and many domestic markets are in the process of becoming more open and competitive. Finance is becoming global.

International Trade and Price Comparisons

Despite the International Monetary Fund, the European Monetary System, and the North American Free Trade Area, the *global financial system* remains based on the fact that there is no true global money, accepted everywhere. In order to conduct international trade and investment, companies must still make payments and borrow and lend money, across systems where different currencies are in use. Out of this need has grown the *foreign-exchange market*, in which one money is exchanged for another. Thanks to foreign-exchange traders' willingness to quote the price of one currency in terms of another (Table 18.1), individuals and businessmen can compare prices across national boundaries. For example, the prices of *The Economist* magazine are listed on the magazine's cover in fourteen different currencies. By using the price quotations in Table 18.2, the reader can verify that what could be bought for $3.50 in the United States cost the equivalent of only $2.76 in England. (Specifically, since £1 is quoted as costing $1.5350, the U.K. cover price of £1.80 translates into $2.76.) Thus the American purchaser was paying more than his British counterpart. More expensive than the price in America was the German cost of DM7.00—that is, US$4.31 at an exchange rate of 1.7130 German marks to the U.S. dollar.

Table 18.1   *Foreign-Exchange Rates.*   Foreign-exchange rates quoted by banks show the dollar price of each unit of foreign currency and its reciprocal, the number of foreign-currency units one dollar will buy.

CURRENCY TRADING

EXCHANGE RATES

Tuesday, May 18, 1993

The New York foreign exchange selling rates below apply to trading among banks in amounts of $1 million and more, as quoted at 3 p.m. Eastern time by Bankers Trust Co., Telerate and other sources. Retail transactions provide fewer units of foreign currency per dollar.

Country	U.S. $ equiv. Tues.	Mon.	Currency per U.S. $ Tues.	Mon.
Argentina (Peso)	1.01	1.01	.99	.99
Australia (Dollar)	.6915	.7020	1.4461	1.4245
Austria (Schilling)	.08746	.08812	11.43	11.35
Bahrain (Dinar)	2.6522	2.6522	.3771	.3771
Belgium (Franc)	.02994	.03013	33.39	33.19
Brazil (Cruzeiro)	.0000279	.0000283	35781.00	35352.05
Britain (Pound)	1.5350	1.5350	.6515	.6515
30-Day Forward	1.5309	1.5309	.6532	.6532
90-Day Forward	1.5237	1.5237	.6563	.6563
180-Day Forward	1.5140	1.5136	.6605	.6607
Canada (Dollar)	.7885	.7835	1.2683	1.2763
30-Day Forward	.7874	.7824	1.2700	1.2781
90-Day Forward	.7847	.7795	1.2743	1.2828
180-Day Forward	.7798	.7744	1.2823	1.2914
Czech. Rep. (Koruna)				
Commercial rate	.0356125	.0356125	28.0800	28.0800
Chile (Peso)	.002544	.002549	393.05	392.24
China (Renminbi)	.174856	.174856	5.7190	5.7190
Colombia (Peso)	.001510	.001510	662.15	662.15
Denmark (Krone)	.1606	.1613	6.2269	6.1990
Ecuador (Sucre)				
Floating rate	.000535	.000535	1870.03	1870.03
Finland (Markka)	.18061	.18072	5.5368	5.5334
France (Franc)	.18248	.18381	5.4800	5.4405
30-Day Forward	.18174	.18299	5.5025	5.4647
90-Day Forward	.18051	.18180	5.5400	5.5005
180-Day Forward	.17902	.18025	5.5860	5.5480
Germany (Mark)	.6159	.6197	1.6237	1.6137
30-Day Forward	.6134	.6171	1.6302	1.6205
90-Day Forward	.6094	.6132	1.6409	1.6308
180-Day Forward	.6046	.6082	1.6540	1.6443
Greece (Drachma)	.004539	.004570	220.30	218.80
Hong Kong (Dollar) ...	.12939	.12937	7.7287	7.7295
Hungary (Forint)	.0115942	.0115808	86.2500	86.3500
India (Rupee)	.03219	.03219	31.07	31.07
Indonesia (Rupiah)	.0004811	.0004811	2078.53	2078.53
Ireland (Punt)	1.5040	1.5105	.6649	.6620
Israel (Shekel)	.3746	.3664	2.6692	2.7290
Italy (Lira)	.0006779	.0006765	1475.14	1478.15
Japan (Yen)	.008973	.008983	111.45	111.32

Country	U.S. $ equiv. Tues.	Mon.	Currency per U.S. $ Tues.	Mon.
30-Day Forward	.008972	.008983	111.46	111.33
90-Day Forward	.008973	.008983	111.45	111.32
180-Day Forward	.008976	.008986	111.41	111.28
Jordan (Dinar)	1.4874	1.4874	.6723	.6723
Kuwait (Dinar)	3.3272	3.3272	.3006	.3006
Lebanon (Pound)	.000577	.000577	1734.00	1734.00
Malaysia (Ringgit)	.3891	.3893	2.5700	2.5688
Malta (Lira)	2.7027	2.7027	.3700	.3700
Mexico (Peso)				
Floating rate	.3201024	.3201024	3.1240	3.1240
Netherland (Guilder) ..	.5493	.5526	1.8205	1.8098
New Zealand (Dollar) .	.5385	.5437	1.8570	1.8392
Norway (Krone)	.1455	.1461	6.8731	6.8469
Pakistan (Rupee)	.0375	.0375	26.68	26.68
Peru (New Sol)	.5287	.5260	1.89	1.90
Philippines (Peso)	.03788	.03788	26.40	26.40
Poland (Zloty)	.00006176	.00006229	16192.02	16055.02
Portugal (Escudo)	.006456	.006445	154.90	155.16
Saudi Arabia (Riyal) ..	.26702	.26702	3.7450	3.7450
Singapore (Dollar)	.6184	.6193	1.6170	1.6147
Slovak Rep. (Koruna) .	.0356125	.0356125	28.0800	28.0800
South Africa (Rand)				
Commercial rate	.3138	.3149	3.1868	3.1753
Financial rate	.2132	.2139	4.6900	4.6750
South Korea (Won) ...	.0012470	.0012473	801.90	801.70
Spain (Peseta)	.008083	.008120	123.71	123.16
Sweden (Krona)	.1363	.1363	7.3391	7.3383
Switzerland (Franc) ...	.6764	.6822	1.4785	1.4658
30-Day Forward	.6752	.6809	1.4811	1.4686
90-Day Forward	.6729	.6788	1.4860	1.4732
180-Day Forward	.6709	.6767	1.4905	1.4778
Taiwan (Dollar)	.038911	.038536	25.70	25.95
Thailand (Baht)	.03964	.03964	25.23	25.23
Turkey (Lira)	.0001012	.0001017	9878.01	9835.01
United Arab (Dirham) .	.2723	.2723	3.6725	3.6725
Uruguay (New Peso)				
Financial	.253742	.253742	3.94	3.94
Venezuela (Bolivar)				
Floating rate	.01165	.01162	85.84	86.07
SDR	1.40580	1.41402	.71134	.70720
ECU	1.20570	1.21000		

Special Drawing Rights (SDR) are based on exchange rates for the U.S., German, British, French and Japanese currencies. Source: International Monetary Fund.

European Currency Unit (ECU) is based on a basket of community currencies.

Source: *Wall Street Journal*, May 19, 1993

These simple examples illustrate the pivotal role of foreign exchange in national economies and in the international financial system. The pattern of international trade should follow the dictates of **comparative advantage**, every country specializing in those goods and services that require factors of production in which the country is relatively better endowed. But currency movements can distort international price comparisons and sometimes have more influence on export competitiveness than a nation's underlying productivity. By extending the magazine-pricing exercise we can compare whole economies to determine the extent to which price parity holds or does not hold between two countries. Germany may find that at current exchange rates its domestic prices are higher across the board than in other countries, thus making it more expensive for foreigners to buy German goods. Because such a loss of export competitiveness hurts domestic employment, the authorities may feel that something should be done. One course of action is to devalue the currency; another, more fundamental, is to use monetary and fiscal measures to deflate the domestic economy.

Table 18.2 **_Multicurrency Pricing._** The *Economist* magazine's quoted prices enable us to verify (using Table 18.1) the absence of price parity across nations.

Australia...............A$6.20	China......................Yuan 22	Hong Kong................HK$30	Japan ....¥850(本体825)	Russia ....US$3.50	Switzerland.................SFr7.00
Bahrain..................Dinar 3.5	France FFr24	India.............................Rs60	Mexico Peso17.50	Saudi Arabia................Rials 22	UK £1.80
Canada.....................C$4.50	Germany....................Dm7.00	Italy ....Lire 6,500	Netherlands FL8.00	South Africa ....Rand 11.75	USA $3.50

Source: *The Economist,* May 15, 1993.

Of course, no country can afford to react to every little change in its currency's value. But if the apparent problem persists, most countries will begin consideration of what policy actions should be taken. Should the government choose to influence the currency market, or the trade and capital flows that traverse the foreign exchanges, these actions will almost certainly concern other countries; hence the need for institutions such as the International Monetary Fund (IMF) and arrangements such as the European Monetary System, to coordinate the international economic policies of national governments. Nobody wants competitive devaluation, where countries push their currencies down in a price war for the spoils of export-market share.

Purchasing Power Parity

It does seem odd that the identical magazine should be so much more expensive in Frankfurt than in New York. In fact, the "law of one price" which is fundamental to economics, says that the same thing should command the same price, for arbitrage would otherwise occur and bring prices into line. If international price differences are big enough, and sufficiently persistent and widespread, the exchange rate and/or the goods' prices will, sooner or later, rectify themselves. So goes the **purchasing-power-parity** theory. That purchasing power parity does not hold continuously is evident, but it should also be common sense to suppose that a country whose prices are rising much faster than those of its trading partners—that is, a country with relatively high inflation—will find its currency's price in terms of other monies falling. For example, in the 1980s, as the Argentinean Austral's domestic buying power fell precipitously, the international value of the Austral fell too.

National prices (and inflation rates) and foreign-exchange rates are inextricably linked. Over time, the trend of the exchange rate between two currencies tends to follow the difference between the inflation rates of the two countries. At any given time, the rate set in the 24-hour currency market, however, may have more to do with short-term capital flows and economic or political expectations than with relative inflation rates.

Fixed Versus Floating Exchange Rates

It is not surprising, therefore, that economic policymakers may feel that the currency is out of line with economic fundamentals or with what political leaders deem to be in the best interests of the country. When this happens, the government has three choices:

1. The authorities can try to influence the value of their currency by buying or selling their currency to compensate for inadequate demand or supply, thus fixing the exchange rate at a desired level. This is called *foreign-exchange intervention.*

2. They may impose regulations on importers and exporters and international investors, seeking to eliminate excess supply or demand administratively. This nonmarket solution is called *exchange controls.*
3. They can let the private market determine the currency's level, devoting their energies instead to domestic budgetary and monetary policies. This is, of course, *freely floating exchange rates.*

Naive as they might seem, these elemental choices form the woof and warp of international economic policy. Although the majority of countries in the world employ some form of exchange control, such as requiring authorization to import goods or to export capital, the developed countries agreed at **Bretton Woods** at the end of World War II that neither currency controls nor unbridled devaluation were conducive to international commerce and prosperity. Instead, each country was to stabilize its currency by foreign-exchange intervention, using the government's reserve stock of gold and foreign currencies. If short of reserves to bolster its currency's price, the country could borrow from its stronger neighbors, often via the International Monetary Fund. In practice, the U.S. dollar came to be the pivot of this Bretton Woods system. By the early 1970s strains on the system precipitated the devaluation of the dollar and ushered in two decades of floating exchange rates, or rather of **managed floating**, which combines floating exchange rates with periodic foreign-exchange intervention.

Fixed versus floating exchange rates—that's the dilemma that governments of modern industrial countries continuously face. Free-market economists and policymakers raise their hands in favor of freely **floating exchange rates**, arguing with some merit that private speculators can succeed only if they bid currency values in the direction of their "true values," those that leave trade in goods and stocks of international investments in equilibrium. But this economic nirvana is an elusive thing, as departures from international price parity disrupt politicians' plans. In a floating-rate system, the only way to achieve relative stability in the currency market is to pursue stable domestic fiscal and monetary policies that command the confidence of investors and traders at home and abroad. Switzerland is one of the few countries that has managed to do so for an extended period. In contrast, when in the late 1970s a floating U.S. dollar was accompanied by flaccid budgetary and lax monetary policies in Washington, the dollar ran an erratic course downhill. Similarly, in the late 1980s, an unfettered pound sterling did nothing to correct, in Margaret Thatcher's Britain, excessive monetary growth and an inflation rate in the teens—hence Britain's eventual decision to join the European Monetary System (see below). Thus a floating exchange rate is not a panacea in and of itself; the currency market reflects, sometimes in magnified form, the bad as well as the good. And when still worse (or better) is expected, foreign-exchange dealers do not normally reserve judgment but buy or sell based on best-guess expectations of future developments. This anticipatory trading in response to ever-changing news is what gives the foreign-exchange market its seemingly impetuous and unpredictable character.

Unsettled, perhaps, by the vagaries of this speculative market and seeking greater discipline than could be exerted by free exchange rates, Britain's more *dirigistic* partners in the European Common Market agreed in 1979 to fix their currencies against one another. The result has been a marked conversion of inflation rates and interest rates. The **European Monetary System** (EMS) permits no more than 2¼ percent movement of any currency against any other, although there are transitional exceptions and, like most so-called fixed-rate arrangements, they are subject to occasional "realignments." The latter entails releasing a pair of currencies whose marriage is under strain and repegging them at a new exchange rate. Obviously, if this were to happen too often the market's confidence in each temporary mooring would flag and the system would disintegrate (as indeed occurred in Europe's earlier attempts at currency unison). So each country must make a serious effort to prevent its currency from dragging anchor at every tide of speculative sentiment. How the country's central bank does so, and the economic consequences of a fixed rate, is a story in itself. Let's try to summarize the sequence of events when a fixed exchange rate comes under strain.

Assume, for example, that the French franc is worth 0.5 German marks (deutschemarks, or DM, for short).[1] Under the EMS, the two monies are fixed at this level.[2] Now, let us say, French inflation picks up, exceeding that of Germany for long enough to hurt French exports and increase imports from West Germany. Foreign-exchange traders, anticipating a weaker French unit in the future, will hasten to cover their franc positions, meaning that no one will want to be caught holding the hot potato (the French franc) at the time of the devaluation of the franc against the DM. The selling of French francs in exchange for DM or other currencies will drive the DM price of the French franc down—to, perhaps, 0.49 DM. The franc depreciation will, in principle, produce some automatic corrective reactions: imports, costing more, will be reduced, and exports stimulated. These effects, however, are slow and unreliable. So to keep the exchange rate fixed, the French central bank will have to intervene in the foreign-exchange market, buying francs with their store of foreign currencies. By reducing the amount of francs in circulation, the French authorities have in effect undertaken contractionary monetary policy. To avoid the embarrassment of a devaluation, the French have imported German monetary discipline. France could try to offset this with domestic stimulus; however to avert continual depletion of France's foreign-exchange reserves, more permanent measures must be taken—such as curbing budgetary deficits and stemming the growth of the money supply, to dampen inflation expectations. These corrective changes in the economy are called the *adjustment process*. This bland term hides some of the harsh effects—high interest rates, economic dislocation, unemployment—that must be considered when a nation chooses which kind of exchange-rate system to adopt. In 1992, Britain made this choice: it opted out of the exchange-rate mechanism, vowing to return only when conditions were right. Most countries face this choice sooner or later. The only alternative is the Albanian road—insulated from the vagaries of the global economy and as poor as a hermit.

Monetary union in Europe, still an elusive goal, would involve the permanent fixing of currencies to one another and in due course their replacement with a single currency managed by a single central bank. The hardest pill to swallow is the loss of monetary and fiscal independence by national governments. Because their debt could no longer be repaid by printing money, governments would have to limit deficit spending to what the capital market deemed an acceptable level, or go, hat in hand, to Brussels.

Foreign-Exchange Trading and Market Efficiency

Currencies are bought and sold in exchange for one another in a 24-hour over-the-telephone market by individuals, corporations, securities firms, and governments, all of which deal with the foreign-exchange traders at commercial banks. The high liquidity of the market stems from the readiness of such banks to trade with other banks as well as

---

[1] Saying that the French franc is worth 0.5 German marks is, of course, the same as saying the DM is worth 2 French francs.

[2] More precisely, they must remain between 3 DM per French franc, plus or minus 2¼ percent—that is, between 2.9325 and 3.0675—or some other specified bounds.

with entities other than banks. Probably over 95 percent of trading occurs between the banks themselves, as they continuously adjust and readjust their positions. Foreign-exchange traders must anticipate changes in government actions by buying and selling currencies for forward (future) or immediate (spot) delivery. The market rates that companies face in doing international business change each time news or expectations of future events alter the outlook for a currency. New technologies may have a profound effect on the foreign-exchange market in the coming years, as more institutions gain the means to monitor market information and transactions, and to execute trades, on a real-time basis via computer linkages.

Forecasting the economic pressures on a currency and the government's actions to stem or stimulate those pressures has become a significant industry. *Currency prediction* involves fundamental economic analysis, political prognostication, and technical analysis, which studies patterns of movement in the currency itself. Modern finance theory, on the other hand, pooh-poohs these efforts as self-destructive; any method that works will become disseminated to the point at which it no longer works! The market will respond more and more rapidly to new information and in time an *efficient market* will prevail: exchange rates will behave as randomly as the arrival of unanticipated information.

Countries frequently change the manner in which they manage their exchange rate or respond to international pressures by adjusting domestic interest rates and other policy variables. It is not surprising, therefore, that currency traders and international money managers are kept busy guessing the direction of the major currencies. Estimates suggest that as little as 5 percent of the trillion dollars of daily foreign-exchange transactions volume is directly linked to exports or imports. Because all monies are domestic monies, every one of these numerous transactions is conducted by means of a transfer of ownership of domestic deposits. The money never leaves home, although the owner may be a nonresident.

The Eurodollar Market

Although all means of payment remain within the home clearing system, the 1970s and 1980s saw enormous growth in the Eurodollar market and its offshoots. These are markets for credit outside the country of the currency in which the credit instrument is denominated. Eurodollars are the money-market gypsies, living side-by-side with their more domesticated neighbors. They are simply bank time deposits, denominated in U.S. dollars but deposited in a bank outside the United States. Euroyen, Eurosterling, and so forth are similar deposits in banks located outside the jurisdiction of the country in whose currency the instrument is denominated. The Eurocurrency market, in other words, permits the separation of the currency of denomination from the country of jurisdiction. International banks and their clients have voted with their pocketbooks in favor of this market because of its freedom from costly and restrictive banking regulation, although the bulk of the market involves banks that are dominant institutions in their home countries and therefore supervised by their home banking authorities. The market for such deposits, and the loans that the Eurobanks make, is called the *Eurocurrency market;* it is centered in London. Eurodollars and Eurocurrencies are traded actively in a global interbank market; indeed, Eurocurrency trading has now become part and parcel of foreign-exchange dealing-room activities.

Interest rates in the Eurocurrency market are the freest in the world, being determined by market forces of supply and demand, although arbitrage ensures their close alignment with domestic money-market rates as long as depositors and borrowers are free to choose between the home and external markets. Notwithstanding their freedom, Eurocurrency rates do offer strict obeisance to a law of the market, one called interest-rate parity.

Spot- and Forward-Exchange Rates and Interest-Rate Parity

Interest-rate parity stems from the fact that Eurocurrency deposits, as well as other credit instruments, can be arbitraged between one another through the spot and forward foreign-exchange markets. We saw in Table 18.1 that some currencies, such as the pound and the yen, are traded for deferred settlement, called *forward* delivery in one month or more as well as the more normal *spot* delivery, which means settlement within two business days. Thus a corporation can purchase Japanese yen for delivery not today but, say, in three months' time.[3] This is a *forward foreign-exchange contract.*

The forward market is frequently used by multinational firms to hedge their future foreign-exchange payments or receipts—or any financial claims, for that matter. In effect, the forward-exchange market allows a firm to manage the currency risk or *exposure* that arises from foreign-currency assets or liabilities. It is also used by banks to arbitrage between Eurodeposits denominated in different currencies. Such arbitrage is the source of the interest-rate-parity linkage. For example, a banker may borrow 3-month *Eurodollars* at 8.5 percent in the interbank market (see the quotations in Table 18.3) and change them into pounds to invest them at a lucrative 15.0625 percent in a 3-month *Eurosterling* deposit. The catch is that Britain's high interest rate reflects its inflation and the currency's weakness. To avoid possible currency losses if the pound were to fall in value, he would sell the sterling invested (plus accrued interest) for delivery in 3 months, at the forward-exchange rate. The proceeds will be used to repay the dollars borrowed. He has undertaken *covered-interest arbitrage.* Unfortunately, this act of covering his foreign-exchange risk

Table 18.3   *Interest Rates in the External Money Market.*   These rates differ because of different domestic monetary conditions, but are linked to one another through the foreign-exchange market.

EURO-CURRENCY INTEREST RATES

May 17	Short term	7 Days notice	One Month	Three Months	Six Months	One Year
Sterling	$6\frac{3}{16} - 6\frac{1}{16}$	$6\frac{1}{8} - 6$	$6\frac{1}{8} - 6$	$6\frac{3}{16} - 6\frac{1}{16}$	$6\frac{1}{16} - 6\frac{1}{16}$	$6\frac{5}{16} - 6\frac{3}{16}$
US Dollar	$3\frac{1}{4} - 3\frac{1}{8}$	$3\frac{1}{8} - 3$	$3\frac{1}{8} - 3$	$3\frac{1}{4} - 3\frac{1}{8}$	$3\frac{3}{8} - 3\frac{1}{4}$	$3\frac{5}{8} - 3\frac{1}{2}$
Can. Dollar	$4\frac{3}{8} - 4\frac{1}{8}$	$4\frac{1}{4} - 4$	$4\frac{3}{4} - 4\frac{1}{2}$	$5\frac{1}{8} - 4\frac{7}{8}$	$5\frac{5}{8} - 5\frac{3}{8}$	$6\frac{1}{4} - 6$
Dutch Guilder	$7\frac{7}{16} - 7\frac{3}{16}$	$7\frac{3}{8} - 7\frac{1}{4}$	$7\frac{1}{4} - 7\frac{1}{8}$	$7 - 6\frac{7}{8}$	$6\frac{11}{16} - 6\frac{9}{16}$	$6\frac{3}{8} - 6\frac{1}{4}$
Swiss Franc	$5\frac{1}{4} - 5$	$5\frac{1}{4} - 5$	$5\frac{3}{16} - 5\frac{1}{16}$	$5\frac{1}{16} - 4\frac{13}{16}$	$4\frac{7}{8} - 4\frac{3}{4}$	$4\frac{5}{8} - 4\frac{1}{2}$
D–Mark	$8 - 7\frac{7}{8}$	$7\frac{7}{8} - 7\frac{3}{4}$	$7\frac{11}{16} - 7\frac{7}{16}$	$7\frac{3}{8} - 7\frac{1}{4}$	$7\frac{1}{8} - 7$	$6\frac{5}{8} - 6\frac{1}{2}$
French Franc	$8\frac{1}{4} - 8$	$8\frac{1}{4} - 8$	$8 - 7\frac{3}{4}$	$7\frac{5}{8} - 7\frac{1}{2}$	$7\frac{3}{8} - 7\frac{1}{8}$	$7\frac{1}{16} - 6\frac{13}{16}$
Italian Lira	$12\frac{1}{2} - 10\frac{1}{2}$	$10\frac{3}{4} - 10\frac{3}{8}$	$10\frac{7}{8} - 10\frac{1}{2}$	$10\frac{5}{8} - 10\frac{1}{4}$	$10\frac{5}{8} - 10\frac{1}{4}$	$10\frac{1}{2} - 10\frac{1}{4}$
Belgian Franc	$7\frac{1}{16} - 7\frac{5}{16}$	$7\frac{1}{2} - 7\frac{3}{8}$	$7\frac{3}{8} - 7\frac{1}{4}$	$7\frac{1}{4} - 7\frac{1}{8}$	$7 - 6\frac{7}{8}$	$6\frac{13}{16} - 6\frac{11}{16}$
Yen	$3\frac{5}{16} - 3\frac{3}{16}$	$3\frac{1}{4} - 3\frac{3}{16}$	$3\frac{1}{4} - 3\frac{3}{16}$	$3\frac{1}{4} - 3\frac{3}{16}$	$3\frac{3}{32} - 3\frac{3}{32}$	$3\frac{11}{32} - 3\frac{7}{32}$
Danish Krone	$9\frac{3}{4} - 9$	$10 - 9\frac{3}{4}$	$9\frac{3}{4} - 9$	$8\frac{1}{2} - 8$	$8\frac{1}{8} - 7\frac{5}{8}$	$7\frac{5}{8} - 7\frac{1}{8}$
Asian $Sing	$3\frac{1}{4} - 2\frac{1}{4}$	$3\frac{1}{4} - 2\frac{1}{4}$	$3\frac{1}{2} - 2\frac{1}{2}$	$3\frac{1}{2} - 2\frac{1}{2}$	$3\frac{1}{2} - 2\frac{1}{2}$	$3\frac{3}{4} - 2\frac{3}{4}$
Spanish Peseta	$12\frac{5}{8} - 12\frac{1}{8}$	$12\frac{5}{8} - 12\frac{1}{8}$	$12\frac{3}{8} - 12\frac{1}{8}$	$12\frac{1}{8} - 11\frac{7}{8}$	$11\frac{9}{16} - 11\frac{5}{16}$	$11\frac{1}{16} - 11\frac{1}{16}$
Portuguese Esc	$15\frac{1}{4} - 14\frac{3}{4}$	$16\frac{1}{4} - 15\frac{1}{4}$	$15\frac{3}{8} - 14\frac{5}{8}$	$15 - 14$	$14 - 13\frac{1}{2}$	$13\frac{3}{4} - 13\frac{1}{4}$

Long term Eurodollars: two years $4\frac{3}{16}-4\frac{1}{16}$ per cent; three years $4\frac{11}{16}-4\frac{9}{16}$ per cent; four years $5\frac{1}{8}-5$ per cent; five years $5\frac{1}{16}-5\frac{3}{16}$ per cent nominal. Short term rates are call for US Dollar and Japanese Yen; others, two days' notice.

---

[3]As the reader may verify by glancing at Figure 18.1, the price for forward delivery will differ from the spot price. Some currencies, like the yen, typically cost more for forward delivery (they are trading at a premium), while others, such as the pound sterling, cost less (they trade at a discount). Which does which is determined by the cost of carry—that is, the net cost (or benefit) from borrowing in one currency and depositing the funds in the other. The forward premium or discount, therefore, is a function of relative interest rates in the two currencies—another expression of the interest-rate-parity relationship.

entails a cost, because pounds for future delivery are priced lower than he paid for them in the spot market. Can he still make money? Probably not; arbitrage of this kind normally ensures that the cost equals the gain—that is, that the difference between the spot- and the forward-exchange rates equal the interest-rate differential between Eurocurrency deposits in different currencies. *This is the interest-rate-parity relationship.*

An Integrated Framework

A currency's Euromarket interest rates provide clues to conditions in its domestic financial system, because interest rates reflect the time value of money in a country. In countries in which the value of the money is expected to fall, either at home (how much the currency will buy in goods and services) or internationally (how much the currency is worth in terms of other currencies), the interest rate will be higher. In countries in which the purchasing power of the money is stable, people will willingly accept a lower interest rate, but if a peso is expected to buy less later, lenders will demand compensation in the form of a higher interest rate. This premium for inflation (the Fisher effect) at home has its international counterpart: a premium for currency depreciation (the international Fisher effect). To summarize, a country whose budget and money supply and hence inflation are under control will have a low interest rate; its currency will be expected to appreciate, and will have a higher price for forward delivery than for spot. At the other extreme, a country like Argentina whose budget deficit and money supply are out of control will have high domestic and Eurocurrency interest rates, to compensate depositors for inflation and corresponding currency depreciation; and interest-rate parity will ensure that the elevated interest rate is accompanied by a correspondingly low value for the currency in the forward-exchange market. Domestic monetary policy, price inflation, interest rates, and the spot and forward values of the currency are all linked in a manner illustrated in Figure 18.1, the *integrated framework* of international finance.

Figure 18.1   ***The Integrated Framework.***   The integrated framework of exchange rates shows how relative interest rates depend on the domestic value of money (inflation) and the value reflected in the foreign-exchange market.

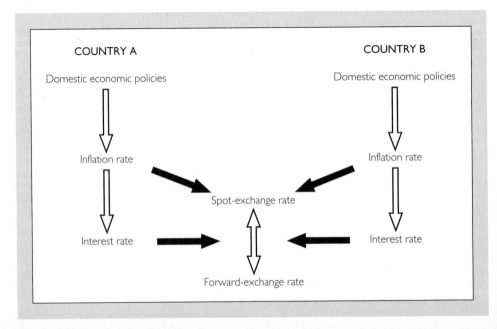

Futures, Options, and Swaps

The forward-exchange market plays the role of linking international interest rates. Today, however, forward contracts have to share the stage with other instruments and markets for arbitrage and for hedging. These so-called **derivative instruments** include futures, options, and swaps.

Futures markets for currencies and Eurodeposits have sprung up in most of the global trading centers. A futures contract is the common man's forward contract; while forwards are available only to banks and others with high credit standing, futures contracts minimize credit risk by daily marking to market of each party's gains or losses. As a result, futures can be purchased or sold by anyone who has sufficient funds to open a margin account. Because they are virtually equivalent, currency futures track currency forwards almost perfectly. Both forwards and futures entail a commitment to exchange two currencies at a certain rate on a given future date. *Currency options*, on the other hand, give the holder the right, but not the obligation, to purchase (or sell) a currency at a prearranged exchange rate in the future. Options are frequently used when international investors or traders want the opportunity to gain if a currency moves favorably but require protection if the exchange rate goes the wrong way. The price of an option, paid up front by the buyer to the seller, is a complex function of market prices, the terms of the contract, and the currency's volatility. Most major international banks now offer options contracts to supplement their forward dealing, but options are also traded side by side with futures on the Chicago Mercantile Exchange, the LIFFE in London, the MATIF in Paris, SIMEX in Singapore, and others.

More recent, but in many respects more important, than futures and options is the market for **interest-rate** and **currency swaps**. For example, the Chinese airline CAAC wishes to obtain long-term, fixed-rate Japanese-yen financing for equipment purchases, but finds that its most efficient access to funds is in the form of dollar-denominated borrowing from banks on a floating-rate basis. By entering into a currency swap, the airline can convert the floating rate, U.S.-dollar debt into fixed-rate, Japanese-yen debt. Swaps are used in a similar fashion by many companies to alter the interest rate or currency characteristics of a debt or an asset. As Figure 18.2 suggests, this is done through an agreement between two parties to exchange one kind of interest rate (and/or principal payment) for another.[4] An interest-rate swap is an agreement to exchange fixed for floating interest payments, or to exchange floating payments linked to two different market benchmarks. Currency swaps, nowadays extensively used in conjunction with new issues in the

Figure 18.2   *Currency Swap.*   Yin has issued a fixed-rate yen bond while Yang has borrowed floating-rate dollar funds. Converting these, Yin pays fixed-rate yen to Yang in exchange for floating-rate dollar coupons.

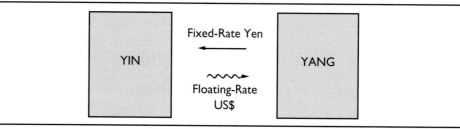

---

[4]In this respect, swaps serve the same function as forward-exchange contracts. They are, in essence, forward contracts tailored to bonds—a package of forward exchanges of currencies matching each coupon and principal payment.

international bond market, entail an agreement to exchange a U.S.-dollar floating interest rate (and the principal amount) for a fixed interest rate (and principal amount) in another currency. The coupon exchange takes place each interest-payment date, such as semi-annually, whereas the principal exchange only occurs at the end of the swap. Bond markets are less liquid and uniform than short-term money markets, so they are slower to form the tight links across national boundaries that the Eurocurrency market has produced. Because market imperfections remain, securities are often priced somewhat differently in different markets. Swaps allow borrowers (and investors, too) to use the capital market in which they have a comparative advantage, and then employ a swap to convert the interest-rate and currency features in those desired. Like forward contracts, swaps can be entered into at any time and reversed at a later date when conditions have changed, so they provide the global financial community with a tool of enormous value in the management of long-term interest-rate and currency risk. On the other hand, like all over-the-counter, as opposed to exchange-traded, derivative contracts, swaps entail *counterparty risk*, the danger that the other party could default on future obligations. Banks, corporations, and regulators continue to seek ways to measure and minimize the credit risk of over-the-counter derivatives.

The International Equity Market

The *international capital market*, of which the swap market is now an integral part, consists of the long-term markets for *intermediated credit* and those for *direct financing*, as well as the related derivative markets, such as long-term forwards, options, swaps, and commodity contracts. In intermediated credit banks intermediate between suppliers and users of credit, while in direct financing issuers sell claims—typically equity or bonds—directly to the investors. Today, the securities markets play a much larger role in the international capital markets than they did a decade or so ago.

International equity investment, always important, has assumed added significance in recent years for at least three reasons:

1. Modern portfolio theory has unequivocally demonstrated that the investor in equities can obtain a clearly superior combination of lower risk and higher return by diversifying internationally rather than only domestically.
2. Cross-border mergers and acquisitions are more evident as the world economy, with Europe at the forefront, becomes more integrated.
3. The performance of foreign markets such as Tokyo means that no modern institutional investor can afford to ignore the opportunities presented by the fast-growing countries of Asia and elsewhere. On the other hand, some of these markets suffer from restrictions and illiquidity, so that many investors have chosen to purchase shares in one of the hundred or more funds or trusts devoted to international investment.

On the issue of whether the global equity market can be thought of as being integrated into a single global market, the academic jury is still out. On the financing side, some firms now list their shares on several exchanges to facilitate round-the-clock trading, but there is no distinct "Euro-equity" market.

International Commodities Markets

Commodities such as gold, oil, and computer memory chips are similarly traded in a world-wide market that ensures price equality across markets and price equivalence across currencies. Most, in fact, use the U.S. dollar as the global currency of denomination no matter where the commodity is traded. Forward contracts, futures, and options are now available for several dozen of the most important commodities. Unhedged, commodities can be viewed as equities of the purest kind by investors and traders. When hedged by means of forward or futures contracts, they assume the character of fixed-income investments. This similarity is the link between interest rates and commodity futures prices: the future and forward price of a commodity equals the spot price plus the cost of financing and other carrying costs, less the convenience yield. Commodity swaps and commodity price indexing are increasingly used in financing.

International Lending Techniques

The *syndicated Eurocredit* market, on the other hand, has probably provided more funding to international corporations, governments, and supranational agencies like the Asian Development Bank than any other single market—at least until dethronement by its offspring, the Euronote market. These and related credit-granting techniques constitute the tool kit of international bankers in the 1990s. *Syndicated Eurocredits* are large loans put together by a group of international banks, each of which takes a participation in the single loan. Most of the defaulted loans to developing countries are of this kind, and many banks have written down the value of their participations and sold them to trade in a fledgling secondary market. Some have been restructured and reconfigured into bonds with guaranteed principal, called Brady bonds. Ordinary Eurodollar loan participations are now usually structured in such a way as to be tradable, too. For this to happen, banks must assign the risks and returns on the loan to another party, employing the legal principles of novation and subparticipation. All these loans are priced on a floating-rate basis, with the interest rate reset periodically, usually at a set margin over six-month LIBOR, which is the rate at which banks offer deposits to other banks in the London Eurodollar market. The lending rates thus reflect the banks' cost of funding.

Today, most creditworthy international borrowers have an alternative to intermediated bank credit: the *Euronote*. Euronotes, also called Eurocommercial paper, are short-term unsecured promissory notes issued and sold in an auctionlike manner periodically, the period ranging from one to six months, or whenever the borrower requires funds.[5] Euronotes are similar to commercial paper issued within the United States but a little less constrained by domestic investors' traditional requirements. The notes are "priced" in relation to LIBOR, like bank loans, but trade at a discount to par and typically reap the issuer money at rates well below those charged on normal bank loans. To give the borrower the added security of availability of funds over a number of years, a Euronote issuance program is often accompanied by an underwriting facility, under which a group of banks agrees to purchase the notes at a higher spread relative to LIBOR, should the borrower prove unable to sell them in the open market.[6] Such underwriting facilities are sometimes used as one element of a *multiple-option facility*, under which the borrower has access to several alternative markets, domestic as well as international, for short- and medium-term credit.

---

[5]A similar instrument but with maturities of one to three years is the medium-term note. Like Euronotes, MTNs are issued under an issuance program or facility.

[6]When Euronotes are sold without the backing of an underwriting commitment, they are called Euro-commercial paper.

Eurobonds, Floating–Rate Notes, and Medium–Term Notes

The *international bond market* comprises the Eurobond and foreign-bond markets, and those markets such as the U.S. market that actively encourage global participation. The *Eurobond market*'s distinctive feature is that the bonds are issued and sold in a jurisdiction outside the country of the currency of denomination. This makes the market freer of certain constraints than the domestic market, constraints such as registration requirements and withholding taxes. *Foreign bonds*, unlike Eurobonds, are issued within the domestic market of the currency of denomination, but they are issued by nonresident borrowers. Eurobonds are quite distinct from Eurodollars, because bond markets enable final borrowers to issue securities to investors directly. In the Eurobond market, no intermediaries intervene between borrower and lender (except during the underwriting and distribution process). Eurobonds represent direct claims on corporations, governments, or governmental entities.

Eurobonds are among the most versatile and variegated of financial instruments. Most are publicly issued and traded, but a growing proportion is privately placed with European or Japanese institutions. Because, as noted in Chapter 12, many are "swapped," borrowers can and do issue them in a variety of currencies to suit investors' preferences. A currency swap then enables the issuer to effectively obtain funds of the currency and kind that he desires. An increasing number placed in Europe, for example, are denominated in the ECU (European Currency Unit). Yet the most dramatic evidence of the market's adaptability is the fact that so few are "plain vanilla" bonds, whereas at one time Eurobonds with periodically reset interest rates (*Eurodollar floating-rate notes*) were the dominant variation.

Floating-rate notes stand to some extent in a category of their own; they are bonds with many of the characteristics of money-market instruments. As far as *interest-rate risk* is concerned, FRNs are like short-term Eurodeposits; however, they are longer-term instruments, so in the *credit-risk* dimension they behave like corporate bonds. Methods of pricing and evaluating the return on FRNs reflect this duality: the value of an FRN is a function of the short-term interest rate to the next reset date, the long-term credit risk of the issuer as perceived by the market, and overall liquidity and demand conditions in the market for floating-rate notes.

In the late 1980s FRNs were supplanted by *Eurobonds linked to equity*—convertible Eurobonds giving indirect access to restricted equity markets, for example, and bonds with detachable equity warrants, and even bonds linked to stock-market indexes such as the Japanese Nikkei index (see Figure 18.3). Other Eurobonds embody currency or commodity options; some are callable, others are puttable, and some are both.[7] In sum, the Eurobond market is fertile ground for the financial innovations that have characterized the global financial markets in the past two decades—and promise to do so for at least the next few years leading to the turn of the century.

Today, a widely used alternative to the Eurobond is the *medium-term note* (MTN). Medium-term notes are in many respects simply fixed-rate corporate bonds, albeit of a generally shorter maturity than Eurobonds or domestic bonds. Unlike conventional bonds, MTNs are offered on a continuous basis in smaller amounts—as little as $2 to $5 million at a time—rather than in single large issues. MTN financing programs are often

---

[7]A callable Eurobond is one where the *issuer* has the right to cancel the bond and repay his debt; a *puttable* bond is one where the *investor* may redeem the bond and demand repayment of the principal.

Figure 18.3   ***Equity-Linked Eurobonds.***   This bond exemplifies only one of the market's many variations.

This announcement appears as a matter of record only.

NEW ISSUE   AUGUST 1989

KANSALLIS-OSAKE-PANKKI
(Incorporated with limited liability in the Republic of Finland)

¥3,000,000,000

8 per cent. Nikkei-Linked
Notes due 1992

Issue Price 101⅝ per cent.

New Japan Securities Europe Limited   Bankers Trust International Limited

Dongsuh Securities Co., Ltd.   IBJ International Limited

Kansallis Banking Group   Takugin Finance International Limited

Source: *Financial Times,* August 1989.

described as investor driven. In effect, the distribution process in the MTN market resembles a commercial-paper issuance program, albeit without the backstop lines of credit that commercial-paper programs typically have. Under a comprehensive MTN-issuance program, an issuer can raise funds by issuing fixed-rate, floating-rate, or deep-discount paper in any of a number of currencies.

Corporate Financing Choices in the Global Capital Market

The preceding discussion has made it evident that companies, banks, and government agencies face a plethora of choices for short-term and long-term financing. How should they select from this cornucopia? This book has offered a framework for financing choices. Debt versus equity, an increasingly blurred distinction, is the starting point. Leverage offers a tax shield and may bring operating efficiencies, but its benefits are limited by the costs of financial distress. For some companies the liquidation value of the firm is far less than the going concern value because of lawyers' fees, lost management time, and other intangibles.

Turning from the question How much debt? to What kind of debt? a useful guiding principle is: *use financial markets to hedge operating exposure, unless the financial markets are biased or inefficient.* The nature of financing should normally be driven by the nature of the business, in such a way as to make debt-service payments match the character and timing of operating earnings. *Because this reduces the probability of financial distress, it allows the firm greater leverage and thus a greater tax shield.* This guideline can be applied to the fixed-versus-floating, maturity, and currency-of-denomination decisions, among others. Derivatives such as swaps and forward contracts as well as hybrid financing techniques can be used to *hedge* a natural exposure that the company has or to take a *position* on the direction or volatility of some market variable.

Having selected the nature of the debt, management can then seek the cheapest source. At the short end, common sources are commercial paper and adjustable-rate preferred stock in the U.S. domestic market or Eurocommercial paper and short-term Eurocurrency loans in the offshore markets. Long-term sources include subsidized credit from national or international agencies, bank loans including nonrecourse project loans, term loans and revolving-credit facilities, various forms of secured and unsecured private placements, and public issues. When individual assets or a self-contained project can be segregated from those of the company, off-balance-sheet financing without recourse—asset-backed finance—may prove more attractive to lenders than general-obligation debt.

New Financing and Investment Techniques

The book is rounded off with an introduction to a practical approach to the analysis and construction of innovative instruments in international finance. Many instruments of the international capital market, new or old, can be broken down into simpler securities or *building blocks.* Once one knows how the instrument is constructed and hence how its value behaves, one can readily compare it against existing instruments that, alone or in combination, produce the same behavior. For example, some instruments' value varies with market interest rates, so that they are bondlike; others are affected by the condition of the issuing company, so that they are more equitylike. Many instruments combine elements of both. Each should be priced in accordance with the price of comparable instruments; if they are not, there may be a mispricing. This approach can be of great practical value to investors and issuers who wish to better understand the risks of instruments offered to them by banks. The method can also be used to identify arbitrage opportunities between instruments and to hedge one instrument with another.

Many, although by no means all, hybrid securities can be broken down into components consisting of: (1) bonds—creditor (long) or debtor (short) positions in zero-coupon bonds; (2) forward contracts (long or short forward positions in a currency, bond, equity, or commodity); and (3) options (long or short positions in calls or puts on a currency, bond, equity, or commodity).

Innovations in finance, as in other markets, evolve. The advantage certain firms have in new instruments is, before long, eroded as uncertainty is reduced and clients can more confidently turn to lower-cost imitators. The high initial returns are eroded by competition from other banks as well as by the market forces that tend to eliminate those imperfections that gave rise to the innovation in the first place. The product may become a "commodity." As new instruments, banks, and countries compete more vigorously with the old, the existing order will break down. This means that any financial insitution or regulatory agency resting on its laurels will come under great competitive threat, and to survive and thrive must change in response to the new order. The winds of change are so sweeping that no market or institution will escape them.

CONCLUSION

The international financial system revolves around the foreign-exchange market. This market links prices in different countries, and governments waver between floating and fixing their exchange rates to manage this interdependence. Domestic money markets are today linked through the Eurocurrency market, which permits the separation of currency of denomination from country of jurisdiction. National interest rates reflect the time value of their respective monies, and the forward foreign-exchange market reflects the time value of the exchange rate between the two monies. Thus the foreign-exchange market links national interest rates, inflation rates, and monetary policies. Currency swaps, used in connection with international bond financing or investment, are the long-term counterparts of the forward-exchange market. Both allow the separation of currency and interest-rate risks of an asset from the asset itself. Eurobonds today may be the most innovative instruments of the global financial market; because they are subject to fewer constraints than the new derivative instruments, they are frequently packaged with future- and optionlike features to match investor and issuer needs in the international capital market. This exemplifies a recurring theme of international finance: because national markets are constrained, international markets evolve to intermediate between them, creating partial but not perfect linkages between them.

CONCEPTUAL QUESTIONS

1. What markets are encompassed in the term *global financial markets*?
2. What considerations might lead a country to fix its exchange rates rather than allowing the currency's value to be determined in free trading?
3. What does exchange-rate theory say about the predictability of exchange rates?
4. In what way are Eurocurrency interest rates linked to domestic interest rates?

5. In what way are Eurocurrency interest rates linked to one another?

6. Summarize the distinction between foreign-exchange forward contracts, futures, and options.

7. How are international syndicated loans transferred from one bank to another?

8. What factors influence the pricing of floating-rate notes?

9. What is a Euronote?

10. What are "Brady bonds"?

11. How does the Eurobond market differ from the Eurodollar market?

12. How does a medium-term note differ from a Eurobond?

13. What is a currency swap? How can it be used in conjunction with Eurobond financing?

14. What are the alternative approaches to hedging currency risk in an international equity portfolio?

15. What links spot and futures prices in the global commodities market?

16. What principles should guide a corporation in selecting the optimal composition of its debt?

17. What are the chief reasons for the use of hybrid (rather than conventional) financing techniques by corporations?

Glossary

Absolute Purchasing Power Parity A theory stating that the exchange rate equalizes the price of a market basket of goods in the two countries. Because the composition of market baskets and price indexes varies substantially across countries, and because many goods are not traded or are subject to tariffs, it is unlikely that absolute PPP will hold in the real world.

Adaptive Expectations A model of price behavior in which expectations of the future spot price are formed from a weighted average of the current spot price and lagged expected prices.

African Development Bank (AfDB) A regional development bank for Africa established in 1964 and located in Abidjan, Ivory Coast.

Agency Theory A theory of firms that deals with the conflict of interest between managers and stockholders.

Agent Bank A bank appointed in a syndicated credit to oversee the loan.

Allocational Efficiency A state in which resource allocation is optimal and further rearrangement of resources would not improve economic welfare.

American Depository Receipts (ADRs) Certificates, traded in the United States, that represent the ownership of foreign stocks.

American Option An option that can be exercised at any time prior to the contract's expiration date.

Amortizing Swap A swap designed to allow a floating-rate borrower with a preset amortization schedule to swap against fixed-rate interest.

Announcement Day The day on which a new issue of bonds is publicly announced, with invitation faxes sent to prospective underwriters and sellers.

Appreciation An increase in the market value of a currency with respect to a second currency or a real asset. The term is used in reference to a market price, as opposed to an official price or par value.

Arbitrage The simultaneous purchase and sale or lending and borrowing of two assets in order to profit from a price disparity.

Arbitrage-Pricing Theory (APT) A theory of asset pricing in which relative pricing on a set of assets adheres to a specific return-generating process.

Arm's Length Price The price that would prevail between unrelated parties.

Articles of Agreement Written specification of the powers and responsibilities vested in the International Monetary Fund by members of that international organization.

Asian Currency Unit A trading department of a bank in Singapore that has received a license from the monetary authorities in Singapore to deal in external currency deposits.

Asian Development Bank (ADB) A regional development bank for Asia formed in 1966 and located in Manila, the Philippines.

Asian Option See Average-Rate Option.

Asked Price The price at which a market-maker in an asset will sell the asset; the price sought by any prospective seller. See Offer Price.

Asset Allocation Determination of the optimal combination of stocks and bonds, domestic and international, in which to invest.

Asset Securitization A financing technique in which a company or bank dedicates the cash flows from selected assets to securing certain liabilities and then creates securities from those liabilities.

Assignment The transfer from one bank to another of the right to receive loan principal and interest from a borrower.

At-the-Money Option An option with a strike price equal to the current market price of the underlying asset.

Average-Rate Option An option on foreign exchange or commodity prices that pays off the difference between the option strike price and the average price of the underlying asset, this average calculated over the life of the option; also called an Asian Option.

Back Bond A Eurobond issued together with or at the same time as a warrant.

Backwardation A relationship in which spot or cash prices are higher than futures (or forward) prices.

Balance of Payments A financial statement prepared for a given country summarizing the flows of goods, services, and funds between the residents of that country and the residents of the rest of the world during a certain period of time. The balance of payments is prepared using the concept of double-entry bookkeeping, in which the total of debits equals the total of credits.

Balance of Trade The net of imports and exports of goods and services reported in the balance of payments.

Baker Plan Policy proposed to reduce the exposure of commercial banks to the debt of less-developed countries.

Banker's Acceptances Drafts drawn on a bank and accepted by the bank, meaning that the bank will honor them at maturity. The maturity date is determined from that date of the acceptance or drawing of the draft plus the period of time indicated in the draft.

Basic Balance The net of the following accounts in the balance of payments: exports and imports of goods and services, unilateral transfers, and long-term capital flows.

Basis The difference between cash and futures prices for the same commodity. Specifically, the cash price minus the futures price of a specific futures contract.

Basis Point One-hundredth of one percent, or 0.0001.

Basis-Rate Swap Similar to the structure of interest-rate swap, except that one floating rate is exchanged for a floating rate calculated on a different basis—for example, U.S.-dollar LIBOR for U.S. commercial paper.

Bear Market A market in which prices are declining.

Bearer Instrument A negotiable instrument payable on demand to the individual who holds the instrument. Title passes by delivery without endorsement.

Best Efforts A form of distribution of securities or loan participations in which the arranging banks make no commitment to purchase the claims at a certain price. The banks' only commitment is to use their "best efforts" to distribute the claims at a prearranged price.

Beta A statistical measure of the risk associated with an individual stock or stock portfolio. The beta of a stock or stock portfolio is the volatility of that stock's or stock portfolio's return relative to the volatility of the overall market return.

Bid Price The price at which a market-maker in an asset will buy the asset; the price sought by any prospective buyer.

Big Bang The 1986 deregulation of British financial markets in which the stock exchange was opened to foreign investment banks and a competitive commission structure was introduced.

BIS (Bank for International Settlements) An international bank located in Basle, Switzerland, which serves as a forum for monetary cooperation among the major central banks of Europe, the United States, and Japan. It monitors and collects data on international banking activity and serves as a clearing agent for the European Monetary System. The bank was originally founded in 1930 to handle the payment of German reparations after World War I.

Black Market Any private market that operates in contravention of government restrictions. For example, such a market may involve the exchange of currencies or goods at prices that are outside government-mandated levels, the trading of prohibited goods, or trading between individuals and/or institutions that are not approved by the government.

Bond Warrant Gives holder the right to buy an existing bond or a new bond at a fixed price during the life of warrant.

Bonds with Warrants Eurobonds are frequently issued with attached warrants that entitle the holder to engage in an additional financial transaction in the future. Some warrants can be exercised only by the bondholder, but others are detachable and separately tradable at times during their lives. The conventional type of warrant entitles the holder to purchase additional bonds of the same issuer at the same issue price and yield as the host bond.

Bons du Tresor (French Treasury Bills) Short-term instruments traded in an interbank market. There are two types: BTF, fixed-rate discount paper with maturity of 13, 26, or 52 weeks; and BTAN, two-to-five-year coupon securities.

Bonus Borrower's option for notes and underwritten standby (same as global note facility). A form of underwritten-Euronote-issuance facility.

Bought Deal A procedure for a new bond issue whereby the lead manager or managers buy the entire issue from the borrower on previously agreed fixed terms, including coupon level and issue price.

Brady Plan A debt-reduction policy for less-developed countries that entailed the conversion of bank loans into more acceptable assets.

Bretton Woods Agreement An agreement signed by 44 nations at Bretton Woods, New Hampshire, in July 1944; the basis of the post–World War II monetary system. Each participating nation declared a par value for its currency and agreed to intervene in foreign-exchange markets to maintain the exchange rate with respect to the U.S. dollar within plus or minus 1 percent of the par value. The United States agreed to the obligation to convert dollars to gold at $35 per ounce. The Bretton Woods fixed-exchange-rate system broke down in 1971.

Bridge Financing Medium-term financing, usually at fluctuating interest rates, that customarily takes the form of renewable overdrafts or discounting facilities. It is used as a continuing source of funds while the borrower obtains medium- or long-term fixed-rate financing, usually from sources other than commercial banks.

Bulldog Bonds Sterling-denominated bonds issued in the United Kingdom by nonresidents. Many are available in either registered or bearer form and most were issued in partly paid form. As with gilts, bulldogs follow an actual/365 day-count convention and pay interest twice a year.

Bund Issues Debt obligations of the Federal Republic of Germany. Most have maturities of 10 years, but there have been some longer-term issues. Bunds are underwritten by a fixed syndicate led by the Bundesbank, which includes both West German institutions and foreign-owned banks. Members of the syndicate are allotted fixed shares of each issue, with 20 percent allotted to foreign-owned banks.

Callable Swap A form of swaption in which the fixed-rate payer has the right to terminate the swap without penalty.

Call-Protection Warrant (or Wedding Warrant) Warrant to give holder an option to buy otherwise identical noncallable bonds. To exercise the warrant during the first half of its life, the holder must sell an equal amount of the original bonds back to the borrower; during the remainder of its life, when the bonds become callable, a warrant can be exercised for cash against purchase of a new bond.

Cap A contract on a short-term interest rate under which the writer of the cap pays the cap buyer the increased borrowing cost for any interest period (occurring prior to cap expiration) in which the short-term rate is fixed at a level above the ceiling rate specified in the cap.

Capital Account A category in the balance of payments of a country that measures the flows of financial and real investments across countries' borders.

Capital-Asset Pricing Model A theoretical model that relates the return on an asset to its risk. The risk is defined as the contribution of the asset to the volatility of the portfolio.

Capital Controls Governmental restrictions (such as prohibitions, taxes, quotas) on the acquisition of foreign assets or foreign liabilities by domestic citizens, or the acquisition of domestic assets or domestic liabilities by foreigners.

Capital Structure The combination of debt (of various kinds) and equity (of various kinds) in a firm's financing.

Capped Floating-Rate Notes Floating-rate notes on which the coupon payment varies directly with market rates when rates are below a predetermined level and payment remains at that level whenever rates exceed this value. Capped FRNs have been issued in U.S. dollars and deutschemarks.

Caption An option on a cap.

Cash-and-Carry Arbitrage An arbitrage-trading strategy in commodity markets that makes forward and futures prices equal to the current spot price plus the costs of carrying it forward to delivery.

Cedel One of two main clearing systems in the Eurobond market. Cedel S.A. is based in Luxembourg and began operations in January 1971.

Central Bank The institution with the primary responsibility to control the growth of its country's money stock. It might also have regulatory powers over commercial banks and sometimes over other financial institutions, and it usually serves as the fiscal agent for the government.

Certificates of Deposit (CDs) Negotiable instruments issued by a bank and payable to the bearer. CDs pay a stated amount of interest and mature on a stated date but may be bought and sold daily in a secondary market.

Charting Interpreting foreign-exchange-market activity and predicting future movements, usually over a short period, from graphic depictions of prices and volumes. It is a primary tool of technical analysis.

Clearing House The organization that assures the financial integrity of futures and options markets by guaranteeing obligations among its clearing members. It registers, monitors, matches, and guarantees trades, and carries out the financial settlement of futures and options transactions. The clearing house can be part of an exchange or can be a separate corporate entity.

Clearing House Interbank Payments System (CHIPS) An automated clearing facility operated by the New York Clearing House Association that processes international transfers among its members. It moves dollars among more than 100 New York financial institutions—mostly major U.S. banks, branches of foreign banks, and Edge Act subsidiaries of out-of-state banks.

Clearing System An institutional arrangement for transferring securities and payment between sellers and buyers subsequent to the establishment of a trading price.

Closing Day The day on which new bonds from the borrower are delivered against payment by members of a bond-issuing syndicate.

Comanager A bank ranking just below that of lead manager in a syndicated Eurocredit or international bond issue. The status of comanager usually indicates a larger share in the loan or a larger bond allotment, and a larger share in the fees, than banks of lower rank. Comanagers may also assist the lead managers in assessing the market or deciding borrower terms.

Collar Swap A swap of fixed-rate dollars against floating-rate dollars with the latter having a maximum and minimum return.

Commercial Paper A short-term unsecured debt instrument issued by a corporation and sold at a discount from its maturity value.

Commitment Fee A fee paid on the unused portion of a credit line.

Commodity Fund An entity in which funds contributed by a number of people are pooled together to trade futures and option contracts under professional management.

Commodity Futures Trading Commission (CFTC) The U.S. federal agency with authority to oversee futures trading.

Comparative Advantage The relative advantage of a country in producing goods and services.

Conditional Expectation The expected value of a variable, conditional on certain information being known.

Conditional Variance The calculation of variance for an economic variable that is conditioned upon a given information set.

Conditionality The International Monetary Fund's practice of requiring members to adopt changes in their domestic economic policies as a condition for receiving balance-of-payments loans from the fund.

Contango Market A market in which futures prices are higher for distant contracts than for nearby delivery months—just the opposite of a backwardation market.

Continuous Tender Panel (CTP) A method of Euronote distribution that combines a dominant note-placing role of the arranger with competitive bidding by facility underwriters against a margin, usually related to LIBOR (or the "strike-offered yield"). The strike-offered yield is set by the arranger. The members of the underwriting group may obtain the protection of being allocated a quantity of notes in proportion to their underwriting commitment.

Convenience Yield The implied yield or nonpecuniary return from holding a commodity. It is also a measure of the degree of backwardation in a market.

Conversion A trading strategy that locks in an arbitrage profit by combining a long put and a short call with the same strike price and expiration date with a long position in the underlying asset.

Convertibility Freedom to exchange a currency without government restrictions or controls.

Convertible Bond A fixed-interest security that is convertible into the borrower's common stock under stipulated conditions. The difference between the price of ordinary shares at the time of the issue of the bonds and the rate at which they can be converted is the conversion premium. The yield on convertibles is usually lower than that on comparable straight bonds, reflecting the value of the conversion option.

Correspondent Bank A bank, located in one geographic area, that accepts deposits from a bank in another region and provides services on behalf of this other bank. Internationally, many banks maintain one account with a correspondent bank in each major country so as to be able to make payments in all major currencies. Correspondent banks are usually established on a reciprocal basis, with the two banks maintaining local currency accounts with each other.

Cost of Capital The weighted rate of return expected by the various parties financing the firm. Bondholders expect a return equivalent to the market interest rate on debt, whereas equity holders expect a return that is a function of dividends received and capital gains as the stock appreciates in value, adjusted for risk. The cost of capital is traditionally used as a hurdle rate that projects must yield in order to be accepted by the firm.

Cost of Carry The costs associated with holding (or carrying) a commodity or an asset. These include financing costs, storage costs, and insurance costs.

Cost-plus Loan Pricing The interest rate on a loan is expressed as a function of some publicly known cost-of-funds measure, such as LIBOR (London Interbank Offered Rate).

Country Risk A broad spectrum of risk, including political as well as economic risk, caused by potential conflict between corporate goals and the national aspirations of host countries. The essential element in country risk is some form of government action preventing the fulfillment of a contract or agreement. Country-risk ratings are assessed annually in publications such as *Euromoney* and *Institutional Investor*.

Covenant Agreement in a syndicated loan or bond contract concerning the borrower's future conduct. Such a covenant may involve, for example, the agreement to maintain a given balance-sheet ratio in the future, or the agreement to adhere to an IMF program.

Covered-Interest Arbitrage Borrowing one currency, converting the proceeds into another currency, where it is invested, and simultaneously selling this other currency forward against the initial currency. Covered interest arbitrage takes advantage of (and in practice quickly eliminates) any temporary discrepancies between the forward rate and the interest-rate differential of two currencies.

Covered-Interest Differential The deviation from interest-rate parity.

Covering Protecting the value of the future proceeds of an international transaction, usually by buying or selling the proceeds in the forward market.

Crawling-Peg System An exchange-rate system in which the exchange rate is adjusted frequently and deliberately, perhaps every few weeks, usually to reflect prevailing rates of inflation. The system has been used by high-inflation countries such as Brazil, Colombia, and Turkey.

Cross Rate An exchange rate between two currencies, neither of which is the U.S. dollar. A cross rate is usually constructed from the individual exchange rates of the two currencies with respect to the U.S. dollar.

Cross Hedging Hedging a commodity by using a futures contract on a different but related commodity. A cross hedge is based on the premise that the price movements of the two commodities are related.

Cross-currency Warrants Bonds with warrants exercisable into bonds denominated in a currency other than that of the host bond.

Cross-default Provision A provision in a loan agreement that allows the lender to declare the loan immediately payable and to terminate any further extension of credit if the borrower defaults on any other debt.

Currency Band A band within which a currency is allowed to fluctuate on both sides of its official parity. The central bank of the country concerned intervenes in order to maintain the value of the currency within the permissible range.

Currency Basket A method for determining the value of a financial asset or currency as a weighted average of market exchange rates. The weights in this average are often defined to be specific quantities of currencies, hence the term "currency basket." A basket can contain two or more currency components, but the number of currencies included is usually limited by practical considerations.

Currency Cocktail Bonds Bonds denominated in a portfolio of currencies.

Currency Swap A contractual obligation entered into by two parties to deliver a sum of money in one currency against a sum of money in another currency at stated intervals. Typically, the exchange of a fixed interest rate (and principal) in some currency for a floating rate (such as LIBOR), and principal, in U.S. dollars.

Current Yield The interest yield on a bond when calculated as the annual amount of money paid on coupons, divided by the current market price of the bond.

Daily Resettlement Also known as marking to market, the requirement in a futures contract that traders realize gains and losses each trading day.

Debt-Equity Swap Process whereby creditors exchange bank debt for an equity interest in assets owned by the debtors. This activity has been extensively conducted by banks holding debt of less-developed countries.

Deferred-Coupon Issues Bonds (or floating-rate notes) in which a predetermined number of coupon payments is deferred to later payment dates, usually for tax purposes.

Deferred Swap A swap arranged now with a specified fixed-rate which will commence at a future date.

Delayed-Cap Floating-Rate Notes Similar structure to capped FRNs, except that the coupon-cap limitation is not effective immediately. The typical grace period is three years.

Delta The ratio of a change in the option price to a small change in the price of the asset on which the option is written. The partial derivative of the option price with respect to the price of the underlying asset.

Demand Deposit Funds in a current account (a checking account) that can be withdrawn at any time without notice, depending on local regulations. Demand deposits might or might not be interest-bearing deposits.

Deposit Notes Medium-term notes issued by banks.

Depreciation A gradual decrease in the market value of a currency with respect to a second currency or a real asset. The term is used in reference to a market price, as opposed to an official price or par value.

Derivative Instruments Contracts or tradable instruments that bear a contractual relationship to some underlying cash instrument or index.

Devaluation A sudden decrease in the market value of a currency with respect to a second currency or a real asset. The term is used in reference to an official price, such as a fixed exchange rate or a declared par value, as opposed to a market price.

Differential Swap A swap in which the net payment between the counterparties is the difference between a floating rate in one currency and a floating rate in another currency. All payments are made in a single currency, such as the U.S. dollar, and no principal is exchanged at maturity.

Dingo A zero-coupon Australian dollar issue created by stripping an Australian government bond.

Direct Investment Cross-border equity investment with control, through the purchase of stock, the acquisition of a foreign firm, or the establishment of a new subsidiary.

Direct Quotation A rate of exchange quoted in units of foreign currency for each unit of the domestic currency.

Discount The amount by which a currency is cheaper for future delivery than for immediate or spot delivery. If sterling is selling for US$2.3940 on the spot market but at US$2.3920 for delivery in three months, then it is selling at a 20-point discount.

Discount Margin A term usually used in the context of floating-rate notes, the discount margin is a measure of the effective spread, relative to LIBOR, that an investor would earn if he bought the FRN at some price on a particular date and held it to maturity.

Disintermediation A process in which savers withdraw deposits from financial intermediaries (like commercial banks and thrift institutions) and lend directly to investors and consumers by purchasing debt instruments such as commercial paper, bonds, and Treasury bills.

Divergence Indicator One aspect of the European Monetary System that measures the departure of a country's economic policies from the European Economic Community "average." The measure of divergence is based exclusively on the movement of a country's exchange rate with respect to the ECU, which represents the community average exchange

rate. In the event of excessive divergence, the country is expected to alter economic policy to conform with the EEC average.

Divergence Threshold The critical value of each European Monetary System member's divergence indicator that, when reached, establishes the presumption that domestic economic policies will be adjusted.

Dragon Bond A Eurobond issued and distributed in Asia, and generally placed with non-Japanese investors.

Drawdown Swap A swap from floating- to fixed-rate interest designed to coincide with a planned drawdown schedule typical of some project financing.

Drop-Lock FRN An FRN carrying a higher-than-otherwise-justified minimum coupon. The "drop-lock" feature would trigger an automatic conversion to a fixed rate if interest rates fell below the minimum coupon rate for a predetermined period.

DTB Deutsche Termin Borse, the German futures and options exchange in Frankfurt.

Dual-Currency Issue An issue denominated in one currency with a coupon and/or repayment of principal at a fixed rate in another currency—for example, an issue denominated and serviced in yen, but redeemed in dollars.

Duration A measure of a bond's price sensitivity to interest-rate changes. The duration of a bond is commonly defined as the weighted average of the maturities of the bond's coupon and principal repayment cash flows, where the weights are the fractions of the bond's price represented by the cash flows in each time period.

Economic and Monetary Union (EMU) A common European currency, central bank, and monetary policy that melds the separate European economies into a single unit (like the United States) that can "enable Europe to negotiate with the U.S. and Japan as an equal, to compete more effectively and to guarantee monetary stability."

ECU See European Currency Unit.

Effective Exchange Rate A rate measuring the overall nominal value of a currency in the foreign-exchange market. It is calculated by forming a weighted average of bilateral exchange rates, using a weighting scheme that reflects the importance of each country's trade with the home country.

Efficient Portfolio One of a set of portfolios that provides the highest level of return for a given level of risk.

Elasticity The degree of responsiveness of one variable to changes in another.

Entrepot Financial Centers World financial centers that play the role of bringing foreign lenders and foreign borrowers together. The countries in which these centers are located might or might not be capital exporters or importers, but they are channels through which international funds pass.

Equity Risk Premium The excess return, over the risk-free rate, for holding equity.

Eurobanks Financial intermediaries that simultaneously bid for time deposits and make loans in a currency or currencies other than that of the country in which they are located.

Eurobond A bond underwritten by an international syndicate of banks and marketed internationally in countries other than the country of the currency in which it is denominated. The issue is thus not subject to national restrictions.

Euroclear One of two main clearing systems in the Eurobond market. Euroclear Clearance System Limited began operations in December, 1968. It is located in Brussels and managed by Morgan Guaranty.

Euro CP (Eurocommercial paper) Bearer-form, short-term, general-obligation notes issued by corporations, banks, and governments outside the country of the currency. A generic term for Euronotes issued on a nonunderwritten basis.

Eurocredits Intermediate-term loans of Eurocurrencies made by banking syndicates to corporate and government borrowers.

Eurocurrency Market The money market for borrowing and lending currencies that are held in the form of time deposits in banks located outside the countries in which those currencies are issued as legal tender.

Eurodollar A dollar-denominated deposit in a bank outside the United States or at International Banking Facility (IBF) in the United States.

Euronote A short-term fully negotiable bearer promissory note, usually issued at a discount to face value of one, three, or six month's maturity.

Euronote Facility A facility that allows the borrower to issue short-term discount notes via a variety of distribution methods, under the umbrella of a medium-term commitment from a group of banks. These agree to purchase notes at a predetermined rate (or "maximum margin"), usually in relation to LIBOR, if the notes cannot be placed with investors at or under that rate.

European Bank for Reconstruction and Development (EBRD) A regional development bank for the transitional socialist economies of Eastern Europe, established in 1990 and located in London.

European Currency Unit (ECU) A currency basket composed of specific quantities of the currencies of European Community members. The ECU is used as part of the system's divergence indicator and provides a unit of account used to value members' exchange-reserve assets and private instruments such as ECU Eurobonds.

European Economic Community (EEC) (also called simply European Community, or EC) An economic association of European countries founded by the Treaty of Rome in 1957. The goals of the EEC were the removal of trade barriers among member countries, the formation of a common commercial policy toward non-EEC countries, and the removal of barriers restricting competition and the free mobility of factors of production. Original members were West Germany, France, Belgium, Luxembourg, the Netherlands, and Italy. The United Kingdom, Ireland, and Denmark joined the EEC in 1973, Greece in 1981, and Spain and Portugal in 1986.

European Free Trade Association (EFTA) Common regulations for tariffs and trade established in 1959 by Austria, Denmark, Norway, Portugal, Sweden, Switzerland, and the United Kingdom.

European Investment Bank (EIB) A regional development bank focusing on intra-EC development, established in 1958 by the members of the European Community.

European Option An option that can be exercised only on the option's expiration date.

European Monetary System (EMS) A structure formed on March 13, 1979, of agreements government the exchange-market activities of participating members of the European Economic Community. Included in the arrangement are a parity grid and a divergence-indicator system. These agreements currently require certain members to closely manage the exchange values of their currencies relative to other members. Ultimately, the agreements envision the creation of a European central bank and monetary unification.

Exchange Controls Governmental restrictions (such as prohibitions, taxes, quotas, or government-set prices) on the purchase of foreign currencies by domestic citizens or on the purchase of the local domestic currency by foreigners.

Exchange-Rate Overshooting Occurs when exchange-rate changes are in excess of some given standard of volatility.

Exchange-Rate Mechanism (ERM) The particular system by which the central banks agree to intervention levels, or upper and lower rates for each currency relative to one another (ERM "floors" or "ceilings"), at which the central banks will conduct market transactions to keep currencies within the limits.

Exchange Risk The risk assumed by a party to an international transaction in which the party could incur an exchange loss as a result of currency movements.

Export-Import Bank An independent agency of the U.S. government that was established in 1934 to stimulate U.S. foreign trade. The Exim Bank supports commercial banks that are financing exports and provides direct financing, loan guarantees, and insurance to foreign buyers purchasing U.S. goods. Similar motivations exist in other countries.

Extendable/Retractable FRN The holder of the FRN can extend or retract its maturity at his option. The investor is given flexibility; the borrower hopes to get cheaper money.

External Debt Public debt owed to nonresidents.

Extrapolative Expectations A pricing model in which expectations are formed such that a change in the current spot price will lead to a further change in the same direction.

Face Value The monetary amount paid on a bond at redemption (excluding any terminal coupon payment). The face value is printed on the bond certificate.

Fair Value The theoretical value of an option or futures contract derived from a mathematical valuation model. It is also referred to as the no-arbitrage value.

Federal Funds Market Federal funds are deposits held by commercial banks at the Federal Reserve System. The federal funds market is the interbank market for borrowing and lending these deposits. Because reserve requirements of commercial banks are satisfied by federal funds, banks with deposits in excess of required reserves will lend the excess deposits to banks with a reserve shortage at a market-determined interest rate, the federal funds rate.

Filter Fule A rule for buying and selling currencies based on the premise that once a movement in a currency's exchange rate has surpassed a given percentage movement, it will continue to move in the same direction. The rule might be that if the currency's price rises by x percent, the trader should buy and hold until the price drops at least x percent from a previous high, in which case the currency should be sold.

Fisher Effect The theory that interest rates in any country rise by an amount approximately equal to the anticipated rate of inflation. If the basic rate of interest is 3 percent a year when there is no inflation, and if inflation is then anticipated to equal 5 percent a year, the rate of interest will rise to approximately 8 percent a year.

Fixed-Exchange-Rate System A system in which the values of various countries' currencies are tied to one major currency (such as the U.S. dollar), gold, or special drawing rights. The term should not be taken literally because fluctuations within a range of 1 percent or 2 percent on either side of the fixed rate are usually permitted in such a system.

Fixed-Rate Currency Swap Exchange between two counterparties of fixed-rate interest in one currency for fixed-rate interest in the other. This swap requires an optional exchange of principal, the ongoing exchange of interest, and the reexchange of principal amounts at maturity.

Floating-Exchange-Rate System A system in which the values of various currencies relative to each other are established by the forces of supply and demand in the market without intervention by the governments involved. In practice, most floating rates are really "managed floating" with periodic ad hoc intervention by central banks.

Floating-Rate CD Certificate of deposit issued by a commercial bank, typically in the Eurocurrency market, paying a floating interest rate like a floating-rate note.

Floating-Rate Notes (FRN) A medium- to long-term security with the quarterly or semiannual interest rate linked to the three- or six-month London interbank rate; the rate is refixed every three or six months at a stated margin above or below the interbank rate.

Floor A contract on a short-term interest rate under which the writer of the floor pays the floor buyer the amount by which the reference rate falls below the floor rate for any interest period.

Fonds D'Etat (French Government Bonds) The most liquid sector of the French bond market, accounting for 60 to 70 percent of all trading activity and around 30 percent of total volume outstanding. Maturities range from 7 to 15 years, and are quoted on a 30/365 day-count basis. Most government bonds are straight bonds with annual coupons, although some floating-rate notes have been issued.

Foreign Bond A long-term security issued by a borrower in the national market of another country. Underwritten by a syndicate from one country alone and sold on that country's capital market, the bond is denominated in the currency of the country in which it is sold

Foreign-Exchange Broker An individual who introduces the two parties in a currency or deposit transaction to each other. The parties could be a buyer and a seller of foreign currencies or a borrower and a lender of a given currency. The broker charges a fee for this service. Brokers seldom take a position for themselves; they only arrange for transactions among other parties.

Foreign-Exchange Exposure The risk that a firm will gain or lose as a result of changes in exchange rates.

Forward Discount Phrase used to describe a currency whose forward price is cheaper than its spot price.

Forward-Exchange Contract An agreement to exchange, at a specified future date, currencies of different countries at a specified contractual rate (the forward rate). Foreign currency traded for settlement beyond two working or business days from today.

Forward-Exchange Rate Price for a currency to be delivered at a certain date in the future.

Forward Option A forward-exchange contract (as opposed to an option contract) that differs from an ordinary forward contract only in that it has a variable, rather than a fixed, maturity date. The buyer of a forward option may, for example, be entitled to take delivery of a currency at any time during a given month as opposed to a specific day.

Forward-Forward FX Swap (or Forward FX Swap) A pair of forward-exchange deals involving a forward purchase and a forward sale of a currency, simultaneously entered into but of different maturities.

Forward Rate The price agreed to by the two parties to a forward-exchange contract.

Forward Swap A forward contract to engage in a swap on preset terms on a particular date in the future; also called a deferred swap.

Forward-Rate Agreement (FRA) A cash-settled interbank forward contract on interest rates. The seller pays the buyer the difference if the interest rate has risen above the agreed rate. In the reverse case, the buyer pays the seller.

Fundamental Analysis A method of analyzing and predicting price movements using information about supply and demand.

Fungible Securities Securities that are not individually designated by serial numbers as belonging to a particular owner. Instead, a clearing system or depository institution credits owners with a given number of a particular bond issue (or other security issue). The owner has title to, say, 50 bonds, but not to 50 specific bonds with designated serial numbers.

Futures Contract A highly standardized foreign-exchange contract written against the exchange clearing house for a fixed number of foreign currency units and for delivery on a fixed date. Because of the high level of standardization, futures contracts can be traded readily in a secondary market.

Futures Option Contract A contract giving the buyer the right to buy or sell a designated futures contract at a certain exercise price through contract expiration.

Gamma The ratio of a change in the option delta to a small change in the price of the asset on which the option is written. The second partial derivative of the option price with respect to the price of the underlying asset.

Gensaki A repurchase agreement of three months or less that is generally collateralized by government bonds, bank debentures, or municipal bonds. Securities companies are the largest fund raisers in the market. The main purchasers are business corporations, pension funds, and financial institutions. Nonresidents are major players in the gensaki market.

Geographic Arbitrage The trading practice of buying a currency in one geographical market and selling it in another in which the price is higher.

German Treasury Notes (U-Schaetze) Zero-coupon securities sold by the Bundesbank under its open-market policy. Maturities may range up to two years.

Gilts (U.K. Government Bonds) Bonds issued as direct obligations of the government of the United Kingdom. Original maturities are 5 to 30 years, although there are a few perpetuals.

Glass-Steagall Act U.S. law separating commercial from investment banking, preventing commercial banks from underwriting corporate bonds and equities.

Global Bond A temporary debt certificate issued by a Eurobond borrower, representing the borrower's total indebtedness. The global bond will subsequently be replaced by the individual bearer bonds.

Global Note Facility The banks' medium-term underwriting commitment is available to back up both the Euronote and a U.S. commercial paper issue. Should the issuer be unable to roll over the U.S. CP, this will trigger a Euronote issuance process by the tender panel. Bridging finance between the time of failed U.S. CP rollover and provision of funds from the Euronote facility is provided by a "swingline."

Gold Standard A monetary agreement under which national currencies are backed by gold and the gold is utilized for international payments. Also called the Gold Exchange Standard.

Gold Warrants Bonds with detachable warrants to buy gold.

Gray Market A forward market for newly issued bonds that takes the form of forward contracting between market participants during the period between the announcement day of a new issue and the day that final terms of the bond issue are signed. Bonds are traded at prices stated at a discount or premium to the (now unknown) issue price.

Gross National Product (GNP) The total market value of all goods and services that are produced in an economy in one year.

GUN (Grantor Underwritten Note) A floating-rate note facility similar to a Euronote facility whereby a group of banks (grantors) commit to purchase any notes put back to them by investors on any FRN interest-rate fixing date.

Hard Currency A strong, freely convertible currency. A strong currency is one that is not expected to devalue in the foreseeable future.

Harmless Warrants A callable host bond with a detachable bond warrant. The warrant can be exercised over the entire life of the bond under the following conditions: (1) Until the call date, the warrant can be exercised only by surrendering the associated bonds. (2) After the call date, the warrant can be exercised independently. Harmless warrants enable the borrower to prevent the exercise of the warrant from increasing the borrower's outstanding debt.

Heaven and Hell Bonds Bonds in which redemption is quoted as a function of the difference between a specified exchange rate and the spot rate at maturity. This can be viewed as a bond with a long-dated option on the principal redemption. Redemption potentially varies between zero and a predetermined maximum value.

Hedging The process of reducing the variation in the value (from price fluctuations) of a total portfolio. Hedging is accomplished by adding to an original portfolio items such as spot assets or liabilities, forward contracts, futures contracts, or options contracts in such a way that the total variation of the new portfolio is smaller than that of the original portfolio.

HKFE The Hong Kong Futures Exchange.

Host Bond A Eurobond issue to which is attached a warrant or similar instrument.

Hot Money Speculative bank deposits that are moved around the international money markets to take advantage of currency and interest-rate movements.

IADB (Inter-American Development Bank) A supranational organization that finances economic development in the Americas.

IBRD (International Bank for Reconstruction and Development) See World Bank.

IMM (The International Money Market of the Chicago Mercantile Exchange) The world's largest market for foreign currency and Eurodollar futures trading.

Implied Forward Rate The rate of interest at which a borrowing or lending transaction of a shorter maturity may be rolled over to yield an equivalent interest rate with a borrowing or lending transaction of longer maturity.

Implied Volatility The future price volatility of an asset that the market currently expects, based on the current price of a particular option contract.

In-the-Money Option An option is "in the money" if it has intrinsic value. A call option is in the money if the current asset price is above the option's strike price; a put option is in the money if the current asset price is below the option's price.

Index-Linked Bonds Bonds in which redemption is quoted as a function of the change in the value of a stock-exchange index over time. Essentially a bond with a long-dated equity option or forward contract written on the principal amount.

Indexed Currency Option Note (ICON) A fixed-rate issue carrying a coupon considerably higher than usual. For this, the investor assumes a currency risk—that is, if the bond currency falls below a certain level, the bond holder will receive a reduced repayment of principal (according to a formula). This option can be stripped off and resold.

Indexing The practice of adjusting asset prices, liabilities, or payments by some measure of inflation to preserve the purchasing power of the original amounts.

Indicator Rules Publicly announced rules that link adjustments in the par values of exchange rates to movements in economic statistics. Par values adjust automatically under this exchange-rate-management policy, while official intervention holds market rates in the neighborhood of the par value.

Indirect Quotation A rate of exchange quoted in units of domestic currency for each unit of foreign currency.

Initial Margin The amount of money that customers must put up when establishing a futures or options position to guarantee their contract obligations.

Interest Equalization Tax A tax imposed on U.S. residents who bought foreign securities between 1963 and 1974. The tax, designed to discourage foreign investment, reduced the after-tax yields on such bonds to the level of yields on U.S. bonds.

Interest-Rate Parity The process that ensures that the annualized forward premium or discount equals the interest-rate differentials on equivalent securities in two currencies.

Interest-Rate Swap An exchange between two counterparties of fixed-rate interest for floating-rate interest in the same currency. The principal amount relating to the underlying assets or liabilities is not exchanged.

International Bank for Reconstruction and Development See World Bank.

International Banking Facilities (IBFs) Legal vehicles that enable bank offices in the United States to accept time deposits in dollars or in other currencies from foreign customers, free of reserve requirements, deposit-insurance fees, and other limitations. Designed to compete with the Eurodollar market, an IBF is a division of an existing U.S. banking operation that is allowed to conduct Eurocurrencylike business but (unlike a Caribbean Eurobank branch) is prohibited from issuing negotiable certificates of deposit. IBFs were allowed by the Federal Reserve Board beginning December 1981, and have since become popular with U.S.-based foreign banks.

International Bonds Collective term referring to both Eurobonds and foreign bonds.

International CAPM Models that account for the influence of world as well as domestic markets on the returns of securities.

International Development Association (IDA) An affiliate of the World Bank (IBRD) established to make long-term low-interest loans to developing countries.

International Finance Corporation (IFC) An affiliate of the World Bank (IBRD) established to make equity investments and development loans to the private sector in developing countries, in forms that can be sold to other investors and/or converted into equity.

International Fisher Effect The theory that the interest-rate differential between two currencies approximately equals the expected rate of change in the exchange rate.

International Monetary Fund (IMF) An international institution created to provide a forum in which nations can jointly examine each other's economic policies, discuss the operation of the international monetary system, and negotiate revisions in international monetary relations. The objectives of the Fund include supervising the exchange-market intervention of member nations, providing the financing needed by members to overcome short-term payments imbalances, and encouraging monetary cooperation and international trade among nations.

International Monetary Market (IMM) A centralized auction market in Chicago in which currency and financial futures contracts are traded. Part of the Chicago Mercantile Exchange.

Intervention The buying and selling of currencies by central banks to influence the exchange rate.

Intrinsic Value The amount by which an option is in the money (see In-the-Money Option).

Issue Price The price, stated as a percentage of face value, at which a new bond is announced. It is used as a basis for calculating investment-banking fees but does not necessarily represent the actual price paid by any investor.

Issuer-Set Margin A note-distribution method whereby the issuer sets the note margin, usually in relation to LIBOR. Underwriters are guaranteed a certain proportion of notes in proportion to their underwriting commitments. Notes not taken up or sold by the underwriters are placed with the facility arranger.

Law of Comparative Advantage According to this law, a country will specialize in producing and will export those goods that it can produce cheaply relative to the costs of producing them in foreign countries. It will import those goods that it can produce only at relatively high cost.

Lead Manager The commercial or investment bank with the primary responsibility for organizing a syndicated bank credit or bond issue. This includes the recruitment of additional lending or underwriting banks, the negotiation of terms with the borrower, and the assessment of market conditions.

Lending Margin The fixed percentage above the reference rate paid by a borrower in a rollover credit or on a floating-rate note.

Letter of Credit A letter issued by a bank, usually at the request of an importer, indicating that the opening bank or another will honor drafts if they are accompanied by specified documents under specified conditions.

Leveraged Buy-Outs (LBOs) The purchase of a controlling interest in a company by means of a large proportion of bank loans.

LIBOR (London Interbank Offered Rate) The interest rate at which prime banks offer dollar deposits to other prime banks in London. This rate is often used as the basis for pricing Eurodollar and other Eurocurrency loans. The lender and the borrower agree to a markup over the LIBOR, and the total of LIBOR plus the markup is the effective interest rate for the loan.

LIFFE (London International Financial Futures Exchange) A London exchange where Eurodollar and other futures and futures-style options are traded.

Listing The formal process required in order to have the price of a bond or other security regularly quoted on a stock exchange. Eurobonds are usually listed to that they can be purchased by those institutional investors who are constrained to invest in listed securities.

Lombard Rate The rate of interest charged on a "Lombard loan"; that is, an advance against the collateral of specific listed securities in Europe.

Long Position To have greater inflows than outflows of a given currency. In foreign-exchange operations, long positions arise when the amount of a given currency purchased is greater than the amount sold.

M1 A measure of the money supply that is composed of demand deposits at commercial banks and currency in circulation.

Maastricht Treaty A treaty agreed to by the 12 EC member countries in December 1991 at Maastricht, Holland, in which the mechanisms by which the EC would proceed toward European Monetary Union (EMU), a common currency, central bank, and monetary policy, by 1999 (at the latest). The treaty also provided for agreement for all member countries to adopt various EC social policies (the U.K. exempted itself).

Managed Float (Dirty Float) A floating-exchange-rate system in which some government intervention still takes place. A government could announce that it will let its currency float, but it might secretly allow its central bank to intervene in the exchange market to avoid too much appreciation or depreciation.

Management Fee The portion of total investment-banking fees accruing to the managing banks in a bond issue. In a syndicated credit, the fee paid to the managing bank or banks for organizing the loan.

Mandate In the context of securities distribution, a formal authorization by an issuer to a bank that allows the bank to negotiate term and conditions of the prospective issue.

Margin The amount of money and/or securities that must be posted as a security bond to ensure performance on a contract. In the futures market, both short and long positions post margin. This ensures that the side with a daily cash-flow loss will meet its payment obligation.

Marking to Market The daily adjustment of an open futures contract to reflect profits and losses on the contract. All futures positions are marked to market using closing (or settlement) futures prices.

Market-Maker An institution that stands willing to buy or sell an asset at some price, or an institution that deals so frequently and in such volume in an asset that it makes it possible for others to buy or sell that asset at almost any time.

Market Portfolio A well-diversified portfolio of risky securities with little or no unsystematic risk, and little or no scope for further risk reduction by means of diversification.

Martingale A price series forms a martingale with drift k if, conditional on today's information, the expected price for next period is equal to $(1 + k)$ times the current price.

Master Agreement Used in swaps and other derivative contracts, the bilateral agreement provides a set of terms applicable to any such transaction between the parties. Parties can tailor the transaction by appending specific terms to the master agreement.

MATIF Marché à Terme des Instruments Financiers, the French futures and options exchange.

Medium-Term Notes Notes issued under a program that authorizes a group of dealer banks to seek investors for amounts up to a specified limit. The notes are often tailored to investors' needs, and may have a wide variety of features such as maturity, currency of denomination, and embedded options.

Merchant Bank A specialist bank that, apart from carrying out a banking business, also acts as an advisor to companies, including assisting with the flotation of new issues of shares on the stock market.

MOF (Multiple-Option Facility) Broader than the classic underwritten Euronote facility (RUF) in that the banks' medium-term commitment is to back up not only the issuance of Euronotes, but also a wide range of other short-term instruments such as bankers' acceptances and advances in a variety of currencies.

Momentum Analysis A technique used to predict short-term exchange-rate changes. Momentum models study the direction and impetus behind past exchange-rate movements to predict future movements.

Monetary Approach An analysis of balance of payments or exchange rates that emphasizes the factors affecting money supply and money demand.

Monetary Base The amount of central-bank liabilities that will potentially serve to satisfy the required reserves of the commercial banking system. In the United States, the monetary base consists of deposits at the Federal Reserve and currency in circulation.

Money Market A financial market for short-term securities; a market in which short-term borrowings and investments are made. Negotiable certificates of deposit, acceptances, and commercial paper are some of the instruments commonly used in the money market.

Money-Market Hedge The reduction of exchange risk by means of debt. Typically a foreign-currency cash inflow is matched with a maturing debt so that cash inflows and cash outflows in a foreign currency are offset.

Money-Back Warrants A bond warrant redeemable for a set amount at different times during the life of the warrant, ensuring the investor a minimum value for the warrant.

Most-Favored-Nation Clause In international business treaties, a provision against tariff discrimination between two or more nations. It provides that each participant will automatically extend to other signatories all tariff reductions that are offered to nonmember nations.

Multicurrency Clause A clause that gives a Eurocurrency borrower the right to switch from one currency to another at an interest-reset date.

Multiple-Exchange-Rate System A system under which a government sets different exchange rates for different transactions.

Naked Warrants An issue of warrants without any host bond.

Negative Pledge A contractual promise by a borrower in a syndicated loan or a bond issue not to undertake some future action. One typical negative pledge is that future new creditors will not be given rights that existing creditors do not have.

Neutral Price On a floating-rate note, the price on the next coupon date that would give a return over the period from settlement to the next coupon date equal to LIBOR plus the discount margin.

Nikkei Index A measure of the level of stock prices on the Tokyo Stock Exchange.

Novation The discharge of one obligation in a debtor/creditor relationship and the creation of an entirely new one.

Offer Price The price at which a market-maker will buy an asset; the price sought by any prospective buyer. See Asked Price.

Offering Day The day on which final terms of a bond issue are signed between the managing banks and the borrower.

Offering Circular A document giving a description of a new securities issue, as well as a description of the firm or entity making the issue.

Official Reserves Government owned international assets that include convertible foreign currencies, gold, and Special Drawing Rights.

Offshore Banking Banking activity that accepts deposits and makes loans in currencies other than that of the country of location of the bank. In other words, Eurocurrency banking.

Open Interest The total number of futures or options contracts on a given commodity that have not yet been offset by an opposite futures or option transaction or fulfilled by delivery of the commodity or exercise of the option. Each open contract has both a buyer and a seller.

Open Position A net long or short foreign currency or futures position whose value will change with a change in the foreign-exchange rate or futures prices.

Open-Market Operations Purchases or sales of securities or other assets by the central bank. Such actions change the monetary base. Usually the term is restricted to purchases and sales of domestic assets (such as government bonds), whereas purchases and sales of foreign exchange are called

"foreign-exchange intervention." Either activity changes the monetary base in a similar way.

Operational Efficiency A market in which transactions are carried out with minimum transaction costs.

Option Contract The right to buy or sell a specific quantity of a specific asset at a fixed price at or before a specified future date.

Option Premium The price of an option, which the option buyer pays and the option seller receives.

Option Writer The person who sells or grants an option in return for a premium, and who is obligated to perform if the option holder exercises his right under the option contract.

Optional-Date Forward Contract A forward-exchange contract in which the rate is fixed but the maturity is open, within a specified range of dates.

Organization for Economic Cooperation and Development (OECD) An organization that provides for intergovernmental discussion among 24 industrialized countries in the fields of economic and social policy. It also collects and publishes data and makes short-term economic forecasts of its member countries.

Out-of-the-Money Option An option that has no intrinsic value: a call option with a strike price above the current asset price or a put option with a strike price below the current asset price.

Outright Forward Rate A forward-exchange rate expressed in terms of the amount of one currency required to buy a unit of another currency.

Overnight In the foreign-exchange market, term used to describe a swap transaction for value today with the reverse transaction taking place the next business day. In the Eurocurrency market, term used to describe a loan or deposit for value today with maturity on the next business day.

Parallel Loan (Back-to-Back Loan) An arrangement in which two business firms in separate countries borrow each other's currency for a specific period of time. At an agreed-upon termination date they return the borrowed currencies. Such a swap creates a covered hedge against exchange loss, because each company, on its own books, borrows the same currency it repays.

Parity Grid The matrix of bilateral par values for the currencies of members of the European Monetary System. Each member government is obliged to maintain the exchange value of currency in terms of every other group currency between the intervention prices that are established by this grid.

Participation The act of taking part in a syndicated credit or a bond issue. In a syndicated credit, participation may involve membership in the original group of lending banks or may involve lending later via a participation certificate. In a Eurobond issue, a participation refers to the size of the underwriting commitment.

Participation Fees The portion of total fees in a syndicated credit that go to the participating banks.

Paying Agent One bank or a syndicate of banks responsible for paying the interest and principal of a bond issue to bondholders on behalf of the bond issuer.

Perpetual FRNs Floating-rate notes with no maturity. They pay an above-market coupon reset margin to compensate investors for the lack of a final maturity date. Issues qualify as primary capital for banks; thus they possess certain quasi-equity features. In most cases, if an issuer cancels a dividend payment within a certain time period, he may also elect to cancel the coupon payment. However, the unpaid interest usually continues to accrue and must be paid at a specified time in the future.

Placement Memorandum A document in a syndicated Eurocredit that sets out details of the proposed loan and gives information about the borrower.

Plain-Vanilla Swap The classic fixed- versus floating-interest-rate swap.

Points The number of units, often expressed in terms of the last two or three significant digits, of an exchange rate. It is customary to state that a currency has appreciated or depreciated by some points from a previous exchange rate. Forward-exchange-rate quotes are often expressed in terms of so many points premium or discount above or below the spot rate.

Portfolio-Balance Approach An analysis of balance of payments or the exchange rate that emphasizes the determinants of demand for, and supply of, the stock of financial assets. It highlights the role of wealth and views assets as imperfect substitutes.

Praecipium In a loan syndication or bond underwriting, the fee charged by the lead manager or managers over and above the normal management, underwriting, and selling fees.

Price Index An index that measures the value of a representative sample of goods and services. The most popular is the Consumer Price Index (CPI).

Privatization The selling of government-owned companies to the private sector.

Product-Life-Cycle Theory A theory that attempts to explain prices and other features of a market over the phases of a product's life.

Purchasing Power Parity (PPP) The notion that in equilibrium the market exchange rate for any two currencies will exactly reflect the relative purchasing powers of the two currencies.

Puttable Swap A swap with an option to terminate early.

Quantity Theory of Money The theory that a proportional increase in the money supply leads to a proportionate increase in the price level.

Quota A restriction on the quantity of an item that can be imported into, or exported from, a country during a specified period of time.

Random-Walk Theory The theory that changes in an asset price, such as an exchange rate, are random—that is, the changes are independent of each other and have an identical distribution.

Rating A letter grade given to a bond by a rating agency (such as Moody's or Standard & Poor's) signifying the amount of credit risk on the bond.

Rational Expectations Expectations of economic variables that fully reflect market information. In the currency market, the forward-exchange rate is often assumed to be "rational" in the sense of incorporating all available information affecting exchange rates.

Real Effective Exchange Rate A rate calculated by dividing the home country's nominal effective exchange rate by an index of the ratio of average foreign prices to home prices. This rate attempts to measure the overall competitiveness of home-country goods in international markets.

Real Exchange Rate The value of a currency in terms of real purchasing power determined by comparing the price of a hypothetical market basket of goods in two different countries, translated into the same currency at the prevailing exchange rate. It is useful for measuring the price competitiveness of domestic goods in international markets and also for calculating the real value of investment projects.

Real Interest Rate The market interest rate is commonly quoted (nominal interest rate) minus the rate of inflation of the price level. The ex ante real rate is calculated by subtracting expected inflation, whereas the ex post real rate is calculated by subtracting actual inflation.

Redemption Discharge of a bond obligation by the issuer by payment of the bond's face value to the bondholder. Redemption may occur at bond maturity or earlier, under conditions stated in the bond contract.

Red Herring A preliminary prospectus (offering circular) giving the expected, but not final, details of a forthcoming securities offering.

Reference Banks The group of banks surveyed in order to determine a reference rate, such as LIBOR.

Reference Rate A market interest rate, such as LIBOR or Prime, that is periodically monitored in connection with a rollover credit or a floating-rate note in order to determine the subsequent interest payment by the borrower.

Registered Term used to refer to bonds that are recorded in the bond issuer's books in the name of the bond owner. Ownership of such bonds can be transferred only by a formal transfer of the ownership name in the issuer's books.

Regulation Q. An erstwhile regulation of the U.S. Federal Reserve that limited the interest rate that U.S. banks could pay on time deposits; phased out in 1986.

Relative Purchasing Power Parity Requires that the percentage change in the exchange rate equal the differential percentage change in the price of a market basket of goods in the two countries.

Rembrandt Bonds Dutch-guilder-denominated foreign bonds issued in Amsterdam.

Representations Statements made by a borrower in a syndicated credit or bond issue describing the borrower's current state of affairs, such as the borrower's financial condition.

Repurchase Agreement An agreement by one party to sell a security with an agreement to buy it back at a specified price on a specified date. The seller gets immediate cash, for the use of which he will in return pay the difference between the repurchase price and the sale price. If the buyer takes possession of the security in the meantime, a repo represents a form of secured lending from the buyer's standpoint, because if the seller defaults on the repurchase, the buyer still has the security.

Reserve Currency A foreign currency held by a central bank (or exchange authority) for purposes of exchange intervention and the settlement of intergovernmental claims.

Reserve Requirements Obligations imposed on commercial banks to maintain a certain percentage of deposits with the central bank or in the form of central-bank liabilities.

Revaluation An official government act that produces a substantial increase in an exchange rate, usually overnight.

Revolving Credit A line of bank credit that may be used or not used at the borrower's discretion. Interest is paid on the amount of credit actually in use, and a commitment fee is paid on the unused portion.

Rho A measure of the change in an option premium with respect to a percentage-point change in the interest rate.

Risk Premium In the context of foreign exchange, a premium embedded in a currency forward or futures price. It stems from the risk-averse nature of market participants, and may be a function of the covariance between the participant's portfolio of assets and liabilities and the exchange rate. Because of the risk premium, the forward rate or futures price may be a biased estimator of the exchange rate expected to prevail at date of delivery.

Rollover A term used in short-term foreign-exchange dealing meaning a short swap designed to employ or borrow foreign currency balances. In a rollover applied to a currency that trades on a two-day spot basis, for example, a trader can sell a currency for delivery in one business day and buy that currency back for delivery in two business days.

Rollover Credit A bank loan whose interest rate is periodically updated to reflect market interest rates. The interest rate in the loan for each subperiod is specified as the sum of a reference rate and a lending margin.

RUF (Revolving underwriting facility) A note-issuance facility that is underwritten. See Euronote facility.

Samurai Bonds Yen-denominated bonds issued in Japan by nonresidents, primarily by supranational and sovereign borrowers. The market is very illiquid.

Schuldscheindarlehen German certificates of indebtedness. These are private loan agreements between borrowers and banks that are resold to other investors with the borrowers' permission. The details of the loan are set on a Schuldschein (debt certificate) held by the bank.

SDR (Special Drawing Right) An artificial reserve asset created and held on the books of the IMF. At the time of first issue on January 1, 1970, the SDR was defined as having a value equal to 1/35 ounce of gold. The definition was altered in 1974 to specify the value in terms of a portfolio of 16 currencies. Since 1981, the SDR has been defined in terms of the U.S. dollar, German mark, French franc, Japanese yen, and British pound.

Seasoned Securities Securities that have traded in the secondary market for more than 90 days.

SEC (Securities and Exchange Commission) A U.S. regulatory agency established in 1934 to regulate the issuing and trading of securities and issuers' reporting practices.

Secondary Market A market in which securities, such as bonds, are traded following the time of their original issue.

Selling Concession The share of total investment-banking fees accruing to the selling group.

Selling Group All banks involved in selling or marketing a new issue of bonds. Sometimes the term is used in reference to dealers acting only as sellers and is intended to exclude reference to underwriters or managers.

Selling Period A period following the signing of terms of a new bond issue during which bonds are bought and sold (in the form of price agreements) prior to actual payment for, and distribution of, the bonds themselves.

Semistrong Efficient Market Hypothesis The hypothesis stating that current asset prices fully reflect all public information.

Settlement Date The day on which the actual transfer of two currencies, or the transfer of money for an asset, takes place at a previously arranged price.

Shogun Bonds Foreign bonds issued in Tokyo and denominated in currencies other than the Japanese yen. The usual denomination is the U.S. dollar.

Short Position A greater outflow than inflow of a given currency. In foreign-exchange operations, short positions arise when the amount of a given currency sold is greater than the amount purchased.

SIMEX The Singapore International Monetary Exchange, a futures and options exchange.

Smithsonian Agreement A revision to the Bretton Woods system that was signed at the Smithsonian Institution in Washington, D.C., in December 1971. Included were a new set of par values, widened bands to plus or minus 2.25 percent around par, and an increase in the official value of gold to $38/ounce. The agreement immediately preceded the collapse of the Bretton Woods system of international monetary relations.

Snake in the Tunnel A system that EC countries agreed on to allow their currencies to fluctuate a maximum of 2.25 percent against one another (the snake) and permitted a 4.5 percent band against other currencies (the tunnel). The tunnel was abandoned in 1973 and the snake ended in 1978, to be replaced by the Exchange-Rate Mechanism of the European Monetary System.

Soft Currency A weak currency whose convertibility is, or is expected to become, restricted.

Sovereign Risk In cross-border contracts, the risk that a country will impose foreign-exchange controls. Also called *country risk,* it can include the risk of government default on a loan made to it or guaranteed by it.

Special Drawing Rights (SDRs) Monetary accounts held at the International Monetary Fund for payments among governments. The rights can be transferred to other countries in exchange for convertible currencies, either voluntarily or for convertible currencies supplied by countries designated by the IMF. At first, SDRs had a fixed value in gold, but later their value was determined by a weighted basket of major currencies.

Speculator A trader whose objective is to make profits by successfully anticipating future price movements.

Spot Foreign-Exchange Market A market involving an exchange of bank deposits denominated in different currencies. A spot contract implies an exchange two business days after the transaction.

Spot/Next In the foreign-exchange market, term used to describe a swap transaction for value on the spot date with the reverse transaction taking place the next working day after the spot date. In the Eurocurrency market, term used to describe a loan or deposit for value on the spot date with maturity on the next working day after the spot date.

Spread The difference between the buying and selling rates or prices.

Stabilization The effort by a lead manager in a bond issue to regulate the price at which bonds trade in the secondary market during the period in which the bond syndicate is still in existence.

Stags/Zebras A zero-coupon sterling issue created by stripping a U.K. government bond.

Standby Facility A Euronote facility set up to act as a standby to the issuance of U.S. commercial paper. Normally, it is not expected to be used.

Startrek A bond priced at a level previously unexplored by the market.

Step-Up, Step-Down Issues Bonds or floating-rate notes in which the coupon rises or falls over time according to a predetermined schedule. Step-down bonds provide more current income for the investor, whereas step-up issues delay the income payments.

Sterilization Intervention in the foreign-exchange market by a central bank in which the change in the monetary base caused by the foreign-exchange intervention is offset by open-market operations involving domestic assets.

Straight Bonds Bonds with fixed coupon payments and without any option features (such as provisions for conversion into equity, other bonds, or other currencies).

Strike Price The price at which an option holder may buy or sell the underlying asset, specified in an option contract.

Strong-Efficient-Market Hypothesis The hypothesis that the current asset price reflects all market information, including any useful "inside" information.

Subparticipation The partial assignment by one bank to another of the right to receive monetary sums from a borrower.

Subscription Period The time period between the day on which a new bond issue is announced and the day on which the terms of the issue are signed and the bonds are formally offered for sale.

Subscription Agreement An agreement between a bond issuer and the managing banks that describes the terms and conditions of the issue and the obligation of the parties to the agreement.

Surety Bond A guarantee that a person or corporation will perform an obligation due another person or corporation. It is issued by a specialized surety company, or an insurance company.

Sushi Bond A dollar issue undertaken by a Japanese company from Japan, designed to be bought by Japanese institutions.

Swap In the interbank foreign-exchange market, the simultaneous purchase and sale of identical amounts of a currency for different value dates. (The currency will be priced in terms of a second currency whose amounts will differ, depending on the relationship between the purchase price and the sale price of the first currency.) More generally, a swap is a contractual obligation entered into by two parties to deliver one sum of money against another sum of money at stated intervals. See also Currency Swap and Interest-Rate Swap.

Swap Lines Lines of credit extended from one government to another that can be drawn on to provide the foreign currencies needed for official intervention in the exchange market. These lines of credit, once drawn, provide very-short-term financing of imbalances in international payments. Swap lines are also referred to as "reciprocal currency arrangements."

Swaps Tender Panel A refinement of the standard tender panel whereby the issuer can ask for currency and/or interest-rate swaps on a particular note issue tranche.

Swaption An option on a swap. The term encompasses the right to enter into a swap on certain terms in the future, and the right to cancel, or to extend, an existing swap.

SWIFT (Society for Worldwide Interbank Financial Transfers) A standardized electronic message-transfer service designed to send and confirm instructions concerning funds transfers associated with international payments.

Swing Line Used in a global note facility or BONUS to allow the issuer to move from the U.S. commercial-paper market to the Euronote market. It is available for short periods of one week or less and is priced over U.S. prime.

Syndicate A group of banks that acts jointly to loan money in a bank credit (syndicated credit) or to underwrite a new issue of bonds (bond-issuing syndicate).

Systematic Risk The risk common to all assets; risk that cannot be diversified away.

Tap Basis A frequent method of issuance in Eurocommercial paper. The dealer approaches the issuer for notes in response to particular investor demand rather than the issuer seeking bids from the dealer.

Technical Analysis A graphical analysis of past prices and trading behavior; used by analysts to predict future price movements.

Tender Panel A group, including Euronote facility underwriters and additionally appointed banks and dealers, who are invited to bid on an issuer's notes in an open-auction format. Notes are awarded to bidders in sequential order from the most competitive bid upwards until the full tranche is allocated.

Term Credit A bank loan that is made according to a time schedule. In the initial period, increasing portions of the total loan amount become available to the borrower. In the final period, the loan is repaid at scheduled intervals.

Term Premium A premium embedded in a futures or forward price that arises from liquidity premia in the term structure of interest rates when participants are risk averse.

Terms of Trade The ratio of export prices to import prices expressed in the same currency.

Theta A measure of the change in an option premium with respect to a one-day change in time to maturity.

Time Value The amount of money that option buyers are willing to pay for an option in anticipation that, over time, a change in the underlying asset price will cause the option to increase in value. An option's premium is the sum of time value and intrinsic value. The amount by which an option's premium exceeds the option's intrinsic value is the option's time value.

Tombstone Advertisement placed in a newspaper or magazine by banks in a syndicated credit to record their participation in the loan, or in a bond issue to record their role in managing, underwriting, or placing the bonds.

Tomorrow/Next In the foreign-exchange market, term used to describe a swap transaction for value tomorrow with the reverse transaction taking place the next working day after tomorrow. In the Eurocurrency market, term used to describe a loan or deposit for value tomorrow with maturity on the next working day after tomorrow.

Tranche French for "slice," this refers to the portion of a loan or security deal that is placed with a particular category of investors at the time of issuance.

Transactions Exposure A measure of a company's vulnerability to currency-related losses arising from known, contractual future cash payments or receipts in foreign currencies.

Translation (or Accounting) Exposure Foreign currency assets, liabilities, revenues, and expenses that are consolidated at current exchange rates into parent-currency–denominated group financial statements.

Triangular Arbitrage The process of buying and selling foreign exchange between three different currencies in order to profit from a discrepancy in cross rates.

Trigger Swap A swap that is triggered if and only if LIBOR or some other market rate reaches a certain level. When triggered, the swap remains in place until some preset termination date.

TRUF (Transferable Revolving Underwriting Facility) A loan facility in which the underwriting banks' contingent liability to purchase notes, in the event of issuer's failure to place them, is fully transferable.

Unbiased Forward-Rate Theory A hypothesis that the forward-exchange rate is an unbiased predictor of the future spot rate.

Underwriting Allowance The share of total investment-banking fees accruing to the underwriting group.

Underwriting Syndicate The banks, in a new bond issue, that agree to pay a minimum price to the borrower even if the bonds cannot be sold on the market at a higher price.

Unsystematic Risk The risk unique to a particular company or country; risk that can be eliminated through diversification.

Value date The contracted date on which the foreign exchange is to be delivered or received. For forward transactions, the value date and maturity date are synonymous.

Value today A special spot foreign-exchange transaction in which delivery and payment are made on the same day as the contract, instead of the normal one- or two-business-day lag.

Value Tomorrow A special spot foreign-exchange transaction in which delivery and payment are made on the next business day after the contract.

Variation Margin The gains or losses on open futures contracts calculated by marking the contracts to the market price at the end of each trading day (or session). These gains or losses are credited or debited by the clearing house to each clearing member's account, and by members to their respective customers' accounts.

Vega The sensitivity of an option's price to changes in volatility.

Volatility A measure of the amount by which an asset's price fluctuated over a given period. Normally, it is measured by the annualized standard deviation of daily returns on the asset.

Warrant A call option to buy a stated number of shares of stock at a specified price.

Warrant Bonds Eurobonds or domestic bonds that are issued together with warrants. The warrants are usually long-term options on the issuer's equity or debt.

Weak Efficient Market Hypothesis The hypothesis that asset prices reflect all information about the history of prices of that asset.

Window Warrant A warrant exercisable on particular days or during particular periods (also European warrant).

Withholding Tax A tax collected by the source originating the income, in contrast to one paid by the recipient of the income after the funds are received. For example, a withholding tax on interest payments to foreigners means that the tax proceeds are deducted from the interest payment made to the lender and collected by the borrower on behalf of the government.

World Bank (International Bank for Reconstruction and Development) A creation of the Bretton Woods negotiations in July 1944, the bank began operations in June 1946. The original intent of the bank was to make postwar reconstruction loans, a role soon supplanted by the Marshall Plan. The bank consequently shifted its attention to development lending. Funds for lending are obtained from the paid-in capital subscriptions of member nations, from borrowings in the world's capital markets, and from net earnings.

Yankee Bond A dollar-denominated foreign bond issued in New York. These bonds are subject to U.S. law and must be registered with the Securities and Exchange Commission.

Yield Curve A diagram of interest rates prevailing on a class of securities that are alike in every respect except term to maturity. A yield curve can slope either upward or downward.

Yield-Curve Notes (Also known as "reverse floaters" or "bull FRNs") Floating-rate notes on which the coupon payment varies inversely with the level of market rates.

Yield-to-Maturity The rate of return earned by a debt instrument if held to maturity and reinvested at that same return.

Zero-Coupon/Deep-Discount Bond Bonds issued at a deep discount from face value, paying no interest (zero) or a lower-than-normal market rate (deep discount).

Index